Beginning SQL Server 2000 DBA: From Novice to Professional

Tony Bain,
with
Baya Pavliashvil
Joseph Sack,
Michael Benkovich,
and Brian Freeman

Apress™

Beginning SQL Server 2000 DBA: From Novice to Professional
Copyright © 2004 by Apress

ISBN (pbk): 1-59059-293-X

Printed and bound in the United States of America 12345678910

Trademarked names may appear in this book. Rather than use a trademark symbol with every occurrence of a trademarked name, we use the names only in an editorial fashion and to the benefit of the trademark owner, with no intention of infringement of the trademark.

Additional Material by: Dan Lampkin, Patrick Gallucci

Technical Reviewer: Craig Weldon

Editorial Board: Steve Anglin, Dan Appleman, Craig Berry, Gary Cornell, Tony Davis, Steven Rycroft, Julian Skinner, Martin Streicher, Jim Sumser, Karen Watterson, Gavin Wray, John Zukowski

Assistant Publisher: Grace Wong

Project Manager: Kylie Johnston

Copy Editor: Mark Nigara

Production Manager: Kari Brooks

Production Editor: Kelly Winquist

Proofreader: Linda Seifert

Compositor: Katy Freer

Indexer: Bill Johncocks

Artist: Christine Calderwood, Kinetic Publishing Services, LLC

Cover Designer: Kurt Krames

Manufacturing Manager: Tom Debolski

Distributed to the book trade in the United States by Springer-Verlag New York, Inc., 175 Fifth Avenue, New York, NY 10010 and outside the United States by Springer-Verlag GmbH & Co. KG, Tiergartenstr. 17, 69112 Heidelberg, Germany.

In the United States: phone 1-800-SPRINGER, email orders@springer-ny.com, or visit http://www.springer-ny.com. Outside the United States: fax +49 6221 345229, email orders@springer.de, or visit http://www.springer.de.

For information on translations, please contact Apress directly at 2560 Ninth Street, Suite 219, Berkeley, CA 94710. Phone 510-549-5930, fax 510-549-5939, email info@apress.com, or visit http://www.apress.com.

The information in this book is distributed on an "as is" basis, without warranty. Although every precaution has been taken in the preparation of this work, neither the author(s) nor Apress shall have any liability to any person or entity with respect to any loss or damage caused or alleged to be caused directly or indirectly by the information contained in this work.

The source code for this book is available to readers at http://www.apress.com in the Downloads section. You will need to answer questions pertaining to this book in order to successfully download the code.

Contents at a Glance

Contents

Contents

About the Authors

Tony Bain is a director of Bain Linwood, a specialist SQL Server services organization (www.bainlinwood.com). He has many years of experience with all areas of SQL Server including proactive database administration, scalable application development, and complex database design. This is the fifth SQL Server book for which Tony has written; other titles are on subjects such as data warehousing and developing SQL Server applications with Visual Basic.NET. Tony is a regular conference speaker with recent appearances at international Microsoft Tech Ed and SQL Server community events.

Tony has MCSE, MCSD, and MCBDA certifications and is also a current SQL Server Most Valuable Professional.

Baya Pavliashvili is a senior DBA with HealthStream. Baya has developed and administered numerous databases and data warehouses. He is an MCSE, MCSD, and MCDBA. Baya has authored many technical articles as well as Quest's Knowledge Xpert for SQL Server, and he has contributed to several other books. He can be reached at baya_baya@hotmail.com.

Joseph Sack is a database administration and developer consultant based in Minneapolis, Minnesota. Since 1997, he has been developing and supporting SQL Server environments for clients in financial services, IT consulting, manufacturing, and the real estate industry. He is a Microsoft Certified Database Administrator (MCDBA). Sack received his bachelor's degree in Psychology from the University of Minnesota. He is the author of *SQL Server 2000 Fast Answers for DBAs and Developers*.

Brian Freeman is a Software Engineer with Carnegie Technologies and Bluewave Computing (www.bluewave-computing.com) in Atlanta, Georgia. His primary role is designing and implementing custom software in Visual Basic with different back end storage platforms. His current project is an insurance program suite utilizing SQL Server and VB6.

Introduction

Have you been considering a career change and thinking about becoming a SQL Server DBA (database administrator)? Perhaps you've been given the responsibility of looking after a SQL Server and you aren't quite sure what this really means or where you should start? Maybe you're just interested in finding out what on earth DBAs do all day long! Many books will teach you the SQL Server DBA functions but being a DBA is more than just simply understanding the tools of SQL Server. It's also about applying solid processes and utilizing those tools for the overall benefit of your business or client.

There are two types of DBAs: the reactive DBA and the proactive DBA. Reactive DBAs understand how to use SQL Server but lack the process skills needed to manage SQL Server in an effective way. Reactive DBAs spend much of their time "fighting fires," that is, fixing problems as they occur, such as adding more disk space when it runs out, trying to improve performance when users complain of poor response times, and implementing security once someone has stolen your customer list. Sure, reactive DBAs fix problems when things get broken, but they do this at a cost to your business–costs measured in idle time as employees sit waiting for the system to become available; costs calculated in missed revenue opportunities. Reactive DBAs are unfortunately common and are often viewed as a necessary evil by many businesses.

The proactive DBA on the other hand takes what they know about SQL Server and applies tested processes to forewarn clients of potential issues so that future problems are avoided before they become an issue. They test contingency plans for those rare occasions when unexpected problems do occur and they plan resource requirements so spare capacity is always available before it's required. They automate the day-to-day maintenance of SQL Server and work to continuously improve their processes in order to ensure that the business they are working gets high, reliable performance from its SQL Server databases. Proactive DBAs are respected and often seen as a valuable asset to their business.

As a DBA and a consultant I have had the pleasure of working with hundreds of DBAs in all types of businesses. I have been lucky to see the outstanding results good practices can make, and the utter shambles bad practices can lead to. Throughout this book I have shared many good practices so you can easily learn as much as possible. This book is about teaching you to be a SQL Server DBA. But most importantly, it teaches you how to be a proactive SQL Server DBA.

Conventions

I've used a number of different styles of text and layout in this book to help differentiate between different kinds of information. Here are examples of the styles used and an explanation of what they mean.

I have represented code in several ways. If I am referring to a single code word in the text–for example, when I am discussing a for (...) loop–it's in this font. If I am discussing code that you can type as a program and run, then I list it on its own line, separate from the rest of the text:

```
DirectoryEntry de = new DirectoryEntry();
```

Sometimes I just refer to one line, but often, we discuss an entire block of code, like this:

```
DirectoryEntries children;
DirectoryEntry de = new DirectoryEntry();
try
{
    Console.WriteLine(de.Name);
}
```

> *Advice, hints, background, and other important information are* *represented like this.*

I have also used several styles and fonts to highlight other types of information.

Important words and words that are defined are in italic type font in the paragraph text; or, when they are defined as part of a list of other terms that are being defined, they may take the following format:

Important word: Followed by definition.

Words that appear on the screen, or in menus like Open or Close, are in a similar font to the one you would see on a Windows desktop.

Downloading the Source Code

As you move through the chapters there will be copious amounts of code available for you, so that you can see exactly how it works. The source code for all examples is available for download. You might decide that you prefer to type all the code in by hand. Many readers prefer this because it's a good way to get familiar with the coding techniques that are being used.

Whether or not you want to type the code in, all the source code for this book is available on the Apress web site, in the Downloads section at the following address:

> http://www.apress.com

If you're one of those readers who likes to type in the code, you can use our files to check the results you should be getting. They should be your first stop if you think you might have typed in an error. If you're one of those readers who doesn't like typing, then downloading the source code from our web site is a must! Either way, it'll help you with updates and debugging.

1

Being a DBA

This book is a guide to the tasks required to install, configure, and maintain a SQL Server database environment. It is assumed that you may not be a dedicated database administrator (DBA); indeed, you may not even consider yourself a DBA at all. Instead, you may be, willingly or unwillingly, responsible for areas of SQL Server administration and maintenance as part of your wider company role. Indeed, it is not uncommon to find system engineers, developers, help-desk staff, and operations staff (among others) responsible for the day-to-day management of a SQL Server installation. This book presents information relevant to all the previously mentioned parties while still remaining a useful tutorial for the dedicated novice DBA.

Over recent years, the role of the DBA has changed significantly, coinciding with the gradual migration of enterprise platforms from large mainframe installations to PC network–based installations. It wasn't that long ago that the quintessential DBA resided in a back room somewhere watching database activity on a green-screen terminal. Thankfully, this change in platform coupled with a significant improvement in database server "self-management" has resulted in DBAs being forced from their burrows to deal with a new range of issues.

This chapter's goal is to introduce the general philosophy of the modern DBA and the many different positions that a DBA may hold. If you're considering moving into a dedicated DBA role, or if you're looking to develop your career further, this chapter contains some interesting information for you.

DBA Responsibilities

Ensuring the validity and recoverability of data in the database are perhaps the most important jobs of the DBA. Nothing else matters, including making the data available to users, if these core responsibilities aren't met.

Understanding this simple point is the first step toward understanding the mind-set and methodology of a good DBA. Everything you do that affects the databases and, possibly even more important, everything that everyone else does that affects the databases, should be assessed for its impact on your primary responsibilities. Some examples of a DBA's responsibilities include

- Giving users ad hoc access to a database

- Allowing developers direct access to the production database

- Applying untested application changes

As it turns out, almost all of the other responsibilities of a DBA either directly or indirectly relate to these primary goals, including ensuring that

- Data is secure and only relevant users can make changes to the data.

- Only valid changes can be made to the data.

- Data is available to users.

- Data is accessible in a timely manner.

DBA Types

"Database administrator" is a broad term that is loosely used to describe a collection of roles within an organization. Every environment will add its own spin on the actual duties and responsibilities of these various roles. Here are some general DBA types and their high-level job descriptions:

- **Junior DBA:** Relatively new, with little to no experience of the DBA profession

- **Senior DBA:** Experienced and may have responsibility over the database environment

- **Production DBA:** Primarily supports the database platform once it has been deployed

- **Development DBA:** Develops database applications for SQL Server while managing the system these applications run on

- **Consultant DBA:** Involved in the actual creation of the database solution

In the next sections, we cover each DBA category in detail. Let us be clear that these aren't hard-and-fast rules; rather, they're simple generalizations. Each organization has its own set of requirements for a DBA; however, the sections that follow should provide a reasonable overview of the main areas of responsibility for each DBA category.

Junior DBA

The junior DBA is someone relatively new to the DBA role. This person may have only a couple years of experience in database technology or in information technology (IT) itself. The junior DBA typically handles the day-to-day operations associated with one or more database servers, including

- ❏ Checking that the database backups have completed without issue

- ❏ Checking that other scheduled jobs and database maintenance jobs complete without issue

- ❏ Giving authorized users access to databases

The junior DBA reports to a senior DBA, which is generally the position the junior DBA aims to advance to in his career. Issues that the junior DBA can't resolve are passed to the senior DBA for attention.

Checking Backups

Backing up a database is one of the most important tasks for a DBA, and thus it should be confirmed in some way. Usually backups can be automated to e-mail on failure and/or on completion, so the process of checking for failed backups may involve scanning an inbox for failure notifications. If a failed backup is found, the junior DBA will usually rerun the backup process to ensure that a good backup of the database has been taken.

However, unless you test backups by restoring the databases, you can't be 100 percent sure that the backups are of any use. As already mentioned, ensuring that data is recoverable is one of the most important responsibilities of a DBA, so the junior DBA will usually test the restoration process on a periodic basis. Any repeated backup failure or other issues involved with restoration would be escalated to the senior DBA.

> For more information on backup and restore with SQL Server 2000, see Chapter 8.

Checking Jobs

Other than backups, most databases run other regular batch jobs. These may be extract jobs for populating a data warehouse, for example, or database maintenance procedures. It's usually the junior DBA's responsibility to ensure that these jobs complete without errors. These jobs, like backups, can be automated to inform the DBA by e-mail if an error does occur. In some cases, the job may be rerun immediately or rerun overnight. Continual job failure will usually be escalated to the senior DBA.

Maintaining Users

To access a database, you need to be authenticated to ensure you're allowed to see the data you want. Authentication requires that your login details be made known to SQL Server and associated with a set of database permissions. The junior DBA usually takes responsibility for assigning and removing the ability of users to access a SQL Server database in line with a business request. Depending on the type of authentication being used, passwords may need to be assigned and maintained.

The junior DBA will normally only be concerned with allowing a user access and assigning that user to a predefined group of database permissions. Typically, the application vendor or the senior DBA defines the actual predefined permissions.

> **An important note about this role: Databases (especially SQL Server) are designed to become more and more reliable and "self-managing" with each major release, so we will gradually see more routine background tasks traditionally undertaken by junior staff becoming redundant.**

Senior DBA

The senior DBA is someone with several years of database experience who has moved into a role in which she has responsibility over the database environment. Usually, the senior DBA will have gained her experience as a junior DBA or a systems administrator (someone who manages the file servers and network) who, as part of her administration role, looked after the day-to-day operation of SQL Server.

The senior DBA is involved more with the management and planning side of the database environment, rather than carrying out the day-to-day operational tasks. The senior DBA interacts with the business managers to identify any potential issues that the business may be experiencing related to the database applications. The senior DBA is also involved with project teams implementing new applications, as she enables them to plan the necessary server requirements and prepare any specific operation procedures that the future application may require.

More specifically, the responsibilities of the senior DBA include

❑   Overall "ownership" of and responsibility for the database environment

❑   Capacity planning and predicting future growth and infrastructure needs

❑   Proactively managing support

❑   Building database servers and installing database server software, or defining the build standards to be used by junior DBAs for building the database servers

❑   Responding to escalation requests from junior DBAs

❑   Managing the junior DBA team and staff

❑   Training and support of the junior DBAs

Ownership of the Database Environment

The senior DBA is considered the owner of the database environment within an organization, as she has overall control and authority over how that environment is implemented. As the owner, the senior DBA takes responsibility for resolving serious problems that prevent users from accessing the database. Also, the senior DBA writes and enforces rules of use so these issues don't happen in the future.

It is the senior DBA's responsibility to establish the processes and procedures to be used by the junior DBA when administering the environment, thereby maintaining control of the overall quality of administration.

Capacity Planning

Planning for new systems or for future growth is one of the senior DBA's more important tasks. Before a database application is implemented, the senior DBA will interact with the client to gain an understanding of how the database will be used over its lifetime. From this information, the senior DBA will determine the hardware, software, and infrastructure requirements to support it.

As very few organizations remain static, the requirements of a database application can change dynamically during its lifetime. To ensure that the application remains well supported, the senior DBA will repeat capacity planning exercises on a regular basis. Early detection of low capacity overhead at a hardware level allows time for the capacity to be increased before the database application begins to suffer from being under-resourced.

Proactive Support

Instead of waiting for a problem to occur, proactive support involves putting measures in place to detect and provide early warning for (and in some cases, a fix) potential problems. Early detection of potential problems significantly improves the reliability of a database environment, as it can allow problems to be resolved before they begin to impact database users. It also significantly reduces the time that the DBA spends fighting fires (that is, reacting to problems as they occur) instead of performing more useful functions such as capacity planning.

Building Servers

The senior DBA typically builds servers for the production environment. In smaller organizations, this may involve installing hardware components, the operating system, and the database server software. In larger organizations, the systems administration team may build the hardware and operating system, and the senior DBA might carry out the installation of the database server software only.

After installation has been completed, the senior DBA configures the server for the appropriate level of security required for the database application and adds any other necessary requirements. If the server is going to be servicing high-transaction workloads, the senior DBA may run some stress-testing software to ensure that the server can adequately meet the load requirements.

Once the server has been configured and tested, it can be installed into the production environment, where the management of backups, jobs, and users will become the responsibility of the junior DBA.

> In some environments, the senior DBA defines the process and standards for building database servers, and the junior DBA uses these standards for building new servers.

Escalation Requests

As covered earlier, it is the junior DBA's responsibility to escalate any issues with his day-to-day tasks, such as repeated backup failure, to the senior DBA for resolution. The senior DBA uses the information provided by the junior DBA to investigate the cause of the problem and to implement any needed remedies.

Team Management

Sometimes a senior DBA has staffing responsibilities over a team of junior DBAs. In such cases, the senior DBA is required to manage the career development path of the junior DBAs, ensuring that the junior DBAs are meeting the requirements placed upon them.

Organizing schedules for staff and schedules for administrative events, such as test restores, is another important component of this role.

Training and Support

A junior DBA can be considered a senior DBA in training. Typically, the junior DBA is keen to learn the skills and gain the experience necessary to move into the senior DBA role. It is often a requirement for existing senior DBAs to provide training to the junior DBAs to help enhance their skill sets. This may be through informal, Q&A-style training, or it may be through more formal approach with a senior DBA providing training to a group of junior DBAs in a classroom-style format.

Although it's the senior DBA's responsibility to resolve issues that have been reported to her by the junior DBA, it's also important for her to feed information on the resolution back to the junior DBA. This would include information on what problem occurred, why it occurred, and what steps are involved in preventing it from occurring in the future.

The senior DBA position encapsulates all issues surrounding the development and deployment of applications within a database environment. However, in a larger organization, the role of the senior DBA may be broken up into two different roles: the production DBA and the development DBA. In addition, consultant DBAs may be brought into an organization to provide specialist skills and advice for specific projects. Let's take a look at the requirements of these three roles.

Production DBA

The production DBA is primarily involved with supporting the database platform once it has been deployed for live use by an organization's users. The production DBA role can be considered a specialized form of the senior DBA role.

> **The production DBA shares many of the responsibilities of the senior DBA. The key difference lies in the areas in which these responsibilities are focused. The senior DBA may look after production, development, and test environments, whereas a production DBA may only be responsible for the production environment. Typically, the size of the organization determines the need to divide the senior DBA role into production DBA and development DBA roles.**

Issues of importance to a production DBA include

❑   Ensuring the database is recoverable

❑   Ensuring the database is secure

❑   Enforcing change management

❑   Ensuring the database is available to users

❑   Ensuring the database performs optimally for its users

Recoverable Data

Production data should be well protected because, once lost, it can be very difficult to regain. The production DBA ensures that the production data is protected fully within a specific environment. This involves setting up appropriate backup plans, which is just one aspect of ensuring recoverability.

> **For more information on ensuring the data is recoverable with SQL Server 2000, see Chapter 8.**

Security

After ensuring that the data is recoverable, ensuring the data is secure is probably next on the production DBA's list of priorities. It's extremely important to ensure that only authorized people can gain access to a database and, once they have access, that they can only view information they're allowed to. Obviously, the importance relates to the type of information retained within the database. Generally, most databases contain some information that an organization doesn't want everyone to be able to view and modify.

Ensuring the correct permissions are assigned is one aspect of good security, but there are many others. Implementing appropriate auditing, using appropriate network communication technologies (such as encryption), and using appropriate application architectures are all issues that can affect the security of a database.

> **For detailed SQL Server 2000 security information, see Chapter 6.**

Change Management

Generally, developers don't have access to the production database environment. All their code and design changes take place in an isolated development environment, are tested in a test environment and, once tested, are made available for implementing in the production environment. The production DBA's responsibility is to implement those changes in the production environment.

As part of implementing the changes, the production DBA considers

- ❑ How urgent the changes are. Are the changes related to a new feature for which users can wait a few days, or are they related to an urgent fix to a problem that is preventing users from doing their work?

- ❑ How changes can be implemented with the least user impact.

- ❑ Whether there are any prerequisites to the changes. Are any other changes being made at the same time that may impact these changes?

- ❑ How changes can be undone if they're found to be faulty (do a backup first!).

- ❑ Whether downtime is required, and when this can be negotiated with the organization.

Availability

Once the database is recoverable and secure, ensuring that users can gain access to it is likely to be high on the list of the production DBA's priorities. Availability is considered from a user's perspective. If a user can connect to the database and carry out his work, then the database is considered available.

The first aspect of ensuring availability includes determining that an adequate disaster-recovery infrastructure exists to support the database application. Examples of this infrastructure are the use of clustering servers to allow for automated failover or the use of standby servers to allow for quick manual failover in the event of server failure. Disaster recovery includes using appropriate disk redundancy to ensure single-disk failure doesn't cause total failure of your database environment. These requirements cross over into the recoverability responsibility, with the key difference being that availability technologies make database recovery fast, without affecting whether or not the database is actually recoverable.

As web applications are driving the availability requirements of databases toward being accessible all day, every day, it's important to note that database management systems are more capable of making changes and performing maintenance tasks while databases remain online. The DBA needs to understand what tasks require data to be taken offline, so that database maintenance doesn't impact work being done by users.

Performance

Having the database performing to users' requirements is another important responsibility of the production DBA. Although ensuring that users can actually gain access to a database is more important, users will only be productive and happy if the database responds to their requests in a timely manner.

Part of this responsibility involves ensuring that the hardware supporting the database application is adequate for the requirements. Another part involves ensuring that the database is optimized through the use of appropriate indexes for the requests it receives from users. Yet another component of this responsibility is ensuring that requests from users are compatible with their workload requirements—that is, ensuring that a small number of users aren't issuing resource-intensive requests that severely impact the performance of requests from the greater user population. Lastly, performance is maintained by monitoring the applications that are used against a SQL Server database. If the applications are poorly optimized, the production DBA may raise the performance issues with the development team or, in the case of off-the-shelf products, the application vendor.

Development DBA

Rather than being concerned with maintaining a database application once it has been deployed into a production environment, the development DBA is more involved with the actual creation of the database solution in the first place. This may involve being part of an application development team or part of a project team testing a potential application for future implementation into production.

Issues of importance to the development DBA include

❑ Ensuring that code written by developers that affects the databases is written optimally

❑ Designing data models and entity-relationship diagrams (ERDs)

❑ Writing Transact-SQL (T-SQL) code, such as stored procedures and triggers (more on this in Chapter 10)

❑ Training application developers in optimal data access techniques

❑ Scalability-testing the proposed database solution to ensure that it will meet the demands of the production environment

Code Review

The term "database code" refers to the T-SQL code that accesses SQL Server, but it also refers to the code that interfaces with SQL Server from higher-level languages (such as a routine constructed to access SQL Server from Visual Basic .NET [VB .NET] using ADO.NET). The development DBA understands database code very well, maybe better than the application developers. It's often a requirement of the development DBA to inspect database code before it's accepted as part of the application. This is an important process, as application developers usually evaluate the code from one perspective, functionality: if the code returns the desired result, then it must be OK. Development DBAs evaluate the code for efficiency, use of resources, compliance with the security policy, impact on other users, and transactional consistency. This evaluation from a nonfunctional perspective can greatly improve the quality of the code that is produced and significantly reduce support issues once the application is deployed into production.

> Because a development DBA needs to understand how other developers are interacting with the database, he needs to understand the programming languages used by his development teams (such as VB .NET, C++, and Delphi). The development DBA may not be an expert, but he should understand the code to a level that he can evaluate whether or not the database is being accessed efficiently.

Database Design

The development DBA is often tasked with the creation of database diagrams to support a set of application requirements. It may be necessary for the development DBA to turn a user requirements document or a technical specification into the first stage of database design, which is a logical data model.

Later in the development processes, once the logical data model has been evaluated and adjusted by the wider application team, the development DBA turns the logical database design into a physical data model for the creation of a database.

> For more information on database design, including database diagrams and logical and physical data models, see Chapter 3.

Database Code Creation

In addition to inspecting developer's database code, the development DBA may be tasked with writing database code. This may be in a specialist area where optimal performance, for example, is critical. The development DBA (or the person most in tune with database performance issues) handles the creation of the code.

However, the code creation may not necessarily be associated with the actual application logic; instead, this is often in areas surrounding the database. Some of these areas include code to import data from other sources, code to perform batch maintenance tasks, or code to perform data validation. As this type of database code can be some of the most complex within a database application, it's often left to the development DBA to construct.

Developer Training

Because the development DBA is responsible for the quality of the database code within the application, it is in his best interest to spend some time training developers in the best ways to write database code. Typically, only one or two development DBAs are involved in a project, whereas there may be ten to twenty application developers. If the development DBA spends his time rewriting the application developer's database code, a serious bottleneck could quickly appear. After spending time training the developers, the development DBA can simply critique code, identify concerns, and send it back to the developers for rewriting.

> **Some developers resist being instructed in "best practices" by anyone. Persistence is required to break through their resistance and help them build better applications that interact with databases. This may be made easier by getting your organization to invest in a set of policies that describe how code that interacts with a database on SQL Server 2000 must operate.**

Scalability Testing

Discovering that the database application can only support a fraction of its intended users and data volumes after it has been deployed into the production environment is too late. Identifying potential scalability issues continuously throughout the development life cycle is critical to successful development and deployment of enterprise database applications.

Typically, scalability testing is performed on the application as a whole, with stress testing software being used to simulate production workloads. As part of this testing, the development DBA generates test data that represents what could be expected in the production environment, both in information and quantity. Once under testing load, the development DBA's responsibility is to monitor the impact of the load and identify any bottlenecks that are limiting the database's performance. Once any bottlenecks are identified, it may be up to the development DBA to resolve these issues by making structural changes to the database design or adding new indexes, for example. Alternatively, the developer of the nonperforming code may be required to rewrite it in a way that causes less impact on performance.

Consultant DBA

Finally, the consultant DBA is someone who provides assistance to project teams or support to other DBAs on a case-by-case basis. Usually, the consultant DBA was a senior DBA with previous experience both as a production DBA and a development DBA.

Skills required by the consultant DBA include

- ❏ The ability to assess complex situations quickly

- ❏ The ability to advise on specialist issues, such as disaster recovery, high availability, and replication

- ❏ The ability to communicate with users, technical people, and management

- ❏ The ability to clearly document the solutions the consultant DBA delivers

- ❏ Experience with the migration of data between different environments

- ❏ A broad range of experience in many different environments

Assessment of Complex Situations

The consultant DBA must be able to quickly gain an understanding of the problems affecting an organization. The consultant DBA is often brought into an organization to diagnose serious problems, such as performance or data consistency issues. In extreme circumstances, the consultant DBA may be brought in as a faultfinder to isolate a problem that is preventing users from accessing the database application. Such situations can cost organizations tens of thousands of dollars an hour in lost revenues and need to be resolved with some urgency. Having a structured, methodical approach to problem solving is immensely valuable when diagnosing and resolving technical issues in the most efficient manner.

Specialist Advice

The consultant DBA requires specialist knowledge in her chosen areas to be effective. As the consultant DBA is an expensive technical resource, the internal DBA and support staff will expect resolution, or steps to resolution, of the complex problems they may be experiencing. A consultant DBA's inability to offer a resolution or, more important, a path to resolution, will leave internal staff questioning the consultant DBA's value.

Of particular value to the consultant DBA is experience and knowledge in areas that internal DBAs may not encounter every day, but are of particular importance to mission-critical database applications that the organization is in the process of implementing. Such areas include designing the infrastructure for high availability, minimizing exposure to data loss in the event of failure, and designing complex data replication topologies. These areas of database applications are critical to get right, and organizations can justify bringing in an external resource to assist with them.

Communication

The consultant DBA communicates on many different levels within an organization. At one end of the scale, the consultant DBA speaks competently with in-house technical staff, and at the other end, she may speak to the upper management to understand the business drivers for their involvement. Effective communication is a must-have—without it, people probably won't feel they're getting value for money from the (usually costly) consultant resource.

Documentation

Along with effective communication, the consultant DBA requires exceptional documentation skills. Although all DBAs should keep good documentation, it's absolutely critical for the consultant DBA to do this. The consultant DBA is usually involved with an organization only for a short period of time to complete a specific project. Once that work has been completed, the consultant DBA steps out and the internal DBA team must handle the ongoing support and maintenance of the work.

Without effective documentation, the internal DBAs will find doing this support and maintenance very difficult and cumbersome. Certainly the company will feel it hasn't been delivered a maintainable solution, so the consultant DBA is unlikely to get repeat business from her clients.

Data Migration

The consultant DBA is often used in application migration projects as an experienced resource in migrating one data platform to another. As application migration doesn't happen very often within an organization, there isn't a lot of opportunity for in-house staff to become experienced in its intricacies. As a consultant DBA will frequently perform this kind of work, she may be brought into an organization either to offer advice to the internal DBAs or to subcontract out the data migration component.

How Does One Become a DBA?

Generally, most DBAs enter their profession as a developer or a junior DBA. Although movement through the roles is very much dependent on the requirements of the organization the DBA is working for at the time, a common career progression plan looks something like this:

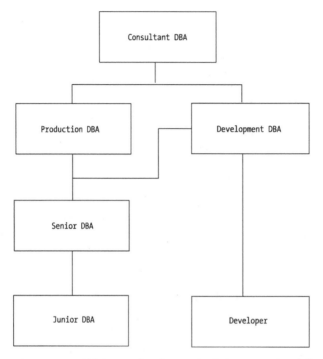

By beginning as either a junior DBA or a developer, the DBA gains the skills necessary to progress in his career into one of the different flavors of DBA role. In the following sections, we examine each of these starting points in more detail and work through a couple of career progression scenarios.

Junior DBA Progression

A person becomes a junior DBA for numerous reasons, including the following common situations:

❑ **Being forced into it:** An organization realizes that it has exposure in the area of database administration and chooses an existing employee to pick up this responsibility.

❑ **A person wants a change:** Someone may have worked as a system engineer or help desk support person and had some involvement with a particular database environment. That person may have enjoyed the database work he did in these positions and decided to pursue database administration as a new career direction.

Starting out in a junior DBA position doesn't necessarily require any previous database experience, although it helps! Instead, potential employers look for the following key qualities that are characteristics of a good DBA:

❑ **A methodical approach to problem solving:** Databases are an organization's centers of knowledge. No one wants a DBA taking a haphazard approach to attempting to resolve issues in these environments. Instead, management looks for a logical thinker who likes to understand why she's doing something before she goes and does it.

❑ **A cautious attitude:** Once again, as databases are the repositories of almost all of an organization's information, someone with a cautious attitude is wanted. Someone who expects the worst situation to occur and creates plans to resolve issues ahead of time will go far as a DBA.

❑ **The ability to communicate effectively:** The days of the DBA in the back room are gone, and this is especially true for junior DBAs. Part of the DBA role is interfacing with users and other IT professionals to answer their questions and help resolve any issues they may have.

In a nutshell, a person who likes order and process suits this type of DBA role well. We've heard the ideal DBA described as a "paranoid control freak." Although this seems harsh, it suits database environments well. Being paranoid, you would prepare mitigation procedures for all the disastrous situations you could imagine occurring. This is good, proactive DBA work. Being a control freak, you would want to know about and question everyone who is doing anything to the database. You'll put in control procedures so you always know what's going on and you'll be able to identify anyone doing anything undesirable to your databases. Again, excellent DBA skills!

If you don't consider yourself a methodical person and prefer more creative involvement with database environments, then perhaps you should investigate pursuing a development DBA career.

Developer Progression

A development DBA usually has one of two backgrounds. First, he may be a senior or production DBA who has gained development knowledge over time and has a desire to move out of the production role into a team designing and creating the database applications.

Second, a development DBA may have metamorphosed from a developer who has gained a great deal of skill, understanding, and interest in the database back-end. Typically, a developer who is skilled at writing SQL (database) code will take on the role of training other developers in optimal database development techniques. Over time, in response to queries from other developers, the developer learns more and more about the intricacies of the database platform. Once he has gained an understanding of the issues that can affect database performance, he uses this knowledge to improve the database design and architecture, and at the same time gain experience and skills in relational database design techniques.

Is DBA Certification Valuable?

The subject of qualifications and certifications is a contentious one. Many people feel that experience is the most important quality and certifications are pointless, whereas others believe the certification is a measure of experience. Personally, we feel that there's merit in certification when it's gained in conjunction with experience, but not instead of it.

Microsoft Certified Database Administrator

The **Microsoft Certified Database Administrator (MCDBA)** qualification is of most relevance to SQL Server DBA professionals. To achieve this qualification, you not only need to know how to administer SQL Server, but you also need to understand database design techniques. In addition, you need to pass core exams on the Windows platform. This is an interesting approach that Microsoft has taken, as most other database vendors avoid operating system topics within their certification program. However, this does make sense for several reasons:

- ❏ SQL Server doesn't try to replace or abstract the operating system (OS), but instead uses it for its benefit. Therefore, issues surrounding the OS, such as security and performance, directly impact the security and performance of SQL Server, and it's important for a DBA to understand such issues.

- ❏ It's common, especially in small- to medium-sized organizations, for the DBA to have responsibility for the entire server. This includes responsibility over the OS. Hence, it's particularly useful for most DBAs to have an understanding of OS administration issues.

- ❏ SQL Server isn't available on multiple platforms; it only runs Windows. Therefore, testing OS knowledge in conjunction with SQL Server is practical because there's only one platform to consider (as opposed to some database servers that run on UNIX, Linux, Windows, OS/400, VM/VSE, and so on).

To gain certification, you need a good understanding of topics in a number of different areas of administration and development, including

- ❏ Administration topics such as backup and restore

- ❏ Relational and dimensional database design

- ❏ SQL code development

To both junior and senior DBAs, the MCDBA certification has a number of benefits, which we outline in the following sections.

The Value of MCDBA Certification for Junior DBAs

Certification demonstrates a couple of things about junior DBAs. First, it shows that they're willing to put in the effort necessary to gain the certification. No matter what a DBA's experience level, certification requires substantial effort in studying, revising notes, and taking exams. The fact that a DBA has made the effort demonstrates that he is committed to his chosen career and is prepared to put in effort and make sacrifices to achieve his goals, which is impressive to any potential employer.

Second, certification demonstrates a minimum level of competency. A junior DBA won't gain a position as a senior DBA simply by undertaking the MCDBA qualification (or at least he shouldn't). However, to achieve this certification, a junior DBA establishes a base of knowledge. Having this base of knowledge makes gaining the practical experience easier, as the DBA already understands the concepts of what he is trying to do.

The Value of MCDBA Certification for Senior DBAs

For the senior DBA, MCDBA certification demonstrates knowledge in a broad range of areas. It's possible to have many years of experience but not a broad range of knowledge. This is especially true if a DBA has worked for one organization while gaining the bulk of her experience. As you've learned, DBAs have a broad role definition; however, a DBA is unlikely to gain all these skills within one organization. Gaining the MCDBA certification gives a DBA a basic understanding of most areas of the administration, design, and development of SQL Server.

Of course, the MCDBA certification may be required for a level of respect from staff that a senior DBA may manage. There's nothing worse than having junior staff who are more qualified than you!

How Long Does It Take to Get Certified?

Well, how long the certification process takes really does depend on your experience, knowledge, determination, and the amount of time available for achieving the certification. We've seen certification take a year or more for junior DBAs, and we've seen a senior DBA get the certification in 4 weeks.

As a recommendation, 6 months is probably average if you have experience as a DBA and a moderate workload. Our advice is that once you've decided to achieve MCDBA certification, don't stretch it out too long. If you have experience as a DBA, then we suggest that you study every night until you've covered all the material needed for the exam (at a guess, 2 to 3 weeks) and then take the exam immediately. We've seen some DBAs study half an hour per week over a period of 6 months and then take the exam. Often they fail because they've long forgotten what they learned early on in their study process.

> Although we don't recommend taking the MCDBA exam without experience, experience alone is often not quite enough to pass. Usually, you won't know and do everything within SQL Server on a daily basis, and you do learn new material while studying for the exam. We see this as being a good thing, as it helps improve your overall product knowledge.

MCDBA Exams

To gain MCDBA certification, you need to pass four exams. The following are the three core exams that you must pass to achieve MCDBA certification.

Exam	Description
Installing, Configuring, and Administering Microsoft SQL Server 2000 Enterprise Edition	Tests your ability to install, configure, and troubleshoot SQL Server 2000 Enterprise Edition.
Designing and Implementing Databases with Microsoft SQL Server 2000 Enterprise Edition	Tests your ability to design, implement, and optimize databases for SQL Server 2000 Enterprise Edition.
Installing, Configuring, and Administering Microsoft Windows 2000 Server	Tests your ability to install, configure, and troubleshoot Windows 2000 Server. This exam isn't exclusive to the MCDBA certification. It covers a wide range of operating system knowledge, not just what a DBA would be expected to have.

The final exam can be your choice from a selection of Microsoft exams. Some of the more common exams people choose to achieve the MCDBA certification are as follows.

Exam	Description
Designing and Implementing Data Warehouses with Microsoft SQL Server 7.0	Tests your ability to design and implement data warehouses on SQL Server 7.0 using OLAP and DTS.
Developing and Implementing Web-based Applications with Microsoft Visual Basic .NET	Tests your ability to build web applications using ASP.NET and the .NET Framework. This exam isn't exclusive to the MCDBA certification, so it covers a wider range of knowledge than what a DBA would be expected to have.
Implementing and Administering a Microsoft Windows 2000 Network Infrastructure	Tests your ability to install, manage, monitor, and configure Windows 2000 networking services, such as DHCP, RAS, DNS, and so on. This exam isn't exclusive to the MCDBA certification.

> You have several other elective exams to choose from. For more information on MCDBA certification requirements, visit the Microsoft training and certification website at www.microsoft.com/mcp.

Summary

In this chapter, we provided a set of definitions for a term used to describe a very broad range of functions within an organization: DBA. Our goal in writing this chapter was to help you understand the common variations of the DBA role and the commonly associated duties of each of these variations. That said, this chapter won't instruct you on what the duties of DBAs within your organization should be or attempt to be the cause of restructuring.

If we dig below the DBA title, we usually find that the duties of the DBA primarily fall into one of the five broad definitions, namely junior, senior, production, development, and consultant. Each of these roles has different characteristics and may appeal to different people for different reasons.

Now that we've covered what a DBA is, let's begin our journey of discovering the specifics of what a DBA does. This begins in Chapter 2 with installing SQL Server.

2

SQL Server Installation

We've covered the DBA's role in an organization and how you might become one. From this chapter onward, we're going to look at the practical, hands-on technical details that DBAs must deal with in their day-to-day life.

Before you can start administering SQL Server, however, you have to install it. In this chapter, we cover

- ❏ The various editions of SQL Server
- ❏ How to determine hardware requirements
- ❏ Preinstallation tasks
- ❏ The actual installation process
- ❏ How to upgrade SQL Server
- ❏ Postinstallation tasks

This is a relatively large chapter to launch into, but detailed technical knowledge isn't required to understand the chapter. Instead, the trick to a good SQL Server installation lies in knowing the best processes to use. Let's get started.

SQL Server 2000 Editions

SQL Server 2000 scales from the smallest of applications on personal or handheld devices right through to large enterprise applications on huge servers. To achieve this diverse application range, Microsoft has created a number of editions of SQL Server 2000, each designed and optimized for its intended application size and platform.

SQL Server 2000 is available in the following editions:

❑ SQL Server CE

❑ SQL Server Desktop (more commonly referred to as MSDE)

❑ SQL Server Personal

❑ SQL Server Standard

❑ SQL Server Developer

❑ SQL Server Enterprise

Applications can be deployed to an organization using any of these editions except the one just for development, which is aptly named SQL Server Developer.

Edition Differences

There aren't many differences between the editions, and most of the database applications that will run on one edition will also run on any other edition, except SQL Server CE. SQL Server CE is a bit of an anomaly, as it's quite a limited implementation of SQL Server whose goal is purely to support low-RAM handheld devices. We examine SQL Server CE and the other editions in more detail in the following sections.

SQL Server CE

As just mentioned, SQL Server CE is a cut-down version, in terms of functionality, that is designed to run on low-RAM devices, such as handheld PCs. It's also quite different from the other editions in its installation process. Instead of running a "setup" program, SQL Server CE is treated more like a component and is installed automatically when you install an application onto your Windows CE device that uses SQL Server CE.

SQL Server CE is also quite different from every other edition in that it isn't functionally equivalent to the other versions of SQL Server. For example, the following aren't available:

❑ Stored procedures

❑ User-defined functions

❑ Triggers

❑ Transaction log backups

SQL Server CE also has limited login and security features. However, SQL Server CE does provide a good query engine for use in mobile devices.

SQL Server Desktop

SQL Server Desktop Edition is often referred to as MSDE (it was actually called this in previous versions). This edition is designed to be a kind of runtime version for application developers who need a reliable repository for their application's data. SQL Server Desktop Edition isn't intended to be used with large mission-critical databases; instead, it should be used as a back-end database to one or more user desktop applications.

SQL Server Desktop Edition doesn't have a graphical tool such as Enterprise Manager supplied with it, so all of the database management functionality must be handled by the application that has been written to use it.

SQL Server Desktop Edition has scalability limits built in to prevent it from being used in unsuitable situations. It can't support individual databases in excess of 2GB in size, and a query workload governor has been built in. This query workload governor slows, exponentially, the performance of queries when more than five are being executed at the same time. This allows SQL Server Desktop Edition to be used when only a handful of users are accessing a small repository of information, but isn't suitable for large user bases or large amounts of data. In these situations, Microsoft requires you to use the Standard or Enterprise editions, which include administration tools that allow them to be managed by a DBA.

SQL Server Desktop Edition can be installed on the following operating systems:

- ❑ Windows 98 (without Windows Authentication)
- ❑ Windows Millennium Edition (without Windows Authentication)
- ❑ Windows NT Workstation
- ❑ Windows NT Server
- ❑ Windows NT Server Enterprise
- ❑ Windows 2000 Professional
- ❑ Windows 2000 Server
- ❑ Windows 2000 Advanced Server
- ❑ Windows 2000 Datacenter Server
- ❑ Windows XP Professional
- ❑ Windows XP Home Edition
- ❑ Windows Server 2003 Standard
- ❑ Windows Server 2003 Enterprise
- ❑ Windows Server 2003 Datacenter
- ❑ Windows Server 2003 Web

SQL Server Personal

SQL Server Personal Edition is provided with the graphical administration tools needed to effectively manage SQL Server. It also features the same query governor as SQL Server Desktop Edition, which makes SQL Server Personal Edition unsuitable for use with large groups of users.

SQL Server Personal Edition is best suited for applications on a user's PC. For example, a salesperson may have an order-entry application that runs on a laptop. With SQL Server Personal Edition, the laptop can be set up to synchronize with a central server and pull customer information into a SQL Server Personal Edition database. When the salesperson goes on the road, the customer information will be available to her, and any orders she entered while in the field can be uploaded into the central server for fulfillment.

Like SQL Server Desktop Edition, SQL Server Personal Edition can be installed on a wide range of operating systems:

❑   Windows 98 (without Windows Authentication)

❑   Windows Millennium Edition (without Windows Authentication)

❑   Windows NT Workstation

❑   Windows NT Server

❑   Windows NT Server Enterprise

❑   Windows 2000 Professional

❑   Windows 2000 Server

❑   Windows 2000 Advanced Server

❑   Windows 2000 Datacenter Server

❑   Windows XP Professional

❑   Windows XP Home Edition

❑   Windows Server 2003 Standard

❑   Windows Server 2003 Enterprise

❑   Windows Server 2003 Datacenter

❑   Windows Server 2003 Web

> **You can't buy SQL Server Personal Edition on its own. You must own a copy of SQL Server Standard Edition or SQL Server Enterprise Edition to be licensed for SQL Server Personal Edition.**

SQL Server Standard

SQL Server Standard Edition is the first of the editions that's suitable for databases that have large volumes of data and numbers of concurrent users. SQL Server Standard Edition doesn't have any of the size or concurrent request restrictions of the editions we've described so far. In fact, SQL Server Standard Edition will scale to support several hundreds of gigabytes of data or more, and many hundreds of concurrent users.

SQL Server Standard Edition runs on only one of the following server operating systems:

- Windows NT Server
- Windows NT Server Enterprise
- Windows 2000 Server
- Windows 2000 Advanced Server
- Windows 2000 Datacenter Server
- Windows Server 2003 Standard
- Windows Server 2003 Enterprise
- Windows Server 2003 Datacenter
- Windows Server 2003 Web

Because Enterprise Edition is more expensive than Standard Edition, you should consider Standard Edition as the default edition of SQL Server unless you require some of the features that are only supported in Enterprise Edition (we look at this edition in more detail in the "SQL Server Enterprise" section).

SQL Server Developer

SQL Server Developer Edition includes almost exactly the same functionality as SQL Server Enterprise Edition, except it will run on workstation operating systems, not just server operating systems. More specifically, it will run on

- Windows 98
- Windows NT Workstation
- Windows NT Server
- Windows NT Server Enterprise
- Windows 2000 Professional
- Windows 2000 Server
- Windows 2000 Advanced Server

- ❑ Windows 2000 Datacenter Server

- ❑ Windows XP Professional

- ❑ Windows XP Home Edition

- ❑ Windows Server 2003 Standard

- ❑ Windows Server 2003 Enterprise

- ❑ Windows Server 2003 Datacenter

- ❑ Windows Server 2003 Web

You're allowed to use it for only one purpose: development. The licensing agreement associated with SQL Server Developer Edition doesn't permit databases to be deployed in a production fashion for use by your organization's users. For this, you'll need either Standard Edition or Enterprise Edition.

SQL Server Enterprise

As mentioned earlier, SQL Server Enterprise Edition is almost the same as SQL Server Standard Edition, and it runs on only the following server operating systems:

- ❑ Windows NT Server

- ❑ Windows NT Server Enterprise

- ❑ Windows 2000 Server

- ❑ Windows 2000 Advanced Server

- ❑ Windows 2000 Datacenter Server

- ❑ Windows Server 2003 Standard

- ❑ Windows Server 2003 Enterprise

- ❑ Windows Server 2003 Datacenter

- ❑ Windows Server 2003 Web

The difference is that Enterprise Edition contains some advanced functionality that isn't available with Standard Edition. We should note that this functionality specifically relates to the implementation of SQL Server, such as scalability and availability, not to the functionality provided by SQL Server to applications via T-SQL code. Database applications that run using SQL Server Enterprise Edition will also run with SQL Server Standard Edition and vice versa. The main additional features of the extra "implementation" functionality provided by SQL Server Enterprise Edition are as follows:

- ❑ **Support for hardware clusters:** Hardware clusters are multiple servers (up to four) that share a common disk array allowing for failover in the event of failure of one of the servers.

❑ **Native log shipping:** Log shipping copies the transaction log backups from one server to another and restores them on a "standby" database.

❑ **Federated servers:** Federated servers are two or more servers that have parts of a database divided between them. Users access the database via one of the servers, but each of the servers in the federation may be called on to process part of the users' query.

❑ **Parallelism with DBCC operations and parallelism with index creation:** Parallelism is the splitting of the workload of a single command across multiple CPUs to allow the command to complete more quickly.

If you don't need these features (you probably won't unless you're implementing a particularly large or highly available database), you should stick with Standard Edition.

> **Most installations require only the functionality provided by SQL Server Standard Edition. Carefully evaluate whether you require Enterprise Edition functionality before you make your decision, as the cost difference can be great.**

Migration Between Editions

One of the major benefits to developers who use SQL Server is that every edition, except SQL Server CE, provides the same functionality to the developer. If you develop a database on SQL Server Developer Edition, it will function on SQL Server Standard Edition and SQL Server Enterprise Edition, and vice versa. The differences in functionality in the editions aren't directly exposed to developers. These functionality differences (overall scalability, clustering support, log shipping, and high-performance index rebuilds) won't impact a particular database application.
Therefore, migration between editions is very straightforward. You can use any of the techniques we discuss later when migrating from SQL Server 7.0 to SQL Server 2000. Migration alone doesn't cause any major changes in hardware requirements, which we discuss next.

Hardware Requirements

As you've seen, a wide range of SQL Server editions is available, with each edition addressing a particular need in terms of the size and usage requirements of the databases that it supports. It's assumed that the Desktop, Personal, and Developer editions will run on the users' PCs due to the size and scalability limitations imposed on these versions.

SQL Server CE Edition requires Windows CE to run, and it will only run on a hardware device that supports this operating system—for example, the Pocket PC. For the rest of this chapter, we concentrate only on SQL Server Standard Edition and SQL Server Enterprise Edition.

Minimum Requirements

The minimum hardware requirements for the SQL Server editions are as follows:

Hardware	Minimum Requirements
CPU Intel	166 MHz (all editions)
Memory	Enterprise, Standard, and Developer editions: 64MB Desktop and Personal editions: 64MB on Windows 2000 and Windows XP; 32MB on other operating systems
Hard disk space	From 95MB to 270MB; 250MB for a typical installation

However, these minimum requirements don't really mean a lot, as it's likely that you'll require more resources than these baseline specifications.

So, what do you need to consider when establishing your hardware requirements?

Few Servers vs. Many Servers

Before you can effectively predict the hardware requirements of your SQL Server installation, you need to make a fundamental decision about the way in which you deploy SQL Server in your environment. There are two schools of thought on this issue: big hardware servers supporting many databases or many hardware servers, with each supporting a few databases. Each approach is valid, but each has its own set of benefits and disadvantages that you need to examine.

Many Hardware Servers, Few Databases

Many hardware servers with few databases is a popular way of deploying SQL Server for a number of reasons. A major reason is the way SQL Server has been introduced into an organization. Microsoft has made progress into businesses with SQL Server, but it has been a gradual process. Very few organizations have made the decision to convert all their applications from their current platforms to SQL Server overnight. Instead, SQL Server has made headway by being the database of choice for many application vendors. The introduction of these applications within organizations has caused SQL Server to become so prevalent.

A vendor may sell an application to an organization that requires a dedicated server to run on and may use SQL Server as its back-end. Therefore, because there isn't a centralized database server, it makes sense to install SQL Server and the database on the same server as the application.

Large organizations can use many applications, so over time a number of similar applications are introduced, leading to a proliferation of SQL Server throughout the corporate infrastructure. At some later time, an organization may take a step back and realize it may have a large number of SQL Server installations, all servicing different applications, and no common policy on disaster recovery or security among them. When this happens, the organization must consider if continuing down this path is a better approach than consolidating the databases on a smaller number of dedicated servers.

Few Hardware Servers, Many Databases

Few servers with a large number of databases is in line with the traditional approach of implementing enterprise database applications. Building high-performing, well-managed, well-monitored, and highly secure servers for the purpose of supporting mission-critical applications isn't so common for those with a purely PC background. For those who have worked with mainframe or mini computers previously, this model is well understood.

Typically, one or two centralized servers are installed with significant hardware redundancy and often server redundancy to provide a high level of availability. These servers are also often multiprocessor with many gigabytes of memory, meaning that they're highly scalable in terms of the number of users that they support.

Pros and Cons of Each Model

Each of the approaches described has advantages and disadvantages that you should consider before deciding on an approach for your deployment of SQL Server. The deployment approach you take needs to be well considered because it will greatly impact the cost and quality of your database environment.

The reduction in administration effort when moving from many to few servers is debatable. It only occurs when you're comparing well-managed servers with well-managed servers. It's common for organizations that embrace the "many servers, few databases" approach to SQL Server deployment to have a number of SQL Servers in production that aren't well looked after. Security, recoverability, and availability may not be much of a concern, so these servers may be deployed and forgotten about until something goes wrong. Is this a true reduction in administrative effort? Maybe, but at what cost? In contrast, a single large server that is housing a number of databases must be well managed; otherwise, all the databases, including those that contain essential information, are exposed. On the other hand, some organizations take all of their corporate information seriously and manage all the servers they deploy in production. In this situation, administration effort will be increased over that of a single server.

Deploying many servers with few databases usually doesn't make the best use of the available hardware resources within an organization. More often than not, a lot of the available hardware resource will be underutilized on one server, whereas on another there may not be enough hardware resources available, resulting in server bottlenecks.

An extreme example of this was a single database server observed recently that had a 20MB SQL Server database on a SQL Server that had 36GB of disk space and 4GB of RAM sitting available. It turns out that the reason this came about was because it was "bundled" in the solution delivered by a third-party vendor. Other database servers within that organization were highly loaded and struggling to meet user demand. Although hardware is cheap, pooling it into a centralized server allows it to be used more effectively.

Under the "many servers, few databases" model, these servers are deployed in stand-alone configurations without using advanced disaster-recovery mechanisms, such as clustering (a high-availability option) or log shipping (an option to automatically maintain an up-to-date copy of a database on a different server). As these features are only available in SQL Server Enterprise Edition, the cost of deployment could be very high in relation to the benefit obtained from doing so. However, in the "few servers, many databases" model, the licensing cost is only incurred a couple of times and the benefit is shared between all of the databases, making it a potentially more cost-effective option.

One server with many databases leads to a single point of failure. Loss of the server will also affect many applications and potentially hundreds of users. Even if the server is clustered, a failure will result in a few minutes of outage. If the server is clustered, the failure of the shared components, such as an external disk resource, can still bring down the entire system. Measures can be taken to mitigate this, such as setting up a remote log shipped server. However, once again, this causes an increase in cost.

If you're deploying many servers for the purpose of supporting a single database application, you can locate the server close to the users. For example, if you're deploying a server to support an application used by a single group of users in a remote office, the server could be located at the remote office to reduce the WAN bandwidth required between the remote office and the central office. Deploying a centralized server, on the other hand, requires the server to be located at some place that's accessible to users of all the various databases. This may mean you need WAN links to connect remote locations to the core database; these WAN links introduce cost and reliability issues you must also consider.

> **Accessing a database over a WAN link doesn't necessarily mean that performance will be poor. Some users are able to access databases hundreds of miles away with acceptable performance. However, the performance usually depends on how much you're willing to pay your telecommunications provider for bandwidth.**

What Happens in the Real World?

The most successful database environments we've been involved with don't exclusively select one of the approaches, but use a combination of the two to best meet the needs to their organizations.

Within any organization there will be some database applications that are absolutely mission critical and must be secure, available, and recoverable. There are other database applications for which security doesn't really matter or for which users aren't going to be too concerned if they can't use the applications for a few hours if the databases are down for maintenance. It makes sense, then, to have a mixed environment in which you don't load up your mission-critical servers with databases that don't matter or waste time locking management down on databases for which security isn't a concern.

By centralizing your mission-critical databases, you're gaining the increased availability, management, and use of hardware resources required by such databases. By distributing your noncritical databases across other servers, you make these more easily accessible to users without incurring the overhead of the stringent management that is needed for the critical databases.

Hardware Redundancy

Everything can break. Be it a $5 cable or a $5,000 disk array controller, no equipment remains perfect forever. Some things, such as disks and power supplies, fail more often than others. We could try and complain about it to the hardware vendors, but we doubt we would get far as it's just one of the facts of life that those in this industry must face. Emphasis has shifted from trying to prevent things from breaking to building in redundancy–"installed spare parts"–for when things do fail.

With a server, the more installed spare parts you have, the better. The latest technological developments include things such as hot-swappable redundant memory banks, in which if one RAM module fails, the server keeps going and you simply pull the failed module out, toss it, and plug in a new one. With server redundancy, you must weigh the risk against the cost and the cost against your budget. The minimum hardware redundancy you should consider if implementing a server into a production environment is as follows:

❑ **Redundant disks:** These are an absolute must. Disks are probably the most common component to fail. Because they're so cheap, don't let the failure of a single disk bring down your entire server. Use a redundant array of independent disks (RAID) controller to build a fault-tolerant array of disks that will survive at least a single disk failing.

❑ **Power supplies:** These are probably the second most common component to fail. Power supplies are also cheap if the server supports redundant power supplies, so it makes sense to include them in your server specification. If you have redundant power supplies, you would power each from separate uninterruptible power supplies (UPSs), which in turn are powered from separate power sources to help combat mains failure.

❑ **Network cards:** The cards themselves aren't prone to failure; rather, failure on the network itself can occur. This requires the necessary LAN infrastructure to support the cards, but most organizations' networks now have redundant LAN networks that allow for network failover in the event of failure of a core network component, such as a router or switch.

Beyond this level of redundancy, it really depends on how critical your business considers the databases that you'll install on the server. If, in fact, the databases must not be unavailable for more than a few minutes at a time, you'll have to consider introducing redundant servers into the configuration. There are two methods that you can use to do this:

❑ **Clustering** involves two servers running a specialized operating system (Windows 2000 Advanced Server or Windows 2000 Datacenter Server) connected to a set of shared disks. The database lives on the shared disks with one server owning the disks at one time and providing access to the databases. The shared disks allow each of the servers to access the database's files. If the server owning the disks was to fail, then the other server would gain ownership of the shared disks and begin providing access to those databases. These servers hide behind a virtual server name that moves from server to server with the disks, so the clients don't need to know the actual server they're connecting to. This requires specialized hardware to install, skilled administration staff to manage, and SQL Server Enterprise Edition. The servers must also be located near each other (usually they have to be almost side by side when using disks connected by copper cable).

❑ **Log shipping** is a great way to provide server redundancy in your database environment. Log shipping involves taking a backup of the transactions that have occurred in a database since the last transaction backup, copying that backup across the network to another server, and restoring the backup on a duplicate copy of the database. If failure of the primary server were to occur, then the secondary server could be brought online as the primary server, and little in the way of data loss or downtime would be incurred.

> **Clustering and log shipping aren't mutually exclusive. As we've explained, they serve different purposes, but often they may be used together.**

Another common method of providing server redundancy is replication, which we discuss in Chapter 9.

> **Clustering and log shipping are advanced topics and are outside the scope of this book. However, Microsoft has some very good resources accessible from the SQL Server website at www.microsoft.com/sql.**

Backups

It's good to have databases located on a server for use by clients within your organization. When things go wrong, however, you need to have a copy of those databases located away from the server so that you can restore them to a new location if need be.

Backups are absolutely critical to any production SQL Server environment, and due to this level of importance we dedicate an entire chapter, Chapter 8, to this subject. When planning your hardware configuration, you need to consider the hardware requirements of your backup scheme. When backing up a SQL Server database, you can choose either to back up directly from SQL Server to disk or tape (you can't back up directly to CD or DVD, but you can use your burning software to copy a disk-based backup to these media).

We get into the pros and cons of each method later, but for now let's consider what has become the best-practice approach for performing SQL Server backups. Because disks are very cheap now, and disk performance can be many times greater than that of tape, you should always purchase additional disks for the purpose of backing up your database. You still need a tape drive to back up the files from disk, but by having the disk available for backing up your databases, you can greatly decrease the backup and restoration times. The process of backing up a SQL Server database involves the following:

❑   SQL Server backs up each database to an individual disk file.

❑   Once a day (or more), tape backups back up the disk files to tape.

To restore the database, the process is as follows:

❑   If the backup files are still on disk, then restore the SQL Server database directly from the backup file.

❑   If the backup files aren't still located on disk, first restore the backup files from tape to disk. Once the files are restored, restore the SQL Server database from the backup file.

If you're still unsure about how to perform backups, we explain the process in full in Chapter 8.

Installation

Before you can go on to become a SQL Server expert, you need to install SQL Server on your computer. Ideally, for the purpose of running the examples in this book, you'll have two computers. One should be running Windows 2000 Server, on which you can install SQL Server 2000 Standard Edition, and the other should be running Windows 2000 Professional (or Windows XP), on which you can install the client tools and connectivity components. If this much hardware is hard to come by, you can install SQL Server 2000 Personal on a computer running a desktop operating system, and most of the examples shown in this book will still be valid.

> **If you don't have a copy of Microsoft SQL Server, you can download an evaluation edition from the Microsoft SQL Server website, www.microsoft.com/sql. This edition has almost all the features of SQL Server Standard Edition, and it will install on Windows 2000 Professional, Windows NT Workstation, and Windows XP.**

Preinstallation Tasks

Although the installation of SQL Server is relatively straightforward, you can make it even easier by considering a few of the following options beforehand and carrying out a small number of preparation tasks.

Service Accounts

SQL Server runs as a service (a software component that runs in the background without a user interface), and as a service it will run in the security context of the Windows user that has been associated with it. By default, SQL Server and the SQL Server Agent services run under the special system account called local system. This may be fine for an installation of a Desktop, Developer, or Personal edition that's being used locally, but for a SQL Server edition that's being used in a multiserver environment, the services should be run under a Windows domain account. This enables you to effectively assign permissions to allow SQL Server to access network resources, and it's a requirement for SQL Mail, which we'll get to shortly.

> *SQL Server Agent is responsible for running scheduled tasks against the SQL Server database engine, which we cover in Chapter 5.*

You should name the service account something like SQLServerService; however, your organization may already have a naming standard for service accounts. If you're creating this account at your workplace on a corporate network, you should discuss this first with your network administrators. Ideally, you should try all the examples from this book (at first, at least) in an isolated test environment.

> **When you decide on a name for the account, make sure you assign a very strong password. You'll have to enter this password only a few times during the installation and configuration of SQL Server, so don't get lazy and assign a weak password to save precious keystrokes. This service account will be able to gain full access to all databases hosted on SQL Server, so we suggest you have a password of at least 12 characters with a mixture of alpha, numeric, and special characters.**

You can choose to run the SQL Server and SQL Server Agent services under different service accounts. SQL Server Agent is responsible for running scheduled tasks against the SQL Server database engine (see Chapter 5 for more information on this). Most installations, for simplicity, use the same Windows account for both the SQL Server and SQL Server Agent services. Unless you have some particularly high security requirements, or you need the Agent service to run under a separate account for a special reason, we recommend that you run these services under the same Windows account because it eases your administration effort.

You can create separate Windows users accounts for each SQL Server you're installing onto your network, but this gets a bit unwieldy over time. A more common approach is to create a Windows user account and use this for all, or most, of your installations of SQL Server. This is highly recommended if your servers are communicating with each other using log shipping, replication, and so on. Although this does decrease administration effort, it also reduces security slightly because, if the password of the service account is breached, access to all the SQL Servers can be gained.

Account Privileges

The Windows user account that you set up for running the SQL Server services is a standard Windows account. It needs some custom permissions and account privileges to function correctly.

The privileges you need to assign to the service are as follows:

❑ Member of the local Administrators group of the server onto which you're installing SQL Server

❑ The Log on as a service privilege

❑ The Act as part of the operating system privilege

❑ The Replace a process level token privilege

In addition, you should set the Password never expires option so the service account won't expire if the password isn't changed regularly. Failure to set this option could result in the SQL Server service failing to start once the Windows user account password has expired.

Try It Out: Setting Up a Windows User Account

For this demonstration, you're going to create a local Windows user account to run the SQL Service under. These instructions are for a Windows 2000 Server computer, but you may choose to use Windows 2000 Professional or Windows XP.

1. Log into the computer on which you want to install SQL Server as a user with administrative privileges.

2. Open the Computer Management tool. This is available under the Settings | Control Panel | Administrative Tools program group on the Start menu.

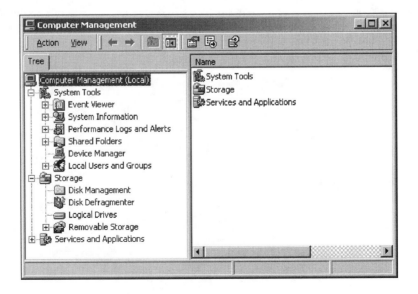

3. Drill down to the Local Users and Groups group and select the Users node. Right-click and select New User. Enter SQLServerService as the username and enter 358tgh@bay09 (or similar) as the password. As this is an example, you may want to enter a simpler password. You'll need this password later in the book, so make sure you remember what you entered here (if you forget this password, you'll have to reset it). Uncheck the User must change password at next logon check box, and check the Password never expires check box. Click Create to add this user, and then click Close to close the creation dialog box.

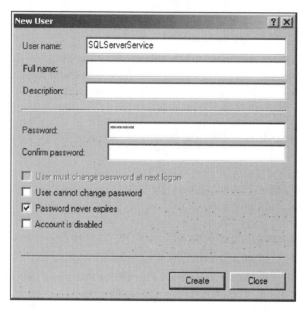

4. Once the Windows service account has been created, you need to add this account as a member of the Administrators group. Right-click the newly created SQLServerService account and select the Member Of tab in the Properties dialog box. Click Add and select the Administrators group. Click Add and then click OK.

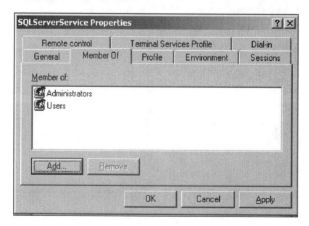

5. Now that you've created the user and set the group membership, you need to assign the appropriate privileges to this account. To do this, you need to open the Local Security Policy tool, which you can find in the Control Panel | Administrative Tools program group on the Start menu.

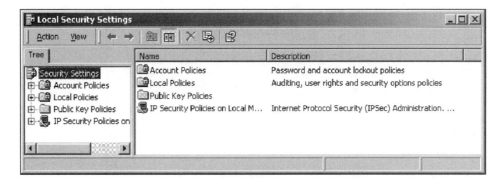

6. Drill down into the Local Policies group, and select the User Rights Assignment node.

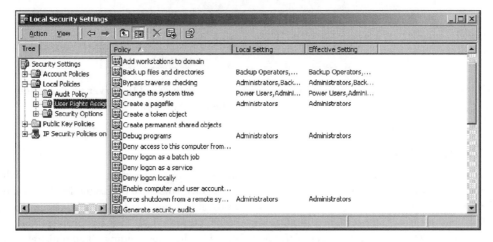

Once you've clicked this node, you'll see a list of user rights appear in the right pane. Ensure that either the SQLServerService user or the Administrators group has been granted permission to each of the following user rights:

❑   The Log on as a service privilege: This allows your SQL Server service account to be used by a service (in this case, the SQL Server service) to authenticate with Windows and acquire server and network permissions.

❑   The Act as part of the operating system privilege

❑   The Replace a process level token privilege

If neither the SQLServerService user nor the Administrators group has been granted permission, then add the correct permission. Select the user right, right-click, and select Security. Click Add and then select the SQLServerService user from the list of Windows accounts. Click OK twice to confirm the changes made to the user right assignment.

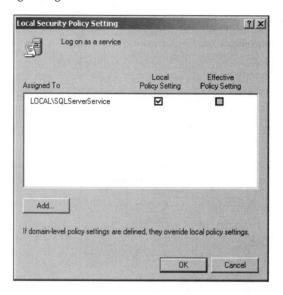

The SQLServerService user account is now ready for use with the SQL Server services. You still have several other tasks to take care of before you begin the installation procedure.

SQLAgentMail

To be able to alert the administrator of critical errors that have occurred in SQL Server or of the failure of a scheduled job to complete successfully, you must configure SQLAgentMail. If you're familiar with earlier versions of SQL Server, you'll probably know this functionality as just "SQL Mail," but this has changed slightly in SQL Server 2000 because SQL Mail has been split into two components. These components are SQLAgentMail, which handles sending all administrative alerts and job failure notifications, and SQL Mail, which sends e-mail when instructed to do so from an application or script running the xp_sendmail T-SQL command.

As you're going to be running both your SQL Agent and SQL Server services under the same Windows user account, you can configure one mail profile for use by both of these services. The first step is to install Outlook 2000 (the normal version of Outlook that people use for their desktop) on the server on which SQL Server is to be installed.

Try It Out: Adding a SQL Mail E-mail Account

To carry out this demonstration, you'll require a server installed within a Windows domain that has a Microsoft Exchange mail server.

Installing Outlook 2000

Installing Outlook 2000 is pretty straightforward, and we don't delve into too much detail here other than to advise you to keep the installation to core components because you don't need any of the extra functionality provided by Office 2000 (in fact, you only need to purchase a copy of Outlook 2000 to use with SQL Server–you don't need to purchase the full Office 2000 suite).

> **SQL Mail and SQLAgentMail work best with Microsoft Outlook 2000 and Microsoft Exchange 5.5 or greater. Outlook 98 and earlier versions don't work well with SQL Server 2000.**

Before you begin the installation, log in to your server with a user that has administrative rights on your computer, as these rights are needed to install the software. The SQLServerService user would be ideal because you'll need to be logged in as this user shortly. Once you've logged in, proceed to install Outlook 2000.

Creating an Exchange Mailbox

Ask your company's Microsoft Exchange administrator to create a mailbox that is associated with the account you created earlier: the SQLServerService user. Nothing fancy is needed here–just a standard Exchange mailbox.

> **Creating an Exchange mailbox isn't usually the responsibility of a SQL Server DBA. Typically, you'll ask your company's network administrator or help-desk staff to set this up for the account you specify. You can't be an expert in everything!**

Creating a Mail Profile

Once the mailbox has been created, log in to the console of the server onto which SQL Server 2000 is to be installed using the SQLServerService account. Start Outlook 2000. Outlook will go through its setup processes and eventually ask you if you want to operate Outlook 2000 in corporate mode or Internet mode. Make sure you select corporate mode, as SQL Mail doesn't support anything else.

Continue setting up Outlook 2000 and, when prompted, enter the information necessary to connect with your Exchange server.

Testing Mail Connectivity

Once you've configured Outlook 2000, you should test out its capability to send and receive mail. The best way to test this is to follow these steps:

❑ Log in as the SQLServerService account.

❑ Start Outlook 2000.

❑ Compose a new e-mail to a known address.

If the e-mail is successfully sent and you don't receive any warnings, error messages, or dialog boxes during this process, you can be pretty confident the mail profile you've configured will work with the SQL Server mail components. If you do have problems, review your configuration and consult with your Exchange administrator. Don't proceed to set up SQL Server until you can carry out the test without incident.

Deciding on Licensing Mode

The licensing mode relates to how you pay for SQL Server and how you pay for users who are connecting to SQL Server. It's important to have this determined in advance, because once you set this, you can't change it easily. The following sections describe the available licensing options.

Per Processor Licensing

When you license SQL Server using the Per Processor model, you have to pay a licensing fee for every CPU in the server onto which you'll be installing SQL Server. This licensing model allows for an unlimited number of clients to connect to SQL Server without any additional costs involved with the purchase of client access licenses (CALs).

If your SQL Server is being used to support an Internet application, such as a website, you must license it using the Per Processor model. Obviously, you can't buy a CAL for every potential user on the Internet, so this is the only option that's available.

Per Seat Licensing

Per Seat licensing requires you to pay a fee for the server, which is lower than with Per Processor licensing, and then purchase a CAL for every user that will be connecting to SQL Server. This is more suited to a corporate environment when you have a known number of users and potentially a large number of SQL Servers. This licensing model works well when you have many SQL Servers, because you only need to buy a CAL once for a user, after which the user can access any number of SQL Server installations.

If you have a middle-tier application (such as a web application), and this in turn communicates with SQL Server, it may be possible that you have only a small number of database connections, whereas your web application may be supporting a large number of users. This is called multiplexing, and according to current Microsoft licensing information, you still need to purchase a license for every device that indirectly accesses information within SQL Server (unless you're using the Per Processor license mode).

The best advice we can offer when you're deciding which licensing model to select is to talk to Microsoft or a Microsoft Certified Partner. Because licensing involves five- and often six-figures, it's worth spending the extra time with a specialist licensing consultant who can analyze your exact requirements and determine the most appropriate licensing option available. After all, do you want to be the person in your organization who spent extra money by making a poor licensing decision?

> Licensing can be complex and costly. Talk to an expert and you may save time and money. Microsoft has some good information available on their website at www.microsoft.com/licensing/.
>
> Alternatively, you can find a Microsoft Certified Partner in your area by visiting http://mcspreferral.microsoft.com/.

Default or Named Instance?

Once you've decided the most appropriate licensing model for your environment, you need to decide if you want a default instance or a named instance.

Instance Overview

We know what you're probably thinking: What's an instance? An **instance** is a complete and independent installation of SQL Server on a given server. What makes instances unique in SQL Server 2000 is that one default instance and any number (up to 16) of named instances can be installed on a single server. Apart from the management tools and client connectivity components that are shared between instances, each instance effectively stands alone. Each instance has its own security, can be started and stopped independently, and can even be service-packed independent of other instances on the same server.

If you're familiar with previous versions of SQL Server, the concept of the default instance won't be new to you. A **default instance** is the first instance you install (if no other installation of SQL Server exists, the situation we look at next), and to access this default instance, clients simply specify the name of the server (for example, MYSERVER). A named instance, on the other hand, has a second naming component that specifies the name of the instance, and it must be unique between instances on a given server. Clients connecting to a named instance must specify the instance name following the server name (for example, MYSERVER\Instance1).

> An instance of SQL Server is an independent installation of SQL Server. One or more instances can exist on one physical server. The first installation of SQL Server you carry out should be a default instance. Any additional installations of SQL Server on that physical server will be named instances.

Instance Interoperability with Previous Versions

If you're installing SQL Server 2000 onto a server with SQL Server 7.0 or SQL Server 6.5, you don't have to upgrade these existing versions. Instances didn't exist in earlier versions, but you can consider an installation of a previous version as the default instance for that server. Instead of upgrading this existing default instance, you can choose to install SQL Server 2000 as a named instance, thereby leaving the existing version untouched. Users can choose to access either the earlier version simply by specifying the server name or the new SQL Server 2000 instance by specifying the server name and instance name.

When SQL Server 2000 is installed in this way, it can coexist with either SQL Server 6.5 or SQL Server 7.0. As SQL Server 6.5 and SQL Server 7.0 couldn't both exist and be active on a single server, only one of these can be active on a server at a time. By using the SQL Server Switch Upgrade utility to interchange between SQL Server 6.5 and SQL Server 7.0, it's possible to configure a server to be running all three versions (SQL Server 6.5, 7.0, and 2000) with either 6.5 or 7.0 running concurrently with the 2000 named instance.

> **Installing SQL Server 6.5, 7.0, and 2000 on the same server is relatively straightforward. Essentially, you must install SQL Server 6.5 first, then you install SQL Server 7.0 (choosing to retain the existing installation of SQL Server 6.5), and finally you install a named instance of SQL Server 2000.**

One Instance, Many Databases vs. Many Instances, Few Databases

The fact that you can install multiple instances provokes the question of whether to install a single instance with many databases or many instances with few databases. As each instance carries the overhead of the binary execution of SQL Server, it's recommended that you install only one instance and create all your databases within this instance if possible.

There's no hard limit to the number of instances of SQL Server installable on a single server. However, for practical reasons you wouldn't want to go above half a dozen instances, because many of the server resources get consumed simply in the "running" of the instance rather than being available for use in accessing your databases. In addition, Microsoft has stated it will only support 12 instances or fewer.

There may be some valid reasons for creating multiple instances and incurring this additional overhead, including

- ❑ **You are a hosting provider, and you want to delegate administration tasks to your clients.** By installing SQL Server 2000 with an instance per client, you can delegate administration rights only on the specific client's instance.

- ❑ **You have databases with different resource requirements.** If you have a multiple-CPU box and you want to divide the resources unevenly between databases, you can only do this by installing multiple instances. Once the instances are installed, you can choose to assign three CPUs to one instance and only one CPU to another instance, for example. This may be useful if you have a database application that carries out a large number of calculations in which processing time isn't too important. By creating this database in an instance that only has access to a single CPU, you won't be preventing other processes in other instances from gaining access to the remaining CPU resources.

- ❑ **You have one test server, but you require multiple test environments.** Creating additional instances allows you to have multiple independent SQL Server environments that don't affect each other during testing (other than impacting the server performance).

Because these requirements are usually valid for only a small number of implementations, most installations have a single default instance.

> **A single instance with multiple databases is the most common scenario. Unless you have a particular, special requirement, we advise you to go with this approach.**

Deciding on File Locations

Before you install SQL Server, you have to decide where you intend the various files to be placed. In particular, you have to decide on homes for the following files:

❑ SQL Server binary files

❑ System databases

❑ The TempDB database

❑ User data files

❑ User log files

You don't necessarily have to find different disks for each of the previously listed components. In fact, you could install these all on the one drive partition, although this isn't advisable for production applications. If you locate your database data and log files on the same disk, and if you lose that disk (due to hardware failure), you'll lose any database changes that have taken place since the last backup. If you separate these, you may be able to recover some information (see Chapter 8 for more information). The other reason you want to separate these files onto multiple disks is performance. Often, data is being read from the data files at the same time data may be in the process of being written to the log files. If these two types of workloads are occurring on the same disk, your application may suffer from I/O contention reducing the performance on each operation. Separating the workloads to separate disks allows each operation to run concurrently with the other without impacting its I/O throughput. So separation of the files is done for two reasons: performance and disaster recovery.

Deciding on Authentication Mode

SQL Server supports two modes of authenticating people who are trying to access information contained within a SQL Server database. The mode that you choose determines how these users can log in to SQL Server and the administration that goes with this.

We deal with more specific information about the security modes in Chapter 6. In this section, we briefly discuss each of the security modes:

❑ Windows Authentication Mode

❑ Mixed Mode

The decision you make during installation isn't binding, so if you decide you want a different setting later, you can change it after installation.

Windows Authentication Mode

When you're using Windows Authentication Mode, SQL Server checks what Windows user account the person connecting across the network has logged into the Windows domain with. If that Windows user account has been granted the right to log in, or if it is a member of a Windows group that has been granted the right to log in, then the user is authenticated and allowed to connect to SQL Server. This is the only way users can authenticate under this mode.

Mixed Mode

Windows Authentication Mode is fully supported under the Mixed Mode, but when you use this mode SQL Server logins can also be created. SQL Server logins have nothing to do with Windows domain authentication; instead, the administrator creates a username and password within SQL Server itself. Users connecting to SQL Server must supply the username and password. If the username and password are valid, then the user is authenticated and allowed to access SQL Server.

Deciding Which Authentication Mode to Use

The first thing you have to consider when you decide the authentication mode is what mode the connecting applications support. Some older or poorly written applications only support SQL Server Authentication. If you're in doubt about the application's authentication capabilities, talk to the application vendor. If you do require SQL Server Authentication, then you'll have to use Mixed Mode, even if only one application out of many doesn't support the Windows Authentication Mode.

If all of the applications that will be connecting to your database server support Windows Authentication Mode, or both Windows Authentication Mode and Mixed Mode, then you have a bit more freedom. Windows Authentication Mode provides the following benefits:

❑ More secure than SQL Server Authentication

❑ Supports password aging

❑ Supports account lockout

❑ Supports single sign-on

You should always try and use only the Windows Authentication Mode if possible. If you have non-Windows clients or you would like to manage users within the database server (not a good idea!), then use Mixed Mode.

> **For more information on authentication modes, see Chapter 6.**

Deciding on Collation Requirements

A **collation** is an option you set that determines how character information is retained and interpreted within a database. Specifically, the collation affects the following:

❑ **The type of characters that SQL Server can store:** Western, Asian, and so on.

❑ **The way characters will be searched:** For example, if (A=a=À) or if (A != a != À !) is determined by a collation setting.

❑ **The way characters will be ordered:** Collations can also affect how character information is ordered. For example, if the collation uses a dictionary order, then you would expect the results of an ordered query to follow dictionary order, such as A, B, G, L, and so on. However, if the collation uses a binary ordering method, then the results are sorted according to the binary representation of each character.

There are many different collations, and many of these exist to support international character data.

Collations have been the bane of the DBA's life with previous versions of SQL Server. Formerly known as "sort orders" and "code pages," collations used to be a serverwide setting that all databases had to use. If one database used a different setting than another, it had to be installed on a different SQL Server.

Fortunately, this is no longer the case. Databases with different collation settings can now share a single installation of SQL Server. It's still important to choose the correct collation during setup, as this determines the collation used for the system databases and the default collation for user databases that you may create.

Installation

Now that you have all the background information you need to install SQL Server 2000, you can begin the installation process. For this demonstration, you'll install a named instance of SQL Server 2000 Standard Edition on Windows 2000 Advanced Server.

You'll use the following options for this installation.

Instance Name	SQLInstance1
Service Account	SQLServerService
SQL Mail Profile Name	MS Exchange Profile
Binary File Locations	C:\Program Files\
Data File Locations	D:\sqlsystemdata
Authentication Mode	Mixed Mode
Collation	Dictionary order, case-insensitive, 1,252 character set
Network Libraries	Named Pipes TCP/IP (discussed in detail in Chapter 7)
Licensing Mode	Per Seat for five connections

Try It Out: Installing SQL Server 2000

1. Insert the SQL Server 2000 Standard installation CD-ROM into the CD drive on the computer on which you're installing SQL Server.

2. Click the SQL Server 2000 Components option on the start-up screen. From the next window, click the Install Database Server option to begin the setup procedure.

3. Click Next to take you past the welcome screen, and you'll see the Computer Name window. In this window you select whether you're performing a local installation or a remote installation. For this demonstration, you only want to perform a local installation. We'll come back to remote installations later on in this chapter, so leave the default Local Computer option selected.

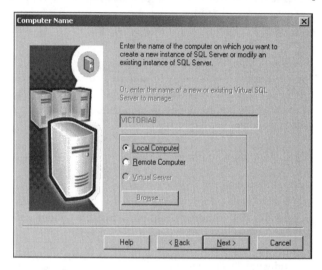

4. Click Next to go to the Installation Selection window. On this screen, you choose what type of installation you want to carry out.

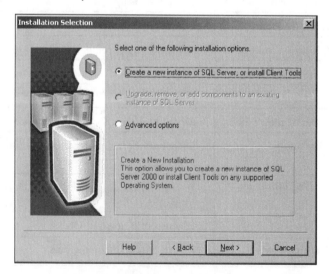

❏ **Create a new instance of SQL Server, or install Client Tools:** Use this option to install SQL Server, either fully or just a selection of the components such as the management tools (if this is a client machine from which you want to manage a remote SQL Server).

❏ **Upgrade, remove, or add components to an existing instance of SQL Server:** Use this option to upgrade SQL Server 7.0, add components to your existing installation of SQL Server 2000, or uninstall SQL Server 2000 from your computer.

❏ **Advanced options:** Select this option if you want to create a scripted installation or rebuild the SQL Server information contained in the registry.

Because you want to install a new instance of SQL Server, leave the default **Create a new instance** option selected and click **Next**.

5.   Now enter the registered user's information and click **Next** to take you to the **Software License Agreement** window. Click **Yes** and you will now be taken to a window that allows you to choose what you want to install.

6.   From this window you can select from three installation options:

❏ **Client Tools Only:** Only installs the tools to manage and develop against an installation elsewhere on your network.

❏ **Server and Client Tools:** Installs SQL Server 2000. This will install the database server software and the tools to manage and develop against it.

❏ **Connectivity Only:** Only installs the components needed by your desktop applications to connect to SQL Server.

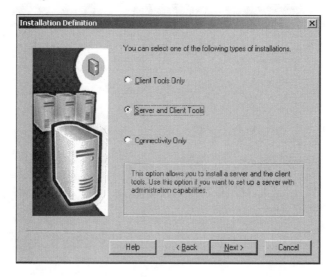

As you want to perform a full installation of both the server and client tools, leave the default option selected and click **Next**.

7. Now you can choose if you want to install a default or named instance (as we discussed before you started the installation). For this demonstration, you'll install a named instance, although more often than not you'll probably install a default instance. Uncheck the **Default** check box and enter the name you want the instance to be known as in the text box provided (for example, SQLInstance1).

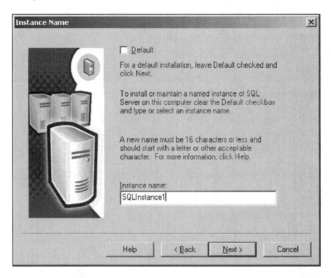

8. Once you've entered your desired instance name, click Next to view the following **Setup Type** window. In this window, you can choose one of the following three options for the setup type:

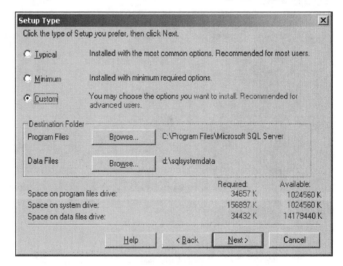

❏ **Typical**: Installs the most common components used by a SQL Server installation. This is what you'll select in most installations. Specifically, the following components are installed using this option:

    ❏ Database Server: The SQL Server database engine itself.

    ❏ Upgrade tools: The Upgrade Wizard, which allows you to upgrade SQL Server 6.5 databases to SQL Server 2000.

    ❏ Replication tools: The script and binary files needed to support replication.

    ❏ Full-text support: The functionality to allow full-text (free text) indexes to be created on character columns within a database.

    ❏ All of the management tools: SQL Server Enterprise Manager, Query Analyzer, Profiler, and Server Manager. These are the tools you need to maintain SQL Server remotely.

    ❏ Client connectivity: The network components needed to establish a connection with SQL Server.

    ❏ Books Online: The product documentation. This is a must-install for every DBA.

    ❏ SQL Server debugger: The server components that allow a stored procedure to be debugged. This should be considered for a development environment, but it's usually not required for a production environment.

❏ **Minimum**: Installs only the components needed to run SQL Server, which is useful if you're running low on disk space. This isn't really an option that you would use except in special circumstances. If you're running low on disk space, then you're probably not installing SQL Server on a machine suitable for running user databases. The components installed with this option are as follows:

    ❏ Database server

    ❏ Replication tools

    ❏ Full-text support

    ❏ Client connectivity

❏ **Custom**: Allows you to select exactly what components you want to install. You use this option to tailor the installation of SQL Server for your exact requirements. Typically, you'll use this option when installing SQL Server onto a production server, so you can ensure that unnecessary components that are part of the Typical option aren't installed.

As you want to see all the options available to you when you install SQL Server 2000, select the Custom installation type, even though you'll probably perform a Typical installation most of the time.

9. In this Setup Type window, you can also specify the location for your SQL Server program files (binary files) and data files. Because you've predetermined the best location for the various files, this isn't a tough decision. For this demonstration, we've decided to leave the SQL Server program files in the default directory structure on the C: drive but move the data files to the `D:\sqlsystemdata` folder. As the installation only installs system databases, you're just specifying the location for these databases now; later, you'll change the default location for your user databases.

10. Because you've selected a custom installation, clicking Next will take you to the Select Components window.

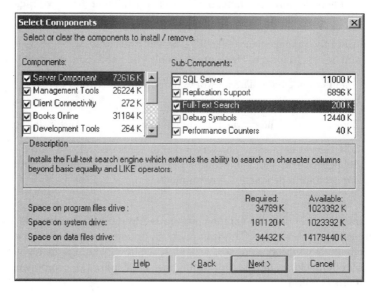

In this window, you can select what components in the following categories you want to install:

❑ **Server Components:** The database server itself and supporting components, such as replication support.

❑ **Management Tools:** The tools you use to administer and support SQL Server, such as Enterprise Manager and Query Analyzer.

❑ **Client Connectivity:** The components required for applications to access SQL Server across the network.

❑ **Books Online:** The SQL Server documentation. Always ensure this is installed somewhere so you can access it easily.

❑ **Development Tools:** Libraries and headers used by C developers to create applications using SQL Server. You wouldn't install these on a production server; usually you'll only select them when you're installing SQL Server on a development server or a developer's desktop.

❑ **Code Samples:** Same as Development Tools. These are for developers creating applications that use SQL Server. You wouldn't install these in a production environment.

For this demonstration, the default options are just fine, so simply click Next to go to the next installation window.

11. The Services Accounts window allows you to either select a separate Windows account for your SQL Server and SQL Agent services to run under or use the same account. As we discussed earlier, it's almost always better, and easier to administer, to use the same account. As you created this earlier, you can simply enter the account information into the fields provided.

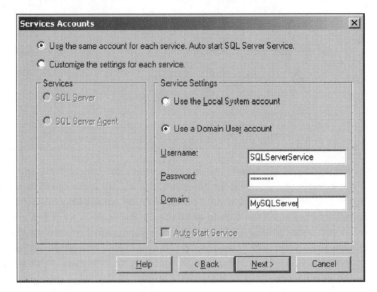

If you were installing SQL Server for use in a stand-alone environment or as a test server that doesn't require interaction with other servers across the network (or SQL Mail support), you could simply select the Use the Local System account option.

Once you've entered the Windows user account, click Next.

12. On the next window, you can choose the authentication mode used to validate users when connecting to SQL Server. Once again, because you're well prepared, you already determined the most appropriate authentication mode before you began the installation process.

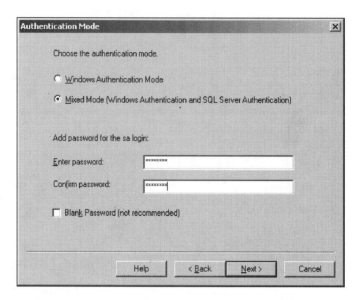

You decided on Mixed Mode authentication, so select this option. Now enter a password to be used for the sa account. As we discussed earlier, the sa user is the system administrator user under SQL Server security. This user has full control over everything that can be done within SQL Server and full access to all the data in all of the databases. You want this user to be secure, so we suggest that you create at least a 12-character password (with a mixture of alpha, numeric, and special characters). Record this password, put it away somewhere safe, and don't use it again. You can grant people who need to administer SQL Server the necessary rights without giving them access to the sa account.

You should never tick the Blank Password check box, even if you're installing a test server. Test servers often contain a copy of production data, and it's usually inappropriate for anyone within your organization, or even someone from outside your organization, to be able to freely access such information.

---

13. Once you've entered a suitable sa password and made a note of it, click Next. In the next window you can select which collation option you want to use for the server-level collation:

❑ Collation designator: Name of the Windows collation to use as the default collation for SQL Server.

❑ SQL Collations: An alternative type of collation to Windows collations that are supported for backward compatibility. These should only be used when necessary, depending on your application requirements, as described earlier.

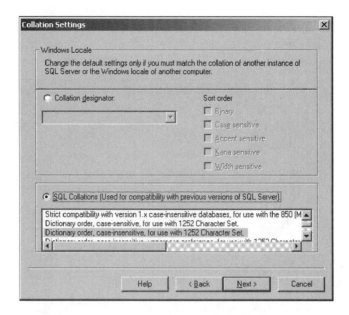

Leaving the default collation as selected is just fine. Clicking Next will take you to the window in which you can choose the network library support you want to install for this SQL Server installation.

14. For this demonstration, you will select (as you probably will for almost all your installations) to leave both Named Pipes and TCP/IP Sockets selected. All of the options for network library support are as discussed in detail in Chapter 7.

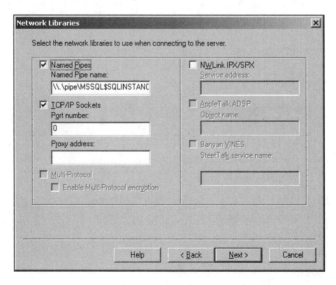

15. Click Next twice, and the installation process will begin. Before the files are installed, you must select the appropriate licensing mode. Remember that we discussed this before you began the installation process, so select the mode that you're licensed to use and click Continue.

The SQL Server installation process will now run through and copy files, install the various applications, and configure the appropriate services. Once setup is complete, you should get a dialog box telling you that everything has gone fine and that you need to reboot your computer.

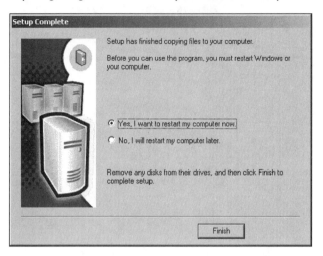

SQL Server is now installed, and after the reboot has completed, it will be available for use.

Installation Problems

If you didn't get the reassuring message informing you that SQL Server was been installed successfully, what should you do? Well, there are a couple of log files that are created as part of the installation process that are worth investigating.

The SQLSTP.LOG file contains a detailed account of actions carried out by the installation process. This file is located in the <SYSTEMROOT>\WINNT directory, and it's a plain text file. If you view it in Notepad, it should look something like this:

If the installation wasn't successful, this file is a good place to start looking for problems. Open it and go right to the end. Here you'll find the last thing that the installation process was attempting to do before it encountered a problem. This is a valuable starting point for trying to determine the cause of the failure.

Remote Installation

In the installation demonstration earlier in this chapter, you may recall a screen that allowed the selection of either a local or remote installation. In the previous demonstration, you were only interested in performing a local installation. However, it's important that we also cover installing SQL Server remotely, as this is a regular requirement. Basically, you have a couple of options for installing remotely:

❑ Use Terminal Services (or other remote control software) to connect to the server, and perform a local installation on that server as you did in the preceding demonstration.

❑ Use the Remote Install option to push SQL Server to the remote server.

As almost every environment will use some form of remote control software for server console management, usually the easiest–and certainly the most common–option is to connect using the remote control software, map a drive to a shared CD-ROM that contains the SQL Server installation media, and perform a local installation.

> **For more information on Terminal Services, see the Windows 2000 Server help information.**

If, for some reason, you don't have the ability to remotely control the console of the remote server, then you can use the Remote Install option provided by the SQL Server setup utility. There are a couple of things to keep in mind when you carry out the remote installation:

❑ The remote machine must be turned on and connected to the network, and ideally it shouldn't have users connected and it shouldn't be running any applications.

❑ The Windows user account that you're logged into locally must have administrator rights on the local machine for the remote installation to run successfully.

❑ Additional software, such as Outlook 2000, can't be deployed and configured remotely in this way, so SQL Mail won't be available until you gain access to the actual server console after SQL Server has been installed.

Try It Out: Performing a Remote Installation

For this demonstration, you're going to remotely install the client tools only to a remote Windows 2000 Professional workstation. The machine you're installing to should not currently have SQL Server components installed (if it does, you should either use a different server or remove the current installation), should be powered up, and should be connected to the same network you are.

1. Start the setup process and choose to install SQL Server database components as before. However, when you're prompted for the name of the computer to which you want to install SQL Server, choose **Remote Computer** and enter the name of the remote Windows 2000 Professional computer on which you're going to install the tools.

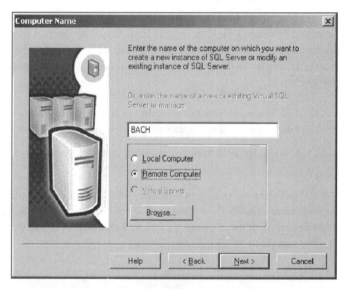

2. Clicking **Next** takes you to the installation selection, as it did when you performed the local installation. You'll notice that the only option enabled is to create a new instance of SQL Server and tools, because you can't upgrade or perform the advanced options of the setup process when you're doing a remote installation.

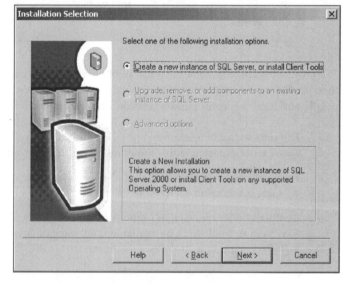

3. Click **Next**, and on the next screen enter the network connection information for accessing the remote machine and installing SQL Server. The first piece of information you need to enter is a Windows user account that has administrator privileges on the remote computer. This can be either a Windows domain account or a local Windows account on the remote computer.

4. Next, you must enter two network Universal Naming Convention (UNC–for example, \\Servername\sharename) paths. The first is the UNC path to the directory on the remote computer on which you'll install the SQL Server components. You shouldn't need to change this.

The second UNC path is to a network share on the computer that you're using to perform the remote installation. This is the UNC path to the location where the SQL Server source installation files are. You shouldn't need to change this unless you've removed the administrative share from your CD-ROM drive or changed it from being the drive letter (for example, E$) to something like cdrom$. If this is the case, change the UNC path to use the correct network share.

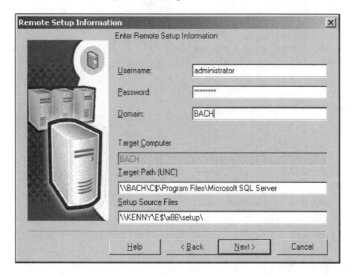

5. Choose the type of installation that you want to perform. For this demonstration, you want to install the client tools only on your remote workstation. Select this option and click Next.

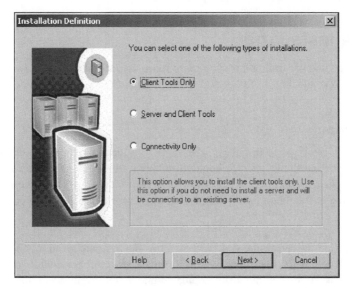

6. On the next screen, you can specifically choose which client components you want to install on your remote computer. For this demonstration, simply leave the default options selected and click Next.

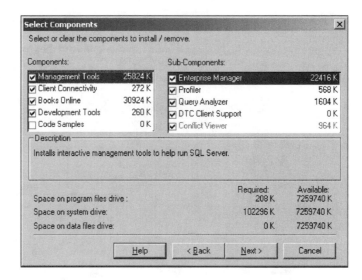

The setup process will now proceed to install the components you've selected onto the remote computer. This involves copying the files across the network from your computer to the remote computer, so the time this takes will be partly determined by the network bandwidth between the two.

Once the installation has finished, you are shown a window confirming that the installation was successful. To validate the installation, log in interactively to the remote computer and check that the SQL Server management tools are available.

Scripting Installation

The SQL Server setup program allows you to do more than simply install SQL Server interactively; it also allows you to create a script to be used by the installation routine at a later point in time.

Using a Script

Using a script is a great way to install SQL Server in a production environment. Why? Well, it ensures that every time you install SQL Server you're installing it in exactly the same way. This helps to eliminate inconsistencies that may occur between server rebuilds, which may result in unnecessary components being enabled in a future installation, or worse required components being missed altogether.

Once you've created the script file, you can retain this file in a safe location, and then all you need to do to install SQL Server to your configuration is run the setup program while referencing the script file. All the options will be automatically populated and you'll simply be notified when the setup has completed.

Try It Out: Installing SQL Server Using a Script File

1. To create a scripted installation, start the SQL Server setup and select **Install the Database Server**. Choose to install a local installation as you did in the earlier installation process.

    Instead of choosing to install a new instance, you should choose the **Advanced options** selection.

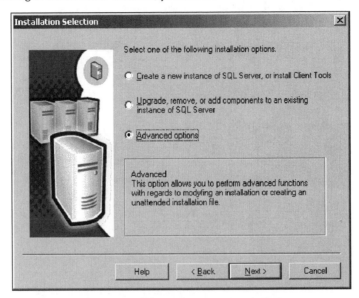

2. Click **Next** and leave the default option of **Record Unattended .ISS** file selected. Click **Next**.

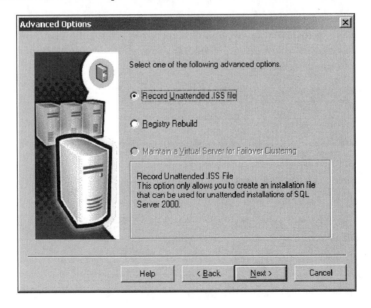

The remainder of the windows will be familiar to you from your previous installation. Basically, just follow the setup process as you did earlier, selecting the options you require for the SQL Server instance that you're installing. Keep in mind that the instance won't actually be installed at this time; instead, the setup utility is just collecting information to create the setup file.

Once you've finished running through the setup options, the following window displays. It's interesting that this window doesn't actually tell you where your .ISS file has been created, but don't worry, we know where it is!

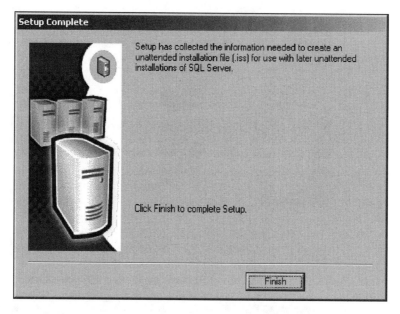

If you look in the <%SYSTEMROOT%>\Winnt directory, you'll find a file named SETUP.ISS. This is the file that has been created by the setup procedure, and if you open it in Notepad, you'll see it's plain text and it looks something like this:

```
[DlgInstanceName-0]
InstanceName=MSSQLSERVER
Result=1
[SetupTypeSQL-0]
szDir=%PROGRAMFILES%\Microsoft SQL Server
Result=303
szDataDir=%PROGRAMFILES%\Microsoft SQL Server
[SQLComponentMult-0]
SQLProg\SQLServr\SCMDev-type=string
SQLProg\SQLServr\SCMDev-count=3
SQLProg\SQLServr\SCMDev-0=SQLProg\SQLServr\SCMDev\SCMh
SQLProg\SQLServr\SCMDev-1=SQLProg\SQLServr\SCMDev\SCMx86Lb
SQLProg\SQLServr\SCMDev-2=SQLProg\SQLServr\SCMDev\SCMALb
SQLProg\SQLServr-type=string
SQLProg\SQLServr-count=6
SQLProg\SQLServr-0=SQLProg\SQLServr\Help
SQLProg\SQLServr-1=SQLProg\SQLServr\SCMDev
SQLProg\SQLServr-2=SQLProg\SQLServr\Rs1033
SQLProg\SQLServr-3=SQLProg\SQLServr\RsIntl
```

All you need to retain is this SETUP.ISS file, as it contains all the information necessary to install SQL Server with all of your installation options already selected.

To run your unattended scripted installation of SQL Server, you simply need to specify this .ISS file at the command prompt of the SQL Server setup utility, SetupSQL.EXE. You can find this in the x86\Setup\ directory on the SQL Server 2000 CD-ROM.

The —f1 parameter is used with the —s parameter of the SetupSQL.EXE command to carry out the unattended installation. Executing this from the command prompt, as shown, will install SQL Server to your predetermined configuration.

Out-of-the-Box Changes

After SQL Server has been installed, you still need to do a few things before you can consider the server ready for use by the users. These tasks include

❑ Setting the sa password

❑ Applying the latest service pack

Setting the sa Password

The sa (server administrator) account is for when you're using Mixed Mode authentication. The sa user has full privileges to do anything within SQL Server, and you should protect it with a strong password and not let anyone other than those responsible for the database server use it.

> If you've installed SQL Server using Windows Authentication Mode, then you haven't been prompted to enter a sa password, because you can't use the sa account under this mode. However, the mode that SQL Server uses is dependent on a registry key, and if it were changed, for example, by a hacker to instruct SQL Server to use Mixed Mode, then your server would become exposed from the sa account having no password.

If you chose to install SQL Server in Mixed Mode and you specifically set a blank sa password, you should change it now to protect your server. Even if it isn't a production server, it will be very difficult to maintain if anyone on your network can alter SQL Server configurations, or worse, look at data that they aren't authorized to see.

Try It Out: Setting the sa Password

For this example, you require SQL Server 2000 to be installed on your computer or on a remote computer on your network.

1. Start SQL Server Enterprise Manager and connect to the server for which you want to change the sa password. If the server in Enterprise Manager is registered using Windows Authentication Mode, you'll need to be logged in as a user with administrator privileges on the computer on which SQL Server is installed.

2. Once you're connected to SQL Server, drill down into the **Security** node and select **Logins**.

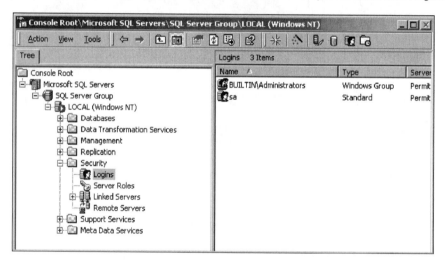

3. Right-click the **sa** login and select **Properties**. Within the **Password** field, enter your new sa password. Because this is a very important login, the password should be at least eight characters long (preferably 12 or more) and made up of a mixture of alpha, numeric, and special characters.

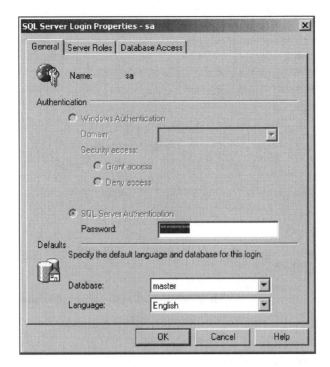

4. Click **OK** and you'll be prompted to reenter the password for confirmation. Enter it again and click **OK**, and the password will be changed.

> Ensure that you record the password in a safe place and you change it regularly. Never give it out to users, developers, or anyone who doesn't have responsibility for the SQL Server installation. Doing so is only asking for trouble. If users require special rights or permissions, they can be assigned to their own logins, as discussed in Chapter 6 of this book.

Applying the Latest Service Pack

Microsoft, like most other software vendors, releases patches and service packs to its applications from time to time, and SQL Server is no exception. After you've finished installing SQL Server, you should install the appropriate service pack. By "appropriate service pack," we don't necessarily mean the latest—here's the guide we use:

❑ If you're installing SQL Server to support a vendor's application database, check with the vendor and find out what service pack the vendor has tested the application with. Apply this to your server.

❑ If you're installing a SQL Server onto a development server, then apply the latest service pack so you can start testing it right away.

❑ If you're installing SQL Server onto a production server, then apply the latest service pack that has been out for over 6 months, and only do this after you've search the Microsoft newsgroups for potential issues. You don't want to be the one finding bugs within a service pack release in your production environment. Although recent service pack quality has been very good, historically there have been some real shockers (SQL Server 6.5 Service Pack 5, for example).

Thankfully, everything from Microsoft that is called a service pack is cumulative–that is, if you're applying Service Pack 3, you don't have to first apply Service Packs 1 and 2.

> **To find the latest service pack from Microsoft, visit** www.microsoft.com/sql.

Try It Out: Applying a Service Pack

For this demonstration, you require a fresh installation of SQL Server 2000 and the latest service pack to be downloaded to your server.

1. Once you've downloaded the latest service pack, expand the download package so the files are decompressed onto your local disk.

   Using Windows Explorer, navigate to the directory to which the package was expanded and run the setup.bat file in this directory. The Welcome window will appear. Click Next to begin the installation.

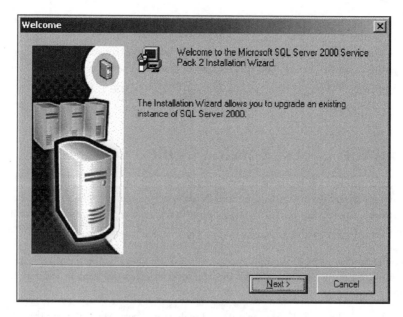

2. Click Yes to agree to the terms of the licensing. On the next screen, you're prompted to enter the instance of SQL Server that you want to install the service pack against. For this demonstration, you're applying the service pack to the Default instance.

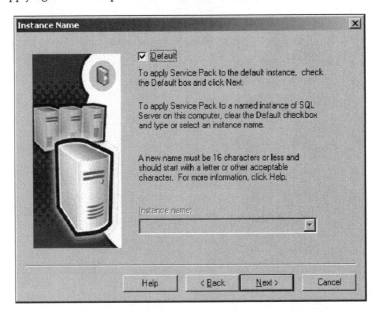

3. Click Next and enter the authentication information needed to connect to the default instance of SQL Server. Accepting the default of Windows authentication should be fine.

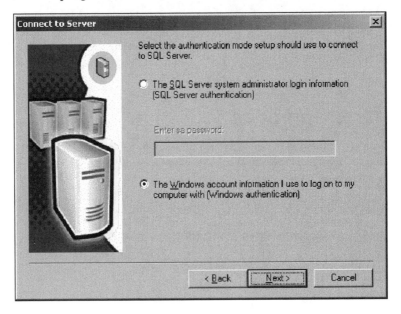

4. Click Next twice to begin installation of the service pack.

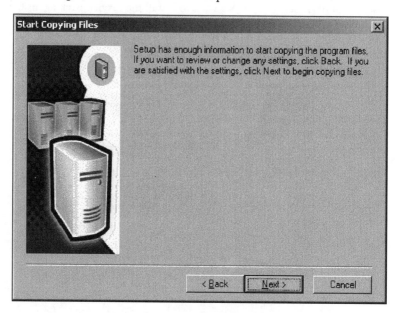

Once the service pack installation has finished, you're prompted to reboot your computer to finish the installation of the service pack.

> In addition to applying service packs, also try running the Baseline Security Analyzer, as this catches some common security problems. You can find out more about this tool at www.microsoft.com/technet/security/tools/tools/mbsawp.asp.

SQL Server Upgrades

Often when you're installing SQL Server, you want to upgrade an existing legacy version of SQL Server with the latest version of the product. You may want to do this for a number of reasons, including the following:

❑ To access support, as older versions are sometimes not supported

❑ To benefit from the improvements in scalability or reliability

❑ To make use of new features included in the latest version

Upgrading an entire server is certainly an option; however, let us offer a bit of practical advice here. We love clean and mean production servers. What this means is, we love knowing that all versions of all components are the latest and we love knowing that only those software components that are required are installed on our servers. Upgrading installations makes us a little uncomfortable as we can't know for sure that everything has been upgraded correctly and there isn't any legacy code hanging around that's going to come back to haunt us later. Now keep that in mind, and let's consider the effort involved in performing a clean installation of a server. The installation and configuration of the operating system, in a well-managed environment, should take about an hour or two. The installation and configuration of SQL Server, in a well-managed environment, should take an hour or two. So for a couple of hours' effort, we can have a clean and fresh installation rather than an upgraded installation.

If you intend not to upgrade an entire server but are instead performing a clean installation on a new server, there are a couple of things to keep in mind:

❑ Login information won't be upgraded. If you're using Windows Authentication, this won't be too much of an issue because you can simply reapply the Windows account logins on the new server. However, if you're using SQL Server Authentication, you'll need to either re-create the logins manually and reset the users' passwords or extract the logins and import these to the new server manually (see Chapter 6 for more information).

❑ If you're upgrading databases from SQL Server 7.0, this is really easy, as no manual conversion will be necessary. However, SQL Server 6.5 databases and earlier will need to be upgraded prior to being migrated to the new SQL Server 2000 server.

Upgrading in a Production Environment

Unless you absolutely have to, don't upgrade a production server. Start fresh and reinstall the operating system and SQL Server. You should have the process to reinstall the operating system well documented for disaster-recovery purposes anyway. Think of the reinstallation as validating your disaster-recovery process.

Upgrade the database on a test server, rebuild your production server, and transfer your upgraded database to the newly rebuilt server. This has another benefit over upgrading using a single server. When dealing with critical production databases, we like to have the database always available on a server somewhere throughout the upgrade procedure. In the event of failure, we can be confident that we have a separate, valid copy of the database available to fall back on. Sure, you should always have backups, but nothing feels quite as safe as having the database you're upgrading available on a server at all times. By upgrading on a separate server, you can simply prevent users accessing your production server while you upgrade on the separate server. Only once you're sure that the upgrade has taken place without problems can you rebuild your production server and then transfer the upgraded database back from the spare server to your production server.

Testing the Upgrade in Advance

When you've organized downtime with your users and you're working within an outage window, it isn't the time to be performing the upgrade for the first time. There are functionality changes between SQL Server 2000 and earlier versions that you must test with your application before you upgrade the production databases. Problems with the upgrade process, or problems with the upgraded database such as T-SQL code compatibility issues, must be identified well in advance with a test environment so you can deal with them in a sensible manner.

When you do actually perform the upgrade within your production environment, you should simply be working according to the process that you've developed, tested, and documented within your test environment. This helps ensure that any impact on the production environment is kept as minimal as possible.

Backup

When you're upgrading your databases, always make sure you perform a full database backup before you begin the upgrade process. It's one of the simplest things in the world to do, and it could save you and your organization much time and effort.

Be sure to read Chapter 8 before you begin any upgrade of an important database.

Upgrading to SQL Server 7.0

Upgrading from SQL Server 7.0 is a relatively straightforward process for a couple of reasons. First, Microsoft has built in good upgrade support for previous versions. Second, the underlying structure of SQL Server 7.0 and SQL Server 2000 is quite similar–the change is certainly not as complete as it was between SQL Server 6.5 and SQL Server 7.0.

Upgrading the Entire Server

We previously mentioned that upgrading production servers isn't the best option, but there are times when you'll need to do this. This could be due to resource constraints (you can't locate a spare server), time constraints (you don't have time for the reinstallation), or simply because it's less effort and you're happy that the upgraded server is going to perform adequately for your requirements (such as a development server, or noncritical production server).

The upgrade process is fairly similar to the installation process, and the easiest way to describe it is with an example.

Try It Out: Upgrading SQL Server 7.0

For this demonstration, you will need an existing copy of SQL Server 7.0 installed on your server. If you don't have this, and you're working on a test server, you may want to uninstall any existing versions of SQL Server that are on your server and then install SQL Server 7.0.

1. Start the SQL Server setup process and choose to install database components again. Choose the local installation option and click Next. On the Installation Selection window, choose the Upgrade, remove, or add components to an existing instance of SQL server option. Click Next.

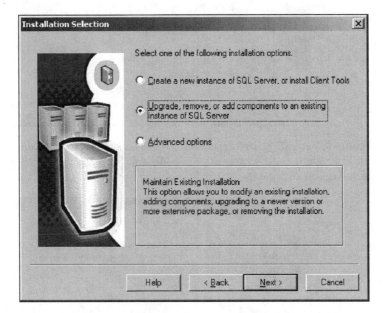

2. When replacing an existing installation of SQL Server 7.0 with SQL Server 2000, you must install a default instance. This is because SQL Server 7.0 can only be a default instance –if you install a named instance of SQL Server 2000, then the existing installation of SQL Server 7.0 will remain intact instead of being upgraded. So leave this option selected and click Next.

3. Select the Upgrade your existing installation option to upgrade from SQL Server 7.0 to SQL Server 2000. Then click Next.

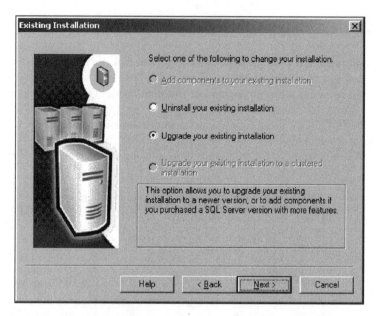

4. The next window simply requests confirmation of what you're about to do. As this can't be easily undone, you should be sure that you really want to upgrade before you do. Check the Yes check box and click Next.

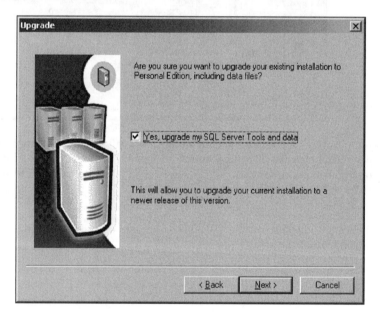

5. Next, you're asked for the authentication information needed to connect to SQL Server. Unless you've changed the way security is configured in SQL Server 7.0, you should just be able to select the Windows Authentication option and click Next.

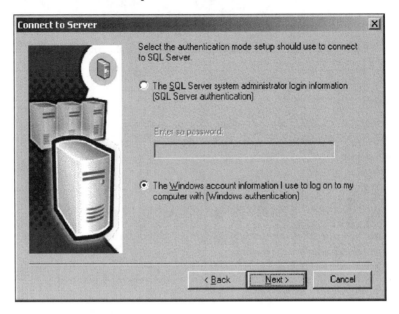

6. Click Next to begin the upgrade process.

Once the upgrade has been completed, you'll probably need to reboot your computer to complete the installation process.

Upgrading Single Databases

An alternative approach to upgrading an entire database server is to upgrade individual databases that you've located on a separate server, or a default instance, to SQL Server 2000. There are a number of different options available to you for achieving this, and the method you choose is really dependent on what fits your situation best, because the end result for each of the methods is the same.

The three most common methods of upgrading single databases are

❑ Backup and restore

❑ Detach and attach

❑ The Copy Database Wizard

The beautiful thing about upgrading SQL Server 7.0 databases to SQL Server 2000 is that you don't need to carry out any database conversion processes. Any conversion necessary is automatically carried out by SQL Server 2000, so all you have to be concerned about is getting the database from SQL Server 7.0 to the SQL Server 2000 server in the format that is most appropriate for your needs.

Other methods of upgrading a database between servers include using DTS to copy all database objects, scripting the schema, and running that script against a new database and BCPing the data out of the old database and into the new. These methods are more complex than the three we mentioned previously and we don't provide details on them. For more information, see Chapter 12.

Backup and Restore

Restoring a SQL Server 7.0 database backup directly into SQL Server 2000 is probably the easiest and most common method for upgrading an individual SQL Server 7.0 database. This method has the following benefits:

❑   Only a single file is needed: the full database backup file.

❑   This method doesn't affect any existing SQL Server 7.0 installation.

❑   This method doesn't require the SQL Server 7.0 installation to still be present. The backup file may be that of a historical backup.

❑   This method tests out your backup routine. This is always a valuable test that helps a DBA sleep at night.

The fact that you have only one file and the upgrade doesn't affect any existing installation of SQL Server 7.0 makes this method very attractive. The disadvantage of the backup and restore method is that no login information will be restored, so any logins will have to be re-created (see Chapter 6 for more information on how to do this).

Restoring a SQL Server 7.0 backup directly into SQL Server 2000 is possible, although restoring a SQL Server 6.5 backup into SQL Server 7.0 is not.

Try It Out: Backup and Restore

To try out the backup and restore example, you'll need SQL Server 7.0 installed as well as SQL Server 2000. If you have only one server, you can achieve this by installing SQL Server 7.0 first and then installing SQL Server 2000 as a named instance, which will allow the installations to coexist on the same server.

You're simply going to upgrade the Northwind database from SQL Server 7.0 to a database named Northwind70 within SQL Server 2000.

1.   Start SQL Server Enterprise Manager and connect to the SQL Server 7.0 system. Drill down into the Databases node and select the Northwind database. Click the Tools menu and choose Backup Database to open a window like the following:

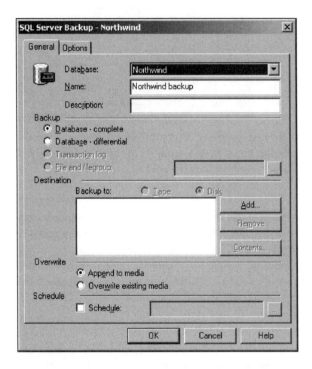

In the backup database window, ensure that the Database – complete has been selected. Click Add within the Destination section. Enter a path for a destination file. For this example, you'll just enter C:\Northwind70.bak.

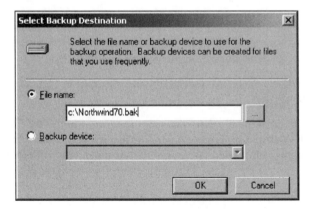

2.　Click OK to accept the destination file and then OK again to begin the database backup. This will run pretty quickly, and very soon you should get a message informing you that the database backup was successful.

Once the backup has finished, you need to get the backup file to the server on which SQL
Server 2000 was installed. If this is on the same server as SQL Server 7.0, then you don't need to do
anything. If this is on another server, you have to copy this across the network to the destination
server.

If you don't want to copy it across the network to the destination server, then you can restore the
database within SQL Server 2000 from a file that's located on a remote server by supplying a UNC
path to the database backup file. The trick here is that the SQL Server 2000 service must be running
under a Windows user account that has the necessary permissions to access the backup file at the
UNC location. If the service account doesn't have these permissions, then the restoration from a file
located on a remote server will fail, even if the account you're currently logged into on the server has
the appropriate permissions.

> **To restore a database across the network, the SQL Server service Windows user
> account requires access to the remote network location, not the account you're
> logged into the server with.**

3. Now move to the computer on which you have SQL Server 2000 installed. Start SQL Server
    Enterprise Manager and drill down to the **Databases** node. Right-click and choose
    All Tasks | Restore Database from the pop-up menu.

4. Give the database a name. As Northwind already exists in SQL Server 2000, call this database
    Northwind70.

5. You need to point to the file that you want to restore. Choose the **From device** bullet and click
    the **Select Devices** button. From the window that appears, click **Add** and enter the UNC path
    to the backup file you created just before–for example, \\tony\c$\Northwind70.bak.

6. Click **OK** twice and a window will appear showing the information you entered, similar to this one:

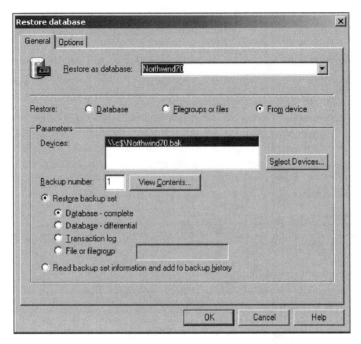

7. Now click **OK** again to commence the restoration process. If everything has gone well, you'll receive a confirmation dialog box informing you of the restoration success.

> **Don't get too concerned with the various backup and restore options at this point. We explain all of these in detail in Chapter 8.**

Detach and Attach

An alternative to the backup and restore method described in the previous section is the detach and attach method. This technique involves detaching the database files from SQL Server 7.0, copying them across the network, and reattaching the database files at the destination SQL Server 2000 server.

The main benefits of this method over the backup and restore approach are time and space. Because you're simply copying the database files, there's no need to create a separate copy of the database as with the backup method. Also, because you don't need to create this backup file, you use less disk space.

The disadvantage of the detach and attach method in comparison to the backup and restore method is that it requires the database to be taken offline, albeit temporarily, from SQL Server 7.0, so you can't carry out or test this method while users are accessing the database. The actual detach and reattach should be almost instantaneous, but if you're copying the database across a network to its new location, this may take some time.

Try It Out: The Detach and Attach Method

To carry out this demonstration, SQL Server 7.0 must be installed on either a remote computer or your local computer, and SQL Server 2000 must also be installed on your local computer.

1. On either your local computer or your remote computer, start SQL Server Query Analyzer. Enter the name of your SQL Server 7.0 computer and also enter the sa user name and password for this server.

2. Once you're connected to SQL Server 7.0, execute **sp_helpdb** followed by the name of the database that you want to migrate from SQL Server 7.0 to SQL Server 2000. The results of this command will be similar to those shown in the following image. You're interested in the path to the database files because you need to know where they are once the database is detached. In this example, you can see that they live in the **C:\MSSQL7\data** directory on the SQL Server 7.0 computer.

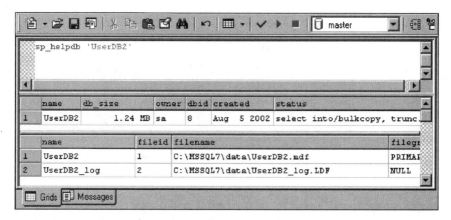

3. Now enter **sp_detach_db** followed by the name of the database that you want to migrate from SQL Server 7.0 to SQL Server 2000. This will remove the database from SQL Server 7.0, but the data files will not be deleted.

4. On your SQL Server 2000 computer, browse to the drive and directory where the database data files were located in step 1. Select the files that relate to the database that you're migrating and copy them to a suitable location on the SQL Server 2000 computer.

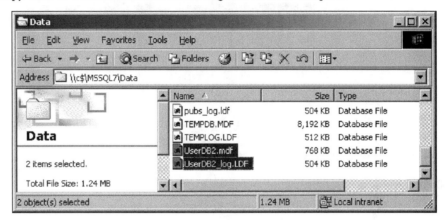

5. Once you've copied these files to the local computer, start SQL Server 2000 Enterprise Manager. Connect to your SQL Server 2000 installation and drill down until you see the Databases node. Right-click the Databases node and choose the All Tasks | Attach Database menu item.

6. Browse to the local directory in which you copied the database files by clicking the ellipsis (...) button. Once you've found this directory, select the file that has an .MDF file extension, as this is the primary database file. Click OK.

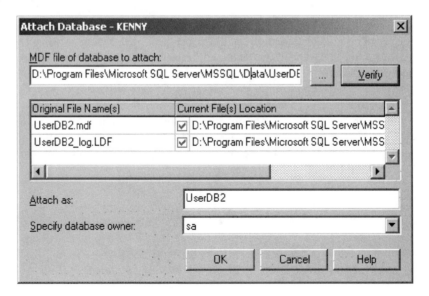

7. Now change the database owner to sa from the drop-down list next to the Specify database owner option. Clicking OK will now attach the database in SQL Server 2000.

As part of the attach, SQL Server 2000 upgrades the data files to the SQL Server 2000 format so this procedure will not work in reverse, from SQL Server 2000 to SQL Server 7.0. If everything went OK, you should see the dialog box confirming the upgrade and attach was successful.

The Copy Database Wizard

In addition to just copying the databases from one server to another, there are a number of associated server objects to also consider that relate to a database, including

❏ **Logins:** Server logins relating to the database being copied

❏ **Stored procedures:** Shared stored procedures within the master database

❏ **Jobs:** Jobs within the SQL Server Agent that relate to the database being copied

❏ **User-defined error messages:** Error messages that have been created to support errors raised in the code of the database being copied

Rather than try to copy the database and all the associated objects manually, Microsoft provides a tool to take care of it. This tool is the **Copy Database Wizard** (CDW) and it's accessible from within SQL Server Enterprise Manager.

To copy the database from your source server to your destination server, the CDW carries out detach, file copy, and attach operations just as you did in the previous sections, so there's little value provided from the CDW from this perspective. However, in addition to simply copying the database, the CDW allows the related server objects to be copied, something that doesn't occur as part of the manual process you performed.

Try It Out: Using the Copy Database Wizard

This demonstration requires SQL Server 7.0 to be installed on a remote computer with a couple of user databases created. On your local computer, you should have SQL Server 2000 installed.

1. On your SQL Server 2000 computer, start SQL Server 2000 Enterprise Manager and connect to your local installation of SQL Server. Once connected, click the Tools menu item and choose the Wizards menu item. Drill down into the Management node and select Copy Database Wizard. Click OK.

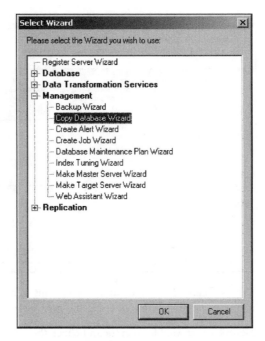

2. Click Next to skip past the introduction screen and you are presented with the Select a Source Server window. Enter the name of the remote SQL Server 7.0 installation and enter the necessary information to authenticate this SQL Server. Click Next.

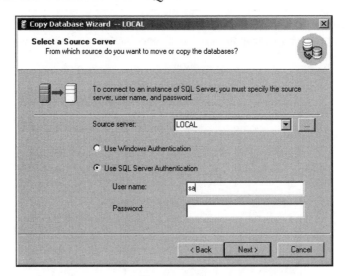

3. Now enter the destination server information (this should be your local SQL Server 2000 installation) and enter the necessary authentication information. Once you've done this, click Next again.

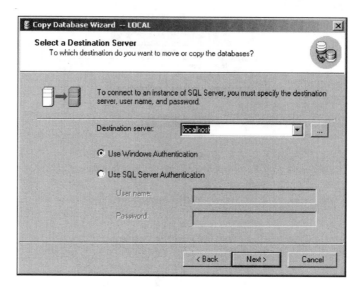

4. On this next window you can select the databases you want to migrate and whether you want to simply copy them or move them completely to the new server.

   Choose the user databases you want to migrate and check the Copy box for those databases. Click Next.

   Always copy the databases! If you want to remove the databases from the old installation, you can drop them manually once you're certain your upgrade was successful.

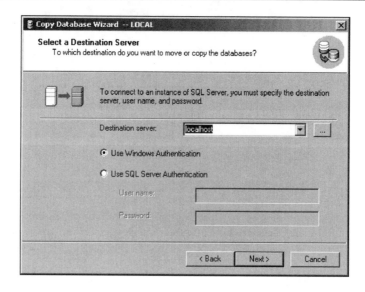

5. Now you can view and modify the location where the database data files will be located after the upgrade. Right now, the default database file location will be used, but if you click the Modify button, you can change this. Click the Modify button.

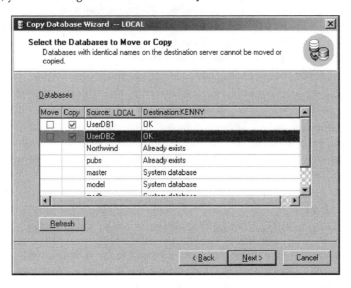

6. In the Database files window, you can change the path where both the database data files and the database log files will be created. This screen warns you if there's a problem with the location you've selected, such as low disk space. The default locations are OK, so simply click OK then Next.

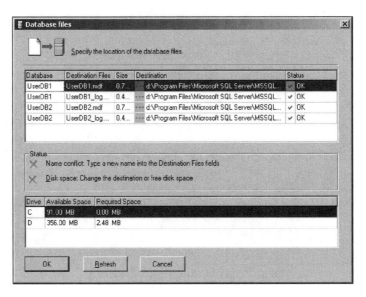

7. Now you can select what other related objects you want to copy from your source server to your destination server. The choices include the following:

❏ **Logins:** For users to gain access to the databases being copied, they need to be able to log in to SQL Server. If the appropriate logins don't currently exist on your SQL Server 2000 server, you can choose that all the logins from the remote server, or only those that relate to the databases you are copying across, should be copied from your remote SQL Server to your new SQL Server.

❏ **Shared stored procedures from the master database:** Although it is bad practice to do so (dependencies in the master database can make recovery more complex, especially when restoring a user database to a different server), developers can create stored procedures in the master database that can then be used from all users' databases. If this is the case, you'll need to bring those shared stored procedures across to your new server and this option will do that for you.

❏ **Jobs from msdb:** Often there are a number of jobs associated with a database. These may be jobs for backing up the database, performing some form of data maintenance, or batch reporting. If you want to bring across the related jobs, choose this option.

❏ **User-defined error messages:** These messages are created on the server for specific application errors. The SQL code within the databases you're copying may reference one of these user-defined error messages, so it may be necessary to copy these to your new server.

For this demonstration, leave the default options enabled and click Next.

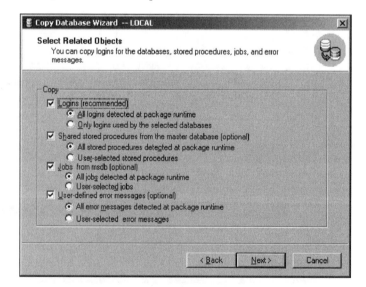

8. You can either run the CDW immediately or schedule it to run later. This may be useful for running the CDW after hours. For this demonstration, choose Run immediately and click Next.

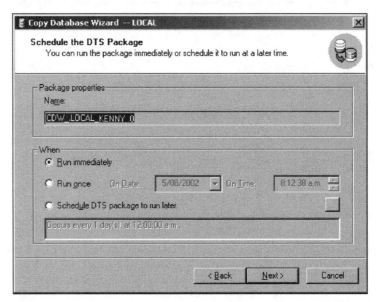

9. Finally, click Finish to start the CDW.

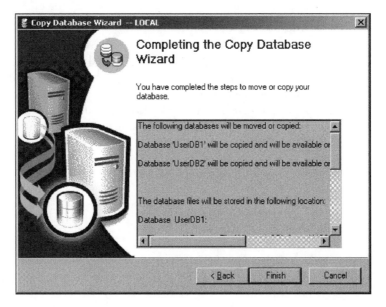

Once the CDW has finished, you'll receive a notification informing you of the outcome of the database copy, either successful or failed.

Upgrading to SQL Server 6.5

Upgrading SQL Server 6.5 is still an automated process supported by the SQL Server 2000 setup tool; however, there are several additional steps that you need to take when you upgrade SQL Server 6.5 to SQL Server 2000. These additional steps include the following:

- ❑ Increase the size of `tempdb` to at least 25MB.

- ❑ Ensure the `master` database has at least 3MB of free space.

- ❑ Ensure that your SQL Server 2000 service is running under a Windows user account.

- ❑ Ensure that the Remote Registry Service is running on the server on which SQL Server 2000 is installed.

Once you've set these options correctly, you can proceed with the upgrade process.

> **You need the Remote Registry Service to be running on the server on which SQL Server 2000 is installed. If this service is disabled or stopped, you'll receive the following error when you attempt to run the Upgrade Wizard:** "The import server MUST be switched to SQL Server 2000".

Try It Out: Upgrading SQL Server 6.5

This example requires SQL Server 6.5 to be installed on a remote server with SQL Server 2000 Standard (or Enterprise) Edition installed on the local machine. When you installed SQL Server, you should have chosen to install the upgrade components. If you didn't, add these to your installation using the SQL Server 2000 setup program. You should also have a user database located on SQL Server 6.5 to upgrade. If you don't have a real one to upgrade, then create a test database for the purpose of this demonstration.

1. From the Start menu, choose the **SQL Server Switch** program group and select the **SQL Server Upgrade Wizard**. You'll see the Welcome screen.

2. Click **Next** and the **Data and Object Transfer** window will appear. Here you can choose your upgrade options, which are as follows:

   - ❑ Export objects and data from SQL Server 6.5

   - ❑ Import objects and data to SQL Server 2000

   - ❑ Select the data transfer method

   - ❑ Verify the object data transfer

For this demonstration, the default options shown are fine. Click Next.

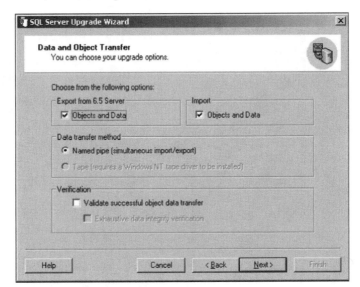

3. Next, you're requested to enter the logon information for connecting to both the remote SQL Server 6.5 installation and the local SQL Server 2000 installation. Enter the sa passwords for both and click Next.

4. Choose the code page to be used for the upgrade. Click Next.

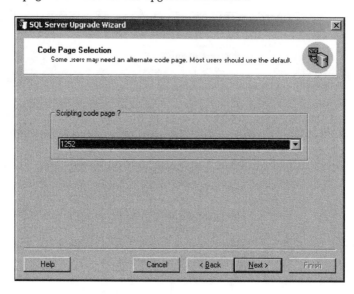

5. Now you can choose the user databases to upgrade. Because the system databases have changed significantly between SQL Server 6.5 and SQL Server 2000, these can't be upgraded. Choose the user databases that you want to upgrade and click Next.

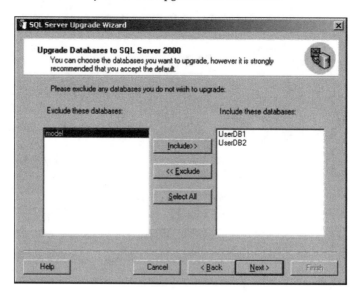

6. Now you can choose how the databases within SQL Server 2000 are to be created. The options are as follows:

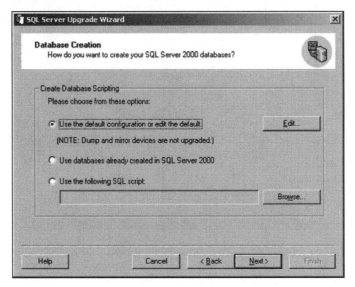

❑ **Use default configuration or edit the default:** This option allows you to update the databases with default file locations. Alternatively, you can edit the default database file parameters (file path, initial size, and growth increment).

❑ **Use databases already created in SQL Server 2000:** When you select this option, the Upgrade Wizard doesn't create any new databases. Instead, the old databases are upgraded into the existing databases on your server.

❑ **Use the following SQL script:** This option allows you to specify a script file that you've previously defined for creating the target databases for the upgrade. If you use this option, the target databases you create *must* have the same name as the existing databases you're upgrading.

7. To view the default configuration, click **Edit**. You can view the proposed location of the data files for the databases that will be created as part of the upgrade process. You can choose to modify this configuration and, when you're satisfied with the file locations, click **Accept**.

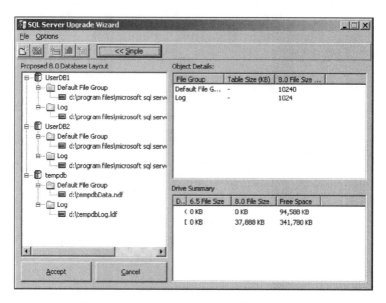

8. Click Next and the System Configuration window will appear. Here you can choose to transfer the system configuration from SQL Server 6.5 to SQL Server 2000. The options available are as follows:

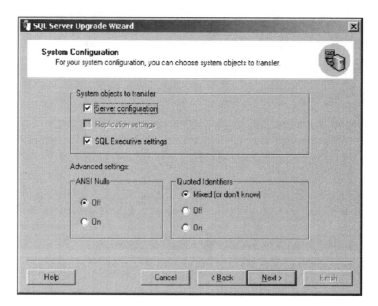

Once again, the default options are adequate for your needs, so click Next.

9. In the final window, you can click the View warnings and choices in notepad button to view the .INI file that was created in the background from your upgrade choices. If the setup process has detected any problems, these will also be visible within this file.

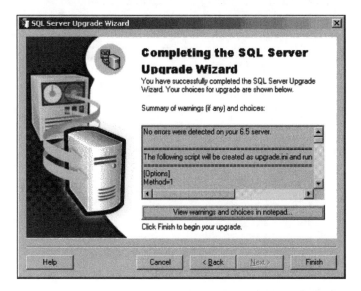

10. Once you're happy with the upgrade, close Notepad and you'll be able to click Finish to begin the upgrade process.

While the upgrade is running, you're able to monitor the process within the window shown. If any part of it is unsuccessful, you're able to view that here.

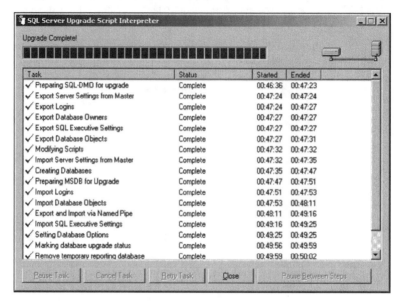

If the upgrade completes without problems, you'll receive a notification that the upgrade was successful. If you now connect to your local SQL Server 2000 installation using Enterprise Manager and drill down into the Databases node, you should find the databases from SQL Server 6.5 that have been migrated.

Upgrading to Earlier Versions of SQL Server

If you have an earlier version of SQL Server, then you're a bit out of luck when it comes to upgrading to SQL Server 2000. This shouldn't bother very many people as there are practically no installations of SQL Server 4.5 or SQL Server 6.0 left anymore.

If you do come across a version of SQL Server earlier than 6.5, you have a couple of options. First, you can choose to upgrade from the early version to SQL Server 6.5, and then upgrade from SQL Server 6.5 to SQL Server 2000.

The other option is probably the preferred option unless your database is quite large: you can re-create the schema in a new SQL Server 2000 database. Once you've done this, you can export the data into flat files from the early version of SQL Server using bulk copy program (BCP, which is covered in more detail in Chapter 12) and import these flat files into SQL Server 2000.

Both options are a lot of work but, as upgrades only need to be performed once, it shouldn't be too frightening. Just remember to document or create scripts for the various upgrade tasks so you can test it a few times to ensure it works, and then carry out the exact same tested process within your production environment.

Postupgrade Tasks

Whether you upgrade from SQL Server 7.0, SQL Server 6.5, or an earlier version, there are a few tasks that you should perform once the upgrade has completed, which we'll now briefly look at.

Taking a Backup

You've done too much work to let an error or a failure of some kind destroy your newly upgraded database. The first thing you must always do is take a full database backup of your SQL Server database and put this backup aside in case you need it at a later point in time. See Chapter 8 for information on how to create a database backup.

Setting the Database Compatibility Level

Databases within SQL Server 2000 have a database compatibility option that specifies the level of backward compatibility SQL Server provides to the database. The compatibility options available are

❑   80: The database is fully compatible with SQL Server 2000. All new T-SQL commands are available.

❑   70: The database is in SQL Server 7.0 compatibility mode. Only the T-SQL commands from SQL Server 7.0 are available.

❑   65: The database is in SQL Server 6.5 compatibility mode. Only the T-SQL commands from SQL Server 6.5 are available.

Once a database has been upgraded, if the compatibility mode defaults to that of the version of SQL Server from which the database was upgraded, it isn't fully compatible with SQL Server 2000. You should verify that the database you've upgraded is fully compatible with the new T-SQL commands included within SQL Server 2000. To carry out these tests, you can change the database compatibility to the 80 option.

Try It Out: Changing the Database Compatibility Level

1.   To change the database compatibility mode for a database, open SQL Server Enterprise Manager and connect to your SQL Server. Drill down into the **Databases** node, right-click the database name, and select **Properties**.

2.   Click the **Options** tab and choose the compatibility level from the drop-down box under the **Compatibility** header. To set the level fully compatible with SQL Server 2000, choose the **80** option.

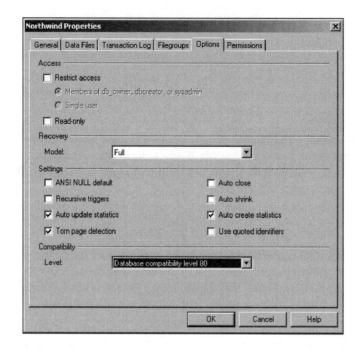

Changing Scheduled Tasks/Maintenance Plans

If you have scheduled tasks or database maintenance plans (both covered in Chapter 5) for carrying out some form of database maintenance, then ensure you update these to include the newly upgraded databases.

Also, be sure to include this database within your backup scheme to ensure it and its transaction logs are regularly backed up.

Summary

The actual process of installing SQL Server 2000 is probably the easiest thing you've done in this chapter. Planning for SQL Server installation, determining hardware requirements, and upgrading existing servers are all going to take many times longer than the installation itself. However, this just highlights that spending time planning provides you with the most effective SQL Server installation and you shouldn't just install it on a server without this sort of preparation.

Now that you're an expert in getting the software onto your server in every different way possible, let's move on to Chapter 3 and make SQL Server do something useful.

3

Creating a Database

Now that you've successfully installed SQL Server, you're going to move on to actually use it and look into creating and using databases. A new database is essentially an empty building–a library. It's the shelving and the books on the shelving that makes it a library, and in this case the shelving is the database **tables**.

In this chapter, you'll see how to create and remove a database from a given instance of SQL Server and how to set the various options associated with a database. Then you'll look at the various database design methods and how to create tables and establish relationships between tables.

Registering a Server

Before you get started, you need to check that the SQL Server that you'll be using for testing is registered within Enterprise Manager, postinstallation. To check this, open Enterprise Manager on your client PC (this resides in the **Microsoft SQL Server** program group in the **Start** menu) and drill down into your list of registered servers:

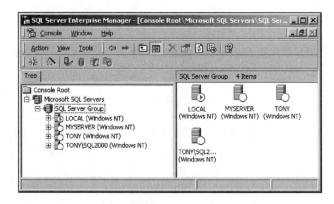

If you don't see the name of the SQL Server that you want to use, follow these steps to register that server.

Try It Out: Registering a Server

1. Open SQL Server Enterprise Manager and right-click the **SQL Server Group** node. From the pop-up menu, select **New SQL Server Registration**. Click **Next** to move past the welcome screen.

2. You should see the name of your SQL Server on the left within the **Available servers** list. If you don't, then you can enter the name of the instance in the space provided. Once you've selected or entered your SQL Server instance name, click **Add** and then click **Next**.

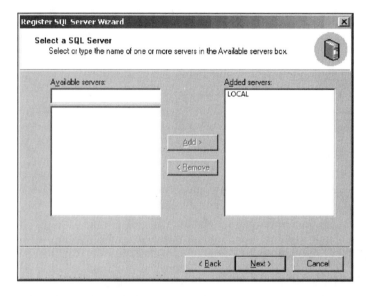

3. Now you need to choose the authentication mode that you'll use to authenticate yourself with SQL Server when you try to connect using Enterprise Manager. Unless you have specific reason not to, such as your Windows account not having the necessary privileges on your SQL Server machine, use the default option of Windows Authentication and not SQL Server Authentication.

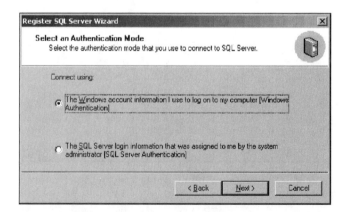

Because Windows Authentication is more secure than SQL Server Authentication, your logins with administration privileges should always be authenticated with Windows Authentication. For more information, see the discussion on authentication in Chapter 6.

4. Next, you can choose the group within Enterprise Manager in which this server registration will appear. You can choose to either use the default SQL Server group or create a new server group. For this demonstration, you'll create a new group called Testing and click Next.

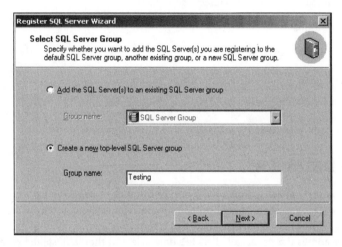

5. Now click Finish to complete the registration process. The server will now appear under your new Testing group within Enterprise Manager.

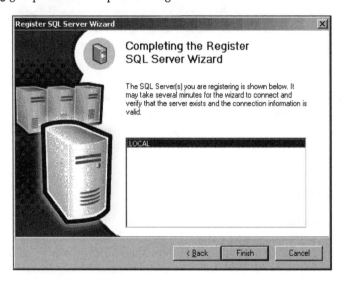

Now that you've registered your server, you can move on to create databases within SQL Server. Before you dive in, though, you need to consider a number of issues.

Planning Database Requirements

Before you create your first database, you must adequately plan for the process. As you'll see shortly, the actual process of creating a database is a rather trivial task. However, if you don't fully plan your requirements in advance, changing the way in which the database has been created will prove much more difficult than creating it correctly in the first place.

So what sorts of things do you need to think about before creating databases with SQL Server 2000? The key considerations are as follows:

- ❏   The model database and how this affects new databases
- ❏   Naming conventions
- ❏   Files, filegroups, and RAID levels
- ❏   Collation type

Although you can change all of these after database creation, thinking about them first will save you work in the long run.

The model Database

When you create a new database within a SQL Server instance, everything isn't created from scratch. Doing so would take a long time, as there are many underlying system objects within every database that are used by SQL Server to make the database perform. Instead of creating everything from scratch, SQL Server copies the preinstalled model database and then adjusts the copy to meet the requirements you specified in your creation request.

> **SQL Server uses the model database as a template for creating all new databases.**

This approach has some benefits for you as the DBA. If you have common objects, such as tables or stored procedures, that you want to be present in every user database that exists within an instance, you can create these within the model database. A common reason for doing this is to store DBA information, such as performance data. Whatever the reason, every new database that is created will receive these user-defined objects as part of its schema automatically.

Naming Conventions

The important thing about naming conventions is that, whatever naming convention you decide upon, it must remain consistent for all databases created within all SQL Server instances throughout your organization. Decide on a standard and then stick to it. This will ultimately result in databases that are more easily identified by you as the DBA and, more important, databases that are more easily identified by the end users.

Some common situations you should avoid when deciding on a database naming convention include the following:

❑ **Don't use spaces in the database name**. Although it's possible to include them, spaces don't always work with the third-party tools on the market. Not all third-party application developers write their applications to handle all the naming formats that SQL Server allows.

❑ **Only use alphanumeric characters**.

❑ **Keep database names short**. Although database names can be up to 128 characters long, it would be pretty silly to create names that long. A lot of administrators went through a period of creating ridiculously long names when this capability was first introduced with SQL Server 7.0 (a similar thing happened when long filename support was added to Windows). Eventually, it was determined that this was unnecessary and caused a lot of problems, especially if you had to key these database names in from time to time. Keeping the database names descriptive, yet short is a much better alternative.

> **Before you decide to implement a new naming convention for your SQL Server databases, check with your IT managers. If your company has been involved in any development in the past, then the managers may already have an established naming standard.**

Files and Filegroups

The most important decision you make when you create a database is what files and filegroups will be created for the database. You can choose to have anything from the default two files (at least one for the data and one for the log) and one filegroup (default) right through to 256 filegroups and over 32,000 data files. Although the latter would be an extreme situation, you can often gain extra performance relating to input/output (I/O) by strategically increasing the number of files and filegroups above the minimum.

Files

Database files are where the information that is contained within a database is physically stored on disk. For example, on my server, the model database is stored at C:\Program Files\Microsoft SQL Server\MSSQL\Data\model.mdf for the data and C:\Program Files\Microsoft SQL Server\MSSQL\Data\modellog.ldf for the log. The concept of files was introduced with SQL Server 7.0. Previously, storage containers, known as database devices, had to be created, and within these devices one or more databases could be created. Database files have replaced the need for database devices and have greatly eased storage administration, making it much more intuitive. Now when you create your database, you specify the number of database files that you want to use with it and their properties. Database files only ever belong to a single database and live in the file system just like any other file within Windows. Every database has at least two files, and these must exist and be accessible for the database to be available.

By default, the database files must be created on disks that are local to the server where SQL Server is installed. This excludes mapped network shares. Although you can locate database files on network shares by using a trace flag (start-up options that modify SQL Server's "normal" behavior), this isn't recommended, as most LANs are much slower than local disks, and this will impact database performance. Also, network-based resources may be unavailable from time to time. If the database files aren't available when SQL Server starts, the database will be marked as corrupted and will have to be manually repaired before it can be used again.

File Types

The two different types of database files that you can specify when creating your database are **data files** and **log files**. Data files are used to permanently store the information and objects that are created within the database. The first data file that is created is known as the **primary data file**, which every database will have. Additional data files are known as **secondary data files**.

> **Every database has one primary data file and zero or more secondary data files. Both the primary and secondary data files store database data. The primary data file also keeps track of all the secondary data files that exist for a database.**

When you create multiple data files within a database, each file will be filled proportionally based on its size within its filegroup, which we cover next. This ensures that data is evenly distributed throughout the various data files of the database.

The other type of data file is the **transaction log file**. Transaction log files are quite distinct from data and must always have separate physical disk files. SQL Server uses transaction log files for recording transactions as they happen within the database, for recovery purposes. Multiple transaction log files can be created for a database, but a database must have at least one. Unlike data files, log files aren't filled proportionally, they're filled in order–that is, when the first file is full, then the second file is populated, and so on.

> **Transaction log files are not human-readable as is the case with text log files (such as an IIS log). These are binary files that SQL Server stores for its own purposes (maintaining transaction consistency) and they aren't intended to be manually inspected.**

Filegroups

When creating data files, you can also specify a filegroup that each belongs to. A **filegroup** is a way of controlling where objects and information are physically located, from within SQL Server. Every database has at least one filegroup, the **primary filegroup**, and you can create additional filegroups. As mentioned, when you have multiple files, SQL Server stores the data proportionally throughout all the various data files so you don't have any way of controlling which objects go to which files (and which objects live on which disks). By assigning one or more files to secondary filegroups, you can gain this control.

The primary filegroup contains all the internal system tables used by SQL Server for maintaining the database information. Primary filegroups may also contain user objects, such as tables and indexes. Secondary filegroups only contain user objects.

Although data is proportionally stored between files within a filegroup, it isn't proportionally stored between filegroups. When you create an object, such as a table, you can explicitly specify the name of the filegroup where it is to be stored. If you don't specify a filegroup, then the object is created on the default filegroup (usually the primary filegroup). However, when you specify a filegroup, you're essentially selecting the group of files where the object is to be stored:

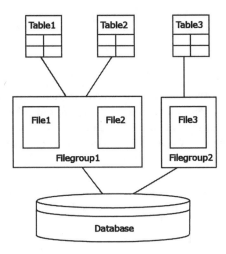

From the preceding diagram you can see that we chose to create Table1 and Table2 on Filegroup1. As Filegroup1 contains two data files, File1 and File2, the information that is stored in Table1 and Table2 will be automatically evenly distributed between these two files by SQL Server. We chose to create Table3 on Filegroup2, and as Filegroup2 contains only one data file, File3, the information that is stored in Table3 will be stored only within File3.

Once a database has been created, it's easy to add new files and filegroups. It's possible to remove files and filegroups as well, but this is not as straightforward; you first must move all objects off those files and filegroups. For more information, see *Adding and Deleting Data and Transaction Log Files* and ALTER DATABASE in SQL Server Books Online.

File Growth

In SQL Server 6.5, the space available to a database didn't expand automatically. Instead, the DBA had to manually allocate space for a database and reallocate more space as needed before activity in the database filled the original allocation completely. If more space wasn't allocated, the database would fill and users wouldn't be able to enter any further information until it had been expanded. Unfortunately, because DBAs are busy people, this happened regularly and running out of space was a common cause of downtime to the end users.

Fortunately, Microsoft introduced the capability for data files to grow automatically with the whole redesign of the way database space was allocated in SQL Server 7.0. When you indicate that you want to add a data file to your database, you must specify the following about the file:

❑ Initial size

❑ Growth increment

❑ Maximum size

The initial size can be any value over 512KB. The growth increment is the amount of space that SQL Server should add when a file becomes full. This can be expressed either as a percentage, such as 10 percent, or as a value in megabytes. Finally, you can specify the maximum size the file can grow to. This can be a value in megabytes or, if you don't specify the maximum size, the data file will continue to grow at the specified rate until all available disk space is used.

Before you create these files, you first need to think about the types of disk where you're going to place these database files, and this involves a discussion of RAID.

RAID Levels

It seems every administration book or article covers the **redundant array of independent disks (RAID)** subsystems in detail, so we won't discuss how RAID works or all the various levels of RAID and what the various redundancy properties of each level are. This information, if you haven't read it many hundreds of times in the course of your career, can be located quickly in most administration manuals, Windows 2000 Help, or the Internet. In this section, we discuss the most common types of RAID levels that are used for database applications and the properties of each level that relate to the performance of read and write operations:

RAID Level	Description	Read Performance	Write Performance	Suitability for Data Files	Suitability for Log Files
0	Disk striping, no redundancy	Excellent	Excellent	Poor	Poor
1	Disk mirroring	Average	Excellent	Good	Excellent
5	Disk striping with parity	Excellent	Poor	Good	Poor
10	Disk striping combined with disk mirroring	Excellent	Excellent	Excellent	Excellent

Although other RAID levels exist, they aren't common when compared to those mentioned. By looking at the various properties of each RAID level, you can quickly decide on the appropriate level for your requirements. In an ideal world, you would simply create RAID 10 arrays for everything; however, as RAID 10 has a 50-percent overhead in terms of usable disk capacity, this is the most expensive option in terms of physical disk requirements. So, it's common to see a mixture of the following situations within production environments:

❏   RAID 1 arrays used for data and RAID 1 arrays used for transaction logs

❏   RAID 5 arrays used for data and RAID 1 arrays used for transaction logs

❏   RAID 10 arrays used for data and RAID 1 arrays used for transaction logs

❏   RAID 10 arrays used for data and RAID 10 arrays used for transaction logs

Notice that you never use RAID 5 for transactions logs due to its poor write performance. Because transactions are written to the transaction log as they occur, by optimizing the I/O performance of the array where the log is stored you help to reduce the impact of I/O bottlenecks.

> **Always try to create your data files and log files on separate disk arrays. This will help optimize writing to the transaction log, which in turn will improve overall database performance.**

Default File Locations

When you create databases in SQL Server, you can specify explicitly where the files are to be located. If you omit this explicit location, SQL Server will create the database files in the default location for the server.

You can specify the default location for the data files when you install SQL Server, and you can change this postinstallation using SQL Server Enterprise Manager.

Try It Out: Changing the Default Location of the Data Files

1. Open SQL Server Enterprise Manager and connect to the SQL Server for which you want to set the default file locations. Right-click the server name within Enterprise Manager and select **Properties** from the pop-up menu. Click the **Database Settings** tab and you'll see two input boxes where you can enter the path information at the bottom of the screen.

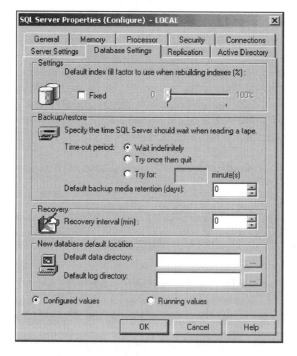

2. Enter your preferred drive and path locations for the new database data files and new database log files. Click **OK** to retain your changes.

Collation Settings

As we mentioned in the previous chapter, you can specify a collation for each database. A collation is used to specify the sort order, case sensitivity, and Unicode collation used by the database when dealing with character data. There is no right or wrong choice for the collation because your choice will be driven by the requirements of the database application you're installing. Check with the vendor or with the developers on what the collation requirements are. If in doubt, the default collation is usually suitable for most situations.

The Create Database Wizard

The Create Database Wizard is a simple way of creating a new database within a SQL Server instance. After you've run it once, you'll probably find it pointless, because creating a database within Enterprise Manager without using the wizard, as you'll see next, is almost as simple and may actually be faster. However, for completeness, we'll quickly run through the Create Database Wizard.

> **The Create Database Wizard doesn't allow you to specify the collation to be used by the database. The database will use the same collation as the server default. If you want to change this, you should do so immediately after creating the database**

Try It Out: Creating a Database with the Create Database Wizard

1. Open SQL Server Enterprise Manager and connect to the server on which you want to create your first database. Click the **Tools** menu and select **Wizards**.

2. In the **Database** node, select the **Create Database Wizard** and click **OK**.

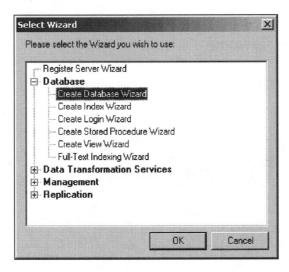

Click **Next** to skip past the welcome screen.

103

3. Now you're prompted to enter some information about the database you want to create. First you're asked to enter your database name. Next you're asked to enter the path to the drive and directory where the database data files will be located, and also the path to the drive and directory where the database log files will be created. Enter this information and click Next.

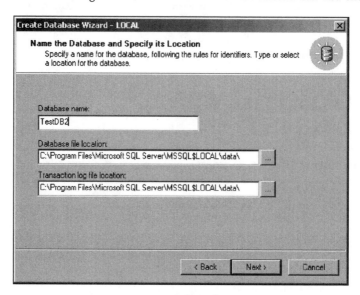

Although we've mentioned that you should create data and log files on separate drives whenever possible, we appreciate that many readers will be testing these examples on a small server or desktop PC that may have only one physical disk. Therefore, we present examples with the data and log on the same drive. If you have additional disk drives, you should consider separating these for performance reasons.

4. You can add additional database data files and set the size of each data file that you want to create. For this example, you need only one data file of the default size, 1MB. Click Next.

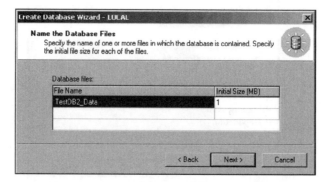

> Unless you've increased the size of the model database from its default, it will be 1MB in size. Because every database you create is actually a copy of the model database, every database you create will be 1MB in size.

5. Now you can set the growth properties of your data files. You can choose whether or not to have the data files grow automatically, the amount by which they will automatically grow, and the maximum size that the data file can grow to. Enter this information (the default is fine for this example) and click Next.

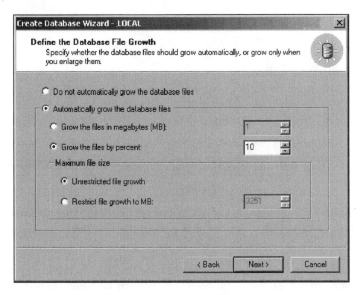

6. Now you need to repeat the previous process for your transaction log files. Enter the name and size of the transaction log files you want to include within your database and click Next.

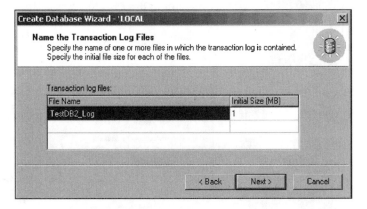

7. Once again, enter the growth increment and maximum size of the transaction log. Remember that all the log files you've asked SQL Server to add to your database will use these parameters. Click Next.

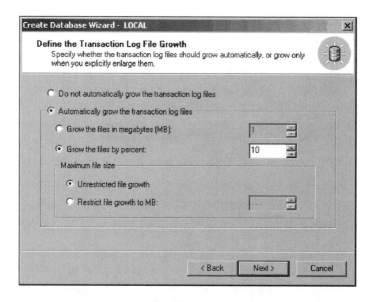

A common "default" starting size of the transaction log is 10 percent of the total size of all your database files. This is a good guide if you're unsure.

8. Finally, click Finish to create the database. In the background, SQL Server creates your database from a copy of the model database and adds any additional files that you've requested.

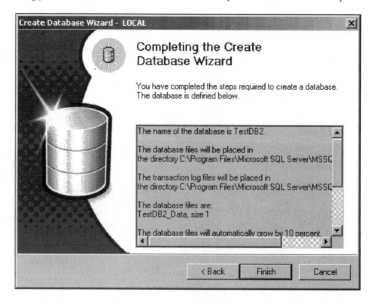

After SQL Server has created the database, it will ask you if you want to create a **database maintenance plan** for this newly created database. If you were doing this in a live environment, it would probably be a good idea, but because this is just a test, and because we cover maintenance plans in Chapter 14, click No.

Creating Databases in Enterprise Manager

Now that you've created a database using the Create Database Wizard, you can promptly forget this information, because it's unlikely that you'll need to do it again. Instead, you're much more likely to create your new databases using Enterprise Manager directly; the Create Database Wizard interface doesn't really simplify the process.

Try It Out: Creating a Database with Enterprise Manager

1. Connect to the appropriate SQL Server using Enterprise Manager and right-click the Databases node. From the pop-up menu, select **New Database**. You are presented with the following window, which contains three tabs for entering information about the database you want to create:

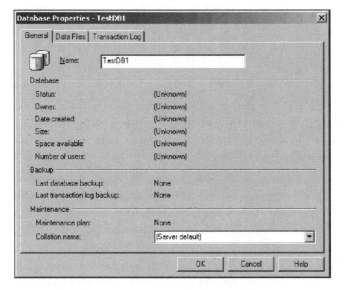

2. On the General tab, you need to enter two options: the database name and the database collation. Enter the database name in line with your established naming standards (see the "Naming Conventions" section earlier in this chapter), and if you have good reason to change the collation do so; otherwise, leave the (Server default) option.

3. Then select the **Data Files** tab. This tab contains information similar to what you saw previously in the Create Database Wizard, albeit in a slightly more verbose format. Within this screen, you enter the information on the data files you want to include within this database. In the top half of the screen, you enter the filename, file location, file size, and filegroup information.

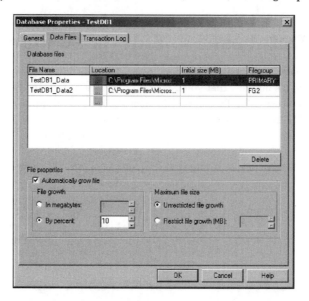

❑ The **File Name** property is the name you'll use to reference this file from within SQL Server when you make changes to the file structure.

❑ The **Location** property is the drive, directory, and disk filename that are used to create the data file physically on disk.

❑ The **Initial size** property is the size SQL Server will expand the file to after the database has been created. It's important to note that a data file can't be reduced in size below its initial size, so it's often a good idea to leave this small and expand it as required later.

❑ Alternatively, if you know the optimal size of the database, enter this into the **Initial size** property. This allows SQL Server to expand the data file to full size after creation, helping reduce the impact of costly file expansions as the data volumes grow and also helping reduce file fragmentation by allowing SQL Server to create the file in contiguous disk space.

❑ The **Filegroup** option allows you to enter the name of the filegroup that the file will belong to. If you want to have more than just the primary filegroup, you don't need to explicitly create a new one–simply type in the name you want to call the filegroup and SQL Server will create it for you.

❑ The bottom half of the screen allows you to set the growth parameters for each file. Here, you set whether you want the file to grow automatically, the growth increment, and the maximum size of the data file (if any). Notice that you can set this for each file in this screen as opposed to a single setting for all files that are available when you were using the Create Database Wizard.

4. On the Transaction Log tab, you enter the transaction log files you want to create within this database. This is similar to the previous Data Files tab, except there is no Filegroup column here because transaction log files don't belong to filegroups. Enter the growth and size information for your desired transaction log files and click OK.

As mentioned earlier, if you're unsure about the size that the transaction log file should be, a common estimate is 10 percent of the combined data files' size. If this proves inadequate, SQL Server will automatically expand the transaction log file as required (based on your file growth parameters):

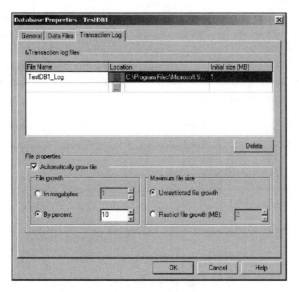

Once you click OK, Enterprise Manager will ask SQL Server to create your database. This usually takes only a few seconds, so very shortly you should have a newly created database listed under the Databases node within Enterprise Manager.

Creating a Database with T-SQL

As with many tasks that you can carry out using SQL Server Enterprise Manager, you can create the database in Query Analyzer using T-SQL code. Although this is a little more complicated than with Enterprise Manager, using T-SQL allows you to save the database creation request as a script that you can reuse in the future. This means you can be sure that each time you create this database, all the filenames, filegroups, file locations, and sizes will be consistent with previous versions of the database.

> By scripting the creation of a database, you can ensure that it's always created in the same way, even on different servers (such as development, test, and production). Also, if you distribute your application to many locations, you can ensure that each location has the same data file settings, which can help reduce administration effort.

To create a database using T-SQL, you use the CREATE DATABASE command with the following parameters:

```
CREATE DATABASE dbname
[ ON <data file information> ]
[ LOG ON <log file information> ]
[ COLLATE ]
[ FOR LOAD | FOR ATTACH ]
```

In the simplest format, only the CREATE DATABASE command, followed by the new database's name, needs to be specified. In this situation, SQL Server will create a database using the default collation with one data file and one log file at the default size in the default file locations for the server. If you want to specify a file location other than the default, you must specify the additional file options. Similarly, if you want to use a collation other than the server default or set the database to a special mode, you must use the appropriate options.

> FOR LOAD and FOR ATTACH are used to create a "placeholder" database to be replaced either by restoring a database backup or by reattaching offline database files. For more information, see CREATE DATABASE in SQL Server Books Online.

Try It Out: Creating a Database with T-SQL

1. Connect to SQL Server with Query Analyzer. Enter the following CREATE DATABASE statement, but remember to alter the physical file paths for your drive and directory structure:

```
CREATE DATABASE Test3
ON PRIMARY
        (NAME = test3_primary_data1,
         FILENAME = 'd:\sqldata\test3_primary_data1.mdf',
         SIZE = 1MB,
         MAXSIZE = 200MB,
         FILEGROWTH = 10%),
        (NAME = test3_primary_data2,
         FILENAME = 'd:\sqldata\test3_primary_data2.ndf',
         SIZE = 1MB,
         MAXSIZE = 200MB,
         FILEGROWTH = 10%),
FILEGROUP FG2
        (NAME = test3_fg2_data1,
         FILENAME = 'd:\sqldata\test3_fg2_data1.ndf',
         SIZE = 1MB,
         MAXSIZE = 200MB,
         FILEGROWTH = 10%)

LOG ON (NAME = test3_log1,
         FILENAME = 'd:\sqldata\test3_log1.ldf',
         SIZE = 51MB,
         MAXSIZE = 200MB,
         FILEGROWTH = 10%)
```

When you execute this script, it will create a database named Test3 on the PRIMARY filegroup that contains two data files, and a FG2 filegroup that contains one data file and a single log file. The default collation for your server will be used and your database will be created normally for immediate use. If the database is created successfully, the following will be displayed:

The CREATE DATABASE process is allocating 1.00 MB on disk 'test3_primary_data1'.
The CREATE DATABASE process is allocating 1.00 MB on disk 'test3_primary_data2'.
The CREATE DATABASE process is allocating 1.00 MB on disk 'test3_fg2_data1'.
The CREATE DATABASE process is allocating 51.00 MB on disk 'test3_log1'.

Database Options

In addition to the database options that you can specify when you create the database, there are a number of options that you can set once the database has been created. In this section, you'll look at available options. Many of these relate to other topics in this book, so they're discussed in more detail elsewhere.

Database Options in Enterprise Manager

Once your database has been created, you can right-click the database name in Enterprise Manager and select Properties from the pop-up menu. You'll see a window similar to the one you saw when you created the database, and the first three Tabs of this window will be very familiar. However, there are some new tabs here, such as Filegroups, Options, and Permissions. The tab you're most interested in at the moment is labeled Options, and if you select it you should see a window similar to the following image:

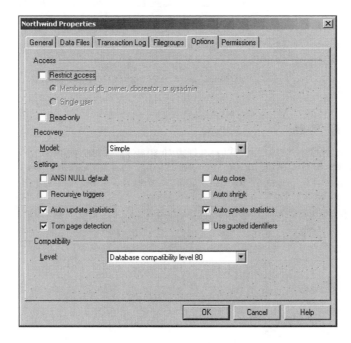

These options allow you to alter the behavior of your database. For now, we'll quickly run through the various options available so you get a good idea of how you can alter the behavior of your database, postcreation.

Restricting Access to a Database

If you want to prevent people from gaining access to your database temporarily, you can select the Restrict access check box. Once you've enabled this option, you can choose to only let administrators or one physical connection (Single user) gain access to the database.

Be careful if you choose Single user, because this single user can be any user, not just an administrator. If you want to be the single user, make sure you establish the connection to the database right away before someone else comes along and snaps it up.

Making a Database Read-Only

If you don't want to prevent people from accessing the database but instead wish to prevent anyone from making changes either temporarily or permanently, you can do this quite easily by enabling the Read-only check box. However, all the database users should be disconnected before you enable the read-only option.

> **If users are connected to your database and you try to set it to read-only using Enterprise Manager, you'll receive an error.**

The Recovery Model

Recovery models are central to the backup and restore strategy of any database, so we cover these in great detail in Chapter 8. However, for the time being you can think of a recovery model as an option that affects the amount of information that is retained within the transaction log files.

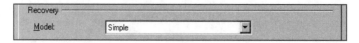

The available recovery models are as follows:

❏ **Simple:** This recovery model uses the least amount of log space, as transactions are removed from the transaction log files after the information has been successfully written to the data files. This greatly reduces the recoverability of backup and restore options.

❏ **Bulk-Logged:** Transactions are retained within the transaction log files indefinitely until you explicitly back up the transaction log. This option can use a lot more log space depending on how regularly you choose to back up the transaction log. However, several operations that affect a lot of information, such as creating an index, record a lot less information in the transaction log than the full model (described next). Using this option impacts how you can recover your database.

❏ **Full:** Transactions are retained within the transaction log until you back it up as in the Bulk-Logged model. However, bulk operations fully log all the changes they make, which means this option can potentially use much more log space than the previous option, once again depending on the backup frequency. Using this option doesn't impact the ability to recover the database.

If you're deciding on the recovery model to use for a production database or an important development or test database, please read Chapter 8 before making this decision.

ANSI NULLs

The ANSI NULL default option affects the way SQL Server treats NULLs in columns within a database. If this option is set ON, and if the table creation command doesn't explicitly specify that the columns allow or disallow NULL values, then SQL Server will create the columns to allow NULL values. When this option is OFF, SQL Server will create the columns (that don't explicitly specify nullability) to not allow NULL values.

Usually this setting shouldn't matter and can be left to its default because all good code will explicitly specify whether or not the column allows NULLs. However, some poorly written code may assume one way or the other, so you may need to alter this option in line with the requirements from the developer/vendor.

Auto Close

Auto close is an option that was intended for use in the desktop edition of SQL Server or for very low-use databases. When SQL Server is running, each database incurs a small amount of resource overhead for it to be online and available for access by database users. This overhead may include SQL Server internally holding the database files open and retaining any recently used data within a cache.

By enabling the Auto close option, SQL Server closes the database files and releases any resources being used by that database when no users are connected to that particular database. Whenever a user attempts to access the database again, SQL Server automatically opens the database files and acquires the necessary resources.

There is quite a bit of performance overhead in closing and opening files, so this is not a suitable option for production databases used regularly by users. If you have an infrequently used database or want to minimize the resources used by SQL Server when it is installed on a desktop machine, you may find this option of use.

Recursive Triggers

Enabling or disabling recursive triggers is another one of those options that requires input from the developer/vendor of the database before you decide what is appropriate. **Triggers** are pieces of code executed automatically by SQL Server when information stored within a table is modified. Triggers are used for a variety of purposes, such as maintaining audit tables (by inserting every changed row into an audit table) or ensuring that certain values within a table are always populated (such as a ModifiedByUsername column).

> **For more information on triggers, see Chapter 10.**

When recursive triggers are allowed, if a trigger on a table, TableA, modifies information within TableA, then the trigger is executed again due to this second modification. This situation isn't usually desirable, as it will lead to circular references, unless you're explicitly expecting and allowing for this situation in your trigger code.

The default and more common setting is to have this option disabled. In this case, when TableA is modified, the trigger is executed, but if TableA is further modified within the trigger itself, then the trigger isn't executed a second time due to this modification.

Automatically Shrinking a Database

You saw that you can specify a growth increment for your data and transaction log files when they become full, but what happens if you take the reverse of the situation: the data files become empty or less full than they once were? Although this isn't really that common in most databases, it can happen from time to time due to periodic archiving of historical information, for example. Also, if you have data that you import from other systems into a staging area and remove it once the production tables have been populated, you may find that the total size of the data stored within the database temporarily increases from time to time.

The issue with this type of system is that, although data files can automatically grow when they become full (up to the maximum size you've allowed them to grow to), they don't automatically shrink when they become less than full. Increasing and decreasing file sizes are expensive operations in terms of I/O, so it's desirable to keep these operations to a minimum. As almost all databases increase in size (very few start off with lots of data and get progressively smaller), it doesn't make a lot of sense to be automatically regularly shrinking the database. Doing so only adds unnecessary overhead.

What about the situation in which you archive large amounts of information from time to time? A much more effective way of regaining this free space is to manually shrink the database as part of the archival job.

> Don't use the Auto shrink option unless you're running SQL Server on your workstation and have limited disk space available. This shouldn't be enabled for production databases on dedicated servers, as it can cause unnecessary performance degradation while SQL Server periodically rearranges the data contained within the database files.

Statistics

Statistics are the information that SQL Server creates about the distribution of data within database tables for the purpose of improving query performance. There are few situations in which you wouldn't want SQL Server to automatically create statistics, so ensure that this option is enabled.

There are also few reasons why you wouldn't want SQL Server to automatically update statistics. One of the few acceptable reasons is if your database is extremely busy; rather than having SQL Server update statistics during peak usage periods (thereby increasing system resource usage slightly), you could disable automatic updating and manually update the statistics during nonpeak periods. This creates more work for you as the DBA, so only consider this alternative if you believe there is good reason to do so.

Torn Page Detection

A **torn page** can occur within a database when a page is only partly written to disk. The common cause of this is when you're using hardware that doesn't have a battery backed-up cache (cheap SCSI controllers and most IDE controllers) and the server fails partway through a disk write operation. As there is no battery backup on the controller cache, the remainder of the disk write is lost. When the server recovers, the physical pages within the database may be left in an inconsistent state.

Enabling Torn page detection doesn't prevent torn pages, but it will alert you when such a corruption is discovered, thus preventing you from unwittingly adding more information into a corrupted database. This adds little overhead, so you should always enable this option if you're working with controllers that don't have battery backup.

> **Torn pages errors are recorded in the SQL Server error log. This can be located under the** Management | SQL Server Logs | Current node **in Enterprise Manager.**

Quoted Identifiers

Quoted identifiers are another of those options that will require advice from the database application developer/vendor.

When this option is enabled, column names within the code can be referred to using the SQL-92 method of placing quotes around them, for example:

```
SELECT "MyCol1","MyCol2" FROM MyTable
```

Instead of being interpreted as column names when the quoted identifiers option is disabled, the values contained within quotes (MyCol1) are interpreted as string literals.

The default is to have this option disabled, in which case you should refer to case identifiers directly, for example:

```
SELECT MyCol1, MyCol2 FROM MyTable
```

Alternatively, you can use square bracket notation (which you must use when your object name contains spaces or other special characters), for example:

```
SELECT [MyCol1], [MyCol2] FROM [MyTable]
```

The quoted identifier setting only sets the default for the database and can easily be overridden by a user's application by specifying, in the connection string, the desired means of identifier referencing.

> **The square bracket notation used by SQL Server is a native method of indicating identifiers and this can't be disabled. Therefore, it's a preferred choice over quoted identifiers, as it will function correctly irrespective of what identifier settings have been set.**

The Compatibility Level

You shouldn't change the database compatibility level from its default value (level 80) for any new databases that you're creating unless you've been specifically directed to do so by the database application developer/vendor.

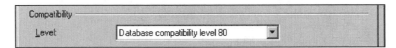

This setting is used for making the SQL Server 2000 database commands compatible with previous versions of SQL Server. Although the majority of commands that were present in SQL Server 6.5 and SQL Server 7.0 are still present in SQL Server 2000, Microsoft has introduced new reserved words and slight changes in the behavior of some commands. These changes in reserved words and command behavior may trip up database applications that were developed for previous versions, and they may not be directly compatible with SQL Server 2000 without modification.

To ease the upgrade process, Microsoft allows you to modify the database compatibility level on a database-by-database basis. By setting this option to 70 or 65 (for SQL Server 7.0 and 6.5, respectively), the reserved words that were introduced with later versions are no longer treated as reserved words, thereby allowing your upgraded databases to function on SQL Server, if this was the cause of upgrade failure.

As the new reserved words aren't available, the new functionality provided by these reserved words, such as CREATE FUNCTION, won't be available in the databases with lower compatibility levels. For this reason, always run databases with level 80 compatibility (for SQL Server 2000), unless there's a conflict that you can't resolve that requires you to drop this level.

> The compatibility level affects command compatibility. This doesn't affect the improvements that were introduced with the underlying storage engine of SQL Server between SQL Server 6.5 and SQL Server 2000. A database in 65 compatibility mode still receives all the storage benefits, such as row-level locking, of any other SQL Server 2000 database.

More Advanced Options

Apart from the options that you can set through Enterprise Manager, there are several advanced options that you can only set through T-SQL. You set these using the ALTER DATABASE T-SQL command, and there are two categories of advanced options: the **SQL options** and the **Cursor options**.

> All of the database options available through Enterprise Manager can be set using the ALTER DATABASE command. In this section, we discuss only the options that aren't available within Enterprise Manager. For a full list of options that you can set using ALTER DATABASE, see the ALTER DATABASE command in SQL Server Books Online.

SQL Options

The SQL options affect the behavior of SQL code, so the need to set these will almost always come from a requirement expressed by the database developer/vendor. The default values are fine for almost all databases, but if you have a specific requirement to change one or more of these values, it's important to be familiar with the ALTER DATABASE command. When using ALTER DATABASE to set database-specific options, you use the following command syntax:

```
ALTER DATABASE dbname SET option ON | OFF
```

The various options you have available are discussed in the following sections.

ANSI_NULLS

If you turn this option ON, a comparison against NULL values will always return NULL—for example, "Does NULL=NULL" will return NULL. On the other hand, if this option is turned OFF, then comparison with a NULL value will return TRUE or FALSE—for example, "Does NULL=NULL" will return TRUE.

```
ALTER DATABASE dbname SET ANSI_NULLS ON
```

ANSI_PADDING

When you set this option to OFF, SQL Server trims trailing spaces from VARCHAR columns when the column data is inserted or updated. Similarly, when this option is set to OFF, trailing zeros are trimmed from VARBINARY columns when the column data is inserted or updated. Setting this option to ON prevents this trimming from taking place:

```
ALTER DATABASE dbname SET ANSI_PADDING ON
```

ANSI_WARNINGS

When you set this option to ON, SQL Server will raise warnings during the processing of a SQL statement if NULL values are included within rows being aggregated (added up) or if a particular condition, such as divide by zero, occurs. When you set this option to OFF, SQL Server doesn't raise these warnings.

```
ALTER DATABASE dbname SET ANSI_WARNINGS ON
```

ARITHABORT

When you set this option to ON, an arithmetic error, such as a divide by zero, will cause SQL Server to terminate the currently executing batch and roll back any transactions that are in progress. If you set this option to OFF, SQL Server will raise warning messages and continue execution.

```
ALTER DATABASE dbname SET ARITHABORT ON
```

CONCAT_NULL_YIELDS_NULL

This option affects the way string values are concatenated within database code. If you set this to ON, then concatenating a string with NULL produces NULL, for example:

```
'ABC' + NULL = NULL
```

When you set this option to OFF, concatenating a string and a NULL value produces a string value, as the NULL is treated as an empty string, for example:

```
'ABC' + NULL = 'ABC'
```

Here's the syntax:

```
ALTER DATABASE dbname SET CONCAT_NULL_YIELDS_NULL ON
```

NUMERIC_ROUND_ABORT

If you set this option to ON and a loss in precision occurs during the assignment of numerical values, then SQL Server will generate an error message. If you set this option to OFF, no error message will be generated.

```
ALTER DATABASE dbname SET NUMERIC_ROUND_ABORT ON
```

Removing Databases

Just knowing how to create a database within SQL Server isn't enough—you also need to know how to remove a database from SQL Server. When you're removing databases, common sense should prevail. Ensure that the database is no longer needed and all information that it contains is backed up so if you discover you need to restore it at a later point in time, you can do so.

Before you're able to remove a database, you must ensure that no users are connected to it. Otherwise, the removal of the database will fail, and SQL Server will inform you that users are still connected. This doesn't mean that the users can't be connected to other databases within the current SQL Server instance; it just means that their connection can't be with the database that you want to remove. To carry out the removal, you can use either Enterprise Manager or T-SQL.

> Always take a full backup of a database before you remove it. Even if you are sure you don't need the database at present, you never know if you might require the information again in the future. Refer to Chapter 8 for information on how to take a full database backup.

Removing a Database with Enterprise Manager

Removing a database using Enterprise Manager is very straightforward.

Try It Out: Removing a Database with Enterprise Manager

Open SQL Server Enterprise Manager and connect to the SQL Server that contains the database to be removed. Drill down into the **Databases** node and right-click the name of the database that you want to remove. From the pop-up menu, select **Delete**.

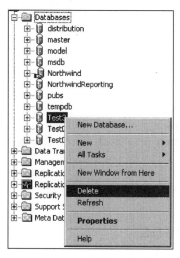

You're asked to confirm the delete, and you're given the option to delete the backup and restore history, which is enabled by default.

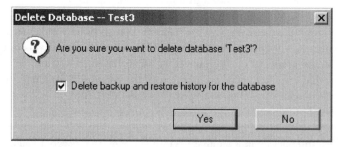

When a database is backed up or restored, these events are recorded within the msdb database. Once you remove the database, the history of when the database was backed up and restored is probably no longer of interest to you, so when you leave this option box checked, Enterprise Manager will also clean out this history information from msdb. If you do want to retain the backup and restore information, uncheck this option box.

Once you click Yes, the database is dropped and the database data files are deleted from the file system.

Removing a Database with T-SQL

To remove a database using T-SQL, you execute the DROP DATABASE statement followed by one or more database names. Don't worry, only the database owner and members of the sysadmin and dbcreator fixed server roles can execute this.

> **Because members of the db_owner database role can drop databases, end users of your database application shouldn't be members of this role. See Chapter 6 for more information on database security.**

Try It Out: Removing a Database with T-SQL

Connect to SQL Server using Query Analyzer and determine the name of the database that you no longer want to keep within your SQL Server instance. You can execute the sp_helpdb stored procedure to get a list of all databases:

```
sp_helpdb
```

```
name
_____

master
model
msdb
Northwind
pubs
tempdb
TestDB1
TestDB2
```

Once you're satisfied that adequate backup precautions have been carried out, run the DROP DATABASE command followed by the name of the database that you want to remove. If you want, you can remove multiple databases by specifying the database names separated by commas.

```
DROP DATABASE TestDB2
```

This results in a message similar to the following:

```
Deleting database file 'D:\SQLdata\TestDB2_Log.LDF'.
Deleting database file 'D:\SQLdata\TestDB2_Data.MDF'.
```

> **A database can't be dropped if there are users connected to it.**

Designing the Database Schema

Now that you're comfortable with creating and removing databases from within SQL Server, you need to start thinking about how you're going to store information within the databases that you create. This can be a complex task and it isn't the aim of this section to trivialize the task necessary to create effective data models. Instead, the aim is to provide you with an introduction to designing databases, and give you enough information to feel comfortable creating simple databases for purposes such as storing your own DBA data (database performance or event information).

After reading this chapter, you may choose to go off and gain further experience with data modeling and read detailed data modeling publications.

> It isn't the goal of this section to be a detailed description of data modeling—rather, this is a light introduction. For further data modeling information, we suggest you read *Data Modeling for Everyone* from Apress (ISBN: 1-59059-213-1).

Database Components

Before you think too much about a design for your particular requirements, let's consider all the various objects that can be components of a database:

- ❑ Tables
- ❑ Views
- ❑ Stored procedures
- ❑ Functions
- ❑ Indexes
- ❑ User-defined functions
- ❑ Triggers
- ❑ Constraints
- ❑ Defaults

Out of all of these objects, only tables are used for storing your data within a database; all other objects exist to access the information within your database tables. We discuss accessing the information in detail in Chapter 4, so for now we'll just concentrate on what you need to do to efficiently and appropriately store data within your database.

Determining the Style of Design You Use

At a high level there are essentially two styles of database design that you can use when designing the tables, columns, and relationships that exist between tables used within the database. These are the **normalized** and **dimensional** models, and each is appropriate for different situations.

Normalized database designs are suitable for Online Transaction Processing (OLTP) databases that SELECT, INSERT, UPDATE, and DELETE information from the database. They're structured to minimize data redundancy so that when someone modifies information, it need only be changed in one place. Also, the number of columns within tables is kept at a minimum to improve performance when modifying rows within the tables.

Dimensional designs are suitable when little or no data modification takes place in an online fashion; instead, changes may be bulk imported from external systems. They're optimized for data retrieval and may contain duplicate or redundant information as well as preaggregated information within the tables. This makes dimensional models particularly well suited for data warehousing and decision support applications.

Normalized Design

A **normalized design** allows the information within your database to be retained within tables that describe a single object or entity. Data duplication within your database is minimized, allowing you to retrieve and modify pieces of data in a single location in your database. This makes it easier to apply changes and also ensures that data is consistent within the database by removing the possibility that data has been updated in one location but not in another.

There are industry rules about how normalization should take place, and these rules are called **normal forms**. There are many different levels of normal forms, starting at first normal form and continuing on to sixth normal form. Each level dictates that the database design complies more strictly with the core principle that the data within each table relates to only a single entity. Most database designers implement database designs that meet the requirements of third normal form because this middle ground provides sufficient data integrity through normalization without overcomplicating the database design to meet the requirements of higher levels of normalization.

Third Normal Form

If you're designing tables to store information within your database, what is third normal form, and why should you design for it? **Third normal form** is a set of rules that attempts to minimize duplicate information within your database to a sufficient level to allow this information to be maintained easily, but without making it difficult to query that information (the more tables in a database, the more difficult it is to query).

The rules of third normal form are as follows:

❑   **There must be a primary key in the table.** A primary key is a set of one or more columns that provides a value that is unique for every row in the table.

❑ **There must be no repeating columns within the table.** For example, in an `Orders` table, a single row shouldn't have `Product1`, `Product2`, `Product3`, and so on.

❑ **Every column in the table must be dependent on the primary key, not another column.** For example, in an `Orders` table, you may have an `OrderNumber` column as your primary key and a `CustomerID` column to refer to a product that has been ordered. The `CustomerID` is dependent on the `OrderNumber`. In other words, the customer who placed the order is dependent on the order itself. However, if you also had a column called `CreditLimit`, this would violate third normal form. As the `CreditLimit` of the customer isn't dependent on the particular `OrderNumber` but is instead dependent on a non–primary key column, the `CustomerID` column.

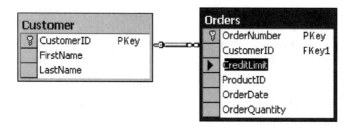

Now, if you moved the `CreditLimit` column into the `Customer` table, then these tables would no longer violate third normal form. This is because all the columns in the `Order` table (`CustomerID`, `ProductID`, `OrderDate`, and `OrderQuantity`) are dependent on the primary key, `OrderNumber`. Similarly, as `CreditLimit` is dependent on the primary key in the `Customer` table, this is also valid.

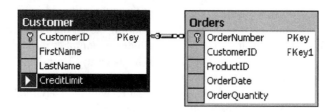

The other conditions of third normal form, such as having a primary key and having nonrepeating fields, are also met.

> Database design can be a complicated subject, and many books are dedicated to this topic. For more information, see *Professional SQL Server 2000 Database Design* from Apress (ISBN: 1-861004-76-1).

Dimensional Design

A normalized design isn't appropriate for all types of databases. Although this style fits well with applications that are entering or updating information regularly, databases designed predominately for reporting and analysis benefit from a structure that is optimized for the identification and retrieval of rows from the database. A common approach to this situation is to use a technique known as **dimensional modeling** to create a star or snowflake schema.

> **Normalized database designs support databases that add and change information regularly. Because of the number of tables involved, they tend to be difficult for users to query on an ad-hoc basis. Also, more tables usually means less performance.**

A dimensional design consists of two key table concepts: **fact tables** and **dimension tables**. A fact table is a core table that contains all the units of measurement from the business process that the database is representing. Surrounding this fact table is a series of dimension tables, each of which contains the descriptive attributes of the dimension that the fact table may reference. Unlike a normalized design, tables aren't necessarily split to minimize data duplication. Instead, the structure is flat and the tables are often wide to incorporate all the attributes of each dimension. This results in increased data retrieval performance, as multiple tables need not be joined to gain a view of all the dimension information.

A star schema contains a single level of dimensional tables surrounding the fact table, and each of these dimensional tables contains the attributes of the dimension in a somewhat denormalized form:

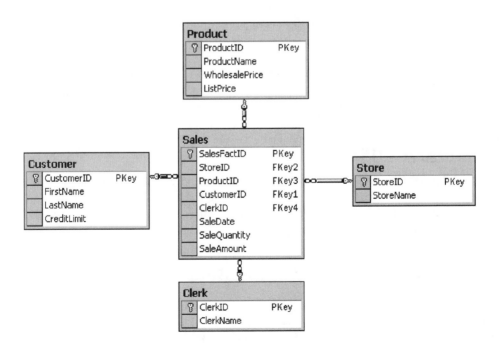

Snowflake schemas may contain additional levels of dimensional tables to separate attributes that are highly duplicated within a given dimension table:

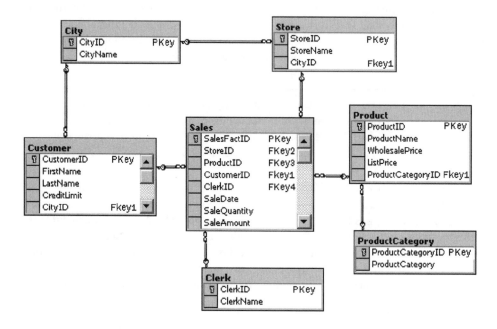

There is much debate as to the benefits of the star or snowflake approach to dimensional modeling. Predominately, this debate centers on the simplicity of ad-hoc reporting for end users. After all, this usually is the sole purpose of a dimensional model, so why make it more difficult for users to query by adding additional levels in the dimensional schema?

Given that a snowflake adds complexity to the database schema from the perspective of those who will be using it (end users running ad-hoc reports, for example), a good approach is to design a star schema and convert it to a snowflake schema if there is a valid reason for doing so.

Creating Tables

Creating a table within a database is one of those things in which actually completing the task is relatively simple, but all the options you need to consider are complex. So, first, we'll go through the issues you need to be thinking about when creating your database tables before we actually look at creating tables through SQL Server Enterprise Manager and T-SQL.

Considerations Before You Create a Table

There are many things to consider when you create a table, and these are issues that you need to consider after you've developed your database design. If you don't yet have a design established, you shouldn't progress to creating database objects. If you do, you'll find yourself continuously modifying the structure within SQL Server or crudely adapting what you create as you gain a better understanding of the application's requirements.

When you have your design established, the following sections should be considered to physically implement your database design within SQL Server.

Naming Conventions Again

We briefly discussed naming conventions when we looked at creating databases. You need to consider naming conventions again when you create database tables, as it's important to have consistent and easily identifiable names for your database tables. These names decide how database developers will reference the tables throughout their code, and this is how users who have ad-hoc access to the database will select the tables to use for their querying requirements. Having convoluted or inconsistent naming standards makes everyone's life more difficult and ultimately leads to mistakes being made.

Determining Which Filegroup Your Table Should Be Created On

When you create your table, you can either let SQL Server create the table on the default filegroup or you can specify another filegroup for the database to be located on. This allows you to balance database load between disks to enhance I/O performance.

There are no hard-and-fast rules for the best placement of database objects on filegroups, but some common situations in which you might create tables on another filegroup include the following:

❏ Placing tables that are commonly joined on separate filegroups (in which the underlying files are physically located on separate disks) can allow rows from both tables to be retrieved in parallel.

❏ Placing tables and the nonclustered indexes of that table on separate filegroups may allow for the index to be searched and rows from the table to be retrieved in parallel.

❏ Placing tables that contain read-only data on their own filegroup allows you to set the filegroup to read-only, which physically prevents changes to these tables and also allows you to back up data that changes regularly independently of the data that doesn't change.

If you don't want to have to explicitly specify an alternative filegroup every time you create a table, you can actually change the default filegroup that objects are created on when no filegroup is specified.

Setting the Default Filegroup

You can set the default filegroup using either Enterprise Manager or T-SQL (via a query tool such as Query Analyzer). If you decide to use T-SQL, you'll use the ALTER DATABASE command with the following syntax:

```
ALTER DATABASE dbname MODIFY FILEGROUP filegroupname DEFAULT
```

Try It Out: Setting the Default Filegroup

To change the filegroup using Enterprise Manager, you should connect to the appropriate SQL Server and drill down into the **Databases** node. Right-click the name of the database you want to change the default filegroup for and select **Properties** from the pop-up menu. Now click the **Filegroups** tab. You'll see a list of filegroups that are within this database. In the check box on the right, you can tick one filegroup to act as the default.

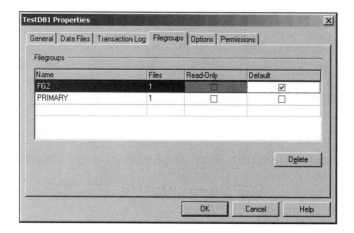

Once you're satisfied with the default filegroup, click **OK** to retain your changes.

Column Data Types

After you've planned your table and column layout in line with one of the database design styles described, you need to determine the most appropriate data type for every column within every table. As a table is nothing more than a collection of columns, it's important to understand the type and nature of the data that's going to be stored in the table so you can select the most suitable column data types.

When choosing the appropriate data type, first you need to establish what high-level type each column will contain:

High-Level Type	Contents
Numeric	Numbers
String data	Numbers, letters, and special characters
Date and Time	Date and time
Binary data	Binary and BLOB data

Once you've established the high-level type for the column, you can examine the various physical column data types to find the one that has the appropriate size and characteristics. Selecting the appropriate data type will help you optimize the retrieval of values within your table columns.

Numeric Data Types

SQL Server supports a wide range of numeric data types. The smallest of them all is BIT, which allows values of NULL, 0, or 1. As you might guess, BIT is most commonly used to store Boolean values (TRUE/FALSE), rather than numbers. TINYINT, SMALLINT, INT, and BIGINT are available to store whole numbers; which one you use depends on the range of values you need to store in your table or variable. Data types with larger ranges require additional storage space.

If you need to store numbers with decimal values, you have a choice of using the exact numeric data type DECIMAL (or NUMERIC) or the approximate numeric data types FLOAT and REAL. The following table summarizes the data types used for storing numeric data, along with the storage requirement for each:

Data Type	Description	Bytes	Precision	Numeric Range
TINYINT	Integer values	1	3	0 to 255
SMALLINT	Integer values	2	5	–32768 to 32767
INT	Integer values	4	10	–2147483648 to 2147483647
BIGINT	Integer values	8	19	-2^{63} to $(2^{63})-1$
BIT	Binary (on or off)	1 byte per 8-bit columns	1	0 or 1
DECIMAL/NUMERIC	Exact numeric values	5 to 17 (depends on precision)	1 to 38	
SMALL MONEY	Money values	4	10	–214,748.3648 to 214,748.3648
MONEY	Money values	8	19	-2^{63} to $(2^{63})-1$
FLOAT	Approximate values	4 to 8 (depends on precision)	7	(1.79E)+308 to (–2.23E)–308 and (2.23E)–308 to (1.79E)+308
REAL	Approximate values	4		(–3.40E)+38 to (–1.18E)–38 and (1.18E)–38 to (3.40E)+38

String Data Types

SQL Server supports several string data types that allow you to store strings of various lengths. Refer to the following table for a summary of supported string data types.

The amount of space required by strings is generally equal to the number of characters contained in the string, plus some overhead. The rule of thumb is to go with the nonvariable length data types CHAR or NCHAR (because these require less overhead), unless you don't know the string length ahead of time or the string length varies greatly from row to row. Notice that the maximum number of characters supported by NCHAR/NVARCHAR is only half those supported by CHAR/VARCHAR.

The TEXT and NTEXT data types should be used only for storing large strings (over 8000 characters) because these can't be queried with the majority of string functions (for instance, LEN, RIGHT, and LEFT) and are generally more difficult to manipulate with T-SQL.

Data Type	Description	Bytes	Number of Characters
CHAR	Fixed-length character values	1 to 8000	1 to 8000
VARCHAR	Variable-length character values	1 to 8000 (varies from row to row based on the number of characters in the column)	1 to 8000
TEXT	Variable-length character values	Up to 2GB	Up to 2147483647
NCHAR	Fixed-length Unicode character values	1 to 8000	1 to 4000
NVARCHAR	Variable-length Unicode character values	1 to 8000 (varies from row to row based on the number of characters in the column)	1 to 4000
NTEXT	Variable-length Unicode character values	Up to 2GB	Up to 1073741823

Date and Time Data Types

SQL Server provides two options for storing date and time data: SMALLDATETIME and DATETIME. The former supports dates between January 1, 1900, and June 6, 2079, which should be sufficient for most business applications. Furthermore, SMALLDATETIME stores dates with times with the accuracy of 1 minute.

If you need to store historical date values or care to track seconds and milliseconds, you'll have to use DATETIME, which allows dates between January 1, 1753, and December 31, 9999. DATETIME tracks time with the accuracy of 0.3 of a second. Because DATETIME allows for a larger range of values, it requires 8 bytes of storage per row, as opposed to 4 bytes required by SMALLDATETIME.

SQL Server doesn't provide data types for storing date and time separately.

Binary Data Types

Occasionally you might need to store binary data. In such cases, you can use BINARY or VARBINARY data types, which store fixed- and variable-length binary strings, respectively. Both data types support specifying the length of the data that will be stored in them, as in BINARY(200), and support up to 8000 bytes. The storage size is equal to the number of bytes entered plus 4 bytes of overhead. If you have a binary string that is 45 characters long, it will require 49 bytes of storage.

Another binary data type is IMAGE, which allows binary representations of images. Reading and writing such data has a high overhead, so typically it's recommended to store images on a file system and store a link to that image in the database instead. The IMAGE data type supports binary data from 0 through $2^{31}-1$ (2147483647) bytes.

Primary Keys

Every table within your database should have a **primary key**, without exception. In SQL Server there's no concept of row numbers or even a way to identify a single row without a unique key. The only way a single row can be individually identified is by a unique value that is composed of one or more columns. To enforce this uniqueness, you create a primary key constraint on those columns that will contain the unique values per row, and the key you use primarily for identifying the row should be defined as the primary key.

> A unique key is a constraint that states that the combination of the values within the columns that are participating in the unique key will be unique for every row within the table. You can have multiple unique keys defined for a table, but only one of these can be defined as the primary key. The primary key is functionally equivalent to nonprimary unique keys, but the one you intend to use to identify the row is known as the primary key.

For example, consider a table with the following rows:

IDCol	VarCharCol
1	Car
1	Car
2	Washer
3	Dryer
4	Desk
4	Desk

In this example, you can retrieve the rows containing Washer and Dryer individually because they have a unique value in the IDCol column. You could tell SQL Server to retrieve the rows with IDCol equal to 2 or 3. However, you can't return only one of the Car rows with the table in its present form. As there is nothing unique about each of the Car rows, SQL Server will retrieve all rows that meet your request.

If you modify your design slightly to make IDCol a unique primary key value (and to remove the duplicated data from your table), then each of the rows can now be individually identified and individually retrieved:

IDCol	VarCharCol
1	Car
2	Car
3	Washer
4	Dryer
5	Desk
6	Desk

Creating a primary key ensures that the value that is stored in the primary key column is different from every other row in the table.

Populating Primary Keys

You have two choices when creating your primary key. First, you can choose to generate a unique value for every row within your table as part of your application's logic. This may map to your business logic—for example, a unique customer identifier may be created for every customer that would also serve as a suitable primary key.

The second option you have available is to use a value that is automatically generated by SQL Server. Although this may have no business meaning, it does serve the purpose of assigning a unique value to every row so every row can be individually identified.

Neither approach is better than the other; you should select the method that works best with your application.

Creating Tables with Enterprise Manager

SQL Server Enterprise Manager provides a simple GUI for creating a table within a SQL Server database. This tool allows you to create and modify table structures, assign constraints and relationships between tables, and create indexes on specific columns to optimize retrieval performance.

Another feature of this interface is that you don't have to apply the changes you make within the designer there and then—you can elect to save the changes you've made as a change script for applying to the database at a later point in time. This could be of use if you're making significant changes to a table and you want the changes to take place outside normal hours of use. By scripting the changes, you can schedule them to take place as a scheduled job within the SQL Server Agent.

Try It Out: Creating a Table with Enterprise Manager

1. Open SQL Server Enterprise Manager and connect to your SQL Server. Drill down into the **Databases** node and select a test database that you previously created. Drill down further into this database, right-click the **Tables** node, and select **New Table** from the pop-up menu. You'll see a window similar to that shown in the following screenshot:

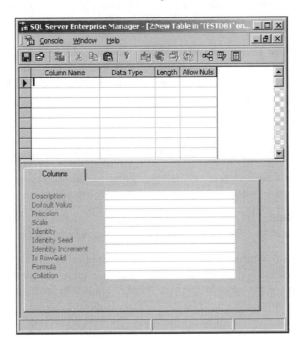

In this window, each row of the grid represents a column within the table you create. For each column you can specify the Column Name, Data Type, Length, and Nullability within the grid:

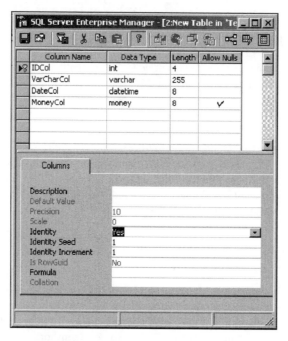

You can also specify additional properties for each column, and these are entered using the various fields located at the bottom of the window:

❑ **Description:** This is column metadata. You can add a small reference for the purpose of making the design self-documenting. This description can be referenced later within the designer or through T-SQL code. This may also be displayed as part of the help system when using a front-end application such as Microsoft Access.

❑ **Default Value:** For each row that is inserted into this table, if no value is explicitly specified for this column, you can specify that a default value be inserted into this column instead of NULL. This is useful if your columns aren't nullable.

❑ **Identity:** You can have one identity column per table. This is an autoincrementing numeric value that increases by the value of Identity Increment for every row that is inserted.

❑ **Is RowGuid:** You can also select one RowGuid column for each table. This is automatically populated for each row with a uniqueidentifer value.

❑ **Formula:** A formula is specified for a computed column. You can't insert a value into a computed column; instead, the value is computed when querying this column. This value is a result of the formula that you specify, and this formula may use the values stored in other columns.

2. As stated earlier in the chapter, every table should have a primary key. A primary key can consist of one or more columns—just bear in mind that each column in the multicolumn primary key must have a value supplied and that the combination of columns used must always produce a unique value. Otherwise the creation of the primary key and subsequent inserts of nonunique rows will fail. To set the primary key, select the columns you want to be part of the key, right-click, and choose **Set Primary Key** from the pop-up menu. A small key will appear next to each of the column definitions within the designer, indicating that these columns form the primary key.

3. In addition to the column properties, there are several table-level properties that you can set through the Enterprise Manager designer. To access the table properties, simply click the **Table and Index Properties** icon on the toolbar:

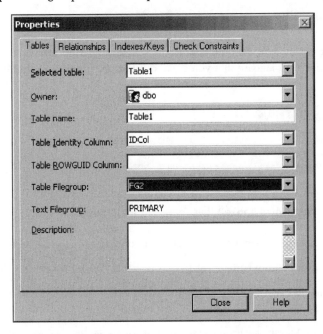

4. In this **Properties** window, you can see a number of options. One of the more common changes you can make here is to change the filegroup that your table is created on. To do this, select the appropriate filegroup from the drop-down list in the **Table Filegroup** property:

5. Click **Close** to close the **Properties** window and return to the table designer. Once you're satisfied with your table design, click the **Save** button to create the table in the database. You'll be asked to enter a name for this table at this point. For this demonstration, name the table as OurFirstTable.

Creating Tables with T-SQL

Creating tables with T-SQL is a little more complicated because you must specify all the column names and property definitions within code. You use the CREATE TABLE T-SQL command, and the syntax of this command is as follows:

```
CREATE TABLE <tablename>
(
  <column definition>,
  <column definition>,
  ...
  [ <tableconstraint>],
  [ <tableconstraint>],
  ...
)
[ ON <filegroup>]
[TEXTON <filegroup]
```

Each column definition can contain the following parameters:

```
columnname datatype [Nullability] [Constraint] [Identity]
```

Try It Out: Creating a Table with T-SQL

Open SQL Server Query Analyzer and connect to your SQL Server. Change the database in the drop-down list to the TestDB1 database that you created earlier in this chapter. Enter the T-SQL statement as shown:

```
CREATE TABLE Table2
(
        IDCol int identity(1,1) PRIMARY KEY,
        Table1_IDCol int NULL,
        VarCharCol varchar(255) NOT NULL,
)
```

This will create a table named Table2 that contains the following:

- ❑ An integer column named IDCol, which is the primary key for the table
- ❑ Another integer column named Table1_IDCol that doesn't require a value to be inserted
- ❑ A column named VarCharCol that requires a character value to be inserted

Once you've entered the CREATE TABLE statement, press F5 to execute the table creation command in your database.

Protecting Data Integrity

Both normalized and dimensional models depend on relationships between tables to maintain data integrity. Although you could leave the client application to enforce these relationships, a much better approach is to enforce these relationships at the table level. This protects the database from erroneous data that the application may attempt to enter due to malfunction, bad coding, and so on. The relationships between tables are defined and enforced using referential constraints.

Referential Constraints

Referential constraints are used to enforce referential integrity. What this means is that after you've separated your information into multiple tables within your database, you need to enforce the intended relationships between those tables to ensure the integrity of your information. For example, you may determine that the structure of your Sales database requires a Customers table, Products table, and Sales table. Sales consist of selling one of your products to one of your customers. To maintain the integrity of your data, you need to enforce this relationship to ensure that a sale references both a customer in the Customers table and a product in the Products table. Anything else is invalid and must not be allowed to be entered into the Sales table.

The constraint that is created to enforce these relationships is called a **foreign key constraint**. For a foreign key to be created successfully, a column in a child table must reference a unique column (usually the primary key) in a parent table. Although these columns don't necessarily need to have the same name, they must have matching data types. Once the foreign key constraint has been created, only a value that exists within the referenced column(s) of the parent table can be inserted into the referencing column(s) of the child table. A NULL value (depending whether the column allows NULLs or not) can also be entered.

There are a number of relationship types, but the two most common are **one-to-many** and **many-to-many**.

One-to-Many Relationships

A **one-to-many relationship** means that a column value that appears in a single row in one table can be referenced in many rows in another table. Taking the sales example we used in the previous section, a CustomerID would be used to uniquely identify **one** customer in the Customers table. However, this CustomerID could be associated with **many** sales, depending on how many purchases that customer made. Similarly, each ProductID would appear in **one** row within your Products table to uniquely identify any given product. And once again, this could be referenced by many rows within your Sales table, depending on the number of times that the product has been sold.

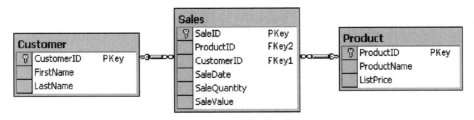

Many-to-Many Relationships

A **many-to-many relationship**, on the other hand, allows **many** rows in one table to be referenced by **many** rows in another table. For example, if you think of product wholesalers, a given product may have **many** wholesalers, and a given wholesaler may provide **many** products. Normalization rules don't allow products or wholesalers to be duplicated within their respective tables, so how do you associate one product with many wholesalers while at the same time associating one wholesaler with many products? Well, you can't directly do it with only the Products and Wholesalers tables. For this, you must create an intermediate table and two one-to-many relationships.

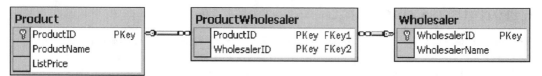

The ProductWholesaler table exists purely to allow the many-to-many relationship to exist; it serves no other purpose. The combination of the ProductID and the WholesalerID is unique in this table, and it allows a single product to be associated with many wholesalers and a single wholesaler to be associated with many products.

> A many-to-many relationship will require an intermediate table to allow this relationship to be formed.

Creating Relationship Constraints with Enterprise Manager

You can choose to create relationship constraints in Enterprise Manager either when you're creating a table or at a later time. To do this, you use the Relationships tab of the table properties window that is available in the table designer.

Try It Out: Creating Relationship Constraints

1. Open SQL Server Enterprise Manager and drill down into your TestDB1 database. Drill down into the Tables node and right-click your Table2 table in the right pane.

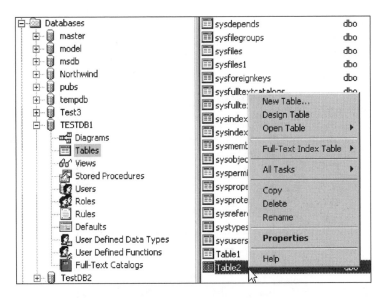

2. From the pop-up menu, select **Design Table**. If you right-click in the table designer and select **Properties** from the pop-up menu, the table properties window will appear. Within this window, select the **Relationships** tab.

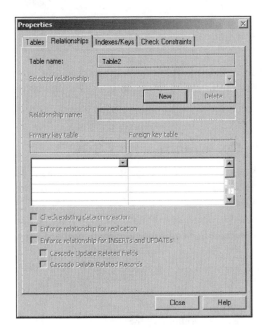

3. Click **New** to create a new constraint. In the **Primary key table** drop-down box, select **Table1** as the parent table. In the box below, select the **IDCol** column from the drop-down list.

4. In the Foreign key table drop-down box, select Table2 as the table. In the box below, select the Table1_IDCol column from the drop-down list. This creates a foreign key constraint where the Table1_IDCol column in your Table2 table references the IDCol column in your Table1 table: ·

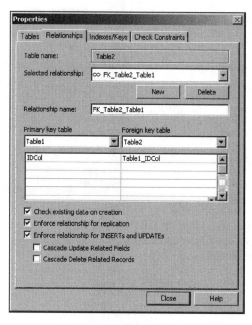

5. To remove this constraint, click the Delete button. Do this now, as you'll create this constraint again using T-SQL. Click the Close button to close the Properties window, and then close the table designer.

Creating Relationship Constraints with T-SQL

As with Enterprise Manager, you can create relationship constraints with T-SQL either at the time of table creation or after table creation. However, you use different T-SQL statements to do each task.

To create a foreign key relationship constraint when creating a table, you embed the foreign key statement within your table definition. For example, when referencing a single column in a parent table, you would use this:

```
CREATE TABLE ChildTable
(
   IDCol INT PRIMARY KEY,
   ParentTable_IDCol INT REFERENCES ParentTable(IDCol)
)
```

If you were referencing multiple columns in your parent table, you would use this:

```
CREATE TABLE ChildTable
(
    IDCol INT PRIMARY KEY,
    ParentTable_IDCol_1 INT,
    ParentTable_IDCol_2 INT,
    FOREIGN KEY (ParentTable_IDCol_1, ParentTable_IDCol_2)
      REFERENCES ParentTable(IDCol_1, IDCol_2)
)
```

To create a foreign key constraint for existing tables, you use the **ALTER TABLE** command with the following syntax:

```
ALTER TABLE ChildTable
ADD CONSTRAINT constraintname
FOREIGN KEY (ChildTableCols)
REFERENCES ParentTable(ParentTableCols)
```

But what better way to understand this than through an example?

Try It Out: Creating a Foreign Key with T-SQL

1. Connect SQL Server Query Analyzer to your SQL Server, and change to your TestDB1 database that you created earlier in this chapter.

2. Enter the following T-SQL command into Query Analyzer. This will create the same constraint as you created in Enterprise Manager in the previous section; a foreign key constraint that references IDCol in your Table1 table from the Table1_IDCol column in your Table2 table.

```
ALTER TABLE Table2
ADD CONSTRAINT fk_table2_table1_idcol FOREIGN KEY (Table1_IDCol)
               REFERENCES Table1(IDCol)
```

Once you've entered the preceding statement, press **F5** to execute it against your database.

Viewing Database Diagrams

Once you have more than a few constraints within your database, identifying what tables reference other tables can be difficult. It's common for a database to have hundreds of tables, and each of these tables may reference several other tables within the database. Fortunately, SQL Server Enterprise Manager includes a feature that allows you to create a diagram of the tables within your database and display the relationships between them. Although this tool is quite crude when compared with available commercial modeling tools, it is included with SQL Server so you should make use of it if you don't have a better alternative.

Try It Out: Viewing Database Diagrams

1. The database diagram tool has its own node in Enterprise Manager under each database. Right-click the Diagrams node and click New Database Diagram.

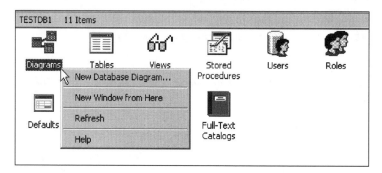

    The Create Database Diagram Wizard will begin. Click Next to skip past the welcome screen of this wizard.

2. On the next screen you're asked to select which tables you want to include within the database diagram. If you have a simple database with few tables, you may want to add them all. If you have a complex database with many tables, you may want to create a number of database diagrams and within each diagram only include the tables that relate to a particular functional area of the database. In this example, as you only have two tables, you'll add all your tables to the diagram. Once you've selected the tables you want to include, click Next.

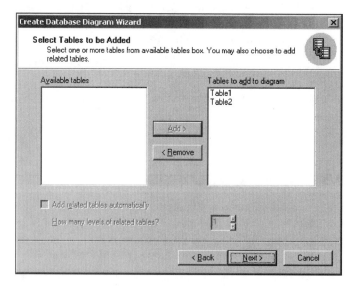

3. Finally, click Finish to complete the Create Database Diagram Wizard. You'll now be able to view your diagram and arrange the layout of the tables within the diagram:

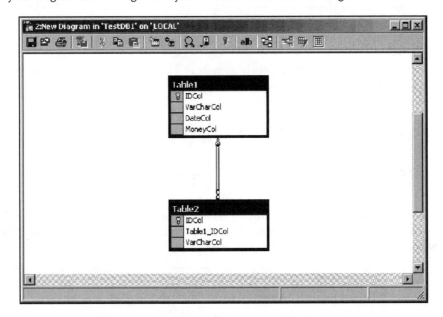

4. You can save each diagram so that you can come back and view it later. Click the Save icon on the toolbar and give the diagram a descriptive and meaningful name.

Deleting Tables

As you now know how to create tables, you should look at how to remove them. But hang on—after you created your tables, you created foreign key constraints, so what happens to these when you remove the tables? Well, as the foreign key constraint is considered part of the child table definition, when you drop the child table, this is also dropped. However, if you try to drop a table that is referenced by a foreign key constraint, you'll get an error, because it can't be dropped while it's referenced. In this case, you'll have to remove the constraint first.

Dropping a Foreign Key Constraint with T-SQL

You saw how to drop a foreign key constraint using SQL Server Enterprise Manager earlier. You simply click the Delete button in the Relationships tab of the Properties window. To do this using T-SQL, you must use the ALTER TABLE statement followed by the DROP CONSTRAINT parameter. This has the following syntax:

```
ALTER TABLE tablename DROP CONSTRAINT constraintname
```

From T-SQL, it isn't always obvious what constraints exist on a particular table. Thankfully, SQL Server provides a command that you can use to identify the constraints that reference a particular table: the sp_helpconstraints stored procedure.

```
sp_helpconstraint tablename
```

By using these two commands, you can easily identify and remove any constraints that are referencing your table before you attempt to remove it.

Try It Out: Identifying Constraints on a Table

1. Open Query Analyzer and connect to your SQL Server. Select TestDB1 database from the drop-down list.

2. Enter the following T-SQL command in the query pane and press F5 to execute it. In the results pane, you'll see a list of constraints that are referencing your Table1 table and the names of the tables in which these constraints exist:

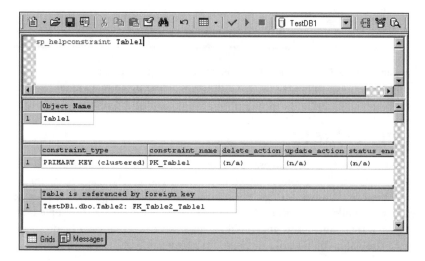

You can see from the results of this command that Table1 table is referenced by a constraint named FK_Table2_Table1, and this constraint exists on the Table2 table.

3. Now that you know the name and location of the constraints that reference your table, you can use the ALTER TABLE statement followed by the DROP CONSTRAINT parameter, as shown in the following screenshot:

4. Press F5 to execute this statement. It will remove the foreign key constraint from your database. You can now move on to remove the actual table.

Dropping Tables with Enterprise Manager

You can use Enterprise Manager to remove tables within your database. This is a straightforward process, so straightforward in fact that you should make sure not to click too quickly. Remember, once you remove a table all the information contained within that table is also permanently removed. Be sure that you're removing the correct table and that you have a full backup of your database before doing this.

Try It Out: Dropping a Table with Enterprise Manager

1. Open SQL Server Enterprise Manager and drill down into the **Databases** node to **TestDB1** database and through to the **Tables** node. In the right pane a list of tables will appear. Right-click the **Test1** table and select **Delete** from the pop-up menu. A dialog box will appear showing a list of the tables that you've chosen to remove:

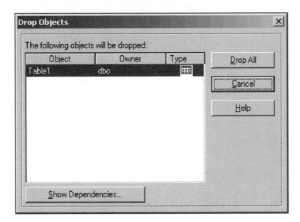

2. Click the **Drop All** button to remove all the tables that are listed. These tables will no longer exist within your database.

Dropping Tables with T-SQL

Dropping a table using T-SQL is just as simple as using Enterprise Manager, but at least it requires you to type the name of the table that you want to remove, and as such it helps to prevent accidental removal of tables. Dropping a table from T-SQL requires you to execute the DROP TABLE command, specifying the table name.

Try It Out: Dropping a Table with T-SQL

Open Query Analyzer and connect to your SQL Server. Select the **TestDB1** database from the drop-down list. Enter the `DROP TABLE` command followed by the `Table2` table name and press **F5**:

```
DROP TABLE Table2
```

This table is now removed from your database.

Summary

You've gone from a clean installation of SQL Server to an installation that contains not only a database but also database tables. Although you have yet to build anything of practical use, the examples you've covered in this chapter demonstrated how you can create tables and relationships between those tables, and how you can drop the relationships and tables when you no longer require them.

In the next chapter you'll look at populating your tables with information and how you can use the T-SQL language to modify and retrieve the information retained within these tables.

DML and Querying

In the previous chapter we discussed the creation of databases and tables; now you need to understand how to get information in and out of those tables. While initially you may think that the querying of tables is a task for developers (not database administrators), in reality you cannot effectively manage a production SQL Server environment without a proficiency in SQL. Over time, SQL will become like a second language to you, and a query tool such as Query Analyzer will become a commonly run application on your workstation.

In this chapter we will cover the following:

❑   Basic use of the SQL data manipulation language commands

❑   Predicates, wildcards, and JOINs

❑   Native SQL Server indexes

❑   Full-text indexes

The Definitions

Before you dive into examples of using the SQL language, let's define the terms you'll be using throughout this chapter and the rest of this book.

Tables

As you learned in the previous chapter, a table is a data storage mechanism consisting of columns and rows. Tables are typically designed (especially in online transaction processing [OLTP] applications) using the rules of normalization, which reduce data redundancy and improve data integrity.

Following is an example of two tables, each containing two columns populated with data in three rows:

Food_Table	Food_ID	Food_Name
Row	1	Bread
Row	2	Steak
Row	3	Milk

Group_Table	Group_ID	Group_Name
Row	1	Grains
Row	5	Meat
Row	3	Dairy

Now, you're going to create those tables in the Northwind database.

Try It Out–Creating Two Example Tables

Connect to SQL Server using Query Analyzer. Enter the following commands and then click the Execute button or press F5:

```
USE Northwind

CREATE TABLE Food_Table
(
   Food_ID INT PRIMARY KEY,
   Food_Name VARCHAR(255)
)

CREATE TABLE Group_Table
(
   Group_ID INT PRIMARY KEY,
   Group_Name VARCHAR(255)
)
```

You'll enter information into these tables a little later using an INSERT statement.

You'll notice that you start out with the USE statement. The USE statement sets the context of the script, or which database the script should run in. When a new database is created, SQL Server uses the model database as a template for the new database, so any object in the model database will be in the new databases you create. If you have a stored procedure or a function for example, that you want in every new database, you can create this object in the model database and it will automatically be in all databases created from that point on.

Rowset

A rowset is the result of a query represented in tabular form. The structure of a rowset is the same as that of a physical table, but the structure (rows and columns) of a rowset is created dynamically at runtime, based on the query that's being executed:

Rowset	Column	Column	Column	Column
Row	Value	Value	Value	Value
Row	Value	Value	Value	Value
Row	Value	Value	Value	Value

A rowset may be generated from columns and rows of a single physical table or many tables when using JOINs, as described shortly.

Data Manipulation Language

Data manipulation language (DML) refers to the SQL statements you use to query and modify data contained within tables in a database. Specifically, the DML SQL statements are as follows:

❑   INSERT

❑   SELECT

❑   UPDATE

❑   DELETE

Using these four statements, you'll be able to retrieve (SELECT), modify (UPDATE and DELETE), and retain (INSERT) all the information that is contained within a table. Of course, Transact-SQL (T-SQL) has many more statements than these four DML statements. Others are used to carry out functions such as defining the schema, workflow, conditional logic, and administration.

> **Transact-SQL is discussed in more detail in Chapter 10.**

Basic SQL DML

SQL as a language is incredibly simple, but powerful. It's easy to construct simple queries using SQL. In fact, almost all data access and modification takes place using the four SQL commands listed earlier. The semantics of the language also allow you to construct complex queries, which is what makes SQL powerful.

INSERT

Let's start at the beginning. Before you can query or update data you need to insert some data into a table. The INSERT statement lets you add data to your tables. You can add row(s) to one table at a time. In its most basic flavor, INSERT contains the list of all columns in a table and values for each column of the row you want to add.

A simple INSERT statement has the following syntax:

```
INSERT table_name(column_name1, column_name2, ...) VALUES(value1, value2, ...)
```

This is the most basic of INSERT statements, as you explicitly pass the values you wish to insert into a single row, in a comma-separated list.

Try It Out–A Simple INSERT

In this example, you'll insert rows into the tables that you created in the last section.

Connect to SQL Server using Query Analyzer. Enter the following commands and then click the Execute button:

```
USE Northwind

INSERT Food_Table(Food_ID, Food_Name) VALUES(1, 'Bread')

INSERT Food_Table(Food_ID, Food_Name) VALUES(2, 'Steak')

INSERT Food_Table(Food_Id, Food_Name) VALUES(3, 'Milk')
```

This enters three new rows into our Food_Table table. For the examples later in this chapter, you also need to INSERT rows into the Group_Table table:

```
USE Northwind

INSERT Group_Table(Group_ID, Group_Name) VALUES(1, 'Grains')

INSERT Group_Table(Group_ID, Group_Name) VALUES(5, 'Meat')

INSERT Group_Table(Group_ID, Group_Name) VALUES(3, 'Dairy')
```

If you have defaults specified on any of the columns, you don't have to specify the value for that column within the INSERT statement. Also note that if you pass an explicit NULL value, SQL Server will not override this value with a default.

Furthermore, if any of the columns in your table allow NULLs, then these columns don't have to be specified in the INSERT statement. The newly inserted row will automatically contain NULL.

It's good coding practice to include the list of the populated columns in the INSERT statement. If you fail to provide the list of columns to be populated, the INSERT statement will break when new columns are added to the table. However, if you're providing values for every column in the table, you can omit the column list. If you happen to provide fewer values than there are columns in the table, SQL Server will return the following error:

Server: Msg 213, Level 16, State 4, Line 1
Insert Error: Column name or number of supplied values doesn't match table definition.

A similar error occurs if you supply more columns in the INSERT list than in the VALUES clause.

SELECT

Once you have data in the database, you'll need a way to get it back out. You use the SELECT statement to do this because SELECT allows you to retrieve data from the tables. There are several basic parts to a SELECT statement. Let's cover these basics and then you'll build your knowledge from there.

The most basic SELECT statement is SELECT <value>, for example, SELECT 'Hello!'. This will always return the same value, so it doesn't do you much good, at least not for getting data out of the database. To retrieve data, you need to tell the SELECT statement what columns to retrieve, and from which table(s):

```
SELECT <column list> FROM <table>
```

The FROM clause specifies what tables are involved in the query, but because it isn't exclusive to the SELECT command (it can be used for both the UPDATE and DELETE commands), first you'll look at it separately.

FROM Clause

The FROM clause is used to specify which table the command is executing against. This clause has the following syntax:

```
FROM table_name [table_alias]
```

The table_name parameter specifies which table you want to retrieve rows from. The table_alias allows you to specify a short name for the table that you can refer to elsewhere in the query as a substitute for the actual table name. This is useful for saving keystrokes and improving the readability of queries when you have tables with long names, such as tblMyVeryBigTableWithTheVeryLongName.

Simple SELECT

In its most basic form, a SELECT statement simply specifies the columns you wish to retrieve from a specified table:

```
SELECT column_name, column_name ... FROM table_name
```

Without a specific predicate (and these are explained in the "Predicates" section) the SELECT statement will simply retrieve all of the rows that are contained within the specified table.

If you wish to retrieve all columns from the tables involved in the SELECT statement, then rather than typing all the column names you can use an asterisk as a shortcut. This has the following syntax:

```
SELECT * FROM table_name
```

Try It Out–Retrieving Data from a Database

In this example, you'll issue a simple SELECT statement against the newly populated base table.

Connect to SQL Server using Query Analyzer. Execute the following command:

```
USE Northwind

SELECT Food_ID, Food_Name FROM Food_Table
```

This retrieves all the rows contained within the Food_Table table. The following command produces the same result:

```
USE Northwind
SELECT * FROM Food_Table
```

Using the asterisk is fine for ad hoc queries, but it will have a slight performance hit, so you should list the columns that you want to retrieve for production code.

You should also avoid the asterisk so that you control the order of the columns that are retrieved. If an application needs to call a stored procedure, the developer of the application needs to know what columns are returned, and in what order. If columns are added, the asterisk can cause problems, so get into the habit of explicitly listing the columns that you need for all but ad hoc queries that won't be used in production.

ORDER BY

ORDER BY is a clause that can be added to the end of a SELECT statement to specify the order of the rows when they're returned in a rowset. This has the following syntax:

```
SELECT * FROM table_name ORDER BY expression1 [ASC | DESC], expression2 [ASC
| DESC]...
```

The ORDER BY clause is always the last clause of a SELECT statement. The ordering takes place using the expression that occurs first in the clause and if the expression resolves to duplicate values, then the second expression is used, and so on. If you specify the ASC option (or specify no option at all because ASC is the default) then the rows are ordered based on the expression in ascending fashion (1,2,3,4). If you specify the DESC option then the rows are ordered based on the expression in descending fashion.

> Unless you explicitly specify the order of the rowset using an ORDER BY clause, no order is guaranteed and the order of the rowset may change over time as the dynamics of the table change.

Try It Out–Ordering the Data Returned from the Database

In this example, you'll issue a simple `SELECT` statement with an `ORDER BY` clause.

Connect to SQL Server using Query Analyzer. Execute the following command:

```
USE Northwind
```

```
SELECT Food_ID, Food_Name FROM Food_Table ORDER BY Food_Name
```

Predicates

Obviously, retrieving all rows may be useful if that table contains 5 or even 50 rows. However, if the table contains 100,000 rows for example, you're more than likely going to want to restrict what is returned to you based on specific criteria. To do this you can specify query predicates as part of a `WHERE` clause.

WHERE Clause

The `WHERE` clause is another SQL construct that is commonly used with `SELECT`, `UPDATE`, and `DELETE` statements. When you use a `WHERE` clause, you specify the criteria that are applied during the query execution to limit the rows retrieved. The `WHERE` clause has the following syntax:

```
FROM table_name
WHERE condition is true
```

Notice that the `WHERE` clause always follows the `FROM` clause. The condition that you'll include is evaluated for every row within the table and can be any valid SQL Server expression, such as

- ❑ >, <, = (numeric comparisons)
- ❑ Calls to system and user-defined functions
- ❑ `IN` (comma-separated list)

and so on. Any valid expression within T-SQL can be used as part of the query predicate.

Try It Out–Specifying a Query Predicate

In this example, you'll execute the simple `SELECT` statement again, but this time, specify a query predicate.

Connect to SQL Server using Query Analyzer. Execute the following code:

```
USE Northwind
SELECT Food_ID, Food_Name FROM Food_Table WHERE Food_ID = 1
```

When this query runs, instead of retrieving all rows from the Food_Table table, only the rows where Food_ID=1 are returned to the user.

Multiple Predicates

More than one predicate can be specified as part of the WHERE clause and you do this with the following syntax:

```
WHERE condition is true
AND/OR condition is true
AND/OR condition is true
...
```

By either AND-ing or OR-ing an additional predicate, you can specify any number of conditions that a given row must meet to be used within the statement. As the order of the AND and OR conditions is important, you can also use brackets to set the order in which predicate conditions are evaluated, for example:

```
WHERE condition1 is true AND (condition2 is true OR condition3 is true)
...
```

Here, SQL Server will evaluate both of the conditions within the brackets first, then the conditions outside the brackets.

Try It Out–Specifying Multiple Query Predicates

In this example, you're going to use a query with multiple predicates.

Connect to SQL Server using Query Analyzer and execute the following command:

```
USE Northwind
```

```
SELECT Food_ID, Food_Name FROM Food_Table
    WHERE Food_ID>1 AND (Food_Name='Steak' OR Food_Name='Milk')
```

This retrieves all rows from our Food_Table table where the value of Food_ID is greater than 1 and the value of Food_Name is either Steak or Milk.

Now, you're going to use one of the core Northwind tables to learn the use of multiple predicates.

Execute the following command in Query Analyzer:

```
SELECT CustomerID, ContactName, City, PostalCode, Country
    FROM Customers
        WHERE City='London' OR (Country='Germany' AND PostalCode='80805')
```

In this example you're retrieving information on all customers who either live in London or Germany and have a postal code of 80805.

You probably noticed that you didn't use the USE command in this second query. The reason you didn't need to include USE Northwind was because you were already in the Northwind database (as you carried out the first query in the Northwind database). Had you used another database or changed databases, then you would have to specify Northwind again with the USE command.

Wildcards

When you retrieve character values from a database table, there may be times when you don't know the complete character string that you need to locate, but have to use a wildcard filter to locate rows. The ability to do this as part of the SQL language is achieved using the LIKE clause, which has the following syntax:

```
WHERE expression LIKE wildcard_expression
```

expression is any valid SQL Server expression (column, constant, function, calculation, and so on). wildcard_expression is similar but is a character value with wildcard operators built into it. These wildcard operators can include the following:

Wildcard Operator	Description
%	Match any string
[ ]	Match any single character within the specified range
[^]	Not to match any single character within the specified range
_(underscore)	Match one character

These can be used on their own or combined to form complex string location logic.

Try It Out–Using Wildcard Operators

In these examples, you'll use wildcard expressions to locate rows within the Northwind database tables.

1. Connect to SQL Server using Query Analyzer. Execute the following command:

```
USE Northwind
```

```
SELECT CustomerID, ContactName, City, PostalCode, Country
  FROM Customers WHERE City LIKE 'L%'
```

Give the following rowset where the entries in the City column begin with the letter L:

CustomerID	ContactName	City	Postal Code	Country
SPLIR	Art Braunschweiger	Lander	82520	USA
MORGK	Alexander Feuer	Leipzig	04179	Germany
FOLIG	Martine Rancé	Lille	59000	France
FURIB	Lino Rodriguez	Lisboa	1675	Portugal
PRINI	Isabel de Castro	Lisboa	1756	Portugal
AROUT	Thomas Hardy	London	WA1 1DP	UK
BSBEV	Victoria Ashworth	London	EC2 5NT	UK
CONSH	Elizabeth Brown	London	WX1 6LT	UK
EASTC	Ann Devon	London	WX3 6FW	UK
NORTS	Simon Crowther	London	SW7 1RZ	UK
SEVES	Hari Kumar	London	OX15	4NB UK
BERGS	Christina Berglund	Luleå	S-958 22	Sweden
VICTE	Mary Saveley	Lyon	69004	France

2. Now if you run the following query you get a different result.

```
SELECT CustomerID, ContactName, City, PostalCode, Country
   FROM Customers WHERE City LIKE '[ABC]%'
```

This retrieves all rows where the first letter of the City column is either A, B, or C. The following list has been abbreviated.

CustomerID	ContactName	City	PostalCode	Country
DRACD	Sven Ottlieb	Aachen	52066	Germany
RATTC	Paula Wilson	Albuquerque	87110	USA
OLDWO	Rene Phillips	Anchorage	99508	USA
GALED	Eduardo Saavedra	Barcelona	08022	Spain
LILAS	Carlos González	Barquisimeto	3508	Venezuela
MAGAA	Giovanni Rovelli	Bergamo	24100	Italy
ALFKI	Maria Anders	Berlin	12209	Germany
CHOPS	Yang Wang	Bern	3012	Switzerland
SAVEA	Jose Pavarotti	Boise	83720	USA
FOLKO	Maria Larsson	Bräcke	S-844 67	Sweden

You could also obtain this result by specifying that you want to retrieve all rows where the first letter of City is between A and C:

```
SELECT CustomerID, ContactName, City, PostalCode, Country
   FROM Customers WHERE City LIKE '[A-C]%'
```

3. Conversely, the following query retrieves all rows where the first letter of the City column is not A, B, or C:

```
SELECT CustomerID, ContactName, City, PostalCode, Country
   FROM Customers WHERE City LIKE '[^ABC]%'
```

The following is an abbreviated list of the results:

CustomerID	ContactName	City	PostalCode	Country
HUNGC	Yoshi Latimer	Elgin	97827	USA
GREAL	HowardSnyder	Eugene	97403	USA
LEHMS	Renate Messner	Frankfurt a.M.	60528	Germany
RICSU	Michael Holz	Genève	1203	Switzerland
ERNSH	Roland Mendel	Graz	8010	Austria
WILMK	Matti Karttunen	Helsinki	21240	Finland
LINOD	Felipe Izquierdo	I. de Margarita	4980	Venezuela
TRAIH	Helvetius Nagy	Kirkland	98034	USA
SIMOB	Jytte Petersen	Kobenhavn	1734	Denmark
OTTIK	Henriette Pfalzheim	Köln	50739	Germany

4. Our final query retrieves all rows where the first letter of the City column is any letter but the second letter of the city column can only be the letter a:

```
SELECT CustomerID, ContactName, City, PostalCode, Country
   FROM Customers WHERE City LIKE '_[a]%'
```

It would return the following (abbreviated) list:

CustomerID	ContactName	City	PostalCode	Country
BLAUS	Hanna Moos	Mannheim	68306	Germany
BOLID	Martín Sommer	Madrid	28023	Spain
BONAP	LaurenceLebihan	Marseille	13008	France
COMMI	Pedro Afonso	Sao Paulo	05432-043	Brazil
DRACD	Sven Ottlieb	Aachen	52066	Germany
DUMON	Janine Labrune	Nantes	44000	France
FAMIA	Aria Cruz	Sao Paulo	05442-030	Brazil
FISSA	Diego Roel	Madrid	28034	Spain
FRANR	Carine Schmitt	Nantes	44000	France
GALED	Eduardo Saavedra	Barcelona	08022	Spain

UPDATE

In addition to inserting new data and retrieving existing data, there are times when you'll want to modify information already in a table. To do this you use the UPDATE statement.

The UPDATE statement lets you modify values of one or multiple columns in a table. In its simplest form, the UPDATE statement has the following syntax:

```
UPDATE table_name SET column_name=expression
```

This UPDATE statement sets the value of the specified column to that of the specified expression for every row within a table. Setting every row to the same value isn't a very common requirement, so you usually use the UPDATE statement in conjunction with a WHERE clause to only update specific rows. This has the following syntax:

```
UPDATE table_name SET column_name=expression WHERE condition is true
```

Now you can specify a WHERE clause (as you did with the SELECT statement) to limit the updated rows to a specific subset. Keep in mind that UPDATE statements can contain a FROM clause, even if only one table is involved.

Try It Out–Using UPDATE

In this example, you update several columns in a couple of rows within the Northwind database.

Connect to SQL Server using Query Analyzer. Execute the following command:

```
SELECT ContactName FROM Customers WHERE CustomerID='FRANR'

UPDATE Customers SET ContactName='Linda Glucina'
   WHERE CustomerID='FRANR'

SELECT ContactName FROM Customers WHERE CustomerID='FRANR'
```

In this example, you first SELECT the current value of the ContactName column for a customer row where the customerID is 'FRANR'. Next you issue an UPDATE statement to modify the ContactName for this customer to the new value. Finally you reselect this row to examine the change that you've made.

DELETE

The final type of command that you can issue against a row within a table is a DELETE operation. As you would expect, this removes the row from the table.

In its simplest form, the DELETE statement has the following syntax:

```
DELETE FROM table_name
```

However, this DELETE statement will remove every row from the specified table. Usually this isn't what you want to do. Instead, you normally use the DELETE statement in conjunction with a WHERE clause to limit the DELETE operation to a set of specific rows:

```
DELETE FROM table_name WHERE condition is true
```

When you use this syntax, only the rows where the WHERE clause condition evaluates to true will be removed.

> **Issuing a DELETE statement without a WHERE clause will delete all rows from the specified table.**

Try It Out–Deleting Data from a Database

In this example, you'll remove a row from a table within the Northwind database. Because you don't really want to remove a row from the Northwind tables, you'll use the test table, Food_Table that you created earlier (if you didn't create it, see the beginning of this chapter).

Connect to SQL Server using Query Analyzer. Execute the following command:

```
USE Northwind
```

```
SELECT Food_ID, Food_Name FROM Food_Table

DELETE Food_Table WHERE Food_Name='Steak'

SELECT Food_ID, Food_Name FROM Food_Table
```

First, you retrieve the current rows from Food_Table. Next you DELETE all rows where Food_Name contains the value Steak. Finally, you retrieve all the rows from Food_Table again so you can view the impact of the DELETE operation.

Because you'll actually need that row for future examples in this chapter, quickly add it back:

```
INSERT Food_Table(Food_ID, Food_Name) VALUES(2, 'Steak')
```

JOINS

A JOIN is the intersection of two tables (a combination of the columns and rows within two tables based on a common column value in both of the tables) in a query, based on given criteria. This intersection allows rows from both tables to be retrieved within a single set of results and is one of the core concepts of relational databases. While information about a concept may be reduced to core attributes and physically stored in more than one table, this information can be brought back together again by joining the tables where the information is located. SQL Server supports three types of JOIN.

INNER JOIN

An INNER JOIN retrieves rows from both tables involved in the JOIN where the join criteria are satisfied. Rows from either table that don't meet the join criteria are ignored and aren't retrieved as part of the query.

An INNER JOIN is specified as part of the FROM clause in a query and has the following syntax:

```
FROM table_name [INNER] JOIN table_name ON join_criteria
```

Try It Out–Using an INNER JOIN

In this example, you join the Food_Table and Group_Table tables using an INNER JOIN with the following syntax:

```
SELECT * FROM Food_Table
    INNER JOIN Group_Table ON Food_Table.Food_ID =
              Group_Table.Group_ID
```

> When joining tables, you can refer to columns within each of the tables by prefixing the column name with the name of the table where that column is located. For example, Food_Table.Food_ID refers to the Food_ID column in the Food_Table table.

The rowset contains values from both tables but only the rows that meet the join condition (Food_Table.Food_ID = Group_Table.Group_ID) will be included in the rowset. When you run this command, the following rowset will be produced:

Food_ID (Food_Table)	Food_Name (Food_Table)	Group_ID (Group_Table)	Group_Name (Group_Table)
1	Bread	1	Grains
3	Milk	3	Dairy

OUTER JOIN

An OUTER JOIN, on the other hand, retrieves all the rows from one of the tables in the join and only the rows where the join criteria are met for the second table. There are three types of OUTER JOIN:

❑ LEFT OUTER JOIN

❑ RIGHT OUTER JOIN

❑ FULL OUTER JOIN

The type of OUTER JOIN dictates from which table all the rows are retrieved and conversely, from which table the matching rows are retrieved.

LEFT OUTER JOIN

For LEFT OUTER JOINs, all the rows from the table specified on the left-hand side of the join criteria are used within the query:

```
FROM table_name LEFT OUTER JOIN table_name ON join_criteria
```

The statement will use only the rows from the right table that meet the JOIN criteria. If there are rows from the left table that have no matching rows in the right table then NULL values are used as placeholders. This will become a little clearer in the next example.

Try It Out–Using a LEFT OUTER JOIN

In this example, you'll join the Food_Table table and the Group_Table table using a LEFT OUTER JOIN.

Connect to SQL Server using Query Analyzer. Enter the following command:

```
SELECT * FROM Food_Table LEFT OUTER JOIN Group_Table ON
           Food_Table.Food_ID = Group_Table.Group_ID
```

Here you're specifying Food_Table as the table you want to retrieve all rows from (on the left side of the join criteria) and Group_Table as the table you want to retrieve rows from when they meet the JOIN criteria (Food_Table.Food_ID = Group_Table.Group_ID).

When you execute this command, you receive the following rowset:

Food_ID (Food_Table)	Food_Name (Food_Table)	Group_ID (Group_Table)	Group_Name (Group_Table)
1	Bread	1	Grains
2	Steak	NULL	NULL
3	Milk	3	Dairy

Notice how all rows from Food_Table are included but only the rows from Group_Table where the join criteria are met are present. For the row in Food_Table where there isn't a row that meets the JOIN criteria in Group_Table (the row where Food_Table.ColumnA=2), you'll notice NULL values used as placeholders in the columns that contain the Group_Table values.

RIGHT OUTER JOIN

RIGHT OUTER JOIN has the same syntax as LEFT OUTER JOIN (except for the change of LEFT to RIGHT):

```
FROM table_name RIGHT OUTER JOIN table_name ON join_criteria
```

The difference with this command is the table roles are reversed. That is, all rows from the table on the right-hand side of the join will be used by the query and only those rows on the left-hand side of the join that match the join criteria will be used.

Try It Out–Using a RIGHT OUTER JOIN

In this example, you'll join the Food_Table table and Group_Table tables using a RIGHT OUTER JOIN.

Connect to SQL Server using Query Analyzer. Enter the following command:

```
SELECT * FROM
    Food_Table RIGHT OUTER JOIN Group_Table ON
    Food_Table.Food_ID = Group_Table.Group_ID
```

Notice, the only change from the previous example is the change from LEFT OUTER JOIN to RIGHT OUTER JOIN. When you execute this command, you receive the following rowset:

Food_ID (Food_Table)	Food_Name (Food_Table)	Group_ID (Group_Table)	Group_Name (Group_Table)
1	Bread	1	Grains
NULL	NULL	5	Meat
3	Milk	3	Dairy

You'll notice that all the rows from the Group_Table table are present. However, only those rows from Food_Table that meet the criteria are included. Where no rows from Food_Table meet the JOIN criteria for the corresponding row in Group_Table, NULLs are once again used as placeholders.

FULL OUTER JOIN

A FULL OUTER JOIN can be thought of as a combination of both the LEFT OUTER and RIGHT OUTER JOIN. It has the same syntax as the previous JOIN types:

```
FROM table_name FULL OUTER JOIN table_name ON join_criteria
```

And the results produced are the same as the LEFT OUTER and RIGHT OUTER JOIN statements merged together; you'll see this in the following example.

Try It Out–Using a FULL OUTER JOIN

In this example, you join the Food_Table table and Group_Table tables using a FULL OUTER JOIN.

Connect to SQL Server using Query Analyzer, and enter the following command:

```
SELECT *FROM
    Food_Table FULL OUTER JOIN Group_Table ON
    Food_Table.Food_ID = Group_Table.Group_ID
```

This command retrieves all rows from both tables. If there are rows in both tables that meet the JOIN criteria, then these are joined, otherwise NULL values are used as placeholders when the JOIN criteria aren't met. So the following rowset will be produced:

Food_ID (Food_Table)	Food_Name (Food_Table)	Group_ID (Group_Table)	Group_Name (Group_Table)
1	Bread	1	Grains
2	Steak	NULL	NULL
NULL	NULL	5	Meat
3	Milk	3	Dairy

You may receive the rows in a different order, but this isn't important.

CROSS JOIN

A CROSS JOIN is the combination of both a LEFT OUTER JOIN and a RIGHT OUTER JOIN for every row in both tables. It has the following syntax:

```
FROM table_name CROSS JOIN table_name
```

Notice that this type of JOIN doesn't have any JOIN criteria.

As every row is combined with every other row, this is often referred to as a Cartesian product.

Try It Out–Using a CROSS JOIN

In this example, you'll join the Food_Table table and Group_Table tables using a CROSS JOIN.

Connect to SQL Server using Query Analyzer. Enter the following command:

```
SELECT * FROM Food_Table CROSS JOIN Group_Table
```

This will produce the following rowset:

Food_ID (Food_Table)	Food_Name (Food_Table)	Group_ID (Group_Table)	Group_Name (Group_Table)
1	Bread	1	Grains
1	Bread	5	Meat
1	Bread	3	Dairy
2	Steak	1	Grains
2	Steak	5	Meat
2	Steak	3	Dairy
3	Milk	1	Grains
3	Milk	5	Meat
3	Milk	3	Dairy

Notice that a relatively large rowset is produced from two tables containing only three rows each. In fact, the formula for determining the number of rows is [number of rows from Food_Table] * [number of rows from Group_Table]. You need to be careful if you're considering using a CROSS JOIN on tables with a large number of rows, because you can easily end up with thousands or even millions of rows in your rowset.

The SQL language, in conjunction with its T-SQL implementation, is much more powerful than the simple cases you've seen so far. These basics are enough for now and you'll learn more advanced use of SQL in Chapter 10.

Using Indexes in SQL Server

Indexes are used in SQL Server to improve the time it takes a particular query to locate the rows needed to satisfy the query criteria. They are purely a performance mechanism and their impact on performance can be dramatic.

What Is an Index?

An index is a tree-like structure that SQL Server maintains internally to allow it to efficiently locate rows matching a query predicate. Without any indexes, the only option SQL Server has to identify rows that match a query predicate is to look at every row within a table. This is known as a table scan.

A table scan doesn't cause too many problems when the table only contains a small number of rows, but imagine the server resources required for SQL Server to look at every row in a table with 10 million rows. If it did that for every query executed, and you had 500 users each generating a query every few seconds, you would have serious performance issues on the database server.

Indexes don't only improve performance; they do so to the extent that most databases would become unusable without them.

As mentioned, an index is a tree-like structure consisting of levels, branches, and leaves. When SQL Server attempts to find rows with a particular value, it starts at the root level of the index structure (the top shown in the diagram) and evaluates the criteria at each level to determine which branch to follow. This continues until it reaches the leaf level (the bottom shown in the diagram). The leaf level contains the actual values within the table.

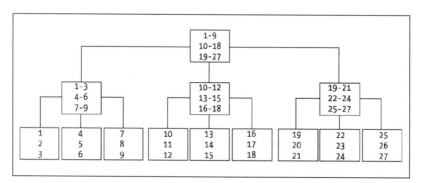

Let's consider how a query would navigate the index tree for the hypothetical index structure, as shown in the diagram. Suppose each block represents a data page (a page is a unit of storage in SQL Server made of eight bytes). When an index exists, a user can issue a query looking for rows where the column in the index equals a specific value, such as 20. The query processor would start at the root node and evaluate the desired value (20) against the criteria for each index branch. As 20 lies between 19 and 27, the third branch is chosen and the query processor follows this branch to the next level in the index tree.

Here the process is repeated. This time 20 is between 19 and 21 so the first branch is chosen. The query processor follows this branch to the page that contains the actual value that the user desires and here it will find a pointer to a row in the physical table that contains this value.

Without the index, the query processor would have to examine every row within the table to see if the specified value of the column is within any of the rows that make up the table.

Index Types

There are two structural types of indexes that affect how SQL Server stores the index internally:

❑ Clustered index

❑ Nonclustered index

The difference is subtle, but important, even if it isn't directly visible to you. Nonclustered indexes store the index structure independently of the base table that the index is created on. At the lowest level of the index structure, the leaf pages, the index retains pointers to the corresponding rows in the base table. With clustered indexes, the leaf level of the index is the base table. The actual rows of the table are logically sorted based on the columns used within the clustered index and the rest of the index tree is built upon this.

What do these differences mean? Well for one thing, they mean there can only be one clustered index per table. There is only one base table and the rows can only be sorted in one way so this makes sense. If there can only be one clustered index, why and when would we use this as opposed to a nonclustered index? Well, as the leaf level of a clustered index is the actual data rows, a clustered index can perform better than a nonclustered index. Remember the nonclustered index stores pointers to the base table rows then uses these to retrieve the rows from the base table, something a clustered index doesn't have to do.

Secondly, because the rows are already logically sorted in order of the clustered index columns, retrieving these rows in that order (by specifying an ORDER BY clause) doesn't require SQL Server to order these rows internally. They can just be picked up in the order in which they occur. A nonclustered index, on the other hand, while it is ordered, doesn't affect the order that the rows within the base table are stored. This results in less efficient I/O than an equivalent clustered index, because the actual base table rows may be stored in an order different to that of the nonclustered index.

A clustered index works best when you're retrieving multiple rows in the order of the clustered index columns, or if you're performing a range scan predicate on a column within the clustered index as the rows are presorted. You carry out a range scan when the predicate you specify isn't searching for a single value (for example, `IDCol=2`), but is looking for rows that have a value within a certain range (`IDCol BETWEEN 1 AND 100`, for example).

> **If you have one index on a table, make sure it is a clustered index. If you have more than one index, you should take some time to work out what indexes your table needs before determining which will benefit most from being clustered.**

Identifying Potential Indexes

Indexes are used to improve the performance of queries, but not just `SELECT` queries. Any type of query that locates rows using a predicate can benefit from an index, including `SELECT`, `UPDATE`, and `DELETE` queries.

If indexes are so great, then why don't we simply create an index on every column? Well there are a couple of reasons:

❑ Indexes maintain a copy of the indexed columns in a separate structure to the base table (except clustered indexes) so every index increases the size of the database.

❑ Every index slightly impacts the performance of `INSERT`s, `DELETE`s, and changes to columns using an `UPDATE` statement. Every time that a change is made within a table that touches a column used within indexes, those indexes also need to be updated so that they reflect the data contained within the base tables.

Only two paragraphs ago, you learned that indexes improve the performance of `UPDATE` and `DELETE` queries. They improve the performance by allowing SQL Server to locate the rows more easily than looking at every row. However, they also negatively impact the performance by requiring the indexes to be maintained by SQL Server as part of the process of carrying out the command. If you have suitable indexes, the negative impact is usually a lot less than the positive impact.

If you don't want to create an index on every column within every table, then how do you identify the columns you do wish to create them on? This is where database administration is more of an art than a science because there are no hard and fast rules, and it depends on each situation. There is a loose process you can use, which is as follows:

❑ Identify critical queries that must run as quickly as possible

❑ Identify queries that are run very frequently by many users

❑ Identify queries that currently run for a long duration

These three groups of queries are a good place to start index optimization. Once you have identified the queries:

❑ Create a list of tables used in these queries.

❑ For each table, identify which columns are frequently used to order the retrieved resultset.

❑ For each table, list the columns that participate in the query predicate or join criteria. For each table, rank the number of occurrences of each column within the queries.

❑ For each column, rank the column selectivity. This is the number of unique values within the column compared with the total number of rows in the table. The better the selectivity the better the index, as SQL Server can narrow down the number of rows that it's dealing with when searching for a value within the tables rows for this column more quickly.

First, consider creating indexes on the columns with high selectivity that are used commonly, especially if they're also used for ordering the resultset. Once you've created indexes on these columns, review the performance of all the queries you've identified and note the impact. You can continue to repeat this process until you're satisfied with the performance of your queries.

Creating an Index

You create indexes in SQL Server using the CREATE INDEX command, which in its simplest form has the following syntax:

```
CREATE [UNIQUE] INDEX  [CLUSTERED | NONCLUSTERED] index_name
ON table_name(column_name, ...)
```

If you specify the UNIQUE option, the index will ensure that every row has a different value in the indexed columns. Any attempt to INSERT a duplicate value will fail.

The index_name is the name you'll use to refer to the index for administration purposes. You'll look at an example of creating an index in the next section.

Using Indexes

Using indexes in SQL Server is straightforward; in fact, you don't have to do anything at all. The query processor (the part of SQL Server that digests your query and works out the best way to carry out the command you have given) automatically inspects indexes on all tables involved in the query to determine if any of them can help the query resolve in a more efficient manner. If they can, then the query processor will automatically make use of the index where appropriate. All you, as the sender of the query, may notice between the situation where a suitable index exists and one where a suitable index doesn't exist, is a change in the time that the query may take to complete.

Try It Out–Using an Index

Now, you'll issue a query against the largest table in the Northwind database, the Order Details table. Then you'll create an index on this table that contains the columns you're using, and execute the query again.

1. Connect to SQL Server using Query Analyzer. Execute the following command:

```
SELECT UnitPrice, Quantity FROM [Order Details]
    WHERE Quantity BETWEEN 10 AND 11 AND UnitPrice > 50
```

Take note of how long it takes to execute. Currently SQL Server will have to look at every row within the table to find the rows that match our query predicates.

2. Now you'll create an index on this table using the following command:

```
CREATE NONCLUSTERED INDEX ix_orderdetails_productid
    ON [Order Details](UnitPrice, Quantity)
```

In this statement, you've called the index ix_orderdetails_productid. This name clearly states exactly what you're creating, as the ix stands for index, which is on the orderdetails table using the productid.

3. This creates a nonclustered index on the Unit Price and Quantity columns, as a nonclustered index is the default. Now reissue the query:

```
SELECT UnitPrice, Quantity FROM [Order Details]
    WHERE Quantity BETWEEN 10 AND 11 AND UnitPrice > 50
```

This time, when the query is executed, SQL Server can simply navigate through the new index structure to locate the rows that match the query predicate without needing to look at every row within the table. Because there is no Order By clause, the resultset may be retrieved in a different order from the previous example.

> **Depending on the performance of the computer that you're using, you may or may not see a significant difference in performance between these two queries.**

Removing an Index

To remove an index, you use the DROP INDEX command with the following syntax:

```
DROP INDEX table_name.index_name
```

You may want to drop indexes from time to time if they are deemed unnecessary (as every index slightly impacts INSERT performance), or if the query requirements change and you've created a more appropriate index. If you're inserting a large number of rows into a table, you may want to drop indexes temporarily while the table is populated and then re-create the indexes once the population has completed. This saves SQL Server having to maintain those indexes for each row that is inserted as part of your data loading process.

Try It Out–Removing an Index

In this example, you use the DROP INDEX command to remove the index you created on the Order Details table.

Connect to SQL Server using Query Analyzer. Execute the following command:

```
DROP INDEX [Order Details].ix_orderdetails_productid
```

This removes the index from the table. No other changes are necessary and SQL Server will no longer consider the index available when the query processor is determining the best way to carry out a query.

Besides these basic tasks, you can also maintain your indexes using the Index Tuning Wizard, which is discussed in detail in Chapter 13.

Full-Text Indexes

Full-Text indexes were introduced in SQL Server 7.0 to allow developers to locate rows by searching free-form text. As you've seen, traditional indexes are a very efficient mechanism for locating rows within a table, based on predicate criteria. However, the effectiveness of these indexes is reduced when you're attempting to locate words or a certain phrase in a given paragraph of text or document. If in fact, the column you want to index contains rows of more than 900 bytes in size, or you're using the TEXT data type, the internal indexes that you looked at cannot be created at all. Full-Text is an attempt to alleviate the limitations of traditional indexes when it comes to searching text.

Why Use Full-Text?

As mentioned, Full-Text is useful for locating snippets of text (words or phrases) within a block of text that is retained in a table row. However, Full-Text doesn't need to be used in all text-locating situations. For example, if you have a table with the following rows

IDCol	CharCol
1	Bread
2	Milk
3	Butter

then a simple query to locate a row based on the CharCol may be:

```
SELECT IDCol FROM Table1 WHERE CharCol='Bread'
```

Because this query is specifying an exact match for the character column, and the character column is relatively short, a traditional SQL Server index will be the most efficient means of locating the desired row(s).

Let's try another example. This time we wish to locate rows based on a wildcard, such as:

```
SELECT IDCol FROM Table1 WHERE CharCol LIKE 'B%'
```

As you're specifying what must be the first character in the character column, SQL Server can once again make use of a traditional index to locate the desired rows relatively efficiently.

Now, consider a table that contains the following data:

IDCol	CharCol
1	The quick brown fox jumps over the lazy dog
2	The slow green goat walks around the smelly cat

If you want to locate all the rows that contain the word "jumps," then you'll have a problem with your traditional indexes. However, it can be done and the query would look like the following:

```
SELECT IDCol FROM Table1 WHERE CharCol LIKE '%jumps%'
```

Although this query will work and return the correct row, SQL Server doesn't use any index that we have on the CharCol column to carry out this query. Because you're instructing SQL Server to search the entire column looking for any matches, using a traditional index to assist with this query isn't beneficial. Because you don't specify a starting point, the index hierarchy cannot be used to reduce the number of rows that need to be physically examined; instead, the only option is for SQL Server to carry out a table scan. Although this may not be too much of an issue for an example table with only two rows, it's likely to have a significant performance impact on any similar tables that contain over a few thousand rows.

When a traditional index cannot assist our query, you should consider using Full-Text.

How Does Full-Text Work?

Full-Text indexes have nothing in common with traditional SQL Server indexes; in fact, they aren't really even part of SQL Server. Instead an external service, the Microsoft Search Service acts as a third-party search provider that is used by SQL Server.

> While SQL Server uses an external service for Full-Text indexing in SQL Server 7.0 and 2000, preliminary information suggests that this functionality will be integrated into the core database engine in the next version of SQL Server. However, there has been no official confirmation of this.

When SQL Server instructs the Microsoft Search Service to populate a search catalog, it connects to SQL Server and examines all the information contained in the columns you've specified as being enabled for Full-Text indexing. The Microsoft Search Service takes a copy of the textual information located in the Full-Text columns and stores it in a proprietary format within data files located in the file system. The Microsoft Search Service structures the data within its files in such a way that it can locate individual words and parts of words very quickly.

When a query is issued against SQL Server that specifies a Full-Text predicate, SQL Server takes that predicate and passes it on to the Microsoft Search Service. The Search Service, using its own copy of the data, locates the rows that match the Full-Text predicate and passes the key values for those rows back to SQL Server. Then SQL Server applies any remaining non-Full-Text predicates, and finally returns the rowset to the user.

Full-Text Administration

Full-Text requires administration effort, not only to set it up but it may require effort to maintain it. Full-Text indexes are not always self-maintaining, meaning that they may have to be periodically refreshed so they reflect any changes that have been made on the base tables. If they aren't synchronized with the base tables, it's possible for incorrect results to be retrieved from Full-Text queries.

Creating a Full-Text Index

Before you can query a Full-Text index, you have to create it. The steps needed to do this are as follows:

- ❑ Install Full-Text indexing support
- ❑ Enable the database for Full-Text support
- ❑ Create a Full-Text catalog
- ❑ Create the table for Full-Text support
- ❑ Enable a Full-Text index on a table column
- ❑ Populate the Full-Text index

You can carry out these steps using SQL Server Enterprise Manager or T-SQL. As both are valid and useful, we'll demonstrate Full-Text indexing using both methods.

Before you begin to use Full-Text indexing, you must make sure that it is supported on your platform. Full-Text indexing is supported on all editions of SQL Server except the following:

❑   SQL Server Desktop Engine (MSDE)

❑   SQL Server CE Edition

In addition, SQL Server Full-Text indexing is supported on all operating systems that SQL Server 2000 is supported on, except Windows 98.

Try It Out–Installing Full-Text Indexing

1.   To install Full-Text indexing support, run the SQL Server Setup wizard.

2.   Click through the various option screens until you reach the Select Components dialog box as shown:

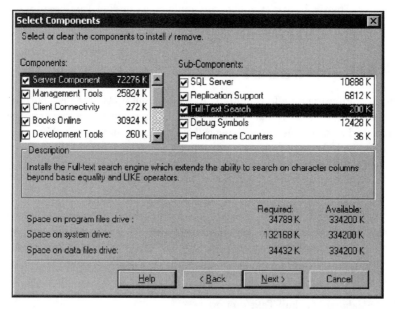

3.   Under Sub-Components, ensure that the Full-Text Search option has been ticked. If it hasn't, then tick it now and click Next. Follow through the remaining windows of the Setup wizard to install it.

Once setup has completed, SQL Server Full-Text support has been enabled. You may need to restart your computer for the changes to take effect. If this is required, the Setup wizard will prompt you to do so.

> **For more information on installing SQL Server 2000 components, see Chapter 2.**

To ensure that Full-Text is started and operational, view the state of the Full-Text Search service within SQL Server Enterprise Manager under the Support Services node. If it is started, you'll see a green arrow as part of the Full-Text Search icon, as shown:

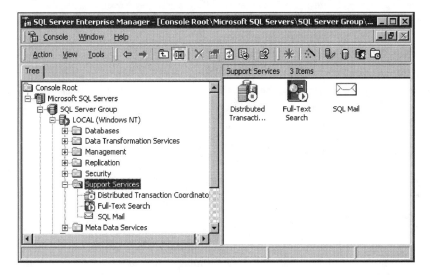

Enabling Full-Text Support for a Database

As mentioned, after installing Full-Text, the next step is to enable Full-Text support for a specific database. This is a relatively trivial task to complete and from T-SQL you simply issue the following command:

```
sp_fulltext_database 'enable'
```

This is executed within the context of the database for which you want to enable Full-Text indexing.

> Be careful when issuing this command. If you execute it against a database that has existing Full-Text indexes, they will be dropped. Although you won't lose any data, you will have to re-create and repopulate the missing Full-Text indexes, which can take a significant amount of time on large tables.

Try It Out–Creating a Full-Text Index

In this example, you'll enable Full-Text indexing support for the Northwind database using T-SQL.

Connect to your SQL Server using Query Analyzer. Issue the following commands:

```
USE Northwind

EXEC sp_fulltext_database 'enable'
```

173

If you get an error, check that the Microsoft Search Service is started on your computer. You can check this from the Services Administration tool (see Windows Help for more information).

When you use SQL Server Enterprise Manager to define a Full-Text index, this step is done for you automatically when you define a Full-Text table, as you'll see in the next section.

Creating a Full-Text Catalog

Once a database has had Full-Text support enabled, you need to create a catalog in which Full-Text will retain the data needed to carry out the Full-Text searches within this database. As we've mentioned, a Full-Text catalog is implemented as a series of files (and directories) located on the file system.

To do this, you execute the following T-SQL statement:

```
sp_fulltext_catalog CatalogName, 'create', path
```

If you don't specify the path parameter, then the catalog is created within the default file location used by Full-Text.

Once again, if you're doing this through Enterprise Manager, this step is carried out automatically when you define a Full-Text index on a table.

Try It Out–Creating a Full-Text Catalog

In this example, you'll create a Full-Text catalog within the Northwind database and call it NorthFTCatalog.

Connect to SQL Server using Query Analyzer. Execute the following command:

```
USE Northwind
EXEC sp_fulltext_catalog 'NorthFTCatalog', 'create'
```

Because you haven't explicitly specified the path parameter, this command creates the Full-Text catalog in the default directory location of Full-Text. By default, this is the path where you installed the SQL Server system data files, for example, in the C:\Program Files\Microsoft SQL Server\MSSQL\FTDATA directory.

Creating a Full-Text Index on a Table

Once you've created the catalog, you can proceed to add individual Full-Text indexes to it. You do this by defining Full-Text indexes on one or more tables within the database using the following statement:

```
sp_fulltext_table table_name, 'Create', catalog_name, unique_key_name
```

The unique_key_name specifies the name of a unique index on the specified table that Full-Text can use to refer to rows within that table. This is usually the primary key for a table.

You can only define one Full-Text index per table, but that Full-Text index may consist of multiple columns.

> You cannot create a Full-Text index on a table that only has a unique constraint comprised of multiple columns. Full-Text only works with single-column unique constraints. If your table only has a composite key, then a single-column artificial key will have to be added to the table.

Try It Out–Creating a Full-Text Index on a Table

In this example, you'll define a Full-Text index on our Products table. You'll tell the Microsoft Search Service to use the primary key of this table for referencing rows within this table.

Connect to SQL Server using Query Analyzer. Run the following command to create the Full-Text index:

```
USE Northwind
EXEC sp_fulltext_table 'dbo.Products',
    'Create', 'NorthFTCatalog', 'PK_Products'
```

This instructs Full-Text to create a Full-Text index on the Products table in the NorthFTCatalog and use the PK_Products key for referencing rows within the base table.

Enabling Full-Text Support for a Column

Now that you've enabled Full-Text support on the database and created a specific catalog repository in which the Microsoft Search Service can retain the necessary catalog data, you can go ahead and create a Full-Text index on a specific column.

To do this, you execute the following T-SQL command:

```
sp_fulltext_column table_name, column_name, 'add'
```

One or more columns can be added to a Full-Text index. They are then collectively searched for any given row in an attempt to match the criteria specified in a Full-Text query.

Try It Out–Enabling a Full-Text Index on a Column

In this example, you'll create a Full-Text index on a column and add this to the catalog you created in the previous step.

Connect to SQL Server using Query Analyzer, and execute the following command:

```
USE Northwind
EXEC sp_fulltext_column 'dbo.Products', 'ProductName', 'add'
```

Populating a Full-Text Index Using T-SQL

You've created a Full-Text index and added the relevant columns to that index, now you need to populate it. Until it has been populated, the Full-Text index will be empty and any queries using a Full-Text predicate will retrieve zero rows. There are two ways in which you can populate an index. First you can populate the catalog, which will populate all the Full-Text indexes on all tables within that catalog. Alternatively, you can select a single table to be populated within the catalog. This is useful when you have many tables within a single catalog, but wish to populate them individually.

A Full Population

A full population is used to fill an empty catalog with the data contained within the table for which you've defined the Full-Text index. You can either populate the entire catalog or populate a single Full-Text index.

To fully populate the entire catalog (all Full-Text indexes within the catalog), you issue the following T-SQL command:

```
sp_fulltext_catalog catalog_name, 'start_full'
```

And to populate a single Full-Text index within the catalog, you issue the following command:

```
sp_fulltext_table table_name, 'start_full'
```

If you instruct Full-Text to carry out a full population on a Full-Text index that has previously been populated, this flushes the existing information retained within the catalog, before undertaking the full population.

> **While a population is in progress, users can be running queries against the database. Users can even run Full-Text queries. However, the results of such queries will be limited to the rows that have been retained within the Full-Text catalog, at the point of query execution.**

Try It Out–Populating a Full-Text Index

In this example, you'll populate the Full-Text index, first by instructing the catalog to populate all indexes within it and then by specifically populating just the Full-Text index that exists on the products table.

Connect to SQL Server using Query Analyzer. Execute the following command to instruct Microsoft Search Service to carry out a full population on all Full-Text indexes within the NorthFTCatalog catalog:

```
EXEC sp_fulltext_catalog 'NorthFTCatalog', 'start_full'
```

Now, carry out another full population but this time you only want to perform a full population on the Full-Text index that exists on the Products table. To do this, execute the following command:

```
EXEC sp_fulltext_table 'dbo.Products', 'start_full'
```

Full populations can take a long time depending on the number of rows in the table and the type and amount of data within each row. The population process runs asynchronously and shouldn't cause any major concurrency issues (such as long-term blocking) for users of your database. Because it can consume most of the CPU resource, you should try to schedule a full population during periods of light database activity.

An Incremental Population

If you had to perform a full population after every row within the database had changed, this would prove to be very resource intensive, especially on large tables. Therefore, Full-Text can perform an incremental population, that is, include any changes since the last population within the Full-Text index.

If you're manually performing an incremental population, you'll have to decide how often you run such a population. Factors to consider are as follows:

❑ How up to date do you need your Full-Text indexes to be in relation to the underlying table's data?

❑ How often does the data within the underlying table change?

❑ What is the impact on server resources of running an incremental update?

For example, if you're using Full-Text indexes to allow the searching of product descriptions, via a website store, then you may determine that the product catalog doesn't change very often; perhaps only half a dozen times in a day. In addition, if the new product descriptions aren't searched immediately, this will not be a major disadvantage. In this situation, you may choose to perform an incremental update every hour to pick up any changes that have been made to the product descriptions within that hour.

For an incremental population to take place, the table must have a timestamp column within it. This timestamp column is used by Full-Text to identify rows that have changed since the last population. A timestamp column is modified automatically by SQL Server whenever a change takes place within a row; however, this means that any changes in the row will cause the row to be included within an incremental Full-Text build, not just changes to the columns that are part of the Full-Text index.

> BLOB operations such as WriteText and UpdateText don't modify the timestamp value, meaning that any changes performed by these operations will not be included within an incremental build.

If your table doesn't have a timestamp column, you can add one using the following command:

```
ALTER TABLE table_name
ADD column_name timestamp
```

A table can only contain a single timestamp column. The column should not be updated directly as it is maintained internally by SQL Server.

> Schema changes, like adding a timestamp column, may impact existing code and applications. All changes to a database schema should be thoroughly tested in a controlled environment before being applied to a production system.

After the timestamp column has been added to your table, you'll need to perform a full population of the Full-Text index. After this has been done, you'll be able to carry out incremental builds by using the following command:

```
sp_fulltext_table table_name, 'start_incremental'
```

Try It Out–Adding an Incremental Full-Text Index

In this example, you'll add a timestamp column to the Products table, carry out a full population, make some changes to the base table, and then carry out an incremental population.

1. Connect to SQL Server using Query Analyzer and run the following command:

```
USE Northwind

ALTER TABLE Products
ADD TimeStampCol timestamp
```

2. This adds a new column named TimeStampCol of type timestamp to the Products table. Next, initiate a full population of the Full-Text index on this table:

```
EXEC sp_fulltext_table 'dbo.Products', 'start_full'
```

3. Now, make a couple of changes to the columns used by the Full-Text index in some of the rows within this table.

```
UPDATE Products
SET ProductName='Marmite Spread' WHERE ProductID=63

UPDATE Products
SET ProductName='Canterbury Beer' WHERE ProductID=60
```

4. At this point, the Full-Text index is out of sync with the base table, because it doesn't reflect the changes that have been made in the base table. Because the table now contains a timestamp column, you can perform an incremental population to update the Full-Text index with the changes that have occurred since the last population:

```
EXEC sp_fulltext_table 'dbo.Products','start_incremental'
```

The Full-Text index is now consistent with the base table.

Full-Text Index Using Enterprise Manager

Now you've learned how to create a Full-Text index the "hard way" (though it wasn't really that hard), you'll look at how to do this using SQL Server Enterprise Manager. Enterprise Manager has all the functionality commonly used for creating and maintaining Full-Text indexes.

Creating a Full-Text Index Using Enterprise Manager

You create a Full-Text index using a wizard that guides you through the entire process.

Try It Out–Creating a Full-Text Index with a Wizard

In this example, you'll create a new Full-Text index on the titles and notes columns of the authors table within the pubs database. As part of the wizard, you'll also create a new Full-Text catalog named PubsFTCatalog.

1. Open SQL Server Enterprise Manager and connect to your SQL Server. Drill down through the Databases node into the pubs database and select the Tables node. Right-click the titles table and select Full Text Index Table | Define Full-Text Indexing on a Table.

2. You'll be presented with the first screen of the wizard as shown. Click Next to move through to the next window.

3. Now you'll be asked to select the unique index that the Full-Text service will use to identify rows within the table. Because there is only one suitable unique index on the titles table, there is only one option in this window. Click Next.

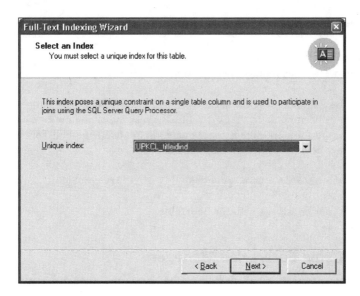

4. Now you enter the name of the catalog where the Full-Text information will be retained. For this example, enter **PubsFTCatalog** and leave the path as the default. Click Next.

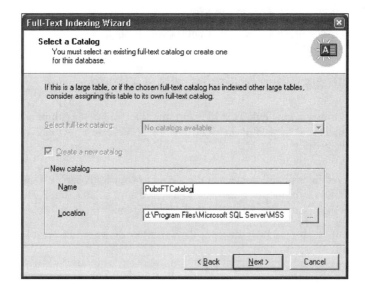

5. Next, you select the columns you want to include in the Full-Text index. For this example, select the title and notes columns and click Next.

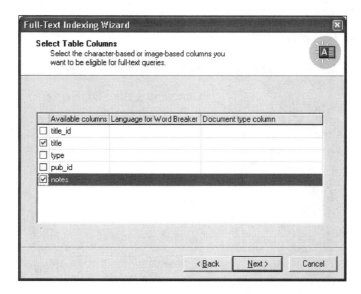

6. Now you can enter a schedule for populating the Full-Text index. For this example, leave this empty and click Next.

And that's it. Review the information shown in the final screen to ensure it is correct and click Finish to create the Full-Text index.

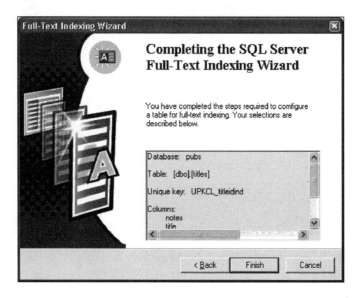

You'll receive a confirmation message letting you know that the index creation has been successful.

Populating with Enterprise Manager

To carry out a full and incremental population using SQL Server Enterprise Manager, simply right-click the table (within the table list view that contains the Full-Text index you want to populate) and select either Full Text Index Table | Start Full Population or Full Text Index Table | Start Incremental Population, depending on the type of population you want to initiate.

Try It Out–Populating a Catalog with Enterprise Manager

In this example, you'll use SQL Server Enterprise Manager to carry out a full population of the Full-Text index that you created on the titles table within the pubs database.

1. Open SQL Server Enterprise Manager and connect to your SQL Server. Drill down into the Databases node. Select the Tables node in the pubs database.

2. In the tables list view, right-click the titles table. From the pop-up menu, select Full-Text Index Table | Start Full Population to commence the population of our Full-Text index.

Information About a Full-Text Index

As part of your administrative activities, from time to time you may need to find information about a Full-Text search, either interactively or through a script. Fortunately, SQL Server has a number of built-in functions for interrogating the Full-Text Search service.

Checking If Full-Text Has Been Installed

If you want to check if Full-Text has been installed, you can do this using the following command:

```
SELECT FULLTEXTSERVICEPROPERTY('IsFulltextInstalled')
```

The results of this function are as follows:

❑   0 – Full-Text hasn't been installed

❑   1 – Full-Text has been installed

Checking If a Database Has Been Full-Text Enabled

You can also check to determine if a particular database has been enabled for Full-Text indexing. Remember that this is important to know because if it has been enabled, and if you enable it again, all existing Full-Text indexes will be dropped.

The syntax for this function is as follows:

```
SELECT DATABASEPROPERTY(database_name, 'IsFulltextEnabled')
```

It produces the following results:

❑   0 – Full-Text hasn't been enabled for the specified database

❑   1 – Full-Text has been enabled for the specified database

> **You may have noticed that there is a mixture of stored procedures and functions for finding out Full-Text information.**

Try It Out–Inspecting Databases for Full-Text Indexes

In this example, you'll inspect a couple of databases to determine if Full-Text has been enabled for them.

Connect to SQL Server using Query Analyzer. Execute the following command:

```
SELECT DATABASEPROPERTY('Northwind', 'IsFulltextEnabled')
```

This should produce the value 1 to indicate that Full-Text has been enabled for the Northwind database. Now execute the following:

```
SELECT DATABASEPROPERTY('msdb', 'IsFulltextEnabled')
```

This should produce the value 0 to indicate that Full-Text hasn't been enabled for the msdb database.

Checking Which Full-Text Catalogs Exist

You can also check to see what Full-Text catalogs currently exist. Unfortunately, there is another command syntax to remember:

```
sp_help_fulltext_catalogs
```

To execute this command, you must be in the context of the database you wish to inspect. If Full-Text catalogs exist, this stored procedure will return a rowset that contains the name, path, and other parameters relating to a Full-Text index. If no Full-Text index exists, this stored procedure will simply return the constant 1.

Try It Out–Inspecting Databases for Full-Text Catalogs

In this example, you'll examine a couple of databases to see what Full-Text catalogs exist within them.

Connect to SQL Server using Query Analyzer. Execute the following command:

```
USE Northwind

EXEC sp_help_fulltext_catalogs
```

You should get a rowset containing the information relating to the NorthFTData catalog. Now execute the following command:

```
USE MSDB

EXEC sp_help_fulltext_catalogs
```

You should simply receive the constant 1 back from this command, indicating that no Full-Text catalogs exist within this database.

Checking Which Tables Have a Full-Text Index

Now that you know which Full-Text catalogs exist, you can also check to see which tables have Full-Text indexes created within those catalogs. To do this, you execute the following command:

```
sp_help_fulltext_tables catalog_name
```

This will return a rowset with the names of the tables that have Full-Text indexes created within the specified catalog.

Try It Out–Examining Full-Text Catalogs

In this example, you'll examine the Full-Text catalog to retrieve information on the tables that have Full-Text indexes created within them.

Connect to SQL Server using Query Analyzer. Execute the following command:

```
Use Northwind

EXEC sp_help_fulltext_tables 'NorthFTCatalog'
```

This will return a rowset that contains information on the Full-Text index that you created on the Products table.

Checking If a Column Has Been Full-Text Indexed

Finally, you can examine a Full-Text index to see which columns from the table are participating in the Full-Text index. To do this, you execute the following command:

```
sp_help_fulltext_columns table_name
```

This command returns a rowset that contains details of the columns that make up the Full-Text index (excluding the unique key that is reported by the prior command).

Try It Out–Checking Columns for Full-Text Indexes

In this example, you'll retrieve a list of columns that are participating in the Full-Text index you created on the Products table.

Connect to SQL Server using Query Analyzer. Execute the following command:

```
Use Northwind

Exec sp_help_fulltext_columns 'Products'
```

This will return a rowset that contains the name of the columns, table, and some additional information about the columns that form the Full-Text index.

Change Tracking

Change Tracking for Full-Text indexes was introduced as a new feature of SQL Server 2000. Up until this point, we've discussed that Full-Text indexes require manual intervention to keep them up to date. Change Tracking is a new feature that allows Full-Text indexes to be more effectively maintained.

Change Tracking can be used to update the Full-Text catalog in the following two ways:

❑ On-demand Updating

❑ Automatically Updating

With On-demand Updating, you must manually instruct SQL Server to update the Full-Text index. Although this is functionally equivalent to the incremental population that we discussed earlier, the way it is carried out is different. When Change Tracking has been turned on, SQL Server maintains a list of all the rows that have been modified since the last update of the Full-Text index. When you issue the command to update the Full-Text index, only the rows that have been identified as modified are sent to the Full-Text service, thereby saving the entire table from being scanned for changes. Although the storage of the modified row information consumes a slight amount of resource (depending on the frequency of change), the improvements in the efficiency of populating the Full-Text indexes often make up for this.

The other mode is Automatically Updating. In this mode of Change Tracking, modified rows are sent immediately to the Full-Text index for updating. This keeps the Full-Text indexes up to date in near real time, but obviously consumes more resource than carrying out a periodic update, especially on tables that are frequently modified.

> **Using Change Tracking is a new alternative in SQL Server 2000 to incremental updates. This is a more efficient manner of updating Full-Text indexes to include changes that have occurred within the database.**

Try It Out–Enabling Change Tracking from Enterprise Manager

1. Using Enterprise Manager, drill down into the Northwind database and select the Tables node.

2. In the detail pane, right-click the Products table.

3. From the pop-up menu, choose Full-Text Index Table | Change Tracking. Selecting this option enables the tracking of which of the rows within this table have been modified since the last population of the associated Full-Text index.

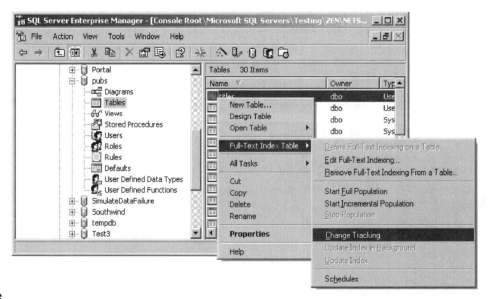

Although you've selected **Change Tracking**, you haven't told SQL Server when to use that change information to update the Full-Text index. With the current settings, the change information will be collected, but the Full-Text index will not be updated to reflect these changes automatically.

4. You can either instruct SQL Server to update the Full-Text index manually (on demand) or tell SQL Server to update the Full-Text index automatically. To do this, open the same pop-up menu as before.

You'll notice now that Change Tracking has been enabled and two new options have appeared. These are as follows:

❑ **Update Index in Background:** Instructs SQL Server to maintain the Full-Text index in real time as the changes occur.

❑ **Update Index:** Instructs SQL Server to update the index immediately with all the changes that have occurred since the last time it was populated (on demand).

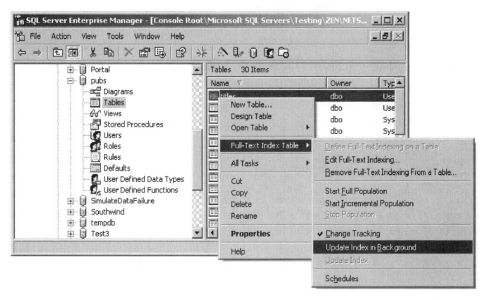

By selecting the **Schedules** menu item, you can schedule the **On Demand** setting so that it is a regular, automated periodic update (as opposed to real time).

Try It Out–Enabling Change Tracking from T-SQL

To enable Change Tracking, you use the sp_fulltext_table stored procedure that you used earlier in this chapter, except this time you specify the following options:

❑   start_change_tracking

❑   stop_change_tracking

For example, to start Change Tracking on the Products table, you issue the following command:

```
USE Northwind
```

```
EXEC sp_fulltext_table 'dbo.Products', 'start_change_tracking'
```

To instruct SQL Server to update the Full-Text index automatically in real time, you use this procedure again but this time you specify the following options:

❑   start_background_updateindex

❑   stop_background_updateindex

For example, to enable real-time updates of the Full-Text index for the Products table, you would issue the following command:

```
EXEC sp_fulltext_table 'dbo.Products',
'start_background_updateindex'
```

If, on the other hand, you simply wanted to update the Full-Text index from the change information on demand, or on a regular schedule (but not real time), you would either issue the following command "ad hoc" or schedule it using a SQL Agent job:

```
EXEC sp_fulltext_table 'dbo.Products', 'update_index'
```

Querying a Full-Text Index

All this talk of administration and we've yet to discuss how to actually construct a query to use a Full-Text index. This has been intentional because, as a database administrator (DBA), most of the time that you spend interacting with Full-Text indexes will likely be from an administration standpoint; querying Full-Text indexes is usually the domain of the application developer. For completeness and because there will be times when it's useful for a DBA to execute a Full-Text search, we'll briefly discuss the various methods of using Full-Text indexes here.

CONTAINS

You can use CONTAINS as a query predicate. It allows you to carry out a precise or fuzzy search based on a set of criteria. CONTAINS has the following syntax:

```
CONTAINS(column_name | *, search_condition )
```

You can either specify a column_name or * to search all Full-Text columns on the table.

> **Even if you're searching multiple columns, you must match the entire phrase within a single column.**

The search condition can be as simple as searching a Full-Text column for a row that contains an exact match of the word or phrase, as follows:

```
"word or phrase"
```

To search for a row that contains a word that begins with the specified prefix, use the following:

```
"prefix*"
```

Search criteria can be used together by separating them using AND or OR, for example:

```
" "fish" AND "chips" "
```

Try It Out–Searching a Full-Text Index

In this example, you'll execute a Full-Text search to locate products based on the search criteria.

Connect to SQL Server using Query Analyzer. Execute the following command:

```
SELECT * FROM Products
  WHERE CONTAINS(ProductName, '"Syrup" OR "Cran*"')
```

This retrieves all rows where the product contains the word "Syrup" or a word starting with "Cran".

CONTAINSTABLE

CONTAINSTABLE is effectively the same as CONTAINS, except that it returns the rows from Full-Text in the form of a rowset rather than being used as a query predicate as with CONTAINS. The syntax is as follows:

```
SELECT *
  FROM CONTAINSTABLE(table_name, column_name | *,
                     search_condition  )
```

FREETEXT

FREETEXT is used as a simple query mechanism and is a lot less precise than CONTAINS. It has the following syntax:

```
FREETEXT(column_name | *, free_text_search)
```

The free_text_search parameter is a string of one or more words. Full-Text will return any row that matches any of the words.

Try It Out–Limiting a Full-Text Index Search

In this example, you'll execute a Full-Text search to locate products based on our search criteria.

Connect to SQL Server using Query Analyzer. Execute the following command:

```
SELECT * FROM Products
   WHERE FREETEXT(ProductName,'Syrup Sauce')
```

This retrieves all rows where the product contains either the word "Syrup" or the word "Sauce".

FREETEXTTABLE

FREETEXTTABLE is analogous to CONTAINSTABLE. It retrieves rows in the same way as the FREETEXT predicate; however, it retrieves the rows within a rowset:

```
SELECT *
   FROM FREETEXTTABLE(table_name, column_name | *,
                      free_text_search)
```

Summary

Your ability to administer SQL Server will be greatly enhanced by knowing how to effectively run queries against a database and, just as importantly, understand what the queries that developers are executing against a database are doing. While this chapter has only laid the foundational concepts of the SQL language, it's a good place to start and will be fleshed out in more detail in succeeding chapters.

We've also discussed native SQL Server indexes and the extra functionality of Full-Text indexing. We discussed how indexes work, which is important when you're optimizing a database for maximum performance.

Full-Text indexing requires a lot of administration so we've also covered this in detail. Once a Full-Text index has been created and populated, it can offer powerful searching functionality to you and your developers.

5

Basic Management Tasks

Basic database management is the core of a database administrator's (DBA) role. These tasks aren't glamorous, difficult, or interesting, but the simple things that are necessary to keep any production SQL Server environment functioning.

You should ensure that you're familiar with all the information provided in this chapter, and that you come back to review it at a later stage, if needed.

Management

There are a number of tools that you can use to help administer SQL Server 2000. The tool you choose is largely based on preference; however, each tool has its own set of benefits and disadvantages, which we'll discuss here.

Enterprise Manager

Without a doubt, Enterprise Manager is the most frequently used tool for database administration. It's easy to use, quick to navigate through, and simple to understand. In fact, Enterprise Manager is one of the core reasons SQL Server has been so successful. By making the process of database administration a point-and-click affair, SQL Server has been able to reach the masses.

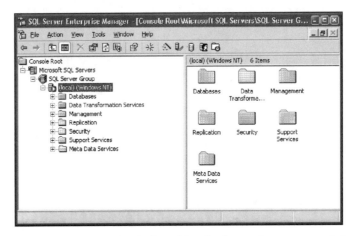

Enterprise Manager isn't the be-all and end-all tool for database administration. It has a number of limitations, such as the following:

❑ It's slow. Well, it's a lot better than in previous versions, but you'll spend a lot of time waiting for Enterprise Manager.

❑ You have more options and more control when you use Transact-SQL (T-SQL) than when you use Enterprise Manager.

If you need to carry out a common database administration task, and you don't want to write code (or remember the command syntax), then Enterprise Manager is a good tool.

Query Analyzer

You've already used Query Analyzer on numerous occasions in this book. Quite simply, it's just a tool for sending T-SQL commands to SQL Server, and displaying the output that SQL Server sends back. Although many of the T-SQL commands are for manipulating data (data manipulation language or DML), many are also for defining the schema (data definition language or DDL) or managing SQL Server in the form of commands and stored procedures.

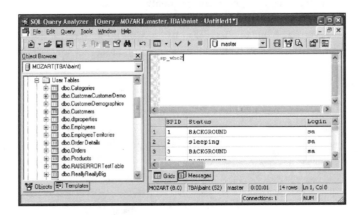

SQL-DMO

You could also choose to do much of the administration using SQL-DMO. SQL-DMO isn't really a tool as such, but more of an interface that you can interact with via a programming language.

Because SQL-DMO is more for use when creating administration applications to be used with SQL Server, we won't cover it within this chapter. However, you should be aware of its existence.

> **For more information on SQL-DMO see SQL Server Books Online.**

Basic Administration Jobs

The job of a DBA is vast and varied and includes tasks discussed throughout this book. However, in spite of how varied the role of a DBA is, there are some core tasks that every DBA should be able to do. These tasks surround the basic functions of a DBA, such as backing up and restoring data, security, and general management.

Basic Database Backup

Backing up a database is *the* most important task of a DBA. It's such an important task that we've dedicated an entire chapter to this subject later in this book (Chapter 8). However, for completeness, we'll briefly discuss how to carry out simple backup and restore procedures.

The most basic database backup is a *full backup*. This takes all the information within a database, including data, schema, and code, and dumps it in a disk file (or tape) for historical retention.

Although backups are primarily used for preserving the information contained within a database at a given point in time, database backups are also a simple way of creating copies of a given database. These copies can either be created locally or e-mailed to a colleague in a remote location for restoration on another server.

> **E-mailing a database should only be considered an option if it's small (a few MB) and the information contained within it isn't highly confidential (due to the "insecure" nature of the Internet).**

Using Enterprise Manager

To create a database backup using SQL Server
Enterprise Manager, you use the Backup Database
option available from the Tools menu. However, you
can also choose to use the Backup wizard, thereby
making the process even simpler. This wizard is
available from the Tools I Wizards menu item, which
opens the following dialog box. Select Backup
Wizard, and it will take you through the entire
procedure.

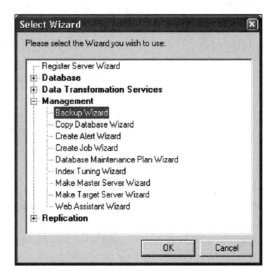

In the example you'll use the Backup Database option from the Tools menu, as this is what you'll
probably choose to use once you're familiar with the backup process.

Try It Out–Backing Up a Database with Enterprise Manager

In this example, you use the Backup Database window in Enterprise Manager to back up the
Northwind database to a local disk file.

1. Open SQL Server Enterprise Manager and connect to the SQL Server. Drill down into the
    Databases node and right-click the Northwind database to open the pop-up menu (you could
    have selected this option by clicking on the Tools I Backup Database menu item as well). On
    the pop-up menu, choose the All Tasks I Backup Database item as shown:

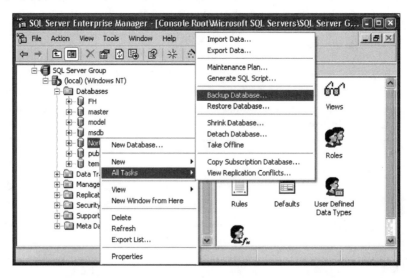

Selecting this menu item will open the **SQL Server Backup** window. In this window you can set all of the information necessary to carry out a backup of the Northwind database.

2. The first thing you need to do is to add a destination location for the database backup. The other options in this dialog box will be explored fully in Chapter 8. The backup location can be a disk or a tape. For this example, you'll be using a disk file so click the **Add** button to enter the appropriate information.

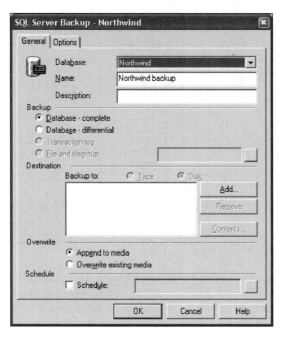

3. Clicking **Add** opens a dialog box, which allows you to enter the path to the location where you want to create the backup file. If you aren't sure exactly where you want to create this file, clicking the ... button will allow you to browse to a directory location.

4. The following dialog box opens when you click the … button. For this example, you'll create the database backup file in the default backup location (unless you have a reason to change it), so leave the default selected. However, in the File name textbox you still need to enter the name you want to call the backup file. In this example, you'll use Northwind.bak.

5. Once you've entered the database backup filename and path, click OK to confirm these details and click OK again to return to the database backup window. For a simple backup, all other options can be left as their defaults. All you need to do now is click OK to start the backup process.

While SQL Server carries out the database backup, you'll see a Backup Progress dialog box similar to the one shown. Depending on the performance of the server, the backup of the Northwind database should be completed within a few seconds.

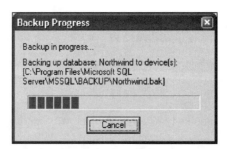

If you had just created a backup of a production database, you would now move that file off the server to a place where it can be retained. One option is to back this file up to tape using the normal file system backup process or by simply copying to CD-ROM or another backup media.

Using Query Analyzer

Almost everything that you do with Enterprise Manager is, under the covers, just sent to SQL Server as T-SQL commands. Often these are the same T-SQL commands that you could send to SQL Server yourself when using a query tool such as Query Analyzer. Backing up a database is a good example of this process, because both Enterprise Manager and Query Analyzer send the BACKUP DATABASE command to SQL Server.

You use the BACKUP DATABASE command to back up a database, and in its simplest form, it has the following syntax:

```
BACKUP DATABASE database_name to DISK=file_path_and_name
```

Try It Out–Backing Up a Database with Query Analyzer

In this example, you'll use Query Analyzer to back up the Northwind database to a file located on a local disk on the SQL Server.

Open Query Analyzer and connect to SQL Server. Once you've connected, enter the following BACKUP DATABASE command:

```
BACKUP DATABASE Northwind
TO DISK='C:\Program Files\Microsoft SQL Server
        \MSSQL\Backup\Northwind.bak' WITH INIT
```

The only thing you'll need to change in the example, when running it against your own SQL Server, is the file location if you've installed SQL Server to a different path or a different disk.

> **When backing up to a disk file, the directory path must exist, because SQL Server won't create it. If the path doesn't exist then the backup will fail.**

The options you can use with the BACKUP DATABASE command will be discussed fully in Chapter 8, but you'll notice we've also included the WITH INIT option at the end of the backup command. All this does is tell the BACKUP DATABASE command to remove any existing backups, if they exist, instead of just appending the backup to the file. As you created a backup to this same file using Enterprise Manager, the WITH INIT option ensures you have one database backup file containing one database backup, instead of one database backup file containing two backups of the same database.

After entering this command, execute it to carry out the actual database backup. Once again this should only take a few seconds to complete and results in the following being displayed (or something similar on your computer):

Processed 528 pages for database 'Northwind', file 'Northwind' on file 1.
Processed 1 pages for database 'Northwind', file 'Northwind_log' on file 1.
BACKUP DATABASE successfully processed 529 pages in 1.202 seconds (3.600 MB/sec).

The output of the BACKUP command provides some basic statistical information on the backup processes. This includes the number of database pages (storage units) backed up, the duration, and the throughput of the backup.

Basic Database Restore

The most basic database restore is the exact opposite of the backup that you just did. It takes a database backup file located on disk (or tape) and restores the information contained within the file into a new database that can then be accessed by database users.

You need to know how to restore a database for that one day (or night) when the database becomes corrupted in some way, or the server crashes, and you need to get the production database online as soon as possible. In a well-managed environment, this situation happens very rarely. Although it's your responsibility as a DBA to restore a database under these circumstances, typically it's rare for you to do so. More commonly you'll restore databases to create copies for test, development, staging, or reporting purposes.

Using Enterprise Manager

Once again, Enterprise Manager provides a simple interface for carrying out database restores. Even though restoring databases is only slightly more difficult than backing up databases, you don't have a wizard to walk you through the process. This time, the only option you have available is the Restore Database tool.

Try It Out—Restoring a Database with Enterprise Manager

In this example, you'll use Enterprise Manager to restore a new database from the backup you created of the Northwind database.

1. Connect to SQL Server using Enterprise Manager and choose the Tools | Restore Database menu item. This will open the Restore Database window where you enter all the information necessary to either create a new database or overwrite an existing database with the information contained within the backup file.

2. You want to create a new database with a different name instead of overwriting the existing Northwind database, so the first thing you need to do is give the new database a name. For this example enter Northwind2 (assuming Northwind2 doesn't already exist).

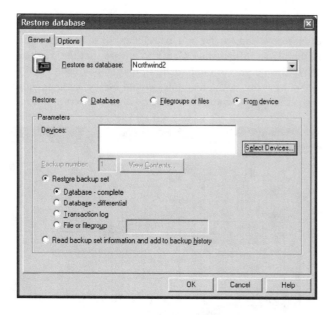

3. Next, you need to tell SQL Server the location of the backup file for restoring the database information. Because this backup file isn't currently associated with the new Northwind2 database, you need to use the From device option in the Restore section.

4. Once you've selected the From device option, click the Select Devices button, which opens the Choose Restore Devices dialog box, which is where you specify the backup file you want to restore from. Click the Add button, select the Northwind.bak file from the files listed, and click OK.

   Once you've selected the Northwind.bak file, it will be shown in the Device name box.

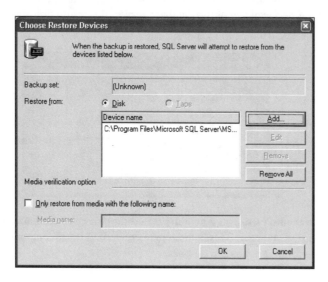

5. Click **OK** to accept this device and return back to the **Restore database** window. Next, click on the **Options** tab. Here you can set the options relevant to restoration, but for now all you're interested in are the physical filenames. Check to ensure that the physical filenames have a 2 appended to the Northwind part of the filenames, that is, **Northwind2_log.ldf** and **Northwind2.mdf**. Without this 2, the filenames would be the same as those currently in use by the existing Northwind database and the restore would overwrite these files.

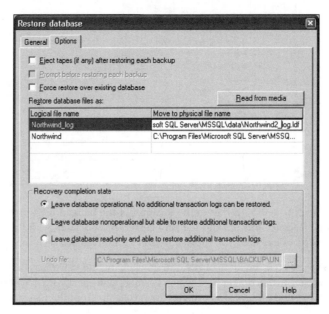

6. Now click **OK** to start the restore process. This should be quick, but not as quick as the backup because writing information to disk is usually slower than reading information from disk. Depending on the performance of the database server, the restoration should take around a minute.

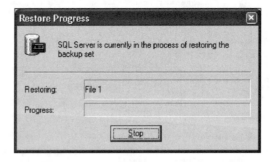

Once the restoration has completed, you'll be able to find the Northwind2 database in the list of databases within Enterprise Manager. This is the newly created, independent, and exact copy (at the time of backup) of the existing Northwind database.

Using Query Analyzer

For restoring a database, you use the RESTORE DATABASE command (under the covers in Enterprise Manager's case). In its simplest format, this command has the following syntax:

```
RESTORE DATABASE database_name FROM DISK=file_path_and_name
```

If you're restoring a database to a new database on the server where it was created (that is, creating a copy of the database) or restoring the database to a different server that has a different directory structure to the one where it was created, you need to be aware of a little more syntax, which is as follows:

```
RESTORE DATABASE database_name FROM DISK=file_path_and_name
   WITH MOVE logical_filename TO physical_filename
```

Using the WITH MOVE option allows you to specify an alternative location for the physical database data files other than the ones used with the database that was originally backed up.

Try It Out–Restoring a Database with Query Analyzer

In this example, you'll restore the Northwind2 database from the backup file using RESTORE DATABASE. Before you begin, remove the existing Northwind2 database if you carried out the previous example. For more information on removing a database, see Chapter 3.

Connect to SQL Server using Query Analyzer and enter the command, as shown:

```
RESTORE DATABASE Northwind2
FROM DISK = 'C:\Program Files\Microsoft SQL Server
            \MSSQL\BACKUP\Northwind.bak'
WITH
   MOVE 'Northwind_log' TO 'C:\Program Files\
        Microsoft SQL Server\MSSQL\data\Northwind2_log.ldf',
   MOVE 'Northwind' TO 'C:\Program Files\
        Microsoft SQL Server\MSSQL\data\Northwind2.mdf'
```

This command specifies that you want to restore the database, named Northwind2, from the backup file, named Northwind.bak. You specify the MOVE option for both the data files that form the backed up database to change the physical filenames to Northwind2_log.ldf and Northwind2.mdf. This prevents the original filenames being used during the restoration, which would result in an error, because the original Northwind database still exists.

When you execute this command, SQL Server will restore the database. If you've specified the parameters correctly, you'll see the completion message as shown, informing you that SQL Server has restored the database successfully:

Processed 528 pages for database 'Northwind2', file 'Northwind' on file 1.
Processed 1 pages for database 'Northwind2', file 'Northwind_log' on file 1.
RESTORE DATABASE successfully processed 529 pages in 1.062 seconds (4.074 MB/sec).

> **Database backups and restores are covered in greater detail in Chapter 8.**

Generating a Database Script

A *database script* is a file that contains all the SQL statements necessary to re-create from scratch the database and the objects within that database, such as, tables, stored procedures, views, and so on.

Scripting is useful for moving object structures between development and test environments as well as creating empty databases that resemble the production or development databases for testing purposes.

Using Enterprise Manager

Fortunately, the tools to generate database scripts are built into Enterprise Manager and are relatively straightforward to use. You can access the tool for creating database scripts using the Tools I Generate SQL Scripts menu item or the pop-up menu available when a database is right-clicked.

Try It Out–Generating Scripts with Enterprise Manager

In this example, you'll use Enterprise Manager to generate a script of all the objects in the Northwind database.

1. Connect to SQL Server using Enterprise Manager and drill down into the Databases node. Select the Northwind database from the list. Right-click and select the All Tasks I Generate SQL Scripts menu item as shown:

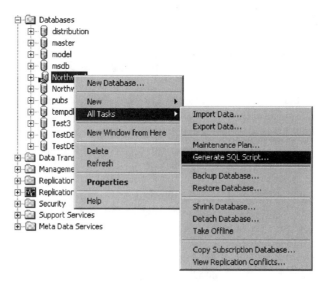

2. This will open the Generate SQL Scripts dialog box. Here you can choose what objects you want to have scripted, and the scripting options you want to use to generate the script. Click the Show All button to allow all database objects to be selected for scripting. Because you want to generate a script of all the database objects, select the Script all objects box. Notice that all the listed database objects now move over into the Objects to be scripted list.

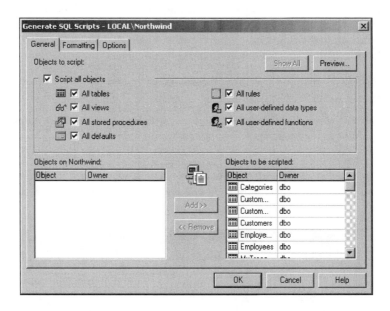

3. Next, click the Formatting tab. This is where you select how you want SQL Server to format the script that is generated.

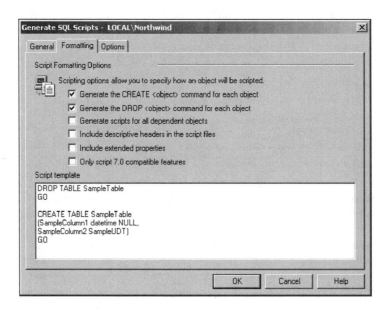

The default options are all you need for this example, but the following are some choices you have:

❑ Including the DROP statement. This statement is useful if you're applying the script to an existing database. Be careful though, because all data within this object will be lost.

❑ Scripting all dependent objects. A dependent object is an object that refers to or needs another object to run successfully. For example, a stored procedure may make use of TableA, so the stored procedure is said to be dependent on TableA. This doesn't matter in the example because you're scripting all the objects in the database anyway.

❑ Including descriptive headers and extended properties (schema metadata). This contains system- and user-generated metadata that describe the option you're scripting.

❑ Only scripting objects that are compatible with SQL Server 7.0. This option is useful if you're creating the script to be applied against a database on the older platform.

4. Once you're comfortable with the options you have selected, click the Options tab. Here, you can choose what additional information you want to be scripted. For this example, you want to include a number of associated objects that aren't selected by default.

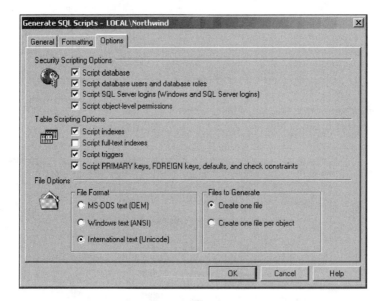

You may have noticed that the Formatting tab contains script options and the Options tab contains a choice of objects to be scripted (indexes, triggers, and so on) but that is just one of those complexities that keeps a DBA awake while doing this sort of task at 2 a.m.

5. The final options on this tab are those relating to how the script file is created. Generally leaving the script file in the Unicode format is the most flexible; however, use an alternative format option if you want. Choose to create one file per object or just one master file, depending on the intentions for the final script. If you want the script to run on another server to duplicate the structure of the existing database, then a single file is probably the best option. If, on the other hand, you want to generate a script that allows you to create specific objects on the other database from the scripted output, then creating a script file per object may be more flexible–although this will result in a large number of files in this example where you are scripting all database objects.

6. Click OK to start generating the script. Depending on the Files to Generate option, you'll be prompted to enter either a specific filename or a path to where the multiple files will be created. In this example, choose to create a single file and save this file at `C:\NorthwindScript.sql`.

If you open this file in Query Analyzer, you'll see it's a script that can be used to create a copy of the Northwind database structure (without any data of course).

Using Query Analyzer

Query Analyzer can also be used to generate scripts for database objects, but unlike Enterprise Manager, it cannot be used to script all objects together with one command. Instead, you can choose to script individual objects to the following:

❑   A Query Analyzer window for modification, review, and execution

❑   A file for saving locally or copying to an offsite location

❑   The clipboard for pasting into documentation

To access the scripting options, you need to have the object browser visible. If it isn't visible, select the Tools I Object Browser I Show/Hide menu item or simply press F8.

Once the object browser is visible, drill down within the object hierarchy to locate the object you want to script and right-click it. The scripting options are located on this menu.

Try It Out–Generating Scripts with Query Analyzer

In this example, you use the scripting capabilities of Query Analyzer to generate a script of a table within the Northwind database.

1. Connect to SQL Server using Query Analyzer. Using the object browser, drill down into the Northwind database, and then into the User Tables node.

2. Right-click the dbo.Categories table and choose Script Object to New Window As I Create.

This will create a T-SQL command that can be used to re-create this particular table's structure.

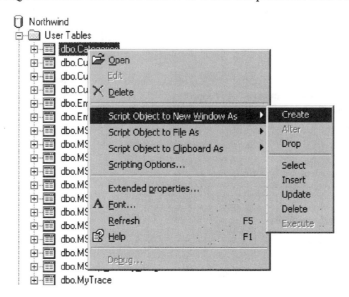

The full script will look something like the following:

```
CREATE TABLE [Categories] (
    [CategoryID] [int] IDENTITY (1, 1) NOT NULL ,
    [CategoryName] [nvarchar] (15) COLLATE SQL_Latin1_General_CP1_CI_AS NOT NULL ,
    [Description] [ntext] COLLATE SQL_Latin1_General_CP1_CI_AS NULL ,
    [Picture] [image] NULL ,
    [rowguid]  uniqueidentifier ROWGUIDCOL  NOT NULL CONSIINT
                                [DF__Categorie__rowgu__08B54D69] DEFAULT (newid()),
    CONSIINT [PK_Categories] PRIMARY KEY  CLUSTERED
    (
        [CategoryID]
    ) ON [PRIMARY]
) ON [PRIMARY] TEXTIMAGE_ON [PRIMARY]
GO
```

There are a number of options you can set to alter the behavior of the scripting functionality within Query Analyzer. These can be accessed from the Tools I Options menu item by clicking on the Script tab. You should notice that they're similar to the options you were given when you created the script using Enterprise Manager.

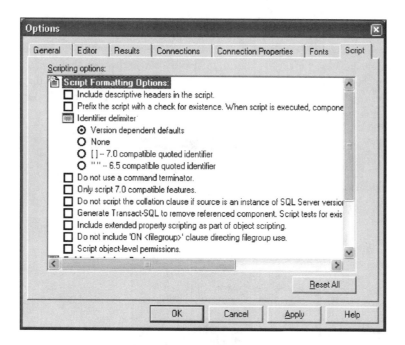

> Database scripts cannot be directly created using T-SQL. You must use one of the graphical tools of the SQL-DMO object library from a programming language such as C# or VBScript.

Generating a Database Diagram

A DBA is often asked to create a database diagram. It may be used by a business analyst who is determining what information is recorded within a particular database, or by a developer who may be making changes to the application code.

Enterprise Manager includes the ability to generate a database diagram. Although this doesn't create the most elegant of diagrams (when compared to professional modeling tools), they can be created quickly and easily. Unlike most other topics discussed in this chapter, there is no equivalent functionality in Query Analyzer; database diagrams are an Enterprise Manager-only option.

> Microsoft Visio Enterprise Architects Edition is included with Visual Studio .NET Enterprise Architect Edition, and this has a more powerful data modeling functionality that can be used with SQL Server.

Using Enterprise Manager

You can create as many database diagrams for a particular database as you like using Enterprise Manager. For small databases, you'll only choose to create a single diagram that contains all the database tables. For large databases (maybe 1000 tables or greater), having a single diagram with all the tables would just be too impractical and of little use. Instead you'll probably choose to create many diagrams, each with a focus on a particular subject area.

Diagrams are created within Enterprise Manager within the Diagrams node under a specific database, as shown in the following screen shot:

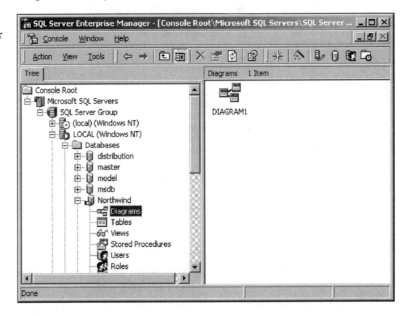

To create a new database diagram, right-click the Diagrams node and select New Database Diagram.

Try It Out—Creating a Database Diagram

In this example you create a new database diagram for the Northwind database.

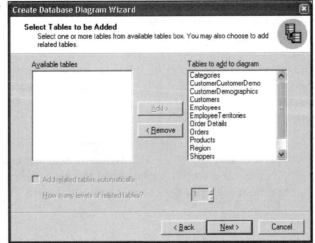

1. Connect to SQL Server using Enterprise Manager and drill down into the Northwind database. Right-click on the Diagrams node and select New Database Diagram. This will start the Create Database Diagram Wizard.

2. Click Next to move past the first screen of the wizard to the screen where you choose the tables you want within the diagram. In this example, select all the tables.

Depending on your server registration settings, within Enterprise Manager you may or may not see system tables listed in this view. If you do see system tables, do not include these in the tables you select to be on the diagram, because they will only confuse your database model. The system tables begin with the sys prefix.

3. Click Next and then Finish to add the tables to the diagram. You should see a diagram similar to the one shown, which can be saved for later use or printed for distribution.

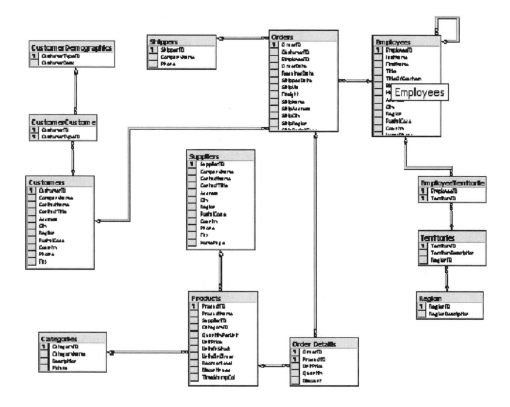

You can print or save the database diagram within Enterprise Manager. However, you cannot export this in a format such as BMP for use in another application.

Questions You Must Be Able to Answer

In addition to the tasks mentioned, there are also questions that you must be able to answer as a DBA. These are questions that a variety of people (CIOs, business analysts, developers, systems engineers, and so on) are likely to spring on you throughout the course of a day and expect you to answer.

How Big Is a Database?

This is one of the most common questions that comes up. Often people want to know this information before meetings when you may be planning server infrastructures, data transfer procedures, backup equipment requirements, and so on. It's really something a DBA should have a good idea of, and check regularly.

Using Enterprise Manager

The easiest way to check the current size of a database is by using Enterprise Manager. All you need to do is right-click the database and select **Properties**. This will show you how big the database is based on the size of its data files (not necessarily the amount of data within those files).

Try It Out–Finding the Size of a Database with Enterprise Manager

In this example, you check the current size of the Northwind database using Enterprise Manager.

Connect to SQL Server using Enterprise Manager. Drill-down into the **Databases** node. Right-click the Northwind database and select **Properties**.

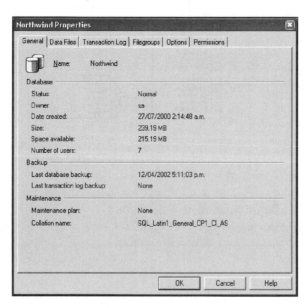

You can see on the General tab that the current size of this particular database is 239.19MB with 215.19MB free. These figures include the size and the free space of both the data and log files.

Using Query Analyzer

The same information can be obtained using the sp_spaceused T-SQL command, which has the following syntax:

```
sp_spaceused @objname=object_name, @updateusage='updateusage'
```

If you specify the object_name, the space used by the specified objects will be displayed. If you omit the object_name then the space used by the entire database is reported. The other parameter, @updateusage, tells SQL Server to run DBCC UPDATEUSAGE on the object or database. This command ensures that the space figures reported have been updated to the latest information. This gives the most accurate information relating to database size.

Try It Out–Finding the Size of a Database with Query Analyzer

In this example, you'll use the sp_spaceused command to report the space used by the Northwind database.

Connect to SQL Server using Query Analyzer. Enter the EXEC sp_spaceused command as shown in the diagram and execute it.

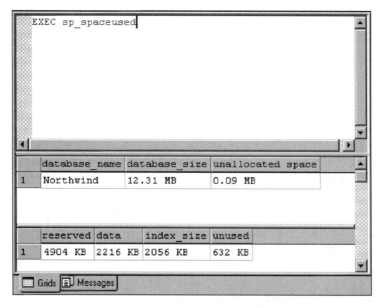

The results show the amount of space used by the database and the free space available. Notice that there is a slight difference between the figures reported in Enterprise Manager and the figures reported here, because the free space figures here only include the free space of the data files and not the free space within the log files.

When Was a Database Last Backed Up?

Another question that you'll need to know the answer to is when a database was last backed up. Unfortunately, it's usually someone who has just corrupted the database in some way who asks this question. So, as a DBA, you'll want to make sure that the database has always been backed up recently.

Using Enterprise Manager

You can see the date and time the database was backed up using the same Properties window that you used within Enterprise Manager to view the size figures.

Try It Out—Finding the Last Backup Date with Enterprise Manager

In this example, you check the date the Northwind database was last backed up using Enterprise Manager.

Connect to SQL Server using Enterprise Manager and drill down into the Databases node. Right-click the Northwind database and select Properties.

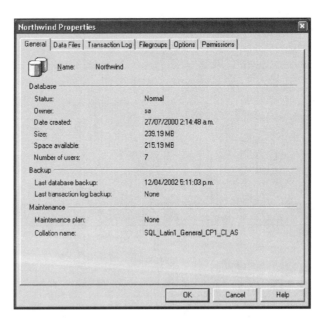

The date that the database was last backed up is shown (assuming the database has been backed up at some point) under the Backup header.

Using Query Analyzer

By using Query Analyzer, you can find out when the database was last backed up. However, there is no command to determine this for us directly. Instead you must execute a simple query that retrieves the information from the msdb.dbo.backupset table. This table contains an entry for every database backup that has taken place.

Try It Out–Finding the Last Backup Date with Query Analyzer

In this example, you'll determine the date the Northwind database was last backed up from the information retained within the backupset table located within the msdb database.

Connect to SQL Server using Query Analyzer and enter the command as shown:

```
SELECT MAX(backup_finish_date)
FROM msdb..backupset
WHERE type = 'D' AND database_name = 'Northwind'
```

This query selects the row with the maximum backup_finish_date where the type of backup was D (full database) and the database was Northwind. In the results pane at the bottom of the window, the date and time of the last backup will be displayed.

Who Is Currently Connected to SQL Server?

Another common requirement is to determine who is connected to a database. The two most common reasons a DBA is asked this are

❑ Someone wants to reboot the server and needs to know who will be affected.

❑ The server has suddenly stopped performing adequately, and you need to see who is connected and who is consuming all the available resources.

Fortunately, reporting this information is straightforward from either Enterprise Manager or Query Analyzer.

Using Enterprise Manager

You can view the currently connected users by drilling down into the Management node, then into the Current Activity | Process Info node. Here you'll see a list of users, the database they're connected to, the last command that they requested to be executed, and the resources they're consuming.

Try It Out–Finding Current Users with Enterprise Manager

In this example, you'll use Enterprise Manager to view the current activity on the SQL Server.

Connect to SQL Server using Enterprise Manager. Under the Management node you'll see a Current Activity node, as shown. Drill down into this and select the Process Info node.

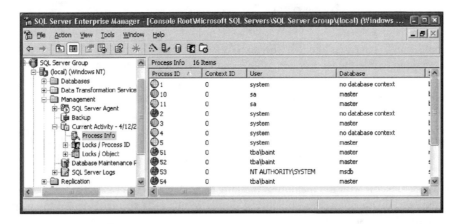

In the right-hand pane, Enterprise Manager displays a list of currently connected user processes, the command currently being executed by those users, and the resources being consumed.

> **To kill any users who are currently connected, right-click the particular user process and select the Kill menu item. Be warned, this command stops any transactions they have in progress by rolling them back. Their connection will also be dropped.**

Using Query Analyzer

The same information can be obtained using Query Analyzer by executing the sp_who2 command. This command has the following syntax:

```
EXEC sp_who2 login_name | SPID
```

You can specify a particular login_name or SPID to view the process information for a particular process. If you omit both of these parameters, the process information will be displayed for all processes.

Try It Out–Finding Current Users with Query Analyzer

In this example, you'll show all process information for all users using the sp_who2 command.

Connect to SQL Server using Query Analyzer and execute the sp_who2 command, as shown:

```
EXEC sp_who2
```

The process information for all user connections will be shown in the results pane.

SQL Server Agent

SQL Server Agent is the job scheduling and notification component of SQL Server. It's used to manage jobs that execute against SQL Server and, depending on the outcome of those jobs, to notify nominated operators about relevant events. In addition, SQL Server Agent includes an alerting component that also notifies the nominated operators when predefined conditions occur.

SQL Server Agent is installed by default with SQL Server and cannot be removed. However, because the SQL Server Agent is a separate physical service to SQL Server, you can start and stop it independently of the SQL Server database engine (as long as the SQL Server service is running).

> **Before configuring operators and alerts, you should configure SQLAgentMail. For directions on how to do this, see Chapter 2.**

Operators

Operators are the people you want to notify if an event of interest occurs. An event of interest may be the completion of a job, the failure of a job, a system error, a threshold being surpassed, and so on.

Operators are created to let SQL Server Agent know the contact details of appropriate people to nominate when an event occurs. The DBA can then associate individual notifications with the relevant people.

You can add an operator using either Enterprise Manager or Query Analyzer. A particular benefit of using Query Analyzer is that you can save the script, thereby allowing you to quickly create the same set of operators on other servers. However, if you choose to use Enterprise Manager this script can be generated automatically later.

Using Enterprise Manager to Add an Operator

To create an operator within Enterprise Manager, drill down into the SQL Server Agent node and select the Operators node. In the right-hand pane, you right-click and select New Operator.

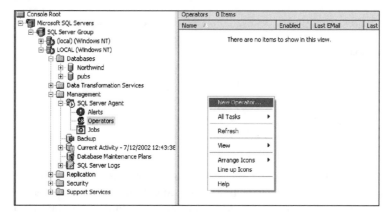

Try It Out—Adding an Operator in Enterprise Manager

In this example, you'll create a new operator within the SQL Server Agent.

1. Once you've selected to create a new operator, the New Operator Properties window will open, as follows:

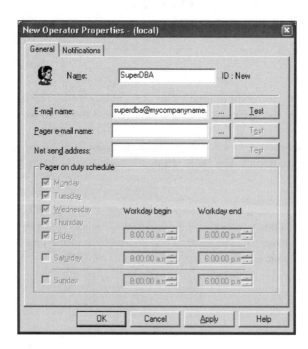

Here you enter all the information necessary to create a database operator. Relevant information in this window is:

❑ Name.
The name of the operator.

❑ E-mail name.
The e-mail address of the operator.

❑ Pager e-mail name.
The e-mail address of the operator's pager.

❑ Net send address.
The operator's Windows username or computer name.

If the operator has a pager, you can select to enter notification times for when this person will be paged. For this example, simply enter an e-mail name, because you only want the operator to be notified by e-mail.

2. On the Notifications tab, you can select which predefined alerts you want the operator to receive. Because you have yet to create any (the ones listed are created by default), you'll leave this information blank for the time being.

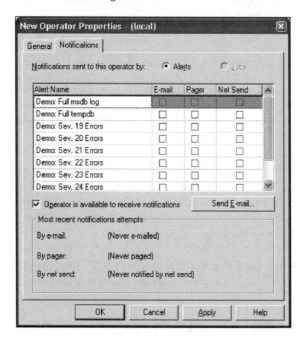

3. Simply click OK to create the operator. The newly created operator will now appear in the list shown in Enterprise Manager.

Using Query Analyzer to Add an Operator

You create operators in Query Analyzer using the `sp_add_operator` command, which, in its most basic format, has the following syntax:

```
sp_add_operator @name=name, @email_address=email_address
```

For a full list of parameters for this command see SQL Server Books Online.

Try It Out–Adding an Operator in Query Analyzer

In this example, you'll create a new operator using T-SQL. If you've already created the operator in the previous example, right-click it and select Delete to remove this operator in Enterprise Manager before carrying out this example.

Connect to SQL Server using Query Analyzer and enter the following command:

```
EXEC msdb..sp_add_operator @name = 'SuperDBA',
                    @email_address = 'superdba@mycompanyname.xyz'
```

When you execute this command, the SuperDBA operator will be created; however, it won't be associated with any jobs or alerts.

Alerts

Alerts are predefined conditions that you instruct SQL Server to watch out for. These predefined conditions can relate to an occurrence of a specific error or a group of errors, by defining the alert around an error-severity level. In addition, you can limit the alert to only a specific database or to all databases on a server.

The second type of alert is based on a performance condition. Depending on the alert's setting, you can decide to have SQL Server Agent notify your operator when a particular performance measure falls outside a predefined range. An example would be when the CPU utilization rises above 90 percent or when the buffer cache hit ratio drops below 90 percent (showing that memory has potentially become limited on the server).

To add an alert, you either use Enterprise Manager or T-SQL. Once again T-SQL allows you to apply the alerts to many servers while Enterprise Manager allows you to create one-off alerts quickly.

Adding an Alert with Enterprise Manager

To create an alert in Enterprise Manager, you select the Alerts node, right-click, and select New Alert.

Try It Out–Adding an Alert with Enterprise Manager

In this example, you'll create a new alert to notify the operator when any Object Not Found error occurs.

1. Connect to SQL Server using Enterprise Manager, drill down into the Management node, and then into SQL Server Agent. From here you can select the Alerts node. Once you've selected to create a new alert, you'll be presented with the New Alert Properties dialog box as shown:

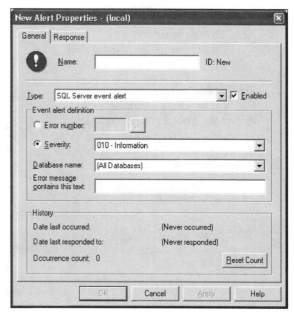

The key information you should enter here is

❑ Name.
A way of identifying the alert

❑ Type.
Either alert or performance condition
Depending on the type of alert, you'll need to enter the following information:

❑ For Alerts

   ❑ Error Number.
   The error that you wish to specifically notify on

   ❑ Severity.
   The group of errors that you wish to notify on

   ❑ Database.
   The database you wish to limit the alert to, if any

   ❑ Error message contains this text.
   A filter condition for searching for in specific error messages

❑ For Performance Conditions.

   ❑ Object.
      Performance monitor object

   ❑ Counter.
      Specific performance counter, which is part of the selected object

   ❑ Alert if count.
      Criteria for generating the alert

2. For this example, you want to create an alert that is generated whenever an **Object Not Found** error occurs within any database. To create this alert, enter the information as shown in the screen shot:

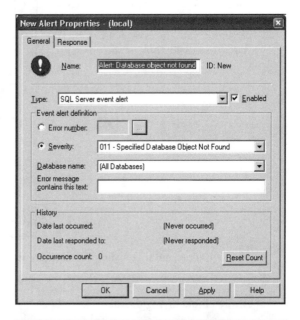

3. The **Response** tab allows you to specify which operators should receive this alert if the event it covers was to occur, and if so, what method of notification should be used. For this example, simply check the E-mail box of the **SuperDBA** operator. Whenever this alert condition occurs, this operator will be notified of the details of this alert.

4. The other fields within this tab allow you to specify a custom message to be included within the alert notification as well as a delay between responses. Setting a delay helps prevent hundreds or thousands of notifications being sent to operators when a condition is recurring at a high frequency. Click OK and the new alert will now appear in the list shown in the Enterprise Manager.

Using Query Analyzer to Add an Alert

As with almost everything else you've done so far, you can also create alerts using Query Analyzer. To do this, you use the sp_add_alert command, which has, in its simplest form, the following syntax:

```
sp_add_alert @name, @message_id | @severity
```

You can choose to enter the message_id parameter if you want to trigger the alert based on a specific condition, or use the severity parameter if you want to trigger the alert based on a severity grouping of error messages.

This command only adds the actual alert component. The notification component of an alert isn't created, but to do this, you use sp_add_notification, which has the following syntax:

```
sp_add_notification alert_name, operator_name,
notification_method
```

For a full list of parameters for these commands see sp_add_alert and sp_add_notification in SQL Server Books Online.

> **Before you run this example, make sure the SQL Server Agent is running. You can start this by right-clicking the SQL Server Agent in Enterprise Manager and choosing Start.**

Try It Out–Adding an Alert with Query Analyzer

In this example, you'll use the sp_add_alert command to add an alert that notifies the DBA, based on a severity criterion. If you created this alert in the previous example with Enterprise Manager, then right-click it and choose Delete before proceeding with this example.

1. Connect to SQL Server using Query Analyzer. Execute the command shown to add an alert named Alert: Object not found, which is fired when any severity 11 error occurs. For a list of all the severity levels, look under *Error Message Severity Levels* in Books Online.

```
EXEC msdb..sp_add_alert @name = 'Alert: Object not found',
                        @severity = 11
```

2. Now execute the following command:

```
EXEC msdb..sp_add_notification 'Alert: Object not found',
                               'SuperDBA', 1
```

This adds the SuperDBA as an enabled operator for this alert. The notification_method option 1 tells the SQL Server Agent to notify this operator using e-mail. For more information on the notification_method options, look up *Notification Method Constants* in Books Online.

Once you've executed these two commands, the alert has been created and will fire whenever code that references an object that doesn't exist is executed.

You can set up any number of alerts and these can notify any number of operators.

Jobs

Jobs are managed by the scheduling component of the SQL Server Agent service, and are used to run certain code at certain times using predefined steps and schedules. Specifically, the major components of a job are as follows:

❑ The job definition.
 The name, category, owner, notifications, and so on

❑ The job step definitions.
 The steps that are executed and their workflow

❑ The schedule definitions.
 The schedule on which the job is executed

Each of these components is created as part of the Create Job dialog box within Enterprise Manager. However, when you create a job using T-SQL, these are all separate commands with different parameters.

Jobs can be added to carry out a number of administration tasks, such as scheduling daily backups and running consistency checks. Jobs can also be added to run DTS packages to import data as well as to run operating system executables to carry out any custom requirements that you may have.

Adding a Job with Enterprise Manager

Jobs can be created using Enterprise Manager by selecting the Jobs node under the SQL Server Agent node, right-clicking, and selecting New Job.

Try It Out–Adding a Job Using Enterprise Manager

In this example, you'll create a job to run a DBCC check on the Northwind database every Monday at 4 a.m.

1. The first tab you see when you have chosen to create a new job is the General tab. Here you enter basic information relating to the job, such as the name of the job and the owner of the job. Enter the name as shown in the following screen shot and change the job owner to sa as follows:

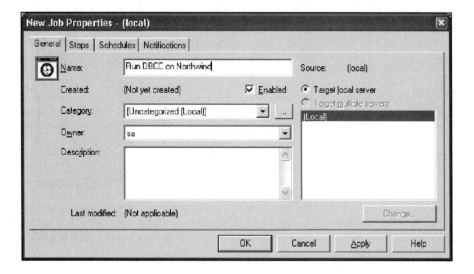

2. On the Steps tab, you enter the steps that form the job. Here you can create one or more steps and associate basic workflow between those steps. Click New to create a new step.

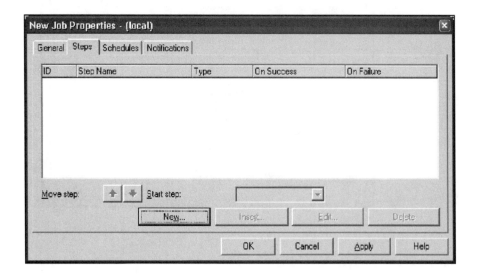

3. Within the New Job Step dialog box, you need to enter the Step name and the Type (use T-SQL for this example, for a full list of types see *Creating Job Steps* in Books Online). The database selected for this example doesn't matter too much because the command that you're using is database insensitive. However, if you were running queries in a specific database as a job step, you would obviously set this to the correct database. Enter the command as shown:

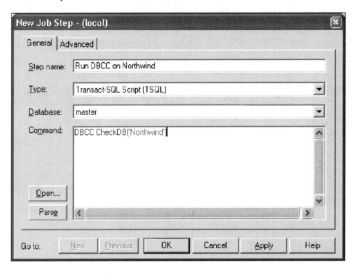

4. On the Advanced tab you can specify how you want this job step to interact with other job steps. Because this is the first step, and you're only creating a single step, this information is irrelevant. Because you want to capture the output of the command into a text file for easy viewing, you specify this in the Output file field as shown:

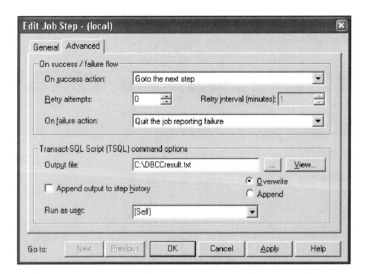

5. You can now create one or more job schedulers for this job and associated job schedules. To do this, click on the Schedules tab and then on New Schedule.

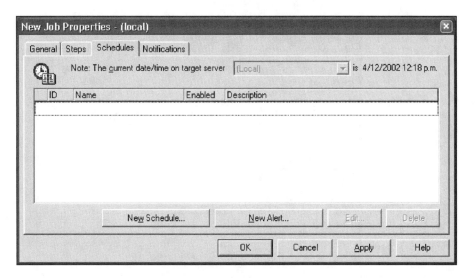

6. In the New Job Schedule dialog box, you set the schedule that the job will run on. First, enter the name of the schedule in the Name text box. Under the Schedule Type header, there are a number of options available; however, the most common option is the recurring schedule. To set a recurring schedule specifically, select the Recurring option and click the Change button.

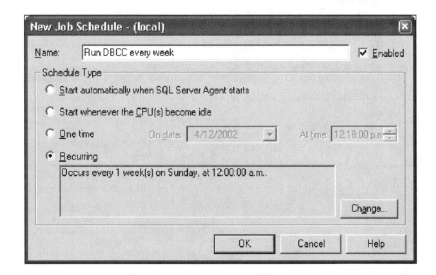

7. Now, you can set the recurrence parameters. Let's say you wanted the DBCC statement to run every week on Monday at 4 a.m. You would set all the relevant options in this dialog box, as shown:

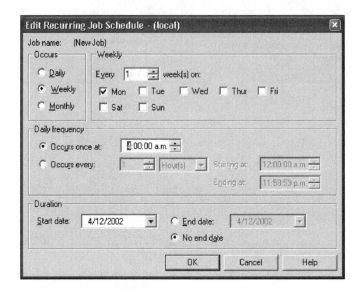

8. Once you've clicked OK to add the schedule, you can click on the Notifications tab of the New Job Properties dialog box. This is where you set the notifications that take place if a specific condition occurs during the job execution. For this particular example, you want to notify the operator if the job fails, and also to write an event to the Windows event log:

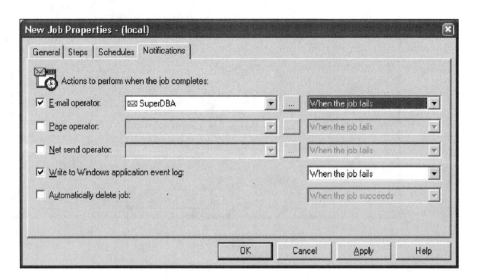

9. Finally, clicking **OK** adds the job to the SQL Server Agent and it will then be shown in the Jobs list.

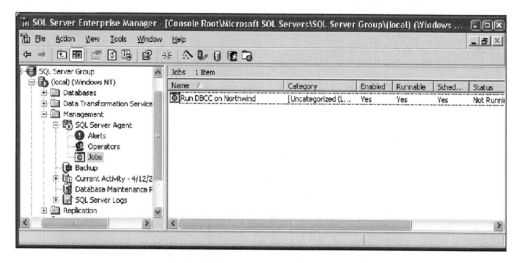

If you do not want to wait until 4 a.m. on Monday to try out the new job, you can simply right-click the job listing and select **Start Job** from the pop-up menu.

Using Query Analyzer to Add a Job

Creating jobs using Query Analyzer requires you to execute a number of commands. Specifically, you need to execute commands to create the job, steps, and schedule.

The commands you use are **sp_add_job** (to create the job), **sp_add_jobstep** (to add the job steps), and **sp_add_jobschedule** (to add the schedule). These commands have an array of parameters that make them highly flexible. For more information, see SQL Server Books Online.

Try It Out–Adding a Job Using Query Analyzer

In this example, you'll re-create the job from the previous example using Query Analyzer. You'll need to remove the previous job before continuing with this example.

1. The first thing you must do is create the job definition by executing the **sp_add_job** command with the following parameters. (Notice that this command contains no information on what or when the job is to occur.)

   ❑ job_name
   The name to be associated with this job

   ❑ enabled
   Set this job to active

- [ ] owner_login_name
  Set the owner of this job to sa

- [ ] notify_level_eventlog
  Create an event log entry if this job fails

- [ ] notify_level_email
  Notify the operator if this job fails

- [ ] notify_email_operator_name
  The name of the operator to notify

```
DECLARE @JobID BINARY(16)

EXEC msdb.dbo.sp_add_job @job_id = @JobID OUTPUT ,
                @job_name = 'Run DBCC on Northwind',
                @enabled = 1, - Active
                @owner_login_name = 'sa',
                @notify_level_eventlog = 2,
                @notify_level_email = 2,
                @notify_email_operator_name = 'SuperDBA'

SELECT @JobID
```

The long hex value presented in the results pane is the unique job identifier that SQL Server has assigned to this job.

2. To add the "what," you need to execute the **sp_add_jobstep** procedure with the following parameters:

- [ ] job_name
  The name of the job that you're adding this step to

- [ ] step_name
  A name for this step that you're creating

- [ ] command
  The actual command that you want to execute

- [ ] subsystem
  The type of command that you want to execute

- [ ] output_file_name
  The filename where you want the output of the command to be retained

```
EXEC msdb.dbo.sp_add_jobstep @job_name = 'Run DBCC on
                                    Northwind',
                    @step_name = 'Run DBCC CheckDB on
                                    Northwind',
                    @command = 'DBCC CheckDB
                                (''Northwind'')',
```

```
@subsystem = 'TSQL',
@output_file_name = 'C: \
                    DBCCResult.txt'
```

You have created the job with the relevant job step that you wish to execute. All that is left now is the job schedule.

3. To add the job schedule, you need to execute the sp_add_jobschedule command. In this example, you pass the following parameters:

    ❑   job_name
        The name of the job to add the schedule to

    ❑   name
        The name of the schedule

    ❑   freq_type
        The occurrence of the schedule (weekly)

    ❑   freq_interval
        In this example, the day of the week (Monday)

    ❑   active_start_time
        In this example, 4 am.

    ❑   freq_recurrence_factor
        In this example this means to execute every week

```
EXEC msdb.dbo.sp_add_jobschedule @job_name = 'Run DBCC on
                                             Northwind',
                    @name = 'Run DBCC Weekly',
                    @freq_type = 8, — Weekly
                    @freq_interval = 2, — Monday
                    @active_start_time = 40000,
                    @freq_recurrence_factor = 1
                                — Every week
```

Once Query Analyzer has executed this command, the process is finished. The job has been created and scheduled to run just as in the previous example using Enterprise Manager.

4. To validate the job information, you can use the `sp_help_job` command to retrieve the job details as shown in the following screen shot:

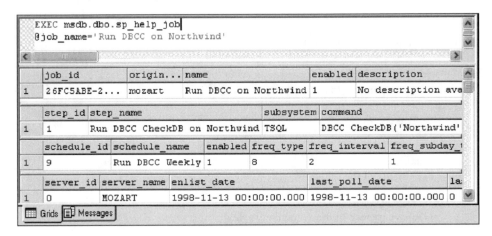

Based on your requirements, you can continue to create multiple job steps or multiple job schedules for a single job.

Summary

As we mentioned in the beginning, we didn't set out to be glamorous in this chapter. It's all about providing the information you need to survive, enjoy, and prosper on a day-to-day basis as a DBA.

Specifically, you need to know about core DBA tasks, such as the following:

❑ How to back up and restore a database

❑ How to generate a database script

❑ How to generate a database diagram

❑ How to determine how big a database is

❑ How to add alerts and operators

❑ How to create jobs, steps, and schedules

Now that we have covered the daily grind, we can move off to more interesting topics within this book.

6

Security

Although performing backups is the most important jobs of a database adminstrator (DBA), implementing security comes a close second. The art of security management lies in finding a satisfactory balance between preventing anyone from doing anything and allowing everyone to do everything. If you're too restrictive in the assignment of permissions then your users aren't going to be able to use the database effectively. If you're too loose in assigning permissions, then the information within your database could be misused or corrupted.

This chapter will provide you with a complete understanding of the way security is handled in SQL Server, so you can suitably design a security solution for your databases.

Terminology

The terminology in this chapter might be a little difficult to understand if you're new to the subject of SQL Server security. This is partly due to the fact that many of the terms are interchangeable or similar. Although you could try to simplify the terminology by creating new names for things, simplification would be a problem because outside of this chapter you'll have to deal with Microsoft's terminology. So, let's start with some definitions. Each of these terms is explained in detail in this chapter, but it's important that you note that each term is different.

❑ SQL Server Login: A mechanism for authorizing access to SQL Server

❑ Authentication methods: The method the login uses for authentication

❑ Authentication mode: The authentication methods that a particular instance of SQL Server accepts

❑ SQL Server Authentication: An authentication method provided by SQL Server

❑ Windows Authentication: An authentication method provided by Windows

❑   SQL Server Authenticated Login: A SQL Server Login that uses the SQL Server Authentication method

❑   Windows Authenticated Login: A SQL Server Login that uses the Windows Authentication method

❑   Windows Login: A security mechanism that a network user uses to authenticate within Windows

❑   Windows group: A mechanism for grouping Windows Logins within Windows

❑   Server role: A mechanism for grouping SQL Server Logins within SQL Server

❑   Database role: A mechanism for grouping database users within a SQL Server database

❑   Database user: A mechanism for allowing a SQL Server Login to access a database

❑   Network user: A person, application, or device on the network attempting to access SQL Server

❑   Authentication: A process to determine whether network users are who they claim to be

❑   Authorization: A process to allow or disallow an authenticated network user the ability to connect to SQL Server

You can see how this chapter may become confusing. However, as you read through it, please refer back to these definitions for clarification as needed.

Logging In to SQL Server

An *SQL Server Login* is a mechanism for validating the authenticity of a client requesting to open a connection with SQL Server. It's important to note that the login step is in two stages: first, is the login permitted to connect to the database? This is known as *authentication*. Secondly, what permissions does the user have within the database? This is known as *authorization*. As authentication comes first, you'll cover it first.

Authentication Methods

Authentication was introduced in Chapter 2. In the following sections, you'll cover this subject in more detail. There are two types of authentication mode in SQL Server:

❑   Windows Authentication

❑   SQL Server Authentication

Although the means used in each of these methods for authenticating someone's ability to establish a connection are different, the result is the same (the connection is either allowed or it's not).

SQL Server Authentication has been with the SQL Server product since its infancy. Windows Authentication was added in more recent versions (and tightly integrated in SQL Server 7.0). Although SQL Server Authentication has been around longer, Windows Authentication is now the preferred method as it's a much more secure authentication mechanism. The following statement from SQL Server Books Online highlights this preference: *"SQL Server Authentication is provided for backward compatibility."*

Windows Authentication

When you use the Windows Authentication method, you're effectively instructing SQL Server to trust your network's Windows domain controller to correctly validate that the user is who they claim to be. Windows can use whatever means you instruct it to (such as a username and password combination, smart card, and so on) to authenticate users. Once Windows has authenticated the user, their Windows Security Identifier (SID) is passed to SQL Server when they try to create a new connection. At this point, SQL Server assumes Windows has correctly identified the user. Now, all it needs to do to determine if the connection is allowed is to check if the SID that is passed by Windows matches the SID of a Windows Authenticated Login that had been previously created within a SQL Server instance. Also, SQL Server checks Windows group membership to see if the user is a member of a group that has been granted the right to connect with SQL Server.

Some of the major benefits of this approach are as follows:

❏ Users have a single sign on or a single set of login credentials.
Users only need to enter login information to use their computer. They don't need to enter further login information again when they wish to establish a database connection.

❏ Account administration is centralized.
Your account administrators don't need to use different tools in different environments to set up appropriate permissions for users.

❏ Windows handles authentication.
SQL Server only needs to worry about allowing or disallowing access to specific database objects. However, SQL Server benefits from the security functionality provided by Windows (2000 and XP) such as:

  ❏ Account lockout

  ❏ Minimum password length

  ❏ Maximum password age

❏ A user can be authenticated once and access many SQL Server installations.
With those credentials (assuming he has been granted the ability to connect to each SQL Server), authentication is handled by Windows externally to SQL Server. If the login credentials change (for example, a change in password), there is no synchronization required because no authentication information is stored within SQL Server other than the SID provided by Windows once authentication has occurred.

As you'll see, these benefits are only available with Windows Authentication, which makes this method very attractive.

> **You should choose to use Windows Authentication unless you have a specific reason not to. Windows Authentication provides the greatest level of security.**

Some of the key reasons for not using Windows Authentication are as follows:

❑ SQL Server installed on Windows 98 or Windows ME.
On these operating systems only SQL Server Authentication is available.

❑ An old application that doesn't allow you to choose Windows Authentication.
Although the applications don't require changes to support Windows Authentication (the actual authentication process is handled outside of the application), many older applications don't provide an option to instruct the application to request Windows Authentication. They simply provide a login screen, and expect a username and password to be entered before they proceed.

SQL Server Authentication

SQL Server Authentication, on the other hand, doesn't delegate the authorization of users to any other source, but instead handles this process within the database server. When using SQL Server Authentication, you must explicitly create a username and password (within SQL Server) for each and every user who needs to establish a connection with SQL Server. In addition, a new SQL Server Login must be created within every SQL Server installation that the user needs to access.

Also, SQL Server Authentication doesn't have the advanced account features of Windows Authentication. The following aren't possible using SQL Server Authentication:

❑ Single sign on.
Users must enter login credentials to connect to Windows and a username and password when they attempt to establish a connection with SQL Server.

❑ Centralized account administration.
If you're using a Windows Domain for managing users "network" accounts, then the use of SQL Server authentication causes account administration to be de-centralized. Account administrators need to use different tools within different environments to set up appropriate permissions for users

❑ SQL Server doesn't benefit from the security functionality provided by Windows.
SQL Server Authentication doesn't provide advanced security functionality, such as the following:

   ❑ Account lockout

   ❑ Min password length

   ❑ Max password age

❑ Multi-installation access
  Each instance of SQL Server requires a separate username and password. It's conceivable (and unfortunately not totally uncommon) for a user to have a different username and different password for each SQL Server installation he accesses.

So is SQL Server Authentication obsolete? Well not completely. All this talk of Windows Authentication integration may make SQL Server sound like a product that can only be used with users who are running Windows on their desktops. However, this isn't true; SQL Server can be accessed from a number of platforms other than Windows (Linux, Mac OS, and so on). This is where SQL Server Authentication is required. Unless you have some means of authorizing your non-Windows users against a Windows domain or server, you need to use SQL Server Authentication to gain this multiplatform capability for your applications. Because a username and password is all that is sent from the client, the platform from where that request is being made is not directly relevant to SQL Server.

> **SQL Server only runs on a Microsoft Windows-based operating system. However, users can access a SQL Server installation from a variety of non-Microsoft platforms using SQL Server Authentication.**

Authentication Modes

We've discussed the authentication mode options you have available; now we'll discuss how you specify which authentication methods SQL Server will accept. Setting the Authentication Mode does this.

The *Authentication mode* is a setting (retained within the registry), which tells SQL Server what type(s) of authentication to allow. The two options you have available are Windows Authentication and Mixed Authentication.

> **Authentication methods and authentication modes are slightly different. The two methods determine "how" authentication can take place. The two modes determine "which" authentication methods are available. This is a subtle but key difference.**

Windows Authentication Mode

When using Windows Authentication Mode, *only* Windows Authentication is available to users establishing connections to SQL Server. Users cannot specify a SQL Server Login username and password and, if they try to, a connection will not be established.

Mixed Authentication Mode

The alternative to the Windows Authentication Mode is to use the Mixed Authentication Mode. When this mode is enabled, users can attempt to connect using either Windows Authentication or SQL Server Authentication.

Use this mode if you require at least one SQL Authenticated Login. Although Windows Authenticated logins are available in both modes, using Windows Authentication Mode explicitly blocks SQL Authenticated logins, which helps to ensure that your administrators don't create, and your network users don't use, SQL Authenticated logins unnecessarily.

> **Windows Authentication is always enabled in any SQL Server installation. You can choose to have Windows Authentication only (in Windows Authentication Mode) or Windows Authentication plus SQL Server Authentication (in Mixed Authentication Mode). SQL Server doesn't have an option to disable Windows Authentication.**

Changing the Authentication Mode

Once you've chosen the authentication mode you want to use, it's a relatively trivial task to change it. Because it's so easy to change between the modes, you should always choose the most restrictive option (Windows Authentication only) and change to the less restrictive later (Mixed Authentication Mode), should the need arise.

SQL Server Enterprise Manager can be used to change the authentication mode of a given SQL Server through the Security tab of the SQL Server Properties dialog box.

Try It Out–Changing the Authentication Mode with Enterprise Manager

Connect to SQL Server using Enterprise Manager. Right-click the server name in Enterprise Manager and select Properties. On the Security tab, you'll see the Authentication option.

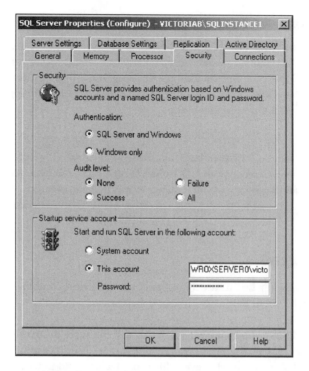

If you change this, a restart of SQL Server will be needed for the change to take effect. You can choose either to restart SQL Server immediately or schedule this for a more convenient time.

> **There is no equivalent T-SQL command that can be used to change the Authentication Mode.**

If you want to carry out all the examples presented in this section, please ensure that you've set SQL Server to operate in Mixed Authentication Mode. If you're currently using Windows Authentication Mode, change this now.

Creating and Managing Logins

Once you've decided on the authentication mechanism that you're going to use, you can set about creating logins that allow users to connect to SQL Server.

You can create logins from Enterprise Manager and by using T-SQL. The type of authentication required dictates the process used; however, you'll look at examples for both.

Logins and Database Users

SQL Server has security entities called logins and database users; each of these is used for a different purpose. A login is an authorization mechanism that is used to validate a network user's attempt to connect to SQL Server. Database users are used for the assignment of permissions within a database. A Database user is associated with a login in a one-to-many relationship (one login can be associated with one database user in zero or more databases).

> Login and user shouldn't be used interchangeably. Logins purely relate to allowing access to establish a connection with SQL Server, and users relate to allowing access to a database and the objects within it once a connection has been established.

SQL Server Logins

As we've discussed, SQL Server Logins are a username and password combination that you give our users so they can connect to SQL Server. SQL Server Logins can be used in a few different ways.

One option is to give all users (who require the same access) the same username and password. This eases account administration, because instead of creating hundreds of individual user accounts you may only need to create half a dozen. However, this is particularly bad practice, because it doesn't allow you to tighten security specifically to each user's requirement. In addition, this doesn't allow the developer to identify the user (for auditing purposes) as unique through code, and it doesn't allow you to identify the user through the DBA monitoring tools (such as Profiler). This removes accountability for the actions that users perform while connected to SQL Server.

Another option (more commonly found than the first) is to use a single username and password for the application to connect to SQL Server. This is especially common for web-based applications where the users may connect to a web server using a browser and the web server connects to SQL Server using the same login information for every user (the users don't need to know this login information). The application then takes the responsibility of identifying the users (through their Windows login information or perhaps by asking them to enter their e-mail addresses and passwords). This application-identified authentication information can be used for auditing purposes within the application. However, this doesn't allow DBAs to monitor who is doing what.

The third option is to create a SQL Server username and password for every network user who requires access to SQL Server. This allows the developers to audit the user activities within the application and allows the DBAs to monitor user processes through DBA tools. However, this option requires the most administration, because a user must be created for every person who uses the application. If this is on an Intranet then it isn't too much of an issue as the number of users is generally limited (although still potentially in the thousands). However, for web-based applications, the number of users could be unlimited. Having an unlimited number of SQL Server database logins will complicate administration somewhat and nullify the DBA's ability to manage security on a per user level.

> The creation, removal, and changing of passwords can be automated from within your application. However, this is generally discouraged, because security is something a DBA likes to manage. After all, it only takes one user with inappropriate access (and bad intentions) to corrupt a database.

The sa Login

Before you look at creating logins, you should discuss the importance of the server administrator, or systems administrator (sa) login. The sa login is the most powerful SQL Server Authenticated user and cannot be removed. This login can gain full access to the information within any databases and carry out any task within SQL Server. It's an account that you want to protect with a strong password and reserve its use for only your trusted DBA team. It is NOT an account you want to give to users or developers to have people connecting via their applications.

> Don't allow your network users or applications to log in to SQL Server using the sa login. Only administration staff should use this.

Unfortunately, many SQL Server installations have had an sa user with no password assigned. Part of the reason for this was that prior to SQL Server 2000, the setup procedure didn't force you to set a sa password. Many people were unaware of the importance of setting this (or were too lazy) and, post-installation, the SQL Server was left with little protection. This ended up being an "oversight" that has been exploited by hackers, especially against SQL Servers that were connected to the Internet. Many businesses have lost information or had their confidential information (such as a client's credit card numbers) compromised simply because the DBA (or another person doing the installation) failed to set this most basic of security measures.

In SQL Server 2000, setup requests that you explicitly set a sa password. Unfortunately, there is still an option box that you can select to explicitly set a blank password. Even after all the warnings, this is still popular with lazy administrators, because we often visit clients who have no password assigned to the sa user.

> Always assign a strong password to the sa user because an sa login without a password is a common means of gaining unauthorized access to SQL Server.

If you install SQL Server using Windows Authentication Mode, you cannot specify a password for the sa user because under Windows Authentication Mode the sa user is not available to be used to log in with. However, you should manually set a password on the sa user post-installation. If at any time you change the authentication mode from Windows to Mixed Authentication Mode, the sa user becomes enabled. Unless you explicitly set a password at this point (which could be easily forgotten because there is no message to remind you), the sa user will be enabled without a password, adding your server to the ranks of the "easily hackable."

You should always assign a password to the sa login even when you're using the
Windows Authentication Mode (in which case the sa login is unavailable).

Creating a SQL Server Authenticated Login

To create SQL Server Authenticated logins, you can use either Enterprise Manager or T-SQL. It may
be a good idea to use T-SQL if you plan to create the same logins against multiple servers, because
this will allow you to rerun the same script in multiple locations. If, on the other hand, you need to
quickly set up a handful of logins, Enterprise Manager provides a fast and convenient interface for
doing this.

Using Enterprise Manager

To create a SQL Server Authenticated Login using Enterprise Manager, you use the Logins node,
which can be located under the Security node as shown.

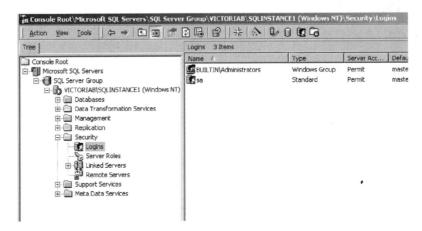

All login administration is done from this location, as you'll see throughout this chapter.

Try It Out–Creating a New SQL Server Login Using Enterprise Manager

In this example, you create a new SQL Server authenticated login named TestSQLUser.

1. Connect to SQL Server using Enterprise Manager and navigate to the Logins node. Right-click
    within the right-hand pane, and select New Login from the pop-up menu. You'll be presented
    with the SQL Server Login Properties – New Login window as shown.

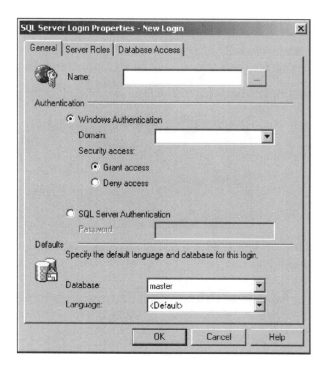

2. By default, the Windows Authentication option is selected. For this example, choose the SQL Server Authentication option. Next, enter TestSQLUser within the Name field. This will be the name of your new login.

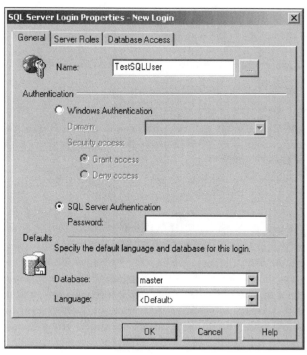

3. Under the SQL Server Authentication option, you need to enter a password for this new login. For this example, enter sqlserverrocks. For this example, the default settings for the rest of the fields are fine.

4. When you click OK, Enterprise Manager will ask you to confirm the password that you have entered.

Once again enter sqlserverrocks and click OK. This new login will be created and will be listed within the Logins detail pane in Enterprise Manager.

Name	Type	Server Acc...	Defaul
BUILTIN\Administrators	Windows Group	Permit	master
sa	Standard	Permit	master
TestSQLUser	Standard	Permit	master

Using T-SQL

Using T-SQL is another method for creating SQL Server Authenticated logins. To do this you use the sp_addlogin stored procedure, which has the following syntax (in its simplest form) when setting a password:

```
sp_addlogin @loginame, @passwd
```

Executing this stored procedure creates a login equivalent to one you could have created from Enterprise Manager.

> **There are other parameters that also allow you to set the default database and default language. For more information on these parameters, see sp_addlogin in SQL Server Books Online.**

Try It Out–Creating a New Login with T-SQL

In this example, you'll use T-SQL to create a new login name of TestSQLUser2. Make sure you're using an account with sufficient privileges to create logins. (For these examples, you should be a member of the sysadmin fixed server role. If you're not sure what this is, don't worry because we discuss it later, in the "Fixed Server Roles" section. For now, connect using Windows Authentication as a Windows user who is a member of the local Administrators group or as an sa.)

Connect to SQL Server using Query Analyzer. Execute the following T-SQL:

```
EXEC sp_addlogin 'TestSQLUser2','sqlserverrocks'
```

When you execute this SQL, it will create a new SQL Server Authenticated Login named TestSQLUser2 with a password of sqlserverrocks.

Testing Your SQL Server Authenticated Login

Now that you've created the test SQL Server Authentication Login, you should test it out.

Try It Out–Connect to SQL Server with a SQL Server Authenticated Login

1. Open **Query Analyzer**. Select the name of the SQL Server you want to connect to from the drop-down list, or manually type it.

2. Select the **SQL Server Authentication** option and enter the **SQL Server Login** information that you created in the last example.

3. Click **OK**, and you'll be connected to SQL Server. If you experience an error, check whether the login information you've entered matches what you specified when you created the SQL Server Authenticated Login.

Removing a SQL Server Authenticated Login

Removing a login is even easier than adding one. Once again, you can do this from either SQL Server Enterprise Manager or by using T-SQL.

Once you remove a SQL Server Authenticated Login, you cannot undo this operation. Any login information, such as name, password, and default database, will be lost.

> **Because you need these logins for the rest of the examples within this chapter, ensure you repeat the creation process if you carry out the following deletes.**

Using Enterprise Manager

You remove SQL Server Authenticated Logins using Enterprise Manager from the same location where you create them (in the Logins node, under the Security node). Simply right-click and select Delete.

Try It Out–Removing TestSQLUser in Enterprise Manager

In this example, you remove the TestSQLUser login.

Connect to SQL Server using Enterprise Manager. Drill down into the Logins node. Right-click the TestSQLUser login and select Delete.

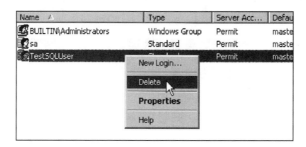

This login has now been removed.

Using T-SQL

The process is just as easy with T-SQL because it's within Enterprise Manager. You use the sp_droplogin stored procedure, which has the following syntax:

```
sp_droplogin @loginame
```

The @loginame parameter must match the name of an existing SQL Server Authenticated Login.

Try It Out–Removing TestSQLUser2 with T-SQL

In this example, you remove the TestSQLUser2 login using T-SQL.

Connect to SQL Server using Query Analyzer and enter the following T-SQL:

```
EXEC sp_droplogin 'TestSQLUser2'
```

Execute this code to remove this SQL Server Authenticated Login.

Changing the Password

Although there is no mechanism built into SQL Server to force password expiration, you'll need to change a SQL Server Authenticated Login's password at times. This may just be good administration (regularly changing administration account passwords) or perhaps because the user has forgotten their existing password (much more likely!). Either way it's a common administration function.

> **You cannot view an existing password. You can only assign a new password to a login.**

Once again, you'll look at how to change a password by using both Enterprise Manager and T-SQL.

Using Enterprise Manager

Changing the password takes place within the Logins node where you have so far created and deleted logins. To change a password, select the desired login for which you wish to change the password, right-click it, and select Properties from the pop-up menu. This Properties window will be the same one you saw when creating a login; however, now all the Authentication fields, apart from the Password field, will be unavailable.

Try It Out–Changing the Password for TestSQLUser

1. Connect to SQL Server using Enterprise Manager. Drill down into our Logins node. Within the details pane, locate the TestSQLUser login and right-click it. Select Properties from the pop-up menu. The Properties window will be as shown.

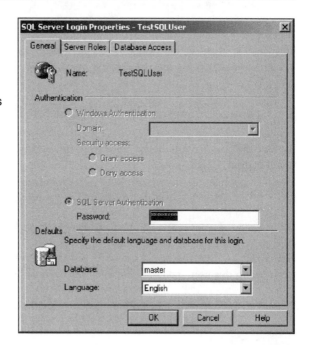

2. Enter a new password in the Password text box, and for this example, use `sqlserverrules`. Click OK.

3. Once you've clicked OK, the Confirm Password dialog box will appear. Once again, enter sqlserverrules and click OK.

The password for this login has now been changed.

> **SQL Server doesn't require a login to even have a password. You could change the password to an empty string if you should so desire; however, this is usually a bad security practice.**

Using T-SQL

To change a password using T-SQL, you must execute the `sp_password` stored procedure. This has the following syntax:

```
sp_password @old, @new, @loginame
```

When you're changing the password for the user that's currently logged in, all three parameters must be specified. When you're changing the password for a user who isn't logged in, only the `@new` and `@loginame` parameters need to be assigned non-NULL values.

Try It Out–Changing the Password for TestSQLUser2

In this example, you use the `sp_password` stored procedure to reset the password of our `TestSQLUser2` login.

Once again, connect to SQL Server using Query Analyzer and enter the following T-SQL command:

```
EXEC sp_password NULL, 'sqlserverrules', 'TestSQLUser2'
```

Notice that you specify the NULL value because, as administrators, you simply wish to assign a new password to this user. You may not even be aware of the old password.

When you execute this code, the new password will be assigned.

Windows Authenticated Logins

As we've previously mentioned, the other method of authenticating users for accessing SQL Server is using Windows Authentication. This is where SQL Server doesn't worry about trying to validate whether users are who they claim to be, because this is the responsibility of the Windows operating system. All SQL Server is concerned about is whether that "validated" user is allowed access to SQL Server.

> **Windows Authenticated Logins aren't available if you're running SQL Server on Windows 98.**

For the purpose of this next section, you need some test Windows users so you can show them how to allow access to SQL Server. Before you dive into this section, let's set up these users. Depending on whether you're using Windows 2000/XP or Windows NT, you'll do this in different places. You're going to look at the 2000/XP method. For information on which versions of Windows the various editions of SQL Server 2000 will run on, see Chapter 2.

Try It Out–Setting Up Windows Users

1. Open the Windows Control Panel and choose Administrative Tools. Next, choose Computer Management. The Computer Management tool will launch.

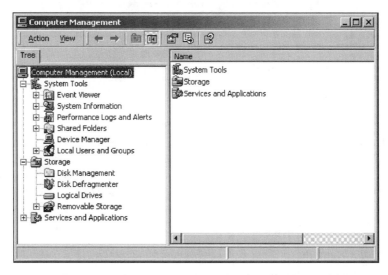

2. Drill down into Local Users and Groups, right-click the Users node, and select New User.

3. The New User dialog box will appear. Enter the information as shown and with the password set as `sqlserveriscool`.

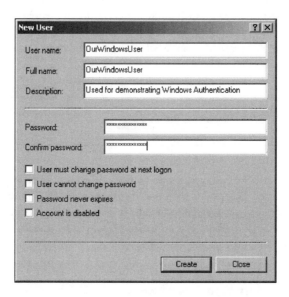

4. Click Create to create this Windows User.

> **Now repeat this process again, except this time create an `OurWindowsUser2`
> account.**

5. Now, you can close the Computer Management application.

Creating a Windows Authenticated Login

As with SQL Server Authenticate Logins, you can use either Enterprise Manager or T-SQL to create Windows Authenticated Logins. However, the information you need to enter differs slightly. The main difference is that when creating a SQL Server Authenticated Login, you are creating a new set of authentication credentials, and must provide a new username and password. When creating a Windows Authenticated Login within SQL Server, you are simply authorizing an existing externally authenticated Windows Login to connect to SQL Server.

Using Enterprise Manager

When creating a Windows Authenticated Login within Enterprise Manager, you still use the familiar Logins node. Here all logins are displayed and managed, whether they are SQL Server or Windows Authenticated.

Try It Out–Creating a Windows Authenticated Login in Enterprise Manager

In this example, you're going to use SQL Server Enterprise Manager to create a Windows
Authenticated Login. You'll be allowing the Windows User you created in the last section the ability
to connect with SQL Server.

1. Connect to SQL Server and drill
down into the **Logins** node, right-
click, and select **New Login**, as
you've done previously. You'll be
presented with the **New Login** dialog
box again. Instead of typing any
information into the **Name** field,
click the ... button.

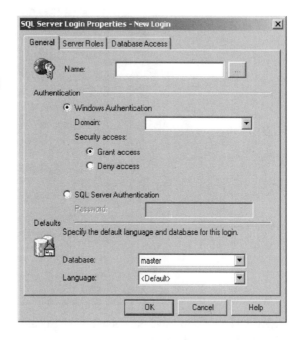

2. This will open the **Login Properties**
dialog box. From the dialog box,
locate and select the
OurWindowsUser account. If your
machine is within a domain, you may
have to select your local machine
from the **List Names From** drop-
down list.

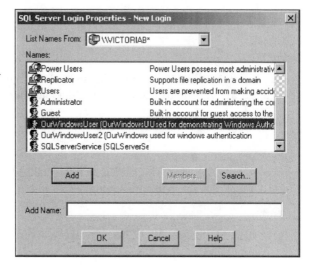

3. Once you've found this account, click **Add** and then **OK**.

249

4. Once you've clicked **OK**, Enterprise Manager will automatically populate the relevant **Name** and **Domain** fields within the **New Login** dialog box. Because you want to allow this login to access SQL Server, leave the **Grant Access** option selected.

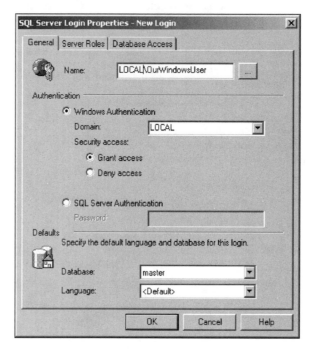

5. Also, you want to leave the default database and language setting as is. Because there is no more information to enter, simply click **OK**.

This new login will be created and displayed within the Enterprise Manager **Logins** node.

Using T-SQL

When granting Windows users the ability to log in to SQL Server through T-SQL, you use the sp_grantlogin stored procedure. This has the following syntax:

```
sp_grantlogin @loginame
```

In the @loginame parameter, you specify the name of the Windows user (or group) that you wish to gain access to SQL Server. This should be fully qualified to include the domain (or machine name for a local account) that the Windows account exists within.

Try It Out–Using T-SQL to Create a Windows Authenticated Login

In this example, you use the sp_grantlogin stored procedure to allow OurWindowsUser2 the ability to establish a connection with SQL Server.

Connect to SQL Server using Query Analyzer, and enter the following command:

```
EXEC sp_grantlogin 'MOZART\OurWindowsUser2'
```

> **My local machine name is Mozart. Use the name of your own computer instead.**

Once you've executed this command, the `OurWindowsUser2` Windows account will be able to establish a connection with SQL Server.

Try It Out–Connecting to SQL Server Using a Windows Authenticated Login

In this example, you'll use Windows Authentication to establish a connection with SQL Server.

1. First log out of Windows, if you're currently logged in.

2. Now log in to Windows using the `OurWindowsUser2` login and password that you created in the previous section.

3. Now open SQL Server Query Analyzer. Because Windows has already authenticated you, you don't need to re-enter any authentication information. Simply select the Windows Authentication option.

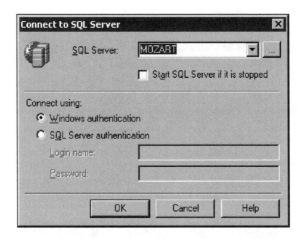

4. When you click OK, a connection will be established, because the Windows user that you're logged in as has been authorized to connect to SQL Server.

Denying Access to a Windows Authenticated Login

It's not only individual Windows users that can be authorized to connect to SQL Server; you can also authorize entire Windows groups. When you authorize a group, all the members of the group gain the ability to establish a connection (this is ongoing, not just for the members at the time the authorization was granted). You do this in exactly the same way as you did in the previous example:

```
EXEC sp_grantlogin 'MOZART\OurWindowsGroup'
```

The group that appears is authorized collectively as one login, which has the name of the group.

A potential problem of this approach appears when you need to authorize a connection to SQL Server for an entire group of people except maybe one or two members of that group. You could decide to authorize them all individually, but this would be a poor solution if you had many hundreds of members within a group. This is where denying a login can be useful.

Any user login that is denied the ability to log in to SQL Server prevents that user from establishing a connection to SQL Server. The login can be denied either explicitly through direct denial of that Windows user, or implicitly through the denying of a group that the Windows user is a member of. If you take the previous scenario, where you wish to grant access to all but a few members of a group, you could grant access to the group and explicitly deny access to individual logins. Another approach is to create a new Windows group named "Denied Users" and add the Windows users that you don't want to allow access to SQL Server to this group. Even if you grant the ability to access SQL Server to the primary group, the denied access to SQL Server for the "Denied Users" group takes precedence over all Windows users who are members of both groups.

> In practice, it's best not to authorize entire groups and deny the members who shouldn't be allowed to connect with SQL Server. It's more efficient to create specific Windows groups especially for grouping only the users who are allowed to connect to SQL Server, excluding those who should not be allowed, and adding an alternative group as a Windows Authenticated Login in SQL Server.

Using Enterprise Manager

To deny a login in Enterprise Manager, you use our SQL Server Login Properties window once again.

Try It Out–Denying Login Access to OurWindowsUser

In this example, you use SQL Server Enterprise Manager to deny the ability to log in to SQL Server to the OurWindowsUser windows account.

Connect using Enterprise Manager and drill down into the Logins node. Right-click the OurWindowUser login, and select Properties. In the Security Access area, select the Deny Access option:

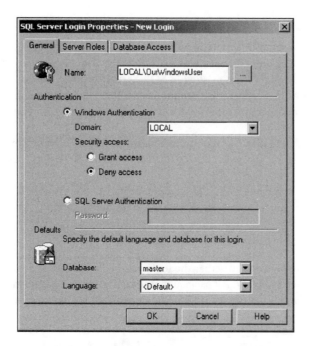

Once you click **OK**, this login will no longer be able to establish a connection with SQL Server even if the login is a member of a Windows group that has been granted access.

Using T-SQL

To deny access to SQL Server for a Windows user (or group), you use the `sp_denylogin` stored procedure, which has the following syntax:

```
sp_denylogin @loginame
```

The `@loginame` parameter is the full-qualified name of a Windows user or group. This login may or may not currently be granted the ability to access SQL Server; either way the end result is a Windows Authenticated Login that cannot access SQL Server.

Try It Out–Denying Access Using T-SQL

In this example, you deny the ability of our `OurWindowsUser2` Windows user account to access SQL Server.

Connect to SQL Server using Query Analyzer. Enter the following command:

```
EXEC sp_denylogin 'MOZART\OurWindowsUser2'
```

When you execute this command, the `OurWindowsUser2` Windows user will no longer be able to access SQL Server even if she is a member of a Windows group that has been granted access.

Removing a Windows Authenticated Login

Finally, you need to understand how to remove a Windows Authenticated Login from SQL Server. You should also be aware of the difference between removing a login and denying a login. Removing a login simply removes the login from existing in SQL Server. It doesn't prevent a particular Windows Account from accessing SQL Server if the account has another means of gaining access to SQL Server, such as through one or more group memberships. Denying access will always prevent access.

To remove a Windows Authenticated Login from Enterprise Manager, you simply right-click the login within the Logins details pane and select Delete (the same as with SQL Server Authenticated Logins).

T-SQL can also be used to remove a Windows Authenticated Login from SQL Server. To do this you use the `sp_revokelogin` stored procedure. This has the following syntax:

```
sp_revokelogin @loginname
```

This removes a login irrespective of whether the login has been granted or denied access to SQL Server, and takes effect immediately. All users authenticated using this login who already have connections established with SQL Server will remain connected, but no new connections using this login will be allowed.

Try It Out–Removing a Windows Authenticated Login with T-SQL

In this example, you use `sp_revokelogin` to remove the `OurWindowsUser2` Windows Authenticated login.

Connect to SQL Server using Query Analyzer and enter the following command:

```
EXEC sp_revokelogin 'MOZART\OurWindowsUser2'
```

Once you execute this command, the login will be removed from existence within SQL Server.

Users

Database users are unique within each database, and as we've mentioned, are different from SQL Server Logins. Although SQL Server Logins and database users are related, they aren't the same thing. SQL Server Logins are analogous to the keys that let you in the front door of SQL Server mansions; database users are analogous to permitting these same keys to unlock the suites where each database lives. Thus whenever a login connects to SQL Server, it will be able to access individual databases with the permission given to the mapped database user for each database.

A database user doesn't necessarily have to be mapped to an SQL Server Login. If this is the case, it's an unmapped (or orphaned) database user. However, no one can make use of the permissions applied to that database user until it's reattached with a SQL Server Login.

Creating Database Users

Database users can be created in a number of ways, but the end result is the same. A database user that is associated with a SQL Server Login can be used for the application of permissions within the given database.

Using Enterprise Manager

One of the easiest ways to create a database user is from the Database Access tab of the Login Properties box that you have dealt with numerous times in the previous sections. This allows you to create database users at the same time you're creating SQL Server Logins. Although this window makes the two tasks appear integrated, bear in mind that they are quite separate steps.

Try It Out–Creating a Database User from the Logins Node

In this example, you use the SQL Server Login Properties dialog box to associate our SQLTestUser with a database user also named SQLTestUser.

1. Connect with Enterprise Manager and drill down into the Logins node. Right-click the SQLTestUser login and select Properties. Click the Database Access tab, as shown.

2. From within this dialog box, select the **Permit** check box for the Northwind database. Enterprise Manager automatically proposes that the login be associated with a database user of the same name (SQLTestUser) within the Northwind database.

3. It's a good idea for the database user and SQL Server Login to have the same name. Although these can be different, it's usually good practice to keep them the same. You can change it here if you wish. Once you're happy with the database username, click **OK**.

You can also create database users from within a given database's Users node. You do this by drilling down into the database where you want to create the particular user, locating the **Users** node, right-clicking, and selecting **New Database User** from the pop-up menu.

Try It Out–Creating a Database User from the Database Users Node

In this example, you use the **Database Users Properties** dialog box to create a new database user named TestSQLUser2 and associate it with out TestSQLUser2 login.

1. Connect using Enterprise Manager and drill down into the Northwind database. Within the Northwind database, select the Users node, right-click, and select **New Database User**.

2. Within the **Database Users Properties** dialog box, select the **Login** name to map the database user to. In this example, choose TestSQLUser2. Ensure that the correct username is shown in the **User Name** text box, in this example it's once again TestSQLUser2.

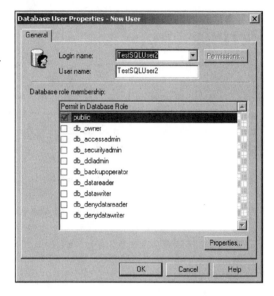

Once you click **OK**, the SQLTestUser2 login will be associated with the SQLTestUser2 database user within the Northwind database.

Using T-SQL

T-SQL can also be used to create a new database user and associate it with a SQL Server Login. To do this you use the sp_grantdbaccess stored procedure with the following syntax:

```
sp_grantdbaccess @loginame, @name_in_db
```

The @loginame parameter is the name of the SQL Server Login you're associating with the database user, and the @name_id_db parameter is the name of the database user you wish to create within the current database and associate with the specified login.

Try It Out–Using T-SQL to Create a New Database User

In this example, you use the sp_grantdbaccess stored procedure to map the SQLTestUser login with a database user of the same name within the pubs database.

Connect to SQL Server using Query Analyzer. Enter the following T-SQL command:

```
USE pubs
EXEC sp_grantdbaccess 'TestSQLUser2', 'TestSQLDBUser2'
```

When you execute this command, a new database user named TestSQLDBUser2 will be created and associated with the TestSQLUser2 login.

Permissions

Now that you have logins mapped to database users, your users can start making use of the information contained within the database, right? Well almost, but not quite. What you have at this point is a security context for a user when they're connected to a database, but you still need to actually apply security to this context. You do this in SQL Server with the assignment of permissions. These permissions are analogous to allowing the user with the key that has entered the database suite in SQL Server mansions to start actually doing things within the room.

Permissions define what activities a specific database user within a database can carry out. Database permissions are local in scope to a database, meaning if you give a user the ability to access an object in one database, they don't automatically gain that ability in other databases.

By default, a database user is created with no permissions. Before they can actually do anything within a database, the user must be given the ability to do so (unless permissions have been explicitly granted to the public role, something you talk about this later in this chapter). Explicitly granting permissions to each database user, or alternatively adding the database user to a role that has been assigned permissions, will do this. You'll examine database roles in the next section.

Types of Permissions

There are two types of permissions that can be assigned within a SQL Server database: object permissions and statement permissions. Although these are managed in a similar way, what they allow is quite different; object permissions manage the access to database objects and statement permissions manage access to certain database related commands.

Object Permissions

Object permissions are used to control access to database objects within SQL Server, including the following:

❑ Tables

❑ Views

❑ Stored procedures

❑ User-defined functions

Using object permissions, an administrator (or object owner; we discuss this a little later in this chapter) can control who can access these objects, and the type of operations they can perform against them. Specifically the types of access that can be controlled by object permissions are as follows:

- ❏ SELECT: Retrieve rows from a table, view, or table-valued, user-defined function

- ❏ INSERT: Add rows into a table or view

- ❏ UPDATE: Modify existing rows within a table or view

- ❏ DELETE: Remove existing rows from within a table or view

- ❏ REFERENCE: Reference rows within a table or view via a foreign key constraint

- ❏ EXECUTE: Run a stored procedure or user-defined function

As you can see, most of the assignable permissions relate to tables and views; only the EXECUTE permission is available for stored procedures.

Statement Permissions

Statement permissions, on the other hand, dictate which administration functions a database user can carry out within a database. This includes tasks like modifying the database schema and backing up the database. Specifically, the available statement permissions are as follows:

- ❏ BACKUP DATABASE: Create a backup copy of the current database.

- ❏ BACKUP LOG: Make a backup of the database's transaction log. This also allows the user to truncate the database log.

- ❏ CREATE DEFAULT: Create a database level, Default, which can be referenced in schema modification operations.

- ❏ CREATE FUNCTION: Create a user-defined function.

- ❏ CREATE PROCEDURE: Create a user-defined stored procedure.

- ❏ CREATE RULE: Create a database level rule, which can be referenced throughout the database schema.

- ❏ CREATE TABLE: Create permanent tables within the current database.

- ❏ CREATE VIEW: Create views within the current database.

In addition, a special kind of statement permission exists within the master database, which is CREATE DATABASE. This allows a user to create a new database. For this permission to be granted, a login must map to a database user within the master database. This statement permission isn't granted in user-defined databases (because it would not make sense to do so).

Assigning Permissions

Both object and statement permissions can be granted, revoked, or denied to database users. GRANT assigns an explicit permission to a database user or role, DENY explicitly removes that permission from a database user or role, and REVOKE removes the explicitly granted or denied permission. If a user is a member of a role that has permissions explicitly granted to them, that user inherits those permissions also. For example, if a user has all permissions revoked, but is a member of a database role that has the SELECT permission on a database table granted, the database user inherits that SELECT permission.

However, if a database user is a member of a role that has a permission granted, but they have had the same permission explicitly denied for that database user, the user doesn't inherit the granted permission. An explicit denial overrides inherited grant permission.

> **Changes in permissions take effect immediately.**

GRANT

You can GRANT permissions using either SQL Server Enterprise Manager or T-SQL. If you're defining permissions for many database objects, it's usually preferable to use T-SQL, because the script used to generate the permissions can be saved and reused. If, on the other hand, you need to set permissions on a handful of objects quickly, Enterprise Manager provides an effective means of doing this.

Using Enterprise Manager

There are several methods for granting permissions within Enterprise Manager. The first method you'll look at is via the **Database User Properties** dialog box. To locate this dialog box, drill down into the specific database and click on the Users node. Right-click the user you wish to apply permissions to and select **Properties**. You should see a window similar to the following:

Try It Out–Granting a SELECT Permission through the User Properties Dialog Box

In this example, you'll grant the TestSQLUser the SELECT object permission on the Summary of Sales by Year view within the Northwind database.

1. Connect to SQL Server using Enterprise Manager. Drill down into the Databases node, and then into the Northwind database. Within the Northwind Database node, select Users. In the details pane you'll see a list of database users.

2. Right-click the TestSQLUser and choose Properties from the pop-up menu. Within the User Properties dialog box, click Permissions. The Database User Properties window will be displayed as shown.

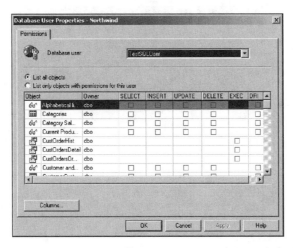

3. Within this dialog box, scroll down until you find the Summary of Sales by Year view. To assign the SELECT permission to our TestSQLUser, click within the SELECT checkbox *once* so a green tick is displayed. This indicates that this permission is explicitly granted.

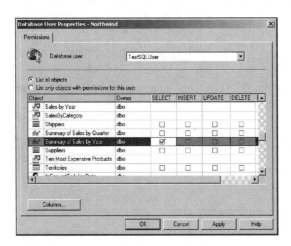

4. Click **OK** to apply this permission, and click **OK** again to close the **User Properties** dialog box.

Another method of applying object permissions is via the **Object Properties** dialog box. This can be accessed from the **Tables, Views, Stored Procedures,** and **User Defined Functions** nodes within a database.

If you right-click the object within the details pane and select **Properties,** the **Object Properties** dialog box will be shown.

Depending on the type of object you have selected to view the properties for, the object properties dialog box may be different from what is shown (which is the **Object Properties** window for a database view). However, there will be a **Permissions** button that you can click to access the **Objects Permission** dialog box.

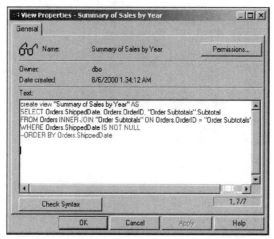

An alternative means of accessing this **Object Properties** dialog box is by right-clicking the object you wish to manage the permissions for in the details pane, and selecting **All Tasks | Manage Permissions** from the pop-up menu.

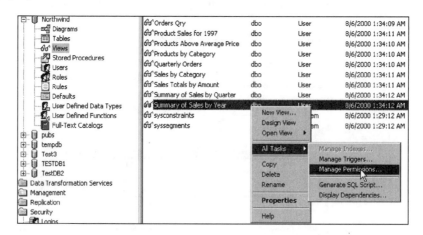

Using either of these methods displays the same **Object Properties** dialog box.

Try It Out–Assign a SELECT Permission Using the Object Properties Dialog Box

In this example, you use the Object Properties dialog box to assign the SELECT permission on the Summary of Sales by Year view to our TestSQLUser2 database user.

1. Connect using Enterprise Manager and drill down into the Views node within the Northwind database. Scroll down the details pane until you can see the Summary of Sales by Year view. Right-click this view, and select All Tasks I Manage Permissions from the pop-up menu.

2. Within the Object Properties dialog box, tick the SELECT permission for our TestSQLUser2 database user.

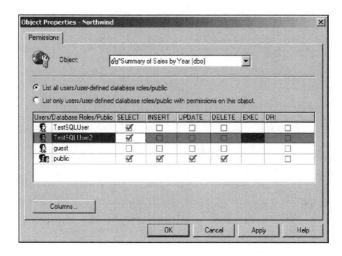

3. Click OK to apply these permissions.

Using T-SQL

To apply GRANT object permissions using T-SQL, you issue the GRANT statement, which has the following syntax:

```
GRANT permission ON object TO user/role
```

The permission parameter will correspond to one of the object permissions we've mentioned in the earlier sections (SELECT, INSERT, EXEC, and so on). The object parameter will contain the name of the SQL Server object that you wish to assign the permission on. Finally, for the user/role parameter, you specify the database user or the user-defined database role that you wish to assign this permission to.

263

Permission to Grant Permissions

To GRANT permission on an object, you must meet one or more of the following criteria:

❑ You must own that object (ownership is discussed later in the chapter).

❑ You must be a member of the db_owner (database owner) fixed database role.

❑ You must be a member of the db_securityadmin fixed database role.

❑ When the permission you're granting was assigned to you, the person who granted you the permission must have specified the WITH GRANT option. This allows you to pass on that permission to others.

The syntax for granting permissions while passing on that permission is

```
GRANT permission [ON object] TO user/role WITH GRANT
```

The WITH GRANT option is valid for object and statement permissions.

Try It Out–Granting Object Permissions Using T-SQL

In this example, you grant the SELECT permission on the Orders table within the Northwind database to our TestSQLUser database user.

Connect to SQL Server using Query Analyzer. Change the current database to Northwind (in the drop-down box above the query window), and enter the following command:

```
GRANT SELECT ON dbo.Orders TO TestSQLUser
```

The TestSQLUser now has the ability to SELECT all rows and columns within this table. If you want the TestSQLUser to be able to choose who can SELECT rows within the Orders table, you can pass on this permission with the WITH GRANT option, as shown in this example:

```
GRANT SELECT ON dbo.Orders TO TestSQLUser WITH GRANT
```

Once you've assigned this permission, the TestSQLUser is free to assign it to anyone.

Try It Out–Granting Statement Permissions Using T-SQL

In this example, you GRANT the CREATE TABLE permission within the Northwind database to the TestSQLUser database user.

Ensure that you're using the Northwind database, and enter and execute the following command:

```
GRANT CREATE TABLE TO TestSQLUser
```

In order to GRANT the CREATE TABLE permission, you must meet one of the following criteria:

❑   You must be a member of the db_owner database role.

❑   You must be a member of the db_ddladmin role.

❑   You must have previously been granted the CREATE TABLE permission with the WITH GRANT option.

> **Statement permissions have different database fixed role membership requirements that determine who can grant a given permission. For a list of all statement permissions and the requirements needed to GRANT them, see SQL Server Books Online.**

DENY

DENY is the exact opposite of GRANT. It explicitly prevents a user from having the specified permission against the specified database object. Typically, you would only deny a permission to a database user if that database user were inheriting a GRANT permission from a role that the database user is a member of. Remember an explicit DENY always overrides an inherited GRANT of permissions.

Using Enterprise Manager

You use the same dialog boxes within Enterprise Manager to DENY a permission as you do to GRANT the permission. The difference is in the symbol that is entered within the permission checkbox. A red cross or an empty box, instead of a green check mark, indicates a denied permission.

Try It Out–Denying Access Using the Object Properties Dialog Box

In this example, you deny the ability of the TestSQLUser to SELECT from the Summary of Sales by Year database view.

Connect to SQL Server using Enterprise Manager and open the Object Properties permission dialog box (as you did within the GRANT example). Click the SELECT permission check box for the TestSQLUser until a red cross is displayed.

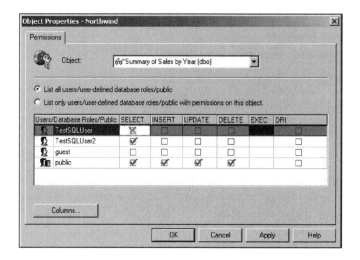

Once you click OK, the denied permission will be applied to this database user.

Using T-SQL

DENY has the same syntax as GRANT:

```
DENY permission ON object TO user/role
```

As with GRANT, multiple permissions can be denied using these syntaxes:

```
DENY permission, permission ... ON object TO user/role
```

Or:

```
DENY ALL ON object TO user/role
```

Try It Out–Denying a Permission Using T-SQL

In this example, you deny the SELECT permission on the Orders table within the Northwind database to the TestSQLUser database user.

Connect to SQL Server using Query Analyzer. Change the database you're using to Northwind, and execute the following command:

```
DENY SELECT ON dbo.orders TO TestSQLUser
```

The TestSQLUser will not be able to SELECT any rows from the Orders table even if a member of a database role that has had the SELECT permission granted.

REVOKE

REVOKE removes any explicitly granted or denied permissions. This isn't used to prevent a user from gaining permission on a database object, but instead to remove previously granted or denied permissions. Revoking a permission doesn't affect permissions that the user inherits from other roles. For example, if you revoke the SELECT permission from a user for a given table, the user may still be able to SELECT from that table if this permission has been granted to one of the database roles that the database user is a member of.

Using Enterprise Manager

You revoke object permissions within the same Object Properties dialog that you used to GRANT and DENY permissions. A revoked permission is indicated by an empty check box (not a cross or check mark).

Try It Out–Revoking the Permission from the TestSQLUser

In this example, you REVOKE the SELECT permission from our TestSQLUser on the Summary of Sales by Year database view.

Connect using Enterprise Manager and open the Object Properties permission dialog box for the Summary of Sales by Year database view, as done in the previous examples. Clear the SELECT check box for the TestSQLUser.

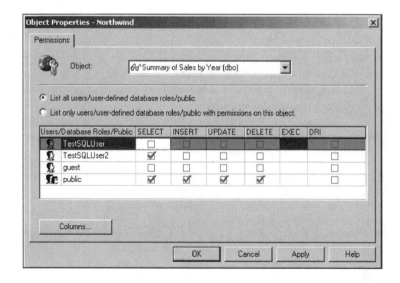

Clicking OK causes the permissions to be revoked.

Using T-SQL

REVOKE is the command used to remove explicitly granted permissions and has a similar syntax as GRANT and DENY:

```
REVOKE  permission ON object FROM user/role
REVOKE  permission, permission ... ON object FROM user/role
REVOKE  ALL ON object FROM user/role
```

If no permission had been explicitly defined, no error is generated (revoking an already revoked permission doesn't cause an error).

Try It Out–Revoking a Permission with T-SQL

In this example, you REVOKE the SELECT permission on the Orders table within the Northwind database from the TestSQLUser database user.

Connect to the SQL Server, and change to using the Northwind database using Query Analyzer. Enter the following command:

```
REVOKE SELECT ON dbo.Orders FROM TestSQLUser
```

Once you execute this command, any explicitly granted or denied SELECT permission will be removed.

Roles

We've mentioned roles a number of times during this chapter and now it's time to discuss these in more detail. Essentially a role can be thought of as SQL Servers term for a group. There are two "levels" of roles in SQL Server, which are as follows:

❑ Server Roles: Roles that Logins can be members of. These roles allow SQL Server-level permissions to be assigned.

❑ Database Roles: Roles that database users (or other database roles) can be a member of. These roles allow database-level permissions to be assigned.

Database roles are available in two types, fixed and custom. Server roles are only available as fixed. The definitions of fixed and custom types of roles are as follows:

❑ Fixed: Predefined by Microsoft and built in to SQL Server. Their permissions are set and cannot be changed. They cannot be dropped and you cannot add new ones. However, you can add and remove members of these roles

❑ Custom: Defined by database developers or administrators. New ones can be added and removed, and the permissions assigned to custom roles can be changed. Also, you can add and remove members of these roles

> **There are only fixed server roles, no custom server roles.**

Roles are used to ease the administration involved with assigning permissions. Instead of having to assign numerous permissions to every login or database user, you can simply add the users or logins to the roles that have the appropriate predefined permissions, and the database user (or login for fixed server roles) inherits the permissions of the various roles that it's a member of.

As you've also seen, you can override the inherited role permission by explicitly denying a permission.

Fixed Server Roles

As we mentioned, only fixed server roles are available and you cannot define your own. This isn't really a limitation because these are intended to allow you to delegate administration privileges only. Database-level security takes place using database roles (or by assigning permissions directly to users), and these roles are user definable.

The following are the available fixed server roles and their intended uses:

- ❑ Sysadmin: System administrators can do anything within SQL Server. This is the level of privilege the sa SQL Server Authenticated login has.

- ❑ Serveradmin: Server administrators can set, configure, and shut down SQL Server. This doesn't give the login permission to access all databases.

- ❑ Setupadmin: Setup administrators can manage linked servers.

- ❑ Securityadmin: Security administrators can add, remove, and modify server logins. They can also grant the CREATE DATABASE login permission.

- ❑ Processadmin: Process administrators can manage (kill) user processes that are running against SQL Server.

- ❑ DBCreator: Database creators can ALTER, CREATE, and DROP databases within a given SQL Server.

- ❑ Diskadmin: Disk administrators can manage database disk files.

- ❑ Bulkadmin: Bulk load administrators can execute statements to BULK INSERT data into a database.

An individual login can be the member of one or more fixed server roles.

> **Normal logins will not be a member of any fixed server roles. These are for use with administration logins only.**

Adding a Login to a Fixed Server Role

You can use Enterprise Manager or T-SQL to add a login to a fixed server role. There are two ways of doing this from within Enterprise Manager, which we'll discuss now.

Using Enterprise Manager—Login Dialog Server Roles Tab

When you create a SQL Server Login using Enterprise Manager within the Login Properties dialog box, there is a Server Roles tab available. Clicking this tab displays a list of the available server roles. Within this tab you can choose the fixed server roles you want the currently selected login to be a member of.

Try It Out—Adding TestSQLUser to the Security Administrators Fixed Server Role

In this example, you add the TestSQLUser as a member of the Security Administrators Fixed Server Role.

1. Within Enterprise Manager, right-click the TestSQLUser login within the Logins details pane. Select Properties from the pop-up menu.

2. Next, click the Server Roles tab to display a list of all of the available fixed server roles. From this list, select the Security Administrators server role.

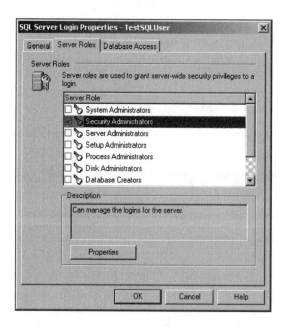

When you click OK, the TestSQLUser will gain the ability to add, remove, and otherwise manage SQL Server Logins.

Using Enterprise Manager—Server Roles Node

The other method of managing server roles is from the Server Roles node. This is located in the Security node for a given SQL Server, underneath the Logins node. When you click on Server Roles, the list of fixed server roles is shown in the details pane. To add a login to any one of the server roles, right-click it and select Properties from the pop-up menu.

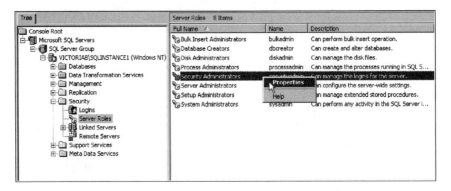

Within the Server Role Properties dialog box, you'll be able to add specific logins as members of that fixed server role.

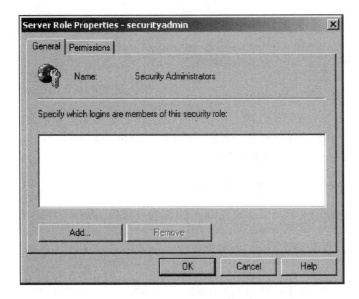

The Server Role Properties dialog box also allows you to see exactly what permissions a login gains by becoming a member of that fixed server role. To see these permissions, click the Permissions tab.

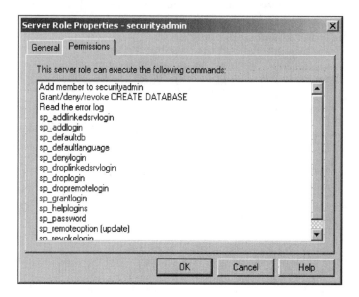

> **Although the permissions are viewable under the** Server Role Properties **Permissions tab, they aren't changeable.**

Using T-SQL

You use the `sp_addsrvrolemember` system stored procedure to add a login as a member of a fixed server role, and this has the following syntax:

```
sp_addsrvrolemember @loginame, @rolename
```

The `@loginame` parameter is the name of the login to add to the server role, and the `@rolename` parameter is the name of the fixed server role. Note that this is the short name that you listed earlier (such as `sysadmin`).

Try It Out–Adding TestSQLUser to diskadmin Using T-SQL

In this example, you add the `TestSQLUser` login as a member of the Disk Administrators server role.

Connect to SQL Server using Query Analyzer. Enter the following command:

```
EXEC sp_addsrvrolemember 'TestSQLUser', 'diskadmin'
```

When you execute this command, the TestSQLUser will gain the permissions of the Disk Administrators role. To see exactly what these permissions are, you can use the sp_srvrolepermission stored procedure with the fixed server role name as a parameter:

```
EXEC sp_srvrolepermission 'diskadmin'
```

Removing a Login from a Fixed Server Role

You can remove a login from a fixed server role within Enterprise Manager or using T-SQL. Once removed from a fixed server role, all inherited permissions are also removed.

Using Enterprise Manager

Within Enterprise Manager, you use either of the dialog boxes that you used to add a login as a fixed server role member.

Try It Out–Removing the Security Administrators Server Role

In this example, you remove the TestSQLUser from being a member of the Security Administrators server role.

Right-click the Security Administrators fixed server role in the details pane of the **Server Roles** node. Select the TestSQLUser and click **Remove**. Click **OK** to apply this change.

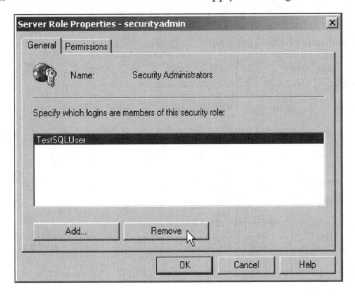

Using T-SQL

To remove a member of a fixed server role using T-SQL, you use the sp_dropsrvrolemember system stored procedure, which has the following syntax:

```
sp_dropsrvrolemember @loginame, @rolename
```

The @loginame parameter is the name of the login to remove from the fixed server role, and the @rolename is the name of the fixed server role from which to remove the login.

Try It Out–Removing TestSQLUser from Disk Administrators

In this example, you remove the TestSQLUser login from being a member of the Disk Administrators fixed server role.

Connect to SQL Server and execute the following command:

```
EXEC sp_dropsrvrolemember 'TestSQLUser', 'diskadmin'
```

TestSQLUser no longer has the permissions that were inherited by the Disk Administrators fixed server role.

Fixed Database Roles

Similar to fixed server roles, fixed database roles exist within each and every database. These are predefined roles that have been assigned predefined permissions by Microsoft. Just like fixed server roles, these cannot be added, removed, or changed; but unlike fixed server roles, you add and remove database users from these roles, rather than SQL Server Logins.

The following fixed database roles exist within every database:

- ❑ db_owner: Performs any operation within a database. Can access any data and take over ownership of any database object.

- ❑ db_accessadmin: Controls which logins can connect to the database.

- ❑ db_datareader: Reads all data within all tables.

- ❑ db_datawriter: Modifies all data within all tables and can also insert new data into all tables.

- ❑ db_ddladmin: Modifies the database schema and creates new schema objects.

- ❑ db_securityadmin: Adds, removes, and manages roles and permissions (object and statement) within a database.

- ❑ db_backupoperator: Initiates a backup of the database.

- ❑ db_denydatareader: Explicitly prevented from viewing any data within any database tables.

- ❑ db_denydatawriter: Explicitly prevented from writing any data within any database tables.

> **For more information on fixed database roles, look in SQL Server Books Online.**

Fixed database roles differ slightly from fixed server roles in that they aren't all for assignment to administration users only. Whereas fixed database roles, such as **db_accessadmin** and **db_owner**, should be reserved for administration users, fixed database roles, such as **db_datareader**, may be used to give a normal database user the ability to view all data within all tables (if this is a valid application requirement).

> **This is a quicker and more easily managed way of granting the SELECT permission on all database tables than explicitly issuing the GRANT SELECT command for every table within the database.**

The Public Role

The public role is a special type of fixed database role. All database users are always a member of the public database role, and this membership cannot be removed. Also, no permissions are predefined for the public database role; instead, you can assign these manually.

The public database role is useful if you wish to grant permissions to every database user. By assigning these permissions to the public database role, you can be sure that every database user will always have those permissions (unless an explicitly denied permission exists for certain database users).

> **Generally, you should avoid assigning permissions directly to the public role. It's a better practice to create a custom database role that you can assign permissions to, and only add the database users who really do need those permissions to this database role.**

Custom Database Roles

Custom database roles are user definable. By default, no custom database roles exist within a database until you explicitly create them. Once created, you can explicitly assign permissions to the custom database role, and any member of that custom role will inherit these permissions.

> **Custom database roles exist to allow us to ease the administration of assigning object and statement permissions within a database.**

Creating a Custom Database Role

You can create a custom database role from within Enterprise Manager or by using T-SQL. You'll examine both of these methods in this section.

To create a custom database role using Enterprise Manager, simply right-click the Roles node within a given database and select New Database Role from the pop-up menu.

You can enter all information necessary to create a database role within the Role Properties dialog box.

Try It Out–Creating a Custom Database Role in Enterprise Manager

In this example, you create a new custom database role name TestDatabaseRole.

1. Right-click the Roles node within the Northwind database and select New Database Role from the pop-up menu.

2. Enter TestDatabaseRole as the name of this database role. This is all the information you need to create a custom database role.

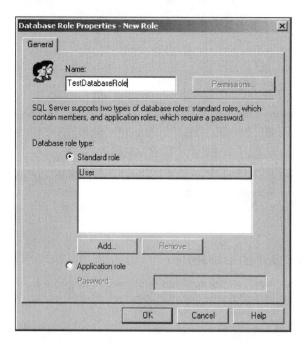

3. Click **OK** and the custom database role will be created. Once it has been created you can assign permissions to this role and members of this role will inherit these permissions (see the next section for information on adding members to a role).

Using T-SQL

To create a custom database role using T-SQL, you execute the `sp_addrole` system stored procedure with the following parameters:

```
sp_addrole @rolename, @ownername
```

The `@rolename` parameter must be specified, because this is the name of the new role you're attempting to create. The `@ownername` parameter is optional and specifies who owns the database role (defaults to `dbo`).

Try It Out–Using T-SQL to Create a Custom Database Role

In this example, you use the sp_addrole system stored procedure to add a custom database role named `TestDatabaseRole2`.

Connect to SQL Server using Query Analyzer. Change the database to the `Northwind` database and execute the following command:

```
EXEC sp_addrole 'TestDatabaseRole2'
```

The `TestDatabaseRole2` has now been created.

Adding a User to a Database Role

To add a database user (or custom database role, as you'll see in the next section) as the member of a database role (either fixed or custom), you can use one of three methods in Enterprise Manager or T-SQL.

Using Enterprise Manager – Via the Login Dialog

The first method available in Enterprise Manager is via the **Login Properties** dialog box again. Once again, you use the **Database Access** tab (as you did when creating a database user mapping for a login); however, now you tick the appropriate database role you wish this database user to be a member of.

Try It Out–Add TestSQLUser to the db_owner Fixed Database Role

In this example, you add the TestSQLUser database user as a member of the db_owner fixed database role.

Open the Login Properties dialog box for the TestSQLUser and select the Database Access tab. In the lower half of this window, click the check box next to the db_owner fixed database role to indicate that you wish TestSQLUser to be a member of this role. Click OK.

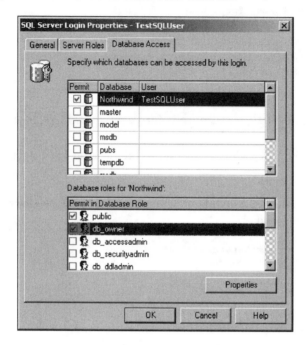

Using Enterprise Manager—Via the Users Node

The second method of assigning a database user to a database role within Enterprise Manager is via the Database User Properties dialog box. This is accessible by navigating to the Users node within a specific database, right-clicking a database user within it, and selecting Properties.

Then you can select the various database roles you wish this database user to be a member of.

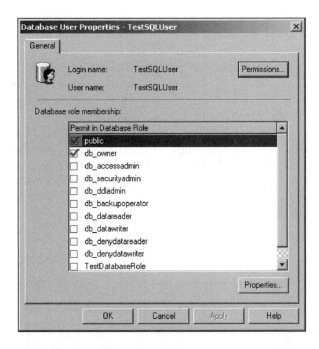

Using Enterprise Manager—Via the Roles Node

The final method of assigning a database user as a member of a database role is under the Roles node within a given database. This can be found directly underneath the Users node.

In this node, a list of available database roles will be displayed in the details pane. To add a member to any of these database roles, right-click the role and select Properties from the pop-up menu.

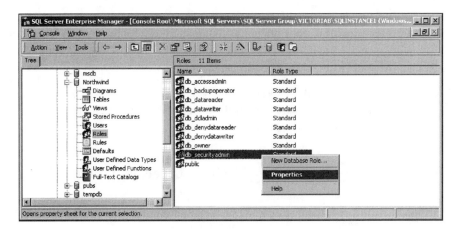

Within the Properties dialog box, you can choose to add database users as members of that database role.

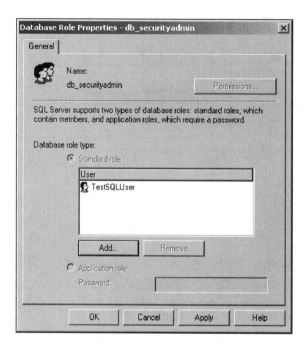

Each of these three methods has the same outcome; they are just different ways of carrying out the same task.

Using T-SQL

To add a database user or existing custom database role, as a member of a fixed or custom database role, you execute the **sp_addrolemember** system stored procedure. This has the following syntax:

```
sp_addrolemember @rolename, @membername
```

Both of these parameters are required. The **@rolename** is the name of the role that you wish to add the member to, and the **@membername** parameter is the name of the database user (or other existing database role) that you wish to add to this role.

Try It Out–Adding TestSQLUser to TestDatabaseRole Using T-SQL

In this example, you execute the **sp_addrolemember** stored procedure to add the **TestSQLUser** as a member of the **TestDatabaseRole2** custom database role.

Connect to SQL Server using Query Analyzer and change the current database to **Northwind**. Execute the following command:

```
EXEC sp_addrolemember 'TestDatabaseRole2', 'TestSQLUser'
```

Removing a User from a Database Role Using Enterprise Manager

To remove a database user (or custom database role) from being a member of a fixed or custom database role using Enterprise Manager, you simply click the Remove button within the Database Role Properties dialog box, and select TestSQLUser in the same window that you used to add role members.

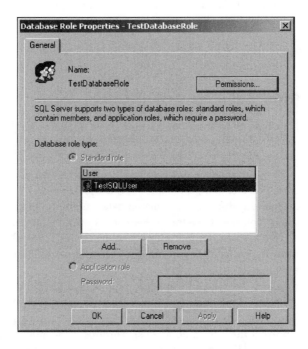

Any permissions inherited from the role will be no longer be available once removed from the role.

Using T-SQL to Remove a User from a Database Role

To remove a member from a fixed or custom database role using T-SQL, you execute the sp_droprolemember stored procedure. This has the following syntax:

```
sp_droprolemember @rolename, @membername
```

Once again, the @rolename is the name of the role that you wish to remove the member from, and the @membername parameter is the name of the database user (or other existing database role) that you wish to remove from the role.

Try It Out–Removing a User from a Database Role

In this example, you execute the `sp_droprolemember` stored procedure to remove our `TestSQLUser` from being a member of our `TestDatabaseRole2` custom database role.

Connect to SQL Server using Query Analyzer and change the current database to `Northwind`. Execute the following command:

```
EXEC sp_droprolemember 'TestDatabaseRole2', 'TestSQLUser'
```

Application Roles

Application roles are the last type of database role. Setting up an application role is a little different compared to the roles you've looked at previously, and they're certainly used in a different manner.

One of the problems with allowing someone to log in to SQL Server is that you don't have control of which application they use to connect to SQL Server. For example, you may grant someone the `SELECT` permissions on the tables within your production database for the purpose of retrieving rows through a specific application. You may have tuned the indexes within your database to be highly optimized for the types of queries that the application issues against SQL Server. Because your database application is highly optimized, you can support a large number of users.

However, suppose a user decides that using the application to look at individual records isn't enough, so instead of using the application, they open up a tool, such as Microsoft Access, and links tables through to SQL Server (because the user has been granted the `SELECT` permission on all database tables, there is nothing to prevent them from doing this). This opens the table in Microsoft Access and the user proceeds to scroll through the table at their leisure. More than likely, this will impact the performance of the database server significantly and end up disturbing the operation of the other users who are accessing the database in the preferred manner.

What can you do to control "how" the users connect to SQL Server, not just "what" they are able to access? This is where application roles come into play. Application roles are a special kind of role that you don't add members to directly; instead you assign a password to that role. You don't tell this password to your database users. Instead, this is a password that you tell your application developers, and they embed the password within the application configuration. The permissions necessary for users to carry out their tasks within the application are assigned to the application role. However, no permissions are assigned directly to the database users.

> **If you embed the application password within your applications, then it's very difficult to change. Doing so may require your application to be recompiled. Therefore, you should always set a long and difficult password for the application password, because this is unlikely to be changed often.**

If a user attempts to connect to SQL Server using a tool like Microsoft Access, they can establish a connection, but they don't have permission to access anything. So what good is this? When those same users connect to SQL Server through the correct means (the client application), the application sends the role name and password to SQL Server.

SQL Server validates the application role name and password, and if these are correct, grants the permissions defined for the application role. All statements executed for the remaining duration of this connection will run with the permissions that have been assigned to the application role, not the connecting user.

> **Although it's considered good security practice to change passwords regularly, this is difficult with application role passwords. Remember that application roles offer another level of protection over the top of authentication and the assignment of permissions, and only logins that are authorized to access a database may attempt to use an application role.**
>
> **However, you must still consider if the inability to regularly change the password fits with your organization's security policy.**

Using Enterprise Manager to Create an Application Role

When creating an application user using Enterprise Manager, you use the familiar Database Role Properties window. However, in addition to specifying the database name, you also select the Application Role option and enter a password that will be used for this application role.

Try It Out–Creating TestApplicationRole Using Enterprise Manager

In this example, you create an application role named `TestApplicationRole`.

1.   Connect to SQL Server using Enterprise Manager and drill down into the `Roles` node within the `Northwind` database. Right-click the `Roles` node and select `New Database Role` from the pop-up menu.

2.   Enter `TestApplicationRole` as the name for our application role. Also, click the `Application` role option and enter `sqlserverisneat` as the application role password.

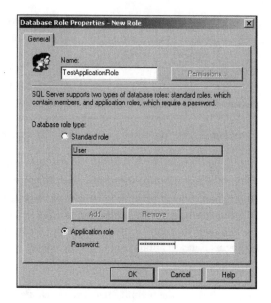

Using T-SQL to Create an Application Role

To create an application role using T-SQL, you execute the `sp_addapprole` stored procedure, which has the following syntax:

```
sp_addapprole @rolename, @password
```

`@rolename` is the name of the application role and `@password` is the password that the application must pass to SQL Server in conjunction with the role name to gain the permissions of the application role.

Adding a Database User to an Application Role

Database users aren't added to an application role, as they are to custom roles. Any user can gain the permissions of an application role as long as the application role name and application role password are known by their client application, and sent to SQL Server.

Assigning Permissions to an Application Role

Permissions are assigned to an application role in exactly the same way that permissions get assigned to database users and custom database roles. See the "Assigning Permissions" section earlier in this chapter.

Enabling an Application Role Using T-SQL

An application role can only be enabled using T-SQL on an existing connection. The permissions inherited from the application role remain in force until the connection is closed.

You should enable an application role within the client application. To do this, you send the `sp_setapprole` command to SQL server with the following syntax:

```
sp_setapprole @rolename, @password, @encrypt
```

@rolename is the name of the application role and @password is the password associated with that role. The @encrypt parameter is optional but, if it's used, it can be set to ODBC, which will cause the application role password to be encrypted before being sent across the network to SQL Server. This will help prevent hackers with network packet sniffers from easily determining the application role password.

Try It Out–Enabling an Application Role

1. Connect to SQL Server using Query Analyzer and log in to SQL Server as the TestSQLUser SQL Server authenticated login.

2. Execute the following command:

```
EXEC sp_setapprole 'TestApplicationRole', 'sqlserverisneat'
```

Our current connection has now inherited the permissions that you've assigned to the application role. These permissions will remain as long as the connection remains open.

Ownership and Ownership Chains

No discussion of SQL Server security would be complete without a discussion of ownership and what happens to security when you have a chain of objects (one object that accesses another, which accesses another, and so on).

Every object that exists within a database is owned by a database user. The user who owns the object has the right to do anything with the object, including removing the object. For this reason, it's generally recommended that "ordinary everyday users" do not own objects that are accessed by users other than themselves.

Because all permissions are implicitly on objects that the accessing user owns, no permission checking is done when the user accessing the object is the same as the owner of the object.

When users access an object that they don't own, then permissions are checked. Only if the appropriate permission has been granted to that user, or to any of the roles that the user is a member of and only if no explicit denial of the required permission exists for that user on that object, may the user gain access.

If the object that the user is accessing accesses another object (such as a stored procedure calling another stored procedure), permissions aren't checked if the owner of both *objects* (not the initial user) is the same.

If the owners of the object that is accessing another object are different then permissions are checked. However, they aren't checked against the initial user who executed the first object, they're checked against the owner of the accessing object. For example, when UserA accesses ObjectA, and ObjectA in turn accesses ObjectB, if ObjectA has a different owner to ObjectB, permissions are checked.

First, permissions are checked for UserA to access ObjectB. Second, permissions are checked to ensure the owner of ObjectA is allowed to access ObjectB. This is known as an ownership chain. The impact on permissions of an ownership chain can be summarized as follows: "Permissions are checked whenever the owner of the object in the access chain changes. The owner of the accessing object is checked to ensure that it has permissions on the object it's attempting to access."

This sounds complicated, so what are the benefits of SQL Server behaving in this way? Well a really simple example is using stored procedures to prevent direct access to the base tables within a database. You can have all your base tables owned by a user, for example, Laura. Then you can create stored procedures, which are also owned by Laura. When you create the stored procedures, you can put T-SQL code in these procedures to query the base tables (with any associated logic).

Now, you can grant the EXECUTE permission on these stored procedures to Linda, William, and Stephanie. When William attempts to access the base tables, he is blocked, because William doesn't have permissions to those base tables. However, William can execute the stored procedure, because this permission has been assigned.

Because Laura owns the stored procedures and the base tables, there is no checking of permissions between the stored procedure and the base table. Laura is implicitly allowed to access Laura's objects. Therefore, the stored procedure can access the base tables and retrieve the appropriate information.

This allows ad hoc access to the base tables to be prevented, while still allowing users to access the data contained within these tables through standard interfaces that you define (such as a stored procedures).

Ownership Chain Best Practices

Having objects owned by many different users can make security management difficult because of the impact of ownership chains. Therefore, it's widely recommended that you should usually (unless you can think of a specific reason not to) ensure that a single user owns all objects within a database. And almost certainly, this should be the database owner.

This allows you to grant permissions directly to users on the objects you want them to access; however, any inter-object accessing will not run into any permission-related problems.

Relinking Database Users

As we've discussed, database users are linked to SQL Server Logins. A user is a means of allowing a login to gain access to a database. This linking isn't done based on name; instead, a database user references an internal unique number of the login known as the SID.

If you restore a database that was created on a different SQL Server, there is a good possibility that users will exist within the restored database that don't map to existing SQL Server Logins, because the SIDs will likely be different between servers. Database users that don't have a corresponding SQL Server Login are known as orphaned users. These orphaned users cannot be used until they are associated with an SQL Server Login again.

There are two approaches to dealing with database users. First, you could execute the following command for each orphaned user within the affected database to remove unlinked database users:

```
EXEC sp_dropuser username
```

Then you could create new database users for existing logins (as in the earlier examples in this chapter). The disadvantage of this approach is that any existing group membership or assigned permission information is lost. In addition, if those users own objects, those objects must be assigned to other users or dropped. Either way, it generally disrupts the existing security configuration of the database.

An alternative approach is to use the sp_change_users_login stored procedure to relink a database user with a SQL Server Login. This has a couple of syntaxes depending on how you want to use it.

The first method explicitly assigns a database user to an existing SQL Server Login. To do this, execute this procedure, as shown:

```
EXEC sp_change_users_login 'Update_One', database_user,
sql_server_login
```

If you have many users with existing logins of the same name to relink, you may consider using the Auto_Fix option. This will automatically link orphaned database users within the current database to SQL Server Logins of the same name. If there is no matching login with the same name as the database user then a new SQL Server Authenticated Login is created that has a name that matches the name of the database user. The password parameter determines the password that is assigned to newly created logins.

```
EXEC sp_change_users_login 'Auto_Fix', database_user, NULL ,
password
```

> You should be careful when using the Auto_Fix option. If the database users do not exactly match existing logins within SQL Server, you may find that you accidentally create new logins for every database user.

Application Security Best Practices

OK, so far we've talked about a lot of different ways to create logins; now let's focus on the real world. What do we consider the best practice? It depends on the type of application that you're using.

In this section, we provide some general SQL Server security recommendations for several styles of application. As always, you should fully consider your options before making a decision; however, you're welcome to use these recommendations as a starting point.

Custom Client Server Application

A custom client server application is a client application that has been developed internally within your organization, which allows you to have some control over changes to the application code to enhance security.

Authentication Mode	Windows only
Authentication Method	Windows Authentication
SQL Server Access	Windows Logins assigned to Windows groups, based on access requirements Windows groups granted login authorization to SQL Server
Database Access	Logins assigned to database users Application roles are members of Custom database roles Custom database roles assigned permissions based on functionality requirements When the user connects to SQL Server using the application, the application role password is sent giving that connection the permissions that have been assigned to the custom database role, of which the application role is a member

Intranet Application

An Intranet application is a web-based application that runs internally on your company's network, rather than on the Internet. The web server and the SQL Server may be on physically separate machines.

Authentication Mode	Windows only
Authentication Method	Windows Authentication
SQL Server Access	Windows Logins assigned to Windows groups, based on access requirements Windows groups granted login authorization to SQL Server
Database Access	Logins assigned to database users Database users are members of appropriate database roles Custom database roles are assigned permissions based on functionality requirements

Legacy Application

A legacy application is a client server application that doesn't support Windows Authentication. The only authentication method you can use with these applications is SQL Server Authentication. This isn't usually an application you have built in-house.

Authentication Mode	Mixed
Authentication Method	SQL Server Authentication
SQL Server Access	SQL Server Logins are created for each user
Database Access	Logins assigned to database users
	Custom database roles created for each discreet subject area and data access requirement (such as read sales, change products)
	Database users are members of appropriate database roles

Additional Security Topics

Besides everything you've looked at so far in this chapter, there are two more areas that are worth looking into briefly: backup passwords, and security in a development environment.

Backup Passwords

Backup passwords help you to protect your backup media by allowing the administrator to specify a password when the backup is performed. That password must also be specified for a restore from that backup to take place. However, this should be used in addition to, not instead of, good file and physical security.

Backup passwords are discussed in more detail in Chapter 8.

> Using a backup password doesn't cause the entire backup file to be encrypted. The password is retained in the header of the backup file and is intended to prevent many "unauthorized" restore attempts by users. However, this isn't a security mechanism that should be considered insurmountable by an experienced hacker.

Security in a Development Environment

It seems obvious when you talk about it, but one of the major security problems today is how to implement security in the nonproduction environments, such as development and test environments.

We commonly work with organizations that have well-implemented security within their production environment. They may use Windows Authentication, assign Windows users to Windows groups, add those Windows groups to database roles, and assign permissions to those database roles. Users can only gain access to the database objects that they're authorized to see, and can only carry out the tasks that they're authorized to.

The problem lies outside this well-maintained server. Most organizations, especially those that develop their applications in-house, have testing and/or development servers that sit outside their production environment. Typically, these servers exist to allow development and administration staff the ability to test changes before these changes are applied to the live production environment.

Often, the only way to effectively test the intended changes is to update the test/development databases with a copy of the production database. This is usually done using backup and restore (see Chapter 8). Although the test/development servers may contain a copy of the production data, the effort and planning of the security of these servers is typically much less than that of the production equivalent. On occasion, I have seen development environments that have no password assigned to the sa user, and all developers connect using this login. Although this makes life easy for the developers because they won't run in to any security issues while they're creating the application, all the effort that has gone into protecting the production application is effectively wasted. A hacker (who may even be someone who works for your organization) can simply gain access to the production data by easily logging in to the development server.

Summary

As you've learned from this chapter, there is a lot involved in the security picture. You have two types of logins, database users, fixed server-level roles, fixed database roles, custom database roles, application roles, object permissions, statement permissions, three methods of permission assignment, and so on.

Initially it's complicated. Security requires planning to get it right, but don't start with roles, users, and permissions when carrying out your security planning. Start with the information within the database and determine how this should be protected. Based on this requirement, determine how these permissions should be applied within SQL Server.

7

Connectivity

The main purpose of the relational database is to provide a means for engineering your data in a productive, reliable, and secure way. However, this data is only of use if the end users can access it—they could be, but aren't limited to applications, services, reports, and data-entry screens. As a database administrator (DBA), you'll be called on to help architect, configure, and troubleshoot a variety of issues related to the connectivity and availability to your database.

In this chapter, you'll explore the tools and technologies that bridge the gap between the database and the consumers of the data as well as different ways of presenting the data to the consumers. You'll learn about the following:

❑ The network architecture and protocols used to communicate with SQL Server

❑ How to configure the SQL Server on a network

❑ How to configure the clients on a network

❑ Monitoring your network traffic

❑ How to administer SQL Server from a remote location

❑ Setting up SQL Server as a web service

Microsoft SQL Server Network Services

Microsoft SQL Server 2000 ships with several tools that allow you to retrieve data from your SQL Server database, including the following:

❏ ISQL (a command-line application)

❏ OSQL (a command-line program that uses the ODBC protocol)

❏ Query Analyzer

OSQL is the replacement for ISQL and should be used instead of ISQL. They're basically the same tool, except that OSQL uses ODBC (Open Database Connectivity) instead of ISQL's DB-Lib (DB Library) to communicate with SQL Server, and ISQL doesn't support the SQL Server 2000 specific functionality. In most cases, these tools are sufficient for the SQL Server DBA, but for a nontechnical end user who needs data presented in a more meaningful way, DBAs and developers will need to write specialized applications. There are two ways to communicate with SQL Server, **APIs** (**application programming interfaces**) and **URLs** (**Uniform Resource Locators**).

As a developer writes applications that request data from the SQL Server database, he needs a hierarchy of channels to communicate with the SQL Server on both the client and the server sides. The following diagram shows the relationship at the different communication layers between the client, Applications, and the server, MS SQL Server 2000.

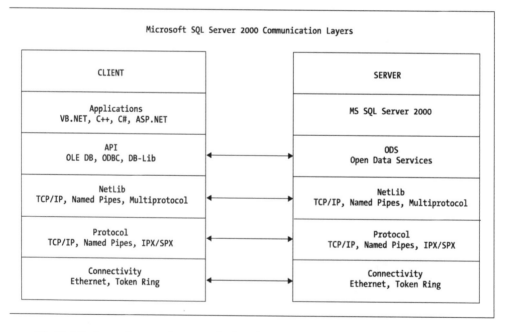

The NetLib *box references the protocols that the client and server use to communicate with each other. They're included just for reference only.*

SQL Server 2000 Application Programming Interfaces

The SQL Server API is considered the top layer of the model and is represented by the API/ODS boxes in the previous diagram. We must call these from our applications to connect to SQL Server and extract data. The main ones are:

❑ ODBC, which allows clients to connect to the SQL Server or other database products or repositories

❑ OLE-DB (Object Linking and Embedding–Database), which is similar to ODBC but usually performs better

❑ SQL-DMO (SQL Distributed Management Objects)

❑ ADO .NET and the .NET managed providers

We'll also discuss the soon-to-be obsolete DB-Lib, which is an API proprietary to SQL Server.

DB-Lib for C

The DB-Lib for C API contains a set of C functions for developers to create applications to interact with SQL Server. Included are functions for sending T-SQL statements and receiving data from SQL Server, handling errors, and converting data.

> **Although the DB-Lib for C API is supported in Microsoft SQL Server 2000, no future versions of SQL Server will provide the tools necessary to develop applications with this API. Microsoft strongly encourages you to remove dependencies on DB-Lib. Instead of DB-Lib, you can use ADO, OLE DB, or ODBC to access data in SQL Server.**

You should only use this API if you have an existing application that requires it.

One common issue with the deployment of the DB-Lib API is the correct installation of system files needed to develop and run the applications. In the next section, we look at the required system files.

Client applications that use DB-Lib must meet the Microsoft SQL Server client system requirements for the operating system they're using. For information about the system requirements for SQL Server, see Chapter 1 of this book or *Installing SQL Server* in Books Online.

To create Win32 DB-Lib applications, you need the client files provided with SQL Server 2000 as well as the following software:

DB-Library Version	Operating System Supported	Compiler
Windows NT	Microsoft Windows NT Workstation version 3.5 or later (version 3.51 or later is recommended)	Microsoft Visual C++ version 2.0 or later, or a 100-percent compatible compiler and linker
	Microsoft Windows NT Server version 3.5 or later (version 3.51 or later is recommended)	Microsoft Visual C++ version 2.0 or later, or a 100-percent compatible compiler and linker
	Windows 95	Microsoft Visual C++ version 2.0 or later, or a 100-percent compatible compiler and linker
	Window 98	Microsoft Visual C++ version 2.0 or later, or a 100-percent compatible compiler and linker
Microsoft Windows 3.11	Microsoft Windows version 3.11 or later, Microsoft Windows for Workgroups version 3.11 or later	Microsoft Visual C++ for Windows version 1.0 or later or Borland C++ version 3.1 or later
MS-DOS	MS-DOS version 5.0 or later	Microsoft Visual C++ for Windows version 1.0 or later or Borland C++ version 3.1 or later

DB-Lib isn't supported on Windows Millennium, XP, and 2000.

DB-Lib uses the client network libraries to communicate with the SQL Server database.

Open Database Connectivity

ODBC is an API developed by Microsoft that allows a client application to communicate with a database. Because each database has its own low-level code used for communication, ODBC insulates you from having to write these specialized layers of communication by providing a common point of entry to each type of database. SQL Server, Access, Fox or Oracle databases can all be accessed using the same ODBC API.

ODBC enables a database to become an integral part of an application. SQL statements can be incorporated into the application, thereby allowing the application to retrieve and update values from a database. Values from the database can be placed in program variables for manipulation by the application. Conversely, values in program variables can be written to the database.

All that you need to do to use this functionality is to install on the client an ODBC driver that is specific to the type of database you'll be using, and then configure the driver with a DSN (data source name) for each different connection.

When defining a data source to connect to the server, there are three types to choose from: user, system, and file.

❑ User data sources.

  Specific to the Microsoft Windows operating system account, they're in effect when they're created. They're stored in the system registry.

❑ System data sources.

  Visible to all accounts and services on a client. They're stored in the system registry.

❑ File data sources.

  Added with ODBC 3.5 and are stored in a file on the client.

Try It Out–Creating an ODBC Data Source

To configure an SQL Server ODBC data source to be accessible by anyone or any service, follow these steps:

1. Load the Microsoft **ODBC Data Source Administrator**. Click the Windows **Start** button, point to **Settings I Control Panel**, and then double-click the **ODBC (32-bit)** icon (in Microsoft Windows 95 or later) or the **ODBC** icon (in Microsoft Windows NT Workstation 4.0 or later). For Windows 2000 Professional and Windows XP Professional, click the **Administrative Tools** icon and then click the **Data Sources (ODBC)** icon. Select the **System DSN** tab as shown.

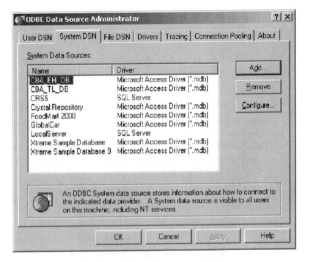

2. Click the Add Button and then in the list box, select SQL Server as shown. Click the Finish button.

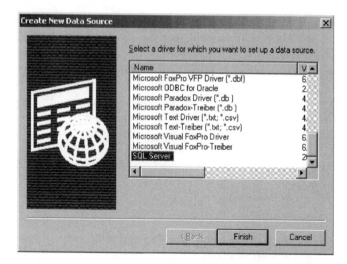

3. This will start the Create a New Data Source to SQL Server wizard.

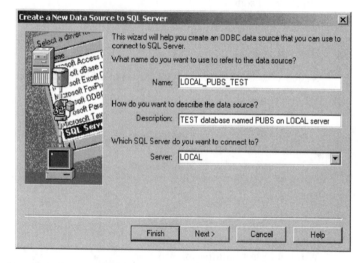

In the Name textbox, enter the name that you wish applications to use to connect to this SQL Server. This doesn't have to be the server or database name. We generally use a naming convention that allows us to easily identify the server, database, and type of database that it is. For example, SERVER_DATABASE_TEST or LOCAL_PUBS_TEST lets us know that the database is a TEST database named PUBS on the LOCAL server.

The Description is just a text version of what the connection is. The Server is a server name resolvable by either DNS or WINS (Windows Internet Name Service) that provides a dynamic replicated database service that can register and resolve NetBIOS names to IP addresses used on your network. Alternatively, the name of a host file located on a local computer or on a central server can be inputted into this box. The host file provides for resolution on both NetBIOS computer names and DNS host names on TCP/IP networks. You can also put in the server IP address, but this isn't advised, due to potential future maintenance problems. After completing the entries, click the Next button.

4. The next window gives you the option of how to connect to SQL Server, by using either Windows Authentication or SQL Server Authentication. Your choice will depend on how the SQL Server that you're connecting to was originally set up. If you used mixed mode, then you can choose either option.

See Chapter 6 for more information on SQL Server security or consult Managing Security in SQL Server Books Online. For this example, you'll choose With Windows NT authentication using the network login ID as shown.

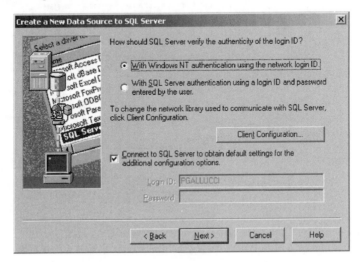

In most cases, you wouldn't have to change the client configuration information. If you did, don't worry, we'll discuss this later in this chapter. Now click the Next button.

5. In the next window, select the database that this connection will connect with.

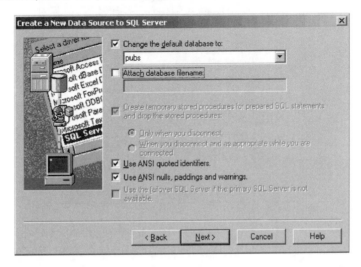

There are some other configuration options that determine how developers will interact with the database. For this example, leave these as the default settings and click Next.

6. On this window, you can specify the language to be used for Microsoft SQL Server character set translation, and whether the SQL Server driver should use regional settings. You can also control the log. You should not enable this log, unless absolutely necessary (for troubleshooting). ODBC logging will result in huge log files and slow down the performance of the client application.

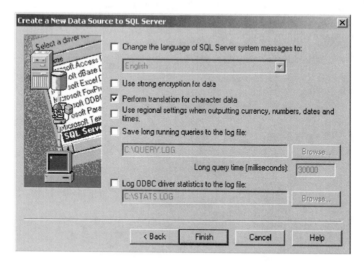

7. Now click the Finish button to test and save your new DSN configuration. This final window will give you the opportunity to review your DSN settings and a button for testing your new entry.

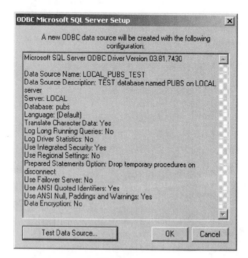

8. Click the Test Data Source button. The following window shows the results of the connection attempt. If the test fails, check the user ID and password that you used to connect to the SQL Server.

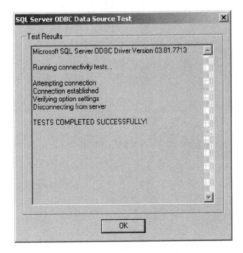

9. Click OK three times and you'll be back to the ODBC Data Source Administrator window, where your new ODBC data source will now be listed.

Configuring DSNs

As an SQL Server DBA, you'll be called on to do DSN configurations on clients of many types. The diagram shows what the typical corporate environment might look like with a development, testing, and production environment.

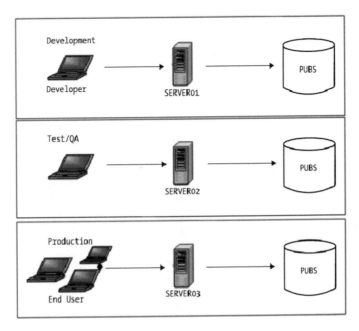

As the developers complete the coding of applications that connect to the SQL Server, the DSN connections that they've been using would be ones that connect to the development environment. Based on the example, you would have a DSN named SERVER01_PUBS_DEV. You might be asked to configure a DSN for the testing and production environments. In doing so you would connect to the correct server, but to the same database for each additional environment.

> **Organizations that you work for may have an established methodology for naming conventions for DSNs. Enquire with other DBAs and system administrators to see if this is the case.**

For the most part, the developer should have configured the application to use the correct DSN and correct properties for each connection for the varied environments. Some of the issues that may occur from the different environments and how to troubleshoot each are listed here.

❑   Unable to connect to SQL Server.

This is a generic error message that SQL Server ODBC and OLE-DB will display in cases where tools and applications are unable to connect to SQL Server. Your first step should be to test the connectivity to the SQL Server machine from a client in the same network. This is important, because developers and TEST/QA personnel may not be separated from the SQL Server via a router or firewall. End users usually have stricter ports access to production servers.

First, use the standard ping command to test TCP/IP connectivity to the server. At the command prompt type the following:

```
C:\>Ping [SERVERNAME]
```

If you get the following error back, then your client is unable to resolve the DNS to the IP address of the server. You'll need to work with your network engineer to resolve this.

Ping request could not find host server. Please check the name and try again.

If you receive a time out response (Request timed out.) then you either physically cannot get to the server or the server may be turned off. Again work with your network engineer to resolve this.

If you're getting a response back from the Ping but still cannot get an ODBC connection to the server then try the ODBCPing.exe utility. The ODBCPing.exe utility tests the integrity of an ODBC data source and the ability of the client to connect to a server. This utility can be found in the SQL Server installation directory under the binn or x:\x86\Binn directory on the Apress website. In this example, you can type the following at the command prompt:

```
odbcping.exe /D SERVER01_PUBS_DEV /Usa /Ppassword
```

> **The complete usage of the ODBCPing utility can be found at:**
> http://msdn.microsoft.com/library/default.asp?url=/library/enus/coprompt/
> cp_odbcping_194p.asp.

❑ DSN names aren't case-sensitive.

You can use both uppercase and lowercase alphanumeric naming conventions for your DSN name, and it doesn't matter if the client connection case doesn't match that of the server.

❑ Be aware of illegal and reserved DSN names.

Stay away from names like 'Table', 'Field', 'Database', and 'Text'. Also, do not include special characters like \ , . - +.

Try It Out–Executing a Command Using an ODBC DSN Connection

The following ASP script shows how a programmer would use the DSN you created earlier in an application. You can execute the script to help test different connection issues between the client and the SQL Server. You can download this file (`createODBCconnection.asp`) from the Apress website.

```
<%
'Declare variables
Dim rs
Dim conn
'handle errors
On Error Resume next
'Set Object reference
Set rs = CreateObject("ADODB.Recordset")

'Open the database and query records
conn = "DSN=LOCAL_PUBS_TEST"
rs.Open "SELECT au_id,au_lname,au_fname FROM authors", conn

Select CASE Err.Number
        CASE 0
            Response.Write "ODBC Connection succeeded."
        CASE Else
            Response.Write "ODBC Connection failed : " & _
            Err.Number & " - " & Err.Description
End Select

'clean up
rs.Close
Set rs = Nothing
%>
```

Remember to change your ODBC connection in the file if you called it something different.

Active Data Objects and ADO.NET

ADO is an API that uses OLE-DB for data access to a diverse set of data sources. ADO has better performance than ODBC and a better support of the SQL Server objects and methods that developers can use. For the most part, the underlying connections still use the same Net-Libs to communicate with SQL Server.

ADO.NET is the enhanced "managed" version of ADO. You'll focus more on the new ADO.NET version because it's the latest release. From a DBA standpoint, the connections are relatively the same. When using ADO you would retrieve data using a recordset object. In ADO.NET, the functionality of the recordset has been broken up into the DataReader, Dataset, and DataAdapter. Microsoft did this to give the developer greater control over the behavior of the different type of data that a developer works with.

> *For more information on programming with ADO .NET, see* Professional ADO.NET Programming *by Apress.*

Try It Out–Executing a SQL Statement Using ADO.NET

The following sample shows an ADO connection using the same server and database used in the ODBC connection sample. Again, you can download this file (`createADONetConnection.vb`), along with all other code in the chapter, from the Apress website.

```
Imports System.Data.SqlClient

Module Module1

Sub Main()
Try
    ' ADO.NET SQL Server-optimized connection object
    Dim conn As New SqlConnection("Initial Catalog=pubs;" _
            & "Data Source =(local);Integrated Security=SSPI")
    conn.Open()

    ' Command object
    Dim command As New SqlCommand("SELECT " _
                & "au_id,au_lname,au_fname" _
                & " FROM authors", conn)
    ' Datareader object
            Dim reader As SqlDataReader = _
        command.ExecuteReader(CommandBehavior.CloseConnection)

    ' Output datareader values
    While reader.Read()
        Console.WriteLine(reader.GetSqlValue(1))
    End While

    ' Tidy & pause
    conn.Close()
    Console.ReadLine()
```

```
        ' Catch any errors
    Catch ex As Exception
        Console.WriteLine("Exception: " & ex.Message)
        Console.WriteLine(ex.ToString)
        Console.ReadLine()
    End Try

    End Sub

    End Module
```

How It Works

You'll notice that the New SqlConnection is where we define the datasource, security, and database or as it is referred to here, catalog. This is called a DSN-less connection. DSN-less connections can be performed with OLE-DB using both ADO.NET and ADO. Using a DSN-less connection eliminates the need for a DSN on the application machine, and can be used to hide the data source connection information from the application end user, thereby removing the possibility of a DSN being viewed or modified.

For a complete listing of ADO.NET connection properties, methods, and other examples of using ADO.NET, consult the MSDN Data Access walkthroughs at http://msdn.microsoft.com/library/default.asp?url=/library/en-us/vbcon/html/vboriIntegratingDataVB.asp.

SQL Server Net-Libraries and Protocols

As mentioned earlier, SQL Server supports a number of Net-Libraries: Named Pipes, TCP/IP, Multiprotocol, NWLink IPX/SPX, AppleTalk, and Banyan VINES. Each Net-Library corresponds to a different network protocol or set of protocols. The network protocol on which you run SQL Server will probably be determined by corporate standards or legacy systems.

Although all SQL Server commands and functions are supported across all network protocols, some protocols are faster than others, or support routing and named services that others do not.

Named Pipes

Microsoft developed the Named Pipes protocol several years ago. Named Pipes is supported in two modes: local and remote. The local Named Pipes protocol is used when the client and server are on the same system, and remote Named Pipes is used when the client and server are on different systems. When a connection is established via Named Pipes, the SQL Server network utilities determine whether to use a local named pipe or a remote named pipe. If local named pipes are used, the network is bypassed, which can potentially improve performance for large data movement operations, such as BCP (bulk copying) operations.

Named Pipes is the default client protocol, and it's one of the default network protocols on Windows NT 4 Server and Windows 2000 systems. Although Named Pipes is an efficient protocol, it isn't usually used for large networks because it doesn't support routing and gateways. It also isn't preferred for use with a slower network. Named Pipes requires significantly more interaction between the server and the client than do other protocols, such as TCP/IP.

> On Microsoft Windows 95 and Microsoft Windows 98 systems, Named Pipes isn't an option. On these systems, the server-side protocols are TCP/IP, Multiprotocol, and shared memory.

TCP/IP

TCP/IP is one of the most popular network protocols because of the number of platforms on which it runs, its acceptance as a standard, and its high speed. It's also the network protocol used for the Internet. The TCP/IP Net-Library is one of the highest performing of the SQL Server Net-Libraries. Unlike Named Pipes, TCP/IP is a routable protocol that allows clients on different networks to connect to your server via a router. TCP/IP's speed and its rich feature set make it a good choice for most networking solutions.

NWLink IPX/SPX, AppleTalk, and Banyan VINES

NWLink IPX/SPX is an ideal protocol to use when you're integrating SQL Server 2000 systems into a Novell NetWare network because it performs the integration seamlessly. IPX/SPX has been around for quite a while, and it has high performance and stability.

AppleTalk is the network protocol developed by Apple Computer and used for Apple systems. Windows NT and Windows 2000 support AppleTalk, which allows Windows NT and Windows 2000 servers and clients to seamlessly integrate into an AppleTalk environment.

The Banyan VINES Net-Library supports systems on a VINES network. This Net-Library allows you to integrate Windows clients and servers into a VINES environment.

VIA (Virtual Interface Architecture)

This protocol comes in two flavors, Giganet and ServerNet II. It's well suited for clustered servers. The VIA protocol is used specifically in large-scale environments, which can be a data warehouse or large webfarms, and is used exclusively for pushing large amounts of data between servers.

> Both the client and server SQL Server VIA Net-Libraries are supported only on Windows NT Server and Advanced Server, and Windows 2000 Server, Advanced Server, and Data Center.

Multiprotocol

The Multiprotocol Net-Library was new with SQL Server 7.0 and carries over to SQL Server 2000. This Net-Library is actually a combination of several Net-Libraries. As such, it isn't as efficient as a single Net-Library, but it offers more flexibility. The Multiprotocol Net-Library supports the TCP/IP, NWLink IPX/SPX, and Named Pipes protocols. When you use the Multiprotocol Net-Library, the first protocol that the client and server have in common is used. When a client might connect to various servers running different protocols, Multiprotocol is an ideal choice.

Choosing a Net-Library

Your choice of Net-Library will be based on the protocols your network is using. During installation of the SQL Server client utilities, TCP/IP and Named Pipes are configured as the default client protocols. As a rule of thumb, TCP/IP generally performs better over slower network connections. Over faster network connections, TCP/IP and Named Pipes perform similarly. As for Multiprotocol, although it provides flexibility for environments that use varying protocols, Multiprotocol doesn't support connections to SQL Server 2000 named instances.

You can change this default protocol via the SQL Server Client Network Utility (reviewed in more detail in the "Network Configuration of Clients" section). You can configure the server-side default protocol by using the SQL Server Network Utility (reviewed in more detail in the next section, "SQL Server Network Utility–Network Configuration of a Server"). Connection problems usually occur when the Net-Libraries on the server and the client aren't in sync. If you have trouble connecting to your server, check the Net-Library definitions on both sides. Also, try connecting to the server using another program, such as the ping command or ODBCPing.exe, to determine whether the problem is SQL Server-related or is caused by the network itself.

SQL Server Network Utility—Network Configuration of a Server

The first tool that you'll use is the SQL Server Network Utility. This tool is used to configure network protocols that you'll use to connect clients to your SQL Server. By default, the Named Pipes and TCP/IP protocols are enabled during the installation of SQL Server.

The following dialog box shows the **SQL Server Network Utility** as it is loaded. You can find this tool in **Programs** | **Microsoft SQL Server** on the **Start** menu.

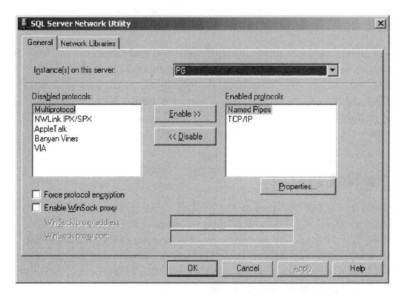

In most situations, you won't need to change the protocols that SQL Server is listening on. However, if your network uses a protocol other than Named Pipes or TCP/IP, you'll need to enable the specific protocol to listen on a given port. It's a good idea to consult your network engineer about the specific port as well as to address any issues that you might encounter with your network appliances, such as firewalls and switches.

The first thing to notice on this dialog box is the Instance(s) on this server drop-down list. If you're running multiple instances of SQL Server on your computer, you'll need to configure each instance separately.

> **This is an important aspect of debugging and troubleshooting connectivity issues with SQL Server, because each server will be using its own network communication paths, including different communication ports that it listens on.**

For example, if you complete the default installation of SQL Server, it will configure the default instance to listen on TCP port 1433. Subsequent instance installations of SQL Server will install and configure TCP on a dynamic port. This window will allow you to select the port that each named instance runs on. This information should be documented and conveyed to the network engineers to ensure that the correct TCP and UDP ports are open on network devices.

> *A UDP (User Datagram Protocol) port is an alternative to TCP and like TCP, it uses IP to get data from one computer to another, but it's much more limited in its service.*

To change the TCP port, highlight TCP/IP on the General tab and click the Properties button. The following dialog box shows the default port that this instance of SQL Server is listening on.

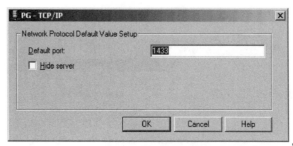

To change the port number, type the new port number in the box and click **OK**. The **Hide server** option allows you to prevent clients from discovering the existence of the SQL Server. This is good for debugging when you need to turn off client access to the server.

Generally you don't need to change the default instance port that SQL Server listens on. By default, Named Pipes are installed to listen on the pipe (\\.\pipe\sql\query). Subsequent instances of SQL Server Named Pipes listen on \\computername\pipe\MSSQL$instancename\sql\Query, as shown.

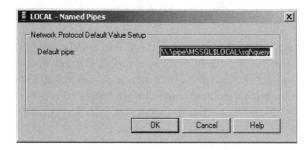

Again it isn't necessary to change the default pipe that SQL Server listens on for Named Pipes.

Back on the **General** tab of the **SQL Server Network Utility** dialog box, the **Force protocol encryption** option allows the server to request that all traffic between the client and SQL Server be encrypted. This ensures the privacy of the data and that the data will be unreadable in any SQL statements that are sent to the server, even if the client has the ability to access the bits in the data stream. If the client is unable to negotiate this type of request, the server terminates the connection.

> **There is a noticeable performance degradation with encryption enabled, as a result of the encryption and decryption that happens at the server and the client. It will be dependent on the amount of data that is in each packet. A way to negate the performance decrease is to add more processing power at the server.**

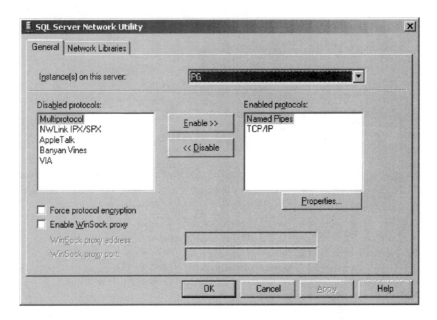

The **Enable WinSock proxy** option allows you to set SQL Server to be configured to listen on a proxy server using Microsoft Proxy Server over TCP/IP. Selecting this option enables the **WinSock proxy address** and **WinSock proxy port** textboxes for the entry of your Proxy server IP address and port number. SQL Server can work hand in hand with your Microsoft Proxy Server to guard against unauthorized access to your SQL Server, and to ensure that SQL Server isn't directly connected to the Internet.

By allowing your external clients to connect through Microsoft Proxy Server, you (as the administrator) can control who connects by limiting users, ports, IP addresses, or domains. This gives you a level of security that allows your instance of SQL Server to operate transparently to the user.

> **For information on setting up Proxy Server, start at**
> http://msdn.microsoft.com/library/default.asp?url=/library/enus/adminsql/ad_1_ser
> ver_1y5u.asp.

The last thing to point out in the SQL Server Network Utility dialog box is the **Network Libraries** tab. This tab provides information about the Server network library, including the filename, path, version, file date, and size of the file. The following figure shows the Network libraries loaded on the PG server:

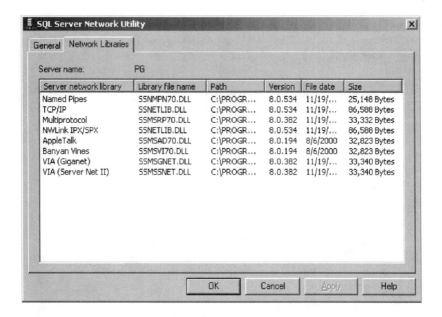

This tab will be useful in providing information to Microsoft if you need to open a support ticket for any issues you might have with connectivity to the server.

Now you'll look at the configuration of the client. Then you'll tie these together by looking at some samples of client connectivity to the server, and general monitoring and troubleshooting techniques that will help you keep your connections up and diagnose problems if they arise.

Network Configuration of Clients

You'll walk through the process and different configuration parameters for client connectivity to SQL Server for Named Pipes, TCP/IP, Multiprotocol, and NWLink IPX/SPX. These are the main protocols that are used to connect to SQL Server. It's important to keep your configuration information handy because new clients are added to your network, and you'll need to resolve issues between connectivity to different clients.

The Net-Libraries for a protocol must be installed before you can set up a configuration. If the client Net-Library for a network protocol isn't installed, it will not be listed on the Network Libraries tab. You can also set up configurations for network protocols supplied by a third party, using the Others option in the Add Network Library Configuration dialog box.

The following image shows the General tab that is used to enable and disable different protocols for clients to connect to the SQL Server. The SQL Server Client Network Utility dialog box is also found in the Programs I Microsoft SQL Server group on the Start menu.

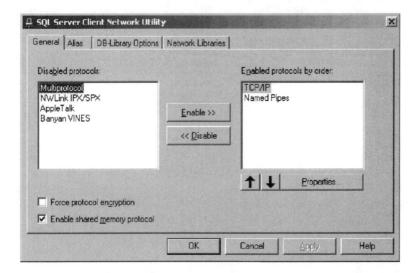

One important aspect of client connectivity and latency to connect to SQL Server is the Enabled protocols by order listbox. The order of the listed protocols gives the sequence the client will attempt to connect to the SQL Server. For example, from the list shown, the client would attempt to connect to SQL Server using the TCP/IP protocol and if that failed, she would then attempt to connect via Named Pipes. The amount of time taken for the client to connect to the server is relatively negligible. We'll discuss this in the troubleshooting section of this chapter.

The other options on this tab are Force protocol encryption and Enable shared memory protocol. This allows SQL Server to use the shared memory protocol for connections from a client that reside on the SQL Server itself. The Force protocol encryption check box enables the client to request that a server use SSL encryption for all communications with the client.

By selecting one of the protocols in the Enabled protocols by order list box, we can select the Properties button and configure the default settings for this client for the selected protocol. The following dialog box shows the settings for the TCP/IP protocol. The value that is shown, 1433, is the default port that SQL Server listens on for client connections via the TCP/IP protocol. In most cases, this value doesn't need to change.

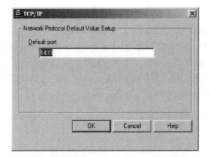

Later in the chapter, you'll see how to configure different ports for different servers and server instances of SQL Server. For the Named Pipes protocol, the default setting is sql\query.

Aliases

The Alias tab is used to configure individual connections to the SQL Server when the default settings will not allow the client to connect to the server. In the following dialog box, you see the configuration information for the PLG server:

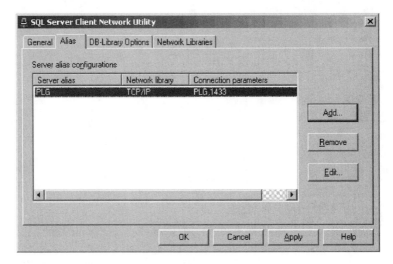

In most cases, you won't need to configure individual connections to the SQL Server. SQL Server will listen to broadcasts on UDP port 1434. The client application will negotiate this with the SQL Server. When the client connects to an SQL Server, only the network name of the computer running the instance and the instance name are needed, provided that there is a clean connection to the server via the UDP port. When a client connects to this port, the server returns a packet listing all the instances running on the server. For each instance, the packet reports the server Net-Libraries and network addresses the instance is listening on. After the Dbnetlib.dll on the application computer receives this packet, it chooses a Net-Library that is enabled on both the application computer and on the instance of SQL Server, and makes a connection to the address listed for that Net-Library in the packet.

If you only have the default TCP port open to connect to SQL Server and there is a firewall or router that may be blocking ports, you can create an alias for the client. The alias gives the information needed to connect to the server without having the server and client negotiate the types of connections that are available.

Configuration of Named Pipes Aliases

By clicking the Add button on the Alias tab, the next window will appear showing the default configuration for the Named Pipes protocol. The Server alias is the name the client application will use to connect to the SQL Server. The Server name is the server name of the instance of SQL Server that you're connecting to.

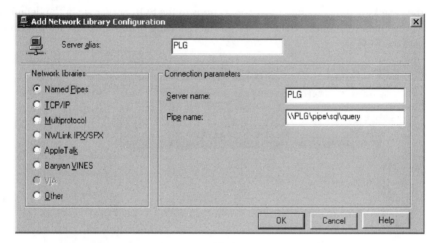

Configuration of TCP/IP Aliases

This next window shows the configuration for TCP/IP. By default, the Dynamically determine port check box is checked. In situations where the SQL Server and client application is separated by a firewall, and the UDP port 1434 is blocked by the firewall, unchecking this setting allows the client to directly connect to the specified server on the configured port without waiting for the reply from the server for the port it's accepting client connections on. This works because port 1434 is used to establish connections from applications seeking to connect to SQL Server 2000 instances.

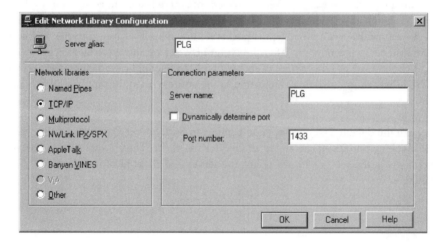

For situations in which the server name isn't resolvable to the IP address by means of a DNS, WINS, or host file entry, as a temporary solution you can put the server's IP address in the Server name text box. You should still try to resolve the underlying issue causing the name resolution failure.

Configuration of Multiprotocol Alias

Configuration using the Multiprotocol option enables the DBA to configure a connection to multiple SQL Servers running a variety of the supported protocols without having to reconfigure the client. The client and server should both be using the Net-Libraries for TCP/IP, NWLink IPX/SPX, or Named Pipes. This will allow the Multiprotocol Net-Library to select the first available network protocol to establish a connection.

The window shows the configuration parameters for the Multiprotocol Network-Library. The Server alias is the name of the server that you want the client to use when connecting. The Server name is the actual server that you'll be connecting to. Leave the Additional parameters setting blank unless your network administrator requests that you enter data here.

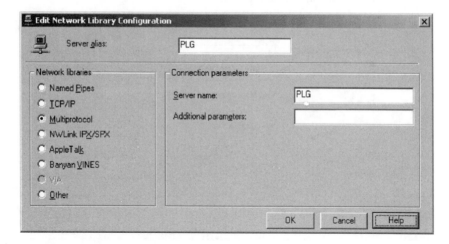

Configuration of NWLink IPX/SPX Alias

NW Link IPX/SPX Compatible Transport is the native protocol of Novell networks. You can configure your client to communicate to the SQL Server using this protocol.

In the following figure, you'll see the configuration settings using the Service name option. The service name can be obtained from the Novell Network Administrator. The Server alias is the name that you want the client applications to use to connect to the server.

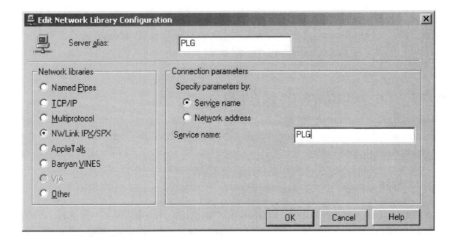

The next window shows the configuration by **Network address**. Consult your network administrator for this information before setting up the configuration.

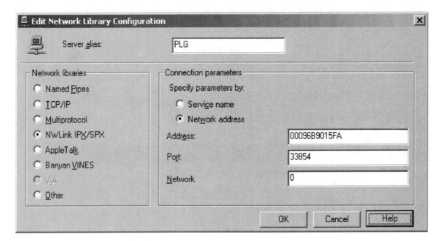

Network Monitoring

As discussed earlier, connectivity problems that arise in your SQL Server environment can sometimes remain undiagnosed until an end user flags it up. As the DBA, you'll be responsible for monitoring and maintaining peak performance of your SQL Server as well as the connectivity to your SQL Server. In most instances, you'll work with your network engineer to maintain this environment and to help you diagnose issues. The following are some of the tools and techniques that will help you monitor your environment and identify issues before they occur.

Using Performance Monitor to Identify SQL Server-Related Network Issues

The Performance Monitor is the DBA's first line of defense in identifying network performance issues as they relate to SQL Server. The Windows 2000 operating system and SQL Server 2000 have many counters that can be traced to help identify common bottlenecks affecting a client application accessing an SQL Server database. By running Performance Monitor, you can select and track some of the following key counters.

Try It Out–Adding a Network Counter to Performance Monitor

1. Click Start | Settings | Control Panel | Administrative Tools | Performance. Click the [+] button located on the toolbar. The following screen shot shows the Add Counters interface for Performance Monitor:

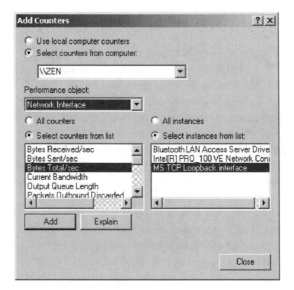

2. Select Network Interface from the Performance object drop-down list.

3. With the Select counters from list checked, select Bytes Total/sec. This countermeasures the number of bytes that are being sent back and forth between your server and the network, and includes both SQL Server and non-SQL Server network traffic. If your server is a dedicated SQL Server, then you can assume that most of this traffic will be SQL Server generated. Because there is no easy way to compute whether or not there is a system bottleneck, work with your Network Engineers to understand the maximum capabilities of the network interface card that the server is using and then identify what percentage of utilization the card is being used at. This counter will actually provide more meaning over time as well. You can increase performance by adding faster or additional network cards, connecting the server to switches, making sure the cards are running in full duplex modes (see the following note), and trying to use only the TCP/IP Network-Library to communicate with the SQL Server.

> To verify the Link Speed & Duplex setting for the network card being used on the
> SQL Server Instance; from the server, select Start I Settings I Network and Dial-up
> Connections. Right-click and select Properties for the network connection you
> wish to verify. On the General, select Configure I Advanced I Link Speed &
> Duplex. In the Value drop-down list, make sure the selected value reflects the full
> capabilities of the network card within the context of your current network
> environment.

After running traces, it's a good idea to save them to a place on your network so that you have a
historical reference to the performance of your SQL Server.

We'll cover Perfmon in more depth in Chapter 13.

SQL Server Remote Administration

With staff downsizing occurring more and more these days, it's critical to be able to administer your
SQL Server remotely. This can be useful if you're away from the office and the performance of
connecting to your server via Enterprise Manager would be too slow. Thankfully, Microsoft has
provided a no-cost solution for this with Windows 2000 Server, Terminal Services. The simplest way
to describe Terminal Services is to compare it with what it is not. In the usual networked PC
infrastructure, all the processing is done locally and the data transfers are handled on the back-end.
Terminal Services, on the other hand, focuses all of the application processing in the server where it's
installed and then shares out the user interface. From the client's point of view, the processing is done
remotely; the only actions handled locally are things like the display, keyboard, mouse, and so on.

You can set up your SQL Server for Terminal Services in administration mode on the Server machine
and connect and manage your servers remotely. When you use Terminal Services in Remote
Administration mode, the server accepts only two Terminal Services client connections. When you use
this mode, you don't require licensing, but only members of the Administrators group can gain access
to the server. It's recommended that you use this mode for non-Terminal Services servers to configure
remote control-type access to remote servers.

To *connect* to Terminal Services hosted servers from your client computer, you can use the Remote
Desktop Connection application software offered by Microsoft. The software download and
instructions are located on http://www.microsoft.com/windowsxp/pro/downloads/rdclientdl.asp.

Try It Out–How to Install Terminal Services in Remote Administration Model

To install Terminal Services in Remote Administration, log on to the server locally as an
administrator, and then follow these steps:

1. Click Start I Settings I Control Panel and double-click Add/Remove Programs.

2. Click Add/Remove Windows Components.

3. After the Windows Components Wizard starts, click the Terminal Services check box, and then click Next.

   For more information about the subcomponents that are included in Terminal Services, click Details. The following subcomponents are displayed:

   ❑ Client Creator Files: Windows uses these files to create installation disks for Terminal Services client computers

   ❑ Enable Terminal Services: Windows uses this component to configure the Terminal Services software on your computer

4. On the Terminal Services Setup page, click Remote Administration mode, and then click Next.

5. If you're prompted, insert your original installation Windows 2000 Server CD.

6. When the installation is completed, click Finish, and then Close.

> **You don't need a Terminal Server Client Access License to run Terminal Services in Remote Administration mode. Therefore, Terminal Services Licensing isn't configured for the scenario that is described. A maximum of two concurrent connections are automatically allowed on a Terminal server in Remote Administration mode.**

Try It Out–Connecting with a Terminal Services Client

To connect to Terminal Services from the client:

1. Click Start I Settings I Control Panel and double-click Administrative Tools. In the Administrative Tools, double-click Terminal Services Items and then Terminal Services Client. Finally, click Terminal Services Client.

2. In the Server box, type a terminal server name, IP address, or select a server from the Available servers box.

3. Under Screen, select the screen resolution for the terminal server window. If you're connecting by using a modem or a slow network, click Use data compression.

4. If you would like to have commonly used bitmaps stored on your local hard disk, click Cache bitmaps to disk.

5. Click Connect.

6. The Log On to Windows dialog box now appears in the Terminal Services Client window. Type your username, password, and domain (if required).

This provides you, as the DBA, with great flexibility in how and when you can connect to your SQL Server database.

SQL Server as a Web Service

Web services, or XML web services, are the building blocks for the construction of distributed computing on the Internet. Open standards, such as HTTP and XML, with a focus on communication and collaboration among people and applications, have created an environment in which XML web services are becoming the platform for distributed application integration. Applications are constructed using multiple XML web services from various sources, which work together regardless of where they reside or how they were implemented.

Some of the characteristics of web services are as follows:

❑ Expose useful functionality to users through a standard protocol, such as HTTP

❑ Provide a way to describe interfaces so that a user can build an application to talk to them. This description is usually provided in an XML document called a WSDL (Web Services Description Language) document

❑ XML web services are registered so that potential users can find them easily. This is done with UDDI (Universal Discovery Description and Integration)

Practical Uses for XML Web Services

Over the years, the IT infrastructure in a company will change many times. New applications must coexist with older legacy systems, and vice versa. Systems architects and engineers are faced with complex integration scenarios as new technologies evolve and integrate into the day-to-day workings of a corporate environment. Usually these tools are from different vendors and have to be coupled with other products or applications.

The issues become even bigger when the applications that you want to work with belong to different organizations. More and more trading partners want to "talk" the same language, but who is going to redo their whole system for just one other partner? The chances are, you have multiple partners all with the same desire to integrate with your applications. The ideal solution would be to be able to exchange information and requests in a common way that has no dependency on the operating system, network protocols programming languages, and database systems of the partners.

XML web services are the vision for making this happen, and XML (eXtensible Market Language) is the core technology that makes this a reality. XML is a self-describing language, whereas SQL Server is a great tool for managing relational data. XML is the tool that can communicate that data without the bounds of an operating system, database server, or programming language.

Making Data Available as XML

To expose our SQL Server over HTTP we use the Configure SQL XML Support In IIS MMC (Microsoft Management Console) snap-in. With this snap-in, you can create and manage IIS virtual directories that publish XML data from SQL Server.

Try It Out–Configure an IIS Virtual Directory

1. From the Start button, click the Microsoft SQL Server I Configure SQL XML Support in IIS. By expanding the server icon you'll be shown all the websites that are currently running on the local server.

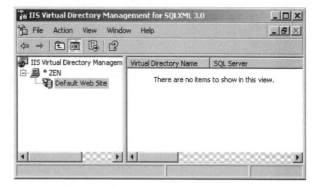

2. To create a new virtual directory for publishing, select the website that you want to publish the directory to, right-click, and select New I Virtual Directory from the menu. This will bring up the New Virtual Directory Properties window, which will allow you to configure your new directory.

   The first tab is used for specifying a name and a path for the virtual directory:

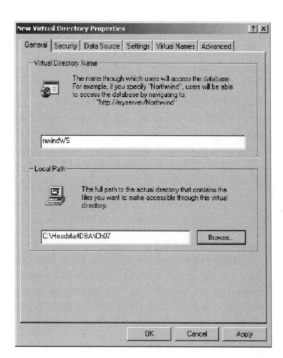

3. In the Virtual Directory Name text box, enter the name that will be used as part of the URL to access the data it publishes. In our example, users will access this as http://ZEN/nwindWS. Try to come up with a naming convention that makes sense for your organization and makes a meaningful reference to the data.

In the Local Path text box, enter the full path to the location of the virtual directory–related folder on your file system.

4. The type of authentication you choose for the users to connect to your virtual directory is configured on the Security tab.

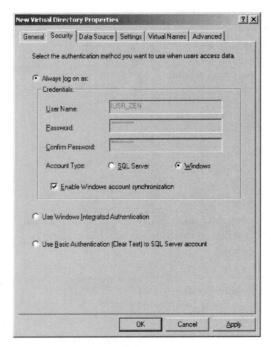

With SQL Server, you can choose one of two ways to connect to the server, the trusted server model or the impersonation/delegation model. In the trusted server model, the web server connects to the database using an "impersonated" anonymous account on behalf of the user. Using the impersonation/delegation model, the user enters an ID and password and the web server passes the credentials on to the SQL Server. The web server poses as the user when accessing the database.

For each authentication model, you can choose from integrated security based on a Windows 2000 user account or SQL Server security based on a separate SQL Server login.

You'll be selecting the trusted server model, by selecting the Always log on as option and selecting Windows for the Account Type. If a Windows account is specified, you can use any local or domain account. (The default is the local IUSR_ computername account used by IIS for anonymous access.) You can specify the password here or allow IIS to synchronize the password automatically. By default, Enable Windows account synchronization is selected.

For our walk-through, you must ensure that the specified Windows account (IUSR_computername) has access to the database and appropriate permissions for such database objects as tables, views, and stored procedures. See Chapter 6 to see how to set permissions.

5. On the Data Source tab, set the server and database that the Virtual Directory will use to get its data.

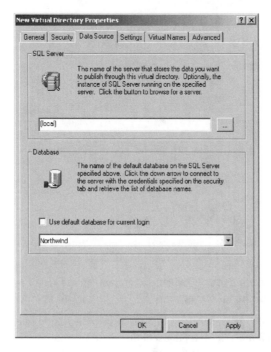

In the SQL Server text box, enter the server name that you'll connect to that has the database on it. In the Database drop-down list, select the database that you'll retrieve data from. This information, along with the security information, is what is used to create the connection string.

6. Next, select the way the users gain access to the data on the Settings tab.

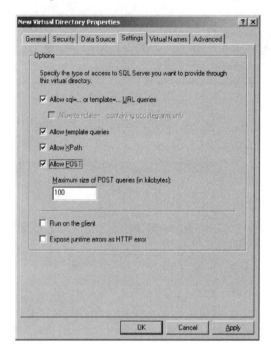

The options are as follows:

❏ Allow URL queries: Execute SQL queries directly at the URL. For security reasons, this option isn't recommended except for testing.

❏ Allow template queries: Execute a template in the URL. A template is a valid XML document, consisting of one or more SQL queries. This option is enabled by default.

❏ Allow XPath. Execute XPath queries against annotated mapping schemas directly at the URL. An annotated mapping schema is used to map XML elements and attributes to SQL Server database tables and columns.

❏ Allow POST. Enable the posting of the data to the database. By default, users cannot send data to the server but can access the data from the server.

> Using the POST method to send templates requires that both the Allow POST and Allow URL queries options be enabled, raising the same security issues that allowing URL queries does (which lets users execute any query against the virtual root and the database).

7. Specify the templates, XPath schemas, or database objects that will be used in URLs with virtual names. These are created and configured on the Virtual Names tab, as shown. Because the files and data elements aren't specified in the virtual names, this adds another layer of security.

You can use virtual names to represent folders containing the XML template or schema files. In the walk-through example, in the nwindWS virtual directory, you can assign the nwind virtual name to a folder that contains a template named customers.xml. This template would then be accessed using the following: http://localhost/nwindWS/nwind/customers.xml.

8. The final tab is used to configure some more advanced properties. Generally, you don't want to change any of the settings on this tab.

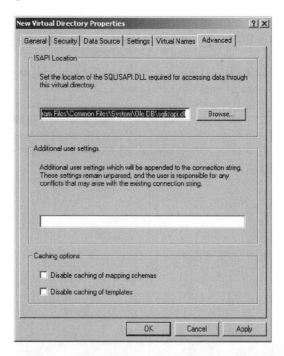

❑ ISAPI Location: Specify the location of the `Sqlisapi.dll`. This file is used to access an instance of SQL Server 2000 via the virtual directory. When the virtual directory is created on a remote server, you may need to provide the location of this file. The default location is Program Files\Common Files\System\Ole DB\. If you do decide to move the file from the default location, make sure that the `Sqlisapi.rll` file is also moved to that same location.

❑ Additional user settings: These settings are appended unparsed to the connection string passed in to OLE DB.

❑ Caching options: Select Disable caching of mapping schemas to prevent caching the mapping schemas. The mapping schemas are reloaded each time a query is executed against the schema.

Your business will greatly influence the exact configuration that you end up using for XML web services. The strengths of SQL Server coupled with XML web services allow you to define different data access methodologies for different situations.

Now, you'll explore some of the ways to access an XML web service with SQL Server.

Using T-SQL to Return XML

In the following examples, you'll look at the ways to access data from your SQL Server. We won't go into a lot of detail, because many a chapter could be spent going over the wonders of using SQL server and XML. Use this as a primer to help you explore the different ways of XML data access.

> *For more detailed information on using SQL Server with XML, please see Professional SQL Server 2000 XML by Apress and SQL Server 2000 XML Distilled by Kevin Williams et al.*

Try It Out–Accessing SQL Server Using an URL Query

The easiest way to access the server is by a straight inline query against your new virtual directory. Load your web browser and enter the following URL:

http://localhost/nwindWS?sql=SELECT+*+FROM+customers+FOR+XML+AUTO&root=customers

If you've followed the steps in the "Configure an IIS Virtual Directory" section earlier, the results of the query should look like this:

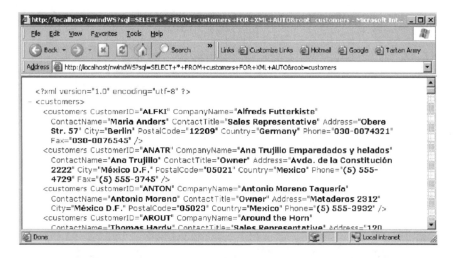

As you can imagine, this opens up endless possibilities of how data can be sent to end users in a more standardized way. You have now returned XML using an URL Query. With URL queries, you can issue SELECT statements using the FOR XML clause (described next), data modification statements (INSERT, UPDATE, DELETE), and stored procedure calls.

Using FOR XML

To retrieve results directly as XML documents rather than standard rowsets, use the FOR XML clause of the SELECT statement. Within the FOR XML clause, specify one of these XML modes:

❑ RAW: Creates each row in the query result set into an XML element with the unique identifier row

❑ AUTO: Returns the query results as nested elements

❑ EXPLICIT: Allows you to control how to output the results

> **These modes are in effect only for the execution of the query for which they're set. They do not affect the results of any subsequent queries.**

The following samples will give you an idea of the differences in the previous modes.

Try It Out–Using the FOR XML RAW Template

Save the following file (`rawhierarch.xml`) to the folder pointed to by your `nwind` virtual directory:

```
<root xmlns:sql="urn:schemas-microsoft-com:xml-sql" >
  <sql:query>
    SELECT Customers.CustomerID, OrderID
    FROM Customers
    LEFT OUTER JOIN Orders
    ON Customers.CustomerID = Orders.CustomerID
    FOR XML RAW
  </sql:query>
</root>
```

Browsing to it returns the following results:

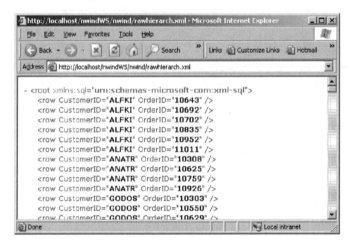

Try It Out–Using FOR XML AUTO

Do the same for the following file (`autohierarch.xml`):

```
<root xmlns:sql="urn:schemas-microsoft-com:xml-sql" >
  <sql:query>
    SELECT Customers.CustomerID, OrderID
    FROM Customers
    LEFT OUTER JOIN Orders
    ON Customers.CustomerID = Orders.CustomerID
    ORDER BY Customers.CustomerID
    FOR XML AUTO
  </sql:query>
</root>
```

Browsing to it produces the following result:

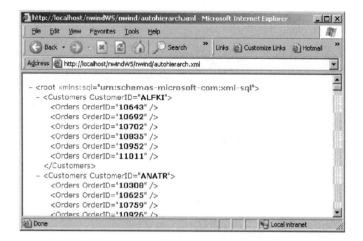

Try It Out–Using the FOR XML EXPLICIT Template

Finally, do the same with the following file (`siblings.xml`):

```
<root xmlns:sql="urn:schemas-microsoft-com:xml-sql" >
  <sql:query>
    SELECT 1 as TAG,
       NULL as Parent,
       CustomerID as [Customer!1!CustomerID],
       NULL as [Order!2!OrderID],
       NULL as [Employee!3!LastName]
    FROM Customers

    UNION ALL
    SELECT 2,
       1,
       Customers.CustomerID,
       Orders.OrderID,
       NULL
    FROM Orders
    JOIN Customers ON Orders.CustomerID = Customers.CustomerID

    UNION ALL
    SELECT DISTINCT 3,
       1,
       Customers.CustomerID,
       NULL,
       Employees.LastName
    FROM Customers
    JOIN Orders ON Customers.CustomerID = Orders.CustomerID
    JOIN Employees ON Orders.EmployeeID = Employees.EmployeeID

    ORDER BY
[Customer!1!CustomerID],[Employee!3!LastName],[Order!2!OrderID]
    FOR XML EXPLICIT
  </sql:query>
</root>
```

Running this returns the following result:

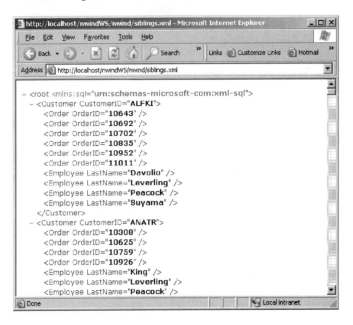

XPATH Query

The last example you'll look at is an XPath Query. XPath (XML Path language) is used to navigate and select a set of nodes from an XML document. For more information on the XPath language, see Books Online or *SQL Server 2000 XML Distilled*.

To run an XPath query, you need to return to the virtual directory and make some modifications. Open IIS Virtual Directory Management For SQLXML 3.0, right-click the nwindWS virtual directory, select Properties, and click the Virtual Names tab.

Earlier, you created a template virtual name called nwind. This is required to run XML template files, but to run XPath queries, you need to add a schema virtual name. Select a schema type, call it nwindXPath, and browse to the location where you'll put the XPath schema file. It can be the same folder as your previous example if you wish. Click Save and OK.

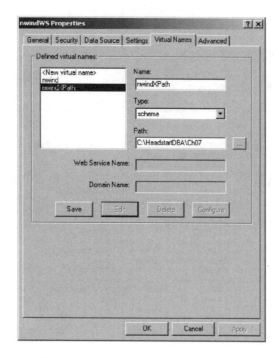

Save the following nwind.xdr file to your virtual directory and browse to it:

```
<?xml version="1.0" ?>
<Schema xmlns="urn:schemas-microsoft-com:xml-data"
        xmlns:sql="urn:schemas-microsoft-com:xml-sql">
  <ElementType name="Customer" sql:relation="Customers" >

     <!- attribute declarations for columns->

     <AttributeType name="ID" />
     <AttributeType name="name" />
     <AttributeType name="Address" />
     <AttributeType name="City" />
     <AttributeType name="State" />


     <!- declare the instances  ->

     <attribute type="ID" sql:field="CustomerID" />
     <attribute type="name" sql:field="CompanyName" />
     <attribute type="Address" />
     <attribute type="City" />
     <attribute type="State" sql:field="Region"/>
  </ElementType>
</Schema>
```

Now that you have the XPath schema in place, run the following query against it:

http://localhost/nwindWS/nwindXPath/nwind.xdr/Customer?root=root

Running this returns the following result:

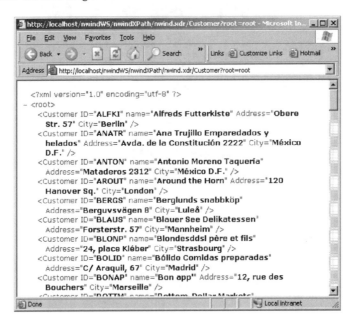

As you can see, there are many options available to provide XML to your consumers.

Other XML Tools and Resources

XML is perhaps the biggest single technology to evolve recently that has gained acceptance from all regions of the technology world. As a result, many vendors have created tools to help you work with XML in a more expedient and productive manner. The following are some must-have tools for working with XML web services and SQL Server 2000:

❑ Microsoft SQL Server 2000 Web Services Toolkit–
   http://www.microsoft.com/sql/techinfo/xml/default.asp. The Microsoft SQL Server 2000
   Web Services Toolkit includes several tools, code samples, and whitepapers related to SQL
   Server 2000 integrated XML Web applications and services.

❑ XMLSpy 5.0–http://www.altova.com/products_ide.html. XMLSpy is an IDE (Integrated
   Development Environment) used for developing applications that use XML-related technologies
   (such as XSL, SOAP, XML Schema, and WSDL).

Summary

Over the course of this chapter you've explored a lot of different topics from client tools to server configuration to programming interfaces to XML. The ability of a client to access your database in a timely and efficient manner will determine the way you're judged as a DBA. In the upcoming chapters you'll utilize a lot of what you've learned here to help you build and manage an efficient available SQL Server database.

8

Backup and Recovery

Backing up a database is **the** most important tasks of a DBA. By definition, this makes this chapter one of the most important in the book. So what do we plan on covering in this chapter?

❑ SQL Server Recovery Models and how these affect your ability to back up and restore a database

❑ Why you should backup a database in the first place

❑ Carrying out Full, Transaction, and Differential backups using Enterprise Manager and T-SQL

❑ The different types of media you can back up to

❑ What is a good "default" backup strategy

❑ Restoring database backups

❑ Planning your backup strategy to meet business requirements

❑ How to approach a disaster

So let's get started with a discussion of database Recovery Models.

Recovery Models

When planning your backup strategy, you need to consider which SQL Server Recovery Model setting you'll use for each of your databases. A **Recovery Model** is a setting that determines how transactions are logged within the transaction log, and how those transactions are retained within the transaction log. The available Recovery Models are as follows:

❑ Full

❑ Bulk-Logged

❑ Simple

Each of the Recovery Model settings affects transaction logging significantly. As you'll see, the most commonly used Recovery Models are Full and Simple, with Bulk-Logged usually being reserved for use during batch operations.

Full

Setting a database to use the **Full Recovery Model** allows a full database backup to be carried out and requires Transaction log backups to take place. The Transaction log backup is "required" because SQL Server purposely holds committed transactions within the transaction log until a Transaction log backup takes place. At this point, these committed transaction log entries are removed (as long as they have been written to the database via a checkpoint). If no Transaction log backup takes place, then the committed transactions are retained indefinitely within the transaction log, which will grow in size until all available space is consumed.

At a minimum when using the Full Recovery Model, you'll need to perform a Full database backup and a regular Transaction log backup. The frequency of each of these depends on your recovery requirements. Additional backup methods, such as Differential, File, and Filegroup, can also take place when using the Full Recovery Model when used in conjunction with the Full and Transaction log backups.

> **The Full Recovery Model is the most commonly used model for production databases, because it offers the most flexibility when restoring from database backups.**

Bulk-Logged

The Bulk-Logged Recovery Model is probably the most misunderstood and least used of the three Recovery Models, mainly because there is little difference between this and the Full Recovery Model.

The primary difference is that when using the **Bulk-Logged Recovery Model**, operations that affect a lot of data have their changes minimally logged (log extent changes rather than individual row changes are logged) as opposed to fully logged (logging of all row changes), thus reducing the amount of log space consumed by this type of statement. This can also result in a performance gain when running bulk logged commands. These commands include the following:

❑ CREATE INDEX: Creating a new index within a database

❑ SELECT INTO: Creating a new table based on the result set of a query

❑ BCP and BULK INSERT: Loading data into a table from an external file

❑ WRITETEXT and UPDATETEXT: Making changes to Text and Image columns

BULK_LOGGED allows you to minimize log space usage and maximize performance when carrying out bulk operations within a SQL Server database.

At first this sounds great, right? Get all the benefits of Full Recovery Model but use less space? Well, not quite. You lose the ability to restore to a given point in time (for that particular transaction log restoration). Note that you don't lose the ability to restore the database, but you do lose the ability to restore a Transaction log backup to a named date and time. This loss of functionality affects only the specific Transaction log backups that contain bulk operations while the database was in Bulked-Logged Recovery mode. You'll look at recovery to a point in time in the "Transaction Log Backup" section.

> **Usually databases should not be left in Bulk-Logged mode. This should be enabled for the duration of the bulk operations and then changed back to the Full Recovery Model once the bulk operations have completed.**

Simple

The **Simple Recovery Model** is, probably, the easiest to use of the Recovery Models. When using the Simple Recovery Model, committed transactions are removed from the transaction log as soon as they have been written to the database data files (checkpointed). Not only does this remove the need to carry out Transaction log backups, but it explicitly prevents them (because there are no transactions retained to back up).

As this effectively limits the backup methods available for the database to Full (a backup of everything in the database) and Differential (a backup of what has changed since the last full backup), this Recovery Model should only be used when recovery to a point in time (allowing for minimal data loss) isn't required, such as in a test environment or a low priority database. Note that File and Filegroup backups are also unavailable, because these must be performed in conjunction with a Transaction log backup (discussed later in the "Transaction Log Backup" section).

> **All production databases should use the Full Recovery Model unless there is a business requirement explicitly stating that recovery to the last full backup is all that is required.**

Recovery Model Matrix

The following matrix is a summary of the information we presented earlier. You can use this to help determine which Recovery Model works best for each of your databases.

	FULL	BULK_LOGGED	SIMPLE
Transaction Logging	The FULL Recovery Model creates the most transaction log entries All changes to individual rows are logged.	The BULK_LOGGED Recovery Model has the same log attributes as for the FULL Recovery Model, unless you're carrying out bulk operations. In this case only minimal information is entered into the transaction log.	Minimal information is entered into the transaction log. Row changes are logged for non-bulk operations.
Transaction Log Size	Transactions are held until you back up the transaction log. Size varies depending on number of transactions, volume or data modified in those transactions and frequency at which you perform Transaction log backups.	The log space requirements for a BULK-LOGGED Recovery Model are the same for the FULL except when doing bulk operations, in which case the BULK-LOGGED Recovery Model will require less transaction log space.	Completed transactions aren't retained in the transaction log. Space is only required for in progress (noncommitted) transactions.
Requirements & Benefits	Transaction log backups must be performed regularly. A database can be recovered to a point in time (assuming all necessary backups have been created).	Transaction log backups must be performed regularly. If a bulk operation has taken place, a database can be recovered to the end of the latest Transaction log backup. Otherwise, a database can be recovered to a point in time.	Transaction log backups aren't possible. A database can only be recovered to the last FULL or DIFFERENTIAL database backup.

For more information on the topics mentioned in this matrix (such as backing up the transaction log) keep reading this chapter.

Changing the Recovery Model

The Recovery Model can be changed using Enterprise Manager or T-SQL. This isn't something you would change on a regular basis, apart from changing between Full and Bulk-Logged before beginning a bulk operation.

You should be aware that if you set a database to the Simple Recovery Model and subsequently change to the FULL Recovery Model, you must perform a full database backup after the change to FULL before the Transaction log backups can be taken.

Using Enterprise Manager

To change the Recovery Model in Enterprise Manager, you use the database Properties window, which can be located by navigating to a specific database within Enterprise Manager, right-clicking, and selecting Properties from the pop-up menu. The Recovery Model setting is available on the Options tab.

Any change to this setting takes effect immediately.

Try It Out–Changing the Recovery Model Using Enterprise Manager

In this example, you change the Recovery Model of the Northwind database to Full.

1. Open the database properties for the Northwind database and choose the Options tab.

2. From the Model drop-down list, choose the Full option.

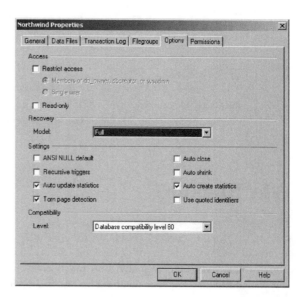

3. Click OK and the database is now using the Full Recovery Model. No other activity is required to set the Recovery Model.

Using T-SQL

To change a Recovery Model with T-SQL, you use the `ALTER DATABASE` command with the following syntax:

```
ALTER DATABASE database_name SET RECOVERY FULL |
                    BULK_LOGGED | SIMPLE
```

To execute the `ALTER DATABASE` command, the login must have one of the following privileges:

❑   `Sysadmin`

❑   `dbcreator`

Or the database user mapped to the login must be a member of the db_owner role.

Try It Out–Using ALTER DATABASE to change the Recovery Model

In this example, you change the Recovery Model being used by the `Northwind` database to the Full Recovery Model.

Connect to SQL Server using Query Analyzer and execute the following command:

```
ALTER DATABASE Northwind SET RECOVERY FULL
```

This immediately changes the Recovery Model to the Full Recovery Model. Transaction log backups can be performed after the next Full database backup has been carried out.

> **The Recovery Model of a newly create database will set to that of the Model database. If you wish future databases to have a specific default Recovery Model, change the Recovery Model of the Model database to your desired setting.**

Why Backup?

This seems obvious, but you do occasionally hear comments like "We have RAID disks, so why do we need to backup our system?" While it's true that many forms of hardware redundancy reduce the need to rebuild systems in the event of hardware failure, there are many types of failure that these measures won't protect you from. No matter how much investment you have in hardware redundancy, you always need to back up your database (unless it contains information that can be easily regenerated).

Hardware Failure

Hardware failure is still one of the most common reasons a database must be restored. Whereas redundancy goes a long way in reducing this, rarely can every component be made fully redundant. Although it's common for most servers to have redundant disks that allow for single disk failure without loss of information or server (when using RAID 1, 5, or 10), it's less common for servers to have redundant disk controllers, redundant CPUs, redundant memory, and so on. Even in highly mission critical environments where this sort of redundancy is more common, this never negates the need for backups.

> While it's relatively uncommon, multiple disks have been known to fail simultaneously. As many RAID levels only allow for single disk failure, multi-disk failure results in the loss of the entire disk array, and all information will require restoration once repaired.

Failure of any one of the nonredundant components can require restoration of the database due to data corruption. Alternately, a hardware failure can require a restoration to a separate server to resume service.

Clustered servers are two (or more) servers sharing a common disk subsystem, so that in the advent of a single server failure, there is another server available to take over the work of the failed server. But even on these high-availability cluster servers, there is a shared disk subsystem between servers that isn't fully redundant (components of the subsystem, such as disks and controllers, may be redundant but the entire disk subsystem itself isn't usually redundant). Failure of this shared disk subsystem can lead to the requirement to restore the database, even if individual server failure doesn't.

> High-availability clusters are considered an advanced topic and aren't discussed in detail in this book. For more information see Microsoft Press's *Microsoft SQL Server 2000 High Availability.*

Software Failure

Software failure can be put into two categories: system software failure and application software failure. These are completely different in cause, but the end result of each is the same–a database with corrupted or inaccessible information.

System Software Failure

The failure of system software (the operating system or SQL Server 2000) is quite uncommon, but does occasionally occur. In many cases, the actual cause can be traced to a third-party component, such as an application service or device driver. Other causes of system failures may be due to bugs within the code that cause exceptions in certain situations.

Whatever the cause (in theory), if the system can fail, then it may be possible for the result of this failure to cause a form of data corruption.

> **SQL Server 2000 running on Windows Server/Advanced Server is very robust. We haven't heard of a case where system software failure has been identified as the cause of data corruption.**

Application Software Failure

Application software failure is a much more common form of software failure, as typically applications don't undergo the same level of testing and bug fixing as system software does. A bug within the application code or an incompatibility with other software components on the user's computer usually causes the failure.

If bugs exist within the application, information may be modified in the database that doesn't meet the business rules imposed by the application. Alternatively, the application may terminate, leaving the data in violation of specific business rules. Both of these situations are a type of data corruption.

User Error

Unfortunately, this is a common cause of data corruption and there is little you, as an IT professional, can do to prevent it. Your IT systems may be in perfect health, the database environment may be stable, application security may be set correctly, and a privileged user may execute a task (that they should have privileges to do) by mistake.

Site Failure

Probably the least common of all types of failure (hopefully) is site failure. This is when the data center where your server is located becomes unavailable. This may be due to communications failure, electricity failure, or manmade or natural disasters. Protecting against this type of failure is more complicated than most. You have to be concerned with creating backups as well as having separate facilities with equipment where you can restore the backups, and a means of getting the backup media to those facilities.

Types of Backup

We've briefly mentioned several types of database Recovery Models throughout this chapter so far (Full, Transaction log, and so on), and now we we you'll look at all the available types of backups in detail. In addition, you'll carry out examples of each of these, so that you gain familiarity with using the appropriate commands and processes.

Full Backup

A **Full backup** is simply that, a full copy of the database as it currently stands. You're able to completely restore a database to the state it was in at the completion of the last Full backup.

A Full database backup is also the most important type of backup. Without it, you cannot run any other type of database backup (Transaction log, Differential, File, and Filegroup). The importance doesn't necessarily impact the frequency on which you should carry out the Full database backup, because this is determined by resource availability, but at some point you must carry out a Full database backup and retain it. Without a Full database backup, you stand to lose all the information within your database if a catastrophic failure occurs.

Using Enterprise Manager

There are several ways you can carry out a Full database backup within Enterprise Manager:

- ❑ The Backup Database dialog boxes
- ❑ The Backup Database wizard
- ❑ Using a maintenance plan

You'll look at maintenance plans later, but you'll discuss the first two methods now.

Backup Database Dialog Box

The Backup Database dialog box is available by right-clicking a database and selecting All Tasks I Backup Database, as shown:

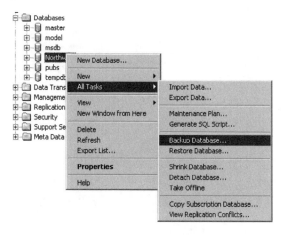

Or by choosing Tools I Backup Database from the Enterprise Manager Tools menu:

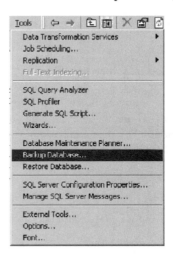

Either way will open the Backup Database dialog box as shown in the next screen shot. You enter all the relevant information needed to carry out a database backup on the following two tabs:

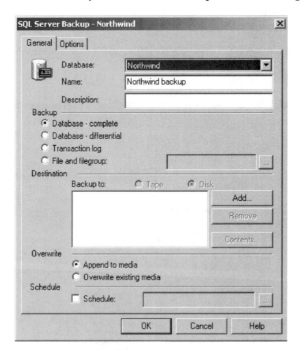

On the General tab, the options are as follows:

❑ Database: Name of the database to be backed up.

❑ Name: Name of the backup (used when selecting the backup to be used for restoration).

- ❑ Description: Place to enter additional "metadata" or notes about the backup.

- ❑ Backup: Backup type selection. For performing a full database backup, use the **Database – complete** option.

- ❑ Destination I Backup to: By clicking the **Add** button, you can specify the destination file or tape drive for this backup. You'll look at this in more detail in the next example.

- ❑ Overwrite: Specify if this backup is appended to a previous backup or if this backup overwrites any previous backups. This option is valid irrespective of whether you're backing up to a tape or disk file. If you specify **Append to media** for a tape backup, the database backup gets created at the end of the previous backups on that tape. If you specify the **Append to media** option for disk-based backups, the database backup gets appended to the end of any previous backups within the same disk file. The **Overwrite existing media** option for both types of media causes any existing backups to be removed by overwriting these with the new backup.

- ❑ Schedule: Allows you to specify when this backup should take place. This is useful if you're defining the backup during working hours but wish it to take place outside of working hours.

The Options tab also contains additional parameters that you can specify:

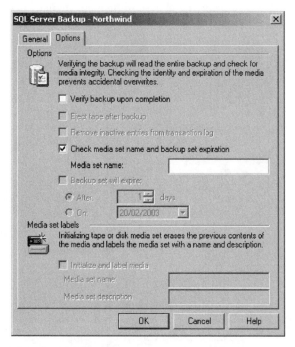

Some of the common options available within this tab are as follows:

- ❑ Verify backup on completion: Once the backup has been completed, SQL Server verifies the backup file that has been created to ensure that it's complete and readable. Verifying backups is a great idea and should always be done as part of your regular backup routines.

❑   Eject tape after backup: If backing up to a tape device, this will cause the tape to be ejected from the tape drive once the backup is completed.

❑   Remove inactive entries from transaction log: This option is available when you're performing a Transaction log backup. This option removes all the committed transactions from the transaction log once they have been backed up. This is normal operation for a Transaction log backup.

Most of the time, when performing an ad hoc backup, you don't need to change the options described previously. All you need to do is simply select the database and specify the backup location.

Try It Out–Performing a Full Backup of the Northwind Database

In this example, you'll be performing a Full backup of the Northwind database to a disk backup file.

1.   Connect to SQL Server using Enterprise Manager. Locate the Northwind database, right-click, and select All Tasks I Backup Database from the pop-up menu.

2.   Ensure the Northwind database is selected in the Database drop-down list. Enter Northwind backup in the Name field. In addition, select the option to Overwrite existing media (this will allow you to rerun this example if you choose without appending a new backup to the backup file every time).

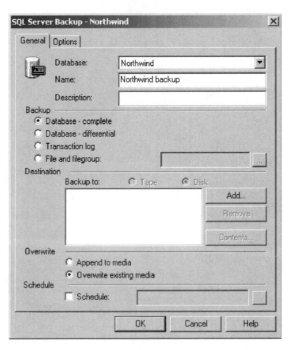

3.   Now you must specify the location where you wish to create the backup. Click the Add button under the Destination heading. The following dialog box will be displayed:

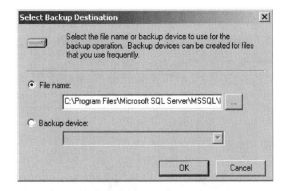

4. Click the ellipsis (...) button to open the backup device location. Navigate to the **Backup** folder under the **Microsoft SQL Server** directory. This depends on where you installed SQL Server, but if you used the default install options this should be under the following:

C:\Program Files\ Microsoft SQL Server\MSSQL\Backup

Now enter **Northwind backup.bak** as the backup file name in the appropriate field and click **OK**.

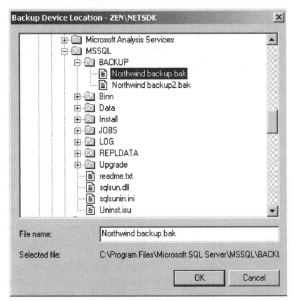

5. This filename and path will be displayed within the backup destination window so click **OK** again to close this window and return to the SQL Server Backup window.

> One physical Backup disk file can hold one or more SQL Server backups. If a SQL Server backup is appended to a physical backup file, the SQL Server backup information is retained in the same file as any previous SQL Server backups made to that backup file.

6. Now click the Options tab. The only option you wish to have checked is the Verify backup upon completion option.

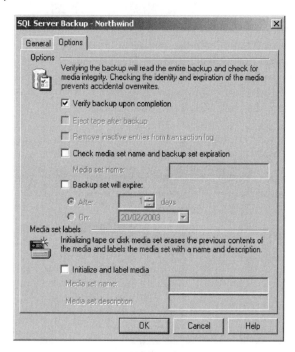

7. Finally, if you click OK, the backup will begin. Depending on the specification of your machine, this may only take a few seconds, or it may take a few minutes. Either way, when the backup is complete, you'll see the following message informing you that the backup was successful:

Note that if the task has been scheduled, you won't receive this message.

Backup Database Wizard

An alternative method of backing up a database is to use the Backup Database wizard. This can be located within Enterprise Manager by opening the Tools menu and choosing the Wizards menu item.

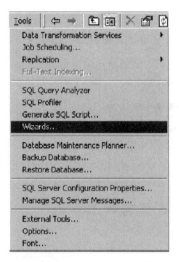

Once you've done this, the Select Wizard window will open. The wizard that you want to use is the Backup Wizard and is located under the Management node, as shown. Clicking OK will open the wizard.

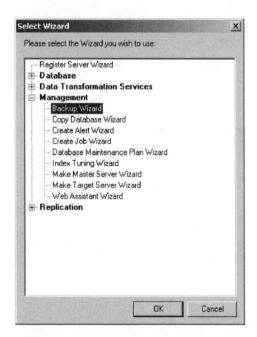

For example purposes, you'll carry out this backup again using the Backup Database wizard. We don't think this is a very useful method, because it doesn't really save any time in setting up a backup.

Try It Out–Creating a Full Backup with the Backup Database Wizard

In this example, you'll create a full backup of the Northwind database using the Backup Database wizard.

1. Open the Backup wizard. You'll be presented with the Welcome screen, so click Next.

2. On the next screen you need to choose which database you want to back up. For this example, choose the Northwind database and click Next.

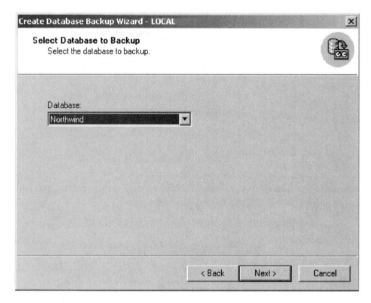

3. Now, enter the name of the backup and a brief description of the backup. Enter the information that is shown in the screen shot and click Next.

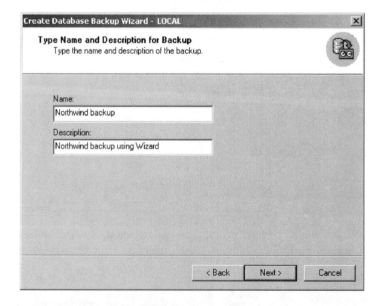

4. Next, you'll be asked to select the type of backup that you want to perform. For this example, choose Database backup – backup the entire database and click Next.

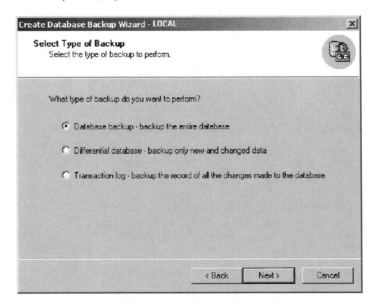

5. Now you'll specify the destination of the database backup. Because you'll want to back up to a file, select this option and enter the name of the file that you used in the last example, which was

C:\Program Files\ Microsoft SQL Server\MSSQL\Backup\Northwind backup.bak

Because you want to retain both the previous backup and this current backup, choose the Append to the backup media option. This will create a new database backup after the existing backup instead of overwriting it.

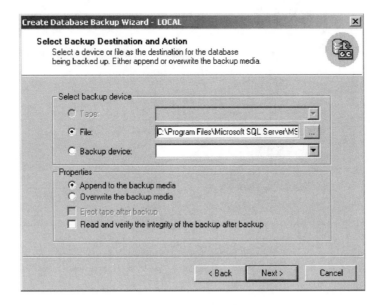

6. When you click Next, you'll be presented with the Backup Verification and Scheduling dialog box. Because you don't want to verify this backup or schedule a backup to run at a later point in time, you can leave these options unselected and click Next again.

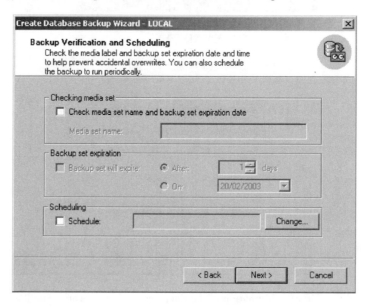

7. And that's it. You're shown a summary of the backup requirements, and when you click Finish, the backup will begin.

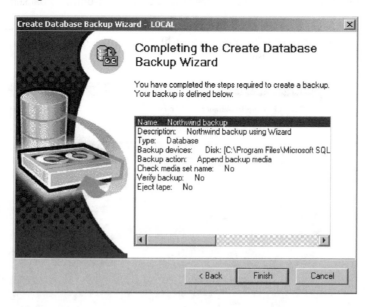

Once the backup has completed you'll be presented with a message that advises of successful completion.

Using T-SQL

You can also back up the database using T-SQL. In fact, behind the scenes Enterprise Manager is translating the requirements you enter graphically into the appropriate T-SQL command needed to back up the database.

To perform a Full backup of a database, you use the BACKUP DATABASE command, which in its simplest form has the following syntax (for disk-based backups):

```
BACKUP DATABASE dbname TO DISK=disk_location WITH option, option ...
```

Or for Tape backups to tape devices:

```
BACKUP DATABASE dbname TO TAPE=tape identifier WITH option, option ...
```

There are numerous option parameters you can specify, but some of the more common ones are as follows:

- ❑ INIT: Causes the current backup to overwrite any existing backups

- ❑ NOINIT: Causes the current backup to be appended to the end of any existing backups

- ❑ NAME: A name for the database backup

There are a number of other options that are available, some of which we discuss in this chapter. But for a full list, see the BACKUP command in SQL Server Books Online.

Try It Out–Backing Up a Database Using T-SQL

In this example, you use the BACKUP DATABASE command to carry out a Full database backup of the Northwind database to a disk-based backup location.

Connect to SQL Server using Query Analyzer. Enter and then execute the following command:

```
BACKUP DATABASE Northwind
TO DISK='C:\Program Files\Microsoft SQL Server\MSSQL\
Backup\Northwind backup.bak'
WITH INIT
```

This command tells SQL Server to create a Full database backup of the Northwind database. This backup is created on disk within the file specified (Northwind backup.bak). The INIT parameter instructs SQL Server to overwrite the existing contents of this backup file as opposed to appending this backup to the end of this file. You should get a status message informing you of the completion of this backup, as shown:

Processed 384 pages for database 'Northwind', file 'Northwind' on file 1.
Processed 1 pages for database 'Northwind', file 'Northwind_log' on file 1.
BACKUP DATABASE successfully processed 385 pages in 0.735 seconds (4.281 MB/sec) .

349

Transaction Log Backup

A **Transaction log backup** takes a copy of the transactions that have been committed within a specified database since the **last** Transaction log backup. Once these transactions have been backed up, they're removed from the transaction log (unless you explicitly specify that they should not be removed).

> **Transaction log backups can only be taken once a Full database backup has been created, and Transaction log backups can only be restored to a database if a valid Full database backup has been restored first.**

Transaction log backups allow you to essentially make incremental backups of the database. As each Transaction log backup contains the transactions that have taken place within the database since the last Transaction log backup (each backup is an increment), to restore from these Transaction log backups, you must make sure that you have each and every Transaction log backup that you've created after the Full database backup (the Full database backup that you're using as the base to restore to).

As long as the database remains in either the Full or Bulk-Logged Recovery Model, you should be able to carry out Transaction log backups. If the Recovery Model changes to Simple, then Transaction log backups aren't available.

You'll now look at several examples of backing up the database transaction log.

Using Enterprise Manager

As you saw when creating a Full database backup, there are a couple methods available for carrying out backups when using Enterprise Manager. Both of these methods are available for performing Transaction log backups, and you'll look at the difference between performing the Full and Transaction log backups here.

Using the SQL Server Backup Dialog Box

You can perform a Transaction log backup from the SQL Server Backup dialog box. The only change you need to make is to select the Transaction log option under the Backup heading. Once this is selected, all other options remain the same as they were for the Full database backup.

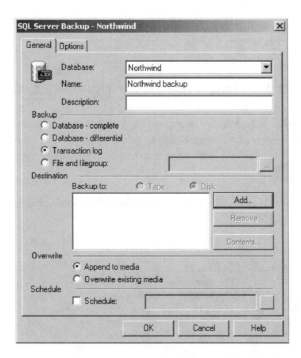

When you select the Destination, you can select to append the Transaction log backup to a destination that you have previously performed a Full database backup to. All backup types can be contained within one physical backup destination.

Using the Backup Database Wizard

The other option when carrying out a Full database backup is to use the Backup wizard. To create a Transaction log backup using this tool, you simply select this option on the Select Type of Backup window.

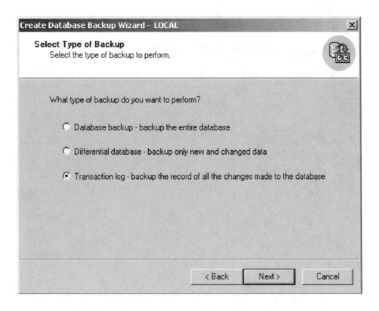

The remainder of the options presented by this wizard are consistent with the options that were available when you were creating the Full database backup.

Try It Out–Creating a Transactional Log Backup with Enterprise Manager

In this example, you use the SQL Server Backup dialog box to create a Transaction log backup of the Northwind database. However, as no transactions have taken place since you created the first database backup, you'll generate some transactions so the Transaction log backup has something to actually backup!

1. Connect to SQL Server using Query Analyzer. Enter the following command:

```
USE Northwind
GO
INSERT dbo.Customers(CustomerID, CompanyName,
                     ContactName, City, Country)
VALUES('TBALG','Tony Bain & Associates',
       'Linda Glucina','Christchurch', 'New Zealand')

INSERT dbo.Customers(CustomerID, CompanyName,
                     ContactName, City, Country)
VALUES('TBALM','Tony Bain & Associates',
       'Laura Major', 'Christchurch', 'New Zealand')
```

This simply inserts two rows into the Northwind database's Customers tables, and will have generated two transactions within the transaction log.

2. To backup these transactions in Enterprise Manager, right-click the Northwind database and choose All Tasks | Backup Database from the pop-up menu.

3. Within the Backup Database window, select the Transaction log option under the Backup header. Also, add the backup file you used to create the Full database backup, under the Destination. In the earlier example, this file was as follows:

C:\Program Files\Microsoft SQL Server\MSSQL\Backup\Northwind backup.bak

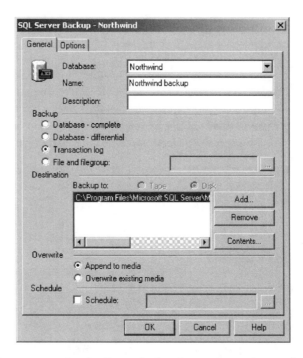

Make sure that you set the option under the **Overwrite** heading to **Append to media** so you don't overwrite the Full database backup (remember you can only restore a Transition log backup if you have a valid Full database backup, and all the Transaction log backups created after that Full database backup).

4. Click **OK** and the backup will commence. When completed you'll see a confirmation message like the following dialog box:

Using T-SQL

The T-SQL command that you use to tell SQL Server to carry out a Transaction log backup is **BACKUP LOG** (log as in transaction log). In its simplest form, it has the following syntax:

```
BACKUP LOG dbname TO DISK=disk_location WITH option, option ...
```

Or for backups to tape devices:

```
BACKUP LOG dbname TO TAPE=tape identifier WITH option, option ...
```

This is pretty much the same syntax as for the BACKUP DATABASE command. And as with that command, there are a number of options you can specify. For a full list see SQL Server Books Online.

Try It Out

In this example, you backup the database transaction log to a disk file using T-SQL. You choose to append the backup to the existing backup file as opposed to overwriting it. Again, you'll first generate a couple of transactions so you have something to backup.

Connect to SQL Server using Query Analyzer. Enter the following command:

```
USE Northwind
GO

INSERT dbo.Customers(CustomerID, CompanyName,
                        ContactName, City, Country)
VALUES('TBASB','Tony Bain & Associates',
        'Stephanie Bain','Christchurch', 'New Zealand')

INSERT dbo.Customers(CustomerID, CompanyName,
                        ContactName, City, Country)
VALUES('TBAWB','Tony Bain & Associates',
        'William Bain', 'Christchurch', 'New Zealand')
```

Once again this simply adds two new rows to the Customers table. Now you have something to backup, so execute the following command to carry out the Transaction log backup.

```
BACKUP LOG Northwind
TO DISK='C:\Program Files\Microsoft SQL Server\MSSQL\
Backup\Northwind backup.bak'
WITH NOINIT
```

As you can see, you're instructing SQL Server to backup the Transaction log for the Northwind database to the previously used database backup file. You're also specifying the NOINIT parameter to tell SQL Server not to overwrite any backups already contained within this file. You should get a status message informing you of the completion of this backup, as shown:

Processed 2 pages for database 'Northwind', file 'Northwind_log' on file 4.
BACKUP LOG successfully processed 2 pages in 0.086 seconds (0.107 MB/sec).

Differential Backup

A **Differential backup** backs up everything that has changed within a database since the last Full database backup. To restore a Differential backup, you need the last Full database backup and the latest good Differential backup.

A Differential backup is often incorrectly called an incremental backup, but this isn't strictly the case. Every Differential backup backs up everything that has changed since the last Full database backup, irrespective of what other Differential database backups have done. Over time, a Differential backup will get bigger and bigger (assuming the database is experiencing modification activity) as the number of "things" that have changed since that last Full database backup increases.

> **You don't require all Differential backups that have taken place to be able to restore, as with the Transaction log backups. To restore a Differential database backup, you just need the last Full database backup and the Differential backup you want to restore (usually this would be the most recent one).**

Using Enterprise Manager

To perform a Differential backup using Enterprise Manager, you can use either the SQL Server Backup dialog box or the Backup wizard again.

Within the SQL Server Backup dialog box, you simply set the Database – differential option under the Backup heading.

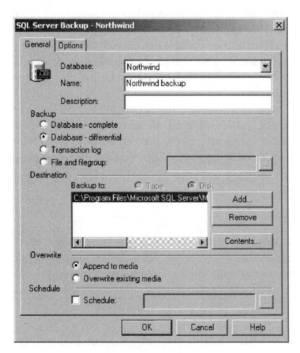

Within the Backup wizard, you simply select the Differential database – backup only new and changed data option.

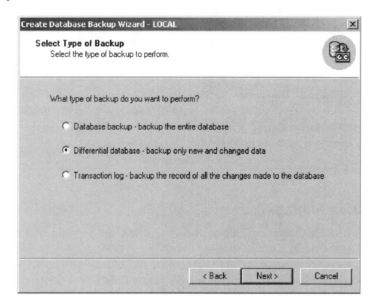

A Differential backup should not really be considered as an alternative to Transaction log backups because these don't clear the transaction log. In addition, each subsequent Differential backup is bigger and takes longer than the last (assuming database activity). Transaction log backups clear the log, and they also back up the transactions that have occurred since the last backup. This means that each backup isn't duplicating already backed-up information, thereby keeping the duration and size of each backup minimal.

Differential backups should be considered as an alternative to a regular Full database backup if there are limiting factors preventing you from carrying out Full database backups as often as you would like (such as the duration of periods of low system usage). You'll still need to perform Full database backups on a regular basis but this may be on a reduced schedule, such as Full weekly backups and daily Differential backups.

> **Always consider using a Full database backup before a Differential backup, because these make restoration simpler. Use a Differential backup if you have time or resource constraints that prevent a Full backup being carried out.**

Try It Out–Making a Differential Backup Using Enterprise Manager

In this example, you carry out a Differential backup using Enterprise Manager.

1. In Enterprise Manager, open the **SQL Server Backup** dialog box for the Northwind database (right-click, **All Tasks I Backup Database**). Select the **Database – differential** option under the **Backup** heading. For the backup **Destination**, enter the location of the backup file you've been using, which is

    C:\Program Files\Microsoft SQL Server\MSSQL\Backup\Northwind backup.bak

2. Once again, ensure that you have the **Append to media** option selected and click **OK**.

Using T-SQL

To perform a Differential backup using T-SQL, you use the `BACKUP DATABASE` command, but you also specify the `DIFFERENTIAL` option, with the following syntax:

```
BACKUP DATABASE dbname TO DISK=disk_location WITH DIFFERENTIAL, option ...
```

You can also use this option if you're backing up to tape.

Try It Out–Using T-SQL for a Differential Backup

In this example, you use T-SQL to create a Differential backup of the Northwind database.

Connect to SQL Server Query Analyzer and enter and the following command:

```
BACKUP DATABASE Northwind
TO DISK='C:\Program Files\Microsoft SQL Server\MSSQL\
Backup\Northwind backup.bak'
WITH DIFFERENTIAL, NOINIT
```

Because you've specified both the `DIFFERENTIAL` and `NOINIT` options, a Differential backup (a backup of everything that has changed since the last Full database backup) is appended to the database backup file. You should get a status message informing you of the completion of this backup, as shown:

Processed 19080 pages for database 'Northwind', file 'Northwind' on file 7.
Processed 1 pages for database 'Northwind', file 'Northwind_log' on file 7.
BACKUP DATABASE WITH DIFFERENTIAL successfully processed 19081 pages in 14.585 seconds (10.716 MB/sec).

Backup Media Types

When you create a backup in SQL Server, you can elect to back up the database directly to a tape device or to a backup disk file. You should carefully consider which option is most appropriate for your needs, because this can affect your ability to recover your database.

SQL Server Tape Backups

SQL Server can store the database on tape in a format that can only be read by SQL Server. When backing up from SQL Server to a tape device, you have a number of benefits and disadvantages that you should consider. First the benefits:

❏ **Retention.**

Tapes can be rotated and retained for long periods of time. Disks are limited in capacity, so only a limited number of historical backups can be retained.

❏ **Offsite storage.**

Tapes can be easily stored offsite to provide protection from disaster (fire, flood, etc.). Disks are usually not removable.

❏ **Cheap media.**

The cost of tape space is less than the cost of disk space. This allows the amount of collective space (combined space available on all tapes) to be increased by adding relatively cheap tapes to the media set.

However, where there are advantages, there are always disadvantages. And when using SQL Server tape backups, some of these are as follows:

❏ **Comparatively slow.**

High-end tape drives have good throughput; however, this is usually not equivalent to the throughput achievable using disks. This can cause backups to take longer.

❏ **Locality.**

SQL Server can only back up (natively) to a tape backup device that is physically connected to the server on which SQL Server is running. Remote tape drives cannot be used. This means you need a tape drive per server.

❏ **Availability.**

Tape backups can only be performed when there is a tape physically located within the server.

❏ **Costly infrastructure.**

If you need lots of tape storage, you may need a tape library. These can be costly, especially if you need to install these on multiple servers.

SQL Server Disk Backups

When using a disk-based backup, SQL Server allows you to specify a disk file location where the backup should be created. This is a disk file that is physically separate from any disk files used by the database itself (such as data and log files). The backup file is in use by SQL Server only for the duration of the backup, once completed the backup file can be moved, copied, removed, and so on.

The benefits of using a disk-based backup are as follows:

❑ **Fast**.

Disks can be considerably faster than tape backups, reducing the amount of time to back up the database.

❑ **Cheap infrastructure**.

Although the cost per GB for tape may be cheaper than the cost per GB for tape storage, the infrastructure required for tape storage can be more costly than that required for disk. For example, if you require 500GB of tape backup capacity, you may need to install a tape library. This can be expensive.

❑ **Always available.**

Tape backups require a tape to be physically within the tape drive before the backup can take place. Disk-based backups can be carried out at any time.

❑ **Network.**

SQL Server can back up to a disk located on another server (via a network share). This allows you to mitigate some of the risk of losing the entire server. However, using this approach normally causes you to lose the performance benefit (networks aren't usually as fast as I/O subsystems).

These benefits make using database file backups an attractive option. Yet there are some downsides, which are as follows:

❑ **Single media**.

A disk is only one device; if it's corrupted you lose all your backups. However, you can have numerous tapes that are rotated to greatly reduce the likelihood of complete loss of all backups.

❑ **Nonmovable.**

Tapes can be housed in secure offsite storage, which means that if you lose your server due to catastrophic disaster you still have your offsite backups to fall back on. Unfortunately, disks cannot be moved offsite, so there is more chance of losing the backups along with the current server.

❑ **Failure rate**.

Disks are perhaps one of the most likely components of a server to fail.

The Middle Ground

IT people are typically quite smart, and when there are two options each with a set of advantages and disadvantages, a common solution is to combine both methods to find the "middle ground." The common approach is to use a combination of native SQL Server Disk Backups and Operating System Level Tape Backups.

Using this combined approach you can do the following:

❏ Backup the database to a disk daily

❏ Backup the transaction log to a disk regularly

❏ Backup the backup disk files daily (or more often if required) to tape

This approach has the following benefits:

❏ Fast backup time: SQL Server can complete its backups quickly.

❏ Always available: SQL Server can perform its backups at any time.

❏ Cheap: You use cheap disks. You still require tape infrastructure; however, disk files **can** be backed up over the network. This means you can purchase the tape library and locate this on one server. You can then use it to back up all of the SQL Servers.

❏ Offsite storage. The tapes can be stored offsite, thus protecting from catastrophic disaster.

❏ Retention: You can use the disk for recent backups and retain backup tapes for historical purposes. This allows you to retain database backups for long periods of time.

But the following disadvantages remain:

❏ Exposure to catastrophic failure: If you're taking tape backups of your SQL Server backups on a daily basis, you still have the potential to lose up to 24 hours of data in the event of catastrophic failure (loss of both SQL Server data disks and SQL Server Backup disks, or loss of entire server).

❏ Administration effort: The tape and SQL Server backups need to be synchronized to ensure that the tape backup doesn't begin before SQL Server has completed the disk backups.

❏ Impact on network: If you have a centrally located tape library that is backing up your SQL Servers over the network, this may heavily impact your network performance for the duration of the backup. In large environments this can be mitigated by implementing a "back-end" network for server-to-server communications only.

Default Backup Strategy

Later in this chapter, we'll discuss how to assess the disaster recovery requirements as specified by your organization for a particular database. But what should you do if you don't have any requirements set by the business? What should you use if the database isn't critical enough for the business to make recommendations about the backup strategy?

In this section, we'll discuss a backup strategy, which can be used when you have no clear guidelines. However, this is by no means something you should implement without using your own judgment. The backup strategy discussed provides a balance between administrative effort, resource consumption, and recoverability; however, you should adjust the individual parameters of this strategy where you see fit.

> **Always try to get senior level business acceptance of any backup strategy. It's the business that is going to suffer, not the IT department, if the strategy doesn't meet the requirements.**

Use Full Recovery Model

The first decision you need to make is what Recovery Model to use. Unless you have been explicitly told otherwise, you should always use the Full Recovery Model. Even if you've been told that recovery to the last full backup is acceptable, you should still consider using the Full Recovery Model. After all, is anyone going to complain that you've restored their database to its state a couple of hours ago instead of 24 hours ago?

Perform Full Database Backups Daily

If you have no clear guidelines on how often a full database backup is required, you may want to carry out a full database backup on a daily basis. This should be done outside "peak" usage periods (such as overnight for a 9 to 5 business, or during the periods of lowest activity for a 24/7 business) as the process of performing the backup will slightly impact the performance of your server. This backup should be a SQL Server file backup to a dedicated disk within your server.

If your database is so large that it cannot be backed up during nonpeak times, you may want to use a combination of weekly full and daily differential backups. However, large databases are "typically" quite important (and the infrastructure required to support them is usually expensive), so you should always try to push the business to come up with a set of hard recovery requirements that you can use to determine your backup strategy.

Hourly Transaction Log Backups

If there are no constraints on recoverability, you may want to consider performing Transaction log backups every hour. This gives you a "reasonable" recovery timeframe (up to one hour of data loss) without over-complicating administrative effort, such as would be the case if you were backing up the transaction log every five minutes.

Nightly Tape Backups

And finally you should consider backing up the database backup files to tape every night after the full database backup has completed. Usually these will be performed by a centralized backup server accessing the network share of the disk, which is used to house SQL Server's database backup files.

These tapes should be included within a media rotation scheme, which causes each backup to be retained for a period of time before being overwritten.

Restores

If you know how to backup the database, you had better know how to restore it! Within this section you'll learn how to restore each type of backup that you created within the backup section. If you haven't carried out the examples in the backup section, you won't be able to carry out the examples shown in this section, so you may wish to go back and run through those examples first.

Full Database Backup Restoration

The first thing you need to learn is how to restore a full database backup. This is both the most common restoration and the most important. Before you can restore either a Transaction log backup or a differential backup, you must restore the full database backup.

Using Enterprise Manager

Unlike backups, there is only one method of restoring databases using Enterprise Manager, and this is using the Restore database dialog box. (There is no Restore Database wizard.) To open the Restore Database dialog box, right-click a database and select the All Tasks I Restore Database menu item from the pop-up menu.

On the General tab, there are a number of options that you can specify. First the database name that you wish the restored database to have. You can either select an existing database from the drop-down list (if you wish the restoration to overwrite an existing database), or you can manually type in a new database name (if you wish to restore the database backup into a newly created database).

> **Restoring a database backup into a new database with a different name to the live database is an effective way of testing the restore process without disrupting your live production database. Just be careful to make sure you're restoring into a different database!**

The remainder of the options on this tab depend on which Restore option you've selected. The choices are: Database, Filegroups or file and From device.

When the Database option is selected, you see a list of backups that have been created on this server for the selected database in the Show backups of database drop-down list. You can see within the figure that the Northwind database has been selected, and the backups that you created earlier in this chapter are listed within the list box.

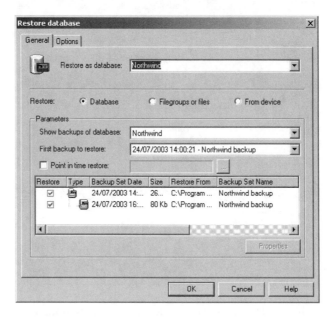

If you select the Filegroups or files option, you'll see a list of filegroups that have been backed up for this database. You'll see this option again later in this chapter.

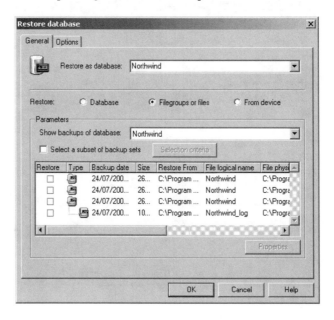

The third option, From device, allows you to locate a database backup that has been created on another server. Here you can locate a physical backup device (disk file or tape), and choose the specific backup within this file to restore.

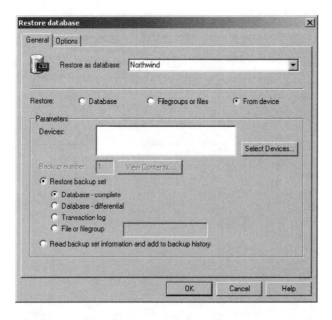

The Options tab within this window allows you to specify general restoration options, no matter how you locate the backup you wish to restore. This is shown in the next figure.

The important options within this dialog are

❑ Force restore over existing database: If a database of the same name exists, then this option must be specified to overwrite the existing database.

❑ Recovery completion state: This option is used to tell SQL Server how it should recover the database once the restore is completed.

   ❑ Leave database operational: Recover the database for normal use; however, no further backups can be restored.

   ❑ Leave database nonoperational: Restore the database, but don't recover it for normal use. Allow additional Transaction log backups to be restored.

   ❑ Leave database read-only: Restore the database and allow it to be used in a read-only manner. Use an undo file so that the recovery can be undone to allow additional backups to be restored.

Now you'll take a look at using this dialog box to restore Full database backups.

Restoring a Database from a Backup Created Locally

The easiest way to restore a Full database backup is to restore an existing database from a backup created on the local server. All you need to do in this example is select the appropriate backup you wish to restore from the backup history listing.

Try It Out

In this example, you'll restore the Northwind database from the backup you created earlier in this chapter.

Open the Restore database dialog box for the Northwind database. Make sure that the Northwind database is the database listed in the Restore as database drop-down list.

Within the Backup History list box, select the first backup (assuming you haven't performed any backups other that those in this chapter) from the History box.

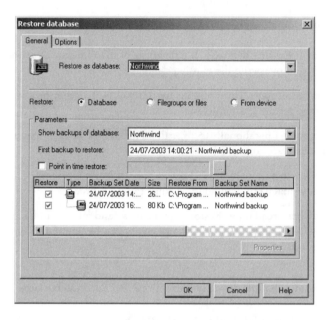

If you click the Properties button, at this point you'll see the available metadata for this particular backup.

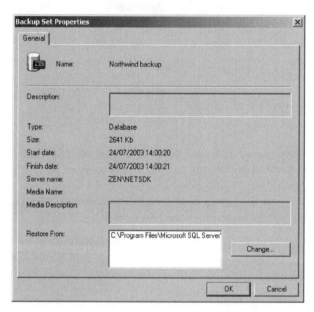

Click OK to close the Properties window, and click the OK button again to begin the database restoration. Depending on your hardware, this may take several minutes. During the restoration, you'll be kept informed of the restoration progress as shown here.

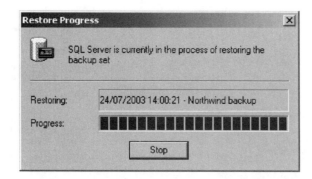

A database can only be restored if no users have an active connection to it. If, for example, you have Query Analyzer connected to SQL Server with Northwind selected as the current database and you try to restore from Enterprise Manager you'll receive an error informing you that a user has a connection to the database and the restoration cannot take place.

Restoring a Database from a Backup Created Elsewhere

If you have a database backup created on another server, you can restore this on any SQL Server just as long as the backup device is accessible by the server you want to restore to. However, because the backup was created on a separate server, your destination server has no information of the backup history of this remote database. So, to restore this database, you have to manually specify the location of the backup file, the specific backup within the file that you wish to restore, and the destination database where you wish to restore the backup to.

Try It Out

In this example, you'll simulate restoring a full database that has been created remotely. In reality, you'll be restoring the Northwind database from the backups you created locally; however, you'll be going through the motions required to restore a database from a backup that was created remotely.

Open the Restore database dialog box for the Northwind database. Ensure that Northwind is selected in the Restore as database drop-down list. Next, select the From device option from the Restore options.

Now click Select Devices to open the Choose Restore Devices dialog box as shown in the next figure. Here, you can add backup devices to restore from by clicking the Add button.

Clicking the Add button opens the Backup Device Location dialog box. Here you can navigate to the database backup file, which contains the backup you wish to restore from. In this example, select the backup file that you have created earlier in this chapter. While these backups were in fact created locally, they could have been created on another SQL Server as well.

Click OK to select the database backup file and then click OK again to accept the list of devices you wish to restore from. Now within the original Restore database dialog, you can click the View Contents button to view a list of all the backups contained within this backup file.

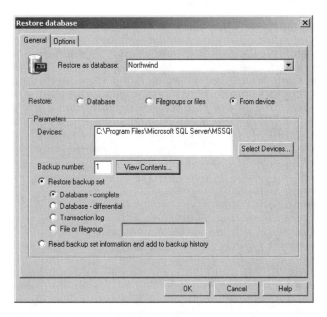

In this particular example, the backup you wish to restore is the first backup in the set.

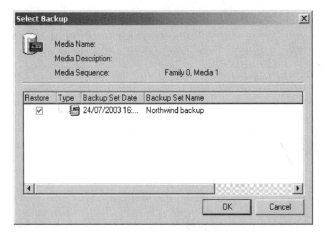

Click OK to close this window, and then click on the Options tab. First you click the Force restore over existing database option. This is because the Northwind database already exists, and you want to restore the database backup that you've just selected over the top of this existing database.

Next you should ensure that the physical filename paths shown under the Restore database files as heading map to physical file paths on the local server. If the backup was created on a remote server with a different disk configuration than the server you want to restore to, this file path parameter will have to be changed to match the file path of the local server. However, because the backup you're restoring was created on the same server, the physical file path is fine.

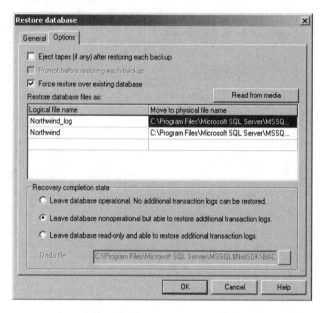

Finally you must select the **Leave database nonoperational but able to restore additional transaction logs** option, because you'll want to restore Transaction log backups in later examples. You can only restore Transaction log backups if you don't recover the database to an operational state after restoration.

Using T-SQL

To restore a database using T-SQL you use the RESTORE DATABASE command. In its simplest form, it has the following syntax:

```
RESTORE DATABASE dbname FROM DISK | TAPE = backup_location
WITH RECOVERY | NORECOVERY, REPLACE, FILE, option, option …
```

As you can see the syntax for RESTORE DATABASE is very similar to what you use when backing up the database using the BACKUP DATABASE command. A key difference is that the dbname parameter can be the name of a database that currently does or doesn't exist. If the database of that name does exist then it will be overwritten with the backup. If the database of that name doesn't exist, then a new database will be created. The options shown in the syntax example are as follows:

❑ RECOVERY: Once the restoration has completed, "recover" the database into an operational state. This allows the database to be used for normal operations, but it doesn't allow any Transaction log backups to be restored. If you wish to restore additional Transaction log backups, you must first restore the full database backup and specify the NORECOVERY option.

❑ NORECOVERY: The NORECOVERY option tells SQL Server not to "recover" the database into an operational state once the database restoration is completed. Instead the database will be inaccessible, but additional Transaction log backups can be restored. You must use the NORECOVERY option for every backup you wish to restore for a database except the very last one. When restoring the last database backup, you specify the RECOVERY option to tell SQL Server to make the database operational on completion of the restore.

❑ REPLACE: Replace must be specified when you're restoring a backup over an existing database. If REPLACE isn't specified, an error will be shown telling you that the database you're trying to restore already exists.

❑ FILE: When a physical backup location (disk file or backup tape) contains multiple backups that have been appended to that backup location, you must use the FILE option to specify which backup you wish to restore. File is a number starting at 1, which is used to indicate the first backup in the backup location.

RESTORE DATABASE has many more options available to help you control database restoration. We've covered the most common options; for more information on the less common options, see SQL Server Books Online.

Try It Out

In this example, you're going to restore the Northwind database from the full database backup using T-SQL.

Connect to SQL Server using Query Analyzer and enter the following command:

```
RESTORE DATABASE Northwind FROM
DISK='C:\Program Files\Microsoft SQL Server\MSSQL\
Backup\Northwind backup.bak'
WITH NORECOVERY, REPLACE, FILE=1
```

> **To restore a database you must first make sure that no one has a connection established to that database.**

This will restore the Northwind database from the Northwind backup.bak file. The NORECOVERY option tells SQL Server not to return the database to the operational state. This means that you won't be able to use the Northwind database after issuing this command (don't worry you'll fix this a little later!). The REPLACE option tells SQL Server to overwrite the existing Northwind database. Finally the FILE option is used to tell SQL Server to restore the first backup in the backup location.

When you execute this command the restoration will begin. This may take anywhere between a few seconds to a few minutes depending on your hardware specification. Once completed, you should see a confirmation message similar to the one shown here:

```
Processed 19080 pages for database 'Northwind', file 'Northwind' on file 1.
Processed 1 pages for database 'Northwind', file 'Northwind_log' on file 1.
RESTORE DATABASE successfully processed 19081 pages in 95.509 seconds (1.636 MB/sec).
```

> **You cannot schedule a database backup to run at a later date and time from T-SQL. However you can add your** BACKUP **command as part of a SQL Agent job that is scheduled to run at the desired date and time.**

Transaction Log Backup Restoration

Once you've restored a full database backup that hasn't been recovered, you can proceed to restore Transaction log backups. Each Transaction log backup applies all the transactions that took place between the last backup (full or transaction log) and the time that the Transaction log backup was created. To successfully restore a series of Transaction log backups, you require a full database backup and every Transaction log backup that was created after the full database backup right through the last Transaction log backup you wish to restore. If you don't have a copy of all of these Transaction log backups, you *cannot* restore past the point where a log file is missing.

Using Enterprise Manager

Once you've restored a full database backup specifying the NORECOVERY option you'll notice that the database is colored gray and has the (Loading) status next to it in Enterprise Manager. If you try to access anything within the database you won't be able to. However, this is the correct state of the database to allow the restoration of Transaction log backups.

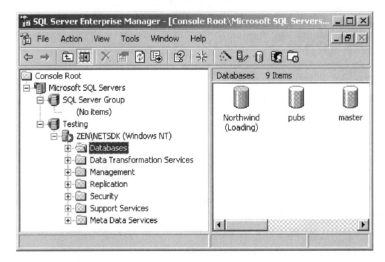

To restore the Transaction log backups in Enterprise Manager, you use the same Restore database dialog box that you used to restore Full database backups. However, instead of selecting the Full database backup to restore, you now select individual Transaction log backups. When you have the Restore: Database option selected (which displays the backup history), Transaction log backups are displayed with an indented icon, as shown in the figure in the "Using Enterprise Management" section earlier.

Once you've selected a Transaction log backup, you can also select the Point in time restore option. Instead of applying all of the transactions within the transaction log, you can choose to only apply the transactions that happened prior to a specific point in time. For example, if a transaction that removed some important data occurred at 10:05 a.m. (and you knew this when it happened), you could choose to restore the backed-up transactions to 10:04 a.m., thereby avoiding the transaction that incorrectly removed data. However, all transactions that occurred after 10:04 a.m. would be lost, and no further Transaction log backups in the sequence can be restored. The next figure shows an example of restoring only the transactions from the transaction log backups that originally occurred before a certain date and time.

> **Point-in-time recovery is a good Data Recovery tool; however, it's only useful if you know the time the corruption occurred.**

Try It Out

In this example you use SQL Server Enterprise Manager to restore one of the Transaction log backups you created earlier in this chapter.

Open the Restore database dialog box for the Northwind database. In the backup history list box, select the first Transaction log backup that is displayed, as shown in the next figure.

Because the database is still in the unrecovered state from the previous Full database restore, you're able to apply this Transaction log backup.

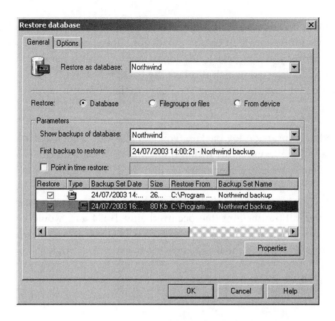

Now on the Options tab make sure you check Leave database nonoperational, because you have another Transaction log backup that you wish to restore a little later on. If you had selected the Leave database operational option, you wouldn't be able to restore additional Transaction log backups.

If you accidentally make your database operational when you still have remaining transaction logs to restore you must start the restoration process again, beginning with the restoration of the full database backup.

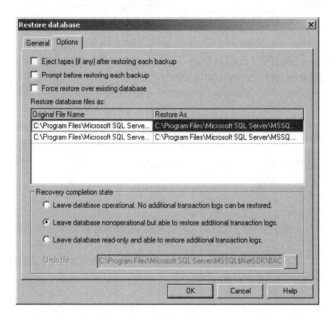

Click OK to carry out the transaction log restore. You'll receive a message letting you know that the restore was successful.

Using T-SQL

You can carry out a transaction log restore using T-SQL as well. You do this by issuing the RESTORE LOG command. In its simplest form, this has the following syntax:

```
RESTORE LOG dbname FROM DISK | TAPE = backup_location
WITH RECOVERY | NORECOVERY, FILE, option, option …
```

As you can see this is very similar to the RESTORE DATABASE command, and once again there are numerous options you can specify (for the full list see SQL Server Books Online).

Try It Out

In this example you'll restore the last Transaction log backup, and recover the database to a usable state.

Connect to SQL Server using Query Analyzer, and enter and the following command:

```
RESTORE LOG Northwind FROM
DISK='C:\Program Files\Microsoft SQL Server\MSSQL\
Backup\Northwind backup.bak'
WITH RECOVERY, FILE=3
```

This will restore the second Transaction log backup (the third backup in the file) and because you have specified the RECOVERY option, this causes the database to be made operational for normal use.

The inserts you made in the customers table a while back are available after the restoration of the Transaction log backups. To do this enter and execute the following T-SQL SELECT statement:

```
USE Northwind
GO
SELECT CustomerID, CompanyName, ContactName
FROM Customers
WHERE CustomerID LIKE 'TBA%'
```

This should produce the following result:

CustomerID	CompanyName	ContactName
TBALG	Tony Bain & Associates	Linda Glucina
TBALM	Tony Bain & Associates	Laura Major
TBASB	Tony Bain & Associates	Stephanie Bain
TBAWB	Tony Bain & Associates	William Bain

Differential Backup Restoration

The final type of backup that you'll need to restore is the Differential backup. A Differential backup contains all the changes that have been made since that last Full backup. To restore this backup, you only need the last Full backup and the most recent Differential backup.

Using Enterprise Manager

To restore a Differential backup using Enterprise Manager, you use the same method that you used for Full and Transaction log backups. All you need to do is select the Differential backup from the backup history, as shown in the figure (although it's hard to see, the icon for the Differential backup is blue).

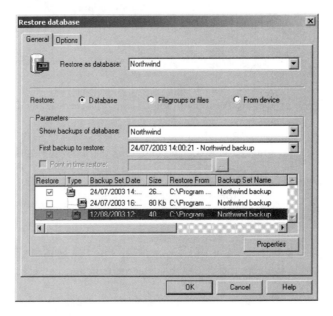

Try It Out

In this example, you restore the Differential backup that you created earlier in this chapter. To restore the Differential backup, you first need to restore the Full database backup (just as happened when subsequently restoring additional Transaction log backups).

Open the Restore database dialog for the Northwind database, and choose the Differential backup from the Backup History list box (this will be the fourth entry in the backup history. The differential backup is indicated by a blue database icon). Because you must first restore the Full database backup, SQL Server will automatically select this for us. So when you click OK, first the Full database restore will take place, and then the Differential restore will take place.

Using T-SQL

You use the RESTORE DATABASE command to restore a differential database. SQL Server knows that it's restoring a differential database based on the information contained in the backup file. This has the following syntax:

```
RESTORE DATABASE dbname FROM DISK | TAPE = backup_location
WITH RECOVERY | NORECOVERY, FILE, option, option ...
```

This is the same syntax you used when restoring a Full database backup.

Try It Out

In this example, you use the RESTORE DATBASE command to first restore the Full database backup, and then use the RESTORE DATABASE command again to restore the Differential backup.

Connect to SQL Server using Query Analyzer, and enter the following command. This tells SQL Server to restore Northwind database from the Full backup that you created earlier.

```
RESTORE DATABASE Northwind FROM
DISK='C:\Program Files\Microsoft SQL Server\MSSQL\
Backup\Northwind backup.bak'
WITH NORECOVERY, REPLACE, FILE=1
```

Now that the Full database has been restored, you can proceed to restore the Differential backup that applies all the changes that occurred after the Full database backup was created.

```
RESTORE DATABASE Northwind FROM
DISK='C:\Program Files\Microsoft SQL Server\MSSQL\
Backup\Northwind backup.bak'
WITH RECOVERY, FILE=4
```

You can validate that the "differential" changes have been applied correctly by rerunning the T-SQL SELECT statement, which retrieves the rows you inserted in the Northwind database after you had carried out the full backup.

```
USE Northwind
GO
SELECT CustomerID, CompanyName, ContactName
FROM Customers
WHERE CustomerID LIKE 'TBA%'
```

This should produce the following result:

CustomerID	CompanyName	ContactName
TBALG	Tony Bain & Associates	Linda Glucina
TBALM	Tony Bain & Associates	Laura Major
TBASB	Tony Bain & Associates	Stephanie Bain
TBAWB	Tony Bain & Associates	William Bain

Advanced Backup & Restore

Next, let's look at some more advanced backup and restore methods.

Backing Up the Log File when the Data Files Are Corrupted

You discussed early on in this book that it's good practice to create your database data files and database log files on different physical disks. Besides performance, this provides benefits in terms of recovery as well. If the disk on which the database data file(s) reside fails, but the disk on which the database log file(s) reside remains OK, then you can back up the database log file to use when restoring the database. This allows you to recover the database **without data loss**. However, this is only possible if the following is true:

❑ The database is using the FULL RECOVERY model.

❑ You have previously performed a Full database backup.

❑ You have all Transaction log backups that have been created since the last good Full database backup was created.

To ensure that there is no data lost, you need *all* the transaction logs from the last Full backup to the point of failure. Therefore if you're performing regular Transaction log backups to disk, it's a really good idea *not* to place these on the same disk as the database data files. Ideally these will be placed on their own physical disk separate from both the disk used for the data files and the disk used for the transaction log.

Try It Out

In this example, you'll create a test database, do some backups, and then simulate data file corruption. After the corruption has occurred, we'll show how you can still backup the active portion of the transaction log, and recover the database fully without the loss of any committed information.

> **For demonstrating this example, you create a test database to specifically demonstrate recovery in the event of corrupted data file. Make sure you use the test database shown in this example. *Don't use* any database that contains valuable information!**

Connect to SQL Server using Query Analyzer. The first thing you need to do is create the test database. To do this you simply execute the CREATE DATABASE command.

```
CREATE DATABASE SimulateDataFailure
```

Next, you need to ensure that you're using the FULL Recovery Model. Remember, you can only backup and restore the transaction log when using the FULL Recovery Model. To do this, you execute the following command:

```
ALTER DATABASE SimulateDataFailure SET RECOVERY FULL
GO
```

Now that you've created the test database, you need to create a table within this database to demonstrate the application of transactions within the Transaction log backups. To do this, execute the following CREATE TABLE command:

```
USE SimulateDataFailure
GO
CREATE TABLE SimulateDataFailure
(
    IdCol    INT    PRIMARY KEY,
    DateCol DATETIME DEFAULT(GETDATE())
)
```

Now you can start inserting data into this table. Make sure you follow closely when you INSERT the data because you'll be doing backups throughout the process to "simulate" the lead up to disk failure that may occur within a production environment.

So at this point, NO backups have been made. First you insert three rows by executing the following commands:

```
INSERT SimulateDataFailure(IdCol) VALUES(1)
INSERT SimulateDataFailure(IdCol) VALUES(2)
INSERT SimulateDataFailure(IdCol) VALUES(3)
```

You now take a FULL database backup. This Full backup contains everything within the database up to this point, that is, the three rows you inserted earlier. To carry out the full database backup, execute the following command. This command creates a new backup file named c:\SimulateDataFailure.bak, which contains a full backup of the SimulateDataFailure database.

```
BACKUP DATABASE SimulateDataFailure
TO DISK='C:\SimulateDataFailure.BAK'
WITH INIT
```

After the Full database backup has taken place, you can proceed to insert another three rows by executing the following three commands:

```
INSERT SimulateDataFailure(IdCol) VALUES(4)
INSERT SimulateDataFailure(IdCol) VALUES(5)
INSERT SimulateDataFailure(IdCol) VALUES(6)
```

Typically in a production environment, a Transaction log backup is done on a fixed schedule. If this demonstration was representative of the production environment, an hour may have passed (depending on the schedule), and many hundreds or thousands of transactions may have taken place during this time.

Once these rows have been inserted, you take a Transaction log backup from the database. This backs up all transactions contained within the log that have been committed, but not yet backed up. Once these transactions have been backup up, they are removed from the transaction log. To carry out the Transaction log backup, you execute the following command:

```
BACKUP LOG SimulateDataFailure
TO DISK='C:\SimulateDataFailure.BAK'
WITH NOINIT
```

Now that you've backed up the current state of the database, let's insert three more rows by executing the following commands:

```
INSERT SimulateDataFailure(IdCol) VALUES(7)
INSERT SimulateDataFailure(IdCol) VALUES(8)
INSERT SimulateDataFailure(IdCol) VALUES(9)
```

At this point in time, NO backup of the last three rows exists. You are now going to simulate the failure of the disk, which contains the user database data files.

To simulate this disk failure, you first need to stop the SQL Server service. In reality the service wouldn't be stopped if a disk failed; however, you need to stop the service for the purpose of this example. This is because SQL Server holds exclusive file locks on the database data files while the SQL Server service is running, so you cannot do anything nasty to them using Windows Explorer until these locks are released (by stopping the service).

Connect to your server using the SQL Server Service Manager tool, and click the Stop button.

Once the SQL Server service has stopped, use Windows Explorer to navigate to the location where your default database data files are kept. The physical disk path depends on where you installed SQL Server. If you left these paths at the default setting, and you've installed a default instance as opposed to a named instance, these files would be located at

`C:\PROGRAM FILES\MICROSOFT SQL SERVER\MSSQL\DATA`

If you've changed any of the default settings, you'll need to navigate to the correct path. Once you find the correct data file location, you should see the `SimulateDataFailure.MDF` and `SimulateDataFailure_log.LDF` files as shown in the figure. The MDF file is the data file and the LDF file is the transaction log file (remember on a production server usually these would be on separate physical disks, not in the same directory as in this example).

You simulate data disk device failure using a simple, but effective method. Right-click the `SimulateDataFailure.mdf` file, and delete it. Removing this file by deleting it is identical to losing this data file by losing access to the disk where it's physically located.

> **Make sure you delete only the `SimulateDataFailure.mdf`. If you accidentally delete any of the system database files, you may prevent SQL Server from functioning.**

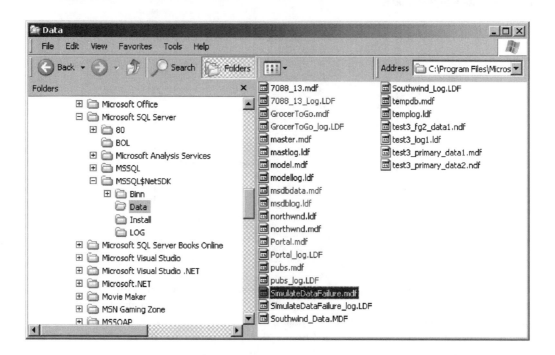

Once you've removed this file, you can restart SQL Server. To do this, open the SQL Server Service Manager and click the green Go button.

Once SQL Server has started, examine the database list within Enterprise Manager. You should see the SimulateDataFailure database in the list of databases. Notice that it's gray in color and marked with the Suspect status (if you don't see this, you probably need to refresh Enterprise Manager. Right-click the Databases node and choose Refresh). The database is marked as suspect because an important part of it, the primary data file, is inaccessible, and the database cannot be used for normal operations. In fact if you try to drill into this database, you'll see that no information about the objects within this database is available.

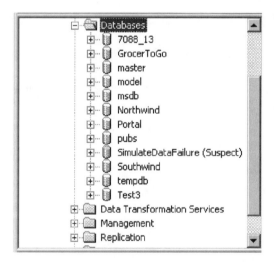

So what can you do? Well. one of the first things you should do in this circumstance is to take a backup of the transaction log (assuming that this is still accessible). The easiest way to do this is using Query Analyzer. Execute the BACKUP LOG command as shown here. This differs slightly from the previous command because you also specify the NO_TRUNCATE parameter. Because the database is "broken," no changes (including the removal of committed transactions from the transaction log) can be made to it. By specifying the NO_TRUNCATE parameter, this backs up the transactions within the transaction log, but doesn't try to remove them thus allowing a Transaction log backup to take place without error. Also, notice that you specify the NOINIT option. This option prevents you from overwriting the historical backups that you've created because overwriting these at this point would not be desirable!

```
BACKUP LOG SimulateDataFailure
TO DISK='C:\SimulateDataFailure.BAK'
WITH NOINIT, NO_TRUNCATE
```

Now remove the damaged database because no more useful information is available in it. To do this you issue the DROP DATABASE command as shown:

```
DROP DATABASE SimulateDataFailure
```

Now that you've dropped the database, there is one more thing you need to do before you attempt to restore it from backup. The DROP DATABASE command physically removes the database from being registered within SQL Server; however, it doesn't physically remove database files from the disk. Before you create a new version of this database, you need to delete the existing SimulateDataFailure.LDF file. Once again, be careful to delete the correct file.

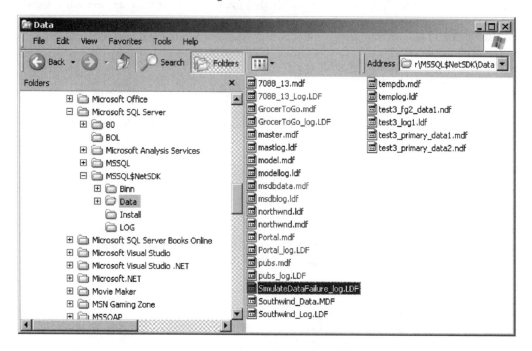

At this point the broken database has been removed form the SQL Server, and any remaining associated data files have been removed as well. You now have the following:

❑   A Full database backup taken soon after database creation

❑   A Transaction log backup taken prior to data disk device failure

❑   A Transaction log backup taken after the data disk device failure

So let's start restoring these database backups. First you must restore the Full database backup (remember you always need a Full database backup). The Full database backup was the first that you created, so you specify the FILE=1 parameter to tell SQL Server to restore the first backup within the backup file. You also specify the NORECOVERY option to tell SQL Server to leave the database in a format suitable for restoring additional backups.

```
RESTORE DATABASE SimulateDataFailure
FROM DISK='C:\SimulateDataFailure.BAK'
WITH FILE=1, NORECOVERY
```

Next, you restore the Transaction log backup that you created after the database backup. Because this was the second backup you created, you specify the FILE=2 parameter and once again specify the NORECOVERY option to allow further restorations.

```
RESTORE LOG SimulateDataFailure
FROM DISK='C:\SimulateDataFailure.BAK'
WITH FILE=2, NORECOVERY
```

Finally you can restore the Transaction log backup that you created **after** the data device had failed. This was the third backup you created, so you use the FILE=3 parameter. This time you specify the RECOVERY option to instruct SQL Server to recover the database into normal operational mode.

```
RESTORE LOG SimulateDataFailure
FROM DISK='C:\SimulateDataFailure.BAK'
WITH FILE=3, RECOVERY
```

To check that you haven't lost anything even after deleting the core database data file, you can execute a simple query against the SimulateDataFailure table, as shown:

```
USE SimulateDataFailure
GO
SELECT * FROM SimulateDataFailure
```

And you should receive a list of rows similar to the one shown here. You've recovered the database fully up to the point where the disk device failure occurred, and you haven't lost a single committed transaction (uncommitted, in-progress transactions would have been lost).

IdCol	DateCol
1	2003-01-22 17:51:07.550
2	2003-01-22 17:51:07.590
3	2003-01-22 17:51:07.590
4	2003-01-22 17:51:08.410
5	2003-01-22 17:51:08.410
6	2003-01-22 17:51:08.410
7	2003-01-22 17:51:08.690
8	2003-01-22 17:51:08.690
9	2003-01-22 17:51:08.690

Restoring the Database to a New Location

When you're restoring a database from a backup that was created previously from that the same database, you usually don't have to worry about changing file options to ensure that the restored database is located in the correct file path. This is because the original location of the database data and log files is part of the metadata retained within the backup. When you come to restore a backup, the original file locations are known from the backup header and this information is used as a default.

> **When you restore a database backup in SQL Server 2000 overtop of an existing database, that existing database is dropped and replaced with the backup image.**

However, you may wish to backup a database to a location different from one contained in the metadata. So SQL Server provides a way to specify the path where you wish the data and log files to be located as part of the restore process.

Try It Out–Restoring a Database to a New Path Using Enterprise Manager

In this example, you use Enterprise Manager to restore a copy of the Northwind database to a new database called Southwind. As part of this restore, you specify where you wish the data and log files of the Southwind database to be located. This example assumes that you backed up the Northwind database in the earlier example.

Before you begin this example, create a new database named Southwind as follows:

```
CREATE DATABASE Southwind
```

When restoring a database, you don't have to select an existing database to replace it; however, you should do that in this example to see the "moving" of restored files when you restore the database using Enterprise Manager.

1. Connect to SQL Server using Enterprise Manager. Drill into your server and right-click the Databases node. Choose **All Tasks | Restore Database** from the pop-up menu.

2. In the **Restore database** dialog box, select Southwind as the name of the database you wish to restore.

3. Next, choose the From device option, and select the backup file you used to backup your Northwind database.

4. Now click the Options tab. Within the Restore Database files as: option box, you'll notice that the database files the SQL Server will attempt to restore have the **same name and file path** as those of the Northwind database when you originally backed it up. But obviously the physical files of the Northwind database still exist and are still being used by the original Northwind database. If you attempt to restore the Southwind database at this point, an error would occur indicating that these files exist and cannot not be overwritten.

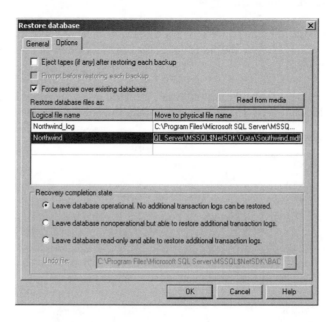

What you need to do is to change these to the **filename path** you require for the data files to be restored for the Southwind database. So, for this example, change the Northwind component of the filename to Southwind as shown. Because you're replacing the existing Southwind database you must select the Force restore over existing database option as shown in the figure.

The Logical and Physical database file information is recorded within the database backup files as part of the database backup. This is why when you try to restore the Northwind backup by default, it tries to restore the database to data files located at their original paths. In this example you're restoring a backup of one database into a new database. In this case the original file locations aren't appropriate (because these are still being used) and you must supply alternative filenames.

5. If you click OK at this point, the restore of the Southwind database from the original backup of the Northwind database begins. This creates new data and log files, which are named appropriately for the Southwind database.

Try It Out–Restoring a Database to a New Path Using T-SQL

You can restore a database and create the data files with a file path that differs from their original file path using T-SQL by specifying the MOVE option with the RESTORE command. But before you can move the database files, you need to know what files are actually contained within the backup itself. To do this you issue the RESTORE FILELISTONLY command as shown.

```
RESTORE FILELISTONLY
FROM DISK='C:\Program Files\Microsoft SQL Server\
MSSQL\BACKUP\Northwind backup.bak'
```

This produces a resultset showing you what files will be restored from this database backup, and their default.

> RESTORE FILELISTONLY **doesn't restore the database. This only shows us information relating to the data files that will be restored when you do attempt to restore the database fully.**

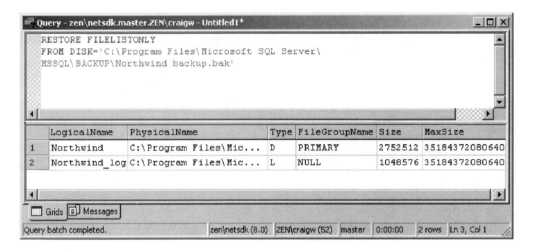

```
RESTORE FILELISTONLY
FROM DISK='C:\Program Files\Microsoft SQL Server\
MSSQL\BACKUP\Northwind backup.bak'
```

	LogicalName	PhysicalName	Type	FileGroupName	Size	MaxSize
1	Northwind	C:\Program Files\Mic...	D	PRIMARY	2752512	35184372080640
2	Northwind_log	C:\Program Files\Mic...	L	NULL	1048576	35184372080640

The LogicalName values are what you use within the MOVE part of the RESTORE command to relocate the database data files. For example, to restore the Southwind database, you would issue the following command:

```
RESTORE DATABASE Southwind
FROM DISK='C:\Program Files\Microsoft SQL Server\MSSQL\
BACKUP\Northwind backup.bak'
WITH MOVE 'Northwind'
    TO 'C:\Program Files\Microsoft SQL Server\MSSQL\
data\Southwind.mdf',
MOVE 'Northwind_log'
    TO 'C:\Program Files\Microsoft SQL Server\MSSQL\
data\Southwind.ldf',
REPLACE
```

Backup and Restore Procedures

So far we've discussed the physical backup and restore techniques that you can use to protect your database environment from failure. However, the combination of backup methods that you choose to use, as well as the frequency you choose to carry out these backups doesn't depend on the "physical" properties of the backup method, but the recovery requirements of that database as determined by your organization. While you may be the most knowledgeable person within your organization on "how" to perform database backups in SQL Server, the methods you use, and the frequency at which you carry out these backups, isn't determined by your judgment, but instead by what is required to meet the recovery requirements of your organization.

Backup Strategy

The backup strategy you use to protect your database environment should be customized for every production database to meet the business requirements. We did present a "generic" backup strategy earlier in this chapter, but this wasn't meant to be a replacement for the strategy you derive from business requirements. The generic strategy is meant as a helpful recommendation that you can use as a base plan.

Basically what you need to determine is how important the particular database application is to the business operation, how much data can be lost without incurring unreasonable costs, and how long can the database application be unavailable without severely impacting the business operations.

> Often, when asked about their downtime and data loss requirements, many organizations will initially say neither is acceptable. It isn't until you budget the cost of coming close to this that these organizations will objectively think about their actual requirements.

Data Loss Requirement

You always have the potential to lose some data. SQL Server on an appropriate infrastructure, can process hundreds of transactions a second. So even if you take a database backup every second (which would be very extreme), you would still have the ability to lose some transactions between the time you took the last backup and the time that the database failed. In some cases (depending on the type of failure), you may not incur any data loss; however, it's very difficult and very expensive to provide 100 percent protection from data loss in all failure situations.

With all business expectations, you're balancing the cost to provide the protection, with the costs in the event of a failure, and how much the users are willing to risk. If, for example, your users calculate that they will lose $100,000 or productivity if their core business transaction system failed, and you had to restore to the last full backup from 24 hours ago. If you could provide protection from this for an extra $10,000, this would seem like a good investment.

However, if the users calculated that they would loose $500 if they lost 5 minutes of data from their production database, and you estimated that it would cost $5,000 to provide protection for this, then this investment may not be justified.

Downtime Requirement

The same balance needs to be met for downtime. The amount of time that an application can be unavailable usually dictates the amount of redundant hardware that you purchase to get the application running again. Once again, if the application being unavailable for two hours costs an organization $50,000 in lost productivity and you estimate that you can provide 99.9 percent availability with your current infrastructure, this calculates to 8.76 hours or $438,000 per year, which isn't very attractive. If you could "reinvest" some of this lost productivity, and provide 99.99 percent availability by spending an extra $100,000 on redundant hardware, this reduces down time to 0.876 hours or $43,800 per year, resulting in a savings of $394,200 per year.

In the real world, calculating the cost of downtime isn't as straightforward because there are many factors that you must consider. However, it's an extremely valuable, and often an eye-opening process that any organization serious about IT should undertake.

> **Zero data loss and zero downtime is very difficult, if not impossible to achieve. In either case, the closer you come to achieving this goal the more costly it usually becomes. Therefore the cost of protection needs to be balanced against the cost of the data loss and downtime to ensure suitable ROI for your organization.**

Meet These Requirements

So once you've determined the organizational requirements, how do you go about meeting them? Well ensuring that you have suitable hardware in terms of specification and redundancy goes a long way in reducing the likelihood of any disaster. Most production-quality servers in use these days have redundant disk arrays (RAID) and redundant power supplies as these are some of the most common forms of hardware failure.

When specifically looking at what you can do within SQL Server to address your organization's data recovery requirements for a given database, you can use a combination of backup methods to allow you to meet these requirements. Let's take a look at several situations and some backup solutions for each of these situations.

Examples

Situation: An organization has an important transaction processing database, which, in the event of failure, they have allowed for up to 20 minutes of data loss and downtime of 5 hours. However, they aren't prepared to have a redundant server available for use in case of complete server failure. This is a risk they are prepared to take.

Solution: You should use RAID disks and have three separate drive arrays at least (additional drive arrays may be required for performance or data volume reasons). One array for the database data files, one for the transaction log files, and one for the database backup file. On the backup disk you should take a full database backup every night and Transaction log backups every 20 minutes. Also, every night after the disk based backup takes place, you backup the backup files to tape.

If the log disk was to fail, you could recover the database off the disk using last night's Full database backup and all the Transaction log backups that had taken place since the Full backup. You would thus get the following:

❑ Max data loss: 20 minutes

❑ Downtime: medium

If the data disk was to fail, you could still backup the transaction log, and recover the database from the Full database backup and all the Transaction log backups since this last Full backup. Thus you would get the following:

❑   Data loss: nil

❑   Downtime: medium

If the backup disk was to fail, you could repair this immediately, and take a new Full database backup giving you the following:

❑   Data loss: nil

❑   Down time: low

If the server was to fail, you would have to go back to last night's backup once the server was repaired resulting in the following:

❑   Max data loss: 24 hours

❑   Downtime: high

Situation: The organization has a very large data warehouse that changes throughout the week. Because all changes happen in batch jobs, you only need to restore to the point after the last batch job. You don't have time during the week to carry out a full database backup every day. The organization wouldn't suffer if they lost a week's worth of data; however, they would want the server available within 7 hours of failure. The organization cannot justify the cost of installing specific disks to perform backups, because this would require a separate disk controller, cabinet, and 700GBs of disk space.

Solution: Back up the database every week to tape using a Full database backup during the weekend. Back up the database to tape once a day using a Differential backup after each batch job.

If the database became corrupted in any way, you could restore the database from the last Full backup, and the last Differential backup resulting in the following:

❑   Data loss: nil

❑   Downtime: medium

Test Restores

This topic is so obvious that it's almost silly, but testing after restoring remains so uncommon that it's a concern. Let's consider the following fictitious but perfectly possible scenario:

Almost every organization performs backups. Most DBAs (database administrators) back up every day, put this backup onto a tape in some way or another, and then store it at some offsite facility. The tape may sit at the offsite storage facility for a few days, weeks, months, or even years (depending on its place in the cycle) until it's retrieved again and overwritten with the most current backup. Then it's back to the storage facility again. This process can continue uninterrupted over the course of years till one day suddenly the server, the disks, or the CPU fails, causing a total loss of all production databases. "No problem," says the DBA "you've got backups." Someone normally brings the tapes in when they're due to be reused, but it's now 6 p.m. on Friday. What is the number of the offsite storage facility? What do you mean, they're closed until Monday? Is there an after-hours emergency number? There is, but they charge a pricey callout fee. Am I authorized to incur this fee? How do I get a hold of my manager after hours? OK, let's just get the tape back....

Three hours later...finally, the offsite provider has arrived with the tape! Overnight batch jobs were supposed to start two hours ago, so you're already seriously behind. But at least you've got the tape back. OK, the server has died, but no problem because you have a spare server that you can use to restore the backup to. Wait a minute, it has a different model tape drive in it that doesn't work with the backup tape you used on the production server! So now you must change the tape drives over....

Four and a half hours later...OK it's now 4.5 hours since the server crashed and you haven't begun the restore process yet. Well at least you have the tape drive installed so you can begin restoring the backup file to disk....gosh you didn't realize how big the backup file had gotten. It's now 5.25 hours since the server failed and the backup file has been restored, but you hadn't noticed how big it had gotten over the last 6 months. It's now 20GB in size but this server only has 36GB of available disk space. This means that you don't have enough space for both the backup file and to recover the actual database. So we'll just have to move the backup file to a network location. The file server has plenty of disk space, you'll move it there...hmmm, it takes a very long time to copy 26GB across a 100Mb LAN...10 hours and 25 minutes since the server failed and you aren't stressed. Ahhhhh. Not stressed whatsoever. Finally you can begin the database install. But first you better install SQL Server on this server. So where is the installation CD? In the software cabinet behind the reception desk. The cabinet the receptionist locks every night when she goes home...You aren't sure how you're going to explain why the software cabinet has the lock broken open and a screwdriver sticking in it on Monday. But at least you've got SQL Server installed and I can begin the restoration. Finally...15 hours 34 minutes and 26 seconds since the server failed and you've almost got the test server functioning again. The status bar is about 90 percent of the way across and you're starting to relax. *Beep*. What was that beep? Hang on a pop-up box has appeared. What does it say, my eyes are too blurry? Restore failed due to corruption in the backup file. What?!?! AHHHHHHHHHHHHHHHHH!

Sounds dramatic? But this isn't far from scenarios we've witnessed and heard of in real production environments for real reputable companies. It doesn't matter how good your backup strategy is, if you don't test it you may find you've been wasting your time all along.

You should test your backups and test them regularly. There are a number of tests that you need to do, and you should do each of these tests on a schedule that fits within your time availability, but as a matter of high priority:

❑   Using a test server, restore a production database into a test database from a backup file and reapply Transaction log backups

❑ Using a test server, restore a database's backup files from tape made a week ago, and restore the database from those files that have been restored off tape

❑ Using a test server, trash the server and rebuild it completely. Reinstall the operating system, SQL Server, and restore the databases from backup

❑ Using a test server, simulate failure of your database data disk. Restore the databases to operational state from this position

❑ Using a test server, simulate failure of your database log disk. Restore the databases to operational state from this position

❑ Using a test server, corrupt some data in a table and restore the database in this situation

Every time you do this, make sure that you time yourself. Also, make a note of how long the restores took, any issues you encounter, and what you've done to mitigate those issues. A schedule may be as follows:

❑ **Every day** (using a test server).

Restore a selected database using Full and Transaction log backups.

❑ **Every other day** (using a test server).

Restore the backup files from tape and restore a selected database from those Full and Transaction log backups.

❑ **Every week** (using a test server).

Simulate disk failure of your database data files and then the log files. Also simulate table corruption. Restore the backups in this situation.

❑ **Every month** (definitely using a test server).

Simulate server corruption and completely rebuild your test server and restore all databases using Full and Transaction log backups.

This may sound like an intensive schedule, but let me remind you that "Backups are the most important activity of a DBA." You should be testing them regularly; doing so helps you sleep a little easier as well!

Approach to Disaster

So once you've established your procedures and you've gotten into a routine of regularly testing of those procedures, you're functionally prepared for disaster. However, when that day arrives, and it likely will at least once during your career as a DBA, how should you approach the situation to ensure you restore operation to your organization with the least amount of fuss, commotion, and emotion?

Don't Panic!

We've seen stable, experienced, respected IT professionals turn into illogical, emotional wrecks when faced with disaster. This state of mind leads to knee-jerk reactions and bad decisions. Rebooting servers, stopping and starting servers, replacing hardware, restoring databases **without reason** and **without proper consideration** may result in an intensification of the present disaster.

Although the users, their managers, and maybe even your manager is stressing out and demanding you fix the problem immediately, the measure of a "good" DBA is someone who can stay calm and collected in spite of the commotion. Taking your time, gathering your thoughts, and using your established procedures will help to resolve the situation with minimal loss of data with minimal downtime.

Assess the Situation

Something has happened to cause the disaster, and you cannot begin to repair the environment if you aren't aware of what the cause was. Doing so may result in the disaster recurring, which will be even more inconvenient for users as well as embarrassing (at the least) for you.

If the situation was caused by hardware fault, get your hardware people to resolve the problem. If the corruption was caused by users, determine which user, or which user action, caused the corruption so you can prevent the task being carried out again post restoration (or at least notify the users not to repeat their action).

Determine the Scale of the Problem

Some problems such as user corruption of valid data may be localized to a few rows within one or more tables. A hardware problem, on the other hand, may have destroyed one or more databases on your server. The scale of the disaster is an important consideration in the course of action you choose to take.

Determine the Course of Action

Once you have assessed the situation, you must determine the course of action to take to resolve it.

Courses of action you may choose to take include the following:

- ❏ Using the application undo function (if one exists)

- ❏ Have the users re-key data (type all the information within your database in again, assuming you have paper records)

- ❏ Restore a parallel environment and extracted corrupted rows

- ❏ Restore the database environment

Using the Application Undo Function

Some applications don't actually UPDATE or DELETE rows, instead they simply add new rows with a current datetime value. This is done to maintain a historical log of activity within the database. Some applications also use this information to allow operations within the application to be effectively undone. It's much more desirable to undo information corruption from within the application than restoring the database.

Have the Users Re-Key Data

If only a small amount of data has been lost or corrupted, then rather than disturbing the entire user population for a period of time while a full restoration of the database takes place (which could be minutes or hours depending on the size of the database), it may be more efficient to have the users repair or re-enter the information from within the application. The point where restoring the database becomes optimal over re-keying the data is objective, but should be determined by talking to key application users.

> **If you need users to re-key information, make sure you make this request to their managers, not directly to the users themselves. Don't become unfavorable with your organization's management by assigning work to their staff without their knowledge!**

Restore to a Parallel Environment and Extract Corrupt Records

If you're familiar with the records that have been corrupted, an alternative approach to restoring over the top of the existing production database is to restore into a temporary database. From this temporary database, you can extract only the records that have become corrupted within the production database, and copy these into the production database.

A common method of doing this is to use the following INSERT–SELECT combination for databases within the same SQL Server instance:

```
INSERT ProductionDatabase.Owner.TableName
SELECT *
FROM TemporaryDatabase.Owner.TableName
WHERE RowPrimaryKey IN (MissingRecordsPK, MissingRecordsPK ...)
```

Alternatively, you can use DTS for databases that are located in separate instances of SQL Server or are located on separate physical servers.

> **Restoring at the table level was available in SQL Server 6.5, but hasn't been available since this version. Only database level restores are available.**

Restore the Database Environment

This is the course of action to take if all else fails. This involves restoring a full copy of your database from the last good Full backup, and restoring as many Transaction log backups in order since the Full backup was created. While this is taking place, no user can access the database.

Notify the Business

Despite popular belief, most users are reasonable creatures. However, they are known to become unreasonable and occasionally irrational if they are left uninformed. Like it or not, a database is a part of the users' systems, not the DBA's. When a problem occurs, there is a strong desire to focus entirely on resolving the problem and to ignore user inquires altogether. Although this may result in the problem being fixed slightly more quickly, you have to be aware that by taking this approach, you may be causing additional loss of productivity to your organization. Without an idea of how long the database is going to be unavailable, users tend to sit and wait, retrying their applications until they become available. This may be minutes or hours because at this point, the users have no idea.

So once you've assessed the situation, you should inform users of the expected duration of the database outage and the course of action being taken. Even if the users aren't thrilled about the expected duration, it gives them the ability to carry out other duties and come back and try the system at a later stage. It also gives users the reassurance that the problem is being taken seriously, and that someone is working on getting the situation resolved.

> **Many organizations have an IT help desk or support groups that have the responsibility of notifying users of system problems. As a DBA it's your job to simply notify the support desk of the expected duration of the outage.**

Preserve the Current Situation

Even if your database environment is in a bad shape, you should always try to take a copy of the environment as it currently stands before you attempt any problem resolution steps. If you can take a backup, take one. This may be a full database backup and/or a Transaction log backup depending on the nature of the problem. If the SQL Server service won't start, you may choose to simply copy the database disk files to a separate location.

This may seem pointless, but if at some point at a later point in time it's discovered that a critical piece of information has been lost during the disaster, at least you have a chance (no matter how small) of getting it back.

> **Make a copy of everything that you can from your production database. Something that you retain from the corrupted environment may prove invaluable during a recovery or at a later time.**

Repair the Current Environment

Once you've saved as much information as possible from the current environment, then you can start to repair it. This may mean replacing server hardware, such as disks, reinstalling the OS, or replacing the server completely.

Use Your Procedures

When you've decided on the course of action, make sure you use your tried and tested procedures. It's tempting, very tempting to dive in and solve the problem quickly, disregarding the formality imposed by following a set of procedures, **but don't fall into this trap**. You created your procedures during quiet, sane times, and now in the midst of a disaster isn't the time to decide to bypass or ignore certain aspects of your procedures. Use them and follow them strictly.

You (should) have tested them well, and you (should) know that they work. However, if you do find a problem with your procedures, note it down and record everything you did outside what is detailed within your procedures. This is essential information for the post-disaster debrief, and is required for solidifying your procedures to help ensure that they don't fail in this situation again.

> In disaster occurs, you don't want to be concerned whether or not your restoration procedures will work. You should have 100 percent faith in your procedures. This faith is established by regular testing of your restoration procedures.

Keep the Business Informed

Once again, it's important to send progress updates to the business. People are a lot less anxious when they're kept up to date when some type of system failure occurs. Keeping the user community calm and patient makes everyone's life easier, including your own.

When doing this, there is no need to confuse the users with intimate technical details. Simple clear statements are the best approach. For example:

> *"An unexpected failure has caused system corruption, which requires us to restore from the backups. We are doing this now, and the expected time to completion is 2 hours; however, we will provide another update in 60 minutes."*

This approach has the added benefit of mitigating the need for users to question their managers for information. This has the unfortunate side effect of flowing up the organizational structure to the point where you get a bunch of senior level executives standing around your desk wanting to known when the system will be available again.

Check the Environment

Once the restoration is complete, don't be too quick to give everyone the "all clear." Perform your initial checks to ensure that the database appears consistent from an IT point of view. Then contact key business users who are able to verify that the database is functioning correctly from an application point of view.

> **Notifying users that the system is again available, only to discover that there is an additional problem that you overlooked, gives the impression of incompetence. Get verification that the system is functioning correctly before the entire user population is notified.**

Once you're sure everything is functioning correctly, notify the users that the system is available.

Notify the Impact of Disaster

In addition to notifying the users that the database is once again available, you also need to notify them of the impact of the disaster. Information of relevance includes the following:

❑ Data loss: This is the most important. If users have lost data and need to re-key information, they need to know about this as soon as possible. Give the time that the database was restored to, and ask users to check any information they were working on around this time.

❑ Reduction in performance due to change in hardware: The database may not perform as well as it did before the disaster if, for example, you have failed over to a lower specification standby server. Give the users an estimate on when the performance will return to normal.

❑ Reduction in performance due to replacement of disk: Similarly the performance of the database may be impacted because you've replaced a disk in a RAID array and the disk is being regenerated. Once again give an estimate for when the performance will return to normal levels.

❑ Functions not to carry out: After restoration you may wish users to only use the database for certain functions while additional checking of the database contents is being carried out by application experts. For example, you may only want users to view existing customer information and not to add any new customer information at present. If this is the case, once again give the estimated duration of this restriction.

Once you've done all these things you can relax a little. You have managed to recover your database environment using your well-documented and well-tested procedures. You kept the business informed of the progress, and you followed up when the restoration was completed by letting the business users know what information, if any, had been lost and would require re-entry. You avoided panicking (hopefully!) and stuck to your procedures, thereby avoiding the temptation to try off-the-cuff activities to try and solve a undiagnosed problem.

Summary

This chapter is large; disaster recovery is an important topic in any IT area. However, when it comes to databases, it's absolutely critical. The important things you learned in this chapter were as follows:

❑ The three backup methods: Full, Transaction, and Differential and when they're most appropriately used

❑ How to restore from these backup methods

❑ How to plan your backup strategy

❑ How to test your backup strategy

❑ How to create and follow your documented procedures during disaster

There are a number of advanced disaster recovery topics that this chapter doesn't discuss, such as log shipping and clustering—so you must research disaster recovery further if you're dealing with mission-critical systems. A good book for further answers when troubleshooting is Apress's *SQL Server 2000 Fast Answers for DBAs and Developers.*

Replication

Replication is the process of copying and distributing user data and some objects (like views and stored procedures) from one database to another. The participating databases can exist on the same or different servers. Depending on the type of replication that you select, data can be modified on the copy of the database, and then resynchronized with the source database.

SQL Server governs the administration and manageability of replication. If a failure occurs during the replication process, SQL Server can usually recover from the point of failure and resume the process. Because of this robust built-in support, DBAs (database administrators) often choose replication as a method for data and object synchronization.

This chapter will review the tasks and concepts relating to replication that a DBA will be expected to be proficient in. This chapter will teach you how to plan, implement, configure, and troubleshoot replication within your environment, and covers. You'll look at the following:

- ❑ **Replication components and topology.**
  Learn about the internals of replication, the different types of replication available, and the various implementation options

- ❑ **Planning for replication.**
  Understand what is needed to use replication

- ❑ **Replication security considerations.**

- ❑ **Replication management.**
  How to set up, monitor, back up (via scripting), troubleshoot, and remove replication

Strategic Planning—Why Use Replication?

Before getting steeped in technical jargon, you may first be wondering what can be achieved by using replication. Replication moves and synchronizes data. Prior to using replication, you should step back and define what you want to do with your data. Replication can make an exact copy of the data at a point in time. It can create static copies of a database on a scheduled basis, or reflect updates made to the source data within a few seconds to the destination database(s). The destination database servers can also initiate a refresh of the destination database. Also, replication can synchronize changes made on both the source and destination databases. It involves migration, but more importantly, synchronization.

Replication is a good fit for the following scenarios:

❑   Providing one or more sites with a copy of the same data.

Distributing a copy of a database can help reduce contention for queries running against the original data source. Replication allows you to "scale out" processing against the source database by spreading traffic across multiple servers.

❑   Moving data closer to the users.

Moving copies of the data to SQL Server instances with better connectivity for local end-users' sites may help improve performance as well as site autonomy (if the original source database goes down, users can access the local copy), while at the same time retaining central control over these remote databases.

❑   Generating a copy of the data for use by reporting or data warehousing applications (Analysis Services\OLAP databases).

The performance of read-intensive applications can often be improved when not having to contend with write-intensive OLTP activities.

❑   Synchronization of data across multiple data sources.

Replication is often used for sales applications, whereby the salesperson is offline and updating data away from the office. Once they're reconnected, that data can be synchronized with the original data sources. Data conflicts can occur when the same data is updated by different users; however, conflict resolution is an automated component included with the data synchronization process, and is used to determine which changes "win" and which ones "lose."

With all that replication *can* do, keep in mind that replication is not a panacea for all your data availability, performance, or recovery needs. Replication can work under the next few scenarios, but with a few caveats attached:

❏ **Disaster recovery.**

Replication is sometimes used to create a second copy of a database on a second SQL Server instance, for use in a disaster recovery scenario. This backup, or "warm" standby, by definition *should* reflect all data and schema changes made on the source, updated within a short timeframe. Although replication can synchronize and copy data and various types of database objects, you cannot guarantee that all objects and changes within the database will be reflected in the copies made to other servers.

The primary flaw with using replication as a disaster recovery method is that it doesn't synchronize all database objects *by default*, just those that you explicitly request. Object modifications, additions, or removals may not be reflected in replication unless you first stop and rebuild your replication configuration. What's more, system tables and databases cannot be replicated. Also, the amount of time between when the updates are requested and when they are actually applied may be too lengthy to meet your needs compared to other solutions, such as Log Shipping, a feature available with SQL Server 2000 Enterprise Edition. Log shipping uses Transaction log backups copied to the "warm" standby server, thus ensuring that all database changes are reflected up until the moment the backup was completed on the source database. (Log shipping is covered in more detail in Chapter 8.)

❏ **Using replication to move data for use in occasional query operations.**

Replication, once set up, needs to be monitored and maintained. If you want to use replication to move data so that it can be queried only occasionally, keep in mind that SQL Server offers linked servers as an option for queries to remote homogenous and heterogeneous data sources. Linked servers may fulfill your needs without having to configure and support replication on an ongoing basis.

❏ **Replicating across slow network connections.**

If you have a slow or unreliable network, replication may be an ongoing problem for you. Depending on the frequency of replication updates, and coupled with large amounts of data, you may find the time spent administering and troubleshooting replication may not justify the benefits of using it.

Now that we've reviewed the different ways that replication can be used, we'll begin discussing the internal workings of replication within SQL Server 2000.

Publications and Articles

SQL Server 2000 uses a publishing industry metaphor by naming the primary components of replication: **publication**, **article**, and **subscription**. A **publication** is a grouping of selected data and database objects that you wish to replicate to another database, and includes one or more of these tables or database objects that you wish to copy. A single object within a publication is called an **article**. A publication can consist of one or more articles, but you may only publish articles from a single user database within a single publication (also, *system* databases cannot be replicated). If you must replicate data or database objects from varying databases, you must have a separate publication for each distinct database.

The following diagram shows the relationship between the database objects, articles, and a single publication:

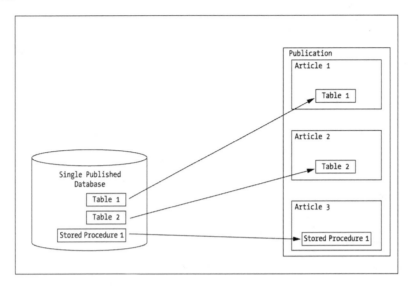

Keep in mind that a single database can have multiple publications defined for it; however, the same article cannot belong to more than one publication. Why would you have two publications for one database? Sometimes, separating publications by subject matter allows you to replicate only the data that individual sites need. For example, in the Northwind database, you could create a publication for order data, and a second publication for employee data. You can then replicate the individual publications to only those sites that require the data.

Notice in the following diagram that the same database is used for two publications, but no article is published twice. If a site required all four tables to be replicated, you would replicate both publications to the site.

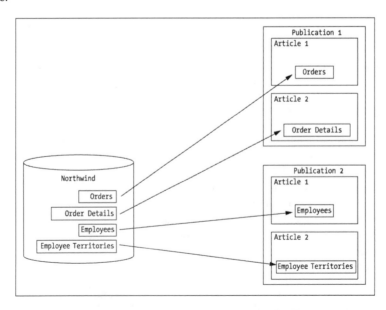

The Role of an SQL Server Instance in Replication

Prior to configuring replication, you must determine what role your participating SQL Server instances will play. The replication process involves three roles: **publisher**, **distributor**, and **subscriber(s)**. One SQL Server instance can fulfill all three roles, but most often two or more SQL Server instances are involved.

A **publisher** makes the data and objects available, and is simply an SQL Server instance that is enabled (allowed) to contain publications. Using the Configure Publishing and Distribution wizard in Enterprise Manager, you can designate your SQL Server instance as a publisher.

The **distributor** manages the replication process, assisting with moving changes and data, as well as tracking the state and history of specific publications. Using Enterprise Manager, you can designate your SQL Server instance as a distributor. When this happens, a distribution database is created. The **distribution database** stores information about the replication configuration (metadata), history data, and transactions to be replicated. Each publisher SQL Server instance must be assigned a distributor when it's created, and a publisher can have only one distributor. An SQL Server instance can be both a publisher and distributor, although it isn't required to be on the same server. In fact, using a dedicated server as a distributor for numerous publisher servers can often provide performance benefits.

The **subscriber** server is an SQL Server instance that contains a user database or databases that receive published data or database objects from one or more publications. For a subscriber to receive replicated data, it must **subscribe** to the publication. Depending on the type of replication selected, subscribers can also make updates to the subscriber database data, which are then updated back at the published database. We'll show you how to subscribe to publications in the "Subscription Types" section.

In the following diagram, the relationships between the publisher, distributor, and subscriber are shown. The subscriber can be any server that contains a database that subscribes to a publication.

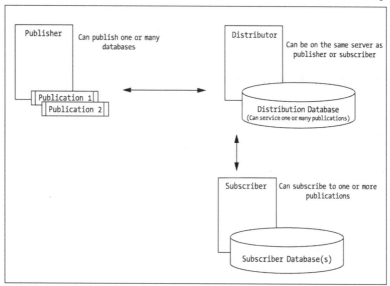

Replication Topology

Your replication **topology** (also called the replication model) is a way of describing how you designate the various replication roles (publisher, distributor, and subscriber) across your SQL Server instances. The topology you choose should be based on what SQL Server instances you have available, how good your network connection between these servers is, and how busy your individual SQL Server instances are.

Central Publisher, Local Distributor

In this topology, the same SQL Server instance is used for the publisher and distributor roles with one or more subscribers subscribing to this publisher. Use this topology if your publisher has plenty of capacity (underutilized), or if you cannot spare a separate machine that can be used as the distributor.

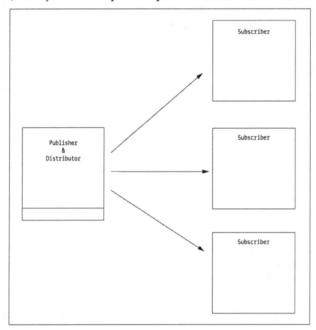

Central Publisher, Remote Distributor

One SQL Server instance acts as the publisher and a different SQL Server instance acts as the distributor. Using a separate instance as a distributor can help improve performance, because the activity of the distributor doesn't compete with the publisher or subscriber database activity. This topology is also useful when the distributor SQL Server instance has a better performing network connection to the subscribers.

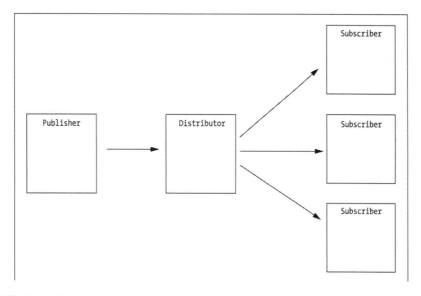

Central Subscriber

The Central Subscriber topology involves having one SQL Server instance subscribe to multiple publications. The publications subscribed to can come from one or more publishers, and the publications from varying databases. This is useful for reporting or data warehousing databases that are used for site-specific data consolidation. One or more databases can subscribe to one or more publications. Note that the publishers can use a remote or local distributor for this topology.

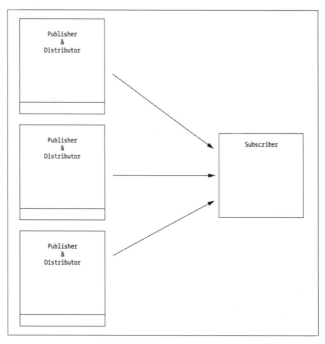

Publishing Subscriber

When a slow (or expensive) LAN or WAN connection connects most subscriber servers to the publisher, you can use a publishing subscriber topology to minimize or reduce the performance overhead. This topology works by having a single subscriber subscribe to a publication (rather than multiple subscriptions directly to the publication). This subscriber then takes on the publisher role and creates a publication based on the subscribed data. The other subscribers, who should be connected to the subscriber, can then subscribe to this publication. This differs from the remote distributor in that a single subscriber–also acting as a publisher and distributor–is responsible for moving the data to other subscribers, rather than the data moving along a direct path from a single publisher and distributor.

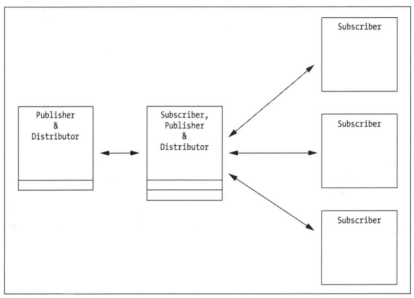

Replication Security Requirements

Before configuring replication on your SQL Server instance, you must ensure that the following appropriate security conditions are in place:

❑   You must be a member of the sysadmin server role to enable replication for the server and a specific database. Once the database is enabled for publishing, any member of the db_owner database role can create publications based on the database. Sysadmin members can also create publications for any database on the SQL Server instance.

❑   The SQL Server Agent service account, which is used to run the SQL Server Agent service, cannot run under "Local System" for those SQL Server instances participating in the replication topology (Publisher, Distributor, and Subscriber), unless the same machine performs all three roles. You must use a Windows domain account or standard account, instead. The SQL Server Agent service account defines the security context of jobs used to configure and maintain replication.

❑ SQL Server replication generates files that contain your schema and data, for intermediate storage prior to distributing to the subscriber database. This storage folder is called the **snapshot folder**, and can be located on an "administrative" share (for example e$\MSSQL\REPL, or a defined Windows 2000 Share). A **Windows 2000 Share** is a folder that is defined on a computer, to be made available for other users on the network. An **Administrative share** includes all drives on the computer that are automatically shared with members of the Administrators group using a drive letter$ format. Administrative shares are hidden by default when you connect to the server remotely. If you choose to use an Administrative share, then the SQL Server Agent account on the publisher and distributor must have administrative group membership on that machine. Otherwise, if using a Windows 2000 Share, be sure to grant read-and-write permissions to the shared folder in which you choose the Windows domain or standard account to run the SQL Server Agent service on.

Try It Out–Configuring Your SQL Server Instance as a Publisher and Distributor

1. Open Enterprise Manager, expand the server group registration, and click the server you wish to configure as a publisher.

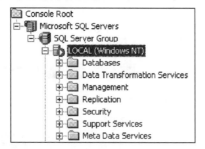

2. From the Tools menu, select Wizards.

3. In the Select Wizard dialog box, expand the Replication node, and select Configure Publishing and Distribution Wizard. Click OK.

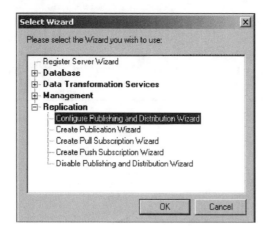

409

4. Click Next to clear the wizard introduction dialog box. On the Select Distributor dialog box, keep the default Make 'ServerName' its own Distributor selected. This distribution database will be created on the same SQL Server instance. Click Next.

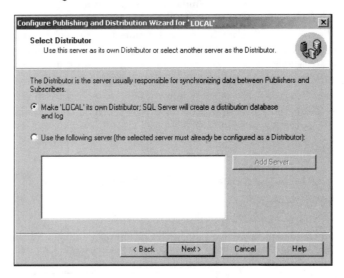

5. In the Configure SQL Server Agent dialog box, select Yes, configure the SQL Server Agent service to start automatically. Click Next.

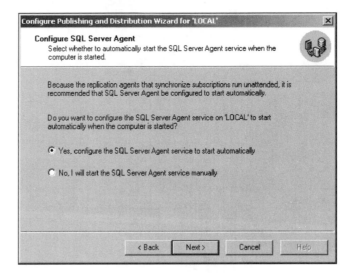

6. In the Specify Snapshot Folder dialog box, select the location of the snapshot folder and click Next.

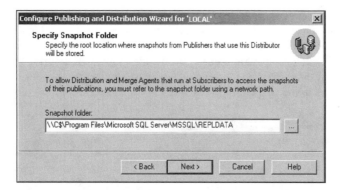

If you choose to use an Administrative share as your folder (where you designate the drive letter followed by a dollar sign, for example C$), you may receive a warning that your SQL Server Agent service accounts involved with replication should all have administrative privileges on the computer you're configuring the Snapshot Folder on. If this is the case, click Yes.

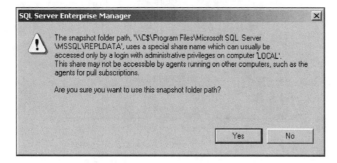

7. In the Customize the Configuration dialog box, select No, use the following default settings to proceed with configuring Publishing and Distribution on your SQL Server instance. Click Next.

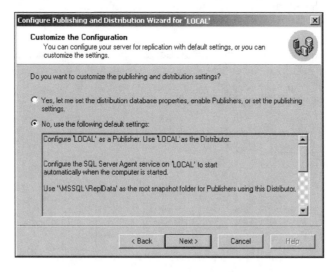

8. In the Completing the Configure Publishing and Distribution Wizard dialog box, select Finish to begin the configuration.

You will see a dialog box reviewing the replication configuration step status, and then a final dialog box indicating that the configuration is complete. At this point, the distribution database will have been created on your SQL Server instance. You will also see a dialog box letting you know that the **Replication Monitor** has been added to your Enterprise Manager console tree. The Replication Monitor is used to view and configure replication. You'll review the Replication Monitor later in the chapter, in the "Using the Replication Monitor" section. Click Close.

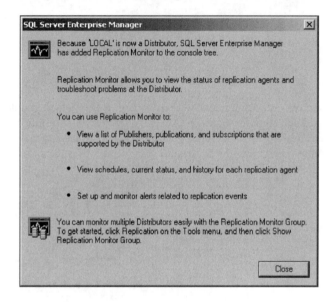

How It Works

In this example, you began by initializing the Configure Publishing and Distribution wizard to enable the SQL Server instance for publishing and distribution. In the dialog box in step 4, the only option was to configure the publisher SQL Server instance as the distributor as well, because you were starting from scratch with the replication topology. This will create the "distribution" database on that SQL Server instance.

In step 5, you selected Yes, configure the SQL Server Agent service to start automatically. This impacts the settings in the Advanced tab of the SQL Server Agent Properties in Enterprise Manager. (To view these settings in Enterprise Manager, expand the SQL Server registration, the Management folder, right-click SQL Server Agent, and select Properties).

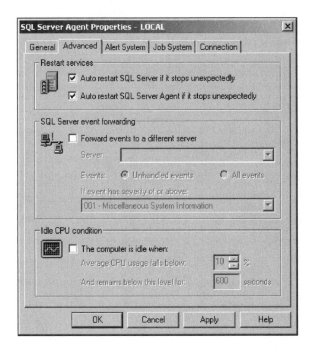

The SQL Server Agent defines the security context (what permissions and actions are allowed) for the jobs used for managing replication. If SQL Server restarts for some reason, you'll want to ensure that your SQL Server Agent is set to start up automatically after SQL Server restarts.

In step 6, you designated the snapshot share for your publication files. Remember to select a share that your SQL Server Agent has permissions for, and one that has sufficient space. If using an Administrative share, use the "X$" standard; otherwise, designate the Windows 2000 share. Be sure there is enough space on the drive where the share is located (the space varies depending on the size and number of articles published).

Step 7 allows you to either use the default settings for the distribution and publishing options, or to configure them in detail. Note that, had you selected Yes, let me set the distribution database properties, enable Publisher, or set the publishing settings, this would have allowed you to do the following:

❑   Change the name and location of your distribution database

❑   Enable other servers to use the new distributor after they are configured as publishers

❑   Enable databases on the SQL Server instance for transactional (includes snapshot) or merge replication (you'll study these in the next sections)

❑   Enable servers that can subscribe to publications from this publisher

After configuring your SQL Server instance as a distributor, predefined alerts will be created for monitoring replication status. To view the alerts in Enterprise Manager, expand the Server Registration, the Management folder, and the SQL Server Agent node. Click Alerts to view the newly created replication alerts, which start with the word Replication. Some of these alerts include the following:

Alert Name	Fires When
Replication: agent failure	The Replication Agent shuts down due to an error (the agent is described next)
Replication: agent retry	The agent shuts down due to an error after unsuccessfully retrying an operation
Replication: agent success	The Replication Agent shuts down successfully
Replication: Subscriber has failed data validation	A Distribution or Merge Agent fails data validation
Replication: Subscriber has passed data validation	Distribution or Merge Agent passes data validation
Replication: Subscription cleaned up	An inactive subscription is deleted
Replication: Subscription reinitialized after validation failure	A subscription has been reinitialized successfully

Most of these alerts involve **agents**, which are executables that are used to perform actions necessary to manage replication. These agents are managed by SQL Server Agent jobs (jobs created after setting up replication with the Replication wizards, which are described later). There are different agents used for different types of replication. Some agents are specific to the type of replication used, and others are created for use by all types of replication.

Replication Types

There are three types of replication in SQL Server 2000:

❑   Snapshot replication

❑   Transactional replication

❑   Merge replication

The next few sections will review how each type of replication operates, and how to set up a publication for each replication type.

Setting up the publication is only part of the process of implementing replication. After reviewing each of the replication types, you'll then examine how to send and receive subscriptions to publications. Once you set up a subscription, the replication process will operate fully.

Snapshot Replication

Snapshot replication is excellent for applications that just need a copy of the data, as it existed at a point in time. An analogy would be taking a picture with a camera. The image is copied and transferred to a print, and the picture doesn't change. This is the same concept as snapshot replication. This replication type is ideal for data that isn't updated frequently, or doesn't need to be kept in sync with the publisher data (and yet is still useful to the subscriber).

This diagram shows the path of the transactions for snapshot replication:

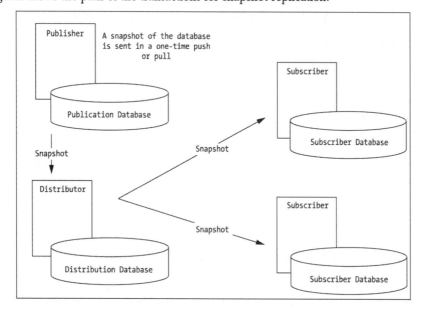

As you can see, snapshot replication takes the data from the publisher and sends it to the distributor, which in turn sends it to one or more subscriber databases.

We mentioned in the previous section that replication takes advantage of agents. Snapshot replication primarily uses two different agents, the **Snapshot Agent** and the **Distribution Agent**.

The **Snapshot Agent** is used for creating and propagating the snapshots from the publisher to the distributor (or snapshot location). The Snapshot Agent creates the replication data (the snapshot), outputs the data via BCP (Bulk Copy Program), and creates the information that is used by the Distribution Agent to propagate that data. One Snapshot Agent is created for each publication, and runs on the distributor.

The Snapshot Agent is dormant most of the time and periodically becomes active, based on the schedule that you have configured to perform its tasks. Each time the Snapshot Agent runs, it performs the following tasks:

❑   Establishes a connection from the distributor to the publisher. If a connection is not available, the Snapshot Agent will not proceed with creating the snapshot (you'll look at how to monitor agent activity in the section "Using Replication Monitor"). Once the connection has been established, the Snapshot Agent locks all of the articles involved in the replication to ensure that the snapshot is a consistent view of the data. (For this reason, it's not a good idea to schedule snapshots during peak periods of usage.)

❑   Establishes a connection from the publisher to the distributor. Once this connection has been established, the Snapshot Agent engineers a copy of the schema for each article and stores that information in the distribution database.

❑   Takes a snapshot of the actual data on the publisher, and writes it to a file in the snapshot folder. Any previous snapshot files created in the folder are removed by default. The snapshot folder doesn't necessarily need to be on the distributor.

❑   Updates information in the distribution database after the data has been copied.

❑   Releases the locks that it has held on the articles, and logs the snapshot into the history file.

The Snapshot Agent should run based on how frequently you want subscriptions to be refreshed using snapshot replication. It's responsible only for creating the snapshot, it doesn't distribute it to subscribers; this is where the Distribution Agent comes in.

The **Distribution Agent** is responsible for propagating the data and schema from the distribution database to the subscriber(s). Each publication has its own Distribution Agent. If you're using a push subscription, the Distribution Agent runs on the distributor. If you're using a pull subscription, the Distribution Agent runs on the subscriber. You'll examine both pull and push subscriptions later in the chapter.

Try It Out–Setting Up Snapshot Replication Publication

1.   Open Enterprise Manager and expand the Server group and Server registration of the **Publisher**.

2.   Expand the Replication folder.

3.   Right-click Publications and select New Publication.

4. In the Create Publication Wizard, click the check box to Show advanced options in this wizard, and click Next.

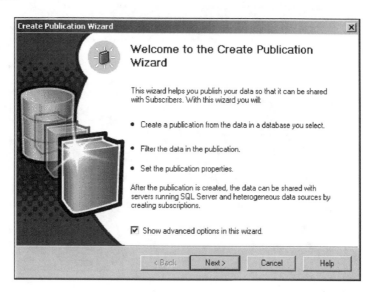

5. Select the database from which you wish to publish articles. In this example, select the Northwind database.

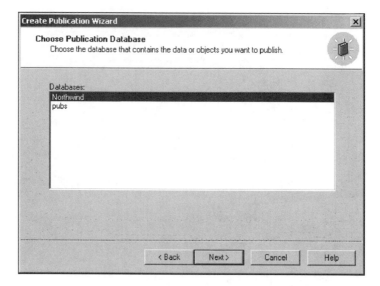

6. Select the publication type.

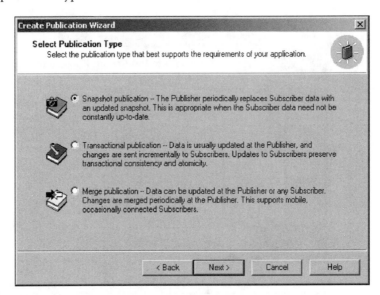

7. Next you'll see an advanced options dialog box allowing you to enable Subscribers to make changes that are replicated back to the publisher and other subscribers. For this example, leave these unselected.

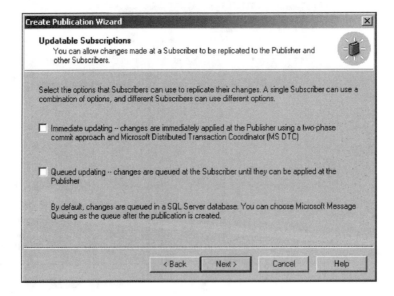

8. In the Transform Published Data dialog box, leave No, Subscribers receive data directly selected.

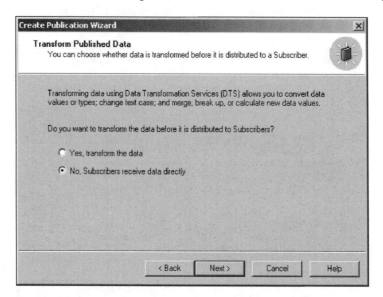

9. In the Specify Subscriber Types dialog box, select the types of subscribers that will be subscribing to the publication. In this example, you'll select Servers running SQL Server 2000.

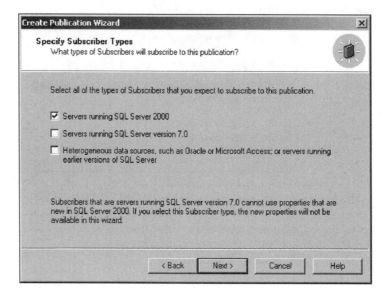

10. In the Specify Articles dialog box, you select the articles to be published. In this example, select the Publish All check box next to the Tables Object Type. This will select all user tables within the database. Click the Article Defaults button.

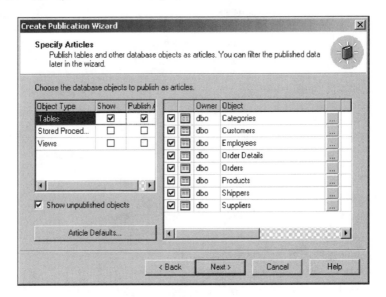

11. Select the Table articles object type and click OK.

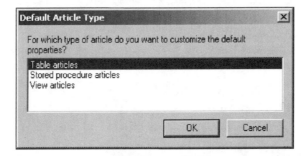

12. Now, you're going to briefly look at what properties are available for table articles, so that you're aware of the many configurable options and defaults. On the General tab, you have the option of adding a Destination table owner (other than the default of dbo). Leave this as it is and select the Snapshot tab.

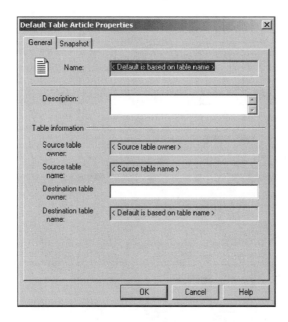

13. Again, you're just looking here. This tab shows you what default table article behaviors will occur once snapshot replication is initiated. In the Name conflicts section, if a table with the same name as the destination table exists on the subscriber, the default is to DROP the existing table on the subscriber. You should leave this option alone.

In the Copy objects to destination area, you can determine what dependent objects should come along with your articles. This includes such dependent database objects as foreign keys, indexes, triggers, extended properties, and column specific collation settings. Leave all the options as they are, and click OK.

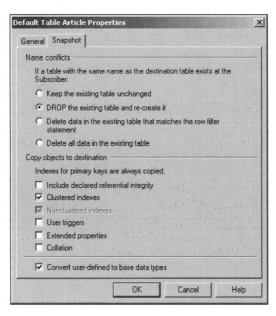

14. After selecting your articles, click Next.

15. The next dialog box lists any warnings or issues about the articles you selected. Read these warnings prior to clicking Next. (We'll discuss these warnings in the following "How it Works" section.)

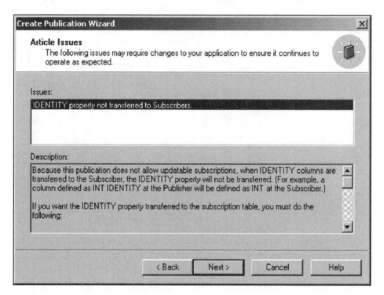

16. In the Select Publication Name and Description dialog box, type in a publication name and description.

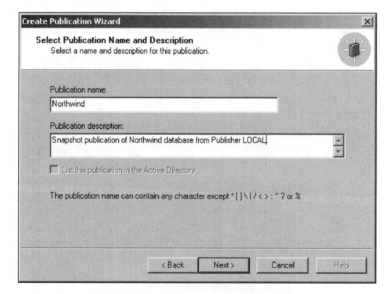

17. In the Customize the Properties of the Publication dialog box, select Yes, I will define data filters, enable anonymous subscriptions, or customize other properties. Once again, you're only looking at the options–not actually changing anything here.

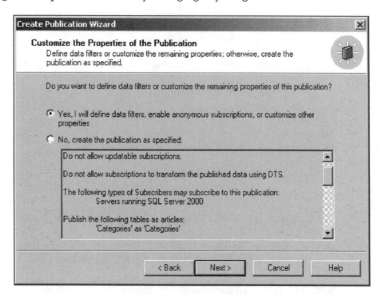

18. In the Filter Data dialog box, you have the option of filtering vertically (what **columns** are published) or horizontally (**rows** published) the data that comes across to the subscribers. For tables in which the full breadth or depth of data isn't necessary on the Subscriber, use filtering to remove columns or rows from the publication. This can reduce the snapshot and distribution processing time. Leave these options unchecked.

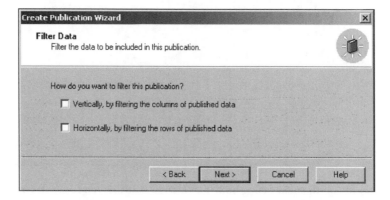

19. The Allow Anonymous Subscriptions dialog box allows your snapshot publication to be used in pull subscriptions without the awareness of the publisher. Pull subscriptions are reviewed later in the "Pull Subscriptions" section. This essentially means that subscribers can subscribe to a publication without the awareness of the publisher, thereby reducing replication history records generated and the performance overhead of maintaining subscriber information in the distribution database. The drawback of this option is that it may allow unintended subscribers to view the published data. Leave the option at the default No, allow only named subscriptions.

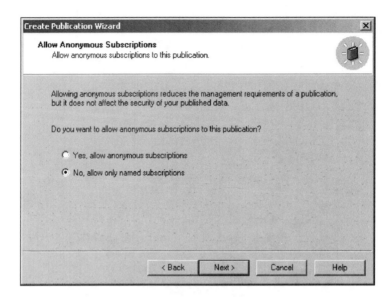

20. In the Set Snapshot Agent Schedule dialog box, you set the schedule that determines when the snapshot files for the publication will be created. Accept the default value.

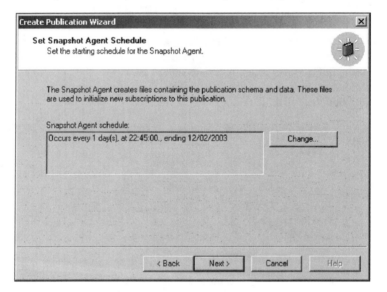

21. Select Finish on the next dialog box. You'll see a status screen for each phase of the publication creation process.

The final dialog box will confirm that the publication was successfully created. Select Close to exit (selecting Publication Properties will allow you to view the properties of your new publication, seeing many of the options that you configured within the wizard).

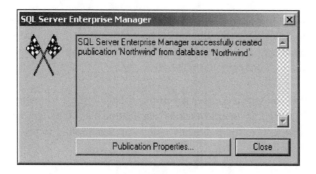

22. In Enterprise Manager, expand the Publications folder to view your new snapshot publication.

How It Works

You have just completed the creation of your snapshot publication. The next step in configuring replication is the pushing or pulling of the publication to subscribers via subscriptions. This will be covered later in the chapter, in the "Pull Subscriptions" section, after you've reviewed each of the replication types.

In the first few steps within Enterprise Manager, you navigated to the registered SQL Server instance that will contain the snapshot publication. On the initial Wizard dialog box (step 4), you selected Show advanced options, allowing you to see the various options that can be configured.

In step 5, you selected the database containing the articles to be published. Remember that a publication can only contain articles from one database. You then selected the replication type "snapshot" in step 6.

Steps 7 and 8 are both dialog boxes that will only be seen if you select Show advanced options. In step 7, in the Updatable Subscriptions dialog box, you can designate whether your subscribers will be allowed to have Immediate or Queued updating. These two types of updateable subscriptions allow changes to be made at the subscriber, which will then be updated back at the publisher. Updatable subscriptions are also available for Transactional replication (looked at in the next section). Updatable subscriptions are best used for those subscribers that perform infrequent updates at the subscriber. **Immediate updating** is ideal when there is a stable connection between the subscriber and publisher. If an update is made to the subscriber, the change is applied immediately to the publisher.

Queued updating, on the other hand, allows modifications at the subscriber without an ongoing connection to the publisher. Queued updating requires that the MSMQ (Message Queuing) service be installed on both the subscriber and publisher. For more details on MSMQ, see Microsoft's MSMQ site: http://www.microsoft.com/msmq/default.htm.

Queued updates utilize the **Queue Reader Agent** to propagate those changes made to subscribers of snapshot replication (as well as for transactional replication too). Changes are queued (held in waiting) until the subscriber connects to the publisher again, and are applied to the publisher and any other subscribers upon reconnection.

> The MS DTC (Distributed Transaction Coordinator) service must be running on both servers (publisher and subscriber) for immediate updating subscriptions to work properly.

The Transform Published Data dialog box in step 8 allows you to designate whether you wish to use DTS (Data Transformation Services) to modify or transform your published data prior to the data being pushed to subscribers. This option allows you to modify the data as per your business needs (for example, transforming OLTP data into OLAP-centric data formats). Using this option can add performance overhead if used in conjunction with larger published tables. In many cases, you may be better served by moving the data without using DTS within replication. Then, you can use the subscriber data as a set of "staging" tables, and transform the data locally on the SQL Server instance.

In step 9, you selected which versions of SQL Server will be used within the replication topology. You selected Servers running SQL Server 2000. If you had enabled Servers running SQL Server version 7.0, only replication options that are compatible with SQL Server 7.0 subscribers would be available in the wizard. If Heterogeneous data sources had been enabled, versions of SQL Server prior to 7.0, Oracle, and potentially other non-SQL Server data sources, would be able to subscribe to snapshot or transactional publications (also, Microsoft Access can subscribe to snapshot, transactional, and merge publications).

> *With Microsoft Access 2000, you can create what is called an Access project, which uses the .adp file extension. Within a Microsoft Access project, you can replicate data with SQL Server 2000. Microsoft Access 2000's project functionality allows other integration points with SQL Server as well. For more information, see Microsoft's Access web site at http://www.microsoft.com/office/access/.*

In step 10, in the Specify Articles dialog box, you selected the articles to be published. Articles available for publication depend on the objects in your database. You can select user tables (and the associated triggers, indexes, primary and foreign keys, and extended properties), stored procedures, the execution of stored procedures, views, indexed views (for the Enterprise Edition of SQL Server 2000), and user-defined functions as articles within your publication. You also examined the article defaults for tables (you can configure article defaults for other article types, such as views and stored procedures).

You looked at warnings about the articles you selected in step 15. You received a warning about tables that use IDENTITY columns. IDENTITY columns automatically generate a numeric value (an integer, for example) for each new row, based on a seed number and increment value. This incrementing occurs on the publisher, and you're warned that this IDENTITY property will not be passed on to the subscriber table. This allows the original values generated on the publisher to be preserved. An IDENTITY column that's being used as a primary key will keep its value preserved on the subscriber by default, rather than regenerating a new value upon insert, thus potentially breaking foreign key references to the primary key values. Next, you selected the name and description for the new publication (step 16). You can name the publication something more descriptive if you want, or use the default of using the database name instead.

In step 17 you selected Yes, I will define data filters, enable anonymous subscriptions, or customize other properties, so that you could look at the breadth of features available for Snapshot replication.

Step 18 shows us the Filter Data dialog box that, when selected, allows you to remove or narrow down which columns or rows are replicated within the publication. Reducing the data sent to the subscriber can result in less network utilization and physical database space used. However, adding filters can also add to the overhead of processing replication, sometimes involving longer locking of larger portions of the tables while the data is processed.

In step 19, you configured the publication to allow anonymous subscriptions, which minimize the overhead of tracking subscribers at the publisher. With anonymous subscriptions, anonymous users can access data using a connection to the Internet (using a virtual private network, Microsoft Proxy Server, or a TCP/IP connection assuming that a firewall or proxy server isn't being used). Unfortunately, anonymous subscriptions may allow unintended subscribers to view the published data.

Finally, you set the schedule for the Snapshot Agent to run (step 20). This job is created to execute the Snapshot Agent at a scheduled time, and can be found under the SQL Server Agent and Jobs nodes in Enterprise Manager.

Once the wizard finished, you either closed the dialog box or checked out the properties of the publication you just created. You selected to close the dialog box and navigate to the new publication in Enterprise Manager.

Now you'll look at Transactional replication.

Transactional Replication

Transactional replication can be used to replicate data modifications made at the publisher database to the subscriber database, as they occur. With Transactional replication, any changes made to published articles are processed and sent on to the subscribers of that publication. Transactional replication is very useful when you need to keep the subscribers closely synchronized with the same data as the publisher at all times (depending on the network and volume of changes, changes can be reflected to subscribers within a few seconds).

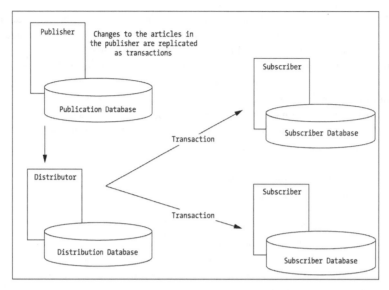

Prior to configuring Transactional replication, make sure that that the transaction log of the database you wish to publish has sufficient space allocated to it. Transactional replication uses the transaction log to identify what changes should be moved to the distribution database (and then on to the subscribers). Completed transactions may not be removed from the log until they've been moved to the distribution database. It's difficult to estimate the space you may need, because it depends on the speed your transactions are moved to the distribution database as well as the availability of the distribution database. If you have sufficient space on a dedicated spare drive, consider allocating a substantial portion of it for use by the publication transaction log. Then, you can monitor the log space used via the `SQLServer: Databases Percent Log Used` System Monitor counter. The same should be done for the transaction log of the distribution database, if resources allow. Also consider using RAID 1 or RAID 10 disk arrays with your transaction logs (one log per array is ideal, but expensive), because these generally are best for sequential write activity (which transaction logs perform).

Like Snapshot replication, Transactional replication makes use of the Snapshot and Distribution Agents. The initial phases of Transactional replication involve the generation of a snapshot (although you can choose to forgo this, should you already have the schema and data on the subscriber) and the distribution of snapshot schema and data to the subscriber database. Transactional replication also uses the **Log Reader Agent**, which is only used with transactional replication. The Log Reader Agent is used to extract change information from the transaction log on the publisher, and then move the data modification commands into the distribution database. Each database that uses Transactional replication has its own Log Reader Agent on the publisher, which is created after the completion of the Replication Setup wizard.

If you chose to allow queued updating for your Transactional replication publication, you'll have a Queue Reader Agent on the SQL Server instance running as the distributor. Unlike the Log Reader Agent, only one instance of the Queue Reader Agent exists to assist queued updates for publications using that specified distributor.

Try It Out–Setting Up Transactional Replication Publication

1. Expand the Server group and Server registration of the database you wish to publish.

2. Expand the Replication folder and then the Publications folder.

3. You'll be creating a Transactional replication publication for Northwind, as you did for the Snapshot example. Prior to doing so, delete the publication you created in the previous exercise. Right-click the Northwind publication and select Delete.

4. Right-click the Publications folder and select New Publication.

5. Leave the Show advanced options unchecked and click Next.

6. In the Choose Publication dialog box, select the database you wish to publish for transactional replication. For this example, select the Northwind database.

7. In the Select Publication Type dialog box, select Transactional publication.

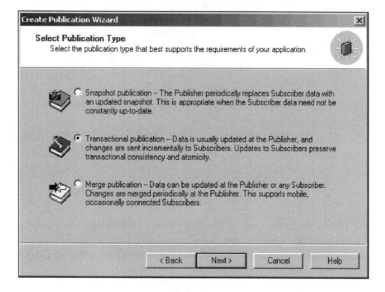

8. In the Specify Subscriber Types dialog box, select which versions of SQL Server your subscribers will be running. The lowest version of SQL Server determines the maximum functionality allowed at the publisher. In this example, select Servers running SQL Server 2000.

9. The Specify Articles dialog box allows you to select which objects should be migrated to the subscribers. In the following screen shot, notice that there are keys with a red x in some of the rows. These are tables without primary keys, which means they cannot be replicated using Transactional replication (the Northwind database doesn't include tables without primary keys, so you should add an extra table to demonstrate this). If you must replicate the table missing the primary key, cancel the Publication wizard and select a primary key for the table or tables prior to creating this publication.

In general, using primary keys is good practice, because you're ensuring that duplicate rows don't exist within the table. Adding a primary key to a table will also add an associated clustered index (if you don't explicitly choose the nonclustered index type and a clustered index doesn't already exist). Tables with clustered indexes can then be rebuilt on a scheduled basis with DBCC (DataBase Consistency Checks) reindexing utilities, which can help reduce table fragmentation.

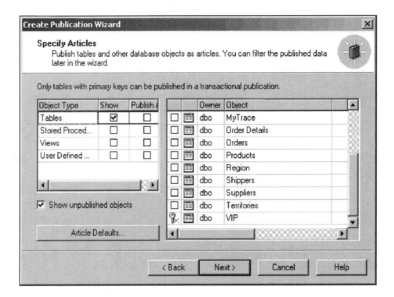

Click the Publish All button on the Tables object type.

10. Click the Show check box next to the Stored Procedures and Views object types. Views will appear in the right pane next to the sunglasses icon. Stored procedures will be seen next to the icon that looks like writing on a card. Select the Employee Sales by Country stored procedure and the Alphabetical list of products view.

If you're replicating views (or other objects that depend on other objects in the database) be sure to include those objects within the same publication. If you don't, users of the subscriber database may raise errors when referencing the view or stored procedure.

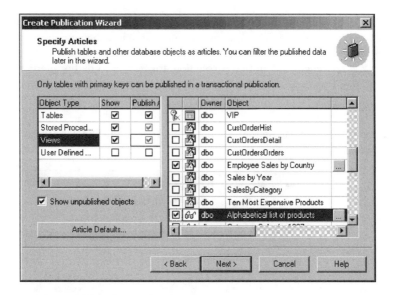

Click the Article Defaults button.

11. Select the Table articles object type and click OK.

12. On the General tab, you can configure different object owners on the subscriber. Watch out when changing ownership for objects that could be referenced by other replicated objects (views, stored procedures, triggers, and so on), as the new owner could cause the existing referencing objects to fail when referenced by subscriber database users.

On the Commands tab, you can replace INSERT, UPDATE, and DELETE commands that are sent to the subscriber with system-generated stored procedures instead. The result is that Transactional replication will call the stored procedures instead of sending the longer INSERT, UPDATE, or DELETE statements, thus improving performance. You can select whether or not the stored procedures are created during the initial synchronization by selecting Create the stored procedures during initial synchronization of subscriptions. If you want the parameters of the stored procedure to be sent in binary format (for faster performance), keep the default check box selected. All of these options are selected by default, so for this example, leave everything checked.

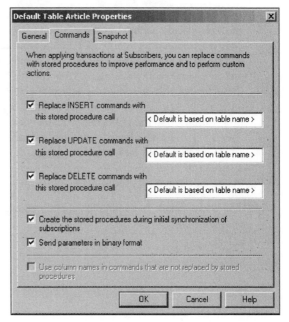

The Snapshot tab (which you see because Transactional replication performs a snapshot in its initial steps) provides you with options for handling objects being published that already exist on the subscriber as well as additional objects that can be replicated with the table (indexes, foreign key references, column level collation, triggers, extended properties). Leave the defaults selected.

Click OK to exit.

13. Click the Article Defaults button again, and this time in the Default Article Type dialog box, select Stored procedure articles.

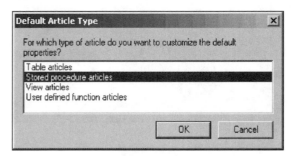

14. The General tab of the Default Stored Procedure Article Properties dialog box is the same as the one for table defaults, allowing you to designate an owner and description on the Subscriber database.

The Other tab, in the Destination name conflict section, allows you to select what actions to take if a stored procedure with the same name already exists on the subscriber. Leave this as the default.

In the Replicate schema and execution section, you can configure whether or not a stored procedure should have only its schema replicated (the default), and whether the actual execution on the publisher should be executed on the subscriber, or executed only if performed within a serializable transaction. "Serializable" refers to the isolation level of the transaction (how it locks objects), where serializable is the strictest possible locking strategy, reducing database concurrency, but ensuring consistent data. Enabling these options allows a stored procedure call on the publisher to actually cause a stored procedure to execute on the subscriber(s). Be sure that if you enable Every time it is executed or Only when it is executed inside a serializable transaction, the procedure call on the subscriber has the necessary objects and references to execute the stored procedure properly. For this exercise, leave this option at the default, Never; replicate the schema only.

The Copy objects to destination section allows you to migrate extended properties associated with the stored procedures.

Click OK to exit.

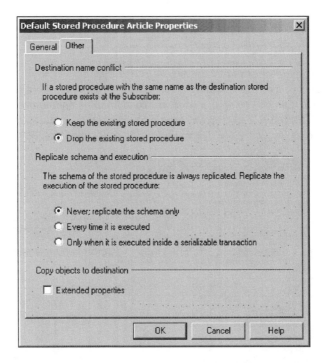

15. Click the Article Defaults button again, and this time in the Default Article Type dialog box, select Views articles.

16. The General tab of the Default View Article Properties dialog box is the same as the one for table defaults, which allows you to designate an owner and description on the Subscriber database.

   Like the table and stored procedure properties, the Snapshot tab for View Article Properties allows you to select what action to take if a destination view exists at the subscriber with the same name. In the Copy objects to destination section, you can select whether triggers and extended properties may be included with the snapshot schema of the view.

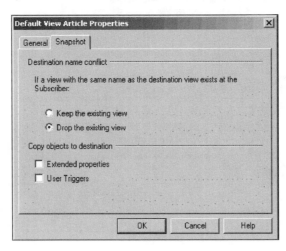

Click OK to exit the dialog box.

17. Back at the Specify Articles dialog box, click Next.

18. Just like the Snapshot example, the Article Issues dialog box lists any warnings about the articles you selected. For this example, you'll see warnings about the IDENTITY column property not being transferred. You're also warned that any tables referenced by replicated views should be included, as well as objects referenced by the stored procedures. Click each warning in the Issues list to see an expanded description of the problem. Click Next.

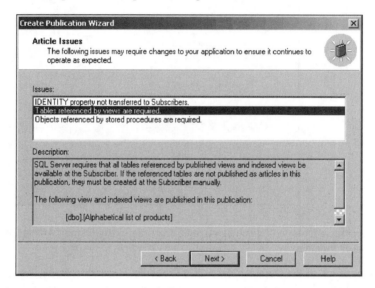

19. In the Select Publication Name and Description dialog box, leave the Publication name and description as default.

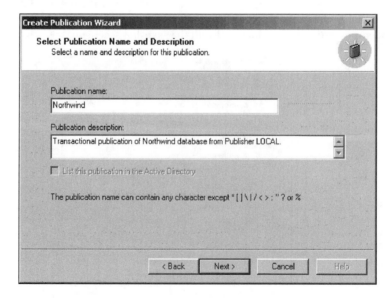

20. In the Customize the Properties of the Publication dialog box, keep the default of No, create the publication as specified. Selecting Yes will provide additional dialog boxes, allowing you to vertically or horizontally partition data in the articles, configure a different snapshot schedule, and/or permit anonymous subscriptions.

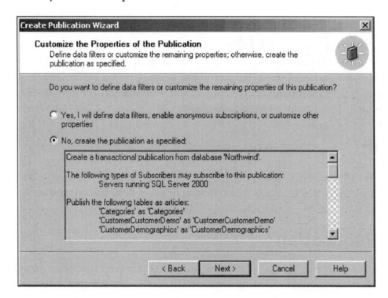

21. Click Finish to create the publication. You'll see a status screen showing the creation of the publication and articles. Click Close to exit the process. Just like the Snapshot replication example, you can view your new publication under the Replications folder in Enterprise Manager.

How It Works

The process of setting up a Transactional replication publication is very similar to that of setting up Snapshot replication, but with a few important distinctions.

The first difference was encountered in step 7, when you selected the Transactional publication replication type.

In step 9, you saw that you cannot replicate tables with missing primary keys. You should also be aware of how text and image columns within your tables are treated within Transactional replication. If your application uses the UPDATETEXT and WRITETEXT commands (used to update text and image data), be sure to include the WITH LOG option for databases not using the Full Recovery Model when using these commands; otherwise, the changes will not be replicated to the subscriber.

In step 12, you explored the Commands tab of the Default Table Article Properties dialog box. It's here that you can configure whether or not data updates are performed at the subscriber using automatically generated stored procedures, or whether the original INSERT, UPDATE, or DELETE is performed instead.

You looked at the Default Stored Procedure Article Properties dialog box in step 14. In the Other tab, you can configure whether or not a stored procedure should have only its schema replicated, whether to have the actual execution on the publisher be executed on the subscriber, or whether this execution should only occur within a serializable transaction.

> **The second and third options involve more planning, so select these options with care. This is because you need to think about what purpose the replication of the *execution* of a stored procedure is used to achieve, on the subscriber. Is it used to make data modifications on the subscriber? Will this put the data out of sync with the publisher, if such a stored procedure is executed? If so, you may not want to select these options.**

In step 16, you explored the Default Article Type dialog box for Views, seeing that on the Snapshot tab you can copy triggers and/or extended properties along with the original view definition.

Merge Replication

Merge replication gives you the ability to send and update changes that have occurred on the subscriber back to the publisher. Changes made at the publisher are also propagated to the subscriber.

Unlike queued updates using Transactional or Snapshot replication, Merge replication propagates data changes on a row-level basis (queued update data modifications are evaluated at a transaction basis). Merge replication should be chosen over queued updating when changes will occur frequently at the subscriber. Queued updating is better suited for environments with only occasional changes at the subscriber.

Merge replication is useful for both connected and disconnected environments. A good example of a disconnected environment would be a salesperson who has a laptop running a local copy of SQL Server and who is out in the field, disconnected from the main office. As the salespeople update their personal contact information, or sales data, these changes can be replicated to the main office once the salesperson is connected back to the corporate office network, thus propagating changes made on the subscriber to the publication database (and changes made at the publisher in turn can also be propagated to the subscribers). The following figure shows the principle behind Merge replication:

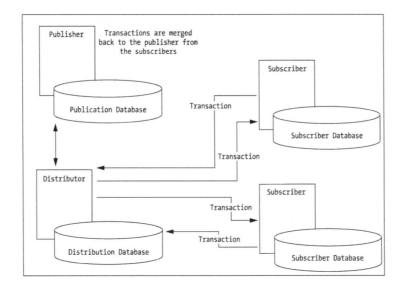

❏ If both the publisher and subscriber have changed the same row or same column within a data row, Merge replication contains built-in "conflict resolvers," which allow SQL Server to automatically handle how change conflicts get handled (someone wins, someone loses). The default is for the publisher's changes to take priority over subscribers, although SQL Server does include other conflict resolution algorithms to choose from, and programmers can also create their own (using Visual Basic, for example).

❏ Conflict resolution, and the ability to modify data at multiple sites, makes Merge replication the most complicated of the three replication types. Merge-conflict information is stored in SQL Server 2000 system-generated tables for each merge article (table) defined in the publication. The names of the merge conflict tables are held in the sysmergearticles table, in the conflict_table column. Also, the Msmerge_delete_conflicts table contains information on rows that were deleted due to a lost conflict.

> Also, you can view replication conflict information by expanding the Replication node in Enterprise Manager, then the Publications node, then by right-clicking the publication you wish to view conflict history for and selecting View Conflict. The utility will then let you view data conflicts that have occurred, as well as reverse a decision made by the conflict resolver.
>
> Conflict resolution works differently for subscribers to queued updating when compared to Merge replication subscribers. Queued updating only allows three forms of conflict resolution: the publisher wins all conflicts and the subscription is then reinitialized (the snapshot is reapplied), the publisher wins but the subscription is NOT reinitialized, or the subscriber wins. When a conflict is detected, the transaction is rolled back (and if you chose "publisher wins with reinitialization," all other transactions in the queue are rolled back). Merge replication, on the other hand, will only reject the specific conflicting row (and apply the "winner").

Merge replication doesn't use the distribution database as much as Transactional replication does. When Merge replication is initialized (by a subscriber subscribing to the publication), SQL Server begins by applying an initial snapshot to the subscriber. After the snapshot is finished, the subscriber can disconnect from the publisher, make modifications, reconnect, and have changes and modifications on both the publisher and subscriber merged into one copy. The subscriber can also stay connected, thus having changes made on both publisher and subscriber reflected more quickly on both (depending on the network and amount of data). When connected, the Merge Agent sends all changed data to the subscriber. Also, the originator of any data changes (publisher or subscriber) sends the changes to the site(s) needing to be updated.

When configuring Merge replication, if a `uniqueidentifier` column doesn't already exist, SQL Server adds one to identify every row in a table published as an article. SQL Server also creates triggers to track changes to data rows and data columns made at the publisher and subscriber.

Stored procedures are also created to update the publisher and subscriber database for use in propagating `INSERT`, `UPDATE`, and `DELETE` operations from the subscriber or publisher, rather than receiving the original update statements. After setting up your publication and subscription, you'll also see many new system tables generated for the exclusive use of Merge replication.

Merge replication uses the Snapshot Agent to generate the original schema and data snapshot on the subscriber. Also, Merge replication uses the **Merge Agent**, which reconciles and propagates incremental changes that occur between the publisher and subscribers. Merge replication uses the distribution database only minimally (and doesn't use the Distribution Agent at all).

Try It Out–Setting Up a Merge Replication Publication

1. Expand the Server group and Server registration of the database you wish to publish.

2. Expand the Replication folder and then the Publications folder.

3. You'll be creating a Merge replication publication for Northwind, as you did for the Snapshot and Transactional replication examples. Prior to doing so, right-click the previously created Northwind publication and select Delete.

4. Right-click the Publications folder and select New Publication. Leave Show advanced options in this wizard unchecked.

5. In the Choose Publication Database dialog box, select the Northwind database.

6. Click Next and select the Merge publication type in the next dialog box.

> **SQL Server 2000 Merge replication allows you to publish data to mobile devices running SQL Server 2000 Windows CE Edition. You must select this merge publication type in the** Specify Subscriber Types **dialog box to enable this functionality. Consequently, selecting this option will automatically allow anonymous subscriptions to subscribe to the publication, which is required for SQL Server CE. See Microsoft's product page for more information on configuring SQL Server CE, at** http://www.microsoft.com/sql/CE/default.asp.

7. In the Specify Subscriber Types dialog box, check Servers running SQL Server 2000.

8. Click the Publish All check box next to the Tables object type. For those tables without a uniqueidentifier column, SQL Server automatically adds one. In step 15, you'll see any warnings in the Article Issues dialog box regarding such added columns, saying Uniqueidentifier columns will be added to tables.

9. Click the Article Defaults button and select Table articles. In the General tab for Default Table Article Properties dialog box, you can specify a description and destination table owner.

   In the When merging changes from different sources section, you can choose to treat any changes to the same *row* on both the publisher and subscriber as a conflict, or you can treat changes to only the same *column* as a conflict. When Treat changes to the same column as a conflict is selected (the default), the publisher and subscriber can modify the same row, as long as the same column isn't modified. Change this from the default for tables in which you do *not* want multiple users modifying different columns on the same row simultaneously.

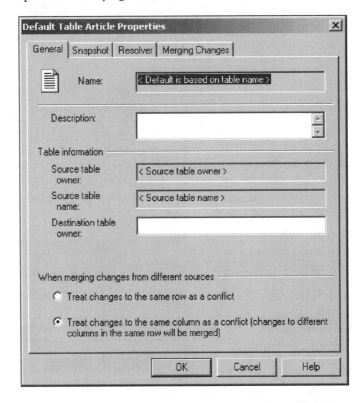

   If Treat changes to the same row as a conflict is selected, any changes to the same row on the publisher and subscriber (even if not updating the same column) are treated as a conflict. Leave the defaults on this tab, and click the Snapshot tab.

10. The Snapshot tab contains the same options as the Snapshot and Transactional replication wizards. Because changes are merged between the publisher and subscriber, the merging process assumes that the same data integrity features apply to **both** sides of the replication topology.

Remember to include triggers and foreign keys within your Merge replication publication to maintain the same business rules and referential integrity on both the publisher and subscribers. Because triggers can be programmed in a variety of ways, be sure to understand how your trigger will act on both the publisher and subscriber (some applications create publisher-specific triggers, and then manually add subscriber triggers, rather than including them in the original publication).

Leave the defaults on this tab and click the Resolver tab.

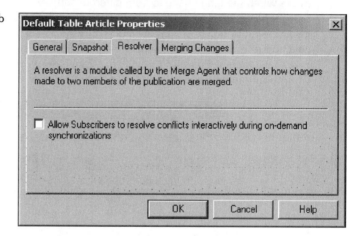

11. This tab allows you to decide whether subscribers can resolve conflicts interactively during on-demand synchronizations. (On-demand synchronization can occur when the subscriber uses WSM (Windows Synchronization Manager) to connect to the publication and synchronize data when they wish, hence on-demand.)

WSM is included with Microsoft Windows 2000 and Microsoft Internet Explorer version 5.0 or above. It allows you to synchronize subscriptions to Snapshot, Transactional, and Merge publications. To launch WSM, go to Start I Programs I Accessories I Synchronize. You'll then see any existing publications or offline web pages listed in the Items to Synchronize dialog box.

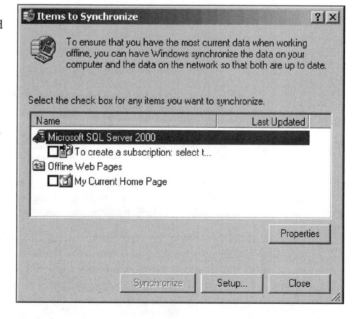

By clicking the first check box under Microsoft SQL Server 2000, you can add a new subscription to your local subscriber server. For more on WSM, see the Books Online topic "Windows Synchronization Manager."

When synchronizing via WSM, if a data conflict is encountered, the interactive resolver (a separate utility) displays the conflicting data rows, and allows you to edit and resolve the conflicting data manually, should you prefer SQL Server not to make the determination automatically. Leave this check box unchecked and click the Merging Changes tab.

12. On the Merging Changes tab, in the Check permissions section, you can select whether the Merge Agent login has permissions to perform INSERT, UPDATE, or DELETE operations. For this exercise, leave all these unchecked.

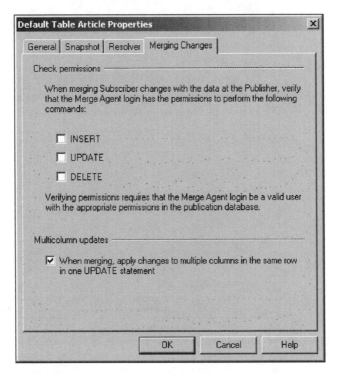

In the Multicolumn updates section, the check box is selected by default to apply multiple column changes for the same row into one UPDATE statement, instead of multiple statements. Leave this default selected and click OK.

13. You can also specify article properties for a specific article. Click the ellipsis button on the article row for the Employees table. (The dialog box you see will depend on the article type you selected properties for. Tables, views, and stored procedures each have different article properties).

		Owner	Object	
☑	▦	dbo	Categories	...
☑	▦	dbo	Customers	...
☑	▦	dbo	Employees	...
☑	▦	dbo	Order Details	...
☑	▦	dbo	Orders	...
☑	▦	dbo	Products	...
☑	▦	dbo	Shippers	...
☑	▦	dbo	Suppliers	...

The General, Snapshot, and Merging Changes tabs are all identical to the Article Defaults dialog boxes. The Resolver tab allows you to specify which Resolver to run when data conflicts occur (a Resolver is a built-in SQL Server algorithm used for determining how to handle update conflicts). For this exercise, leave the default Resolver selected. The default resolver will resolve conflicts based on a priority value assigned to individual subscribers. The default is for the publisher's changes to take priority over subscribers. SQL Server provides other resolvers, along with programming hooks that allow you to program your own resolver (in Visual Basic, for example).

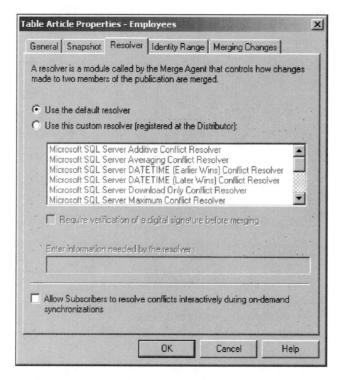

The Identity Range tab allows you to define the range of values permitted for the IDENTITY column of each subscription article. For this exercise, check the Automatically assign and maintain a unique identity range for each subscription check box, and click OK.

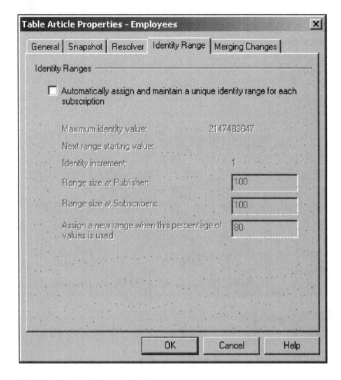

14. Click Next on the Specify Articles dialog box.

15. In the Article Issues dialog box, you'll be warned about any issues relating to the use of selected articles in the publication.

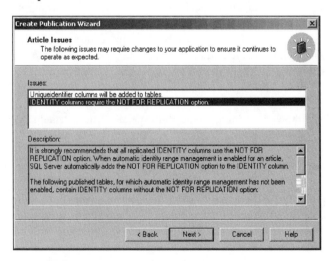

16. Click Next to get to the Publication Name and Description dialog box. Leave the default of Northwind.

17. In the Customize the Properties of the Publication dialog box, choose No, to bypass the addition of data filters, anonymous subscriptions, and the configuration of a different snapshot schedule.

18. In the Completing the Create Publication Wizard dialog box, click Finish to begin the process of creating the Merge publication. You'll see the progress of the publication creation, addition of articles, and starting of the Snapshot Agent.

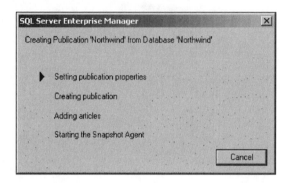

19. Click Close in the final dialog box.

How It Works

In this exercise, you began by starting up the Create Publication wizard. You selected the Northwind database, and then the replication type of Merge.

In step 8, you selected those articles that you wanted to use within the publication. Tables without a uniqueidentifier column will automatically have one added for Merge replication. We included all tables. Remember to include only the data that is needed by the subscribers as a best practice in creating your own publications. However, to avoid lookup or integrity errors, remember to include objects that are dependent upon each other (for example, primary and foreign key table relations). Also, any views or stored procedures should also have the referenced objects included in the same publication.

In step 9, you viewed the various merge replication specific article defaults. You also reviewed merge replication article configurations for a single table, the Employees table. From the Resolver tab, you left the default to resolve conflicts based on a priority value assigned to individual subscribers (you'll see where this is assigned when you review the push and pull subscriptions, in the next section).

You looked at the Identity Range tab (step 13), which permits you to define the range of values allowed on the IDENTITY column of each subscription. Designating ranges allows you to prevent duplicate IDENTITY values from being replicated back to the publisher and other subscribers. For example, if a new row (containing an IDENTITY value) is inserted on the subscriber, it may not be updated on the publisher right away. So if the row insert on the subscriber generates an IDENTITY value of 10, for example, this value may have already been used on the publisher by a different transaction. If an attempt to insert the value 10 occurs when the subscriber synchronizes queued updates to the publisher, the row will be rejected.

Defining ranges helps reduce the danger of this occurring. In this example, you used the default range size of 100 for both the publisher and subscribers. This means that one clump of 100 values are preserved for use by the publisher (for example, identity values 101–200), and another clump of 100 values for each subscriber (for example, identity values 201–300 for subscriber A and 301–400 for subscriber B). When the value ranges reach 80 percent usage, a new identity range is automatically created for new inserts for the publisher or subscriber that has reached the threshold.

In step 15, you looked at the Article Issues dialog box, which listed warnings about adding uniqueidentifier columns to tables as well as warnings about the NOT FOR REPLICATION option for IDENTITY columns. When NOT FOR REPLICATION is configured, SQL Server 2000 maintains the original IDENTITY values on rows added by the publisher to the subscriber and vice versa, but increments those rows added by users at the source database (where the original increment occurred) as usual. This keeps the publisher and subscriber data in sync, which is particularly important when the IDENTITY column is used as a primary key (and/or referenced by a foreign key).

> **Timestamp columns, on the other hand, have the exact opposite behavior. Timestamp data types automatically generate binary numbers, which are guaranteed to be unique within the database. This data type is used to version-stamp a table row. Microsoft's version of the timestamp data type isn't functionally equivalent with the SQL-92 standard, but will be made compliant in future versions of SQL Server. For now, timestamp columns replicated from the publisher to the subscriber are regenerated and not preserved.**

Lastly, if your Merge replication contains text or image data, any calls to UPDATETEXT and WRITETEXT will not cause changes to be replicated because the system triggers that monitor data changes don't detect these operations. Unlike Transactional replication, you cannot use WITH LOG because these commands don't cause the Merge replication system triggers to fire. To continue using these functions, you must follow them with a "dummy" UPDATE statement within the same transaction, so the values will be replicated, as the UPDATE trigger will then be fired, propagating the changes accordingly.

Subscription Types

There are two types of subscriptions: push and pull. In the following sections, you'll look at each of these subscription types and what happens when you use them.

Push Subscriptions

With **push subscriptions**, the distributor is responsible for sending updates to the subscribers. The subscriber will receive updates from the distributor without requesting them. Centralized administration is one of the advantages of a push subscription methodology. Push subscriptions should also be used for those subscribers that require frequent updates from the publisher and are normally continuously connected to the network.

Try It Out—Setting Up a Push Subscription

In this example, you'll push a subscription using the Merge publication you created in the previous Try It Out example. To push a subscription, in Enterprise Manager, do the following:

1. Expand the Server group, Server registration, Replication folder, and Publications folder.

2. Right-click the publication and select Push New Subscription.

3. For this exercise, in the Push Subscription Wizard introduction dialog box, leave Show advanced options unchecked and click Next. Checking the Show Advanced Options check box for Transactional or Snapshot replication publications would have allowed you to set configuration options for immediate or queued updating, as well as set the location of the Distribution Agent. If you're performing a push of a Merge subscription, you'll see the option to set the location of the Distribution Agent regardless of selecting Show Advanced Options.

4. Select the SQL Server Instance where your subscriber database is located on your network.

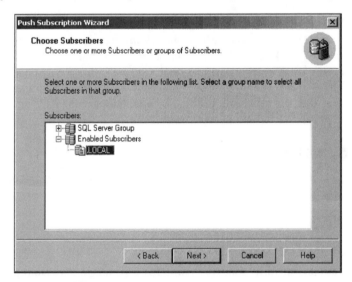

5. In the Choose Destination Database dialog box, click the Browse or Create button to select an existing database or create a new database.

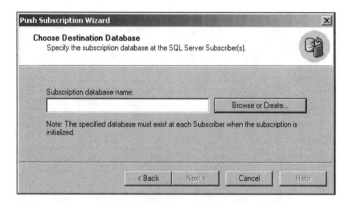

6. You can select a database to replicate to on your subscriber SQL Server instance. In this example, you select NorthwindReporting as the subscribing database.

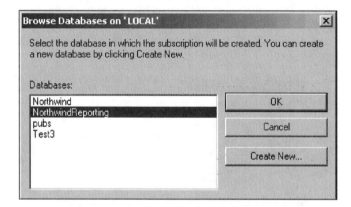

On this dialog box you can also create a new subscriber database by clicking the Create New button. If you haven't created NorthwindReporting, you can click this button now to create it. For this exercise, click OK to exit the Browse Databases dialog box, and Next to continue past the Choose Destination Database dialog box.

7. On the Set Merge Agent Location, select Run the agent at the Distributor. Had you chosen to Run the agent at the Subscriber, you would be offloading some of the agent processing to the subscriber server while still keeping administration control at the publisher and distributor. You won't see this dialog if subscriber and distributor are on the same SQL Server instance.

8. In the Set Merge Agent Schedule dialog box, select Continuously. Continuously running Merge Agents will cause more frequent polling of the publisher and subscriber, but also keeps changes made between the participating databases up to date. Scheduled updates would work well for data that is allowed to remain out of sync for a defined period of time (in between updates).

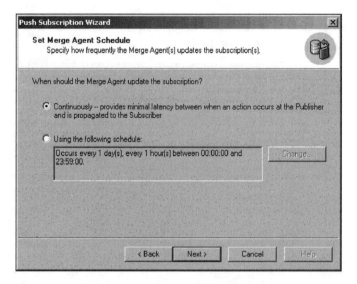

9. In the Initialize Subscription dialog box, leave the Yes, initialize the schema and data bullet selected, and then check the Start the Snapshot Agent to begin the initialization process immediately check box. If you don't see the check box, this means that the Snapshot Agent has already created the snapshot. That snapshot will be applied automatically when the subscription is created.

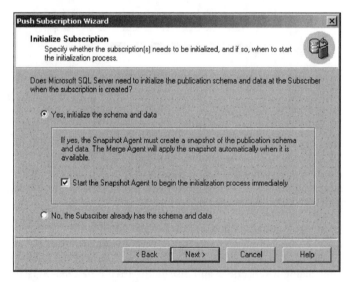

10. In the Set Subscription Priority dialog box, leave Use the Publisher as a proxy for the Subscriber when resolving conflicts selected. A subscription that uses this option is called a **local subscription**, which means that all subscribers have the same priority. With this setting, the first subscriber to merge with the publisher wins the data conflict.

You'll often see this setting for anonymous subscriptions, or those publications with many subscribers, as assigning individual priority values can be a burdensome task. A subscription that has a set priority is called a **global subscription**, which means that those subscribers with higher priorities win data conflicts.

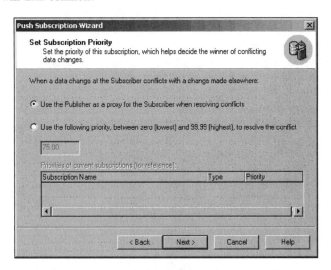

11. Click Next in the Start Required Services dialog box.

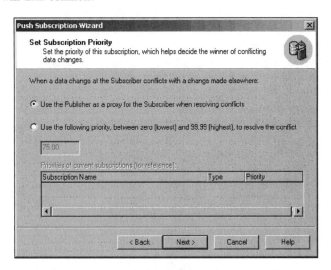

12. Click Finish in the final dialog box, and then Close.

How It Works

Checking the Show Advanced Options check box for Transactional or Snapshot replication publications would have allowed you to set configuration options for immediate or queued updating, and also would have set the location of the Distribution Agent. If you're performing a push of a Merge subscription, you will see the option to set the location of the Distribution Agent regardless of selecting Show Advanced Options.

In step 7, you selected whether or not to run the Merge Agent at the distributor or subscriber. By running the agent at the subscriber, you're able to offload processing overhead to a different server, while still keeping control with the publisher and distributor. On the other hand, if the subscriber server has less capacity, running the agent on the publisher and distributor may be a better choice. For Snapshot and Transactional replication, you'll see the Distribution Agent Location dialog box; while for Merge replication, you select the location of the Merge Agent. In general, for publications with few subscribers, run the agent from the SQL Server instance with the most available capacity and performance. Otherwise, if you have hundreds of subscribers, you may have better performance running the agent from the subscriber computers.

In step 8, for Merge replication, this dialog box determined the schedule and frequency for when the Merge Agent would run (the dialog box is similar for the Distribution Agent when using Transactional or Snapshot replication). If both continuous and scheduled update frequencies are an option for your topology, try out both frequencies to see which performs better (if a difference is seen).

In the Initialize Subscription dialog box (step 9), you checked the Start the Snapshot Agent to begin the initialization process immediately check box to kick off a new snapshot of the schema and data. This means the process will begin immediately after finishing the wizard. (The No option is grayed out for Snapshot replication.)

In step 10, in the Set Subscription Priority dialog box, you left the Use the Publisher as a proxy for the Subscriber when resolving conflicts selected. Also, you can set varying priorities for each subscriber if you want some subscribers to have greater (or lesser) priority when a merge conflict occurs.

The status of the required services for the subscriptions was listed (in this case, the SQL Server Agent) in the Start Required Services dialog box. The MS DTC service is also required to enable Immediate Update functionality for Transactional replication.

After configuring push subscriptions, the initial snapshot should be created, and associated agents (depending on the replication type) should be started as well. After reviewing pull subscriptions, you'll learn how to monitor the status of your publication and subscriptions.

> **One last important note on push and pull subscriptions.** Your Snapshot Agent may take a longer time to run based on the size and number of tables being replicated. If the Distribution Agent begins running without an available snapshot, it will shut down if it isn't configured to run continuously. The distribution and Merge Agents will not run until this process is complete. If you chose to run the Distribution or Merge Agents continuously, these agents should start up automatically. Be sure to review the "Replication Monitor" section to learn how to view the status of these agents as well as how to manually start these agents when necessary.

Pull Subscriptions

Pull subscriptions are subscriber initiated. This allows disconnected subscribers to control when and how they connect. For example, mobile office users can connect with a modem and synchronize when they have the opportunity. Connected sites may wish to use pull subscriptions for subscriber servers that have more capacity than the publisher and/or distributor.

Try It Out–Setting Up a Pull Subscription

1. In the previous example, you pushed a Merge publication subscription. In this example, you'll be pulling a Transactional publication subscription. Prior to beginning these steps, drop the merge publication for Northwind and re-create the Transactional replication publication. After you're finished re-creating this publication, expand the Server group and Server registration of the server with the publication you wish to subscribe to. You'll first check to make sure you have access to the publication you're trying to pull.

2. Expand the Replication folder and right-click the publication you wish to pull and select Properties.

3. Be sure the login that is used by your SQL Server Agent on the pulling SQL Server instance will have access to pull this publication. Otherwise, click the Add button to add the appropriate login (this will list any login with access to the published database that is defined on the publisher and distributor). Unlike other settings in Publication Properties, you can add new logins to access the publication even when other subscribers are actively subscribed to the publication. Click OK when finished.

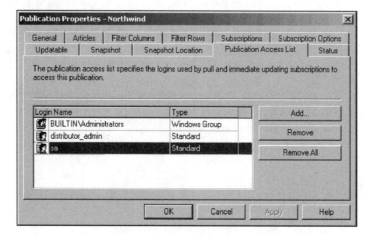

4. Expand the Server group and Server registration of the SQL Server instance pulling the subscription.

5. Expand the Replication folder and right-click Subscriptions. Select New Pull Subscription.

6. In the Pull Subscription Wizard dialog box, check the check box to Show advanced options, and click Next.

7. In the Look for Publications dialog box, select Look at publications from registered servers.

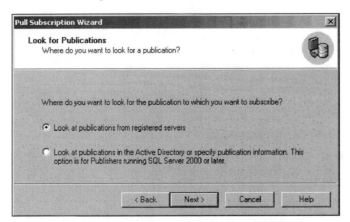

8. Expand the server and select a Transactional replication publication (since you did Merge replication last time) to subscribe to, in the Choose Publication dialog box.

9. If your SQL Server Agent is not included in the publication access list you looked at step 3, you'll get the Specify Synchronization Agent Login dialog box, which offers two options for connecting to the distributor—impersonation of the SQL Server Agent, or specifying another SQL Server login.

10. In the Choose Destination Database dialog box, select the database from which the subscription will be pulled.

11. Keep the setting of Yes, initialize the schema and data, in the Initialize Subscription dialog box.

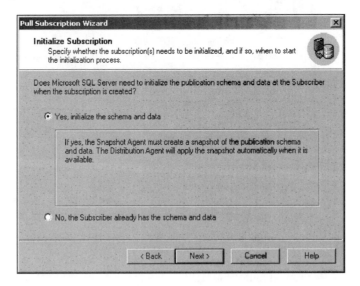

12. In the Snapshot Delivery dialog box, leave the default of Use snapshot files from the default snapshot folder for this publication. The other option would allow you to download snapshot files from an alternative location. Alternate snapshot locations are often used to download snapshot files over the Internet.

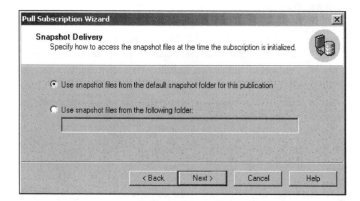

13. Because this is Transactional replication (although you'll see this for Snapshot as well), next you'll see the Set Distribution Agent Schedule dialog box. Leave Continuously selected.

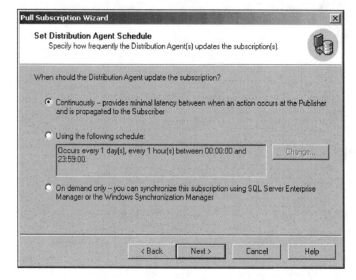

14. In the Start Required Services dialog box (which was also seen in the push subscription example), you're shown the status of required services on the subscriber server. Click Next.

15. Click Finish to begin pulling the subscription. You'll be shown a status screen listing each step of the build process. Click Close when finished.

How It Works

First, you verified that the security account controlling the SQL Server Agent on the subscriber SQL Server instance had permissions to pull the publication. Remember that group membership counts toward this, so members of the Administrators group on the publisher would have permissions via the BUILTIN\Administrators group (assuming this wasn't removed).

In step 7, you selected whether to look for publications from registered servers, or through Active Directory and/or specification of publication information. Had you selected Active Directory and the publication specification, you would have seen a dialog box allowing you to type in the Publisher server name, database, and publication name, along with the authentication method (how to connect) or the option to look up registered publications via Active Directory. Instead, you chose to search for publications on servers registered on the computer.

In step 10, you selected the database where the subscription will be pulled, and in step 11, you chose the schema and data to be created on the subscriber (since it didn't already exist).

> **Foregoing this option adds more complexity, because you must ensure that the subscriber reflects the schema and data at a time immediately prior to moving data via the Distribution or Merge Agents. Doing so can be tricky when you have several concurrent updates to the published database.**

In step 12, you used the default directory for storing snapshot files, and in step 13 you opted for the updates to occur continuously (although pull subscriptions are often used on a scheduled basis, or on demand).

Using Replication Monitor

Replication Monitor is the primary tool used within Enterprise Manager to monitor your replication topology. It allows you to view the status of Replication Agents based on the polling interval, which you can configure, and it helps you gather troubleshooting information in the event of problems (more on this in the "Troubleshooting" section). Replication Monitor, as you saw earlier in the chapter, is added automatically for the distributor SQL Server instance. Only members of the sysadmin server role or members of the replmonitor database role (a database role automatically created in the distribution database) may view activity using Replication Monitor.

1. In Enterprise Manager, expand the Server registration and the Replication Monitor node.

2. Expand the Publishers folder, and then the name of publisher and publication you want to view. Click the publication, and in the right pane, you'll see the list of agents associated with the publication and any subscribers subscribing to it.

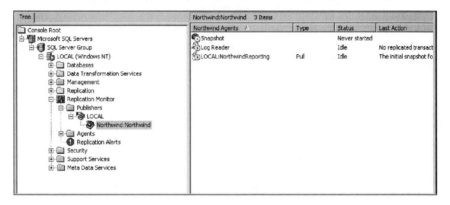

From this view, you can check the status of your Replication Agents. The Last Action column shows the last replication update status. If you see red Xs on any of the nodes in the branches of replication, this indicates issues with replication. Common errors are described in the "Troubleshooting" section.

How It Works

Within this view of agents, you perform the following actions:

❑ **View agent history.**
Right-click the agent in the right pane and select Agent History. Use this to help troubleshoot your replication issues. Once in the Agent History dialog box, you can double-click the individual rows in the History view to see more detailed information about the event.

❑ **Use Replication Monitor to view any error details.**
When you see red Xs, right-click the agent and select Error Details. If it's grayed out, it means there are no error details to see. Also, you can see error messages in the Agent History view.

❑ **View the properties of the SQL Server Job that invokes the Replication Agent.**
Replication Agents are actually executables located on the SQL Server instance. SQL Server
Agent jobs are used to manage these executables. To view the associated job from within
Replication Monitor, right-click the agent and select Agent Properties.

❑ **Start or stop synchronizing between the publisher and subscriber for merge or Distribution
Agents.**
Right-click the agent and select Start Synchronizing or Stop Synchronizing. If you're stopping
the agent, changes will stop flowing between the publisher and subscriber(s) until you restart
the agent again (changes will be queued and won't be lost).

❑ **Start or stop the log reader or Snapshot Agents.**
Right-click them and select Start Agent or Stop Agent.

❑ **View or modify agent profiles.**
Replication Monitor allows you to configure the individual settings of the Replication Agents.
These settings are grouped together in a "profile," and each agent has a "default" profile. If you
want to change the settings, you can create a new profile, change the values of the new profile,
and change the profile the agent will use once it's restarted. In the "Troubleshooting" section,
you'll look at some applied uses for doing so. To view or modify the profile, right-click the
agent and select Agent Profile.

Try It Out—Viewing the Profile of the Snapshot Agent

1. Expand Replication Monitor on the publisher.

2. Expand the Agents folder and click the Snapshot Agents folder.

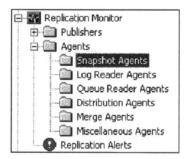

3. In the right pane, right-click the Snapshot Agent for the publication you wish to configure, and
select Agent Profiles.

4. Click the View Details button in the Snapshot Agent Profiles dialog box (this is the same dialog
box where you can add new profiles for your agent to use instead).

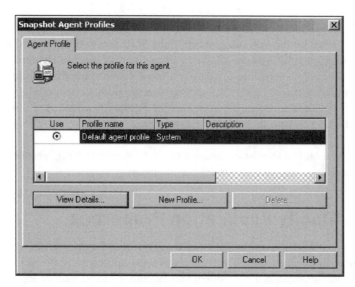

5. The various settings your agent uses during operation are shown in the Replication Agent Profile Detail dialog box. In some cases, you may want to change these settings, but we'll address this in the "Troubleshooting" section.

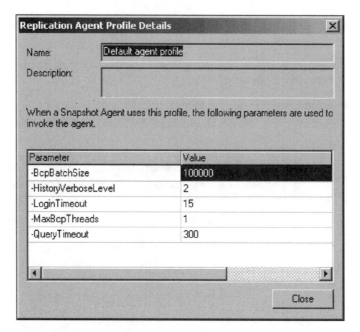

How It Works

Agents are executables on the operating system of the SQL Server instance, and are controlled via switches in the associated SQL Server job. Sometimes you may need to change the settings of the agent, either to improve performance or remedy a specific error (more on this in the "Troubleshooting" section). To modify the settings, you would have selected New Profile in step 5. After changing the associated settings, you change the Profile the agent uses box by changing the bullet point in the Use column in the Agent Profile dialog box.

In this example, you looked at existing settings. In the "Troubleshooting" section, we'll show you which settings may help you with certain replication issues.

View and Modify Publication Properties

You can view or modify the properties of a publication within Enterprise Manager. Some changes to a publication cannot be performed until you drop any subscriptions subscribing to the publication. Once subscriptions for the publication are dropped, you can modify most publication settings that you originally configured within the wizard. (You cannot change some properties, such as the name of the publication, database referenced by the publication, or the type of publication—merge, transactional, snapshot. If you need to do this, drop and re-create the publication from scratch.)

Try It Out—View and Modify Publication Properties

1. Expand the Server group and Server registration of the publisher. Then expand the Replication folder and Publications folder.

2. Right-click the publication you wish to view or modify properties for, and select Properties. If there are still subscribers subscribing to this publication, you'll receive a warning. Click OK to continue.

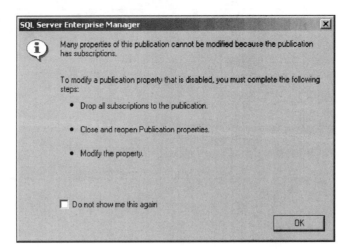

3. The Publication Properties dialog box shows tabs for many of the features you originally configured when setting up the publication via the Create Publication wizard.

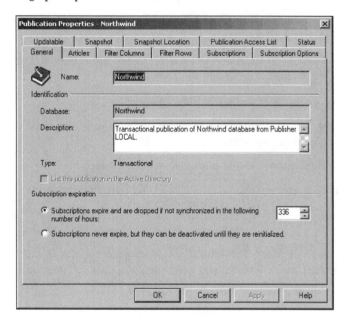

How It Works

This Properties dialog box contains several tabs that allow you to make modifications to the publication. For example, you can add or remove articles (in the Articles tab), add horizontal or vertical filters (Filter Columns or Filter Rows), change whether or not you allow pull subscriptions (in the Subscription Options), and more.

Reinitializing a Subscription

In the previous example, you may have noticed the Subscription expiration setting on the General tab. The Subscriptions expire and are dropped if not synchronized in the following number of hours: option controls the number of hours without synchronizing (not running distribution or Merge Agents) before the subscription is marked as expired and dropped. For Merge replication, you can designate the number of days before subscriptions are expired and dropped. If you select the Never expire option, subscriptions will be deactivated only after transactions have been kept in the distribution database for a maximum retention period (72 hours for Transactional replication).

Expired subscriptions must be re-created from scratch, either by using the Enterprise Manager wizards or, if you scripted the subscriber, executing the script to re-create the subscription. Replication scripting is reviewed later on in the "Scripting Your Publication and Subscriptions" section. Deactivated subscriptions must be reinitialized, meaning a new snapshot must be applied to the subscriber before replication can continue for the subscriber.

1. For push subscriptions in Enterprise Manager, expand the Server registration and Server name of the publisher SQL Server instance.

2. Expand the Replication folder and Publication folder. Select the publication for the subscriber you wish to reinitialize.

3. Right-click the subscriber and select Reinitialize.

4. For pull subscriptions in Enterprise Manager, expand the Server registration and Server name of the subscriber SQL Server instance.

5. Expand the Replication folder and the Subscriptions folder.

6. Right-click the subscription to be reinitialized and click Reinitialize.

How It Works

After selecting the subscription to be reinitialized, the snapshot schema and data will be applied to the subscriber the next time the Snapshot Agent prepares a snapshot and the distribution or Merge Agent runs.

Scripting Your Publication and Subscriptions

You can use Enterprise Manager to generate a T-SQL script of your publication and subscription configurations. This is useful in case your publication or subscriptions are erroneously dropped or modified, or if you wish to temporarily remove replication to perform an upgrade or migration. Scripting saves you time by allowing you to reexecute the script in Query Analyzer rather than stepping through the entire setup wizard.

There are two methods for scripting replication. In the first method, you'll be shown how to script the publication along with replication and distributor settings configured on the SQL Server instance. The second method is written to script for just the specific publication and the subscribers subscribing to it.

1. Expand the Server Group and registration for the publications and distributor settings you want to script.

2. Click the Databases folder and go to Tools I Replication I Generate SQL Script.

3. In the Generate SQL Script dialog box, on the General tab, select the check box to designate whether distributor properties should be scripted, which publications to script, which pull sub-scriptions to include (if any), and whether to script the creation or the dropping of the existing components. You can also script the creation of the replication jobs. The Preview button allows you to see what is scripted. Select the File Options tab.

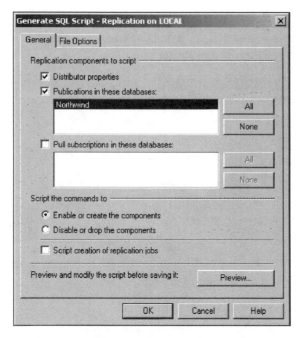

4. In the File Options tab, choose the preferred file format, and decide whether or not the script should be appended to an existing file. Click OK to create the file. You will then be prompted for the file location. The resulting file can be opened in Query Analyzer and executed from the publisher SQL Server instance to re-create the publications and settings that have been scripted.

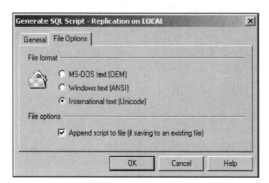

Try It Out–Script Out a Specific Publication and Associated Subscribers

1. Expand the Server Group and registration for the publication and subscriptions you want to script.

2. Expand the Replication folder, and the Publications folder. Right-click the publication you want to script, and select Generate SQL Script.

3. In the Generate SQL Script dialog box, select whether to create the publication, or to delete it. Select the file format, and whether or not you wish to append the script to an existing file. Click the Preview button to view the script.

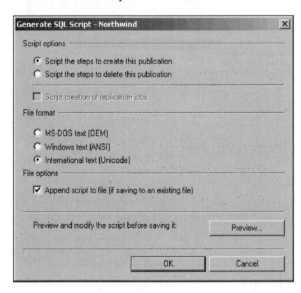

4. In the Replication Component Script Preview dialog box, you can view the stored procedures necessary for rebuilding the publication and associated subscriptions. If you want to just recover a specific subscription, these procedures will be located toward the end of the script, and are commented for readability.

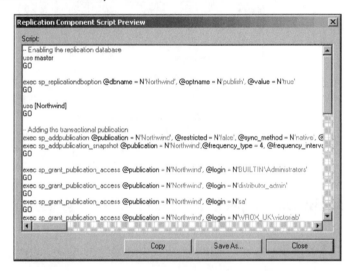

5. Select Close, and then OK to generate the script. You'll be prompted for the script output location. The resulting file can then be used in Query Analyzer to restore or delete (if that's what you selected) your publications and subscriptions.

Remove Publications or Subscriptions

Enterprise Manager can be used to remove existing subscriptions and publications.

Try It Out–Remove a Publication and Subscription

1. To drop a subscription to a publication, expand the Server registration and Server name of the publisher SQL Server instance.

2. Expand the Replication folder and Publications folder. Click the publication containing the subscriptions you wish to delete.

3. In the right pane, right-click the subscription you wish to delete and select Delete.

4. To drop a publication, right-click the publication under the Publications folder and select Delete.

How It Works

Deleting a publication and subscription removes the definition of the publication and subscription in the replication system tables as well as jobs that are used to control the Replication Agents. If you remove replication while there are outstanding updates in the queue, these pending transactions may not be migrated to the associated subscribers.

Disabling your Publisher and Distributor

You may decide that you no longer wish to use your SQL Server instance as a publisher or distributor. Also, you may want to remove the publisher and distributor properties before an SQL Server upgrade (removing replication prior to an upgrade can sometimes translate to cleaner or faster upgrades). Regardless of the reason, you can remove the publisher and distributor roles quite easily within Enterprise Manager.

Try It Out–Disable Publishing and the Distributor

1. Expand the server group and click the SQL Server registration.

2. Select Tools | Replication | Disable Publishing.

3. At the introductory dialog box, click Next.

4. Select Yes, disable publishing on 'ServerName'.

5. You will then be warned about publications and subscriptions that will be dropped if publishing is disabled. Click Next.

6. In the final dialog box, click Finish to remove publications and subscriptions. You'll receive a final dialog box telling you that the removal is complete.

How It Works

Replication is disabled in this exercise by using the Disable Publishing and Distribution Wizard. This wizard disables all components on your SQL Server instance, cleans up system table entries, and removes any publications and subscriptions referencing them. To publish on this server in the future, you must run the Configure Publishing and Distribution wizard again.

Troubleshooting

First and foremost, when troubleshooting replication, make sure you're running the latest service pack available for SQL Server. Service packs often include replication bug fixes. The latest service pack offered by Microsoft is Service Pack 3a, and can be downloaded from www.microsoft.com/sql/downloads/2000/sp3.asp.

Other errors you may see often aren't related to bugs, but rather environment or configuration issues. The following table reviews the more common issues you may see, as well as the reason they occur and potential resolutions. Also, when it comes to troubleshooting, familiarize yourself with the Microsoft Product Support Services site, at support.microsoft.com/. Knowledgebase articles on this site are very helpful for troubleshooting known replication issues.

If This Goes Wrong	Cause and Resolution
In the Create Publication wizard, Transactional Replication is grayed out; it cannot be selected.	The Microsoft SQL Server 2000 Personal Edition and Desktop Engine versions do not support Transactional replication publishing. These versions DO support Transactional replication **subscriptions** however.
When I try to change the data type column in a published table, I get the following error: "Server: Msg 4929, Level 16, State 1, Line 1 Cannot alter the table "TableName" because it's being published for replication."	When changing the data type of an existing table of a column, you will need to do the following: ❑ Drop referencing subscriptions ❑ Remove the article from the publication ❑ Perform the data type change ❑ Add the article to the publication again ❑ Add the subscriptions again When adding or deleting columns on published tables, these changes should be made through the Replication Publication Properties dialog box, on the **Filter Columns** tab. Via this interface, you can add additional columns to the publication, or delete columns. Changes made here will be propagated to subscribers. If you're adding or removing existing columns from the article (publishing some and not others), keep in mind that your subscriptions will be reinitialized, and the schema and data will need to be re-sent.

If This Goes Wrong	Cause and Resolution
When I try to create a publication, I get the following error: "Because SQL Server Agent on 'ServerName' uses the system account, SQL Server replication between servers will fail. To use replication between servers, select another server to be the Distributor for 'ServerName'."	Your SQL Server Agent service account should not be using the Local System account. Rather, you should be using a Domain or Standard Windows 2000 account with Administrator access to all SQL Server instances in your replication topology.
When I try to enable my SQL Server instance to be a publisher, I get the following error: "You must be a member of the sysadmin fixed server role to complete this operation."	You need to be a member of the `sysadmin` fixed server role to configure replication. Be sure to check the properties of your Server Registration in Enterprise Manager, making sure the login you use (authentication or a SLQ login) is associated with the `sysadmin` server role membership. To check your method of connection, right-click the server in Enterprise Manager, and select **Edit SQL Server Registration Properties**. Check the connection method here. This is the security context from which you'll be attempting to configure the SQL Server instance as a publisher.
Your Distribution Agent in Replication Monitor keeps showing message "Timeout expired."	This error usually occurs when replicating over slow networks. The remedy is to increase the amount of the time the Distribution Agent has to complete its operation. This is configured via the Query Timeout property within the profile of the Distribution Agent for your publication. Experiment with increasing this value (the default is 300 seconds).

Table continued overleaf

If This Goes Wrong	Cause and Resolution
When viewing my Replication Agents within Replication Monitor, the agent (could be Snapshot, Distribution, Log Reader, Merge), keeps saying, "never started," even though I keep restarting it.	Replication Agents are executables on your SQL Server computer; however, they are actually managed and started by SQL Server Agent jobs. When you see "never started," it's often due to insufficient permissions of the job owner Often, you're best off assigning the replication job owners to sysadmin or a member of the sysadmin role. To change this, follow these steps: 1. Expand Replication Monitor 2. Expand the Publishers folder 3. Expand the publisher encountering the issue 4. Click the publication 5. Right-click the agent encountering the issue and select Agent Properties 6. This brings up the SQL Server Agent job's General tab, where you can change the Owner to "sa" or another job owner with sufficient access
Within Replication Monitor, my Distribution Agent displays the following error: "The process could not connect to Subscriber 'ServerName'. Login failed for user 'UserName'." My agents are displaying errors about not being able to connect to the subscriber server.	Be sure that the service account running the SQL Server Agent has access to the subscriber database. If you originally did this, check the permissions on the subscriber to ensure that the account security hasn't been modified. (Security is covered in detail in Chapter 6.) There are many variations of this error message, but most of the time, you should check the following: 1. Make sure that the subscriber is up and available. Is the SQL Server instance encountering problems (errors or outages)? Is there a network issue? If the answer is no to the first question, or yes to the second, you should troubleshoot these issues first. 2. Does the SQL Server Agent service account running the agent encountering the issue have access to the subscriber server? If not, this should be resolved first.
My pull subscription is failing for my Merge Agent with the error: "The subscription has been marked inactive and must be reinitialized at the Publisher. Contact the database administrator."	Earlier we discussed how to reinitialize subscriptions that have been marked as inactive. This error indicates that you should reinitialize the subscription.

If This Goes Wrong	Cause and Resolution
I keep seeing the following error: "The agent is suspect. No activity reported within the last 10 minutes." in Replication Monitor for my distribution or Merge Agents.	You may see this error appear when the Replication Agent is too busy to respond to polls from SQL Server Enterprise Manager. This error is problematic only when associated with other errors. If this is the only error, you usually only need to check the history of the agent, any error details, and whether or not the agent is running. You can potentially reduce the frequency of the error by increasing the inactivity threshold that the Replication Monitor uses to poll the agent. Do the following: 1. Right-click Replication Monitor, and select Refresh Rate and Settings 2. Increase the value of the Inactivity threshold to a larger value (greater than the 10 minute default)
My Log Reader Agent is returning the following message: "The process could not execute 'sp_replcmds' on servername."	This error may occur when the transactions marked for replication by the Log Reader Agent aren't moved quickly enough to the distribution database. Setting the Log Reader Agent profile `QueryTimeout` value to 0 (which means that the query will wait indefinitely for a response) alleviates this. Otherwise, you can increase the value of `QueryTimeout` to a higher value and reduce the size of the `ReadBatchSize` setting (which controls the maximum transactions read from the transaction log of the publisher at a time, thus decreasing the time it takes for the Log Reader Agent to process a batch to the distribution database).

Summary

In this chapter, we began by defining what replication is, why you would use it, and when you should not use it. You learned about the components that make up replication (publications and articles), and the role that SQL Server instances play within the replication topology (publisher, distributor, subscriber). You then reviewed the various replication topology combinations that can be used.

Next, you looked at the replication security requirements that should be addressed prior to first configuring replication. After that, you went through how to configure an SQL Server instance as a publisher and distributor. Once the publisher was configured, you learned about the three types of replication: Snapshot, Transactional, and Merge. You looked at how each works and how to set them up.

Next you examined the two subscription types: push and pull. You ran through an exercise on each type, highlighting the variations between the two. Once the publication and subscription were set up, you learned how to monitor their progress using Replication Monitor.

You studied how to view and modify an existing publication, how to reinitialize a subscription that has been deactivated, how to remove a subscription and publication, and how to disable the publisher and distributor on your SQL Server instance.

Finally, you went through the various things that can go wrong when setting up replication, and what you can do to resolve issues when they occur.

10

Development with Transact-SQL

As a database administrator (DBA), writing Transact-SQL (T-SQL) code may or may not be your direct responsibility. However, as a DBA it's your responsibility to ensure that database routines do what they're supposed to do, and that these routines are as efficient as possible. Knowledge of T-SQL will provide you with the ability to determine which code is acceptable for your database. It will also allow you to set coding standards for your organization's developers.

This chapter will build on what was looked at in Chapters 3 and 4, and give you a good understanding of some more advanced T-SQL syntax. Complete coverage of the syntax is beyond the scope of this book, but we'll give you everything you need to start developing. We'll point out some common pitfalls along the way and try to provide you with some good practices and advice as well. We'll also give references that will provide more depth than we can provide here, where appropriate. One thing that we won't do is try to convince you that T-SQL is always the best tool for every job. T-SQL is a set-based language, and although you can use it like other programming languages, it isn't always a good idea to do so. There are often many ways to accomplish the same task using T-SQL, and we'll try to show you several ways, along with some considerations of why one way may be a better choice than the other.

Programmable Components

In addition to Data Definition Language, Data Modification Language, and Data Control Language statements (which you'll continue to look at in the following sections), T-SQL offers numerous programmable components that let you write powerful database routines. In this section we'll give you an overview of how each construct works.

Other Data Types

There are a few data types that don't exactly fall into any of the groups discussed in Chapter 3.

The TABLE data type is used to store a table in memory. This data type cannot be used to create a column within a table. Rather, it's used to create in-memory tables within your stored procedures. Such tables are similar in concept to temporary tables, but instead of residing in the TEMPDB database as temporary tables, in-memory tables are generated in RAM and are destroyed as soon as your code module has finished executing. We'll discuss table variables later in the chapter.

The CURSOR data type holds a reference to a cursor—a temporary object used to loop through a set of records. Cursors are discussed later in the chapter. The CURSOR data type cannot be used to create a column.

The SQL_VARIANT data type stores values of other Transact-SQL data types. SQL_VARIANT can be used if the range of variable values is unknown when the variable is declared. SQL_VARIANT can also be used to create a table column.

The TIMESTAMP data type holds a binary value that tracks the sequence of row modifications. SQL Server automatically maintains columns with a TIMESTAMP data type. Contrary to what you might think, a TIMESTAMP data type isn't associated with the storage of date or time values.

The UNIQUEIDENTIFIER data type holds GUIDs (**globally unique identifiers**). Columns or variables of a UNIQUEIDENTIFIER data type can be populated by using the NEWID() system function, which creates a new GUID each time it's executed, or by supplying a string with xxxxxxxx-xxxx-xxxx-xxxx-xxxxxxxxxxxx format where each x can be a digit or a letter between a and f.

Variables and Parameters

As you've seen in the previous section, T-SQL provides a rich set of data types for storing values in tables and in temporary holding areas. Variables and parameters happen to be just that: a temporary holding of a value, or a set of values.

There are two types of variables: **local** and **global**. Local variables are denoted with a single @ sign, as in the following:

```
DECLARE @my_variable
```

Global variables, on the other hand, are internal values tracked by SQL Server itself, and are denoted with two @ signs. For example, @@TRANCOUNT shows the number of open transactions on the current connection. When you write code, you can only declare and modify values of the local variables. Unless specified, when we refer to variables in this chapter, we mean the local variables.

There are a few subtle differences between the local variables and parameters that you should keep in mind while developing database code. Parameters are passed into stored procedures or user-defined functions to limit the scope of their execution to a certain table or a certain set of values. Variables, on the other hand can be declared in any query or batch (set of queries), including stored procedures, triggers, and user-defined functions. Views don't take parameters and cannot contain variable declarations.

> **Also, keep in mind that local variables cannot be declared with data types of TEXT, NTEXT, or IMAGE, while parameters can. We'll show you plenty of examples using variables and parameters when we talk about stored procedures and user-defined functions.**

Data Definition Language

As the name implies, DDL is used to **define** objects in SQL. An object in SQL Server can be a table, trigger, stored procedure, view, or function, among others; and a SQL Server database can contain over 2 billion objects. A search for "*specifications-SQL Server objects*" in BOL (Books Online) will give you all the details that are common among all versions of SQL Server and some that are specific to the version that you use.

If you'd like to follow along, open up an instance of Query Analyzer. You'll go through the syntax to create a simple database with some of these objects inside. Although you could use Enterprise Manager (EM) to do what you're doing here, it's good to know how to script all of this as well.

A big reason to use T-SQL scripts is so that you can easily re-create the database. You can check the scripts in and out of version control applications (like Microsoft Visual SourceSafe), retain the complete history of your work, and go back to any version you've had. Scripts can be a lifesaver, and it can't be stressed enough that you should create, use, and back up these scripts. Some good habits to get into are to always make changes using scripts, and test and apply your scripts, and once they're bug-free, check them in. If you don't have time to finish the script, find a good stopping point, document it clearly, and check in what you have. Don't get into the habit of manipulating your objects directly in EM. Some people are willing to make minor tweaks directly in EM, but this should never be done in production. A tweak here and there adds up over time, and your scripts will be unlikely to reflect the actual objects.

If you're the DBA that creates the database and its objects, you should have scripts for everything in the database. If you're working on a database that you've inherited, it's likely that you won't have these scripts. For large databases, generating these scripts can be time-consuming, but there are some shortcuts. You can generate scripts for everything in your database from Query Analyzer or EM, but be warned, creating a single script for all objects doesn't mean that this same script will run error- or warning-free all of the time. A single script like this may be a good idea to start off with, but at a minimum you should at least go through and reorganize it. Many scripting tools, including Enterprise Manager create objects in alphabetical order. Therefore, stored procedures, triggers, views, and other code modules might be scripted before the tables that these code modules reference. Hence, if you attempt to run the script generated by the scripting tool, you might encounter many errors.

CREATE

CREATE is used to create objects in SQL Server. To begin with, you're going to create a database and populate it with objects to work with.

Try It Out–Creating the Southwind Database

Let's create a database called Southwind. You'll use CREATE DATABASE to do this as follows:

```
USE master
GO
CREATE DATABASE Southwind
GO
```

Of course, there are many other options you can use, but this is CREATE DATABASE in its simplest form. This simple CREATE DATABASE statement creates a very small database with default options: default sizes for data and transaction log files, default collation, and so forth.

Before moving on, we wanted to discuss GO statement briefly. GO separates batches within the script, and sends the statements to be processed together. GO cannot be commented with other statements using multiline style comments (/*...*/) unless the GO line is the first line in the commented section; otherwise, use single-line style comment markers (–).

Next, you use CREATE TABLE to create a table:

```
USE Southwind
GO

CREATE TABLE dbo.Employee (
    EmployeeID INT NOT NULL IDENTITY(1, 1) PRIMARY KEY,
    [Group] VARCHAR(50) NULL,
    EmployeeName VARCHAR(50) NULL
)
GO
```

First, you tell SQL Server that you want to use the Southwind database, and then you use CREATE TABLE to create the Employee table. Objects in the database must have an owner; if the owner isn't specified, then by default, the owner is the creator of the object. Let's create all of the objects with dbo as the owner. For more on Ownership chains, see Chapter 6.

There's a lot going on in this simple script, so let's dive into it. The first item on the first line after the CREATE statement is the name of the column, EmployeeID in this case. You give its data type (as discussed in Chapter 3), an INTeger, and indicate that the column should not allow NULLs (meaning that the column has to have a known value). The next column is Group. You'll notice that it's delimited with square brackets because the column name is also a reserved word and has a special meaning in a SQL statement. Anytime you use reserved words or special characters for column names (like spaces or backslashes, for example) you have to enclose them in delimiters. You should try to avoid using reserved words as column names not only for this reason, but because some SQL statements can get confusing this way.

Lastly, we'll discuss the IDENTITY keyword. SQL Server can automatically add values in columns. For this example, you have a primary key column, the EmployeeID that identifies the whole column. Instead of having to keep track of the values for this column, you'll let SQL Server handle it for you. Here you tell SQL Server that you want the values to start with 1 and increment by 1. There are other restrictions and uses for an IDENTITY column; you can find more in BOL.

CREATE VIEW

You use CREATE VIEW to create views on one or more tables. For example, if you have a table that contains a salary, this data should be kept confidential from all but a select few people. You can build a view on this table that has all of the other data, but leaves out the salary data. Then you would grant the permission to read the view to those few people who need access. Also, you can create a view to read data from multiple tables to remove complexity for end users (and other programmers) as well.

Try It Out–Creating a View

In the Employee table, you don't want users to be able to see the group that an employee is in. To create a view limiting users from seeing the group, you would use the following:

```
USE Southwind
GO

CREATE VIEW dbo.vEmployee AS
   SELECT EmployeeID, EmployeeName FROM dbo.Employee
GO
```

Now you can treat this view as you would a table–you can read and modify data through the view. Note however, that you can only change data through the view if it references a single table. The main difference between Employee table and vEmployee view is that you don't see the group that the employee is in.

```
SELECT * FROM dbo.vEmployee
```

If SELECT permission is denied to users on the Employee table but granted on the vEmployee view, then users are unable to tell which group employees are in.

One quick word about using the * in the SELECT statement, the asterisk tells SQL Server to retrieve all columns, in this case, EmployeeID and EmployeeName. In testing single-use and some development situations, using the asterisk is fine. However, there is often a performance hit when you use it, because SQL Server has to resolve the column names. You can also break applications that rely on specific columns or column order if you add or alter columns for the table(s) in the select statement. It's always better to list the columns that you want to retrieve, even if you do actually want to retrieve all of them. So, if this statement were in a stored procedure that is used again and again, you would use it like this:

```
SELECT EmployeeID, EmployeeName FROM dbo.vEmployee
```

For ad hoc queries, testing, and so on, the asterisk is fine. But it should not be used in production code.

CREATE PROCEDURE

A **stored procedure** is like a method in other programming languages. You can build complex stored procedures and then users can call these procedures to perform work, such as gathering, manipulating, and returning specific data. Stored procedures can have parameters, and they can return values of parameters, single values, or resultsets.

An advantage of using a stored procedure over an ad hoc query is that SQL Server will compile information about this procedure and cache it in memory. So the next time the procedure is called, much of the work of retrieving the data doesn't have to be performed again, thus giving you better performance.

Try It Out–Creating a Stored Procedure

Let's create a stored procedure to retrieve all of the data from the Employee table:

```
USE Southwind
GO


CREATE PROCEDURE dbo.GetEmployees AS
BEGIN
   SELECT EmployeeID, [Group], EmployeeName FROM dbo.Employee
END
GO

EXECUTE dbo.GetEmployees
```

This seems like it doesn't have much benefit over just using the SELECT statement, but it does have a performance benefit. Even though the code for this particular stored procedure is very simple, the query is precompiled on the server, rather than having to be interpreted at runtime thus providing performance advantage. Of course most stored procedures are much more complex than this, so the benefit is even greater.

You can also create stored procedures with parameters. This allows you to make the stored procedure more generic and flexible. For example, you could have made the previous stored procedure take a single CHAR(1) parameter and return only employees with an EmployeeName that begins with that character, or pass in the group and return only employees within the specified group. SQL Server only allows 2100 parameters for a stored procedure, but in practice you should rarely, if ever, need so many parameters. A stored procedure with that many parameters would be difficult to maintain.

Here's the modified procedure that takes a parameter to limit the resultset:

```
CREATE PROCEDURE dbo.GetEmployees (@EName CHAR(1)) AS
BEGIN
  SELECT EmployeeID, [Group], EmployeeName FROM dbo.Employee
  WHERE EmployeeName LIKE @EName + '%'
END
GO


EXECUTE dbo.GetEmployees 'D'
GO
/* We can still get all employees by supplying a wildcard as the parameter */
EXECUTE dbo.GetEmployees '%'
```

The % in the procedure is a wildcard that can be used with the LIKE clause in SQL Server meaning "match 0 or more of any character." Since you must have a parameter for this procedure, you can still get all of the values from the underlying table because LIKE '%%' means to match 0 or more of any character.

CREATE FUNCTION

SQL Server 2000 introduced UDFs (**user-defined functions**), which allow you to simplify code. There are several different kinds of functions: ones that return a single value (**scalar functions**) or ones that return a resultset (**table functions**). One of the problems of stored procedures is that you cannot insert the recordset returned by a stored procedure into a table with a single SELECT statement, but table functions overcome this problem. SQL Server actually breaks down table functions into single statement and multistatement types. Table functions are like views that you can pass a parameter into, so this gives you more flexibility. Functions also have limits on number of parameters as stored procedures; you can only have 1024 of them, but again, you'll probably never need this many.

Try It Out–Creating a Scalar User-Defined Function

Here you create a function to convert a date to the ISO standard of yyyymmdd (see "Convert" in BOL for more options for the Convert function).

```
USE Southwind
GO


CREATE FUNCTION dbo.fnConvertDateToISOStd(@DateToUse DATETIME)
RETURNS CHAR(8)
AS
BEGIN
  RETURN CONVERT(CHAR(8), @DateToUse, 112)
END
GO
```

And here's how you would call it:

```
SELECT dbo.fnConvertDateToISOStd((GETDATE())
```

This would return a value of 20030201 (if ran on 02/01/2003).

Try It Out–Creating a Table User-Defined Function

This function just returns the contents of the Employee table. After calling it, you would see the contents of the table, or a row returned for each row in the table.

```
USE Southwind
GO

CREATE FUNCTION dbo.fnTest2()
RETURNS TABLE
AS
   RETURN SELECT EmployeeID, [Group], EmployeeName
   FROM dbo.Employee
GO
```

Here's how to call the table function:

```
SELECT * FROM dbo.fnTest2()
```

These are very simple functions that don't really give you any benefit, but we'll get into functions much more in the "Functions" section of this chapter.

DROP

If you no longer need an object in the database, you can get rid of it by using a DROP object statement. If you drop a table, the table and the data within it will be removed; any triggers and constraints that you have on the table will also be dropped along with the table. Be careful with this statement, because there is no undo statement to reverse it.

Try It Out–Dropping Objects

Let's drop the stored procedure that you created earlier:

```
USE Southwind
GO

DROP PROCEDURE dbo.GetEmployees
```

If you had multiple stored procedures that you wanted to drop at the same time, you could list them separated by commas:

```
DROP PROCEDURE sp1, sp2, sp3
```

Now let's drop the view you had created on the `Employee` table:

```
DROP VIEW dbo.vEmployee
```

Let's drop the `Employee` table. You didn't have to drop these objects in this order, but it's a good idea to drop the table last so that you don't leave orphaned views and stored procedures:

```
DROP TABLE dbo.Employee
```

Now that all of the objects are gone, you have an empty database, so let's drop it as well:

```
USE master
GO

DROP DATABASE Southwind
GO
```

You will notice that you changed the context to the `master` database. This is necessary because you must get out of the context of the database you are dropping before it can be dropped. Dropping the database removes the database and deletes all files associated with it.

Data Manipulation Language

You already looked at some basic DML statements in Chapter 4. Here we'll continue this discussion with more advanced SQL statements.

SELECT

Once you have data in the database, you need a way to retrieve it. You use the SELECT statement to do this because SELECT allows you to retrieve data from the tables. You can also get data from related tables. Typically, you relate the tables using foreign key constraints, although this isn't mandatory.

Try It Out–Obtaining Data from Related Tables

In the `pubs` database, the `titles` table lists the book titles, and this table is related to the `authors` table through an associative table, called `titleauthor`. The three tables are related in the following manner: `authors` is related to `titleauthor` through the au_id column, and the `titleauthor` table is related to the `titles` table through the title_id column.

> **Notice how the tables are related to each other with the same column name in the related tables. This isn't required, but it results in an easy-to-understand data model. Always use the same name for a given attribute in all your tables. This means that when you relate two tables using foreign key constraints, the referencing and referenced columns will have the same name.**

Now let's get some author and title data:

```
SELECT authors.au_lname, authors.au_fname, titles.title,
titles.price
FROM dbo.authors
   INNER JOIN dbo.titleauthor ON authors.au_id =
titleauthor.au_id
   INNER JOIN dbo.titles ON titleauthor.title_id =
titles.title_id
ORDER BY authors.au_lname, authors.au_fname
```

This gives you the following abbreviated results:

au_lname	au_fname	title	price
Bennet	Abraham	The Busy Executive's Databa...	19.9900
Blotchet-Halls	Reginald	Fifty Years in Buckingham P...	11.9500
Carson	Cheryl	But Is It User Friendly?	22.9500
DeFrance	Michel	The Gourmet Microwave	2.9900
del Castillo	Innes	Silicon Valley Gastronomic ...	19.9900
Dull	Ann	Secrets of Silicon Valley	20.0000
Green	Marjorie	The Busy Executive's Databa...	19.9900

Here you see first and last names of the authors and the title and price for each book the author wrote. The data is ordered by the author's last name, and then by the author's first name to keep the authors together. In this case you used a JOIN to get the related data.

JOIN

As discussed in Chapter 4, there are several types of joins, and in the last example, you used an **inner join**, indicating that you want all rows from both tables where the columns in the ON section of the clause match (are equal in this case). Inner joins are the default join if no join type is specified, but you also have **outer joins** and **cross joins**. Inner joins are the most common, but outer joins are used often as well.

Aliases

If you look closely at the last query, you'll see that you had to retype the table names several times. Some of these were not necessary, for example, the column names that you selected were only in one specific table, so you could have left out the table name in this particular query. If you wanted the au_id column for example, specifying the table would be mandatory, since that column is in two of the tables. SQL Server would not know which column you wanted and throw back an error telling you that the au_id column is ambiguous, meaning that it cannot determine from which table to pull the data for that column.

Although you certainly don't have to type in the table names for each column, doing so makes the table that they come from clearer, but typing the table name can often be very cumbersome. You can give tables an **alias** with which to refer to them. Once you've done so, you can (and must) refer to that table by its alias. Let's rewrite the preceding query giving each of the three tables an alias:

```
SELECT a.au_lname, a.au_fname, t.title, t.price
FROM dbo.authors a
   INNER JOIN dbo.titleauthor ta on a.au_id = ta.au_id
   INNER JOIN dbo.titles t on ta.title_id = t.title_id
ORDER BY a.au_lname, a.au_fname
```

You can see that this is a little easier to type, and is a bit more concise. You still could have eliminated the table prefixes on all of the column names in the SELECT statement and in the ORDER BY, but this does make it clear what table each of them came from.

GROUP BY

You can group data from the query with a GROUP BY statement. If you want to get the price of all of the books for each author, you can modify the preceding query a little to get this data:

```
SELECT a.au_lname, a.au_fname, SUM(t.price) AS TotalPrice
FROM dbo.authors a
   INNER JOIN dbo.titleauthor ta on a.au_id = ta.au_id
   INNER JOIN dbo.titles t on ta.title_id = t.title_id
GROUP BY a.au_lname, a.au_fname
ORDER BY a.au_lname, a.au_fname
```

Resulting in the following (abbreviated):

au_lname	au_fname	TotalPrice
Bennet	Abraham	19.9900
Blotchet-Halls	Reginald	11.9500
Carson	Cheryl	22.9500
DeFrance	Michel	2.9900
del Castillo	Innes	19.9900
Dull	Ann	20.0000
Green	Marjorie	22.9800

> Note we put the GROUP BY before the ORDER BY. All of the clauses for the SELECT statement have a specific order (refer to BOL for a full listing of the clauses, their descriptions, and orders).

This query now gives you the author's last and first name along with the total prices for all of their books. To get this total, you used the SUM() built-in function, and grouped the data by the author's last and first name. This told SQL Server how you want to group the data for the SUM() function. Also, you used an alias for this column. If you had left the AS TotalPrice off, the column would have come back with no column name. The AS word is optional, and you can give this column (as well as any column) any name you choose, the same rules apply here as they do in real column names.

TOP

The next part of the SELECT is the TOP keyword. Using the TOP keyword will limit your resultset to the number specified after the TOP keyword. For example, let's get authors and the prices of the books they've written ordered by the price of the book, from highest to lowest:

```
SELECT a.au_lname, a.au_fname, t.title, t.price
FROM dbo.authors a
    INNER JOIN dbo.titleauthor ta on a.au_id = ta.au_id
    INNER JOIN dbo.titles t on ta.title_id = t.title_id
ORDER BY t.price DESC
```

This returns 25 records starting with Cheryl Carson, as shown (again this list is abbreviated):

au_lname	au_fname	title	price
Carson	Cheryl	But Is It User Friendly?	22.9500
MacFeather	Stearns	Computer Phobic AND Non-Pho...	21.5900
Karsen	Livia	Computer Phobic AND Non-Pho...	21.5900
Panteley	Sylvia	Onions, Leeks, and Garlic: ...	20.9500
Dull	Ann	Secrets of Silicon Valley	20.0000
Hunter	Sheryl	Secrets of Silicon Valley	20.0000
White	Johnson	Prolonged Data Deprivation:...	19.9900
del Castillo	Innes	Silicon Valley Gastronomic ...	19.9900
Green	Marjorie	The Busy Executive's Databa...	19.9900
Bennet	Abraham	The Busy Executive's Databa...	19.9900
Straight	Dean	Straight Talk About Computers	19.9900

Now let's modify it to only give you the ten highest-priced books:

```
SELECT TOP 10 a.au_lname, a.au_fname, t.title, t.price
FROM dbo.authors a
    INNER JOIN dbo.titleauthor ta on a.au_id = ta.au_id
    INNER JOIN dbo.titles t on ta.title_id = t.title_id
ORDER BY t.price DESC
```

If you run this query, you'll see that you now have the top 10 highest-priced books, or do you? If you ran the first query, you may have noticed that the lowest priced book out of the top 10 was 19.90, but that number 11 was also 19.90. This may or may not be a problem depending on what you're doing with the data you're retrieving. If you were bringing back the top 10 salespeople and numbers 10 and 11 were tied, you better bet that number 11 wouldn't be happy that he was left out.

WITH TIES

To remedy this situation, you have a WITH TIES option that can be used with the TOP keyword. This option will bring back the top x number of records, and any records that tie with the last one. If you change the statement from the TOP 10 to TOP 10 WITH TIES, you'll see that number 11 is now returned as well. With TOP, you don't have to specify a specific number of records: You can specify a number relative to the total number of records that would be returned.

PERCENT

In this last example, you would get 25 records without using the TOP keyword. If you change the TOP 10 to TOP 20 PERCENT, you'll get back 20 percent of the 25 that would be returned, or 5 records. With TOP, SQL Server sorts the order of the records first, and then returns the TOP x of those sorted records. Also, using a TOP without an ORDER BY doesn't make sense for the most part. If you tell SQL Server to give you the top 10 records, you should usually tell it what you mean by top 10; that's what is done by the ORDER BY. If you fail to provide ORDER BY clause to the SELECT statement that includes TOP keyword then data is retrieved according to its physical order. This means that TOP 10 records will be chosen based on how records are stored in the table. The physical order of records depends on a table's clustered index.

INSERT

The INSERT statement lets you add data to your tables. You can only add row(s) to one table at a time. In its most basic flavor, INSERT contains the list of all columns in a table and values for each column of the row you want to add to this table.

Identity Columns

When you create a table, you can define a column with an IDENTITY property. SQL Server automatically populates IDENTITY columns according to the SEED and INCREMENT values you provide when defining the column. For instance, suppose you have the following table:

```
CREATE TABLE table_with_identity (
   My_id INT IDENTITY(1, 1) NOT NULL
   My_name VARCHAR(50) NULL
)
```

In this case, the my_id column has an identity seed of 1 and an increment of 1. That means the first value inserted will be 1, then 2, then 3, and so on.

If you have an IDENTITY column defined on the table, you can't specify the value of that column within the INSERT statement, unless you explicitly set the IDENTITY_INSERT setting ON. If you attempt to provide a value for the identity column without setting IDENTITY_INSERT ON, you'll get the following error:

Server: Msg 8101, Level 16, State 1, Line 1
An explicit value for the identity column in table 'table_name' can only be specified when a column list is used and IDENTITY_INSERT is ON.

Try It Out–Inserting Data from Other Tables

Instead of supplying an explicit list of values, you might be populating a row with values from other tables, variables, or functions. In such cases, the VALUES clause is replaced with a valid SELECT statement, as in the following:

```
INSERT sales (
stor_id,
ord_num,
ord_date,
qty,
payterms,
title_id)

SELECT stores.stor_id,
       'neworder',
       GETDATE(),
       55,
       'net 439',
       titles.title_id
FROM stores, titles
  WHERE stores.stor_name = 'news & brews'
    AND
  titles.title = 'you can combat computer stress!'
```

In this example you're simply looking up the store identifier in the stores table and the title identifier in the titles table. In addition, you're using the GETDATE() system function to provide the current date and time as the order date for the newly placed order.

INSERT and Stored Procedures

There is one more flavor of INSERT that you should be aware of. This kind populates a table based on the output from a stored procedure or a set of dynamic SQL statements. This variation of the INSERT statement comes in handy if you'd like to manipulate the resultset returned from a stored procedure.

Try It Out–Inserting the Results of a Stored Procedure

Suppose you have a stored procedure that returns a list of author names and their respective cities within the specified state, which you then pass in as a parameter. The code of the procedure is as follows:

```
CREATE PROCEDURE dbo.author_name_city(@state CHAR(2))

AS

SELECT au_lname, au_fname, city FROM authors
WHERE state = @state
```

Now you can populate a table based on the execution of the author_name_city procedure as follows (this example uses a temporary table). Please refer to the discussion of temporary tables later in the chapter. The following code snippet will populate a temporary table with results of a stored procedure execution:

```
CREATE TABLE #author (
au_lname VARCHAR(50),
au_fname VARCHAR(50),
city VARCHAR(50)
)

GO

INSERT #author EXEC author_name_city @state = 'ca'
```

Notice that you passed the parameter of ca, so the procedure will only return authors that reside in the state of California. Notice also that you didn't have to specify the column list for the temporary table because the table has the same number and data types of columns as the resultset returned from the procedure. Keep in mind that to populate a table with results of a stored procedure, you must have the same number of columns in a table as in the resultset, and the respective columns must have compatible data types.

Similarly, you can use an INSERT statement to populate a table based on executing a dynamic set of SQL statements, as in the following:

```
DECLARE @sql VARCHAR(600)
SELECT @sql = 'DECLARE @state CHAR(2)'
SELECT @sql = @sql + 'SET @state = ''ca'''
SELECT @sql = @sql  + 'SELECT au_lname, au_fname FROM authors
WHERE state = @state '

INSERT #author (au_lname, au_fname)

EXEC (@sql)
```

UPDATE

The UPDATE statement lets you modify values of one or multiple columns in a table. Simple UPDATE statements provide the new value for the column(s). More complex UPDATE statements look up the value in the SET clause or the WHERE clause from multiple tables.

Try It Out–A Complex UPDATE

For example, the following statement changes the pay terms to COD (cash on delivery), only for purchases of business titles:

```
UPDATE sales SET payterms = 'COD'
FROM sales INNER JOIN titles ON sales.title_id =
                                titles.title_id
WHERE titles.type = 'business'
```

To ensure that you're about to run a correct UPDATE statement, it's prudent to first examine the SELECT statement with the same criteria. In the previous example, you wanted to change payment terms only for the business titles; you could ensure that you were doing just that by running the following SELECT statement first:

```
SELECT sales.*
FROM sales INNER JOIN titles ON sales.title_id =
                                 titles.title_id
WHERE titles.type = 'business'
```

The result of this is as follows:

stor_id	ord_num	ord_date	qty	payterms	title_id
6380	6871	1994-09-14 00:00:00.000	5	Net 60	BU1032
7067	neworder	2003-09-04 11:57:30.470	55	net 439	BU2075
7896	QQ2299	1993-10-28 00:00:00.000	15	Net 60	BU7832
7896	X999	1993-02-21 00:00:00.000	35	ON invoice	BU2075
8042	423LL930	1994-09-14 00:00:00.000	10	ON invoice	BU1032
8042	P723	1993-03-11 00:00:00.000	25	Net 30	BU1111

Now that you know which rows should be affected, you can run the UPDATE and double-check the results, which now show the pay terms as being COD.

stor_id	ord_num	ord_date	qty	payterms	title_id
6380	6871	1994-09-14 00:00:00.000	5	COD	BU1032
7067	neworder	2003-09-04 11:57:30.470	55	COD	BU2075
7896	QQ2299	1993-10-28 00:00:00.000	15	COD	BU7832
7896	X999	1993-02-21 00:00:00.000	35	COD	BU2075
8042	423LL930	1994-09-14 00:00:00.000	10	COD	BU1032
8042	P723	1993-03-11 00:00:00.000	25	COD	BU1111

CASE

You could make UPDATE statements even more sophisticated if you include CASE statements or subqueries within them.

Try It Out–Using CASE

The following statement modifies payment terms for all sales based on the title type, as shown:

```
UPDATE sales
SET
payterms = CASE WHEN titles.type = 'business' THEN 'cod'
                WHEN titles.type = 'mod_cook' THEN 'net 30'
                WHEN titles.type = 'popular_comp' THEN 'net 40'
                WHEN titles.type = 'trad_cook' THEN 'net 35'
                WHEN titles.type = 'psychology' THEN 'net 0'
```

```
                        ELSE 'CASH'
              END
      FROM sales

  INNER JOIN titles ON sales.title_id = titles.title_id
```

Try It Out–Keeping a Running Total

In the next example you'll add a column to the sales table to keep a running total of the copies of a particular title sold so far. Then you'll update the newly added column with the number of copies of each title sold so far:

```
ALTER TABLE sales ADD sold_so_far INT NULL
GO

UPDATE sales
SET sold_so_far = (
  SELECT COUNT(*) FROM sales s2 WHERE s2.title_id =
                              sales.title_id)
```

If you run a SELECT * query on the sales table, you'll see the following (abbreviated list):

stor_id	ord_num	ord_date	qty	payterms	title_id	sold_so_far
6380	6871	1994-09-14 00:00:00.000	5	cod	BU1032	2
6380	722a	1994-09-13 00:00:00.000	3	net 0	PS2091	4
7066	A2976	1993-05-24 00:00:00.000	50	net 40	PC8888	1
7066	QA7442.3	1994-09-13 00:00:00.000	75	net 0	PS2091	4
7067	D4482	1994-09-14 00:00:00.000	10	net 0	PS2091	4
7067	neworder	2003-09-04 11:57:30.470	55	cod	BU2075	2
7067	P2121	1992-06-15 00:00:00.000	40	net 35	TC3218	1
7067	P2121	1992-06-15 00:00:00.000	20	net 35	TC4203	1
7067	P2121	1992-06-15 00:00:00.000	20	net 35	TC7777	1

Notice that you used a subquery to look up the number of copies sold. To differentiate between the two instances of sales table in this UPDATE statement, you provided an alias of s2 for one of them.

DELETE

The DELETE statement removes a row or a set of rows from a table. Remember, if your DELETE statement has no WHERE clause, then **all** rows are deleted from the table. Note also that you can only delete rows from one table at a time.

More complex DELETE statements determine the rows to be deleted through joins or subqueries. Much like the UPDATE statement, each DELETE can contain a FROM clause, so the following two statements are equivalent:

```
DELETE authors WHERE state = 'ca'
```

```
DELETE FROM authors WHERE state = 'ca'
```

The DELETE statement is often used with data-archiving operations, which is what you're going to look at now.

Try It Out–Archiving Records

For example, to keep a database to a manageable size, you might archive all sales records that are older than two years. To do so, you'll create a second database that contains historic sales records and copy old records to that table. Once you've got a copy of the old records, you can delete them from the main sales table. The archiving procedure would look like this (this file is called ArchiveSalesTable.sql and can be found in this book's download):

```
/* create the history table */
CREATE TABLE sales_history (
stor_id INT,
ord_num VARCHAR(15),
ord_date SMALLDATETIME,
qty INT,
payterms VARCHAR(20),
title_id VARCHAR(10)
)

GO

/* enclose all data modification statements in a transaction
** just in case we encounter errors
*/

BEGIN TRANSACTION

/* populate history table first: */

  INSERT sales_history (
  stor_id,
  ord_num,
  ord_date,
  qty,
  payterms,
  title_id
  )

  SELECT
    stor_id,
    ord_num,
    ord_date,
    qty,
    payterms,
    title_id
  FROM sales
  WHERE
    DATEDIFF(YEAR, ord_date, GETDATE()) > = 2

/* handle any errors: */
IF @@ERROR <> 0
  BEGIN
```

```
         RAISERROR('error while populating history table', 16, 1)
         ROLLBACK TRANSACTION
         RETURN
      END

   /* now that we have a copy
   ** get rid of the old records:
   */

   DELETE sales
      WHERE DATEDIFF(YEAR, ord_date, GETDATE()) > = 2

   IF @@ERROR <> 0
      BEGIN
         RAISERROR('error while deleting old records', 16, 1)
         ROLLBACK TRANSACTION
         RETURN
      END

   /* commit transaction if no errors: */
   COMMIT TRANSACTION
```

This script uses a transaction to carry out its activity. We'll be discussing transactions in detail later in this chapter.

TRUNCATE TABLE

TRUNCATE TABLE is a handy tool if you wish to get rid of all rows in a table. It's true that you can do the same by executing a DELETE statement without specifying the WHERE clause. However, there are a couple of advantages to using TRUNCATE TABLE instead:

❑ TRUNCATE TABLE adds only one entry to the transaction log. If you execute a DELETE against a huge table with millions of rows, the DELETE statement will log each deleted record in the transaction log.

❑ TRUNCATE TABLE resets the identity to its original seed. So, if you're testing a system with tables that have identity columns and you wish to reset the identity values, use TRUNCATE TABLE. The DELETE statement, on the other hand, doesn't reset the identity. For example, suppose you create a customer table with an identity column seeded at 1 and with an increment of 1, and then you add a thousand entries to this table. The next record added to the customer table will have the identity of 1001. Now if you delete all rows from customer, the next inserted row will still have the identity of 1001; however, if you use the TRUNCATE TABLE syntax, the next inserted row will have the identity of 1.

Data Control Language

Data control language allows a DBA to assign permissions to database objects and T-SQL statements. DCL statements are used for defining security within a database. A complete discussion of security is beyond the scope of this chapter; for further details, refer to Chapter 8. Here we'll introduce the syntax of these statements, and show you a few examples where each might be used.

DCL can be used to administer statement- and object-level permissions. Statement-level permissions include privileges to execute certain SQL statements, such as CREATE TABLE, CREATE VIEW, ALTER FUNCTION, and so on. Object-level permissions, on the other hand, allow a user to read or write data to and from a certain object. Object level permissions also allow users to execute stored procedures.

GRANT

Unless you're a database owner, if you want to execute SELECT, INSERT, UPDATE, and DELETE statements against tables, you first need a permission to do so. Not surprisingly, the GRANT statement grants a statement or object permission to a database user or role. For instance, the following statement permits Mary to read data from the authors table:

```
GRANT SELECT on authors TO Mary
```

The next statement grants CREATE VIEW permission (a statement permission) to Chuck:

```
GRANT CREATE VIEW TO Chuck
```

You can use a single GRANT statement to assign permissions to more than one user; however, permissions to only one object can be assigned, for instance:

```
GRANT SELECT, INSERT on authors to Chuck, JohnDoe
```

This is a valid statement permitting JohnDoe and Chuck to add records and read data from the authors table. However, if you try to assign multiple permissions, the statement will fail; for example, the following statement is incorrect:

```
GRANT SELECT on authors to Chuck, INSERT on authors to JohnDoe
```

Also, SQL Server allows you to define SELECT and UPDATE permissions at the individual column level. For instance, the following statement allows JohnDoe to read and modify only author last names and first names:

```
GRANT SELECT, UPDATE on authors(au_lname, au_fname) to JohnDoe
```

You can allow some database users to transfer their permissions to other users. This is accomplished by adding WITH GRANT OPTION to the GRANT statement. For instance, you could grant Mary permissions to read data from the sales table and allow her to transfer such permissions to other users:

```
GRANT SELECT on sales TO Mary WITH GRANT OPTION
```

Note: You can only use WITH GRANT OPTION for object-level permissions.

REVOKE

The REVOKE statement takes away previously granted or denied permissions from a user or role (DENY is discussed shortly). Continuing from the previous example, you can revoke the permission to read or update author last names and first names from JohnDoe with the following statement:

```
REVOKE SELECT, UPDATE (au_lname, au_fname) on authors
FROM JohnDoe
```

Similarly, you can revoke previously granted (or denied) statement permissions:

```
REVOKE CREATE VIEW FROM Mary
```

Try It Out–Revoking Selected Privileges

Suppose you had granted a SELECT permission using WITH GRANT OPTION (discussed earlier). You can revoke the permission to transfer permissions (to take away administrative capabilities, for example) without revoking the SELECT permission itself. To do so, use the following syntax:

```
REVOKE GRANT OPTION FOR SELECT on sales FROM Mary CASCADE
```

The CASCADE keyword at the end ensures that any users that Mary granted permissions to using WITH GRANT OPTION will lose such administrative capabilities as well.

DENY

The DENY statement has an effect similar to REVOKE–it takes away permission(s) from the user. However, DENY is stricter than REVOKE, in that DENY explicitly restricts a user from inheriting permissions from any database roles that the user might belong to. (Database roles are a concept similar to Windows groups) For instance, suppose JohnDoe is a member of the ACCOUNTING role. Further, suppose that you grant ACCOUNTING and JohnDoe a permission to read data from sales. Now, if you REVOKE the permission to read data from the sales table to JohnDoe, he can still read data from sales because he is part of the ACCOUNTING role. Instead, you should use the DENY statement to prevent JohnDoe from reading data in sales, as follows:

```
DENY SELECT on sales TO JohnDoe
```

The reverse is also true; if you DENY permission to read sales from ACCOUNTING, but JohnDoe still happens to have such a permission; he still won't be able to read from sales. The most restrictive statement, in this case DENY, takes precedence over GRANT and REVOKE.

Conditional Logic

Every programming language has a way of constructing conditional statements and T-SQL is no exception. If you've programmed in any other language, IF statements will look very familiar to you, with the exception of the THEN keyword, which is always implied and therefore, omitted in T-SQL. The general syntax for an IF statement is as follows:

```
IF [condition is true]
   BEGIN
     [do some processing here]
  ·END
ELSE
   BEGIN
     [perform alternative logic]
   END
```

Although the BEGIN...END construct isn't required with the ELSE portion of the IF statement, you should get into the habit of always enclosing your conditional logic in BEGIN...END. Doing so will save you many hours of code debugging and wondering why your program doesn't behave as expected.

You're also allowed to nest your IF statements.

Try It Out–Nesting IF Statements

The following code snippet will retrieve different sets of rows from the authors table in the pubs database, depending on the day of the week:

```
-- declare local variable
-- to determine weekday number:
DECLARE @day INT

SELECT @day = DATEPART(DAY, GETDATE())

IF @day = 1
  BEGIN
    SELECT * FROM authors WHERE state = 'ca'
  END
ELSE
  BEGIN
    -- nested IF logic:
    IF @day = 2
      BEGIN
        SELECT * FROM authors WHERE state = 'tn'
      END
    ELSE
      BEGIN
        SELECT * FROM authors WHERE state = 'or'
      END
  END
```

Since today is Tuesday, the following row was returned:

au_id	au_lname	au_fname	phone	address	city	state
648-92-1872	Blotchet-Halls	Reginald	503 745-6402	55 Hillsdale Bl.	Corvallis	OR

Checking a False Condition

You can also use IF constructs to verify that the condition is FALSE. This is accomplished with the following pseudocode:

```
IF NOT [condition]
  BEGIN
    [some statements here]
  END
```

Try It Out–Checking for False Conditions

For example, the following statement ensures that there are no authors from the state of Texas:

```
IF NOT ((SELECT COUNT(*) FROM authors WHERE state = 'tx') > 0)
  BEGIN
    PRINT 'There are no authors from Texas'
  END
```

Which results in the following being displayed on your Query Analyzer Messages pane: There are no authors from Texas. Alternatively, you can check for the existence of a record with certain criteria using the EXISTS keyword, as follows:

```
IF EXISTS (SELECT * FROM authors WHERE state = 'tx')
  BEGIN
    PRINT 'There ARE authors from Texas'
  END
```

CASE

Now if you're savvy in VB or some other procedural language, you must be asking, "IF statements are cool, but couldn't you use a CASE statement to do something similar?" Very true; Transact-SQL also supports the CASE statement, but the implementation is slightly different.

Try It Out–Using CASE

The following statement will return authors from a particular state depending on the weekday:

```
-- delcare local variable
-- to determine weekday number:
DECLARE @day INT

SELECT @day = DATEPART(DAY, GETDATE())
```

```
SELECT * FROM authors
WHERE
   state = CASE
     WHEN @day = 1 THEN 'ca'
     WHEN @day = 2 THEN 'tn'
     ELSE 'or'
   END
```

T-SQL also supports another variation of CASE, which allows you to replace a value within a column with another value, depending on a condition. For example, the following query translates the state abbreviation into the full spelling of the state's name for California, Tennessee, and Oregon; for all other states the state abbreviation is returned:

```
SELECT DISTINCT state = CASE
             WHEN state = 'ca' THEN 'California'
             WHEN state = 'tn' THEN 'Tennessee'
             WHEN state = 'or' THEN 'Oregon'
             ELSE state
          END
FROM authors
```

The condition within the CASE statement can be more complex and can contain an examination of variable values or system functions as well. For instance, the following statement will create a custom greeting based on time of day and day of the week:

```
SELECT greeting =
   CASE WHEN DATEPART(HOUR, GETDATE()) < 12
          THEN 'Good ' + DATENAME(WEEKDAY, GETDATE()) +
' Morning!'
        WHEN DATEPART(HOUR, GETDATE()) BETWEEN 12 AND 17
          THEN 'Good ' + DATENAME(WEEKDAY, GETDATE()) +
' Afternoon!'
        WHEN DATEPART(HOUR, GETDATE()) BETWEEN 18 AND 22
          THEN 'Good ' + DATENAME(WEEKDAY, GETDATE())  +
' Evening!'
        ELSE
          'Good ' + DATENAME(WEEKDAY, GETDATE()) + ' Night!'
   END
```

Here's the result:

greeting
Good Thursday Afternoon!

Transactions

There are often times when you'll want to perform several units of work, but want to make them behave as a single unit. For a classic example, consider a banking application; with a process that withdraws money from a person's savings account, and then credits that money to that person's checking account. You wouldn't want one of those processes to work if the other one failed.

In this example, if you withdrew the money out of the savings account and the credit to the checking account failed, you would want the money to go back into the savings account. You can do this with a **transaction**. A transaction is a group of statements that will all pass, or all fail.

Transactions should pass what's called an **ACID test**; that is they should be all of the following:

❑ **Atomic**

All or none of the statements work

❑ **Consistent**

Reliable and maintain data integrity

❑ **Isolated**

Any other process should see the data in the all or none state, and that no other process can use the data while it's being modified

❑ **Durable**

As the saying goes "when it's done, it's done," in other words once the changes are finished, they are permanent

You may have noticed that, earlier in this chapter when you were archiving data, you used a transaction so that if any part of the archiving failed, everything would be returned to its previous state. Actually, you've already been using transactions, implicitly. Every unit of work is implicitly a transaction. If you do an INSERT into a table, SQL Server implicitly puts that work into a transaction, the INSERT (or UPDATE, or DELETE) all works, or it all fails.

Transactions can also be valuable for testing. If you have data that you don't want to modify, but you need to test a set of statements, you can put them in a transaction, perform the work, check the results, and then roll back the transaction. For example, say that you're building some statements in Northwind, but you don't want to modify the data. You could do the following:

```
Use Northwind
BEGIN TRANSACTION

SELECT UnitPrice, * FROM Products WHERE ProductID = 3

UPDATE Products SET UnitPrice = UnitPrice * 1.05
WHERE ProductID = 3

SELECT UnitPrice, * FROM Products WHERE ProductID = 3

ROLLBACK TRANSACTION

SELECT UnitPrice, * FROM Products WHERE ProductID = 3
```

You put the code, along with some test statements to see the data before and after the work, within a transaction.

Transactions should be as short as possible. When you perform data modifications, SQL Server has to lock rows to make sure that it can roll the data back in the event of a failure, so the more statements that are in the transaction, the more data rows it locks and for a longer period of time. This reduces the concurrency of the database (or the number of people that can concurrently access data) because the more data rows you've locked, the fewer users can access that data. So, keep transactions short and to the point; don't put a lot of unnecessary logic (such as variable declarations, for example) and code within them.

Transaction Syntax

To begin a transaction, use the BEGIN TRANSACTION statement. You can abbreviate the TRANSACTION and just use TRAN for short. In this chapter, we'll spell it out for clarity, but be aware that either will work. Once you start a transaction, you can perform the work. If you perform all of the work and everything goes as expected, you use a COMMIT TRANSACTION statement to commit the work and make it permanent. If you encounter an error, or some other situation that shouldn't be allowed, you can roll back the transaction with the ROLLBACK TRANSACTION statement. You usually do a test after the work, and do something like the following:

```
BEGIN TRANSACTION
...
Do Work
...

Test for error

IF error
   ROLLBACK TRANSACTION
ELSE
   COMMIT TRANSACTION
```

You can give the transactions names as well. You can say BEGIN TRANSACTION transname, and then use COMMIT or ROLLBACK TRANSACTION transname, accordingly. These names are optional, and in fact, the TRANSACTION keyword is optional as well for committing and rolling back transactions, but it's a good idea to use them for clarity.

Transactions can also be nested. Each time you start a new transaction, SQL Server increments an internal transaction nest-level value; you can access this value by using the @@TRANCOUNT function. Nested transactions can be a bit confusing, so let's go over them a little here. If you begin an outer transaction and then begin an inner transaction, and you perform the work for the inner transaction, commit the inner transaction, and then the outer transaction encounters an error and rolls back, then the inner transaction is also rolled back. Remember that a transaction is an all-or-nothing unit of work, so it makes sense that it would happen this way.

At this point, you may be wondering why you would ever use a nested transaction. Here's an example to show one reason why. Say that you have a stored procedure, sprocA, that calls another stored procedure, sprocB. sprocB performs some work, and this work must be treated as a single unit, so it's wrapped in a transaction.

Now, when sprocA calls sprocB, if sprocA is already in a transaction when it calls sprocB, sprocB's transaction is a nested transaction, so if the transaction in sprocA is rolled back, then the work that was performed in sprocB will be rolled back as well. If sprocA isn't in a transaction when sprocB is called, then sprocB's work will still be an all-or-nothing unit of work. Each time a BEGIN TRANSACTION is used, @@TRANCOUNT is incremented by one, and each time a ROLLBACK TRANSACTION without a transname is used, @@TRANCOUNT is reset to 0.

If you try to roll back a transaction, but you're not in a transaction, an error will occur, so you can use the @@TRANCOUNT function to see if you're within a transaction before attempting a rollback. A return of 0 from @@TRANCOUNT means that you're not within a transaction; any other value indicates that you are.

You can save transactions at a particular point, and then roll back the work to that point using a SAVE TRANSACTION statement. For example, you perform some work, create a save point with the SAVE TRANSACTION statement, and then do some more work. You could roll back the transaction to the save point, and then proceed from there, doing more work, committing or rolling back the transaction, and so on.

Isolation Levels

An **isolation level** is the level at which a transaction is isolated from other transactions. You can go from isolated (other transactions cannot access the data being accessed by the current transaction) to minimal isolation (other transactions can access the data along with the current transaction).

SQL Server has the following four isolation levels, going from the most to the least isolated:

❏   **Serializable**

The most isolated. Serializable means that other transactions cannot INSERT or UPDATE data that is being accessed by this transaction. Because this level locks the most data rows, you should only use this if you absolutely need to.

❏   **Repeatable read**

Similar to the serializable level, except that phantom records can be inserted by other transactions. What this means is that if you perform a SELECT on a set of data and get, for example, ten records, another transaction could INSERT a record that would have been included in your current record set if it were there. This is called a phantom record, since it will be picked up if you were to run the same SELECT statement. A serializable read prevents this kind of data from being inserted

❏   **Read committed**

Specifies that only committed data is read, meaning that data from other transactions that hasn't been committed will not be read. This level allows the data within the dataset to be modified, meaning that this level can produce phantom reads as the repeatable read level does, but it also means that you can have a nonrepeatable read, meaning that if you run the same SELECT statement at a later time, you may not get all of the records that were in the first read. This level is the default for SQL Server

❑ **Read uncommitted**

The least restrictive. It allows you to read uncommitted data, meaning that you can read data that has been inserted or modified by another transaction that hasn't committed yet. This level ignores the locks placed by the more restrictive reads. One advantage of this approach is that you can read all data in the current state of the database, so it's good for data that doesn't change much or data for which you don't care if it's out of date (for example, a report that shows the average amount of orders for the past year, so one or two more orders wouldn't change the average by much). The cons are that you can have nonrepeatable reads and phantom records. Use this level only if it isn't important for the data you read to be absolutely accurate.

The level of isolation you need depends on what is being done with the data, and how important it is that a specific transaction takes priority over other transactions that may want to access and modify the same data.

In SQL Server, you can set the transaction isolation level for a batch of statements with:

```
SET TRANSACTION ISOLATION LEVEL {level}
```

If you wanted a batch to run at the serializable level, you would use the following at the beginning of your batch:

```
TRANSACTION ISOLATION LEVEL Serializable
```

This level stays in effect until it's explicitly changed within a connection.

This table was taken from BOL to show the differences between the levels:

Isolation Level	Dirty Read	Nonrepeatable Read	Phantom
Read uncommitted	Yes	Yes	Yes
Read committed	No	Yes	Yes
Repeatable read	No	No	Yes
Serializable	No	No	No

Locking

To ensure the integrity of the data, SQL Server locks specific data rows at times. For example, if you set your batch to the serializable transaction isolation level and SELECT data, SQL Server locks the data rows that you've read to make sure that if you run the same SELECT statement again, you get the exact same data. No data that would meet your SELECT criteria can be inserted or updated. To do this, SQL Server uses different kinds of locks. Here we'll give a brief overview of how SQL Server locks data.

SQL Server will handle the locking of the data by itself, and can usually do a better job at handling the locking than you can. There are times when you may want to specify your own locking hints to try to improve performance or concurrency; for example, if you're writing a lot of read-only queries for reporting, you can specify a NOLOCK hint to tell SQL Server to not place, or honor, any locks on the data. There are several types of locks that SQL Server uses (share, update, exclusive, intent, schema, and bulk update) so you can search on any of these on BOL.

Do this with care. The more you lock the data, the lower the level of concurrency you have. If you're only accessing or updating a single record, SQL Server can lock only the one row, but if you're modifying a large proportion of the records in a table or even the database, SQL Server can escalate locks up to the entire database.

Error Handling

Error handling in T-SQL is accomplished by checking the value of the @@ERROR global variable. If this variable has a value other than zero, your code has encountered some kind of error and you should provide an alternative course of action.

Errors can be raised to the calling program or to the client with the RAISERROR statement or xp_logevent extended stored procedure. The former should be used for returning an error to the client application, whereas the latter can be used to add an entry to the application event log. Let's discuss each of these separately.

RAISERROR

The basic syntax of the RAISERROR statement is rather simple:

```
RAISERROR (message_id | message_string, severity, state )
    [ WITH option [ ,...n ] ]
```

message_id is the identifier for the message stored in the sysmessages system table. The sysmessages table resides in the master database and contains error strings for all user-defined and system-supplied errors. You can use the system-stored procedure sp_addmessage to define your own errors; alternatively, you can add errors through EM as well. Please refer to online documentation for syntax of sp_addmessage. If you have a common error string that you intend on using in multiple procedures, it makes sense to add such a string to sysmessages and refer to it by message identifier, rather than writing it out each time. User-defined errors must have IDs greater than 50000.

message_string, on the other hand, is any string up to 400 characters long that you might wish to return to a client. severity tells the calling application how severe the error was, and can range from 0 to 25. Severity levels between 19 and 25 can only be raised by members of the sysadmin role, and are required to be logged in to the event log. Severity levels of 20 and above are considered fatal, which means the session that encountered the error will be disconnected.

Finally, the state is an integer you can use to specify the invocation state of the error. This parameter allows values from 1 to 127; unless you have a compelling reason to do otherwise, keep the error state equal to 1.

Options supported by RAISERROR are as follows:

❑ WITH LOG

Records the error in the event log

❑ NOWAIT

Sends the error immediately to the client

❑ SETERROR

Sets the value of the global variable @@ERROR to message_id, if specified, or 50000 if message_string is used

Of the three options, you're most likely to use WITH LOG in the majority of your development. As mentioned earlier, you should avoid using RAISERROR (and use xp_eventlog instead) to record errors in the event log. The reason is that the WITH LOG option requires administrative privileges on the server—only the members of the sysadmin fixed server role can use this option. Therefore, to use RAISERROR WITH LOG, your developer must have administrative privileges, which might not be such a good idea. Instead, you can grant permission to execute the xp_logevent extended procedure to your developers without granting administrative privileges.

Try It Out–Using RAISERROR

Here you'll send a custom error message to the client as follows:

```
SELECT CAST('23/34/20' AS SMALLDATETIME)

IF @@ERROR <> 0
  BEGIN
    RAISERROR('An error occurred', 16, 1)
  END
```

The xp_logevent Extended Stored Procedure

The xp_logevent extended procedure also has fairly simple syntax. You can specify the error number (again, this number must be greater than 50000), error string, and, optionally, the severity. Severity can take one of three values: INFORMATIONAL, WARNING, or ERROR. The severity value is used to classify the error within the event log; if you're familiar with the Windows NT or Windows 2000 event log, you know that informational messages are identified with a circled "i"; warnings have a yellow exclamation point and errors have a red cross.

Try It Out–Logging a Warning

The following statement will log an entry in the event log with a yellow exclamation point as follows:

```
RAISERROR('ouch', 16, 1) WITH  SETERROR

IF @@ERROR <> 0
  BEGIN
    EXEC master..xp_logevent 50002,
         'An error of type warning has been encountered',
         WARNING
  END
```

Notice that because all extended procedures reside in the `master` database, you must prefix `xp_logevent` with `master..` when executing from any database other than `master`.

Looping Structures

As we mentioned at the beginning of this chapter, T-SQL is a set-based language. This means that the language is optimized for operations that involve sets of data, as in rows from the table, multiple tables joined together, and so on. Approximately 80 percent of all T-SQL code can be written without using loops. However, at times you encounter situations where looping mechanisms are unavoidable, say, to repeat an operation on one row at a time.

Even though T-SQL supports loops, you should strive to avoid them, because looping structures in T-SQL aren't very efficient.

There are two looping structures supported: `WHILE` loops and cursors.

WHILE Loops

The syntax for `WHILE` loops, is as follows:

```
WHILE [condition is true | false]
  BEGIN
    [do some processing]
  END
```

Try It Out–Running a WHILE Loop

For instance, the following loop will print the last name of the first author, whose identifier contains the value of the counter, as long as the counter is less than ten:

```
SET NOCOUNT ON
DECLARE @counter TINYINT

SET @counter = 0

WHILE @counter < 10
  BEGIN
    SELECT TOP 1 au_lname FROM authors
    WHERE au_id LIKE '%' + CAST(@counter AS VARCHAR) + '%'
    SET @counter = @counter + 1
  END
```

The results (abbreviated) are as follows:

au_lname
Straight

au_lname
White

au_lname
White

au_lname
White

au_lname
Green

BREAK

Within the WHILE loop you might want to stop processing when a certain condition occurs. This can be accomplished with the BREAK keyword.

Try It Out–Using BREAK

The following loop will stop processing as soon as the counter is greater than two:

```
SET NOCOUNT ON
DECLARE @counter TINYINT

SET @counter = 0

WHILE @counter < 10
  BEGIN
    SELECT TOP 1 au_lname FROM authors
```

```
        WHERE au_id LIKE '%' + CAST(@counter AS VARCHAR) + '%'

        SET @counter = @counter + 1

        IF @counter > 2
           BEGIN
              BREAK
           END
     END
```

Nesting WHILE Loops

Note that WHILE loops can be nested. If so, the BREAK keyword only breaks the innermost loop and transfers processing to the next outer loop. The CONTINUE keyword can be used to continue processing.

Try It Out–Nesting WHILE Loops

The next example uses the BREAK keyword to break the inner loop; however, the CONTINUE keyword will keep the loop processing until the counter reaches the value of ten:

```
SET NOCOUNT ON
DECLARE @counter TINYINT

SET @counter = 0

WHILE @counter < 10
   BEGIN
      SELECT TOP 1 au_lname FROM authors
      WHERE au_id LIKE '%' + CAST(@counter AS VARCHAR) + '%'
      SET @counter = @counter + 1

      WHILE @counter = 2
         BEGIN
            PRINT 'now breaking!'
            BREAK
         END

      IF @counter = 2
         BEGIN
            PRINT 'now continuing!'
            CONTINUE
         END
   END
```

GOTO

The other trick with the loops is the GOTO keyword. GOTO isn't as despised in T-SQL as it is in some other languages—it doesn't hurt performance. GOTO simply transfers processing to a different point within a T-SQL program. To use GOTO, you must label the portion of the code where the processing needs to continue. To label a portion of the code, simply give it a name and follow it up with a colon, as in the following:

```
My_label:
```

Try It Out–Using GOTO

This next example exits the loop with a GOTO statement and continues processing further down the program:

```
DECLARE @counter TINYINT

SET @counter = 0

WHILE @counter < 10
  BEGIN
    SELECT TOP 1 au_lname FROM authors
        WHERE au_id LIKE '%' + CAST(@counter AS VARCHAR) + '%'
    SET @counter = @counter + 1
    WHILE @counter > 2
      BEGIN
        BREAK
      END

    IF @counter > 1
      BEGIN
        GOTO my_label
      END
  END

my_label:

SELECT 'The processing continues here!'
```

The results are as follows:

au_lname	
Straight	

au_lname	
White	

(No column name)
The processing continues here!

Try It Out–Using GOTO for Error Handling

GOTO can also be used effectively to centralize error handling. Instead of providing error handling blocks after every INSERT, UPDATE, and DELETE statement, you could simply forward the code to an error-handling block at the end. The following example performs two UPDATE statements within a transaction. If either of these fails, you issue an error and roll back the transaction as follows:

```
BEGIN TRANSACTION

UPDATE authors SET au_lname = 'Ringer'
WHERE au_lname = 'Whiter'

IF @@ERROR <> 0
  BEGIN
    GOTO error_handler
  END

UPDATE titles SET title = 'new title'
WHERE title = 'old title'

IF @@ERROR <> 0
  BEGIN
    GOTO error_handler
  END

COMMIT TRANSACTION

error_handler:
IF @@ERROR <>0
  BEGIN
    RAISERROR('An error occurred, rolling back', 16, 1)
    ROLLBACK TRANSACTION
  END
```

Cursors

Cursors are the slowest method of manipulating data in Transact-SQL. A cursor is a temporary physical structure built in the tempdb database. The cursor life cycle can be described as follows:

1. The cursor is declared with a DECLARE statement.

2. The cursor is populated with the results of the SELECT statement.

3. The cursor is opened and prepared for processing.

4. The cursor rows are fetched into local variables.

5. A WHILE loop is initiated for the duration of successful fetches of rows from a cursor.

6. The global variable @@FETCH_STATUS maintains the status of the fetch. The majority of cursors simply check for a successful fetch. The list of possible values is as follows:

- ❏ 0
  Successful fetch.

- ❏ –1
  The FETCH statement failed or the row is beyond the resultset.

- ❏ –2
  The row that was fetched is missing.

7. Within the WHILE loop certain processing takes place.

8. The cursor is closed–at this point the cursor is still alive, but isn't available for processing. The cursor can be further reopened if needed.

9. The cursor is deallocated–that is, when the cursor dies–and it cannot be resurrected.

> Some DBAs think cursors are difficult to write. We wish they were more difficult to write, so that developers would stay away from using them because of the performance penalty they incur. Indeed, once you've written a cursor a few times, it's really easy.

Try It Out–Writing a Cursor

Have a look at the following example:

```
/* turn off messages of how many rows are returned */
SET NOCOUNT ON

-- declare local variables for further processing:
DECLARE @last_name VARCHAR(40),
        @first_name VARCHAR(40)

-- declare the cursor with a SELECT statement
DECLARE author_cursor CURSOR FOR
  SELECT au_lname, au_fname FROM authors

-- open cursor
OPEN author_cursor
-- attempt to fetch a row from a cursor
FETCH NEXT FROM author_cursor INTO @last_name, @first_name

/* initialize a WHILE loop for successful fetches*/
WHILE @@FETCH_STATUS = 0
BEGIN
   -- do some processing:
   SELECT 'Current author is ' + @first_name + ' ' + @last_name

   -- go to the next row:
   FETCH NEXT FROM author_cursor INTO @last_name, @first_name
```

```
END

-- close and deallocate the cursor
CLOSE author_cursor
DEALLOCATE author_cursor
```

The results are as follows (reduced list):

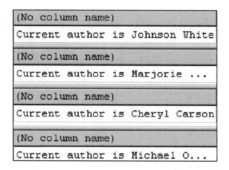

Unless you declare the cursor using the FOR UPDATE clause, it defaults to read-only. This simply means that rows within the cursor aren't updateable. Even so, you can issue DML statements within cursors.

See BOL for more information on cursors.

Temporary Tables and Table Variables

Temporary tables are built in the tempdb database and represent a way of holding intermediate query results that you can further manipulate. It's often difficult, or impossible, to write code that performs all the required data manipulations as a single query. In such cases, a temporary table is an indispensable tool that can make your life (and query performance) much better.

There are two types of temporary tables: **local** and **global**. Local temporary tables are prefixed with a single # sign, whereas global tables take two # signs. The difference is that the global temporary tables can be shared among different connections, whereas local temporary tables can only be used by the connection that created them. Internally, SQL Server appends an identifier to each local temporary table, so that it knows which local temporary table belongs to which connection. Each temporary table must be explicitly dropped to be removed from tempdb. Otherwise, they stay in tempdb until the session that created the temporary table disconnects. The exception to this rule occurs when a temp table is created within a stored procedure. In such a case, the temp table is destroyed as soon as the procedure has finished execution. Even so, go ahead and get into habit of dropping each temp table explicitly as soon as you're done with it. Doing so will save you many headaches.

Table variables represent a great alternative to temporary tables. The advantages to using a table variable are that they don't take up precious space in the tempdb database, and you don't have to drop them explicitly once you're done working with them. However, there is a flip side to the coin too.

Temporary tables look, act, and feel just like real tables. You can create keys, constraints, and even indexes on them. Table variables, on the other hand, don't support indexes, although you can create constraints on them. Therefore, a temporary table, if indexed, can actually provide better performance than a table variable. Another disadvantage to using table variables is that you can't use INSERT...EXECUTE syntax to populate such a table, which you can do with a temporary table.

Try It Out–Using Temporary Tables and Table Variables

The following example shows you how to use temporary tables and table variables–for this simple example both behave identically:

```
CREATE TABLE #temp_table (
last_name VARCHAR(40),
first_name VARCHAR(40)
)

DECLARE @table_variable TABLE (
last_name VARCHAR(40),
first_name VARCHAR(40)
)

INSERT #temp_table
   SELECT TOP 3 au_lname, au_fname FROM authors
   ORDER BY au_lname

INSERT @table_variable
   SELECT TOP 3 au_lname, au_fname FROM authors
   ORDER BY au_lname

SELECT * FROM #temp_table
SELECT * FROM @table_variable

-- must explicitly drop the temp table:
DROP TABLE #temp_table
```

Functions

SQL Server comes with a multitude of functions that you can use. These functions save developers the time and hassle of performing many different kinds of data manipulations. SQL Server 2000 also introduced user-defined functions. If there's a function that you need that SQL Server doesn't provide, you can build it yourself. Here we'll discuss built-in and user-defined functions, give examples, and try to explain when you should and shouldn't use them.

Built-In Functions

SQL Server gives you many different built-in functions in several different categories. There are math functions like LOG, PI, POWER; aggregate functions like SUM, AVG, MIN, MAX; date functions like DATEADD, DATEDIFF, and GETDATE; plus more. These functions save you the time of doing these types of thing manually, and are very convenient.

Another nice enhancement to the tools that come with SQL Server 2000 is the object browser for Query Analyzer. Along with allowing you to view your database and its objects, the object browser has templates for you to use to create almost any object with a variety of options. It also shows you a list of the most common objects. If you're in Query Analyzer and don't see the object browser, press *F8* to toggle it on and off, or choose Tools | Object Browser | Show/Hide.

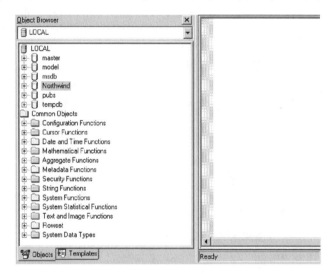

You can see that it breaks the functions down into several different categories, making it easy to decide what function to use. Also, if you need help with the syntax, you can right-click a function and then choose one of the scripting options to see the syntax of the function.

Try It Out–Built-In Functions

For example, if you want to know the average value of orders for all orders in 1997 in the Northwind database, you would use the AVG function to do so as follows:

```
USE Northwind
GO

SELECT STR(AVG(OD.Quantity * OD.UnitPrice), 6, 2) FROM Orders O
   INNER JOIN [Order Details] OD ON O.OrderID = OD.OrderID
WHERE DATEPART(YY, O.OrderDate) = '1997'
GO
```

Several functions are used here. The first one you come to, STR, is a function that allows you to format the numeric value. The AVG function takes the average of all of the values passed into it. This time you take the Quantity multiplied by the Price of all of the order-detail lines. The last function you use is the DATEPART function, which allows you to pull a specific part of the DATETIME value of the OrderDate column (the year) so that you can get only orders that were ordered in 1997.

Try It Out—Creating Unique Values Across Multiple Servers

You can also use some functions for defaults of columns. The NEWID function is a good example. You can create a UNIQEUIDENTIFIER column and use the NEWID function to automatically populate it. This can be useful when you want to create a GUID key that, like an identity column, is automatically populated, but that is unique across multiple servers. If you had a company with offices in many different locations, you could let each location add their own people to their database. If you were to replicate these databases, you wouldn't have conflicting IDs for these people. Here's an example of a small table that does something like that:

```
CREATE TABLE dbo.VIP(
VIPID UNIQUEIDENTIFIER NOT NULL CONSTRAINT DF_VIP_VIPID DEFAULT(NEWID()),
VIPName VARCHAR(50)
)
GO

INSERT INTO dbo.VIP(VIPName)
SELECT 'Melinda' UNION ALL
SELECT 'Letha' UNION ALL
SELECT 'Autrey' UNION ALL
SELECT 'Scott' UNION ALL
SELECT 'Craig' UNION ALL
SELECT 'Shabbir'
GO
```

This creates the table and puts a few rows into it. If you now SELECT the data out of it, you can see that each of the VIPs has an ID that is guaranteed to be unique across the system:

```
SELECT * FROM dbo.VIP
```

This returns the following recordset (Note: Because the VIP IDs are globally unique, your values will be different for this column):

VIPID	VIPName
EFA6C169-8AFF-4044-8912-734...	Melinda
4F42DCC3-2BFD-4846-8D63-630...	Letha
DAE8F992-3F8E-44A9-8C7A-C51...	Autrey
610D1846-021D-4F2A-9C7D-E93...	Scott
8A58F9BF-FFFE-4921-8C7E-677...	Craig
47379CB4-FC48-4E20-8DBC-6E5...	Shabbir

To be more robust, you would probably want to either make the VIPID column the primary key, or at a minimum make this column UNIQUE. Since people can still manually populate the column, without a UNIQUE constraint, someone could create a GUID and use it over and over when inserting new records into the table.

User-Defined Functions

If you can't find the function that you need, don't despair because you can create your own functions, beginning with SQL Server 2000. These are known as **user-defined functions** or UDFs for short. UDFs can be very useful, but you must be careful. You can create UDFs that are very slow or resource-intensive, but this would detract from your attempts to make the database easier to use. Let's look at a few examples of some UDFs.

Scalar UDFs

UDFs can be of two basic types. The first type of UDF is a **scalar** type, which means that the UDF returns a single value. This is similar to scalar built-in functions, like ABS or DATEPART. You use scalar UDFs much like you would use a scalar built-in function.

Try It Out–Writing a Scalar User-Defined Function

Perhaps you want a function to give you the date in the format of a Julian date. A Julian date is a five-digit date, consisting of a two-digit year, plus the day of the year; so January 15, 2003 would be 03015, and March 23, 2003 would be 03082, and so on. You could even extend this to be a seven-digit format and use four digits for the year, so the two previous dates would be 2003015 and 2003082, respectively. Now that you have a grasp of the Julian date format, let's build a scalar UDF in Northwind that gives you the date in this format, since SQL Server doesn't provide you with one.

```
USE Northwind
GO

CREATE FUNCTION dbo.fnConvertToJulianDate(
   @inDate AS DATETIME
)
RETURNS VARCHAR(7)
AS
BEGIN
   RETURN CAST(DATEPART(YY, @inDate) AS CHAR(4)) +
   RIGHT('00' + CAST(DATEPART(DY, @inDate) AS VARCHAR(3)), 3)
END
GO
```

Then, let's get some order information, using the new function:

```
SELECT TOP 5
    O.OrderID, O.CustomerID,
    dbo.fnConvertToJulianDate(O.OrderDate) AS OrderDate,
    dbo.fnConvertToJulianDate(O.RequiredDate) AS RequiredDate,
    dbo.fnConvertToJulianDate(O.ShippedDate) AS ShippedDate,
    STR(SUM(OD.UnitPrice * OD.Quantity), 8, 2) AS Amount
FROM Orders O
    INNER JOIN [Order Details] OD ON O.OrderID = OD.OrderID
GROUP BY O.ORDERID, O.CustomerID, O.OrderDate, O.RequiredDate,
            O.ShippedDate
ORDER BY Amount DESC
```

This will give you the required information for the top five orders, based on the amount of the order. If you run this, you'll get the following results:

OrderID	CustomerID	OrderDate	RequiredDate	ShippedDate	Amount
10865	QUICK	1998033	1998047	1998043	17250.00
11030	SAVEA	1998107	1998135	1998117	16321.90
10981	HANAR	1998086	1998114	1998092	15810.00
10372	QUEEN	1996339	1997001	1996344	12281.20
10424	MEREP	1997023	1997051	1997027	11493.20

You can see that this shows you the three dates as Julian dates.

Inline UDFs

Inline UDFs are just functions that return a table. When you create these UDFs, you can SELECT from them like you can a table, but you can pass parameters, so you can think of it like a view that can take a parameter. The main difference between inline and table UDFs is that the former can only consist of a single SELECT statement.

Try It Out–Writing an Inline User-Defined Function

Here is an inline UDF that gives you the same columns as the previous UDF, but without the use of the Julian date (but you do strip off the time data for clarity). The user can call this with a specific date range and get the only the records that fall within that range as follows:

```
Use Northwind
GO

CREATE FUNCTION dbo.fnGetCustInfoByAmount (
    @StartDate DATETIME,
    @EndDate DATETIME
)
RETURNS TABLE
AS
RETURN SELECT
```

```
      O.OrderID, O.CustomerID, CONVERT(VARCHAR(12), O.OrderDate,
                                  101)
   AS
      OrderDate,
      CONVERT(VARCHAR(12), O.RequiredDate, 101) AS RequiredDate,
      CONVERT(VARCHAR(12), O.ShippedDate, 101) AS ShippedDate,
      STR(SUM(OD.UnitPrice * OD.Quantity), 8, 2) AS Amount
   FROM Orders O
      INNER JOIN [Order Details] OD ON O.OrderID = OD.OrderID
   WHERE OrderDate BETWEEN @StartDate AND @EndDate
   GROUP BY O.ORDERID, O.CustomerID, O.OrderDate, O.RequiredDate,
            O.ShippedDate
   GO
```

Then you select from this inline UDF as if it were a table, as follows:

```
SELECT * FROM dbo.fnGetCustInfoByAmount ('9/30/1997',
                                         '10/02/1997')
```

You now get all of the records that were ordered between the two dates (inclusive) passed into the function, as shown:

OrderID	CustomerID	OrderDate	RequiredDate	ShippedDate	Amount
10686	PICCO	09/30/1997	10/28/1997	10/08/1997	1638.45
10687	HUNGO	09/30/1997	10/28/1997	10/30/1997	6201.90
10688	VAFFE	10/01/1997	10/15/1997	10/07/1997	3490.00
10689	BERGS	10/01/1997	10/29/1997	10/07/1997	630.00
10690	HANAR	10/02/1997	10/30/1997	10/03/1997	1150.00

Table UDFs

SQL Server 2000 introduced the TABLE data type. It's often convenient to create a table variable, populate the variable, and then return the contents of the variable.

Try It Out–Writing a Table User-Defined Function

In the following function, you use a table variable, just to show its use. This is the same function as the last one, but it uses the table variable. Keep in mind that this is just for show; the earlier function is more practical:

```
CREATE FUNCTION dbo.fnGetCustInfoByAmount2 (
   @StartDate DATETIME,
   @EndDate DATETIME
)
RETURNS @JustForShow TABLE (
   OrderID INT NOT NULL,
   CustomerID NCHAR(5) NULL,
   OrderDate VARCHAR(12) NULL,
   RequiredDate VARCHAR(12) NULL,
   ShippedDate VARCHAR(12) NULL,
   Amount VARCHAR(8) NULL)
```

```
      AS
        BEGIN
          INSERT INTO @JustForShow (
            OrderID, CustomerID,
            OrderDate, RequiredDate, ShippedDate, Amount)
          SELECT O.OrderID, O.CustomerID,
                  CONVERT(VARCHAR(12), O.OrderDate, 101) AS OrderDate,
                  CONVERT(VARCHAR(12), O.RequiredDate, 101)
                      AS RequiredDate,
                  CONVERT(VARCHAR(12), O.ShippedDate, 101)
                      AS ShippedDate,
                  STR(SUM(OD.UnitPrice * OD.Quantity), 8, 2) AS Amount
          FROM Orders O
            INNER JOIN [Order Details] OD ON O.OrderID = OD.OrderID
          WHERE OrderDate BETWEEN @StartDate AND @EndDate
          GROUP BY O.ORDERID, O.CustomerID, O.OrderDate,
                    O.RequiredDate, O.ShippedDate

          RETURN
        END
      GO
```

You would use this UDF in the same way as the previous one, so if you ran the following:

```
SELECT * FROM dbo.fnGetCustInfoByAmount2 ('9/30/1997',
                                          '10/02/1997')
```

You would get this:

OrderID	CustomerID	OrderDate	RequiredDate	ShippedDate	Amount
10686	PICCO	09/30/1997	10/28/1997	10/08/1997	1638.45
10687	HUNGO	09/30/1997	10/28/1997	10/30/1997	6201.90
10688	VAFFE	10/01/1997	10/15/1997	10/07/1997	3490.00
10689	BERGS	10/01/1997	10/29/1997	10/07/1997	630.00
10690	HANAR	10/02/1997	10/30/1997	10/03/1997	1150.00

Not-So-Good UDFs

UDFs aren't always a good idea. If the UDF that you create performs a lot of calculations or is resource-intensive, then you should try to rework your function or find a different way to do the work. Whenever you build a UDF or a stored procedure or view for that matter, you should run a few performance metrics on it to make sure that it performs in a satisfactory manner.

Many developers and DBAs make a mistake of joining the output of a scalar UDF to tables. The fact that you can join the output of UDF's to other tables in the query is great for functions that return tables. Keep in mind, however, that scalar UDFs are executed once per each row they're joined to. Therefore, if you join the output of a scalar UDF to a table with million rows the UDF will be called million times – much like a cursor. Always ensure that your scalar UDF's are as efficient as possible and avoid joining their output to large tables.

Stored Procedures

A stored procedure is like a method, that is, a group of SQL statements that perform one or more units of work. Stored procedures can return one or more recordsets, one or more output parameters, or values (they don't have to return anything). A stored procedure can range from one simple SQL statement to a very complex set of statements. They can call other stored procedures, COM objects, or the operating system. Stored procedures allow you to hide logic and complexity from application developers, and can protect sensitive data from prying eyes.

You can hide the underlying data structures with stored procedures as well. A user can call a stored procedure and get a resultset back from a mix of tables. You can create stored procedures to return only the columns or data a user requires for their application.

Many times, a developer will build the front-end of an application in VB, C#, or ASP, and many of these applications rely on databases for much of their data. As a DBA, you should do all that you can to make sure that this data is reliable and safe. Ad hoc queries by these applications usually aren't a good idea, especially for production code. Ad hoc queries open the database up to more vulnerability and expose the structures and data more than should be allowed; they're also invariably slower than stored procedures.

SQL Server will build an execution plan for a stored procedure and keep it in cache so that when it's run again, it will use the same execution plan and run faster on subsequent calls. Granted, SQL Server will also create and store execution plans for ad hoc queries, but a stored procedure is more likely to reuse an execution plan than ad hoc queries that may vary too much to benefit from reusing this execution plan.

Stored procedures can also reduce network traffic. If a user has to send a large set of SQL statements to the server, or if the user has to send many statements for the server to process and send back, a stored procedure can be called. Much less data will be sent over the network, because the stored procedure can perform much of the logic and work on the server. There is also no need to send intermediate results to the client to process.

Stored procedures give you many advantages over using ad hoc queries, and good programming practices will help to thwart would-be attackers who are attempting to gain access to your valuable data. You can secure all of your tables from users and only allow them access to the database through stored procedures. As a matter of fact, many companies do this; the only way into their database is through stored procedures.

User Stored Procedures

User stored procedures are simply stored procedures that a user creates. A user can build stored procedures for developers to access the data in the underlying tables. These stored procedures can be complex, thus allowing an application developer to call the stored procedure, treat it as a black box, requiring no knowledge of how the work was done. All that developers need know is that this black box requires certain input and returns the data they need. Common stored procedures allow a user to INSERT, UPDATE, or DELETE columns from tables, but many also do specific tasks, or may do a combination of INSERT, UPDATE, and DELETE operations. Stored procedures also allow you to build specific logic once, and reuse it for other similar processes.

Stored procedures are a good place to put much of the business logic for the data. Let's look at the Northwind database. If you go to either Query Analyzer or Enterprise Manager, you can see all of the stored procedures listed. Let's look at the SalesByCategory stored procedure (note that you aren't looking at the Sales By Year stored procedure; we'll discuss this in a moment). In Query Analyzer, the stored procedures are listed in the Objects window.

And in EM, the stored procedures are found under the specific database, such as Northwind here.

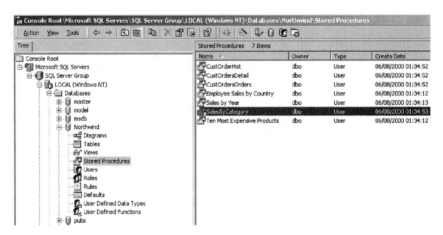

If you're in EM, you can double-click the stored procedure to examine it.

And if you're in Query Analyzer, you can see the contents in several ways. The first way is to right-click the procedure name, choose one of the Script ... As options, and then script it to a new window or the clipboard.

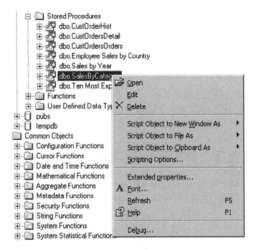

Another nice way to see it is to use the sp_helptext system stored procedure (system stored procedures are discussed in the next section). This stored procedure will produce the text of a stored procedure, function, or trigger. It may be easier to view it if you set the output to Results in Text by choosing the Execute mode button (or the Query menu) and then Results in text (or press *Ctrl+T*).

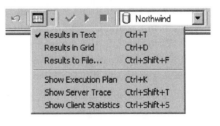

Then type the following to see the contents of the procedure:

```
sp_helptext SalesByCategory
```

515

You can see that this places a report that will give the sales, grouped by category for a given year. You could have put this code into a front-end application, maybe even in several places where it may be needed, but it's convenient and efficient to have it stored on the database server where it can be reused over and over.

Note that the name of the `Sales By Year` stored procedure has spaces in it. For the previous stored procedure, you can simply call it by its name and parameters: `EXEC SalesByCateory parm1, parm2`. But with any object with spaces or odd characters in the name, you must tell SQL Server to use all of the words separately for the name of the object, as mentioned earlier in the chapter, so you would have to call this one like this:

```
exec [Sales By Year] parm1, parm2
```

```
exec "Sales By Year" parm1, parm2
```

Save yourself, and those you work with, the hassle of dealing with objects with names like this. `Northwind` does this in several places; my guess (and hope) is that Microsoft wants to show you that it can be done, and isn't leading by example here.

Another good practice to get into is scripting your objects and code and keeping them in Microsoft Visual SourceSafe. This not only allows you to go back to a previous stable version if you wander off the path trying to improve your code, but also allows you to easily re-create your database when the need arises, provided you keep some kind of a `make` file, or a file that indicates the order to call your scripts in. Please note: This is intentionally for "when the need arises" and not "if the need arises."

System Stored Procedures

System stored procedures are stored procedures that come with SQL Server; they're predefined and allow you to perform many administrative functions on the databases. In the last section, you saw how to use the `sp_helptext` system stored procedure to give you the text of a stored procedure. You have access to many stored procedures that carry out tasks such as this.

BOL gives a reference to most of them, but not all of them. Go to the index tab of BOL and then type in "sp_"; this is where they start. Use undocumented procedures at your own risk, since they can change at any time. If you look at the stored procedures in the `master` database, you'll see a list of more than what BOL covers. In this section, you'll go over some commonly used system stored procedures to get you started, but it would take a chapter by itself to go into detail on all of them. Here are a few of our favorite ones:

Stored Procedure	Description
sp_helptext	Gives the text of a trigger, view, or stored procedure.
sp_help	Provides some information about an object. Parameters can be a table name, view, stored procedure, user-defined function, user-defined data type, and so on, to get more information about the object.
sp_helpdb	Shows information about a specific database.
sp_columns	Shows detailed information about columns in a table or view.
sp_statistics	Shows the indexes and statistics for a given table (or indexed view).
sp_who2	Allows you to see all of the users on the databases on a server.
sp_configure	Allows you to set different options on a database server.
sp_dbcmptlevel	Allows you to get or set the compatibility level, or the behavior particular to a specific version of SQL Server. This is a good item to look at if your database gives you unpredictable results. We were working with a database for a client and had the TOP clause in a SQL statement. We received a syntax error, and after playing with it for a little while, we looked at this setting to find that the compatibility level was at 6.5. The available options are 60, 65, 70, and 80, and they correspond with the various versions of SQL Server (80 is SQL Server 2000).
sp_lock	Returns information about locks. Use this when you're having locking problems and want to see what processes are locking other processes.
sp_changedbowner	Allows you to easily change the owner of a database.
sp_addmessage	Allows you to define your own system messages and numbers that you can use in your code. You can pass it parameters to make the messages more readable and customizable at runtime.

Note that most of the system stored procedures start with sp_ (you'll discuss the xp_ ones next). When you see a stored procedure that starts with these three characters, you can usually safely assume that it's a system stored procedure. Most of the functionality in these stored procedures can also be achieved using EM, but you should learn how to do everything via a script so that you can back up and version your script.

> **For this reason, among others, you should not start your stored procedure names with these three characters (sp_), because it will lead to confusion between user stored procedures and system stored procedures.**

Another reason to not start your procedures with sp_ is that when SQL Server sees a stored procedure with a name like this, it assumes that this is a system stored procedure and that it's stored in the master database. You may have noticed that when you called a system stored procedure earlier, you didn't have to prefix it with the master database; SQL Server knew where it was because of its naming convention, so naming yours like this will have an affect on performance as well.

If you want a good learning tool for stored procedures, look at some of the system stored procedures; you can view their content and get some good ideas for your own user-defined stored procedures.

Extended Stored Procedures

Extended stored procedures are also stored procedures that come with SQL Server. These stored procedures extend the capability of SQL Server and allow you to do things that T-SQL can't. You can write your own extended stored procedure in a programming language like C, but that is beyond the scope of this book. Extended stored procedures allow you to interact with resources external to SQL Server; resources like COM objects and the operating system.

For example, there are a group of stored procedures that allow you to instantiate COM objects and call their methods. These are the sp_OA methods. Although these start with sp_, they are extended stored procedures. Most of the extended stored procedures start with xp_.

The extended stored procedures make calls to DLLs, so you can't see their contents like other stored procedures. There are several that allow you to interact with the operating system as well. You can use the xp_cmdshell extended stored procedure to run a string as you would on the command line. There's xp_fileexist, which checks for the existence of a file or directory; xp_dirtree, which gets a complete directory listing for a specific directory; and xp_sendmail, which sends an e-mail message.

Views

A view is a virtual table, based on one or more tables and can be treated in many ways like a table. Views can hide the complexity of code and table structures. For example, if you have a query with a complex join or complex logic, you can create a view with that query. This hides the complexity of the tables, and keeps others from having to reinvent the wheel if they need that same logic in their queries.

In SQL Server 2000, you can create indexes on views, and because of availability of the INSTEAD OF triggers, you can even update views. You can create a view that is based on tables on different servers, and you can hide certain data from users with views. To create a view, you just write the query and put it into a CREATE VIEW statement. Once you have a view, you can select from it, or join to it just as if it were a table.

Views can also help you split and manage tables that you want to separate. For example, imagine you have two sales tables, one for the current year and one for all past years. Let's call them Sales_Current and Sales_Past. Sales_Current contains all of the current year's sales data and

`Sales_Past` contains all sales data prior to the current year. Instead of making the user decide on which table to pull data from, you can create a view that will pull data from these two tables, and all the user has to see (and `SELECT` from) is the view. This is called a **partitioned view**.

Tables that the partitioned view uses can even be on different servers. This is called a **distributed partitioned view**. These partitioned views can be used for updates so that the user can `UPDATE` the view, and the view can then update the correct table.

Indexed Views

Beginning with SQL Server 2000, you can place indexes on the views. Placing an index on a view means that SQL Server will physically store the data from the view. These views are often called **materialized views,** because SQL Server materializes the data for these views.

Indexed views work best when they're based on tables in which the data changes infrequently or when the SQL statement that creates the view will result in a lot of records. When you create an indexed view, SQL Server manages the indexes on the underlying tables and on the indexed views as well. You need to balance the overhead of maintaining these indexes so the view doesn't become an indexed view. Indexed views can significantly affect performance, either positively or negatively, so make sure that you design and test your views thoroughly.

Advantages and Drawbacks of Views

Views offer the following advantages:

❏ They can be used to hide the complexity of the data model.

❏ They can be used to enforce security by allowing users to read data only from certain columns.

If you already have a clustered index on a table and you really need another clustered index on a different column, you can create a view on a table and add a clustered index on the view.

Unfortunately, you must use views with the following disadvantages in mind:

❏ Views affect performance negatively if they're built on top of other views, which in turn are built on top of other views, and so on. Keep in mind that a view is just another `SELECT` statement that isn't precompiled—it's simply stored in a system table and is executed each time it's accessed. So in essence, if the `SELECT` statement in `CREATE VIEW` becomes complex, it's time to rewrite the view as a stored procedure or user-defined function.

❏ Views don't allow any conditional statements, parameters, temporary tables, table variables, and much more that can be accomplished through UDFs and stored procedures.

Triggers

Triggers are like stored procedures that run automatically when data in a table (or view) is modified. If there's an action or actions that you want to make happen whenever table data is modified, a trigger is the place to do it. You can create triggers to fire when a table is inserted into, updated, deleted from, or any combination of these. When you create a trigger to fire when records are inserted into the table, it's called an **insert trigger**.

Triggers can be used for many purposes. The main use of triggers is to enforce business rules, for example if you have business rules that dictate that an action should occur when a table is modified. Triggers are also used for cascade actions. If you have an order and order details table, a trigger can delete order-detail records if the order is deleted. Triggers can also be used to check constraints in order to insert default values, and in order to ensure data integrity by guaranteeing that a specific record exists before allowing the current one to be inserted. For example, you could verify that a specific order exists before allowing a related order detail record to be created.

There are two basic types of triggers on SQL Server 2000: AFTER triggers and INSTEAD OF triggers. Up until SQL Server 2000, all triggers were AFTER triggers, running after the modification of the table. For example, if you have an INSERT statement that inserts into a table with a trigger on it, the data is inserted into the table and then the trigger fires, so if the insert fails, the trigger doesn't run.

With SQL Server 2000, you can now specify instead of triggers, which are triggers that run instead of the data manipulation code. You have to actually write the code to do the data manipulation. If you don't specify what type of trigger you're writing, AFTER is the default.

In every trigger, you have access to two special tables. These tables are called inserted and deleted and they have the exact same structure as the table that the trigger is for. The inserted table contains all of the new records that were inserted into the underlying table and the deleted table contains all of the records that were deleted from the underlying table. These two tables have scope only within the trigger.

Well, what about an updated table, you ask? An UPDATE is really just a DELETE and an INSERT; the original record is deleted and then a record with the new values is inserted, so when there's an UPDATE, the deleted table contains the original values of the record and the inserted table contains the new values of the table.

AFTER Trigger

Like the name suggests, an AFTER trigger is executed after the data manipulation that fired the trigger occurs. AFTER triggers can only be written for tables, not views, and you can have multiple AFTER triggers for each action (INSERT, UPDATE, or DELETE) for a single table. To specify that a trigger is for multiple actions, just separate the actions by commas, for example FOR INSERT, UPDATE.

Earlier, we mentioned that you have some control over what order triggers fire in. You don't have total control; you can set the first and last trigger to fire, but not the order of any triggers in between. With this capability, you have control of the order of up to three triggers. You set the order of the triggers with the sp_settriggerorder system stored procedure.

Try It Out–Writing a Trigger

Let's create a simple trigger on the Northwind database for the Territories table. First let's create an audit table to track when some territories are inserted or deleted:

```
CREATE TABLE triggertest(
TestID INT NOT NULL IDENTITY(1, 1) Primary Key,
TestDate DATETIME NOT NULL DEFAULT(GETDATE()),
TestData VARCHAR(256) NOT NULL
)
```

Then create the INSERT trigger:

```
CREATE TRIGGER trInsTerritories ON dbo.Territories
FOR INSERT
AS
INSERT INTO dbo.triggertest(TestData)
SELECT 'New Territory added: ' + TerritoryDescription
FROM INSERTED
```

And then the DELETE trigger:

```
CREATE TRIGGER trDelTerritories ON dbo.Territories
FOR DELETE
AS
INSERT INTO dbo.triggertest(TestData)
SELECT 'New Territory removed: ' + TerritoryDescription
FROM DELETED
```

Now, you'll INSERT a few territories:

```
INSERT INTO Territories(TerritoryID, TerritoryDescription,
                        RegionID)
VALUES(11111, 'TestTerritory1', 4)
INSERT INTO Territories(TerritoryID, TerritoryDescription,
                        RegionID)
VALUES(22222, 'TestTerritory2', 4)
```

And then DELETE them (you'll do it in a single statement to show that the trigger works for multiple rows):

```
DELETE FROM Territories
WHERE TerritoryDescription LIKE 'TestTerritory%'
```

Now, let's look at the triggertest table:

```
SELECT * FROM triggertest
```

You've tracked when new territories were added and deleted to give you the following resultset:

TestID	TestDate	TestData
1	2003-09-05 09:29:44.677	New Territory added: TestTerritory1
2	2003-09-05 09:29:44.687	New Territory added: TestTerritory2
3	2003-09-05 09:29:47.630	New Territory removed: TestTerritory1
4	2003-09-05 09:29:47.630	New Territory removed: TestTerritory2

You could add UPDATE triggers, or even put them into a single trigger, and then look at the inserted and deleted tables to determine what to write out to the triggertest table.

INSTEAD OF Trigger

INSTEAD OF triggers run in place of the actual data manipulation. These types of triggers can be written for views as well as tables. INSTEAD OF triggers can be pretty powerful, because you can completely control what happens when an action triggers them to run. Unlike AFTER triggers, there can only be one INSTEAD OF trigger for each trigger action for a single table.

INSTEAD OF triggers also fire before constraints are checked, so you could actually INSERT records that violate constraints, as long as you correct the error within the trigger. The syntax for INSTEAD OF triggers is to use the INSTEAD OF clause to replace the FOR keyword of an AFTER trigger, so it would be something like this:

```
CREATE TRIGGER trTest ON dbo.Territories
INSTEAD OF INSERT
AS
...
```

The Good, the Bad, and the Ugly

Triggers can be used for many reasons, some of which were listed at the beginning of this section. But with SQL Server 2000, many of these reasons are no longer valid, because there are better ways of doing much of this than with triggers. For example, you can create a default constraint, which is much better than using a trigger, because it's easier to write and maintain, and it's a part of the table creation, where triggers aren't.

Foreign key constraints, rather than triggers should be used to enforce referential integrity; with SQL Server 2000 and cascading actions for DELETE and UPDATE operations, you don't even need to use triggers for cascading actions either. Triggers were more useful in the past for these items than they are now. That's not to say that they shouldn't be used at all, but used with discretion. There are still occasions during which triggers can enforce business rules; just ensure that the code wouldn't be better served in a stored procedure. If you want to use triggers, make sure that a trigger is the best place for the code.

A good example of when a trigger is still a good choice is when you wish to perform an action when data in a certain column is updated in order to create an audit trail. Within a trigger you can issue a statement such as the following:

```
IF UPDATE (column_1)
  BEGIN
    INSERT audit_table ('column_name', 'old_value', 'new_value')
    SELECT 'column_1',
           deleted.column_1,
           inserted.column_1
  FROM inserted INNER JOIN deleted


    ON inserted.key_column = deleted.key_column
```

> Stay away from cursors within triggers. The performance of a trigger lies in what the trigger does, and as mentioned earlier, cursors are slow, so putting them in triggers is just asking for trouble. Keep in mind that a trigger fires each time an INSERT, UPDATE, or DELETE is executed against the table. Furthermore, the implicit transaction associated with INSERT, UPDATE, and DELETE isn't committed until the trigger has finished executing. So a cursor within a trigger has the potential to force SQL Server to hold locks for a very long time, thereby causing all other users to wait until the trigger has finished executing.
>
> Another thing to remember when coding a trigger is that there can be more than one row being updated when the trigger is fired. We've seen triggers that can handle only single row updates. Be sure to test your triggers for single and multiple row updates.

T-SQL XML Extensions

XML has made its way into most coding languages and T-SQL is no exception. In fact, SQL Server 2000 was one of the first database engines to provide support for reading and writing data as XML. Although SQL Server 2000 doesn't support native XML data types, the next version of SQL Server is very likely to provide such functionality.

In this section, we'll discuss the FOR XML clause of the SELECT statement, which provides you with a way to return data as XML instead of a resultset, and the OPENXML function, which allows you to parse XML documents. Because this chapter isn't intended to be the full-blown T-SQL or XML reference, we advise you to pick up an excellent book from Curlingstone, *SQL Server 2000 XML Distilled* for additional information.

The FOR XML clause of the SELECT statement supports three modes: AUTO, RAW, and EXPLICIT. Each of these modes can be beneficial for certain coding needs.

AUTO Mode

The AUTO mode of the FOR XML clause treats the table name as a parent, and each column in the table becomes a child of the table name tag.

Try It Out–Returning XML

For instance, the following query retrieves the first two rows in the customers table from the Northwind database in XML format:

```
SELECT TOP 2 * FROM customers FOR XML AUTO
```

Here are the results:

```
<customers
    CustomerID="ALFKI"
    CompanyName="Alfreds Futterkiste"
    ContactName="Maria Anders"
    ContactTitle="Sales Representative"
    Address="Obere Str. 57"
    City="Berlin"
    PostalCode="12209"
    Country="Germany"
    Phone="030-0074321"
    Fax="030-0076545"/>

<customers
    CustomerID="ANATR"
    CompanyName="Ana Trujillo Emparedados y helados"
    ContactName="Ana Trujillo"
    ContactTitle="Owner"
    Address="Avda. de la Constitución 2222"
    City="México D.F."
    PostalCode="05021"
    Country="Mexico"
    Phone="(5) 555-4729"
    Fax="(5) 555-3745"/>
```

Try It Out–Returning XML Elements

By default, the AUTO mode treats the columns as attributes, but you can easily override this setting by appending the ELEMENTS option, as follows:

```
SELECT TOP 2 * FROM customers FOR XML AUTO, ELEMENTS
```

Which returns the following results:

```
<customers>
<CustomerID>ALFKI</CustomerID>
<CompanyName>Alfreds Futterkiste</CompanyName>
<ContactName>Maria Anders</ContactName>
```

```
<ContactTitle>Sales Representative</ContactTitle>
<Address>Obere Str. 57</Address>
<City>Berlin</City>
<PostalCode>12209</PostalCode>
<Country>Germany</Country>
<Phone>030-0074321</Phone>
<Fax>030-0076545</Fax>
</customers>

<customers>
<CustomerID>ANATR</CustomerID>
<CompanyName>Ana Trujillo Emparedados y helados</CompanyName>
<ContactName>Ana Trujillo</ContactName>
<ContactTitle>Owner</ContactTitle>
<Address>Avda. de la Constitución 2222</Address>
<City>México D.F.</City>
<PostalCode>05021</PostalCode>
<Country>Mexico</Country>
<Phone>(5) 555-4729</Phone>
<Fax>(5) 555-3745</Fax>
</customers>
```

Try It Out–Multitable Queries and XML

Multitable queries with FOR XML AUTO return hierarchies of XML elements that depend on the order in which table columns are specified in the query. For instance, if you select a couple of rows from the customers and orders tables, the XML hierarchy returned depends on the order of columns specified in the query. Let's look at an example to make things easier to grasp:

```
SELECT TOP 2
    Orders.OrderDate,
    Orders.ShipCity,
    Customers.CompanyName,
    Customers.Country
FROM orders INNER JOIN customers ON
    orders.customerid = customers.customerid
FOR XML AUTO
```

Which returns the following:

```
<orders OrderDate="1996-07-04T00:00:00" ShipCity="Reims">
  <customers CompanyName="Vins et alcools Chevalier" Country="France"/>
</orders>

<orders OrderDate="1996-07-05T00:00:00" ShipCity="Münster">
  <customers CompanyName="Toms Spezialitäten" Country="Germany"/>
</orders>
```

Notice that, since you specified columns selected from the orders table, SQL Server returned <orders> as the parent tag and <customers> as the child. Note also that T-SQL isn't case sensitive, whereas XML is. Because you specified table names in lowercase, the elements were also returned in lowercase.

Now let's see what happens if you switch the order in which the columns are specified and capitalize the table names:

```
SELECT TOP 2
    Customers.CompanyName,
    Customers.Country,
    Orders.OrderDate,
    Orders.ShipCity
FROM Orders INNER JOIN Customers ON
    orders.customerid = customers.customerid
FOR XML AUTO
```

Here are the results:

```
<Customers CompanyName="Vins et alcools Chevalier" Country="France">
  <Orders OrderDate="1996-07-04T00:00:00" ShipCity="Reims"/>
</Customers>

<Customers CompanyName="Toms Spezialitäten" Country="Germany">
  <Orders OrderDate="1996-07-05T00:00:00" ShipCity="Münster"/>
</Customers>
```

The same query with a slight change returns a different hierarchy; <Customers> is now the parent and <Orders> is the child.

RAW Mode

The RAW mode appends the <row> tag to the output and doesn't include table names. If you need to know which table the data is coming from, the RAW mode won't help you. On the other hand, the RAW mode is very useful when you don't really care about the source of the data so, if you have a query joining multiple tables and you just want to grab the data without mentioning table names, use the RAW mode.

Try It Out–Returning XML in RAW Mode

The following example returns the data from the Orders and Customers tables as XML in RAW mode:

```
SELECT TOP 2
    Customers.CompanyName,
    Customers.Country,
    Orders.OrderDate,
    Orders.ShipCity
FROM Orders INNER JOIN Customers ON
    orders.customerid = customers.customerid
FOR XML RAW
```

Which returns the following:

```
<row CompanyName="Vins et alcools Chevalier"
Country="France" OrderDate="1996-07-04T00:00:00" ShipCity="Reims"/>

<row CompanyName="Toms Spezialitäten" Country="Germany"
OrderDate="1996-07-05T00:00:00" ShipCity="Münster"/>
```

Notice that the RAW mode doesn't support the ELEMENTS option; instead, you're limited to retrieving data as attributes.

EXPLICIT Mode

You've seen that neither RAW nor AUTO provides much flexibility for customizing the XML output when reading data out of SQL Server tables. Fortunately, the EXPLICIT mode provides this flexibility, even though at first it might seem cumbersome to use.

The EXPLICIT mode is implemented through UNION ALL queries. The UNION ALL clause combines the results of two or more SELECT queries. Each query combined using the UNION ALL clause has to contain the same number of columns. The corresponding columns in each query must also have compatible data types. In other words, you cannot UNION an integer and a string (unless you explicitly convert one of them first). For instance, you could combine the names of customer contacts and employee names in the Northwind database with the following query:

```
SELECT ContactName FROM customers

UNION ALL

SELECT FirstName + ' ' + LastName AS FullName FROM Employees
```

Which returns the following results (abbreviated):

ContactName
Maria Anders
Ana Trujillo
Antonio Moreno
Thomas Hardy
Christina Berglund
Hanna Moos
Frédérique Citeaux
Martín Sommer

Notice that even though you combined two queries with different column names, the output has a heading of the top query. In fact, the UNION ALL clause always gives you the column names from the top query regardless of how many queries are involved.

The EXPLICIT mode of FOR XML works similarly; you define your XML hierarchy in the top query, and then grab data for each of the XML nodes from the queries that follow. Keep in mind that each query will have to contain the same number of columns with compatible data types.

The XML structure to be returned is stored in what is referred to as the **universal table**. The universal table contains information about the XML tag names as well as how the tags need to be nested. Let's look at an example to make things a bit clearer.

Try It Out–Returning XML in EXPLICIT Mode

The following query returns titles written by the author Green and respective royalty percentages from the pubs database:

```
USE pubs

SELECT 1 AS TAG, NULL AS PARENT,
authors.au_fname            AS      [author!1!au_fname],
authors.au_lname            AS      [author!1!au_lname],
NULL                AS      [titleauthor!2!royaltyper],
NULL                AS      [titles!3!title]
FROM
authors WHERE au_lname = 'green'

UNION ALL

SELECT 2 AS TAG, 1 AS PARENT,
au_fname,
au_lname,
royaltyper,
NULL
FROM authors INNER JOIN titleauthor ON
authors.au_id= titleauthor.au_id
WHERE au_lname ='green'

UNION ALL

SELECT 3 AS TAG, 2 AS PARENT,
au_fname,
au_lname,
royaltyper,
title
FROM authors INNER JOIN titleauthor ON authors.au_id =
                                    titleauthor.au_id
INNER JOIN titles ON titles.title_id = titleauthor.title_id
WHERE au_lname ='green'
ORDER BY [author!1!au_fname], [author!1!au_lname],
         [titleauthor!2!royaltyper]
FOR XML EXPLICIT
```

The results are as follows:

```
<author au_fname="Marjorie" au_lname="green">
  <titleauthor royaltyper="40">
    <titles title="The Busy Executive&apos;s Database Guide"/>
  </titleauthor>
  <titleauthor royaltyper="100">
    <titles title="You Can Combat Computer Stress!"/>
  </titleauthor>
</author>
```

If you haven't used FOR XML EXPLICIT before, the previous query might seem overwhelming, but we'll go though each part in detail now.

As you saw earlier, you have to specify the XML structure to be returned in the top query. The topmost tag in the XML hierarchy doesn't have a parent. That's why every query using the EXPLICIT mode has to start with the following:

```
SELECT 1 AS TAG, NULL AS PARENT
```

The rest of the first SELECT statement constructs the XML hierarchy you want to see in the output. You'd like <author> to be the outermost tag, followed by <titleauthor> and then <titles>. The <author> tag should contain the first and last names of the author. The <titleauthor> tag, which is the child of <author>, should contain a single attribute of royalty percentages. Finally, the <titles> tag is the child of <titleauthor>, and should contain the title of the book(s) the author has written. Hence, the hierarchy defined in the topmost query looks as follows:

```
authors.au_fname AS [author!1!au_fname],
authors.au_lname AS [author!1!au_lname],
NULL AS [titleauthor!2!royaltyper],
NULL AS [titles!3!title]
```

Now the only part of the query that should still be puzzling you is the NULLs involved in the top query. Recall that each SELECT statement participating in the UNION ALL must contain the same number of columns. An alternative to using NULLs is to join all tables in each query. However, doing so would negatively affect the performance of the query. The example you looked at here returns only a couple of rows, but if you have three tables with thousands of rows in each, joining the three tables for each SELECT would make your query rather slow.

Although you might be familiar with the ORDER BY clause in regular SELECT statements, FOR XML EXPLICIT plays a slightly different role. In this case, ORDER BY sorts the XML hierarchy instead of the resultset. Let's examine the output of the same query executed without the ORDER BY clause:

```
<authors au_fname="Marjorie" au_lname="green">
  <titleauthor royaltyper="40"/>
  <titleauthor royaltyper="100">
  <titles title="The Busy Executive&apos;s Database Guide"/>
  <titles title="You Can Combat Computer Stress!"/>
  </titleauthor>
</authors>
```

Notice that now you have no way of telling which title is earning the author Green 40 percent of royalties and which one earns 100 percent. If you only have a couple of nodes in your XML hierarchy you might be able to get away without the ORDER BY clause. However, as a rule of thumb, be sure to include ORDER BY in all queries using the EXPLICIT mode.

It might sound obvious but, if you haven't already guessed, you can test your FOR XML EXPLICIT queries first by running SELECT statements without FOR XML clause.

OPENXML

As mentioned, the OPENXML function allows you to parse an XML document and turn it into a rowset. OPENXML can be used effectively to pass XML strings from the front-end or middle-tier programs to stored procedures. These stored procedures can in turn store data in table format after parsing the XML strings.

The full syntax of OPENXML is as follows:

```
OPENXML(idoc int [in], rowpattern nvarchar[in],
        [flags byte[in]]) [WITH (SchemaDeclaration | TableName)]
```

Just as with FOR XML, OPENXML might seem rather convoluted at first; however, deciphering a couple of examples should make this function relatively easy to understand.

The OPENXML function must be used with two system stored procedures: sp_xml_preparedocument and sp_xml_removedocument. As the names of these procedures suggest, the former prepares an internal representation of the XML document in memory and the latter removes such representations from memory to free up resources.

sp_xml_preparedocument accepts two parameters: the XML document, which is an input parameter, and an output parameter with the integer data type. Once the document is prepared with sp_xml_preparedocument, OPENXML can translate it into a rowset.

Try It Out–Using OPENXML

Consider the following example:

```
USE PUBS
DECLARE @xml_text VARCHAR(4000), @i INT

SELECT @xml_text = '
<root>
<authors    au_id="172-32-1176"
            au_lname="White"
            au_fname="Johnson"
            phone="408 496-7223"
            address="10932 Bigge Rd."
            city="Menlo Park"
```

```
                state="CA"
                zip="94025"
                contract="1"/>
    <authors    au_id="213-46-8915"
                au_lname="Green"
                au_fname="Marjorie"
                phone="415 986-7020"
                address="309 63rd St. #411"
                city="Oakland"
                state="CA"
                zip="94618"
                contract="1"/>
    </root>'

    EXEC sp_xml_preparedocument @i OUTPUT, @xml_text

    SELECT * FROM
        OPENXML(@i, '/root/authors')
    WITH (
                au_id       VARCHAR(11),
                au_lname    VARCHAR(20),
                au_fname    VARCHAR(30),
                phone       VARCHAR(12),
                address     VARCHAR(50),
                city        VARCHAR(20),
                state       CHAR(2),
                zip         CHAR(5),
                contract    BIT)

    EXEC sp_xml_removedocument @i
```

Which returns the following results:

au_id	au_lname	au_fname	phone	address	city	state	zip	contract
172-32-1176	White	Johnson	408 496-7223	10932 Bigge Rd.	Menlo Park	CA	94025	1
213-46-8915	Green	Marjorie	415 986-7020	309 63rd St. #411	Oakland	CA	94618	1

So what happened? First you declare the variable to hold the internal representation of the XML document (@I), and then you parse the XML string with sp_xml_preparedocument. At this point you're ready to use OPENXML, which takes @I and the path to where the data can be found within the XML string ('/root/author') as parameters. The WITH clause specifies the data types for each data element to be found within the XML string. Finally, you use sp_xml_removedocument to remove the XML string from memory.

Notice that in this example you're specifying each column found in the authors table within the XML string, so the structure of the rowset generated by OPENXML is identical to the structure of the authors table. If this happens, you can take a shortcut in coding and simply specify the database table whose structure is identical to the rowset generated by OPEXML. You could get the same results by writing the OPENXML portion of the previous query as follows:

```
    SELECT * FROM OPENXML(@i, '/root/authors')
    WITH authors
```

So you've seen that the basics of OPENXML statements are fairly simple. There are plenty of other options that might come in handy while using this function. Please refer to the online documentation for the explanation of each advanced option (search under OPENXML).

Summary

T-SQL is a powerful language, and has many tools for reading, writing, and manipulating data. Knowledge of T-SQL is essential for performing the duties of a DBA, whether or not you develop database code yourself. This chapter gave you a good overview of T-SQL, and what you can do with the database routines within SQL Server.

11

Data Warehousing and Analysis

Data warehousing has been around for over two decades. Yet, until a few years ago, only large companies could afford to build and maintain data warehouses. Microsoft changed this by introducing OLAP Services with SQL Server version 7.0 (in SQL Server 2000, OLAP Services are referred to as Analysis Services). What this means to you, as a DBA (database administrator), is that you and your colleagues are now more likely to develop and maintain a data warehouse than ever before.

This chapter will give you a general overview of what data warehousing is about as well as what it takes to build a data warehouse. We'll introduce Microsoft Analysis Services and MDX—the language for querying multidimensional data sources. Becoming a data-warehousing guru takes many years of research, study, and hands-on work; in this chapter, we'll begin the process by introducing the main concepts and terms through easy-to-understand examples.

Data Warehouses

In simple terms, a **data warehouse** is a data repository that is optimized for high-level reporting. If you've worked with databases for a while, you know that databases that support reporting applications are typically referred to as a DSS (decision support system). Unlike a DSS, a data warehouse is typically populated from multiple data sources. Furthermore, a data warehouse schema is dimensional, rather than relational. (We'll review the dimensional modeling principles shortly.) Although you could query tables in the dimensional model, a preferred way to query a data warehouse is through Microsoft Analysis Services cubes with MDX (Multidimensional eXpressions) queries, which are far more efficient than running T-SQL queries.

Why Build a Data Warehouse?

A majority of computer systems are built to collect data. In fact, for most organizations, data is the most valuable asset. To make use of this data, one has to have a way to retrieve the data from the database. DSS applications are great for generating long reports containing every transaction that has occurred in your OLTP (online transaction processing) system. However, deciphering mile-long reports isn't the most efficient way to run a business. Furthermore, decision makers often cannot derive much value from long reports. More valuable is a quick summary of the transactions broken down from various angles. A data warehouse happens to provide just that–a way to "slice and dice" the summarized data across various dimensions that make up the data.

It's important to understand that a data warehouse isn't a "data dump" from various data sources that a programmer or an Excel or Access expert has to manipulate further. It's true that you can use Excel for reading data out of the warehouse. In fact, we'll show you how you can read data from Analysis Services cubes later in the chapter. However, a data warehouse keeps the data organized in a format that is optimized for quick summary reporting over various functions of the business. Excel or Access reports must be distributed to individual users; Access is a single-user database although it's often misused by sharing a network file to multiple users. Data warehouses can serve numerous users and provide ways of customizing the output without the need for being an Access or Excel guru.

What Is Online Analytical Processing?

As mentioned in the previous section, DSS applications usually provide long, detailed reports, which tend to be paper-based and cannot be easily customized. Every time decision makers try to customize the report, they'll have to pay a programmer to make certain coding changes. Again, there are ways to create reports in MS Access without any programming; however, if you need to customize such reports, you have to hire someone (whether programmer or "click here" expert) to achieve what is needed.

OLAP allows easy customization of reports, based on summarized data. OLAP allows such flexibility due to the fact that it isn't based on a traditional two-dimensional approach; rather, OLAP is multidimensional.

As it pertains to OLAP, the concept of dimensions has nothing to do with length, width, and height; instead, dimensions are the variables within the business data. For example, an OLAP application for a grocery store chain might contain the customer, time, and item dimensions. Each sale in a grocery store happens at a particular instance in time; sale items are sold to a certain customer, and each sale consists of at least one item.

The terms data warehouse and OLAP are often used interchangeably, but there is a difference. A data warehouse is where the data actually resides–a multidimensional database. OLAP, on the other hand, is the suite of tools that let the decision makers query the data with multidimensional queries.

Microsoft Analysis Services supports three types of OLAP cubes–MOLAP, ROLAP, and HOLAP. We'll discuss the differences among these when we show you the example of building a cube later in the chapter.

Common Misconceptions and Misuses of Data Warehouses

As mentioned earlier, the data-warehousing concept has been around for quite a while. Because only a few companies could afford to build a data warehouse, many people still use the term wrongly. Let's have a look at a few common mistakes:

❑ A data warehouse isn't a transactional (OLTP) database. Just because OLAP provides a way to run queries efficiently doesn't mean that it can or should be used to speed up your transactional application. If you have problems with an OLTP system, you need to make an effort to optimize or rewrite the application. A data warehouse won't help in this case.

❑ A data warehouse isn't a reporting (DSS) database, because it isn't meant to produce long reports. If you feel like you have a need for long reports that will be printed and stored, OLAP isn't the right tool for you (hence the term **Online** Analytical Processing).

❑ A data warehouse will not solve data consistency problems. People new to the data warehouse and OLAP world think it's the cure for all of their problems, including data that is severely out of shape. For instance, if you collect names and titles of your customers in a free-form text field, you might have any of the following in your database:

❑ John Doe, Sr., Doctor

❑ Mr. John H Doe, MD

❑ Dr. John H Doe

❑ Dr. John H Doe Sr.

❑ Doe, John H, M.D.

To the human eye, it's quite clear that all of these entries denote the same person. However, for a database, each of these entries is different. Sticking all of these entries into the data warehouse will not solve the problem of such inconsistent data entry. Instead, you should improve your data entry application so that it accepts the title, last name, first name, and salutation in separate fields.

Building a Data Warehouse

As a beginner DBA or database developer, you won't have to build a data warehouse by yourself. Still, it makes sense to introduce the skill sets and support necessary, in case you become involved with a project that involves building or maintaining a data warehouse.

❑ **Business knowledge and business analysis.**

Just like any business application, a data warehouse project should start with gathering requirements from the users. Since data warehousing is a fairly new term for technical people, it comes as no surprise to expect confusion about a data warehouse from the business people. So, in addition to asking questions, you might have to explain what you're about to build. Be careful not to promise too much; once business users see the value of having a data warehouse, they often want to use it for all of their data—be sure to limit the scope to as few features as possible, since building a data warehouse isn't a trivial task and takes a lot of time.

❑   **Programming**.

If all of your data sources are limited to SQL Server databases, you're in luck. More than likely though, you'll have multiple data sources: SQL Server, Oracle, Sybase, Access, third-party databases, or even spreadsheets and text files. If you're strictly a T-SQL programmer, this is the time to find developers who are savvy in procedural languages. Such skills will be necessary to write the data extraction routines discussed later in the chapter.

❑   **Relational and dimensional modeling skills**.

If you've developed transactional systems, you'll be familiar with the normalization rules used for relational modeling. Dimensional modeling is somewhat different, and will be discussed later in the chapter–please refer to the "Creating a Dimensional Model" section. It's important to have both of these skills, because you'll probably store data extracted from various sources in relational format first, and then transform it into a dimensional database.

❑   **Management of the changing dimensions.**

Managing changing dimensions is perhaps one of the most difficult tasks associated with maintaining the data warehouse. Simply put, as your data changes, you'll need to make decisions on how much change you would like to track in the data warehouse. Management of the slowly changing dimensions is an advanced topic and will not be discussed in this chapter.

❑   **Knowledge of Microsoft Analysis Services and SQL Server.**

Building and maintaining a data warehouse isn't a trivial task, so be sure you have up-to-date knowledge of Analysis Services and SQL Server. If you don't have a full-time, dedicated DBA on staff, get one.

❑   **Knowledge of DTS and T-SQL.**

Although you can develop your own transformation tools, DTS (Data Transformation Services) does much of the groundwork for you, and provides helpful graphical utilities. If you care about saving time and money, be sure you have an expert in DTS on your staff.

❑   **Knowledge of Multidimensional eXpressions.**

Yet another huge challenge with building an effective data warehouse is learning MDX–the language used to query Analysis Services cubes. The complexity enters in because most developers are used to thinking in two-dimensional terms–rows and columns. MDX, on the other hand, operates on multidimensional concepts like cells, tuples, and sets. To complicate matters further, there is very little documentation of MDX available.

❑   **Knowledge of VB and ASP to develop front-end tools.**

Although you can use the Pivot Table Service with Excel to present cube data to users, it might be beneficial to develop or purchase more flexible tools. Again, knowledge of procedural and scripting languages would be required to develop such tools.

❑   **Support of executives and business users**.

Most data-warehousing projects will last at least several months and cost a fairly large sum of money. Due to this fact, the executives and business users tend to get rather impatient with developers and DBAs working on the data warehouse. To avoid undue hostility, you need to get the support of your users, and let them know early on in the project that they're in for a long ride.

Steps Involved in Building a Data Warehouse

In this section, we'll go over the steps involved in building a typical data warehouse. Although the effort your company might undertake could involve more (or less) work, you'll generally have to perform the tasks in the following sections. We'll also cover a small example of building a data warehouse to enhance your understanding of the material.

Gathering Requirements

What do you need to know before you begin?

Identifying Data Sources

Most companies will have their data dispersed in multiple data sources. Along with major RDBMS (relational database management systems) such as SQL Server, Oracle, DB2, and so on, your organization might store data in mail systems, flat files, spreadsheets, and other sources. The first step in building a data warehouse is determining the data sources you'll have to work with. For each data source involved, you (or your colleagues) will have to define data extraction and transformation routines; therefore, this step needs to be taken very seriously. Discovering new data sources 75 percent of the way into the project isn't an option because this could add several weeks or even several months of design and programming work.

For this mini-example, you have two data sources: a text file and an Access database.

Defining Reports to Be supported by the Data Warehouse

Business people like reports. Depending on the size of your organization, you might have to work with a handful or dozens of business users while building a data warehouse. Therefore, it's extremely important to limit the scope for each phase of your project and set the reasonable expectations for your data warehouse. There might be thousands of reports that your users would like to have, but not all of those reports have to be delivered at one time. Further, data for some of the desired reports might not be available in electronic format. To avoid failing to meet business users' expectations, meet with them and define a list of reports your data warehouse will support.

Defining Dimensions and Measures

The next step is to come up with a list of **measures** and **dimensions** for your data warehouse. For instance, suppose you work for a grocery store chain and you need to provide a report of total sales by store, customer age groups, zip code, and product description. The total amount of sales is your measure; store, customer, zip code, and product description are your dimensions.

Once you've identified your dimensions and measures, look at your data sources and ensure that you have all the data needed to support your data warehouse. Continuing with the previous example, if none of your data sources collect customer addresses, you can't provide a breakdown by zip code. If you find yourself in such a situation, go back to the business users and ask where the address data is being collected. More than likely, they have a separate data source that contains such information.

537

Building the Staging Area

The following quote is from the SQL Server Online documentation:

A cube is a set of data that is usually constructed from a subset of a data warehouse and is organized and summarized into a multidimensional structure defined by a set of dimensions and measures.

The OLAP cubes you'll build for your data warehouse will get their data from the database with a dimensional schema. However, when you first get your data from your sources, it might be easier to put such data in a staging database. The staging database doesn't have to be normalized, but if you're used to relational modeling, it might be beneficial to build a relational staging database.

Keep in mind that whichever method you use to get your data, it will have to be reused over and over again. Contrary to a common belief among business people, building a data warehouse isn't a one-shot operation. To refresh the data in your warehouse, you'll have to regularly update the data in your staging and dimensional databases as well as rebuild the dimensions and cubes in Analysis Services.

There are two points at which you can transform your data, giving it a shape or form needed for the data warehouse:

❑   While extracting data from various sources into the staging database

❑   While populating the dimensional database

Extracting data can be performed with a built-in tool such as DTS, or through custom procedural code; this depends on the types of data sources you must work with. Personally, we prefer manipulating data into a SQL Server database, but this is a matter of coding preference. If you're a VB or C++ programmer, you might find it easier to build your data transformations while getting the data from its original source.

Building Logical and Physical Data Models

If you're new to data modeling, you should learn the difference between the logical and physical models. The **logical model** isn't specific to the RDBMS used to implement the database. You don't have to be an SQL Server guru to build a logical model. The logical model contains the entities and attributes and relations between the entities. The **physical model**, on the other hand, will be specific to the RDBMS used.

For instance, this grocery chain data warehouse might contain a store entity with attributes of store identifier, store name, address, number of employees, and manager. This will remain the same however you implement it; in SQL Server, the physical implementation might contain tables, primary and foreign keys, default and check constraints, indexes, views, and more. While building a data warehouse, you should document your logical and physical data model for the staging database as well as the dimensional database.

For more information on data modeling, refer to *Data Modeling for Everyone* by Curlingstone Publishing.

Defining Data Transformations and Creating Transformation Routines for Each Data Source

At first glance, defining and creating data transformation routines might look like the same task. However, the definition of data extraction involves figuring out the mappings of data columns in the original data source and your staging area. If you aren't the owner of the original data source, you need to find the person responsible for collecting and maintaining data in that source. The data owner will have to confirm that your data mappings are correct. This is important because data columns might not always be appropriately named.

Creating transformation routines can be done with DTS if your data sources are OLE DB and ODBC compliant, and if you have appropriate drivers. Otherwise, you might have to write code in a language, such as VB, that allows you to write procedural code.

Building Data Cleansing Routines

Cleaning the data stored in OLTP databases could very well be the most annoying and tedious task in the whole data-warehousing project. As mentioned earlier, free-form text data entry can generate all kinds of data anomalies. Your business user is well aware that "Dr. John Doe" is the same person as "John Doe, Jr. M.D."; however, you can't convince the computer that those two values are equal–they aren't.

If you only have a few anomalies such as these in your data sources, you're in luck–you can easily write code that modifies the `customer_name` column and makes it "Dr. John Doe" wherever there is "John Doe, Jr. M.D." The following T-SQL statement will accomplish such a task:

```
UPDATE customers
SET
    customer_name = 'Dr. John Doe'
WHERE
    customer_name = 'John Doe, Jr. M.D.'
```

Keep in mind, that if you have such anomalies for almost every customer in your database of hundreds of customers, writing such routines could be a nightmare. The data entry clerk, who knows each customer by name, might be able to correct such data issues with much less effort. So, one alternative is to allow data entry clerks to correct mistakes. Another alternative is to write an SQL statement that brings back all occurrences of customer names that are similar to John Doe, as in the following:

```
SELECT DISTINCT customer_name FROM customers
WHERE customer_name LIKE '%john%doe%' OR customer_name LIKE '%doe%john%'
```

Unfortunately, there is no definitive approach to data cleansing. You'll have to use good judgment and decide which approach makes the most sense.

Creating a Dimensional Model and Populating a Dimensional Database

A dimensional database is the source for building the Analysis Services cubes, and must be optimized accordingly. Two variations of dimensional models are referred to as **star schema** and **snowflake schema** (discussed in more detail in Chapter 3). Both star and snowflake schemas are based on the concept of the fact table and dimension tables.

The dimension tables contain various values for each dimension as well as dimension keys. For example, the time dimension might contain the following columns:

```
Time_key
Date
Time
```

In the snowflake schema, adding the attribute keys might further normalize the dimension tables. So this time dimension might consist of multiple tables, as follows:

`time_dimension`

```
date_and_time_key
date_key
time_key
```

`date`

```
date_key
Date
```

`time`

```
time_key
Time
```

The fact table, on the other hand, tends to have the same structure in both the star and snowflake schemas. A fact table contains facts—measurable occurrences in your transactional systems. For instance, a fact table in a grocery store might contain the fact that Jeremy Gonzalez made a purchase at the 3rd National Store on January 2, 2003 at 5:40 pm for $5.49. The fact table will record this fact by containing all dimension keys and measures, as in the following:

`sales_fact`

```
customer_key
store_key
time_key
product_key
sales_amount
```

In the `sales_fact` table, `customer_key`, `store_key`, `time_key`, and `product_key` refer to their respective dimensions. `sales_amount`, on the other hand, refers to the measurable amount of dollars and cents ($5.49). Therefore, `sales_amount` is the measure. You could have a measure of `product_amount` as well, for measuring the amount of product (two boxes, one carton, three pounds, and so on). Such measures aren't additive, but we'll save the discussion of such measures for a more advanced book.

In summary, a dimensional model consists of one or more fact tables and multiple dimension tables. The fact table contains foreign keys to the dimension tables. In addition, the fact table contains at least one measure.

At first, building a dimensional data model might be a challenge if you're used to building relational models. The main concept behind the dimensional approach is that you have to store dimensional data and measures associated with each value of each dimension. The physical model for a dimensional database should contain indexes. Generally, dimensional databases perform the best with a few indexes on dimension tables (dimension keys) and many indexes on the fact tables.

Transforming Data from the Staging Area into the Dimensional Database

As mentioned earlier, you can skip the staging area and populate the dimensional database directly from your data sources. However, performing some of the transformations specific to the dimensional model might be easier in T-SQL. For business users, normalization is a foreign concept; when they see data on the report, they need a full description along with the name. For instance, "store 15" might not be sufficient; a business user might desire "Store 15 on 2nd Avenue South in Franklin, OH." Therefore, the store dimension might combine the `store_name` and `store_address` columns in the staging area into a single column, referred to as `store_name_and_address`.

Where you perform your data transformations is entirely a matter of preference and convenience.

Creating MS Analysis Services Cubes

Before you look at how to create a cube in Analysis Services, you should first create a database called `grocery` on your SQL Server, and run the `CreateTablesAndConstraints.sql` script (from the download accompanying this book on the Apress website) to create the fact and dimension tables. This will help you follow along as you create a cube.

After you've created the database and the fact and dimension tables, you could easily build a diagram similar to the following in the Enterprise Manager Diagrams view:

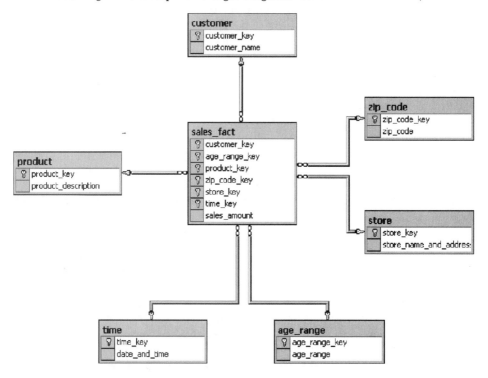

Before you go any further with the example, you need to populate the database. Run the PopulateTables.sql script (also downloadable from apress.com) to add the data to your grocery database.

Try It Out–Creating a Data Source

1. Open Analysis Services by choosing Start I Programs I Microsoft SQL Server I Analysis Services I Analysis Manager.

> **Analysis Services aren't installed by default. They can be installed from SQL Server CD.**

2. Connect to your local server, right-click, and choose New database. In the dialog box that appears, enter the information as shown.

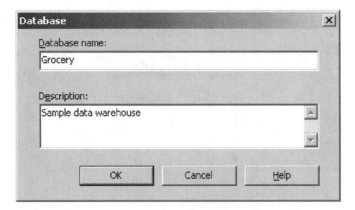

3. Now you can connect to the newly created **grocery** database in Analysis Manager. Right-click the **Data Sources** folder and choose **New Data Source**. This brings up the **Data Link Properties** dialog box, as shown.

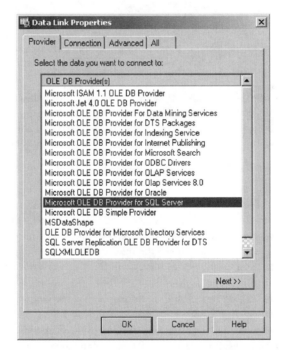

4. On the **Provider** tab, choose **Microsoft OLE DB Provider for SQL Server**. Click the **Connection** tab and specify your server name, log on details, and the **grocery** database.

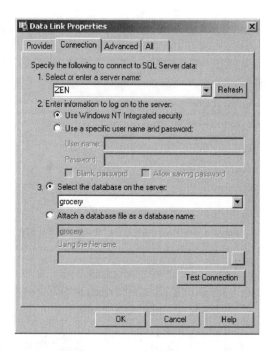

Note that if you choose to connect using a username and password, you must check the Allow saving password box, unless you have a blank password (you should not); otherwise, you'll get numerous errors when creating a cube.

As you can see, there are many other options available on each tab; however, for this example, the default options will suffice.

5. You can click the Test Connection button now to see if you successfully connect to your server. If you don't see the Test Connection Succeeded message, you've provided the wrong authentication information or selected the wrong database. Please ensure that you provide the correct username and password. If you do see the message box indicating success and click OK, you'll see that the connection to your local server will be added to your data sources folder.

Once you click OK in this dialog box, you'll be informed that the password for the user you supplied will now be stored in the MS Repository database on your local SQL Server in an unencrypted format. If you have other users with permissions to msdb, then your security might be compromised. To avoid such issues, simply disallow access to the msdb database for nonadministrative users.

Now that you have a connection to work with, you can create your cube.

Try It Out–Creating a Cube

1. Right-click the Cubes folder in Analysis Manager, and then select New Cube I Wizard. Click Next.

2. The next window in the Cube wizard allows you to choose the fact table. Notice that you have an option to browse the data in the selected table. You also have an option to add a new data source. If you have tables owned by different users in your database, then the tables on this screen will be ordered according to the owner name. For now, select **sales_fact** and proceed to the next window.

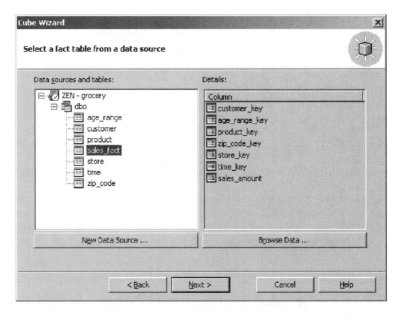

3. The following window lets you define the column containing your measures. In this case, the only measure is **sales_amount**. Select **sales_amount** and click **Next**. Notice that the measure name is currently Sales Amount, without an underscore. You'll have an option to change the name of the measure later.

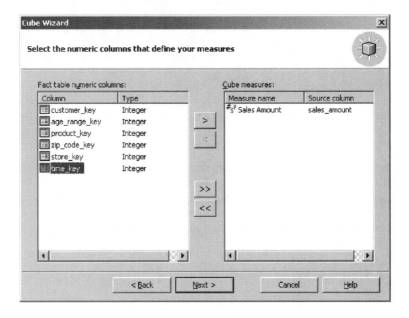

4. Next, you can add dimensions to the cube. There are two types of dimensions in Analysis Services: **cube dimensions** and **shared dimensions**. The shared dimensions can be shared among different cubes, while cube dimensions cannot. The advantage of having a cube dimension is that you aren't dependent on other cubes; you can rebuild cube dimensions at any time without affecting any other cubes on your server.

Since you haven't created any dimensions yet, you won't see any dimensions in this window. Click New Dimension to create a new dimension, which brings up the Dimension wizard. Check Skip this screen in the future option, and then click Next.

5. The following window lets you define the type of dimension you're building. You have several options: single table from a star schema, multiple related tables from a snowflake schema, parent-child relationship, Virtual Dimension, and a mining model.

We discussed the differences between the star and snowflake schemas earlier in the chapter. The parent-child dimension relates two columns in the same table–this could be useful for hierarchies (where one organization is the parent of another), or parts (where one part is a parent of another). Virtual dimensions and mining models are advanced topics, and will not be discussed here.

6. For now, simply select Star Schema: a single dimension table, and click Next.

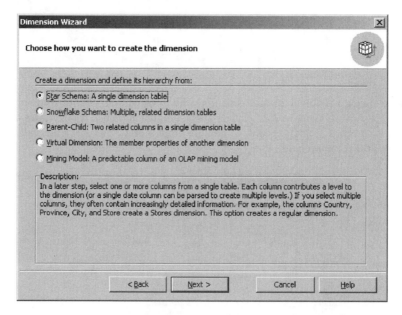

7. The next window allows you to select a dimension table. You can also browse the data in the selected table–feel free to do so. Select the zip_code table and click Next. This brings up the window where you get to select the dimension levels. The zip code table contains only one level of hierarchy; in more complicated dimensions you could have multiple hierarchy levels. For example, a job_title table might contain job titles and job categories, both of which would be considered as dimension levels.

Notice that this window has a check box for Count level members automatically. This is useful if you have multiple levels and don't know which level has more members (in other words, which level is the parent and which one is the child). If this were to happen, the Dimension wizard would automatically warn you if you selected the wrong parent and child. Select zip_code and click Next.

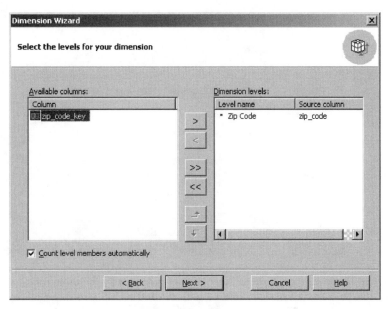

8. The next window allows you to Specify the member key columns. The second column on the window has a drop-down list, from which you can choose the key. In this case, the key is zip_code_key. Select "dbo"."zip_code"."zip_code_key" and click Next.

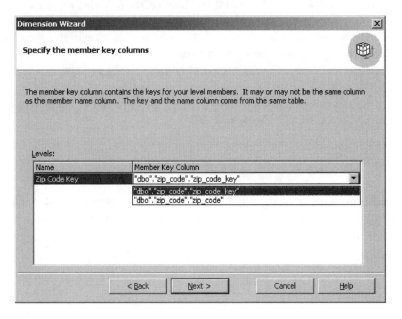

9. The next window allows you to select some of the advanced options for the new dimension. For now, let's skip all of these advanced options, and continue to the final window.

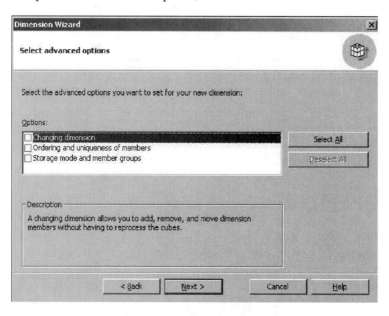

10. The final window in the Dimension wizard lets you specify the dimension name and whether you'd like to make it a shared dimension. This window will also show you some of your new dimension members. Call the dimension **zip_code**.

> **If you're using Windows XP, you'll probably get the following error message:** "Unable to browse dimension 'New Dimension'. Unspecified Error." **This is a bug in Windows XP, and this only works with Windows 2K. Simply give the dimension a name and don't worry about the message.**

11. This completes the Dimension wizard. Repeat these steps and create dimensions for age_range, customer, product, and store.

Try It Out—Creating a Time Dimension

Creating a time dimension is slightly different. When you check New Dimension in the Cube wizard and choose the time table within the Dimension wizard, a new screen appears.

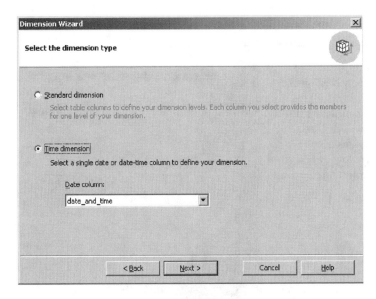

The Dimension wizard in Analysis Manager automatically guesses that you're about to build a time dimension. The reason why this matters is that many data warehouse implementations have multiple time dimensions, each starting on a different date (for instance calendar time and fiscal time). Furthermore, the time dimension might consist of year, quarter, month, and day; or it might be more granular and include hours, minutes, and seconds as well.

1. This time dimension contains a single SMALLDATETIME column date_and_time, so select Time dimension and click Next.

2. This window lets you determine the structure of your time dimension or, in other words, how granular you want your time dimension to be. You have the option to account for week numbers as well as hours and minutes, if you so desire. Notice also that the wizard allows you to change the start date for the year. For this example, just accept the default options (Year/Quarter/Month/Day, Year starts on January 1), and click Next.

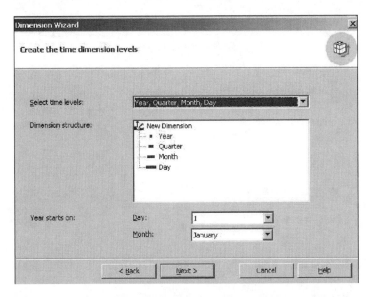

3. This brings up the Advanced Options window, which you can skip, and then the wizard will let you name the dimension. Please name the time dimension time.

4. This brings you back to the Cube wizard, which by now shows all the new dimensions just created. Click Next, and you'll be taken to the final window, which allows you to name the cube.

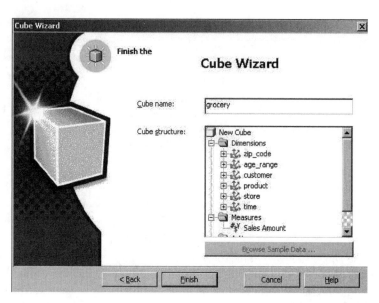

Processing a Cube

Now that you've built a cube, let's continue with processing the cube.

Try It Out—Processing a Cube

1. If you right-click the cube and choose Edit from Analysis Manager, you'll get a picture similar to the following:

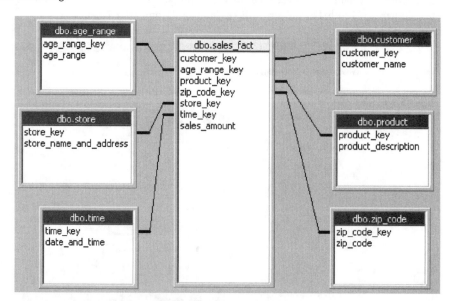

This diagram shows you how the dimension tables are joined to the fact table. The fact table shows up in yellow, and the dimension tables have a blue heading. If you attempt to close this window, you'll get a dialog box asking you whether you want to design storage options for this cube. The dialog box also warns you that you cannot view cube data until it's processed. If you decide to design box storage options, you'll be taken to the Storage Design wizard.

Right-clicking the cube and choosing Design storage will also let you access this wizard.

2. The first window in the Storage Design wizard is the usual welcome window. Check the box to skip this screen in the future and click Next.

3. This window lets you choose between various OLAP options available within Analysis Services.

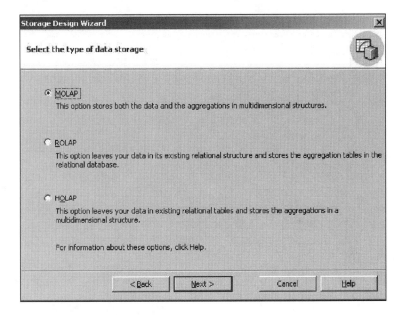

❑ **MOLAP (multidimensional OLAP).**
Stores data and aggregations (From SQL Server Online documentation: "an aggregation is a table or a structure that contains pre-calculated data for a cube") in multidimensional structures. This is by far the most efficient option as far as storage space is concerned.

❑ **ROLAP (relational OLAP).**
Creates all aggregations (summary values) in the relational tables–if you choose this option don't be surprised to see dozens of new tables within your SQL Server database.

❑ **HOLAP (hybrid OLAP).**
Combination of ROLAP and MOLAP. HOLAP leaves data in relational format but creates aggregations in multidimensional format.

For now, select MOLAP and click Next.

4. The next window lets you set aggregation options. Even the tiny cube you're creating in this example will have numerous aggregations, and not all of these aggregations will be used in your queries. This is why the wizard gives you the option to choose between size of aggregation, number of aggregations, or performance gain. My personal recommendation is to build aggregations until performance gain reaches 80 percent. Feel free to experiment with these options within the Storage Design wizard, and see which one provides the best performance in your environment.

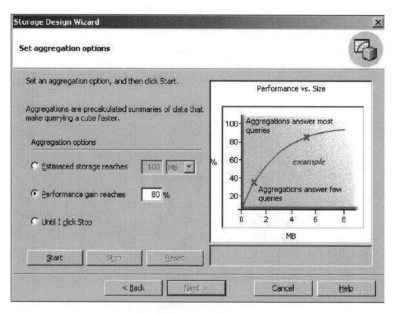

5. When you click the Start button, the wizard will define aggregations and alter the chart on the right-hand side of this window accordingly. Once you've defined the aggregations, click Next and you'll be taken to the Process window.

6. Here you can specify whether to process the cube now or later. Select the Process now option, and you should see something similar to the following:

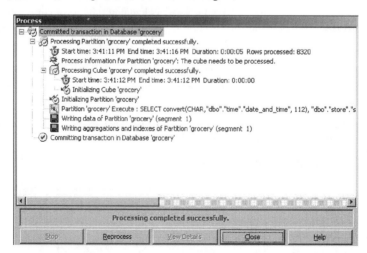

If you get any errors while processing a cube, ensure that all of your dimensions are processed prior to reprocessing the cube. Typically, errors will be associated with the dimensions that aren't processed. This means that data within the dimension has changed, but the dimension hasn't been reprocessed within Analysis Services. Simply right-click the dimension within Analysis Manager and click Process.

Keep in mind that cube processing is time-consuming and resource-intensive. The more memory you have on the server, the better performance you can expect from the cube-processing tasks. A data warehouse should most definitely reside on a dedicated server. Do not fool yourself by putting a data warehouse on a desktop with less than 0.5GB of RAM.

7. Now that you've built and processed a cube, you can view the data in the cube by clicking the cube in Analysis Manager, and choosing the Data tab on the right-hand side of the screen, as shown.

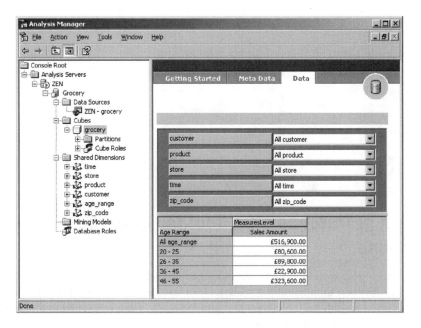

Automating Data Warehouse Population through Database Routines

What you've just done is built a cube from the dimensional database. Of course, because the stores sell more products each day, you need to refresh this cube and recalculate the aggregations to keep the cube current. So, building a cube is only the tip of the iceberg.

The data warehouse population and cube-rebuilding tasks need to be automated through stored procedures and DTS. For example, you could have a routine that grabs data from each of your data sources and puts data into the staging database. Next, another routine could populate the dimensional database from the staging area. Finally, you can use DTS tasks to rebuild Analysis Services dimensions and cubes to keep them up-to-date.

The following screen shot shows a sample DTS package that grabs data from two sources (a text file and an MS Access database) and puts it in a staging database. Afterward, the package transfers data from the staging database to the dimensional database. The package goes on to refresh a couple of dimensions within the Analysis Services cube (the product and customer dimensions) and processes the cube. If the cube processing task or transformation task fails, the package sends an e-mail to the DBA notifying of the failure. This is just an example; you can automate this routine as you like.

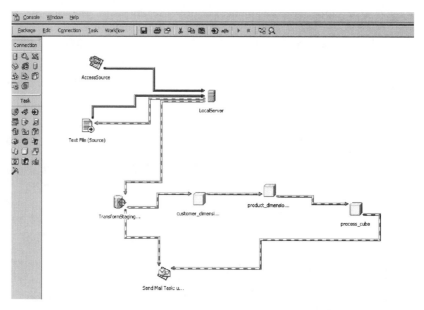

Creating or Purchasing a Tool for Querying the Data Warehouse

You can program your own tools and utilities for getting data from a data warehouse by using the DSO (Decision Support Objects) object model. However, developing such tools isn't an easy task. There are third-party tools on the market that you can use to retrieve data from the data warehouse, but such tools tend to be rather expensive.

Fortunately Microsoft provides an option for querying cube data through Excel and the Pivot Table Service.

Try It Out–Querying a Cube

1. Open MS Excel, choose Data | Pivot Table and select PivotChart Report. This opens up the PivotTable and PivotChart wizard. On the initial window, choose External Data Source and click Next. The following dialog box asks you to define the location of the external data source.

2. Click the Get Data button, which will open up the dialog box to let you select the data source. Choose New Data Source and click OK.

3. This opens yet another dialog box, which allows you to name the data source and choose the OLAP provider. Provide a data source name of your liking and select Microsoft OLE DB Provider for OLAP Services 8.0; then click Connect.

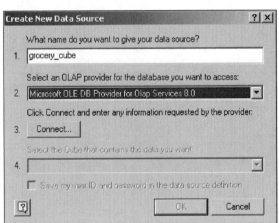

> To get these examples working, you must have Microsoft Query and Pivot Table Service (Full version) installed on your computer.

4. Clicking the Connect button opens the final dialog box, which lets you supply the Analysis Server name. Enter the Analysis Server name, and click Next.

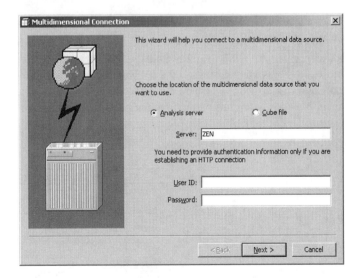

5. The final window lets you select the cube that you'd like to query with the pivot table. Select grocery (if you've been following along with the examples in this chapter), and click Finish.

6. Doing so takes you back to the New Data Source dialog box—click OK there, and again click OK in the next dialog box. Now the PivotTable and PivotChart wizard should state: Data fields have been retrieved.

7. Clicking Next takes you to the final step of the wizard, letting you specify where you want your pivot table to reside. Select the desired location within the spreadsheet, and click Finish.

Now you should see the following toolbar and an outlined section in your spreadsheet.

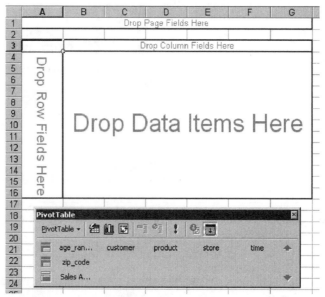

At this point, the pivot table is easy to use. Simply drag and drop data items (**measures** in data warehouse terms; in this example Sales Amount is the only measure) where shown. Then drag and drop page fields (dimensions in data warehouse terms; age_range, customer, product, store, time, and zip_code in this example) where indicated. Once you've dropped all items, you should see the drop-down lists for dimensions and total amount of sales, as shown.

A	B	
age_range	All age_range	▼
customer	All customer	▼
product	All product	▼
store	All store	▼
time	All time	▼
zip_code	All zip_code	▼
Sales Amount	Total	
Total		516900

A pivot table is easy to manipulate; you can move entire dimensions down into the "row fields" to get a full breakdown of that dimension. In this screen shot, age_range, customer, product, store, time, and zip_code are dimensions; Sales Amount is the measure. Alternatively, you can select a particular dimension member from the dimension drop-down list to get the sales amount for that particular member. For example, if you drop the age_range dimension in the row fields, you'll see the breakdown of sales amount as per each age_range. You'll further drop the time dimension in the column fields, so that you can see the breakdown by time as well, as shown in the following screen shot.

customer	All customer ▾		
product	All product ▾		
store	All store ▾		
zip_code	All zip_code ▾		
Sales Amount	Year ▾		
Age Range ▾	2002	2003	Grand Total *
20 - 25	79184	1416	80600
26 - 35	88200	1600	89800
36 - 45	22540	360	22900
46 - 55	317520	6080	323600
Grand Total *	507444	9456	516900

Notice that you can further expand the pivot table to get the breakdown by quarter, month, or even individual days, because you have those members in this time dimension. To do so, simply expand the Year drop-down list and select the appropriate members. The more you play with pivot tables and use them to query against Analysis Services cubes, the more you'll realize how powerful and useful a data warehouse can be.

So far you've gone through the steps required for building a data warehouse and deploying the solution using pivot tables. Although easy to use, a pivot table might not be the best tool for the job. The next section will introduce you to MDX–a powerful programming language used to query multidimensional cubes.

Introduction to Multidimensional eXpressions

You saw the power of pivot tables in the previous section. However, using pivot tables won't always be the best choice, especially when supporting custom reports for business users. As an example, simply connecting to a cube with the pivot table service won't tell your executives who their top-two customers were in the first quarter of 2002. In the tiny data warehouse example presented in this chapter, you can play with the pivot table for a few minutes to figure this out, but if you have millions of customers and hundreds of stores to manage, clicking through Excel for several months isn't an option.

MDX is the language used to run queries against Analysis Services cubes. MDX isn't specific to Analysis Services, and it has been around for a while. Analysis Services implements a particular flavor of MDX, and might not support some options available in MDX with other OLAP tools.

MDX is a complex language that presents a challenge to anyone trying to learn it. Part of the challenge comes from the fact that most people are used to thinking in two-dimensional terms; you're used to analyzing spreadsheets and databases that have rows and columns. Analysis Services cubes, on the other hand, can have many dimensions, and querying such constructs requires thinking in multidimensional terms. Some people like to compare multidimensional cubes to spreadsheets with multiple worksheets. In such a case, to locate a particular cell, you must specify the worksheet, the row, and the column.

A complete overview of MDX is beyond the scope of this book; however, we would like to introduce the main concepts involved in querying Analysis Services cubes, and give you a few examples to get you started.

Simple MDX SELECT

Microsoft supplies an MDX sample application with Analysis Services. You can use this tool for testing your MDX queries. The sample application can be accessed by choosing Start | Programs | Microsoft SQL Server | Analysis Services | MDX Sample Application. The sample application's look and feel is similar to Query Analyzer. It has a query window in which you type in your MDX statement as well as a results pane where you see the output.

You might find the Syntax Examples section in the right-hand portion of the Sample Application window helpful when developing your MDX queries. If you forget the syntax of a particular construct, you can drill down to that construct and double-click it–the syntax will be copied to the query window.

If you've been following the examples in this chapter and would like to continue to do so, connect to your OLAP server and select the grocery cube in the Cube drop-down list. You should see dimensions and measures available in the grocery cube.

The simplest MDX statements look similar to SELECT statements in T-SQL. Each MDX SELECT consists of SELECT, FROM, and possibly WHERE clauses. Even so, don't expect too many similarities between T-SQL and MDX.

For instance the following statement will generate a list of total sales per customer:

```
SELECT
    {[Measures].[Sales Amount]} on COLUMNS,
    {[customer].members} on ROWS
FROM grocery
```

Here are the results:

	Sales Amount
All customer	£516,900.00
bubba smith	£22,900.00
jane doe	£89,800.00
john doe	£80,600.00
john smith	£323,600.00
tabiry karesi	

If you've been writing SELECT statements in T-SQL for years, MDX SELECT may look a bit strange to you. MDX explicitly specifies the dimensions or measures that need to be displayed on rows and on columns. In fact, MDX can map measures and dimension members on more than two dimensions (rows, columns, pages, chapters, and so on). However, the sample application only supports returning data in rows and columns.

In MDX you must enclose a set of elements from a given dimension in curly brackets. Hence {[Measures].[Sales Amount]} in the previous query. Square brackets, on the other hand, are only necessary when a particular dimension or member contains numbers, special characters, or spaces. For instance, in the following query you must enclose [Sales Amount], [2002], and [quarter 1] in square brackets, as follows:

```
SELECT
    {Measures.[Sales Amount]} on COLUMNS,
    {customer.members} on ROWS
FROM grocery
WHERE time.year.[2002].[quarter 1].January
```

Although the syntax is rather particular, MDX isn't case sensitive.

Whether you put measures on rows and dimensions on columns, or the other way around, is entirely up to you. Also, in MDX, it doesn't matter whether ROWS or COLUMNS is specified first. You could have easily written the previous query as follows:

```
SELECT
    {[Measures].[Sales Amount]} on ROWS,
    {[customer].members} on COLUMNS
FROM grocery
```

Here are the results:

	All customer	bubba smith	jane doe	john doe	john smith	tabiry karesi
Sales Amount	£516,900.00	£22,900.00	£89,800.00	£80,600.00	£323,600.00	

You can go one step further and limit the output to sales that have occurred in 2002 by adding the WHERE clause. The WHERE clause is one of the several ways of limiting the output of MDX statements; we'll discuss the FILTER function briefly in the "Filter" section to show you another way. Although it's similar to its T-SQL cousin, the WHERE clause doesn't take "=", ">", "<", or any similar conditions. Instead, you specify the range of the dimension that you wish to limit the output by doing the following:

```
SELECT
    {[Measures].[Sales Amount]} on COLUMNS,
    {[customer].members} on ROWS
FROM grocery
WHERE [time].[year].[2002]
```

Here are the results:

	Sales Amount
All customer	£507,444.00
bubba smith	£22,540.00
jane doe	£88,200.00
john doe	£79,184.00
john smith	£317,520.00
tabiry karesi	

Dimensions, Levels, Members, Tuples, and Sets

To understand MDX queries, you must become familiar with some additional multidimensional terminology. We've already discussed dimensions and measures. Each dimension can have multiple **levels**; for instance, the time dimension can have levels of year, month, day, and so on. Each level within a dimension can have many **members**; for instance, the month level will include 12 members (January, February, and so on). As far as MDX is concerned, measures is just another dimension, each measure being a member of the measures dimension.

You can get a list of dimension members in MDX by specifying the .members operator. This operator brings back either all members of a dimension, as in [customers].members, or members of the specified level within a dimension, as in customers.[customer name].members. In one of the previous examples, MDX gave you the grand total for all customers even though you didn't explicitly ask for it, because you didn't specify the level of dimension you wanted. If you wanted to eliminate the All customer summary level from the output, you could specify [customer].[customer name].members instead.

Tuples

Tuples consist of one or more members from different dimensions. A tuple can have only one member per dimension. For example, (Measures.[Sales Amount], product.[product description].[turkey]) is a tuple consisting of the Sales Amount measure and the turkey product. Note that if a tuple consists of a single dimension member, then it doesn't have to be enclosed in ordinary brackets. If a tuple is made up of members from multiple dimensions, then a comma must separate each member and the tuple must be enclosed in parentheses.

The following query retrieves any turkey purchases in January of 2003:

```
SELECT
    {(Measures.[Sales Amount],
      product.[product description].[turkey])}
      on COLUMNS,
    {customer.[customer name].members} on ROWS
FROM grocery
WHERE time.year.[2003].[quarter 1].January
```

Which returns the following results:

	Sales Amount
	turkey
bubba smith	£115.00
jane doe	£450.00
john doe	£404.00
john smith	£1,620.00
tabiry karesi	

Sets

Sets in MDX can be thought of as an ordered collection of tuples. For instance, the following set contains the sales amounts of turkey and chocolate (in that order):

```
{(Measures.[Sales Amount],
   product.[product description].[turkey]),
  (measures.[sales amount],
   [product].[product description].[chocolate])}
```

561

Sets must be enclosed in curly braces. You can use the set you just defined to change the previous example slightly:

```
SELECT
    {(Measures.[Sales Amount],
      product.[product description].[turkey]),
      (measures.[sales amount],
       [product].[product description].[chocolate])}
      on COLUMNS,
    {customer.[customer name].members} on ROWS
FROM grocery
WHERE time.year.[2003].[quarter 1].January
```

The results are as follows:

	Sales Amount	
	turkey	chocolate
bubba smith	£115.00	£15.00
jane doe	£450.00	£250.00
john doe	£404.00	£204.00
john smith	£1,620.00	£1,220.00
tabiry karesi		

Calculated Members

Calculated members let you calculate the values of a cube cell. The calculated members aren't the only way to calculate values, but they're used very frequently. Calculated members must be defined using the WITH MEMBER keywords prior to being used in the SELECT statement. For instance, in the following query, you'll define a calculated member called [measures].[Sales in 2002]. This calculated member shows only those sales that have occurred in 2002. You'll also add a WHERE clause to the query to limit the output to the sales of chocolate:

```
WITH MEMBER  [measures].[sales in 2002] AS
'([Measures].[Sales Amount], [time].[year].[2002])'

SELECT
    {[Measures].[Sales in 2002]} on COLUMNS,
    {[customer].members}  on ROWS
FROM grocery
WHERE  [product].[product description].[chocolate]
```

You get the following results:

	sales in 2002
All customer	£93,786.00
bubba smith	£1,960.00
jane doe	£14,700.00
john doe	£12,446.00
john smith	£64,680.00
tabiry karesi	

Notice that to define a calculated member, you had to specify the measure that you wanted to limit as well as the dimension and dimension member you wanted to limit the output by.

You can also define a calculated member by limiting the measure with more than one dimension. In the following query, you further wish to limit the output to sales of chocolate by customers that are between the ages of 20 and 25:

```
WITH MEMBER  [measures].[Sales in 2002] AS
'([Measures].[Sales Amount], [time].[year].[2002],
[age_range].[age range].[20 - 25])'

SELECT
     {[Measures].[sales in 2002]} on COLUMNS,
     {[customer].members}  on ROWS
FROM grocery
WHERE [product].[product description].[chocolate]
```

Which returns the following results:

	Sales in 2002
All customer	£12,446.00
bubba smith	
jane doe	
john doe	£12,446.00
john smith	
tabiry karesi	

You can use more complex calculated members to construct formulas. For instance, the following query returns a comparison of sales in January 2002 and January 2003:

```
WITH MEMBER  [measures].[january sales comparison] AS
'([Measures].[Sales Amount],
   [time].[year].[2003].[quarter 1].january) -
 ([Measures].[Sales Amount],
   [time].[year].[2002].[quarter 1].january) '
SELECT
   {[measures].[january sales comparison]} on COLUMNS
FROM grocery
```

Which returns the following results:

january sales comparison
£9,456.00

Functions

MDX provides numerous functions that help you customize the output of your queries. Going through each function or even giving a full overview of a few functions is beyond the scope of this book. We'll briefly introduce a few of the commonly used functions.

NON EMPTY

In several of the previous examples, you've seen that Tabiry Karesi hasn't bought anything; therefore, having this person in the query output is useless. The NON EMPTY function helps us filter out all members that have no output, as in the following example:

```
WITH MEMBER  [measures].[Sales in 2002] AS
'([Measures].[Sales Amount], [time].[year].[2002])'

SELECT
    {[Measures].[sales in 2002]} on COLUMNS,
    NON EMPTY {[customer].members}  on ROWS
FROM grocery
WHERE  [product].[product description].[chocolate]
```

The results of this query will be as follows:

	Sales in 2002
All customer	£93,786.00
bubba smith	£1,960.00
jane doe	£14,700.00
john doe	£12,446.00
john smith	£64,680.00

TOPCOUNT

Another function that you'll encounter frequently is TOPCOUNT. This function lets you select only the top N members within the dimension, based on the criteria you provide in a query. For instance, the following query will return the top two customers in 2002:

```
WITH MEMBER  [measures].[sales in 2002] AS
'([Measures].[Sales Amount], [time].[year].[2002])'

SELECT
    {[Measures].[sales in 2002]} on COLUMNS,
    {TOPCOUNT([customer].[customer name].members, 2)}  on ROWS
FROM grocery
```

Which returns the following:

	sales in 2002
bubba smith	£22,540.00
jane doe	£88,200.00

BOTTOMCOUNT

Analogous to TOPCOUNT is the BOTTOMCOUNT function, which retrieves the bottom N members. To retrieve the two customers with the least sales amount in 2002, you would run the following query:

```
WITH MEMBER  [measures].[sales in 2002] AS
'([Measures].[Sales Amount], [time].[year].[2002])'

SELECT
   {[Measures].[sales in 2002]} on COLUMNS,
   {BOTTOMCOUNT([customer].[customer name].members, 2)}  on ROWS
FROM grocery
```

Which would return the following results:

	sales in 2002
tabiry karesi	
john smith	£317,520.00

CROSSJOIN

At times you'll need to get a cross-product of dimension members or tuples. This can be accomplished with the CROSSJOIN function. CROSSJOIN is extremely powerful and can map the cross product of sets on columns or rows. For example, the following query maps out age_range and product description on rows and shows the amount of sales in 2002 for each combination of age_range and product description on columns:

```
SELECT
   CROSSJOIN ({[age_range].[age range].members},
              {product.[product description].members}) on ROWS,
   {[Measures].[sales amount]} on COLUMNS
FROM grocery
WHERE time.year.[2002]
```

Which returns the following results:

		Sales Amount
20 - 25	chocolate	£12,446.00
	cranberry sauce	£17,346.00
	pumpkin pie	£27,146.00
	turkey	£22,246.00
26 - 35	chocolate	£14,700.00
	cranberry sauce	£19,600.00
	pumpkin pie	£29,400.00
	turkey	£24,500.00
36 - 45	chocolate	£1,960.00
	cranberry sauce	£4,410.00
	pumpkin pie	£9,310.00
	turkey	£6,860.00
46 - 55	chocolate	£64,680.00
	cranberry sauce	£74,480.00
	pumpkin pie	£94,080.00
	turkey	£84,280.00

Keep in mind that CROSSJOIN can take only two sets as inputs at a time. However, you can nest CROSSJOIN functions if you wish to map more than two sets on columns or rows. For instance, the next query will add the store name and address to the results of the previous query:

```
SELECT
    CROSSJOIN ({store.[store name and address].members},
            CROSSJOIN ({[age_range].[age range].members},
                    {product.[product description].members})
        ) on ROWS,
    {[Measures].[sales amount]} on COLUMNS
FROM grocery
WHERE time.year.[2002]
```

Here are the results of this query (reduced list):

			Sales Amount
store 1 on Wilson street	20 - 25	chocolate	£1,323.00
		cranberry sauce	£3,773.00
		pumpkin pie	£8,673.00
		turkey	£6,223.00
	26 - 35	chocolate	
		cranberry sauce	
		pumpkin pie	
		turkey	
	36 - 45	chocolate	£1,960.00
		cranberry sauce	£4,410.00
		pumpkin pie	£9,310.00
		turkey	£6,860.00
	46 - 55	chocolate	£1,470.00
		cranberry sauce	£3,920.00
		pumpkin pie	£8,820.00
		turkey	£6,370.00
store 2 on Market street	20 - 25	chocolate	£11,123.00
		cranberry sauce	£13,573.00
		pumpkin pie	£18,473.00
		turkey	£16,023.00
	26 - 35	chocolate	
		cranberry sauce	
		pumpkin pie	
		turkey	
	36 - 45	chocolate	
		cranberry sauce	
		pumpkin pie	
		turkey	
	46 - 55	chocolate	£11,270.00
		cranberry sauce	£13,720.00
		pumpkin pie	£18,620.00
		turkey	£16,170.00
store 3 on East Main street	20 - 25	chocolate	
		cranberry sauce	
		pumpkin pie	

FILTER

You looked at the WHERE clause of MDX statements earlier in the chapter, and mentioned that it wasn't the only way to restrict the output of the query. The FILTER function presents yet another way to reduce the resultset. This function takes a set and a condition as parameters. For example, the next query brings back only those age ranges that have purchased groceries of over $30,000 in 2002:

```
SELECT
    FILTER ( {[age_range].[age range].members},
             measures.[sales amount] > 30000) on ROWS,
    {[Measures].[sales amount]} on COLUMNS
FROM grocery
WHERE time.year.[2002]
```

Which returns the following results:

	Sales Amount
20 - 25	£79,184.00
26 - 35	£88,200.00
46 - 55	£317,520.00

ORDER

Finally, the other function that you'll find useful is ORDER. This function sorts sets based on a numeric or character expression. ORDER accepts a set and a character or numeric expression as parameters.

For example, the following query orders customers based on the amount of their purchases in descending order:

```
SELECT
   ORDER ( {[customer].[customer name].members},
           measures.[sales amount],
           DESC) on ROWS,
      {[Measures].[sales amount]} on COLUMNS
   FROM grocery
```

The results are as follows:

	Sales Amount
john smith	£323,600.00
jane doe	£89,800.00
john doe	£80,600.00
bubba smith	£22,900.00
tabiry karesi	

Summary

In this chapter, we introduced the concept of data warehousing. Although fairly new to SQL Server, data warehousing has been around for a couple of decades. Because building a data warehouse has recently become affordable to small- and medium-sized companies, a good knowledge of data warehousing concepts is a very hot skill. You learned what it takes to build a data warehouse, and the steps involved in building one. We also provided an introduction to Microsoft Analysis Services and MDX.

Data warehousing and related technologies aren't for the faint of heart, because they require much effort and dedication, not to mention intelligence and willingness to learn. If you think you possess such qualities, be sure to get several books dedicated to data warehousing and OLAP (for example, *Professional SQL Server 2000 Data Warehousing with Analysis Services* by Apress).

12

Data Transformation Services

At some point in the life of most databases, there is a need to transfer large amounts of data into or out of the database. The two tools SQL Server provides for this task are **BCP (bulk copy program)** and **DTS (Data Transformation Services).**

In my opinion, DTS has two major advantages over BCP–increased functionality and a superior interface. BCP is optimized for importing and exporting large amounts of data between a single table and a single text file. While DTS can import and export text files, it can also transfer data or objects between other databases (such as Access or Oracle) and flat files (Excel, Text, dBase). DTS can also manipulate the data during transfer and operate on multiple tables and files in one operation. Furthermore DTS is implemented using COM and a graphical interface, thereby allowing a more intuitive and rich environment than running BCP from the command line.

Because there are more comprehensive references on DTS and how to use it, this chapter isn't geared to make you an expert in DTS; here you'll gain a basic understanding of what DTS is and how to use it. By the end of the chapter you should be able to use the Import/Export wizard and create and modify packages through the package editor.

The DTS Package Editor

Because DTS is a graphical application, let's first examine the interface. You can create a new set of DTS VBA commands (called a package) in several ways, one of which is to right-click the node for Data Transformation Services in Enterprise Manager to view the pop-up menu.

The two main options are to open an existing package or to create a new package. Choose New Package to see the environment.

Let's first cover the main items on the toolbar on the left. There are two primary groupings titled Connection and Task.

The Connection Group

As mentioned in the introduction, part of the power of DTS lies in its ability to connect and transfer data between multiple platforms from relational databases such as Oracle and SQL Server to flat files such as, Access, Text, Excel, and dBase. The following figure shows all the systems you can connect to, including any system with an OLEDB or ODBC driver. If your list is different, you may have a different version of MDAC (Microsoft Data Access Components) installed.

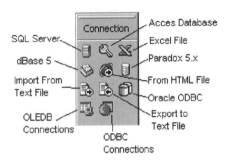

Most of your packages will contain at least one connection to an SQL Server. Often this server is the one you're creating the package on. It's worth noting here that this isn't an essential requirement. We've used DTS to transfer data between two Access databases with transforms. We've also known companies that purchase SQL Server just to utilize DTS to transfer data between other database systems such as Oracle and Sybase.

Most of the properties required for connections are pretty intuitive. In general the connections can be classified into relational database management systems (SQL Server, Oracle) and flat files (such as Text, Excel, dBase). Each type requires similar yet unique information, as follows:

❑   RDBMS: In general for relational database management systems, you'll need to input the server name, user information, and possibly the default database.

❑   File based: File-based systems range from single file options such as Access, text files, and Excel to multifile options such as dBase and paradox. For single file options, DTS will ask for the path and the filename. For multifile options, DTS will ask for the path to the folder, and will treat each file as if it were a table.

When you're designing your package and adding connections, think about how much work is going to take place and then decide the number of connections required. Although adding connections adds overhead, throughput speed can be increased with parallel connections. As a general rule, use one new connection per large-throughput action.

The Task Group

Connections define where the data is from and where it's going; **tasks** define how it gets there. In a practical sense, they're the workhorses of the package. We'll give you a brief overview of the different items here, and in the later examples, we'll elaborate on some of the regularly used tasks.

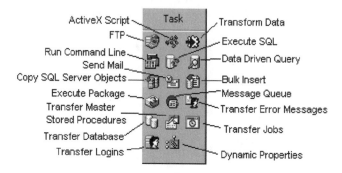

ActiveX Script

The **ActiveX script task** allows you to use an installed scripting language, such as VBScript or JScript to perform custom actions within the package. This can be anything from a complex transformation, to invoking outside COM objects, to even modifying or creating tasks within the current package. This is a very powerful tool.

FTP

The **FTP task** allows you to download and upload files to an FTP site. This includes logging into the site, changing directories, and retrieving the appropriate file to any specified local directory. This allows an automated method for transferring files between remote systems, including legacy mainframe applications.

Execute Process (Run Command Line)

The **Execute Process task** allows you to run executable program files and batch files that you would normally run from the command line or a DOS shell. This task also allows you to specify any command-line parameters that may be needed.

Send Mail

The **Send Mail task** allows you to send mail to any recipient(s). The only caveat is that in order to use it, you need a MAPI client on the SQL Server, with a mail server and login information that will be accessible to the user account under which SQL Server runs the DTS package.

Copy SQL Server Objects

The **Copy SQL Server Objects task** is a quick way to copy any scriptable object within a SQL Server database to another SQL Server database or server. The task defaults to copying all objects, but can be used for individual objects as well.

Execute Package

New to SQL Server 2000, the **Execute Package task** allows DTS packages to be modularized and called from other packages. This also allows you to specify values for global variables and reduce duplication of common tasks.

Transfer Error Messages

The **Transfer Error Messages task** allows the transfer of system messages between SQL Servers, where the destination server must be SQL Server 2000.

Transfer Databases

The **Transfer Database task** is used to copy or move databases between different servers. You can specify a different path for the database files to allow for different file structures between the systems. This task must occur between two distinct servers, because the transferred database name will remain the same as the source database(s). Again, the destination server must run SQL Server 2000.

Transfer Logins

The **Transfer Logins task** moves or copies logins between databases or servers (on the same domain if the Windows Authenticated security model is used). The destination server cannot be SQL Server 7.0, but can be SQL Server 2000.

Transform Data

The **Transform Data task** is the general method for transferring data from tables, views, or queries to other databases, tables, or views. In addition to simply copying the data, this also allows you to manipulate the data, log errors, or even to skip particular information. For example, if you needed to change date formats between different systems, and not import rows with incorrect dates, the transform data task enables you to do so.

Execute SQL

The **Execute SQL task** allows you to execute one or more T-SQL statements. We can also specify parameters for the queries based on data within the package.

Data Driven Query

The **Data Driven Query task** allows you to execute different query statements depending on conditions in the source data. If, for example, you needed to perform an UPDATE, INSERT or DELETE query depending on particular conditions within the incoming data, you could use this task.

Bulk Insert

New to SQL Server 2000, the Bulk Insert T-SQL statement is similar to BCP. The **Bulk Insert task** performs this new command.

Message Queue

The **Message Queue task** allows you to insert one or more messages into a Microsoft Message Queue. As expected, the message queue client must be installed to use this task properly.

Transfer Jobs

The **Transfer Jobs task** allows the transfer of one or more scheduled jobs between servers, where the destination server must be SQL Server 2000.

Transfer Master Stored Procedures

The **Transfer Master Stored Procedures task** allows you to copy system stored procedures that reside in the master database between servers. While the source can be SQL Server 7.0 or 2000, the destination server must be 2000.

Dynamic Properties

The **Dynamic Properties task** allows you to retrieve data from outside the package for use during execution of the package. Examples include values to use as defaults during transformation, or even what database you're importing into. Sources to retrieve data from include .ini files, queries or system information such as host_name or @@ServerName. The only restriction is that each separate task can only operate on a single value. Therefore, care must be taken that any query referenced should return a single row and single column and single line.

Analysis Services Processing

The **Analysis Services Processing task,** along with the **Data Mining Predictions task,** are available on a server with the optional Analysis Services installed (not shown in figure). The **Analysis Services task** (discussed in Chapter 11) performs an update task. All three update models are supported (full process, refresh data, and incremental update).

Workflow

So far you've seen how to specify the data sources (connections) and what you can do with them (tasks). Now, **workflow** allows you to specify the order in which tasks are completed. Workflow also allows you to specify branching or conditional processing. There is no toolbar for workflow; instead it's manipulated via the workflow menu, which is part of the top menu bar.

Each option allows you to specify a dependency between tasks, enabling one task to execute before another task begins. You can also specify the condition to be met for the dependent (or successive) task to run.

On Completion

Using the **On Completion** option specifies that the second (or dependent) task will execute after the first task completes, regardless of success or failure.

On Success

If you choose **On Success**, the second task will only start if the first task has completed successfully. For example, you could use this option to ensure that parent tables were imported prior to importing dependent or child tables.

On Failure

On Failure is used to ensure that the second task will only execute if the preceding task ends with a failure. This can be used for cleanup, or for sending a mail message indicating the failure.

With the coverage of workflow, you've completed the overview of the editor environment. Now it's time to start the first of two examples.

Creating a DTS Package Using the Import/Export Wizard

There are a number of ways you can create a DTS package—you can manipulate the connections, tasks, and workflow objects in the DTS editor, you can directly program a Visual Basic file to be the package, or you can run one of SQL Server's wizards. Running a wizard is the easiest way to create a DTS package, and you'll see how to do this next.

Try It Out–Import/Export Wizard

In the first hands-on example, you'll use the Import/Export Wizard to generate your first package. This will show you how powerful even a simple package can be.

1. Like most other SQL Server tasks, there are several ways to start this wizard. For now, right-click the **Data Transformation Services** node in Enterprise Manager and select **All Tasks** and then **Import**.

    After you click through the first screen, you're presented with a dialog box in which you can choose a data source.

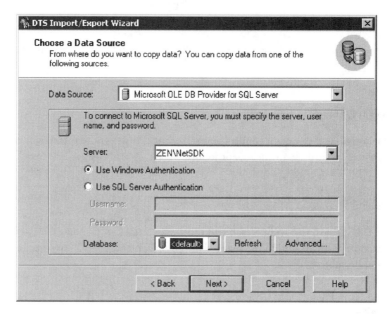

This dialog box collects the information to create a **connection** as discussed earlier. For this example, you're going to connect to SQL Server, so leave the default selected. However, if you click the down arrow by Data Source, you'll see all the possible sources.

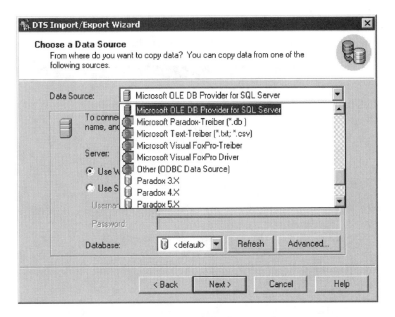

The important point to note in this dialog box is that some sources have different versions listed separately (such as Paradox 3.x, 4.x, and 5.x). Go ahead and select SQL Server, choose your server, and select the pubs database. Also enter the appropriate login information to match your server security model.

2. After clicking Next, the only change in the dialog box is that it states Choose Destination. Enter the information for the connection to the destination server here. You could choose a different destination such as Oracle, but for this example, choose the same SQL Server and the pubs database.

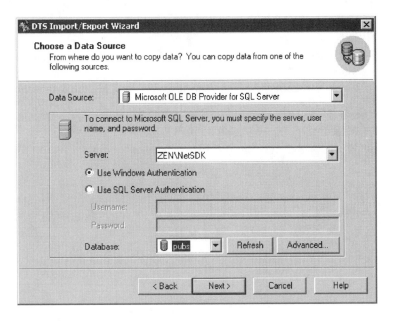

3. Move on to the next dialog box by clicking Next. This dialog box allows you to choose what
process SQL Server will apply to the data between the source and the destination:

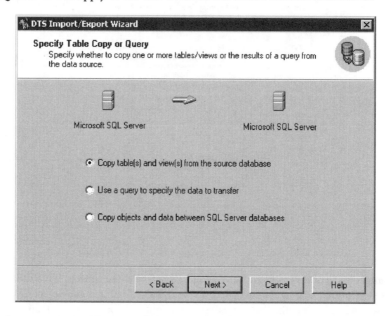

There are three categories of options that summarize the basic transformations available:

❑ **Copy tables and views**: This allows you to copy the data from one or more tables. By
default, the destination tables are an exact match of the source tables (although in another
screen you have the option to edit the create table statement).

❑ **Specify query**: As the name states, this allows you to specify a single query as your source.
This option allows you to do some initial manipulations on the data exclusively through
script.

❑ **Copy SQL Server Objects**: This option is used to copy more than just tables and views,
including logins, UDFs (user defined functions) and stored procedures between SQL
Servers. You can use this when you want more than just the data within the table or view.

Choose Copy table(s) and view(s) from the source database. When you click Next, you're
presented with the options for selecting the source tables and views.

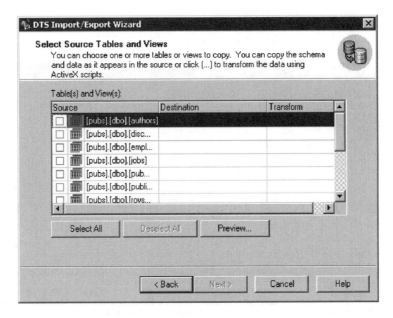

4. You'll probably need to expand the source column to see the names. For this example, you're going to "import" three tables: authors, titles, and titleauthor. You can select or deselect a table or view by clicking the check box in the first column. Next, you'll need to select a destination table or view. Since you're importing back into the same database, you'll need to create three new tables in the transform. Type in a new name for each table by adding "_DTS" to the original names. Therefore the destination tables will be authors_DTS, titles_DTS, and titleauthor_DTS.

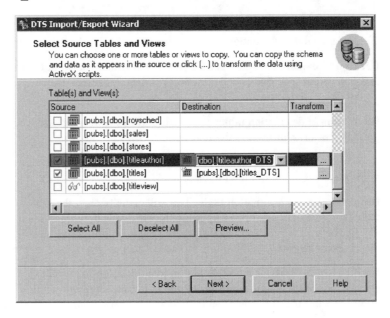

Next, let's preview the Transformation dialog box information. You get there by clicking the ellipsis (...) button in the Transform column.

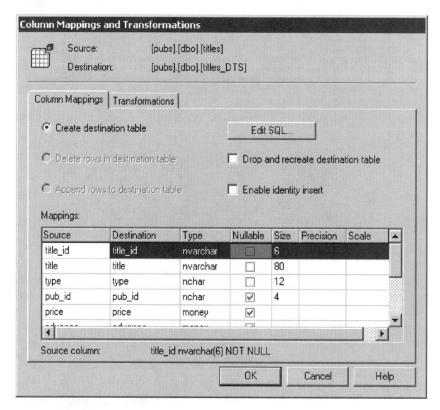

5. There is a great deal of information in this dialog box. Briefly, the options are as follows:

    ❑   **Create destination table**: This is used in cases in which you want to create a new table and populate it with the data. To modify the default CREATE TABLE query, you can click on the Edit SQL button.

    ❑   **Delete rows in destination table**: This option will execute a DELETE query on the destination table prior to importing the new data.

    ❑   **Append rows to destination table**: This simply appends the new data to the data that already resides in the destination table.

    ❑   **Drop and recreate destination table**: This will actually drop the table, and then run a CREATE TABLE query prior to importing the data. When you use this option, be aware that any object-level permissions are lost due to these actions. In addition, other dependencies may prevent the successful implementation of this option.

    ❑   **Enable identity insert**: If the table has an identity column, this allows you to insert the data and maintain the current identity value. If data is present within the table, this will only succeed if the imported identity values don't conflict with values that already exist within the table.

6. The second available tab is the **Transformations** tab. Selecting this tab shows the two options within the wizard, which allow you to either perform a straight copy of the data between source and destination columns, or modify the data with an ActiveX script (either VBScript or JScript).

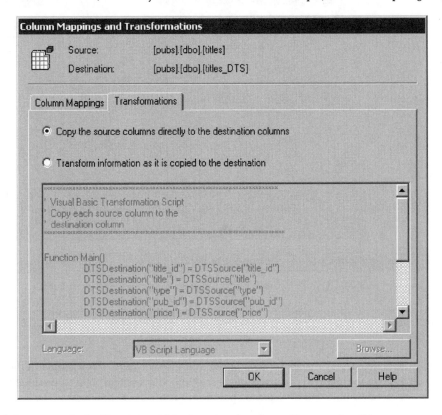

The ability to use ActiveX scripts within the wizard and transforms makes this a very powerful option. It allows everything from simple field testing and replacing to invoking a COM object and interacting with it during the transformation. For this example, leave it as default to perform a direct copy. You can return to the **Select Source Tables and Views** window by clicking the **OK** button.

7. Click **Next** to go the next screen, which allows you to save and or run the package that you just created.

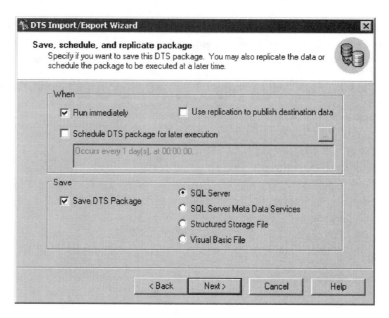

Let's just briefly describe the various options:

❑ **Run immediately**: The package is run as soon as the wizard completes.

❑ **Use replication to publish destination table:** This allows you to set up the destination table for replication after importing the data. The Create Publication wizard will start up after the Import/Export wizard completes to create the replication.

❑ **Schedule DTS package for later execution**: Choose this if you wish to run the package at a later time. This option allows for specifying either a single delayed execution or multiple executions; the default is for the package to run daily at midnight.

❑ **Save DTS package**: There are several formats and destinations to choose from when you save a package, whether it's created by the Import/Export wizard or via the package editor. We'll discuss these options in more detail later. As shown, you can save to the server, or to a structured storage (.dts) file, or even create a Visual Basic module to re-create the package.

For now, choose to run your package immediately and also save it to the server. When you click Next, you'll need to choose a name for the package and a server to save the package to.

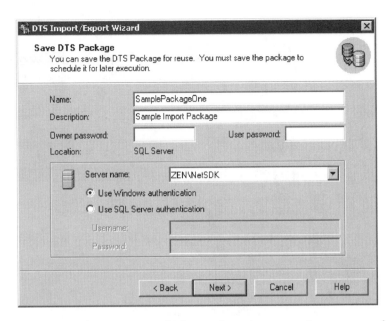

8. Here you can give the package a name, which must be unique on a given server and also, if desired, a description of what the package is accomplishing. Name this package SamplePackageOne.

9. Click Next, and review the summary of the options you've chosen.

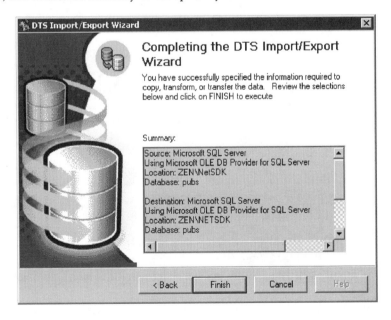

When you click on the Finish button, the package will immediately be saved and then run.

This screen shows you the progress of the executing DTS package. The icons to the left of each task indicate their status. Tasks that are currently running have a green arrow; tasks waiting for execution have a yellow clock. If a task fails for some reason, a red X appears and if a task doesn't run, due to a workflow constraint or being disabled, a black circle with a white X appears.

> **Notice that there are three tasks running in parallel. In the absence of any workflow constraints, DTS will execute multiple tasks simultaneously. The number of concurrent tasks can be set in the options for a given package. Just be aware of this behavior and specify any constraints on task execution order via workflow.**

10. When the package is complete, the following dialog box appears.

This dialog box will only appear when the package is run right after creation by the wizard. It will not appear if you open the package and run it again. Once you click OK, you'll return to a more informative screen.

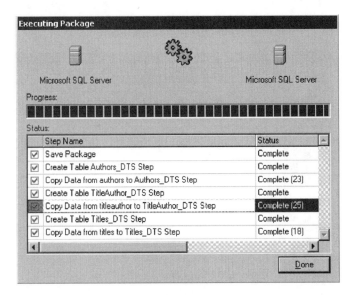

11. This screen shows you the status of each of the tasks within the package. It also shows the number of rows transformed when applicable. If a task failed due to an error, you could double-click the task to view detailed information on the error that occurred.

12. Close the Executing Package dialog box by clicking Done. Now open this new package and see what the wizard created. Next, select Local Packages in the Enterprise Manager. It should look similar to this:

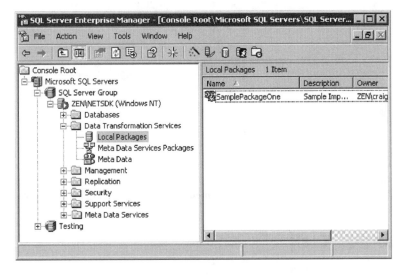

13. Bring up the editor by double-clicking the package.

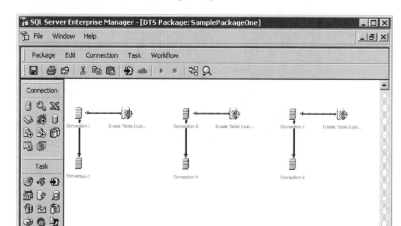

Examining the Package

Take a look at the package you've just created. There are three similar groupings of items in the package, one for each table that you imported. Let's look at one of these groups of five items.

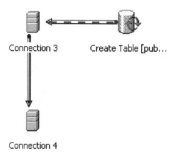

The five items in each group are as follows: the Execute SQL task to create the table, two connection objects, a transform task, and the workflow connecting the Execute SQL and the transformation.

Execute SQL Task

As mentioned earlier, the **Execute SQL task** can execute almost any SQL command or commands, including parametric SQL commands. For now, double-click the Create Table task to view the properties.

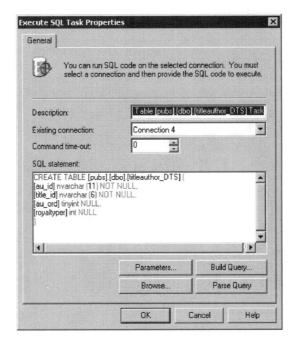

This screen shot shows the connection being used for the commands and the SQL statement(s). This task uses Connection 4 to execute a basic **CREATE TABLE** command for your new `titleauthor_DTS` table.

> **Note the absence of any constraints, indexes, or even primary keys on the new table.** The Copy table(s) and view(s) from the source database **option you selected earlier only copies the data and the column data types. It doesn't transfer other table information such as indexes, primary constraints, or default constraints. To do this, you would have to specify** Copy objects and data between SQL Server databases.

The Workflow

The workflow in this package is represented by a blue dashed arrow, representing an On Completion workflow. This ensures that the transformation into the `titleauthor_DTS` table (the dependent task) doesn't start until the **CREATE TABLE** (the preceding task) completes.

The Connection Object

As discussed earlier, when you open the Connection object it shows that you're connecting to a SQL Server, the name of the server, and that you're referencing the pubs database.

The Transform Task

The black arrow between Connection 3 and Connection 4 is the transformation task. When you double-click the arrow, you see the properties as shown here.

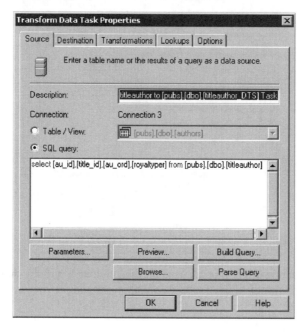

Notice that the wizard used a SQL statement, and not the table directly. If you were building this package from scratch, you could choose either one. The actual performance of each is about the same. Close the transformation for now. The next example will cover the other tabs in greater detail.

Creating a DTS Package Using the DTS Editor

Now that you've seen how to create a package via the Import/Export wizard, it's time to create a package from scratch using the graphical DTS editor, looking into the data transformation in more detail.

Try It Out–Creating a Simple Package

In this example, you'll transfer part of the pubs database (the titles, authors, publishers tables and dependent tables) to a new database. Along the way, you'll denormalize some data for easier reporting.

1. First create an empty database to work with called Pubs_DTS. For this, enter the following command in Query Analyzer:

```
Create database Pubs_DTS
```

In this example, you'll connect to the same server as the original pubs *database. You could just as easily connect to a database on another server.*

2. Now that the database has been created, right-click the Local Packages node in Enterprise Manager and start a New Package. The first step is to create the connections. Click the SQL Server connection icon in the toolbar to the left. SQL Server will display the Connection Properties dialog box (the same one that you saw in the Import/Export wizard). Name the connection Pubs Source, and set the database to pubs. When you click OK, the editor will place the icon for the connection on the package.

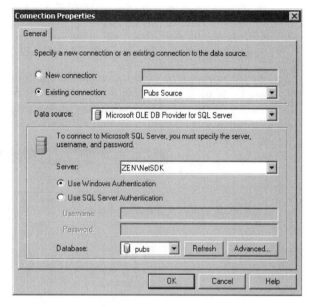

3. Create another connection. This time name it Pubs_DTS Destination and set the database to the newly created database Pubs_DTS.

4. Now that you've specified where to go, you need to specify how to get there. The first transform will be on the employees table. You'll want to copy all the data and combine the name fields (First, last, middle initial) into one field.

5. Drag the Transform Data Task icon onto the package from the toolbar. At this point, the cursor changes to a database icon with an arrow pointing right and says "Select Source Connection." Click Pubs Source and the cursor changes to have the arrow pointing left, which says "Select Destination Connection." Click Pubs_DTS Destination, and a black arrow appears between the connections, which looks something like the following screen shot.

6. You now have a transform between the two connections, but it doesn't know what to do. Double-click the black arrow, and the property pages for the transformation will appear. The first step is to give the transformation a meaningful name, say EmployeeTransform. Next select the employee table in the drop down Table/View list. After that is completed, you can specify the destination table. When you select the Destination Table tab, the editor opens a dialog box for creating the destination table. This dialog box appears because the destination database is empty. In the future, if you need to create a table, simply click the Create button.

As you saw with the wizard example earlier, this default create statement matches column name and column types, but doesn't create any constraints, not even a primary key. Now modify this statement to combine the three employee name fields into one varchar field named FullName with a length of 60 that will not accept NULLs and add a primary key.

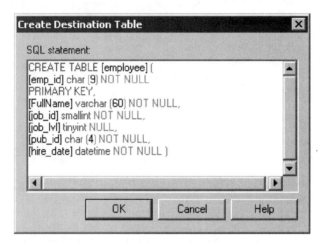

7. The final modified SQL statement should look like the screen shot above, and you can click OK to create the table and return to the Destination Table tab.

> As soon as you click OK in the Create Destination dialog box, the table is created. This means that, unlike the initial wizard, the table isn't created as part of the package. When the package executes, it expects the table to already exist. Be aware of this if you want to run this package again against a different database.

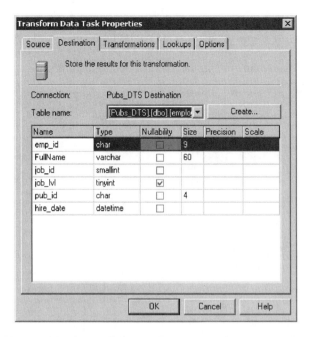

Note that the destination table shows all the newly created columns, including the new
FullName column.

8. Now move ahead to the Transformations tab. DTS will prefill default transformations as shown
below.

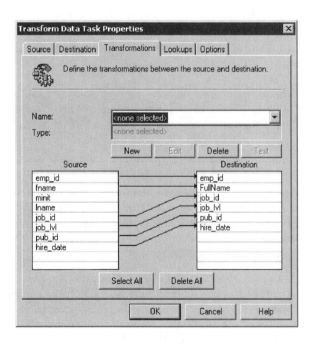

The editor will make its best guess to match each source column with a destination column. Notice that it only places the first name (fname) in the new FullName column and doesn't transform on Last Name (lname) and minit. Another point to mention here is that each column is transformed individually. This can be seen by clicking the down arrow beside Name.

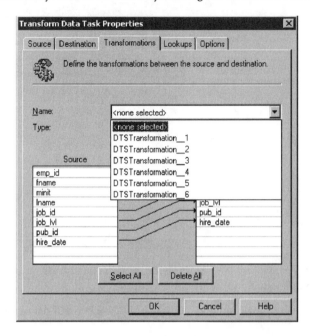

There are a couple of things we don't like about this, the first being the names. Without descriptive names, there is no easy way to find what DTSTransformation_1 does without opening it up. Having each column in its own transformation also incurs unnecessary overhead.

> **We should stress again that for performance, individual transformations incur a large penalty and will run slower than a single transformation that includes all the columns.**

In an inconsistent way, if you reopen the SamplePackageOne that you created with the Import/Export wizard and view any of the transformation tasks, you'll see that they're grouped into a single transformation, yielding the better performance. On these small sample tables, the time difference is negligible, but if you're transforming hundreds of thousands of rows, there will be a noticeable performance difference.

9. Start with a clean slate and remove the existing transformations by clicking the Delete All button. Now you'll start with your transformation of all non-name columns. As with most things, choosing the columns for a given transformation can be accomplished in several ways. If the transformation will occur on all columns, you can click the Select All button to select all Source columns and all Destination columns. Alternatively, you can perform a multiselect on the two

column lists prior to clicking the New button. For this example, you'll see another method of specifying the columns. Click the New button to open the Transformation dialog box.

10. The first dialog box allows you to choose the type of transformation.

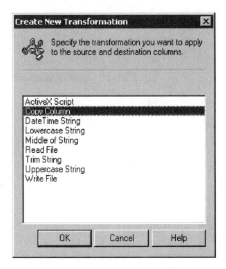

There are several transformation types available. They consist of the more general Copy Column and ActiveX Script, to specific transforms that apply to a single column, such as DateTime String, or To LowerCase String. The first transformation to create will be a basic Copy Column. After you select the transformation type, the Transformation Properties dialog box opens.

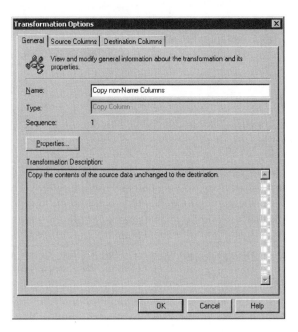

11. The first step is to give the transformation a meaningful name. For this example, choose Copy non-Name Columns.

12. Next, you'll need to specify the columns for this transformation. Click the Source Columns tab, and use the arrow buttons (>, >>, <, <<) between the two lists to move all but the name columns into the Selected columns list. After they're selected, they should appear in the same order as shown.

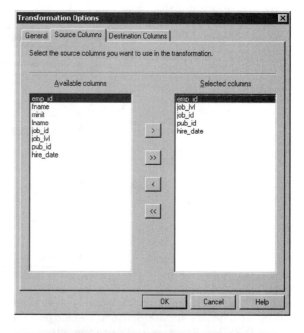

13. After specifying the columns, click the Destination Columns tab and use the arrow buttons to specify the destination columns as shown.

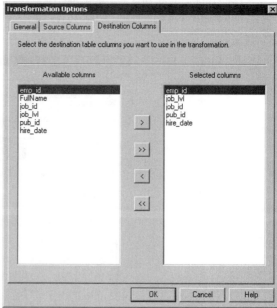

14. Now that the columns are specified, make a final check that the columns are being transferred to the proper destination. Click the General tab and then click the Properties button. The following box will appear.

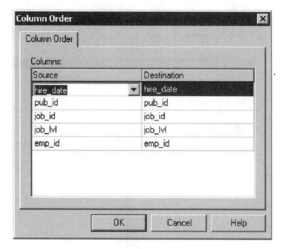

15. Ensure that the source and destination columns match properly. If they don't, you can select an item on either side and set the available columns to make them match. Finish this transformation by clicking OK, and then click OK on the General tab. When you return to the Transform Data Task Properties, it will look like the following screen shot.

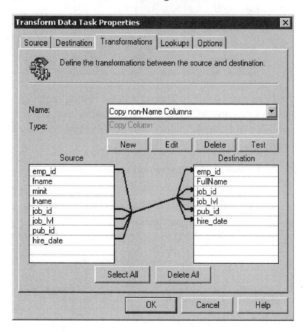

16. This shows the preferred setup with the transformation of multiple columns occurring in a single transformation. Now you need to perform the transform on the name columns to merge the three name fields into one. While holding down the *Ctrl* key, select the three Source name fields (fname, minit, and lname) and the one Destination name field (FullName) and click New. For Transformation Type, select ActiveX Script. On the General tab, enter the name Merge Name Fields. Click the Properties button to show and edit the ActiveX Script.

17. On the top left of this page you can choose what scripting language to use; the default is VBScript, but JScript can also be used if desired. Below that is a list of functions. Below the functions is a tab labeled Browser, which can be used to select key DTS information such as source or destination columns.

DTS starts with the following auto-generated script:

```
'***************************************************************
'   Visual Basic Transformation Script
'***************************************************************


'   Copy each source column to the destination column
Function Main()
    DTSDestination("FullName") = DTSSource("fname")
    Main = DTSTransformStat_OK
    End Function
```

Before you modify this script, let's discuss the key lines:

```
Function Main()
```

Each script transform must have at least one function called Main. Like it says, this is the main function that is called for the transform. The script can contain additional subroutines or functions, but they will only be executed if they're called from Main.

```
DTSDestination("FullName") = DTSSource("fname")
```

The values within the source and destination columns are accessible from the DTSDestination() and DTSSource()collections. The previous line sets the destination field FullName to the value in the source field fname.

```
Main = DTSTransformStat_OK
```

The return value on the Main function lets the package know the status. The previous line is stating that the transform occurred without error. There are constants available on the Browser tab to skip a row or end the transform with an error, or even to stop processing the current row.

In this case, you'll want to merge the first name, middle initial, and last name into one full-name field. You also need to account for any null values in the middle initial column. The following code accomplishes this.

```
'**********************************************
'  Visual Basic Transformation Script
'**********************************************

'  Copy each source column to the destination column
Function Main()
    if ISNULL(DTSSource("minit")) then
        DTSDestination("FullName") = DTSSource("fname") _
                                & " " & DTSSource("lname")
    elseif Len(trim(DTSSource("minit"))) = 0 then
        DTSDestination("FullName") = DTSSource("fname") _
                                & " " & DTSSource("lname")
    else
        DTSDestination("FullName") = DTSSource("fname") _
                                & " " & DTSSource("minit") _
                                & ". " & DTSSource("lname")
    end if
    Main = DTSTransformStat_OK
End Function
```

This script tests for and handles names with a middle initial and no middle initial. By clicking the Test button you can preview the results and whether the script generates any errors for the initial rows of the table. Click OK twice to complete the transformation.

18. This ActiveX transformation completes the transformations for the `employee` table. Next, you'll want to copy the `titles` and other dependent tables. Return to your DTS package editor and click the Copy SQL Server Objects Task. This will open a dialog box to choose the source and destination server and database. Call the task Copy Dependent tables. As with your other connections, select the pubs database for the source and Pubs_DTS as the destination. After entering those, select the Copy tab. Fill in the dialog box as shown.

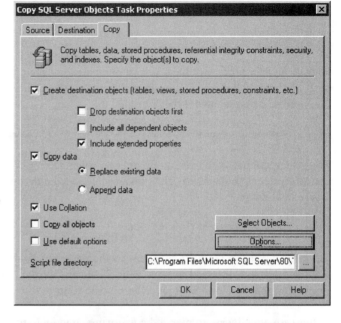

Most of these options are self-explanatory. Because the destination database is blank, you need to create the destination objects, and you don't need to drop the existing objects. Although the default is to copy all objects for this example, you don't want to do that, so click the Select Objects button to choose the tables.

19. Select all the user tables except `employee`, and the three example tables created in the previous example (authors_DTS, titles_DTS, titleauthor_DTS). Also select the user-defined data type id. Click OK.

20. Now click Options button to display the advanced options. Notice that you have the options of copying constraints, including primary and foreign key constraints and even triggers. Click OK twice.

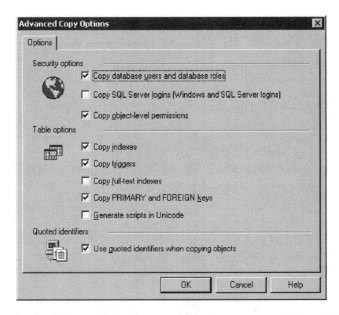

21. The package is now almost complete. All you need to do now is to add a workflow. Because you're copying foreign key constraints, if you import the `publisher` table prior to the `employee` table, the copy would fail due to the dependency on the `employee` table. So you need to add a workflow between the EmployeeTransform task and the Copy Dependent tables task. To do this, hold down the *Ctrl* key, and select the Pubs_DTS destination connection, then select the Copy Dependent tables task in the DTS editor. Next, choose On Completion from the Workflow menu.

Now the completed package looks like the following figure.

All you need to do now is save the package and run it.

Save Package

As you saw when saving the package Import/Export wizard example, there are several options of where to save a package. When you first choose Save on a new package, the following dialog box appears.

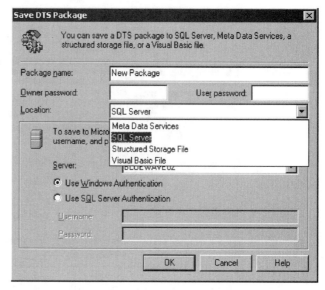

The different locations for saving are as follows:

- ❑ **Meta Data Services**: This option not only allows you to save version information, but also catalog which tables and columns are affected by what version.

- ❑ **SQL Server**: This is the default option. This option saves the package into the msdb database on the specified server.

- ❑ **Structure Storage File**: This is a file-based system that stores the package in a proprietary format. This option is good when you need to move packages between SQL Servers.

- ❑ **Visual Basic File**: This is a cool option that in essence scripts the package into Visual Basic. This file can be used as a starting point for more advanced packages, or run on another server to re-create the package there. We would caution you to check the re-created package against the original because we've found discrepancies before.

Save your package to SQL server with the name Sample Package Two.

After saving the package, you can run the package. When a package is open, you can run (execute) the package from the package menu. If the package is closed from local packages, you can right-click the package and select Execute Package.

Summary

You've now taken a whirlwind tour of DTS. Along the way, you've visited the Import/Export wizard and created a package from scratch. You've copied SQL Server objects, including tables, and user-defined data types. You've created a basic ActiveX script and manipulated your data to suit your needs. You've also seen some of the powerful options available, and hopefully you'll feel a little more comfortable when the time comes to move data into or out of a database or server.

13

Monitor, Profile, and Tune

Using a tool and understanding how the tool should be used are two very different things. Even the most expensive tool won't get a job done any faster unless you know how to take full advantage of its features. In this chapter, you'll fine-tune a SQL Server instance for performance, identify some areas to look at proactively so that you can prevent situations in which people complain that the database is slow, and lay out some practical approaches for resolving performance problems. In this chapter, you'll look at how to do the following:

❑   Measure performance

❑   Identify likely bottlenecks causing sluggish responses

❑   Look inside SQL Server and see what's going on

❑   Use tools provided by Microsoft to get better performance

What Tuning Can Do for You

In the early 1990s, we had a client who had recently invested in a relational database management system and was in the process of determining how to take advantage of the benefits it promised. Because the client was in the health care industry, we ran reports against millions of records at a time and summarized in different ways on large mainframe computers, at significant cost. If the analysis could be completed in a timely fashion, responses to market changes could be made quickly.

One such report was taking more than ten hours to run. Because it was a critical piece of information, the client felt justified in investing in newer technologies in order to get it to run faster. Following a consultant's advice, the company purchased a bigger and faster server and was able to cut over two hours from the runtime. Our company was brought in to see if anything else could be done. After spending some time looking at how the client was using the database, we came up with a list of various items that would likely improve performance.

The consultant's response was that each item wouldn't make that big of a difference, so why bother? He had a good bit invested in the way things were working, and we were new to the client. After a week of arguing about it, we went ahead to see what would happen. Once we made the changes that we had suggested, the report ran in eight minutes.

Tuning is the art of making small adjustments to gain a large effect.

Where to Start

Database tuning is generally addressed as a result of poor performance by one of the applications running against the server. The question of why it's running slowly requires that you step back and look at the whole picture before jumping in with a quick solution. You need to understand the problem before you can give your answer. Generally, poor performance is the result of poor design either in the hardware, schema design (in other words, bad normalization), the network, or the way the application uses the database.

A good place to start, then, is to conduct a quick interview with those who use the system. We generally start by talking with the person who brought up performance tuning. Why is performance a concern, and what do they expect to achieve from the exercise? Do they have an idea of what the problem is, or are they grasping at straws? Is their application running more slowly than it used to? Maybe it has always been slow, or it runs slower on one server than on another one that supposedly has a similar configuration?

Before you jump in and start recoding SQL statements, you need to determine what the real nature of the problem is: whether it's hardware, software, or something else. We've heard from the sponsor of our efforts what they perceive the issue to be; now our job is to look at the facts and make an informed diagnosis. One way is to take a top-down approach to the problem (start at the application level and work down to the hardware). The areas to look at include the following:

- ❑ Database design
- ❑ Application architecture
- ❑ Operating system configuration
- ❑ Hardware
- ❑ Network

Poor design in any of these areas can result in poor performance. The questions you ask can give you an insight into what you're looking for. Some good questions include the following:

- ❑ Is the poor performance localized to a single application or is it widespread, affecting any program that uses the database?
- ❑ Has the application always run slowly, or has the performance noticeably degraded over time?
- ❑ What new applications have recently been added to the server load?

- ❑ Has the volume of data changed recently?

- ❑ How is the database engine configured for memory, disks, and so on?

- ❑ Does the application perform better on a different server?

- ❑ Has the application been upgraded or changed recently?

- ❑ Are new applications causing contention for access to data?

- ❑ What has been done to address performance problems?

Application Issues

If the application used to perform well but now has problems, find out what has changed in its environment. Determine if unexpected volumes of data being processed might cause the perceived change in performance. Has the number of users increased recently? In most corporate situations, no database is an island; find out what other applications share the server. Specifically you should be interested in those that share the same tables as the suspect application. If there are time outs in the application, then you might want to determine whether blocking is an issue. Another approach is to look at the timing of the problems. Is performance notably better or worse at a particular time of the day? What else is going on against the server at those times? When an application that used to run well has problems, the issue might be outside the application.

If the problem is chronic, or the application has never run well, even though other similar systems do, this is an indicator of application issues. One likely cause is poorly designed queries that pull too much, or unwanted, information. This isn't uncommon among less-experienced developers who are newer to building software. As a result of doing whatever it takes to get it to work, a lot of legacy code may have been left in and is now wasting resources. Even though the program might have run fine in development, when there was only one user and limited amounts of information, you still have to put it into a multiuser environment with full data volumes in order to make the program show its warts. A code review at this point would make some sense if time allows, but you just want to fix the problem.

Select What You Need

When selecting information from the database engine, determine whether you really need all the records and columns that you requested. Rather than performing aggregation and summarization of large numbers of records within the application, push the work onto the database and use the built-in functions and features of T-SQL to do the work for you. One developer we worked with decided to remove duplicate values from the result set within his code because he didn't know about the DISTINCT keyword.

Furthermore, if you're selecting from the database, try to avoid the SELECT * FROM ... statement, because it returns all columns and adds to the volume of data transferred between the server and the client. SQL Server provides some excellent extensions to ANSI SQL like the TOP expression, which puts the limit of the number of records in the resultset on the server instead of on the client workstation.

Avoiding Blocking Situations

Blocking occurs when one process needs a lock on a table that another process already has. This can result in time outs and a perceived locking up of the application if the condition isn't handled gracefully. This condition is caused by long-running queries, by not completely retrieving the resultset from a cursor-based query, and by canceling queries without performing commits or rollbacks.

What can you do to prevent blocking situations? Because the database is driven by the application and the types of query submitted by the client determine what types of locks are required, well-designed and coded applications are key to preventing these types of problems.

When using cursors, ensure that the resultsets are fetched to completion. Locks are held by the database on open cursors and will block other applications that share the data. If possible, consider using set-based queries instead of cursors. This isn't to say that you shouldn't use cursors, but should just avoid using them inappropriately.

Avoid long-running queries by designing the application to use existing indexes wherever possible to prevent excessive table scans on nonindexed columns. During the design of the application, try to determine the required pathways for accessing the data and create indexes where it makes sense.

Confirm that the application developers have provided a means for the user to cancel a query and gracefully handle it when requested. A commit or rollback must occur, because it isn't appropriate to leave the database in an indeterminate state.

The Effect of Indexing

Indexes speed up the performance when querying information from tables. Adding indexes will make reading the contents of the database quicker by reducing the number of operations required to access a specific record. While the speed of reading data is increased, every time data is added or changed, these structures must be updated as well. This will affect the performance of transaction-based systems that require the ability to quickly write to the database. Also, there is the additional cost of storing the indexes, which can be significant.

It's good practice to separate OLTP (**online transaction processing**) systems from the decision-support reporting-type analysis systems by placing them on different servers. Imagine what could happen if a cash register wasn't able to write sales transactions to the database because someone was reporting on last quarter's sales.

Database Design

The best database design won't ensure a successful project, but a poorly designed one will almost always ruin it. Applications that are migrated from a legacy data store often don't do justice to the modifications made over time to accommodate new business requirements. Legacy applications often used databases that weren't relational, and the developer who got it to work once will attempt to treat SQL Server just like the old database and not take advantage of the functionality the new one provides.

We once worked with a colleague who was a great COBOL programmer and was able to write wonderful code. The trouble was, we were developing in C, and he didn't grasp the difference in language. The result was that his code read a lot like COBOL, and didn't take full advantage of what the new language offered.

A good design makes all the difference. Proper normalization and documentation, following the shop standards for things like column names, helps to ensure that the application being built today will not only be running, but also be supportable tomorrow.

Normalize for Efficient Storage, Denormalize for Performance

After working through the data requirements, using all the techniques learned at DBA school, and normalizing to third normal form and beyond, you finally have created the perfect schema. You implemented the physical model, and now the developers are complaining. Too many joins, dependent tables, database contention, and excessive blocking. What can you do?

Depending on the nature of the system, it's appropriate to use different levels of normalization. When working with databases used primarily for reporting, in which information is written once and read many times using many different access paths, you should consider denormalizing your model to reduce the number of tables that need to be joined to return a resultset. On the other hand, storing the same information in multiple places means that all of them need to be kept in sync if the resulting reports are to provide valid information.

Configuration Issues

The SQL Server installation CD will make a number of assumptions about how to configure the engine and where to put the data and log files. While working with small development and test server environments, with small volumes of data and users, the default options work well. However, planning a large database server for performance of the system requires careful consideration on how you use the hardware. Decisions you make at the beginning of the process will have long-lasting implications on a production server, particularly if it's used to support critical enterprise functions.

Transaction Log

The **transaction log** is used to recover the database in case of failure or if you need to roll back to a point in time. Thus, if you plan to use the transaction log in case a disk fails, having the log file on that same disk might be a problem. A second reason for not having the transaction log on the same disk as the data files is that you'll have less contention for disk I/O.

Finally, check the size of the transaction log to ensure that it won't be growing over time. A single contiguous file will give better performance than an excessive number of extents (an **extent** is an additional amount of disk space that is logically part of an existing file). Also, make sure to have a backup strategy that runs periodically, so that the transaction log gets cleared out before it exceeds its size and needs to grow. What that timing is depends on a number of factors, but a database that is used to capture new information will use the transaction log faster than a database whose primary function is reporting.

Effects of Memory

Not having enough memory will slow down any computer system, but adding an excessive amount of RAM won't guarantee faster performance. SQL Server is designed to dynamically allocate and release memory as it needs it, depending on the workload, so it's possible to add more memory than will ever get used. On the other hand, sizing the amount of memory to ensure that you have enough to handle the peak workload without it becoming a bottleneck is an easy fix.

How much is enough? Given current hardware configurations, and the reduced cost of RAM, you should have at least one GB available to you. SQL Server does allow you the option of setting hard limits on the maximum and minimum amounts, but you generally don't need to. If you have a server on which the database will be competing for resources with other services, you will eliminate some of the problems if you ensure that there are sufficient resources to run the database.

Each database connection will use 24KB of memory to start with, and then for each object opened, additional memory is used. There is a connection pooling option at the ODBC level in which connections are shared between users. If you're working with a system that supports a large user base (such as an e-commerce solution), using connection pooling and a messaging architecture may be worth the additional cost to get the scalability.

Disk Format—NTFS vs. FAT32

SQL Server will run equally well on both NTFS and FAT32 formatted drives, but Microsoft recommends you use NTFS unless you need to be able to boot to Windows 95/98. Microsoft's reasons for using NTFS include improved recoverability and better security. If you're going to use NTFS, SQL Server will perform better if you format the drive with 64KB extent sizes.

RAID Sets

RAID (**redundant array of independent disks**) describes a named configuration scheme for the disk subsystem. There are several types of RAID, each of which specifies a means for achieving performance and recoverability. Type 0 involves striping the data sets across the disks, and because the disk reads can be performed concurrently, it has the highest performance, but if one disk fails you're out of luck. RAID 1 specifies mirrored drives, so you have recoverability. Microsoft recommends using RAID 0 for the data files and RAID 1 for your transaction log. This way you should have a comfortable level of recoverability and performance. RAID 5 provides a redundant solution, such that if one disk fails, it can be replaced with no downtime. SQL Books online provides in-depth coverage of this topic.

Measuring Performance

Poor performance can mean a lot of different things depending on who you're talking to. Identifying discrete measurements that are quantifiable, and then using them to compare new applications to old ones, will help you to effectively communicate the true nature of performance to your customers. These measurements can include time to complete common tasks, the maximum number of users, and how long it takes to generate reports. Things to keep in mind when choosing measurements are the nature of the system and what you're trying to optimize. For example, you may want to focus more on responsiveness than user volume or handling extreme data loads.

If you're replacing or upgrading an existing system, start with gathering facts about the number of records added daily to the system, the typical number of users, and a measurement of the time to perform common tasks. For example, in a point-of-sale system, these would include the expected number of sales transactions per day, the number of cash registers, and how many cashiers are running concurrently. Peak volumes from holiday periods and performance behavior at these times will help give you an idea of what type of performance is expected.

Importance of Perception

They say that one happy customer will tell four of their friends, but an unhappy one will tell many more. The squeaky wheel gets the grease, and you won't necessarily hear the good stories. Depending on the user's familiarity with the system and experience with similar applications (or lack thereof), what one person would describe as good or even adequate can be called horrible by another. Being the victim of a deadlock or a time out on the database just once may give a user a bias that will be tough to break. That is why it's important to know what you're talking about, and to be able to back up your findings with facts.

Importance of Facts

A national retailer has a complex pricing system that responds to their competitor's prices. The time between setting the prices and having it visible in the stores was taking too long, and the guy in marketing was fuming. Why is it so slow he asked? When we started looking into it, we asked him to describe what he saw and what he expected. Then we laid out the various steps required for the price to be called in from the store, the time to get it relayed to the right people in marketing, the time for the manager to approve the prices, and the time for the prices to be downloaded to the stores, with each step dependent on the previous one.

The system time involved the time between the instant when the prices were approved until the instant they showed up at the stores on the cash registers. We looked at the time from when the download at the corporate office occurred up to the completion of the data load at the stores. We didn't just look at one run, or even a day's run; we looked at all the data from the previous month, by day and by run, and found that on average, there were 400 price changes at a store for each run, for a total of about 2,000 per day. Moreover, these were running at about 350 stores, which meant the system was updating 140,000 per run, or 700,000 updates per day. The average time for a pricing download to be applied was less than eight minutes.

When we presented these facts, it became obvious that the majority of the time required to manage the pricing system wasn't consumed by the pricing and replication applications, but rather by the human processes of communications and approvals.

Knowing When to Quit

By defining what you want to accomplish with some hard numbers in terms of the type of performance you need, you have a way to know when you're done. You need not only to define measurements, but be diligent to take them after each iteration through the tuning process, so you can tell whether you're getting closer to the desired end result. One approach is to create service-level agreements with your customers in which you explicitly write down what is acceptable.

Tools for Monitoring SQL Server

Microsoft provides several tools with SQL Server for monitoring and tuning the database. These include system-based utilities like Performance Monitor (commonly called PerfMon) and Task Manager, as well as SQL Server specific utilities like Enterprise Manager, Query Analyzer, SQL Profiler, and the Index Tuning wizard.

Query Analyzer

You may be familiar with the Query Analyzer, but there are several new features you may not have used that can help you tune your SQL Server. Prior to SQL Server 2000, the Query Analyzer tool simply provided a way to show the query and the resultset, but not much else. There was a basic Show Plan option, but this has been much improved. With the release of SQL Server 2000, Microsoft has gone a long way to show how the database engine does its work. All of this is neatly packaged in a series of tabs at the bottom of the screen.

By turning on the options, the developer can see where resources are being spent relative to the total cost, and can get an idea of what optimization choices the database engine is making.

Execution Plan

You can view the execution plan by selecting Show Execution Plan from the Query menu or by pressing *Ctrl+K* on the keyboard. Query Analyzer adds a tab at the bottom of the screen that provides a graphical display of the steps the database engine takes to resolve a query. The display uses icons for each of the forty-three physical operations and six cursor operations, along with some statistical information on the cost of each operation as a percent of the total query. If there is more than one statement in a batch, the relative cost of each statement is listed.

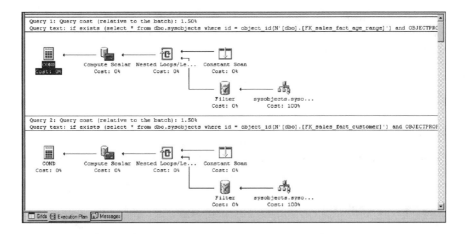

Although this book doesn't go into depth on all the operators, what you're looking for are the ones that are most expensive and may benefit from a change in the indexes, or by adding a query hint to specify the index to use. Good candidates to look for include table scans.

Server Trace

The trace option provides server-side statistical information to the Execution plan, and is turned on by selecting Show Server Trace from the Query menu or by typing *Ctrl+SHIFT+T*. This is similar to what is captured using SQL Profiler, but it's specific to the single query being executed. If you're running several statements in a batch, you can use this data to identify problem queries.

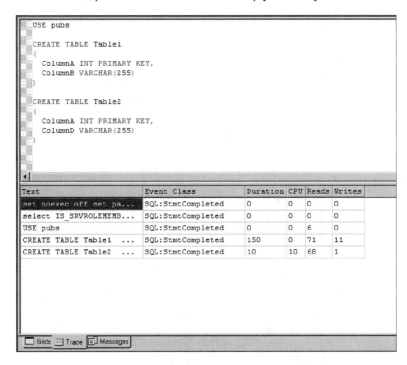

The Text of the statement being executed is shown along with the Event Class, Duration, CPU, Reads, and Writes to disk. In this batch of statements, you can see that the first CREATE TABLE statement involves many more writes to disk than the second, and therefore takes much longer.

Client Statistics

The Show Client Statistics option captures three types of client-side statistics from the executing query or batch of queries, including application information, network, and cumulative time statistics. This option can be selected by clicking Show Client Statistics in the Query menu. Application statistics show how many rows were affected, the number of INSERT, UPDATE, and DELETE statements executed, and the number of user transactions that have been processed, as well as information about how quickly the data retrievals were completed.

The network statistics tell you the number of round-trips to the server that were required, the packet information, and the number of bytes sent and received. This is useful in determining whether the network is causing the bottleneck.

The final group of statistics includes the total time it took from when the query started until it completed, and how much of that time was spent waiting for the server to finish its work.

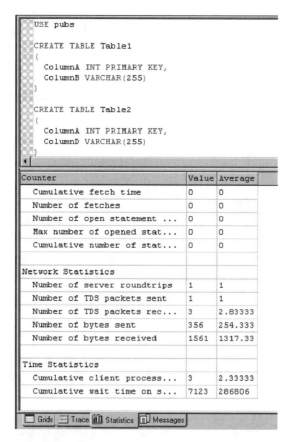

SQL Profiler

Formerly known as SQL Trace, this tool displays what is happening within the database engine as it happens. Using SQL Profiler, you can capture the activity to a file or another database for analysis and use it when tuning the system. With this information, you can identify queries that use large amounts of resources as well as see all the activity going on in the database engine.

Be careful not to go overboard. Running the profiler does use up system resources, and it requires at least 10MB of free disk space. Capturing all events without any filter on a server while active users are running applications against it may result in more information than you expect. For this reason, it's a good idea to limit what you monitor to just what you need.

Try It Out–Capturing Output with SQL Profiler

1. SQL Profiler can be started from the Start menu by choosing Start I All Programs I Microsoft SQL Server I SQL Profiler (with a standard installation).

2. After opening the program, click the File menu and select New I Trace. You'll be prompted to make a connection to the target server you'll be profiling. To use SQL Profiler against a server, you need to be a member of the administrators group or you need to log in as sa.

3. Then, you're presented with the Trace Properties window for the trace. You can select from one of the available templates, or you can start from scratch. For this example, you'll select the SQLProfilerStandard template.

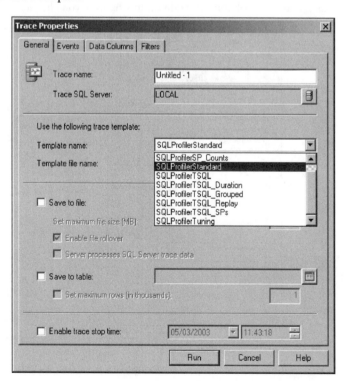

To make use of the trace information, you can either capture it to file or to a table. If you're running a general trace and don't plan to use it for detailed application-specific analysis, capturing to a file will suffice. Otherwise, capturing the information to a table and using some creativity will allow you to provide the application team with good information about how effectively they're using the database. By saving the information in this fashion, it's possible to report which SQL is being executed so that you can present each page of a website or form of an application.

4. Click the Save to table check box, and you're presented with a logon dialog box to determine where to store the information. You can name the table whatever you want, although if you plan to use it in the future for comparison purposes, picking a naming standard for the tables will help you find the right trace later.

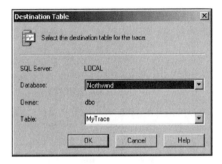

5. After the table has been named, you're returned to the Properties pages for the trace you're creating. Select the Data Columns tab and make sure you're capturing the SPID (process id), Reads, Writes, and CPU columns, in addition to whatever you choose.

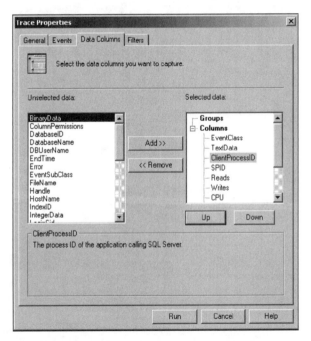

An application typically has a number of points of interaction at which the user opens a screen, clicks a button, or does some other action that the system responds to. You'll use the SPID column later to denote the point of interaction so that you can generate a report of how the application interacts with the database.

6. The standard profile includes a lot of good information. You can customize the capture to filter out other applications and users so you can get a clear view of your application. Specifying filters is similar to the WHERE clause in SQL. Use semicolons to separate lists of items, and the % character as a wildcard, which will find any-thing beginning with the preceding letters (like SQL%), similar to the way it works in standard T-SQL.

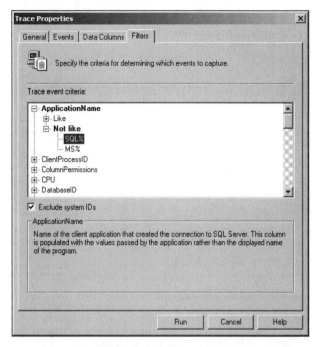

7. You can also specify which types of event you're interested in. SQL Books Online provides information about the various events so we won't go into them here (open the topic *SQL Profiler Terminology* for an overview of events, data columns, and so on).

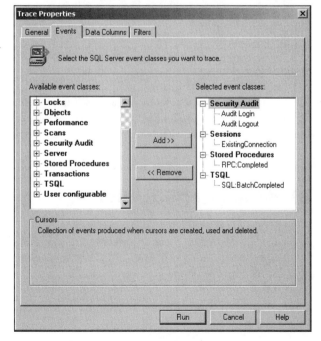

8. When you've set up the parameters of how you want to run the capture, click the Run button. The profiler window will open and display what is happening.

At this point, the events are listed as they happen, and selecting one by clicking it displays the details of the query in the lower part of the window. If you let the trace run for a while, you can get an idea of what is going on. You can pause, stop, and restart the trace by clicking the appropriate buttons on the toolbar.

Capturing Point of Interaction Data

When you're ready to capture information about a specific application or form, start a trace in which you're filtering out events not associated with your application by filtering on the user name (LoginName, or NTLoginName if you're using trusted connections), or the name of your machine (HostName). Next, open a Query Analyzer session and delete all data from the table into which you plan to capture the trace data. Then start the trace and begin the application.

Trace information from the application will be shown each time you do something, such as change forms, run commands, or open different pages (if the application is web-based). Each time you perform an action with the application, run an update command to set the SPID equal to an arbitrary sequence of numbers, as shown:

```
UPDATE MyTrace set SPID = 10001 where SPID < 10000
```

The SPID is usually a fairly small number so 10,001 will work; although you can choose any base number you want. By executing this command after each point of interaction, in which 10001 will be incremented to 10002, 10003, and so on, you'll be able to link the SQL commands to a specific action done by the application.

Capturing this type of information may not be easy because you have to work with your filters and events, and you may even need to find a place where you have exclusive access to the development systems, but the value can be enormous. Later, you can generate reports for the application team in which you highlight inefficient database use. You can summarize which points of interaction are most expensive, and identify redundant queries that the developers may not even realize are being run. In short, with very little knowledge of how an application was written, you can learn a great deal about how well it uses the database.

Other Uses for SQL Profiler

Identify Problem Queries.
If you have performance issues and want to find the offending application, you can use SQL Profiler to capture events relating to T-SQL and stored procedures (including RPC:Completed and SQL:BatchCompleted), and group the results by query duration. It's recommended that you add a filter so that you limit the results to only those queries that run for more than one thousand milliseconds, thus isolating problem queries.

Deadlocks.

If you want to identify the queries that are causing deadlocks, then set up the trace to capture the start of SQL and RPC events (`RPC:Starting` and `SQL:BatchStarting`), and the Locks events (`Deadlock` and `Deadlock Chain`).

Monitor User Activity.

If you know of a particular user that is having problems, you can create a trace to capture information from the `Sessions` and `ExistingConnection` classes, and then group the events by the `DBUserName`.

Tuning Wizard

Tuning a database schema for performance has traditionally required extensive knowledge of both the schema and the DBMS's optimizing engine. The analyst had to spend time reviewing the table structures and comparing these to the queries taken from the application code to find where indexes made sense. Using experience, judgment, and a little bit of luck, the perfect combination of indexes and denormalization was implemented and the users of the application paid homage to the database expert for a job well done.

Because you can't depend on luck, Microsoft provided a tool with SQL Server 2000 called the Tuning wizard, which takes an actual sample captured with SQL Profiler and uses that information to perform the analysis to determine what index changes will provide the maximum benefit.

Tuning for Application vs. Tuning for System

Be careful to avoid being pushed into tuning a database server for a specific application, because this can have an adverse impact on other applications that rely on the shared data store. You want the users to be happy with the performance of their application, but you need to be aware of the higher-level view.

For example, suppose a user wants to summarize the sales information, and has written an application that runs against the store database. Because the store's primary purpose is to allow the people who bring items to the front to be able to give money when they leave, anything that slows the performance of this primary application is foolish. A better approach is to build another server, load sales data on it periodically during off peak hours, and then create summarization tables and schemas to optimize reporting.

Try It Out–Running the Index Wizard

Start the Tuning wizard from the **Enterprise Manager Wizards** tab, or you can run it from the **Query** menu in Query Analyzer. Either way, this wizard will take you through the process and provide you with useful information to make your decisions.

1. Drill down into the database and select **Tools | Wizards**. In the dialog box that opens, drill down to **Management | Index Tuning Wizard**.

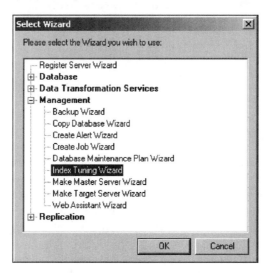

2. The first thing you need to decide is how thoroughly you wish to analyze the indexes. The first window after the splash screen gives you the opportunity to select a **Fast, Medium,** or **Thorough** processing plan of analysis.

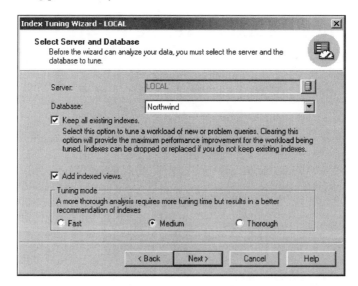

Selecting the **Fast** option puts limits on the types of recommendations the wizard will make. For instance, it will not recommend new clustered indexes or indexed views. The **Thorough** mode will take longer to run, but should yield better results. The default is **Medium**.

3. You also have the choice of whether or not the wizard should assume that you plan to keep existing indexes. This allows the optimizer to generate its recommendations without the overhead of legacy, and possibly underused, indexes.

4. After you've selected the plan for using the Tuning wizard, you're asked for the workload file. You'll use the table to which you captured the profile earlier, but you can use a file if you choose not to save it to the database.

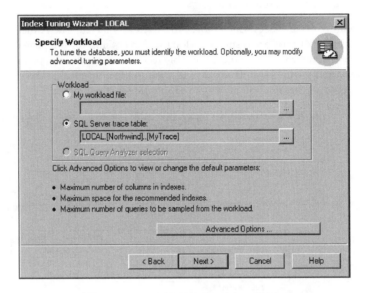

5. Clicking the **Advanced Options** button opens up a dialog box in which you can further specify how the wizard should use the input.

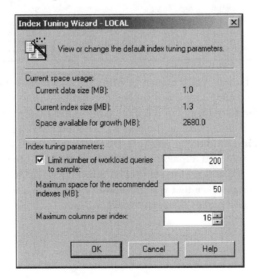

The queries are chosen at random from the workload file. Increasing the number to sample or opting to not limit the number will give a more thorough analysis, but will take longer to process. Also, you can limit the amount of space for storing the new indexes as well as the maximum number of columns to consider indexing.

Remember that in a transactional system in which data insertion and updating is the primary job of the database, more indexes mean more overhead in processing. Conversely, if the system is primarily used for reporting, and the data doesn't change after it has been loaded, then more indexes will improve response time.

6. At this point you can select which tables you want to analyze. The names of the tables and the current number of rows are displayed, along with a column for the projected size of the tables (that is, how many rows you expect the table to have when it's fully populated in production). If you're working with a test database, and want to scale up to what the expected production data volumes will be, this will allow you to simulate that condition.

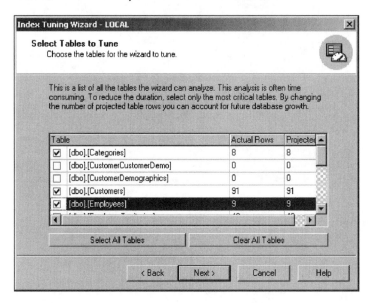

7. Clicking the Next button runs the analysis using the parameters you set in the previous steps, which may take several minutes to complete depending on the number and complexities of queries whose effects are logged in the trace table. After loading the data, the wizard will identify candidate indexes and calculate the benefit to be expected from each. It proceeds from selecting one-column candidate indexes to two-column indexes and so on until it reaches a point where it has achieved a maximum projected benefit. At that point, it displays its recommendations to you. Of course, the results are only as good as the test data, but if you've done a good job of capturing a trace that is representative of typical usage, you'll find that the recommendations the wizard makes are pretty good.

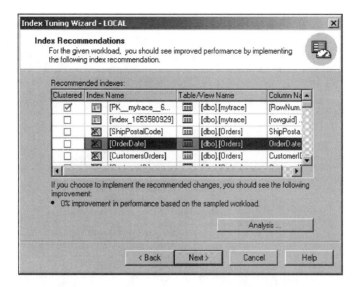

8. Clicking the Analysis button displays a dialog box with reports of what the wizard was able to determine.

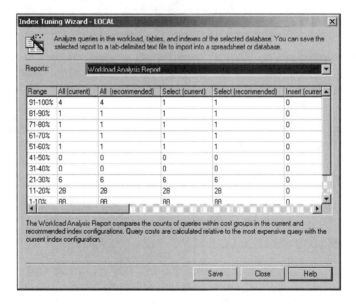

You can save the reports to file for future reference if you need. These reports contain a lot of information and also explain why the recommendations were made.

9. After you close the analysis report dialog box and continue the wizard, you're prompted to apply the changes now, or schedule them to be implemented later. Note that you need to have SQL Agent running to schedule the changes. You can also save the modifications to a file for future use.

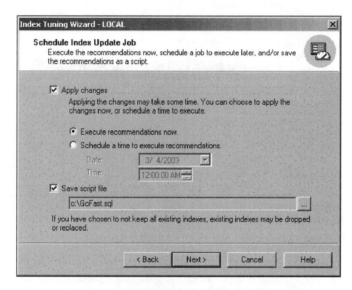

10. Clicking Next will exit the Tuning wizard. If you've applied the recommended changes, test the application to check whether there really has been a benefit. If the database has been tuned before, improvement may not be as noticeable.

The Tuning wizard helps you to determine the likely impact that changes like this will have. If the performance is still slow, and you've exhausted the application and configuration options, it's time to look deeper. This is where you start to learn about the hardware level and use NT's Performance Monitor to capture statistics and do further analysis to determine whether the hardware is a bottleneck.

Performance Monitor

This tool, referred to as "PerfMon" or "System Monitor," provides a graphical view of what the server is doing. It goes to the lowest level and can help you determine whether aged hardware is causing system problems. Again, like the SQL Profiler, it's event based, and can show you a realtime version of what is happening, as well as open an existing log for analysis. Capturing a large amount of information can degrade system performance, so use it only for what you need.

Try It Out–Running PerfMon

1. PerfMon can be started from the command line by entering PERFMON at a command prompt, or from the **Administrative Tools** in **Control Panel**. This tool has been a part of the NT OS since it was first released. It reads information captured to the registry on various system counters. SQL Server registers a variety of counters that can be monitored. The goal of the analysis here is to determine whether or not the disk is acting as a bottleneck.

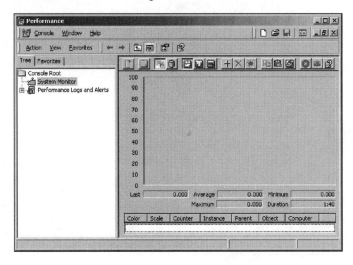

2. Clicking the + button opens the **Add Counters** dialog box, from which you can select items of interest. If you're part of another computer's administrative group, you can view information from that machine. Then you select the performance object and counters of interest to be added to the graph.

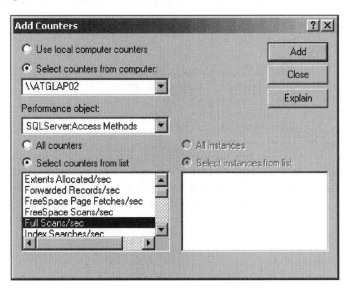

More information about each counter is available by clicking **Explain**. A Help dialog box tells you what the counter is and gives some information about it.

3. Adding all counters results in a confusing view, but you can delete them from the graph easily. Use the Highlight option to emphasize a particular counter. By using this tool, you can spot upward trends in memory usage that might point to an application with a memory leak, or peak information in which contention for system resources between applications is apparent.

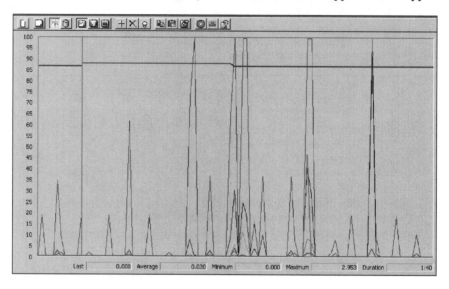

Counters of Interest

As you can see from a cursory glance at the **Add Counters** dialog box, there are a large number of counters you can monitor. In this section, you're just going to look at a couple of the more useful ones.

Free Disk Space

Microsoft suggests a threshold of 15 percent free disk space. SQL Server must be able to grow files, especially if the database is configured to automatically grow.

Disk Queue Length

This is the number of reads or writes waiting to be completed. The recommendation is the sustained value for this counter, and should not be higher than twice the number of spindles (physical disks). For example, if you were working on a server that has three disks, a queue length greater than six would point toward disk I/O problems. Increase the number of disks, or reconfigure the disks to get better performance.

Summary

Tuning a database can be a very complex and daunting task to undertake, and fortunately SQL Server provides a lot of good tools to help you do it. In this chapter, you looked at how you can measure performance and set some benchmarks for attaining that goal. You looked at Query Analyzer, SQL Profiler, and PerfMon as tools that can help you see what is going on inside the database engine. But you've only skimmed the surface of monitoring and tuning; for a more in-depth view, read Sajal Dam's *SQL Server Query Performance Tuning Distilled* from Apress. Microsoft's SQL Server Books Online is another great place to get more specific information about each tool.

Remember to look at the big picture when you're engaged in tuning a system. Beginning with an end in mind helps you to know where to stop.

14

Keeping the Plates Spinning

Well here it is, the final chapter of this book. We've covered all the major subject areas that a DBA must be familiar with before getting his hands (too) dirty on a production SQL Server environment, namely, the following:

- ❑ Installation
- ❑ Creating and querying a database
- ❑ Maintenance tasks
- ❑ Security
- ❑ Networking
- ❑ Backup and recovery
- ❑ Replication
- ❑ Data analysis and warehousing
- ❑ Migration
- ❑ Monitoring and tuning

To top off this vast collection of knowledge, we'll finish up by discussing the day-to-day tasks that rely on the knowledge built up throughout this book. These are the tasks that a DBA carries out regularly to keep the database environment functioning. A DBA must also keep the users and business running smoothly.

Inspecting Activity

Knowing what activity is occurring within SQL Server is essential to all DBAs. The reasons for this may include isolating a problem, such as a rogue query causing performance problems, or monitoring usage over time for the purpose of capacity planning.

There are several tools available for inspecting activity at various levels of detail within SQL Server. Each has a different purpose, but they all share the common goal of allowing a DBA to gain visibility of the work that SQL Server is currently doing.

> There are also a number of useful third-party tools that you might want to explore; unfortunately, we don't have the space to cover them all here.

Profiler

You've looked at examples of the SQL Server Profiler within this book already (see Chapter 13). The Profiler is a front-end tool that allows you to view all the requests made to SQL Server. We use the term "front-end tool" because SQL Server Profiler is a display tool for the data captured by the SQL Trace functionality of SQL Server. SQL Trace is the back-end capture tool that allows the recording of events that occur within SQL Server.

> You can use SQL Profiler from a client machine to capture event information occurring on a remote SQL Server.

SQL Profiler allows you to choose a myriad of events that you're interested in as well as numerous columns that contain individual pieces of event data. The collected information generated by these events can be retained within a database, stored in a disk file, or simply displayed to the screen for ad hoc analysis. The collected data can also be used as source data for the Index Tuning wizard, or used to "replay" prior SQL Server activity.

> Replaying SQL Server activity allows you to collect a series of events as they take place in real time in the SQL Server environment and then later rerun this series of events on the same, or another, SQL Server (such as a test or development SQL Server).

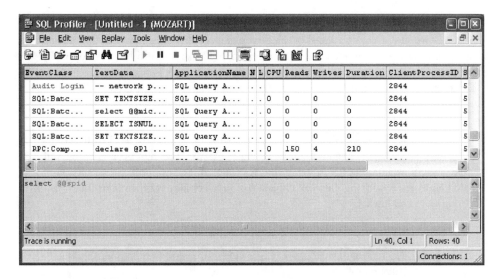

As great as SQL Server Profiler is, its use is limited. SQL Server Profiler captures the start and end of events as they occur within SQL Server, but it's not a real-time tool. If you start Profiler, you'll see the activity as events finish and start, but not events that are currently in progress until they complete. Therefore, if a problem is in progress, such as a long-running query that is consuming a high percentage of system resource, this may not be viewable until the event completes (which may not be for seconds, minutes, or maybe hours later). Don't worry; SQL Server provides other tools for inspecting the activity currently in progress.

Current Activity in Enterprise Manager

To inspect the current activity within a database, you can use either T-SQL or Enterprise Manager. Within Enterprise Manager, you can view the current activity by drilling down into the Current Activity node and selecting Process Info. In the details frame of this node, you'll see a list of all the current connections to SQL Server and relevant metadata.

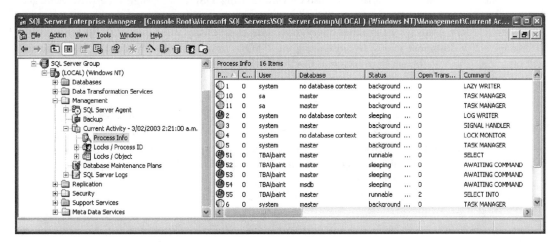

If you double-click any one of the process rows within this view, you'll open the **Process Details** dialog box as shown in the next screen shot. Here you can see the last command that this current process requested SQL Server to execute. Within this dialog box, you also have the option of "killing" this current database connection. Doing so will result in the end user being disconnected from SQL Server and any transactions on this connection that are in progress being rolled back.

> **Killing a process and causing SQL Server to roll back any in-progress transactions can take a long time, depending on how long the transaction had been running and the amount of data modified during that transaction. For example, a transaction that had been modifying data for the last five minutes may take three or four minutes to roll back.**

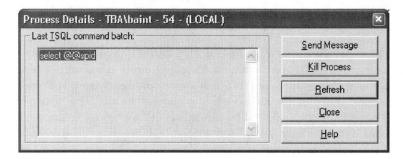

The information within the Current Activity details frame isn't self-refreshing. To update this information, you must right-click the Current Activity node within Enterprise Manager and choose the Refresh menu item from the pop-up menu.

Current Activity with T-SQL

The current activity within a database can also be viewed using T-SQL. Although Enterprise Manager provides a simple way of viewing activity, it's often more convenient to inspect such activity directly from within Query Analyzer (or another query tool). This is especially true when SQL Server is suffering from performance issues, because using the T-SQL commands directly from Query Analyzer will often prove more efficient than trying to use the GUI interface.

> **Remember that Enterprise Manager isn't part of the SQL Server database engine. Behind the scenes it talks to SQL Server the same way you can, using T-SQL. Sometimes Enterprise Manager spends a long time trying to display the information received from SQL Server graphically, and it's often quicker to issue the T-SQL commands directly through Query Analyzer.**

SP_WHO2

The sp_who2 T-SQL command (resident in the master database and therefore a global system-stored procedure) displays the current activity within the SQL Server instance. The information produced by this procedure is similar to that displayed by the Current Activity node of Enterprise Manager. Essentially, a list of database connections (processes) is created, along with information regarding their resource consumption and current status.

> **During times of very heavy activity and locking, the sp_who2 procedure may be blocked and may take a long time to run. In this situation, try using sp_who, a subset of sp_who2, because this requires fewer resources, thereby allowing it to execute more quickly.**

Sp_who2 produces a list of processes for the whole server and is database-independent. This system-stored procedure can accept one parameter, and depending on its value, it will take one of two actions. First, when the parameter is active, as shown in the following screen shot, this will display a list of processes that are currently executing a command:

```
sp_who2 active
```

If the parameter is a number, then the parameter is interpreted as a specific SPID (process identifier), so only that particular processes information is shown.

```
sp_who2 SPID
```

To get a complete list of current SPIDs, execute sp_who2 without any parameters.

Try It Out–Displaying Current Processes Using T-SQL

In this example, you use sp_who2 to display a list of current processes in SQL Server.

1. Connect to SQL Server using Query Analyzer. Execute sp_who2 as shown in the next screen shot to return a list of all processes connected to SQL Server.

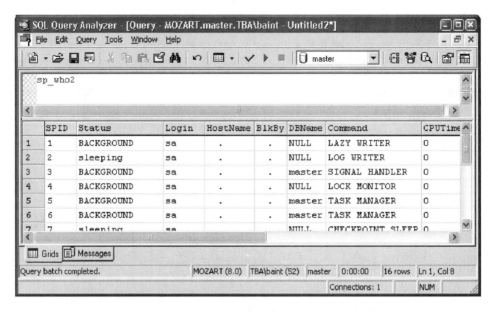

2. Now execute this procedure again; however, this time specify the `active` parameter to show a list of processes that are currently executing a database command.

> The `active` parameter tells the `sp_who2` command to filter its results to only include processes that are presently executing a T-SQL command. Although an application may have a connection established with SQL Server, most applications tend to issue database commands intermittently in response to user requests.

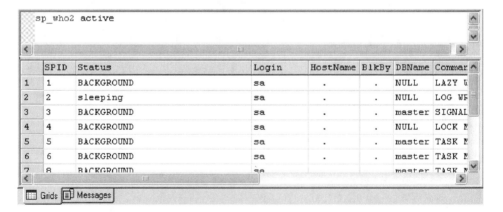

3. Finally, execute this procedure and specify a specific process number as a parameter. Only information for that process is displayed.

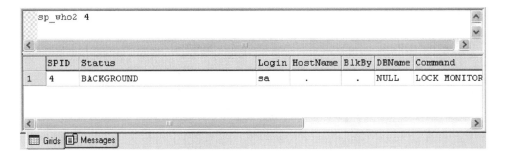

DBCC INPUTBUFFER

DBCC (Database Consistency Checker) commands are a special class of commands used to inspect the internal operations of SQL Server. We'll cover only a representative sample here; for a complete list, see DBCC in Books Online.

The DBCC INPUTBUFFER command shows the last batch that a particular process sent to SQL Server to execute. This is useful when you're attempting to determine why a command for a given process is heavily consuming resources (and you haven't had SQL Server Profiler running).

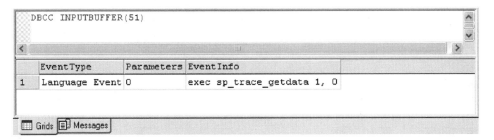

DBCC OpenTran

Transactions cause blocking, a normal function of concurrency handling within SQL Server. Blocking is what happens when one transaction is modifying a particular row and another transaction attempts to access that row. The second transaction is "blocked" until the first transaction has completed its change, thus preventing the second transaction from seeing values that are in the process of being changed, and thereby maintaining data integrity. When the first transaction has completed the second transaction is no longer blocked and proceeds with its access of the previously blocked row.

Typically, developers write code to keep transactions as short as possible in order to minimize blocking. However, if a "bug" exists within a piece of code, a transaction may be kept open for a long period of time, maybe indefinitely (if the code has got itself into an infinite loop, for example). As the sp_who2 procedure shows which processes are blocking other processes, determining the cause of the blocking is usually quite straightforward. The output of the sp_who2 command shows if the command being executed on one connection is being blocked by a command being executed on another connection.

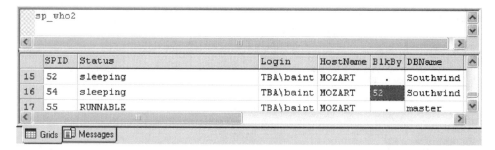

This figure shows that the connection with the SPID (process id) of 54 is currently being blocked by the command being executed by SPID 52. Once the command that is causing the blocking has completed, SPID 54 will continue unless it's kept waiting so long that a time out occurs. The length of the time out varies by application because this is set in the application connection string.

However, if you have a cascading effect of processes blocking other processes, it may be difficult to quickly determine the root cause of such blocking. This is where the DBCC OPENTRAN command can help. Executing this command displays information relating to the oldest running transaction. Assuming this isn't an expected process in another database on the same server, typically the oldest running transaction is the one at the root of the blocking problems. Of course, once you've identified the cause of the blocking problem you can decide what action to take.

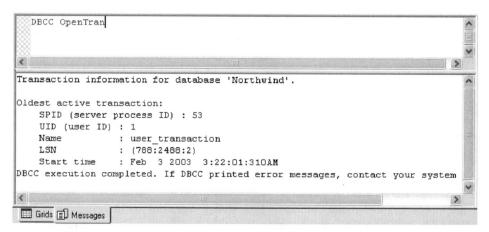

DBCC Checks

The physical integrity of the information within your database is of critical importance to ensure the quality of your database environment. The physical integrity has less to do with the actual values contained within individual tables, and more to do with the integrity of the underlying page structure in which those tables exist.

> A page is a unit of storage that SQL Server uses internally to allocate space to
> database objects.

SQL Server 2000 is usually very reliable when it comes to maintaining the integrity of the database data files. Corruption is quite rare and often this is traced back to faulty hardware instead of problems with SQL Server itself (such as a disk drive that's beginning to fail). Whatever the reason why corruption is occurring, the sooner you're aware of it, the sooner you can do something about it.

The following DBCC commands allow you to check the physical consistency of the database.

DBCC CheckDB

DBCC CheckDB is a command that's used to check the physical consistency of a database by inspecting the allocation of pages within the database to ensure that they're correctly linked. Also, the command checks the structure of objects within the database to ensure that they're correctly formed.

```
DBCC CheckDB(dbname)
```

DBCC CheckDB has the ability to fix minor problems by specifying repair options, as follows:

```
DBCC CheckDB(dbname,{ REPAIR_ALLOW_DATA_LOSS |
                      REPAIR_FAST |
                      REPAIR_REBUILD })
```

Which have the following descriptions:

❑ REPAIR_ALLOW_DATA_LOSS: Attempt to fix the problem within the database even if the fix results in some data being lost

❑ REPAIR_FAST: Only attempt to repair minor problems and only if the repairs don't result in data loss

❑ REPAIR_REBUILD: Attempt to repair problems within the database, but only if the repairs don't result in data loss

> If your database is corrupted, we doubt whether time is more important than a full recovery, so we would suggest that there really isn't a need to use the REPAIR_FAST option. If corruption occurs we would use the REPAIR_REBUILD option first to attempt to fix the problem. If this doesn't work and you don't have any viable alternative (such as restoring from a backup), we would attempt the REPAIR_ALLOW_DATA_LOSS option. This isn't a great situation to be in, as you may have lost some data but you have no way of determining what data has been lost, but it's better than having no data at all. Always take regular backups!

In addition to these repair options, you can control what the DBCC CheckDB command checks using one of the following options:

```
DBCC CheckDB(dbname, NOINDEX) WITH { ESTIMATE_ONLY |
                                     PHYSICAL_ONLY }
```

633

Which have the following descriptions:

❑ NOINDEX: Nonclustered indexes will not be checked by the DBCC command. This helps to improve execution time.

❑ ESTIMATE_ONLY: Doesn't carry out the DBCC checks; instead, gives an estimation of the space required in TempDB to perform the checks.

❑ PHYSICAL_ONLY: Only checks the page allocation and cannot be used to make repairs.

> **Repairing a corrupt database isn't something that should happen often. In fact we've only seen half a dozen occurrences of this type of failure out of hundreds of database environments that we've been involved in over the last six years. And on almost every one of those occasions, the database corruption was linked to some form of pending hardware failure. While the repair options of the DBCC CheckDB command may help you recover your database to a usable state, you should still try to identify the cause of the corruption to help stop it from occurring again (for instance, by replacing the faulty hardware if it's traced back to a hardware-related problem).**

Try It Out–Check the Northwind Database for Physical Errors

In this example, you use the DBCC CheckDB command to check the Northwind database for physical errors.

Connect to SQL Server using Query Analyzer. Execute the DBCC CheckDB command as shown in the next screen shot. This command may take several minutes to run, depending on your machine, but when it completes, the output of the DBCC command will be presented within the results frame.

```
DBCC CheckDB(Northwind)
```

```
DBCC results for 'Northwind'.
DBCC results for 'sysobjects'.
There are 177 rows in 4 pages for object 'sysobjects'.
DBCC results for 'sysindexes'.
There are 159 rows in 6 pages for object 'sysindexes'.
DBCC results for 'syscolumns'.
There are 637 rows in 11 pages for object 'syscolumns'.
DBCC results for 'systypes'.
There are 26 rows in 1 pages for object 'systypes'.
DBCC results for 'syscomments'.
There are 183 rows in 16 pages for object 'syscomments'.
```

Grids Messages

The DBCC CheckDB command is very verbose; however, if you scroll through this output, you'll see any errors highlighted with the error caption. Unless you have some major problems with your SQL Server installation or your computer, you wouldn't expect to see any error information listed here in this example.

634

DBCC CheckAlloc

DBCC CheckAlloc is similar to DBCC CheckDB; however, it only checks the allocation of pages within a database, not the physical structure of objects. This is a useful check if DBCC CheckDB is proving too time consuming, and you wish to provide basic allocating checking.

DBCC CheckAlloc has all the options of DBCC CheckDB, except the PHYSICAL_ONLY option.

```
DBCC CheckAlloc(dbname, NOINDEX | {REPAIR_ALLOW_DATA_LOSS |
                                  REPAIR_FAST|
                                  REPAIR_REBUILD } )
               WITH ESTIMATEONLY
```

> DBCC CheckDB **does everything** DBCC CheckAlloc **does (however the opposite isn't true). You don't need to execute them both.**

Try It Out–Checking the Page Allocation of Northwind Database

In this example, you use DBCC CheckAlloc to check the page allocation of the Northwind database.

Connect to SQL Server using Query Analyzer. Execute the DBCC CheckAlloc command as shown. Again, this may take several minutes to complete (the DBCC CheckDB is still faster) and again the results frame will be full of verbose output. If you scroll through this output, any errors will become apparent with the error keyword.

```
DBCC CheckAlloc(Northwind)



DBCC results for 'Northwind'.
*******************************************************************
Table sysobjects                    Object ID 1.
Index ID 1. FirstIAM (1:10). Root (1:11). Dpages 4.
Index ID 1. 6 pages used in 0 dedicated extents.
Index ID 2. FirstIAM (1:25). Root (1:15). Dpages 2.
Index ID 2. 4 pages used in 0 dedicated extents.
Index ID 3. FirstIAM (1:33). Root (1:31). Dpages 1.
Index ID 3. 2 pages used in 0 dedicated extents.
Total number of extents is 0.
*******************************************************************
```

Grids | Messages

WITH TABLERESULTS

As an alternative to the flat file verbose output, you can choose to specify the TABLERESULTS option with most DBCC commands. This causes the output of the DBCC command to be formatted into a resultset. This resultset can then be inserted into a table for automated processing of the outputted DBCC results.

Try It Out–Using the WITH TABLERESULTS Parameter with DBCC CheckAlloc

In this example, you reissue the DBCC CheckAlloc command, but this time, you specify the WITH TABLERESULTS parameter.

Connect to SQL Server using Query Analyzer and enter the DBCC command as shown. This is the same command you issued in the last example; however, this time you're also specifying the WITH TABLERESULTS parameter.

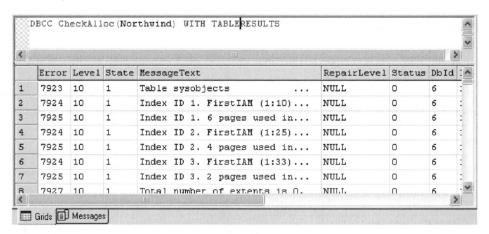

Once the execution of this command has completed, instead of the verbose text output, you'll be presented with a resultset of the output of the DBCC command. Although this isn't as easy to read with your eyes, it's a lot more manageable if you were to build some automation around the interpretation of the DBCC command results.

Maintenance Plans

A maintenance plan in SQL Server is a mechanism for bringing together a number of the DBA tasks that must be carried out on a routine basis, including the following:

❏   Integrity checks

❏   Index optimizations

❑ Full database backups

❑ Transaction log backups

Maintenance plans can be configured only within SQL Server Enterprise Manager. This functionality is located within its own node under the **Management** node in Enterprise Manager.

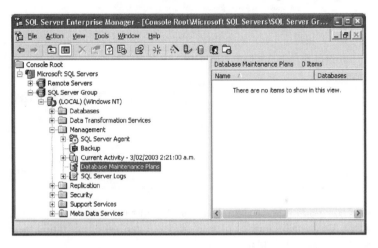

Try It Out–Create a Maintenance Plan for Northwind

In this example, you'll create a simple database maintenance plan to look after the Northwind database.

1. Connect to SQL Server using Enterprise Manager. Drill down into the **Management** node then right-click the **Database Maintenance Plans** node and choose **New Maintenance Plan** from the pop-up menu. This will start the Database Maintenance Plan wizard, the first window of which is the welcome screen.

2. Click **Next** to move on to the **Select Databases** window. Here you'll choose which databases you want *this particular* maintenance plan to look after. The options are self-explanatory, and for this example you only want the Northwind database to be involved with this maintenance plan, so select the check box next to this database name.

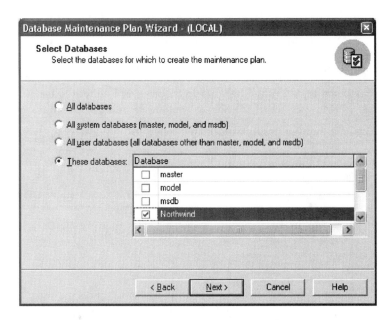

3. Click Next to take you to the Update Database Optimization Information window. Here you choose options for the maintenance plan to carry out general optimization tasks for each database participating within this plan.

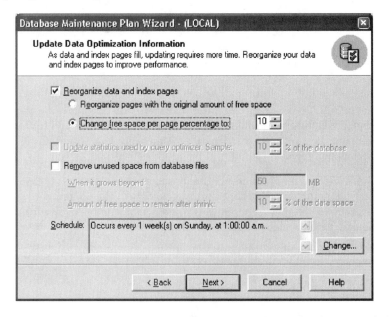

For this example, you want to reorganize the data within the data and index pages (rebuild clustered and nonclustered indexes), and when rebuilding these indexes, you want to leave 10 percent free space to allow for future growth (fill factor). You want this reindexing to take place once a week at 1 a.m. on Sunday.

4. Clicking **Next** takes you to the **Database Integrity Check** window. Here you set the options for processing integrity checks against the databases participating in this plan.

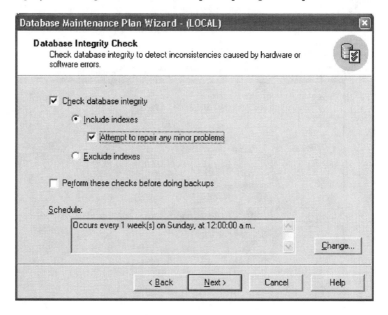

In this example, select to carry out integrity checks every Sunday at 1 a.m., include indexes in these checks, and if any minor problems exist within the index structures, then SQL Server should try and fix these minor problems.

5. Next you specify whether or not you want this maintenance plan to carry out a Full database backup for the databases participating in this plan.

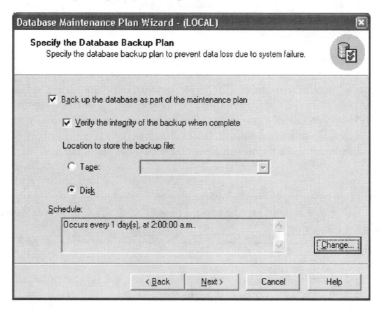

In this example you want to back up the database every day at 2 a.m. to disk, and once the backup has finished, to verify that the backup was successful (with RESTORE VERIFYONLY).

6. Click Next and you can specify where on the disk you want the Full database backups to be located. For this example, leave the Default Directory option selected. An alternative is to specify a different path.

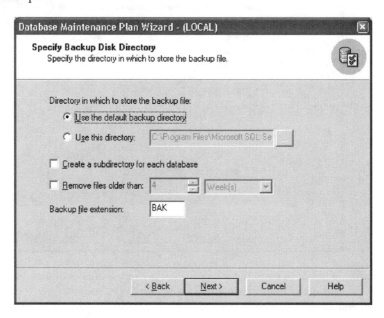

You can also choose to create a new subdirectory per database, or have all the backup files created within the same directory. If you're backing up a large number of databases, or if you're retaining a large number of database backups per database, then using a separate subdirectory (named after the database) is usually a good idea. However, you don't need to do this for this example.

The next option you have on this screen is to instruct the maintenance plan to delete database backup files once they become a certain number of days, weeks, or months old. In theory in a production environment, the disk backups are written to tape backup regularly so you don't need to keep this on disk indefinitely. If you're backing up to tape every night, you may only want to keep a couple of days' worth of Full database backups on disk (depending on available space) to provide protection against database failure (keeping a couple of days of backup on disk also provides some protection from on-off tape backup failure).

> **Remember to schedule the tape backup to start after the SQL Server backup to disk has completed!**

7. Click Next and you'll specify the same options as you did for the Full database backup, but this time you're dealing with transaction log backups.

> If you choose to enable Transaction log backups for this maintenance plan, then all databases must be using the Full or Bulk Logged Recovery Model or else this step will fail. For more information see the discussion on Recovery Models in Chapter 8.

Select the options and the schedule as shown in the following screen shot.

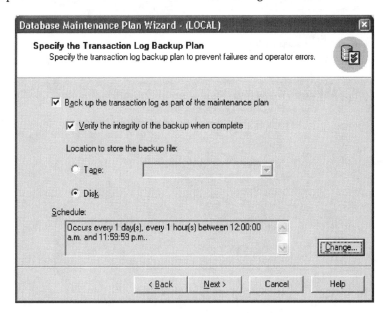

8. Ensure the schedule is set to back up the transaction log to disk every hour by clicking the Change button.

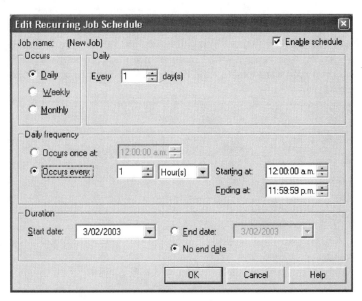

It's important to remember that a Transaction log backup only backs up what has been entered into the transaction log since the last transaction log backup. The frequency at which you run the Transaction log backup doesn't affect the amount of disk space used by the Transaction log backup files. The total amount of information being backed up remains the same regardless of the frequency at which you choose to back it up.

9. And retain the Transaction log backups within the same directory as the Full database backups with the same options.

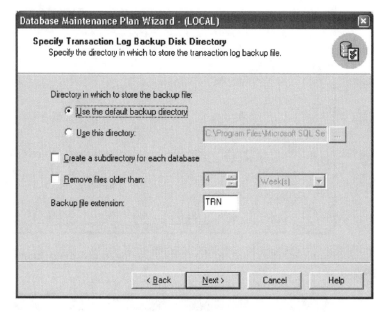

10. Click Next and you'll be asked if you want to create a report file and send a notification to an operator after every execution of the maintenance plan. If you installed SQL Agent Mail (see Chapter 2) you may want to select the SuperDBA operator to receive a message every time this maintenance plan completes.

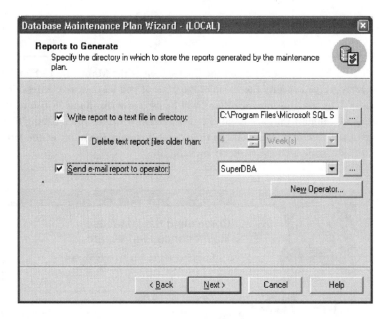

11. Click Next again, and you can specify the execution history that is retained for this maintenance plan. The default options are fine for this example.

> The history options don't affect the function of the maintenance plan but instead
> affect how many historical plan execution logs are retained. These logs may be of
> use if you're diagnosing a problem.

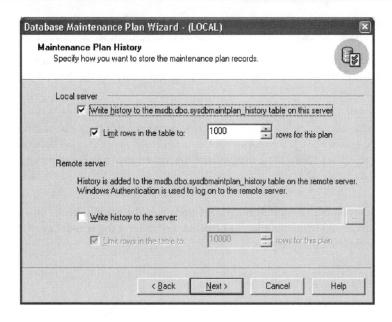

12. And in the final window, you must give the maintenance plan a name. Click Finish to create it.

> **Don't click Finish too quickly on the final screen of the Maintenance Plan wizard. This is where you specify the name of the plan. If you leave it as the default, a name such as DB Maintenance Plan1 will be used and this name is also used for naming all the jobs that are created in association with this plan. Changing the name of the plan at a later point in time doesn't change the name of the jobs, and this default name isn't particularly meaningful.**

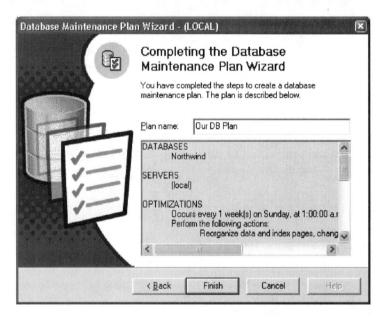

In the detail pane within Enterprise Manager you'll see the newly created maintenance plan. This is where you maintain the plan, for example, by adding and removing databases from participating within the plan.

> **Usually many of the databases on a single server require the same backup and maintenance plan. It's common for DBAs to create one or two maintenance plans on a server and have these maintain all the databases.**

If you look under the SQL Server Agent – Jobs node, you'll see a number of new plans. These were automatically generated when the plan was created, and control the scheduling of the various tasks you selected in the maintenance plan.

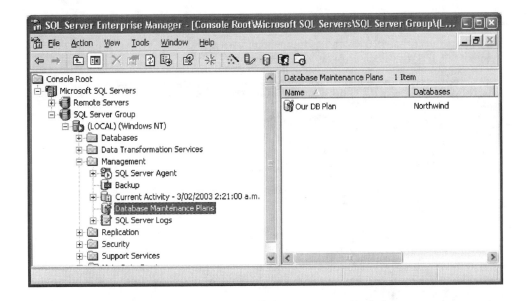

> The jobs associated with the maintenance plan aren't intended to be modified
> directly through the SQL Server Agent. You should make all changes, such as
> scheduling, through the Maintenance Plan node in Enterprise Manager. Making
> changes directly may prevent you from being able to make future changes to the
> database maintenance plan.

Monitoring Error Logs

Regular review of the error logs associated with SQL Server is an important task of a DBA. While (in
theory) major system events should automatically be sent to SQL Server via alerts, this doesn't
completely replace the need for the error logs to be checked. Consider the SQL Mail service for
example. If this fails, a note will be made in the error log, but no alerts will be sent to the DBA.

There are three error logs you should inspect regularly (at least daily for a database server). These are
the SQL Server error log, the SQL Agent error log and the Windows event log.

SQL Server Error Log

The SQL Server error log is the most important of the error logs. This maintains information about
any important event that takes place within the SQL Server database engine. This should be inspected
regularly by a DBA, because this is the most likely place you'll receive messages of impending
problems surrounding your SQL Server environment.

Using Enterprise Manager

You can inspect the SQL Server error log from within Enterprise Manager. This is under the Management I SQL Server Logs node, as shown next.

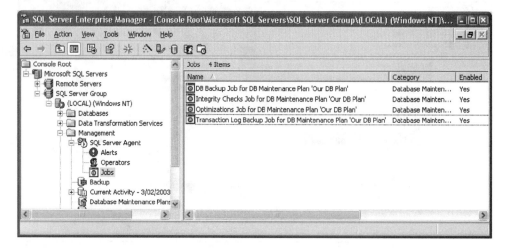

SQL Server retains the six most recent log files plus the current log file. A new log file is generated when SQL Server starts.

> **If you're experiencing problems with your SQL Server, make sure you don't restart it more than six times before you inspect the error log. If you do, all historical error logs will be replaced, and the source of the problem may have been in one of those error logs.**

The number of log files that SQL Server retains can be changed if you find the default value of six inadequate for your environment. To do this, right-click the SQL Server Logs node in Enterprise Manager and choose Configure from the pop-up menu. Here you can change the default number of retained log files to any number required.

Cycling the Error Log

If your SQL Server has been running for a long time, you may find the error log becoming very large in size (depending on the number of events logged). This large file may take a long time to load due to the sheer number of events within it. This will be especially true if you've enabled login auditing (on success or even on failure), because all audit events will be recorded as a separate event in the SQL Server error log. It isn't uncommon to come across large-MB error logs that contain tens of thousands of events for busy servers that have been running for a long period of time.

In this situation you can choose to cycle the SQL Server error log. Cycling the error log means to generate a new error log and remove the oldest one (as SQL Server does when it starts up). To do this you use the `sp_cycle_errorlog` system stored procedure; this has no parameters.

```
sp_cycle_error_log
```

Try It Out

In this example you execute the `sp_cycle_errorlog` stored procedure to replace the current SQL Server error log.

Connect to SQL Server using Enterprise Manager and inspect the current error log. Notice how the first few lines contain information about the version and build of SQL Server you're running. This information is always entered in the log file when SQL Server starts up.

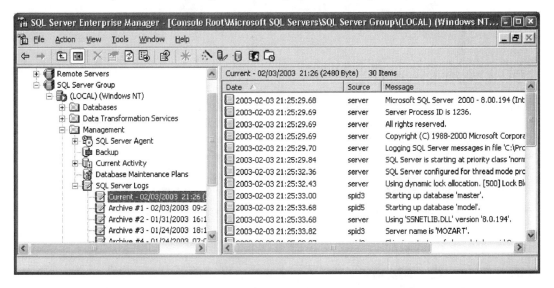

Next connect to SQL Server using Query Analyzer and execute the following command:

```
sp_cycle_errorlog
```

If you return to Enterprise Manager, right-click the **SQL Server Logs** node, and choose **Refresh** from the pop-up menu, you'll see the date and time of the current error log file change. If you select this current error log, you'll see that this only contains a few events, the first of which shows that the log file has indeed been cycled.

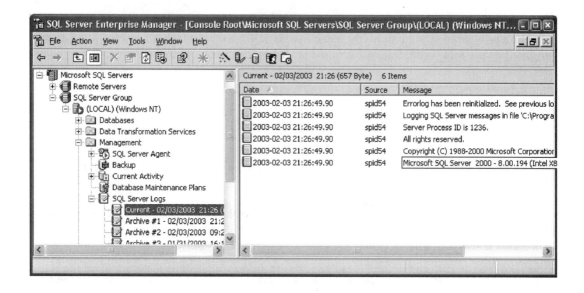

SQL Agent Error Log

The SQL Agent Error Log is the other SQL Server specific error log file, and this one contains error information relating to the running of the SQL Agent service and associate processes such as SQL Agent Mail. This is a useful log file to inspect when you have a particular issue with the SQL Agent; however, it isn't necessarily one that must be inspected on a daily basis.

> Errors in the SQL Agent error log are usually related to the failed startup of the SQL Agent or SQL Agent–related services such as SQL Agent Mail.

Using Enterprise Manager

To view the SQL Agent error log, drill down into the Management node within SQL Server, right-click the SQL Server Agent node, and choose Display Error Log, as shown in the following screen shot.

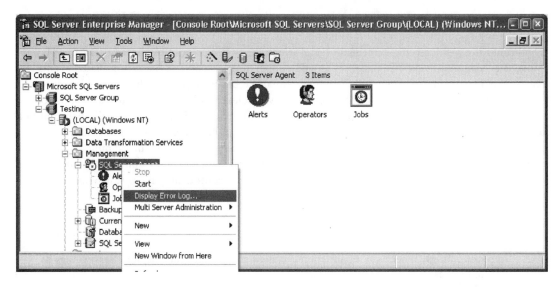

The initial view of the error log only shows errors. However, you can choose to change the filter on the error log to show all events, as in the next screen shot.

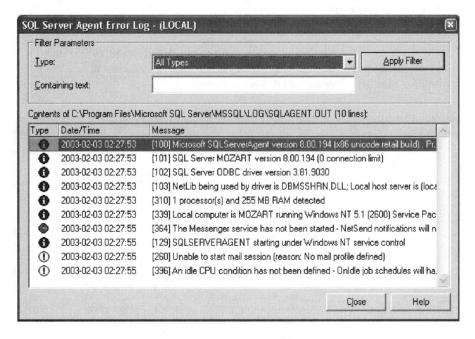

Windows Event Log

The Windows event log is the other main log of which the SQL Server DBA should be aware. This contains events generated by SQL Server as well as operating system- and hardware-related events that a DBA may be interested in. Although many organizations have people who are dedicated to looking after the operating systems and hardware, nevertheless as a DBA, it's still useful to monitor any serious events in either of these areas. After all, a failure of the OS or hardware will often lead to a disruption of your database environment in some way. Even if these don't result in server failure, they may impact your database environment in other ways, such as performance. For example the failure of a disk within a RAID (redundant array of independent disks) set may not result in any data being lost, however your database environment may process queries considerably more slowly until the failed disk has been replaced and the RAID set has repaired itself.

Windows events are separated into at least three logs:

❑ Application logs: Where any nonoperating system component (such as SQL Server) logs its error messages

❑ Security logs: Entries relating to security auditing

❑ System logs: Operating system events

> Your Windows server may have more than three logs depending on the services it's running. For example, if it's also acting as a DNS server, there will be a DNS server log specifically recording DNS-related events.

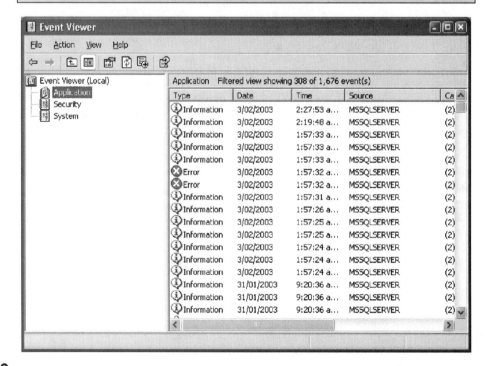

The Windows error log can become quite large, thus locating specific messages of interest can become a tedious task. Thankfully, this tool includes the ability to filter the messages displayed on screen. For example, if you only wish to view the error-log entries generated by SQL Server, you would choose the Application node. Then from the Action | Filter Events menu item you could limit the events shown to those that have a source of MSSQLSERVER, as shown in the figure.

Summary

Thank you. We appreciate the effort you've put into this book, as you worked through each of the chapters and finally reached the end. We hope you've become more knowledgeable about the life and duties of a DBA and we encourage you to take this newfound knowledge and apply it in the real world as you grow in your career as a DBA. Remember, walk before you run, look before you leap, and back up before you modify!

Index

X

forums.apress.com

JOIN THE APRESS FORUMS AND BE PART OF OUR COMMUNITY. You'll find discussions that cover topics of interest to IT professionals, programmers, and enthusiasts just like you. If you post a query to one of our forums, you can expect that some of the best minds in the business—especially Apress authors, who all write with *The Expert's Voice*™—will chime in to help you. Why not aim to become one of our most valuable participants (MVPs) and win cool stuff? Here's a sampling of what you'll find:

DATABASES
Data drives everything.

Share information, exchange ideas, and discuss any database programming or administration issues.

INTERNET TECHNOLOGIES AND NETWORKING
Try living without plumbing (and eventually IPv6).

Talk about networking topics including protocols, design, administration, wireless, wired, storage, backup, certifications, trends, and new technologies.

JAVA
We've come a long way from the old Oak tree.

Hang out and discuss Java in whatever flavor you choose: J2SE, J2EE, J2ME, Jakarta, and so on.

MAC OS X
All about the Zen of OS X.

OS X is both the present and the future for Mac apps. Make suggestions, offer up ideas, or boast about your new hardware.

OPEN SOURCE
Source code is good; understanding (open) source is better.

Discuss open source technologies and related topics such as PHP, MySQL, Linux, Perl, Apache, Python, and more.

PROGRAMMING/BUSINESS
Unfortunately, it is.

Talk about the Apress line of books that cover software methodology, best practices, and how programmers interact with the "suits."

WEB DEVELOPMENT/DESIGN
Ugly doesn't cut it anymore, and CGI is absurd.

Help is in sight for your site. Find design solutions for your projects and get ideas for building an interactive Web site.

SECURITY
Lots of bad guys out there—the good guys need help.

Discuss computer and network security issues here. Just don't let anyone else know the answers!

TECHNOLOGY IN ACTION
Cool things. Fun things.

It's after hours. It's time to play. Whether you're into LEGO® MINDSTORMS™ or turning an old PC into a DVR, this is where technology turns into fun.

WINDOWS
No defenestration here.

Ask questions about all aspects of Windows programming, get help on Microsoft technologies covered in Apress books, or provide feedback on any Apress Windows book.

HOW TO PARTICIPATE:
Go to the Apress Forums site at **http://forums.apress.com/**.
Click the New User link.